Multicultural Children's Literature

fourth edition

Multicultural Children's Literature

Through the Eyes of Many Children

DONNA E. NORTON
Texas A&M University, Emerita

LIBRARY
FRANKLIN PIERCE UNIVERSITY
RINDGE, NH 03461

PEARSON

Boston • Columbus • Indianapolis • New York • San Francisco • Upper Saddle River
Amsterdam • Cape Town • Dubai • London • Madrid • Milan • Munich • Paris • Montreal • Toronto
Delhi • Mexico City • São Paulo • Sydney • Hong Kong • Seoul • Singapore • Taipei • Tokyo

Vice President, Editor in Chief: Aurora Martínez Ramos
Editor: Erin Grelak
Editorial Assistant: Michelle Hochberg
Vice President, Director of Marketing: Margaret Waples
Executive Marketing Manager: Krista Clark
Production Editor: Mary Beth Finch
Editorial Production Service: Electronic Publishing Services Inc.
Manufacturing Buyer: Megan Cochran
Electronic Composition: Jouve
Cover Designer: Jennifer Hart

Credits and acknowledgments borrowed from other sources and reproduced, with permission, in this textbook appear on appropriate page within text.

Copyright © 2013, 2009, 2005, 2001 Pearson Education, Inc., publishing as Allyn & Bacon, 501 Boylston Street, Boston, MA, 02116. All rights reserved. Manufactured in the United States of America. This publication is protected by Copyright, and permission should be obtained from the publisher prior to any prohibited reproduction, storage in a retrieval system, or transmission in any form or by any means, electronic, mechanical, photocopying, recording, or likewise. To obtain permission(s) to use material from this work, please submit a written request to Pearson Education, Inc., Permissions Department, 501 Boylston Street, Boston, MA, 02116, or email permissionsus@pearson.com.

Library of Congress Cataloging-in-Publication Data

Norton, Donna E.
Multicultural children's literature : through the eyes of many children / Donna E. Norton.—4th ed.
p. cm.
Includes bibliographical references and index.
ISBN-13: 978-0-13-268576-4 (pbk.)
ISBN-10: 0-13-268576-0 (pbk.)
1. American literature—Minority authors—History and criticism. 2. Minorities—United States—Intellectual life—Study and teaching. 3. Minorities in literature—Study and teaching—United States. 4. American literature—Minority authors—Study and teaching. 5. Children's literature, American—History and criticism. 6. Children's literature, American—Study and teaching. 7. Children—Books and reading—United States. 8. Children of minorities—Books and reading. 9. Cultural pluralism in literature. 10. Ethnic groups in literature. 11. Minorities in literature. 12. Ethnicity in literature. I. Title.
PS153.M56N675 2012
810.9-9'28208693—dc23

2011041770

10 9 8 7 6 5 4 3 2 1 16 15 14 13 12

www.pearsonhighered.com

ISBN-10: 0-13-268576-0
ISBN-13: 978-0-13-268576-4

Contents

Preface

This text is intended for any adult who is interested in evaluating, selecting, and sharing multicultural literature written for children and young adults. The text focuses on the most outstanding examples of children's and adolescent literature in the following areas: African American, Native American, Latino, Asian, Jewish, and Middle Eastern. Written for use in university and college classes and by classroom teachers, it is also a valuable source for workshops and seminars for those leading discussions in adult education. My hope is that those who read this text receive a deeper appreciation and understanding of the rich cultural heritage embedded in authentic multicultural literature and share that appreciation and heritage with children and young adults.

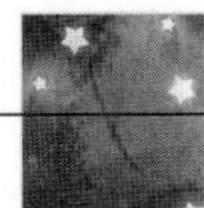

HIGHLIGHTS

Two-Part Chapter Organization

Each chapter has two distinct sections. The first section of each chapter includes a discussion of specific literature, nonfiction and fiction, that develops a historical perspective of the culture. The second section in each chapter develops the techniques and methodologies that adults can use to help children, young adults, and interested adult learners develop an understanding of the culture and an appreciation for its literature. This is typically accomplished by providing five phases of learning experiences in the following order: phase one, general approach to traditional literature; phase two, folklore from a narrower region; phase three, historical nonfiction; phase four, historical fiction; and phase five, contemporary literature.

Criteria for Evaluating Literature

Each chapter discusses criteria that could be used when selecting and evaluating the literature. The criteria may be used in a historical perspective so that students understand the various changes in evaluation that may have occurred over time.

Authentication

Throughout the book, there are strategies that model how to authenticate the literature from that culture. The text explains how to authenticate multicultural literature to verify that the literature accurately depicts the values, beliefs, and cultural backgrounds of various cultural groups. Individual chapters provide authentication models.

Issues

Each chapter discusses various issues that are associated with writing, publishing, selecting, and evaluating the literature. These issues are written in such a way as to encourage discussion or debate on various viewpoints.

Annotated Bibliographies

Chapters 2 through 7 conclude with annotated bibliographies that describe multiple literature recommendations. These annotations provide a short description of the book, readability level, and an interest level.

New to This Edition

- Chapters 2 through 7 include a new section titled "**Survival.**" These sections focus on the literature that reflects the skills, strategies, values, and beliefs that allow people in that culture to survive. Characters in books frequently rely on survival techniques and strategies that are embedded deep within their cultures or they may use survival strategies that are common to all cultures. These books are among the strongest for literary quality and frequently depict the harsh realities experienced by people within the culture. Analyzing these books encourages considerable use of critical thinking skills.

- Sections in each chapter relate possible responses of cultural personages to **current news articles and issues** within the culture. This section asks students to consider: "What might a particular person do in response to this event or crisis? What evidence did you find in the literature of the culture that made you believe that this would be a logical response?"

- Several new sections have been added to the "**Involving Students**" portions of each chapter. For example, a section in the African American chapter asks students to analyze why particular pieces of African American literature were chosen as favorites by children's book authors. A chart of examples is included. In the same chapter is a research and writing activity that asks students to use music to develop an understanding of civil rights.

ACKNOWLEDGMENTS

I wish to thank the adults who were in my "Survival Seminar" in Madison, Wisconsin. Many of the participants already had advanced degrees in medicine, architecture, business, library science, and education. Their interest in the subject made me realize that gaining an understanding of multicultural literature is a topic that appeals to many people of all ages. Their reading and discussions also highlighted the need for high-quality literature that is also authentic. I would like to thank Stefanie Rose, the head librarian at Beth Israel Center in Madison, Wisconsin, for her recommendations of Jewish literature that are authentic and that appeal to her readers. I would like to thank the reviewers of this manuscript for their insights and comments: Stanley E. Bochtler, Buena Vista University; Mi-Hyun Chung, Mercy College; Patricia E. Murphy, Arkansas State University; and Wilma Robles-Melendez, Nova Southeastern University.

Multicultural Children's Literature

Chapter 1

Introduction to Multicultural iterature

states and Canada are multicultural nations, including Europeans, Native , African Americans, Latinos, and Asians. The United States and Canada also people from different religious groups such as Christian, Jewish, and Muslim. A ghtened sensitivity to the needs of all people has led to the realization that literature plays a considerable role in the development of understanding across cultures.

The school-age population of minority children is increasing rapidly. This rapid change makes the understanding of and ability to use multicultural literature even more necessary. For example, Sabrina Tavernise (2011) reports that America's population of white children will be in the minority during this decade. She states, "The Census Bureau had originally forecast that 2023 would be the tipping point for the minority population under the age of 18. But rapid growth among Latinos, Asians, and people of more than one race has pushed it earlier to 2019" (p. A14). Don Van Natta, Jr. (2011) reports that the Latino population in Orange County, Florida, jumped 84 percent since the last census, while Jennifer Medina (2011) states that one-third of the population in Orange County, California, is Latino and one-fifth of the county is Asian.

To aid in developing understandings of other cultures, many educators and researchers emphasize the need for high-quality multicultural literature. Hazel Rochman (1993) states the need for multicultural literature very well when she concludes: "The best books break down borders. They surprise us—whether they are set close to home or abroad. They change our view of ourselves; they extend that phase 'like me' to include what we thought was foreign and strange" (p. 9). This changing view of ourselves is especially important to researchers who are investigating minority children's responses to literature. For example, M. Liaw (1995), after analyzing Chinese children's responses to Chinese children's books, called for more cultural sensitivity in the stories and a need for researching children's responses to literature. Grice and Vaughn (1992), following research in which they analyzed responses to African American literature, also identified the need for culturally conscious literature.

Rena Lewis and Donald Doorlag (1995) present the following reasons for developing multicultural education:

1. Commonalities among people cannot be recognized unless differences are acknowledged.
2. A society that interweaves the best of all of its cultures reflects a truly mosaic image.

3. Multicultural education can restore cultural rights by emphasizing cultural equality and respect.
4. Students can learn basic skills while also learning to respect cultures; multicultural education need not detract from basic education.
5. Multicultural education enhances the self-concepts of all students because it provides a more balanced view of U.S. society.
6. Students must learn to respect others.

Christina P. DeNicolo and Maria E. Franquiz (2006) recommend developing literature discussions that allow students to discuss the literature by using their life experiences as linguistic and cultural tools to help them understand the selections. Renea Arnold and Nell Colburn (2007), early-childhood specialists and librarians, recommend that non-English speakers have fun with their first language through songs, books, rhymes, family stories, and word games. They conclude: "The most important message we can share with parents is to embrace your native language and celebrate your culture—your children will flourish!" (p. 33). Critics of literature for children and young adults maintain that readers should be exposed to multicultural literature that heightens respect for the individuals, as well as the contributions and values, of cultural minorities.

Positive multicultural literature has been used effectively to help readers identify cultural heritages, understand sociological change, respect the values of minority groups, raise aspirations, and expand imagination and creativity. This author has found that multicultural literature and activities related to the literature also improves reading scores and improves attitudes among students from varying cultures. When the literature and literature-related activities are part of the curriculum, and when adults know how to select this literature and develop strategies to accompany the literature, they encourage students to see commonalities and value in literature different from their own culture (Norton, 1981, 1984, 1990, 2001). In contrast, merely placing the literature in a classroom or a library without subsequent interaction does not change attitudes.

The importance of multicultural literature is shown in the summer reading programs required of students entering many colleges. Tamar Lewin (2007) reports that a survey of 100 college programs identified the types of reading required. For example, many reading lists deal with diversity, especially multicultural encounters, global understanding, political turmoil in the Middle East, and the rift between rich and poor in the United States. Lewin quotes several college administrators who express the importance of such reading. An administrator from the University of Florida wants books that show that "one person can make a difference" (p. C13) and the president of the University of Vermont describes this reading as "an opportunity to voyage together on the sea of thought" (p. C13). An opportunity for this voyage of discovery is also the goal of the literature discussed in this textbook.

Although we can find numerous authorities who identify the need for multicultural literature, the selection of literature that is of both high literary quality and culturally authentic is a formidable task. The tasks involved in the process are enormous. Universities are beginning to require that students in education, library science, and English take courses that focus on choosing, analyzing, evaluating, and effectively using multicultural literature. Library selection committees, university professors, public school teachers, librarians, and administrators must all become involved in this process of evaluating and choosing multicultural literature.

An example of the complexity of the problems facing the collection of multicultural literature is emphasized when we consider the evaluation of Native American literature. When developing the Native American collection, librarians and educators must meet the basic requirements for students, scholars, and general readers who are interested in the study of Native American people, their culture, and their literature. They must also, however, be equally concerned with the quality and authenticity of the literature and reference materials. A special sensitivity is required when approaching the selection of materials, the categorizing of the materials, and the possible issues related to those selections. A case in point is *The Education of Little Tree,* written by Forrest Carter. When the book was reissued in 1991, it received that year's American Booksellers Association's ABBY award, given annually to the book that booksellers most enjoyed recommending directly to customers. At this point, it was advertised as a sensitive, evocative autobiographical account of a Cherokee boyhood in the 1930s and was on the *New York Times* Best Seller list for nonfiction. After revelations about the author's background, the book was moved from nonfiction to fiction on the same best-seller list of the *New York Times.* The book has carefully developed characterizations, historical settings, and believable conflict, but it is not an autobiography of a Cherokee boy. Instead, it is historical fiction. Such distinctions are important for scholars and students who are studying Native American literature.

In addition to the sensitivity required in selecting materials, educators are also emphasizing the moral dimensions related to sharing and discussing literature associated with various cultures. Johnston, Juhasz, Marken, and Ruiz (1998) define morality as "judgments of what is right and what is wrong, what is good and what is bad. These judgments, moreover, are produced at the meeting point between personal values, beliefs, and standards, and their negotiation in social settings. Morality then crucially includes both individual and social judgments" (p. 162). Consequently, the nature of the discussions between students and adults, the questions asked, the reactions to responses, and the choices of materials to be read and discussed may reflect differences in cultural values and portray moral messages.

Johnston et al. (1998) conclude with the following advice to teachers or other adults who work in multicultural settings: "Observe classroom events carefully and reflect upon their significance while suppressing the urge to criticize or condemn. The overall message that emerges from our analysis is that what teachers do and say in class does matter—their words and their actions carry great moral weight. Teachers, unavoidably, act as moral agents; how they choose to direct this action is a crucial part of what it means to be a teacher" (p. 180). This is excellent advice for anyone who is selecting, evaluating, and using multicultural literature, especially if the literature reflects cultural values and beliefs that are different from those of the educator.

Numerous articles in newspapers and journals stress the importance of developing educational systems that allow all children to succeed. For example, David M. Herszenhorn and Susan Saulny (2005) describe how a New York City school raised literacy scores by "specifying a literacy genre to focus on each month like autobiography or mystery, and weekly skills like making inferences" (p. 30). John M. Broder (2006) reports on "[a] state deadlocks on non-English-speaking children." Sam Dillon (2006) highlights falling achievement scores in science. Daniel Golden (2006) presents an issue associated with multicultural education when he states "[p]ublishers use quotas in images to win contracts in big states, but they may be creating new stereotypes" (p. A1). Total issues of some educational journals focus on multicultural themes. The November 2006 issue of *Language Arts* is titled "Multilingual and Multicultural: Changing the Ways We Teach." Special features in journals frequently discuss the importance of specific types of multicultural literature or provide recommended books. For example, the October 2010 issue of *School Library Journal* includes Lauren Barack's article "Islam in the Classroom" and the journal provides recommended "Resources for Teaching About Islam" and "SLJ's Recommended Titles."

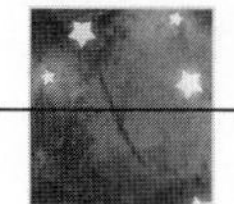

Developing a Study of Multicultural Literature

My own interest in multicultural literature as a scholarly subject began over twenty years ago when I was attending a conference on researching and writing biography. One of the speakers, a Native American author, spoke about his difficulty in researching the life of a Native American chief who lived in the 1800s. As an example of the problems he encountered, he explained how there were three differing interpretations of the chief's last statement given before his execution. The interpretation by a military officer was that the chief called on his people to lay down their arms and live on the reservation. A missionary translated the same message to be one in which the chief asked his people to give up their own beliefs and worship the white-man's god. The third interpretation was given by the chief's brother. In this version, the chief reminded his people of his accomplishments and what he would like them to remember about his life. This example illustrates the need for careful research if the author is to present an authentic viewpoint.

Shortly after this experience, I began my own research into the authenticity of the multicultural literature used with children and young adults. I also developed a university course in which students who were mostly from the fields of education, liberal arts, and library science could gain insights into multicultural literature. After several years of trying different methods for teaching the course, I developed a five-phase multicultural literature study that proceeds from ancient to contemporary literature. The sequence of study is summarized in Chart 1.1. This procedure is based partly on the one described in Franchot Ballinger's article, "A Matter of Emphasis: Teaching the 'Literature' in Native American Literature Courses" (1984): he begins with a general study of the oral tradition associated with Native American folklore, extends the study to the literature from specific Native American cultures, continues with biography and

CHART 1.1 Sequence for Studying Multicultural Literature

Phase One: Traditional Literature (Generalizations and Broad Views)	
A.	Identify distinctions among folktales, myths, and legends.
B.	Identify ancient stories that have common features and that are found in many regions.
C.	Identify types of stories that dominate a subject.
D.	Summarize the nature of oral language, the role of traditional literature, the role of an audience, and the literary style.
Phase Two: Traditional Tales from One Area (Narrower View)	
A.	Analyze traditional myths and other story types and compare findings with those in Phase One.
B.	Analyze and identify values, beliefs, and themes in the traditional tales of one region.
Phase Three: Historical Nonfiction	
A.	Analyze nonfiction for the values, beliefs, and themes identified in traditional literature.
B.	Compare adult autobiographies and children's biographies (if possible).
C.	Compare information in historical documents with autobiographies and biographies.
Phase Four: Historical Fiction	
A.	Evaluate historical fiction according to the authenticity of the conflicts, characterizations, settings, themes, language, and traditional beliefs and values.
B.	Search for the role of traditional literature in historical fiction.
C.	Compare historical fiction with autobiographies, biographies, and historical information.
Phase Five: Contemporary Literature	
A.	Analyze the inclusion of any beliefs and values identified in traditional literature and nonfictional literature.
B.	Analyze contemporary characterization and conflicts.
C.	Analyze the themes and look for threads that cross the literature.

autobiography, and concludes with contemporary writings. Throughout this study, he searches for the emergence of critical themes, basic symbols, and shared values that tie the ancient and contemporary literature together.

A modification of this approach proved to be the most valuable for my own students, both graduate and undergraduate, who chose to do in-depth studies of African/ African American, Asian/Asian American, Latino, Native American, Jewish, or Middle Eastern literature or to develop instructional units to be used with children.

As you read this book and conduct your own research, you will discover that the literature is discussed in a way that focuses on a five-phase approach. The conclusion of each chapter includes a section titled "Involving Children in _____ Literature," with the blank filled with the name of the culture covered in that chapter. These sections provide suggestions showing some of the ways that the literature from various cultures may be used with children and young adult audiences.

Five-Phase Approach for the Study of Multicultural Literature

Phase One This phase is a broad introduction to the ancient myths, legends, and folktales of a culture. The literature, discussions, and assignments encourage students to understand the nature of the oral language in storytelling and to appreciate the role of oral tradition in transmitting the culture, the philosophy, and the language of the people.

Activities for Phase One. Identify the ancient myths, legends, and folktales from a culture. Find the commonalities among them and identify those that are found in different regions within the cultural group. Also identify the types of stories that dominate, the characteristics of the traditional literature, and variants of the same tale. Consider the history of the recording of the tales and problems that the interpretations and translations created. Finally, summarize the broad generalizations and understandings: What did you learn about the people, their belief and value systems, and their language?

Phase Two This phase narrows the study to the ancient myths, legends, and folktales from one specific area. For example, this may involve the study of traditional literature from Native Americans of the Great Plains or the Southwest or the Inuit; tracing African tales from West Africa to southern plantations in the United States, or comparing tales from the Aztec or Inca or Latino cultures to the tales of the Hispanic Southwest. The literature, discussions, and assignments encourage students to consider how the generalizations from Phase One apply to one specific segment of a wider culture, how and why the literature may diverge from the generalizations, and what traditional values are reflected in the literature.

Activities for Phase Two. For one specific group or area, identify examples of ancient myths, legends, and folktales. Look for the characteristics and the story types that arose out of the study during Phase One. Identify stories that reflect differences from the characteristics identified in Phase One and consider any reasons for the differences. Comparative assignments are excellent ways to help students analyze literature. Identify examples of stories that reflect interference of an alien culture or changes that resulted because people were forced from their homelands: What are the changes? What might have caused these changes? Finally, summarize the philosophy, values, beliefs, and literary styles of the specific people as reflected in their myths, legends, and folktales.

Phase Three This phase involves study of nonfiction selections such as biographies, autobiographies, and informational literature of one group of people or culture. The literature, discussions, and assignments should encourage students to understand the early experiences and the social and political history of the specific people. This is an opportunity to verify the beliefs, values, and traditions identified in Phase One and Phase Two and to evaluate the accuracy of literature by comparing biographies, autobiographies, and informational writing.

Activities for Phase Three. Search for evidence that the philosophy, values, and beliefs depicted in myths, legends, and folktales are also depicted in biographies and autobiographies. Do the values, beliefs, and philosophies appear to be authentic? Use nonfiction informational texts to evaluate the authenticity of biographies. You may even be able to use autobiographies to evaluate the authenticity of both informational texts and biographies. If possible, compare an adult autobiography with a juvenile biography written about the same character. Or compare an adult biography with juvenile biographies that are written about the same character. What are the similarities and the differences? Evaluate the authenticity of the literature. Finally, summarize the historical happenings that influenced the culture and the people. Identify the literature that accurately presents this history.

The nonfiction selections in Phase Three encourage students of all ages to become what Marc Aronson (2007) calls detectives. As detectives, the students go from investigating what they know or they can easily discover about a people, such as geography, chronology, clothes, weapons, and available food, to discovering things they may not know, such as what a people believe and how they think about and experience the world. According to Aronson, fact checking is crucial because it allows readers to fill in the missing pieces about a people and their culture. By conducting this type of investigation, readers travel in time and see the world through the eyes of a culture that may not be known to them.

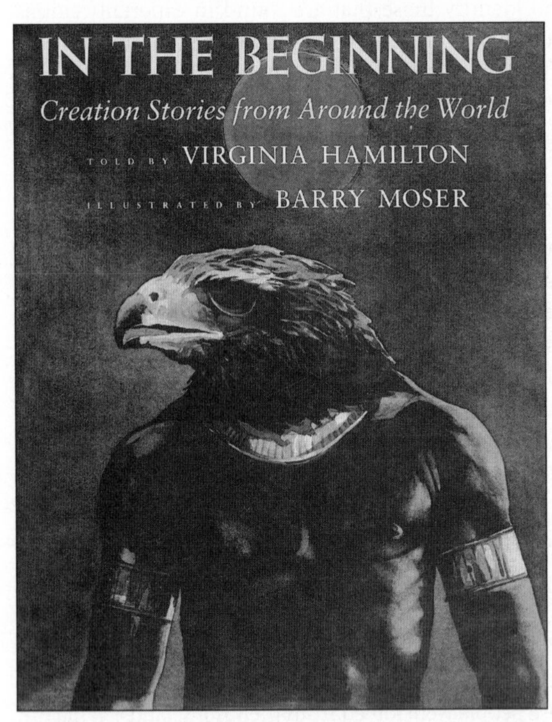

The myths in this book include creation stories from many parts of the world.

Cover from *In The Beginning: Creation Stories from Around the World* by Virginia Hamilton. Cover illustrations copyright © 1988 by Pennyroyal Press, Inc. Reprinted by permission of Harcourt Children's Books, an imprint of Houghton Mifflin Harcourt Publishing Company. All rights reserved.

Phase Four This phase is a study of historical fiction selections based on characters from the specific culture or on interactions between the people and another cultural group. The literature, discussions, and assignments encourage students to use the background information gained during the previous readings and discussions to evaluate the authenticity of historical fiction.

Activities for Phase Four. Analyze historical fiction for authenticity of settings, credibility of conflicts, and believability of characterizations, as well as for authenticity of the presentation of traditional beliefs, for the appropriateness of theme, and for the effectiveness of the author's style.

Phase Five Phase Five is a study of contemporary literature including realistic fiction, poetry, biography, and autobiography. The literature, discussions, and activities encourage students to search for continuity among traditional literature, nonfiction, historical fiction, and contemporary writings and to consider the themes, values, and conflicts that emerge in contemporary writings.

Activities for Phase Five. Search for any continuity within the literature as the literature proceeds from ancient to contemporary. Search for images, themes, values, style, and sources of conflict in writings by contemporary authors who are members of the group. Compare contemporary literature written for adult and juvenile

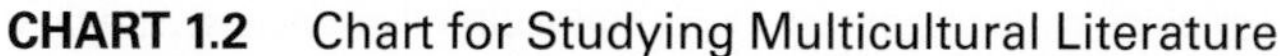

CHART 1.2 Chart for Studying Multicultural Literature

Phase One					
Examples	Characteristics and types of folklore	Cultural knowledge gained		Beliefs and values of the people	Variants, interpretations, notes
Phase Two					
Examples	Values and beliefs	Commonalities, characteristics, and story types	Differences from Phase One	Interference of alien culture	Variants, interpretations, notes
Phase Three					
Examples	Values and beliefs from Phases One and Two	Historical happenings that influenced culture		Authenticity of historical information	Comparisons among biographies
Phase Four					
Examples	Setting Conflicts	Characterization	Traditional values, beliefs, and behaviors	Themes and style	Historical happenings and connections with previous phases
Phase Five					
Examples	Continuity and changes within literature	Images, themes, values, style	Sources of conflict	Comparisons between children's and adult literature	Comparisons between writings of members and nonmembers of group

audiences. Compare contemporary literature written by members of the group with contemporary literature that focuses on the group but is written by authors who are not members of the group.

University students find it helpful to detail some of their findings in chart form before they summarize their discoveries about the literature. They also find these charts to be extremely helpful when they are evaluating the authenticity of the literature. For example, you may find Chart 1.2 to be helpful in your own research.

Each of the following chapters includes examples of various assignments or research developed by students. There are also excerpts from the summaries of each phase of the literature developed by students.

Authenticating the Literature: A Summary

As can be inferred from this discussion, authenticity is very important in the selection of literature that depicts the values, beliefs, and cultural backgrounds of various groups. Marc Aronson (2007) warns that history is getting to know the language, customs, and culture of a people. He concludes, "Fact checking is crucial because it is pretty easy to get history wrong" (p. 31). The need for accuracy and authenticity is emphasized in numerous articles about multicultural literature. For example, two articles by Betsy Hearne emphasize the importance of authenticity in picture books. In "Cite the Source: Reducing Cultural Chaos in Picture Books, Part One" (1993a), Hearne states,

> How do you tell if a folktale in picture-book format is authentic, or true to its cultural background? What picture books have met the challenge of presenting authentic folklore for children? These two questions, which dominated a recent program at the Harold Washington Library in Chicago, are

> especially pressing in light of our growing national concern about multicultural awareness. And they generate even broader questions: How can an oral tradition survive in print? How do children's books pass on—and play on—folklore? (p. 22)

In her second article, "Respect the Source: Reducing Cultural Chaos in Picture Books, Part Two" (1993b), Hearne discusses the importance of establishing cultural authority, citing the sources for folklore, and training adults who select and interact with the literature. She concludes her article with the following statements:

> We can ask for source citations and more critical reviews; we can compare adaptations to their printed sources (interlibrary loan works for librarians as well as their patrons) and see what's been changed in tone and content; we can consider what context graphic art provides for a story; we can make more informed selections, not by hard and fast rules, but by judging the balance of each book. . . . We can, in short, educate ourselves on the use and abuse of folklore at an intersection of traditions. (p. 37)

Hearne's concerns about cultural authenticity are valid with any of the genres of literature. After reading this book and critically evaluating the literature discussed in the various chapters, you will be able to make critical decisions about choosing and evaluating the literature more effectively. Authenticating various examples of multicultural literature is one of the favorite assignments of both my undergraduate and graduate students. It has also been shown to be a favorite assignment when used with schoolchildren. Or like many of my students who express their own desires, you will be able to write your own stories that authentically depict a cultural group.

A Process to Use to Authenticate a Book

It is difficult to teach about a culture if the information in the book is not accurate for that culture. As you consider the five phases for reviewing the authenticity of books from varying cultures or one culture, you will want to consider using the following approach, based on Altick and Fenstermaker's *The Art of Literary Research* (1993). The method has been modified for use with students at all levels. It works especially well for authenticating historical fiction, biography, and informational literature.

Categories for evaluating literature—geographical and social settings, values and beliefs, political ideologies, major events, themes, major conflicts, summary of reactions and responses—have been placed in question format to help younger students conduct their authentication. Questions help children critique literature as a way to authenticate what they read. Also notice that these questions provide an excellent outline to aid students in a writing activity as they respond to the various questions. (The categories are shown in depth later, as we consider the authentication of literature in various chapters.)

1. What are the geographical and social settings for the book, and are they authentic? Students should use nonfictional sources to evaluate this area. Pictures found in sources such as *National Geographic* are especially good for authenticating geographical settings.
2. What are the values and beliefs of the people in the book, and are they authentic?
3. What are the major events that make up the plot of the story? Are they possible for the time period and the culture?
4. What are the major conflicts in the book, and are they authentic for the time period?
5. What are the major themes, and are they found in other literature written about the time period or the people?

Ask the students to develop their own reasons for reading a book that is authentic. Why would they prefer not to read an inauthentic book? Ask them to consider the personal consequences if they accept as true a book that is not authentic. They may choose to add authenticity questions to the ones here or to change these questions as desired.

Activities for Involving Children in the Study of Literature

In addition to the activity sections that use the five-phase approach for the study of the literature, the literature studies in each chapter of this text include ideas for "Involving Children in the Study of That Literature." For example, each of the "Involving" sections includes an activity that focuses on storytelling and on the authentication of the literature. In addition, each includes ideas for developing writing connections with the literature, visualizing the culture and the literature through illustrated texts, and developing an analytical reading of a literature selection.

Writing Connections with the Literature A report from the National Commission on Writing in America's Schools and Colleges (http://www.writingcommission.org) identifies writing as the neglected "R" and calls for a writing revolution. The report recommends that writing should be the center of the school agenda. The report indicates the current neglect of writing with the following statistics:

1. Most fourth-grade students spend less than three hours a week writing. (This is 15% of the time they spend watching television.)
2. Nearly 60% of high school seniors do not write a three-page paper as often as once a month for their English teachers.
3. Seventy-five percent of seniors never receive a writing assignment in history or social studies.

At grades 4, 8, and 12, about one in five students produces completely unsatisfactory prose, about 50% meet basic requirements, and only one in five rate proficient in writing. Unfortunately, the report shows that more than 50% of college freshman are unable to produce papers relatively free of language errors or to analyze arguments or synthesize information.

The vice chair of the commission, Arlene Ackerman, summarized the need for a writing revolution very clearly when she stated, "Writing is how we teach students complex skills of synthesis, analysis, and problem solving. These skills will serve them well throughout life" (2003, p. 4).

The literature discussed and the activities related to the literature developed in this text provide many opportunities for students to synthesize, analyze, and solve problems through written papers and arguments. Consequently, this text highlights ways that writing may be used with the literature. Many of the activities such as authenticating the literature are natural methods for adding writing to the curriculum.

Visualizing the Literature Multicultural literature includes many contexts that may be outside students' experiences. Consequently, using illustrated texts and encouraging students to visualize what is written in texts that do not include illustrations are two very important techniques for increasing comprehension of the texts.

Anne Nielsen Hibbing and Joan L. Rankin-Erickson (2003) state, "In our work with struggling readers we have found that the use of sketches, illustrations, picture books, and movies provides students with information on which to build internal images, by supporting students with essential elements necessary for responding to the text" (p. 769). In addition, these authors recommend teaching students to create their own images on the television screens in their minds as they read.

Although Hibbing and Rankin-Erickson are especially interested in using visual imagery with lower-ability readers, the technique is an important tool for all readers, especially as they are trying to visualize and understand a setting or a situation outside of their experiences. These authors recommend discussions that check students' ability to create visual images, modeling imagery strategies with students, drawing pictures to clarify texts, using students' drawings to help them make predictions, and encouraging students to authenticate the accuracy or inaccuracy of the illustrations.

As we proceed through this multicultural literature text, we will discover many occasions to use illustrated picture books and to create images for nonillustrated books. The writing in many of the award-winning books provides considerable opportunities to use visual imagery to imagine settings, conflicts, and character analysis. These range from the images of a segregated South created in the writing of Christopher Paul Curtis in *The Watsons Go to Birmingham—1963* to the setting in 1847 as an Ojibwa girl experiences the seasons of the year and many traditional cultural experiences in Louise Erdrich's *The Birchbark House.* The settings and conflicts generated by Nancy Farmer in *The House of the Scorpion* are especially detailed for a setting along the Mexican-American border. The customs and settings associated with the Hindu culture of India are vividly depicted in Gloria Whelan's *Homeless Bird.* The World War II setting for two characters, one a Jewish refugee boy and one an American girl living near the refuge camp in Oswego, New York, in Miriam Bat-Ami's *Two Suns in the Sky,* provides many opportunities to visualize a historical fiction setting. The setting of the Cholistan Desert in Pakistan is developed by Suzanne Fisher Staples in *Shabanu: Daughter of the Wind.* Current news reports include numerous depictions of the places in the text. Students can compare the television reports with the settings described by Staples.

Analytical Reading of Literature Selections. The literature discussed in the various chapters in this text, especially the literature written for students in the middle- and upper-elementary grades and in middle school, frequently includes complex issues and concepts that require in-depth reading and analysis of the books. This type of analysis and understanding requires adult assistance and modeling if the students are to comprehend what they read.

In the 1970s, Mortimer J. Adler and Charles Van Doren wrote the best-selling *How to Read a Book: The Classic Guide to Intelligent Reading* (1972). This guide includes steps students can use when outlining a book and later when applying informed criticism of the book. This approach is currently being used by university students in this author's classes. It is very helpful for both university students and for teaching students in the upper-elementary grades. Each of the "Involving Children in _____" sections presented in this book includes an example of how the approach may be applied to literature from that culture. As you read and analyze each of the following stages, identify how the technique increases both analytical and critical reading abilities. Also notice how the approach increases and improves student involvement in discussion and writing about a book.

These are the stages in analytical reading identified by Adler and Van Doren:

First Stage: Rules for Finding What a Book Is About

1. Classify the book by subject matter (genre of literature and characteristics of that genre).
2. Briefly state what the book is about (summarizing).
3. List and outline the major parts of the book.
4. Define the problems the author has tried to solve.

Second Stage: Rules for Interpreting a Book's Content

5. Identify and interpret the author's key words (vocabulary).
6. Identify and discuss the author's most important sentences.

A Featured Book for Discussions with Older Readers and Young Adults

Each chapter includes an in-depth discussion of a book that is appropriate for young adult readers. Many of these books include issues, plot developments, and themes that are more appropriate for discussions with older readers. For example, the African American chapter discusses *The Astonishing Life of Octavian Nothing: Traitor to the Nation* by M. T. Anderson. This National Book Award winner is a historical novel set during the Revolutionary War. The hero is a slave who is caught up in the contradictory beliefs demonstrated by the Sons of Liberty. They fight for equality and freedom from English rule, but they own slaves, consider them property, and frequently treat them cruelly.

The featured book in the Native American chapter is Joseph Bruchac's *Code Talker*. This fictional story is based on the experiences of Ned Begay, who was one of the Navajo marines who used his native language to develop an unbreakable code that helped defeat the Japanese during World War II. The novel includes both interesting facts about the conflicts during World War II and the cultural heritage and values of the Navajo people. One of Bruchac's major themes is that it is important to respect other languages and cultures.

Red Hot Salsa: Bilingual Poems on Being Young and Latino in the United States, edited by Lori Marie Carlson, is the featured book in the Latino chapter. This collection of poems written in both English and Spanish presents experiences, feelings, and issues that face Latinos today. The collection includes poems both by well-known poets such as Gary Soto and also by Latino students who are attending New York City public schools.

The featured book in the Asian chapter is David Patneaude's *Thin Wood Walls* set in the Tule Lake Relocation Camp in California during World War II. The author develops both credibility for the time period and themes similar to many books with like settings. Book discussions may relate to how the author-developed themes such as prejudice and hatred are destructive forces and moral obligations and personal conscience are strong forces.

The Book Thief by Markus Zusak is the featured book in the Jewish chapter. The book, narrated by Death, is set in Nazi Germany. The theme, books have the power to nourish the soul, is highlighted as the protagonist collects books before Nazi burnings, comforts neighbors as she reads orally from the books during bombing raids, and reads to a Jewish man who is hidden in her basement. As students read the book, they may trace the development of the author's powerful themes and discuss why the author develops the conflicts as seen through Death's viewpoint.

The featured book for the Middle Eastern chapter is Kathy Henderson's *Lugalbanda: The Boy Who Got Caught Up in a War*. This legend was originally translated from ancient Sumerian fables believed to be between 4,000 and 5,000 years old. This book could easily accompany a study of traditional literature. The language has the cadence of an oral story, the format follows that from many traditional tales, and the themes are found in tales from other locations that focus on cultural heroes. Two themes are important for discussions and comparisons. First, a hero must keep promises. Second, peace is the ultimate goal of any cultural hero.

7. Know the author's arguments by identifying them in the text.
8. Determine which of the problems the author has solved and which have not been solved.
9. Do not begin critiquing the book until you have completed your interpretation (suspend judgment until you understand the text).
10. When you disagree with the author, do so reasonably.
11. Respect the differences between knowledge and personal opinion by giving reasons for critical judgments.

Share each of these stages with upper-elementary students or in your college classes. Why are these stages critical? What do you discover about the book by analyzing it according to each stage? Why is the approach identified as an approach for fostering and improving analytical reading? Why is analytical reading important? This approach to analytical reading is developed in each of the chapters using an award-winning book, such as the Latino literature chapter that focuses on Nancy Farmer's *The House of the Scorpion,* a Newbery Honor recipient and a National Book Award winner.

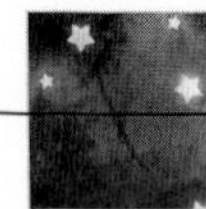

Survival

This fourth edition of *Multicultural Children's Literature: Through the Eyes of Many Children* includes a new section in each of the chapters. This section focuses on the skills, strategies, values, and beliefs that allow people in that culture to survive. When considering survival there are many types of survival. For example, women and minorities may need to overcome prejudices to survive. There may be survival following physical accidents or emotional survival as characters overcome person against self or society conflicts. Or, the survival may result as characters are stranded in nature. These characters frequently rely on survival techniques and strategies that are embedded deep within their cultures or they may rely on survival strategies that are common to all cultures.

Survival is the focus in both news articles and in books written for young adults. Newspaper articles in 2011 stressed survival following earthquakes, nuclear-power meltdowns, and tsunamis. Or, survival may be closer to home as students try to survive bullying (Parker-Pope, 2011). An article describing the trapped miners in Chile has the headline: "With Life Skills and Leadership, Trapped Miners Forge a Refuge" (Barrionuevo, 2010, p. A1). In the article, the author stresses how one of the miners used his nursing background, while others relied on leadership skills or prayed and read the Bible. The power of nature to help with personal survival is emphasized in Matt Richtel's "Outdoors and Out of Reach, Studying the Brain" (2010, p. A1). Survival may also be important for political careers as expressed in Kirk Johnson's "Message of Survival Won Denver Race for Mayor" (2011, p. A15).

The books discussed under survival in this text are among the strongest for literary quality and frequently depict the harsh realities experienced by people within the culture. Some books are historical fiction, while others are set in contemporary times with contemporary issues that must be at least partially resolved if the characters are to survive. A brief introduction to some of the books that will be discussed within the chapter reveals the range of materials.

One of the books discussed in the African American chapter is Laurie Halse Anderson's *Chains,* both a National Book Award finalist and the winner of the Scott O'Dell Award for Historical Fiction. In a story set in New York during the Revolutionary War, the character Isabel, who is a slave, discovers that while her body may be in chains, no one can chain her soul. The author develops strong survival techniques as Isabel realizes that she must have a map or plan for her life if she is to survive.

The Native American chapter includes a contemporary realistic fiction book that is a Boston Globe and a National Book Award winner for young adult literature, Sherman Alexie's *The Absolutely True Diary of a Part-Time Indian.* As the main character faces prejudice and problems when he leaves the reservation to attend an all-white school, he discovers that it is important to develop self-esteem and to search for a dream. He also realizes that his grandmother's values of forgiveness, love, and tolerance are all essential for his own survival.

The Latino chapter includes an autobiography, Francisco Jimenez's *Reaching Out.* His books have won both a Pura Belpré Honor and a Tomas Rivera Mexican American Children's Book Award. This true story emphasizes how the son of illegal immigrants worked hard for the opportunity to go to college, developed a strong work ethic, relied on his hope and faith to develop a sense of personal responsibility, and retained pride in his heritage.

The Asian chapter includes a 2010 Newbery Honor, Grace Lin's *Where the Mountain Meets the Moon*. The author's style in this book relies on folktales. Each time Minli asks a question, the author tells a folktale to answer the question. Consequently, readers gain an understanding of the cultural values and beliefs through the Chinese folktales as well as survival techniques such as a belief that nothing is impossible and the importance of curiosity, patience, wisdom, and happiness.

The Jewish chapter includes a heartwarming true story, Louise Borden's *The Journey That Saved Curious George: The True Wartime Escape of Margret and H. A. Rey*. This survival story tells how a skillful talent for writing and illustrating about a mischievous little monkey rescued the Reys by convincing the police that they were not spies but authors of books for children. The characterizations reveal the importance of spunk, fearlessness, and retaining a dream even in times of the worst peril. Would you, like the Reys, bike across Europe to escape capture in WWII?

The Middle Eastern chapter also includes a book about responses during wartime. Deborah Ellis's *Children of War: Voices of Iraqi Refugees* is a true account of the author's interviews with children. These interviews include responses to current social conditions as well as emotional and physical reactions to wartime conditions. Now survival may include the need to join a political party when told, having no choice when instructed to join the military, and being careful about trusting people. There are also more positive survival skills such as retaining one's religion, thinking about a future in which there is peace and freedom, and relying on music and stories to help in times of fear. A strong survival theme develops through these interviews as many individuals conclude that the people of Iraq must be responsible for making their own lives better.

What Would ___________ Do? is a new section added to the "Involving Children" portion of each chapter. Teachers and librarians have asked for more opportunities to involve students in current events. The "Survival" sections emphasize how the characters in many of the books use skills and strategies that are important within their cultures. This new section will ask students to use their increased knowledge of a culture to consider how an influential member of the culture might respond to a current issue or crisis. For example, one of the books discussed in the Asian chapter is Kimiko Kajikawa's *Tsunami!*. This book is based on the actions of a real person who in 1854 set his own rice harvest on fire to warn the people of a coming tsunami. A news article published in 2011 is titled "Japanese City's Desperate Cry Resonates Around the World" (Fackler, 2011). After reading articles such as this one, students may consider how the Japanese hero from 1854, Hamaguchi Gohei, might respond to the mayor of this Japanese city in 2011.

As part of an African American study, students might consider how Martin Luther King, Jr., would respond to current racial issues or how Muhammad would respond to fighting in the Middle East. As part of the Asian culture students could identify current news articles and consider what advice might be given by Confucius, Buddha, or the Dalai Lama.

International issues related to each cultural group are found in any major newspaper. For example, a search of the front page of the "International" news section for two days of the *New York Times* resulted in the following articles that could be used in such an activity: Jeffrey Gettleman's "U.N. Officials Warn of a Growing 'Panic' in Central Sudan as Violence Spreads" (p. A5), Neil MacFarquhar's "Social Media Help Keep the Door Open to Sustained Dissent Inside Saudi Arabia" (p. A5), Ethan Bronner's "Israel Warns of Using Force if New Flotilla Heads to Gaza" (p. A4) and Alexei Barrionuevo's "Plan for Hydroelectric Dam in Patagonia Outrages Chileans" (p. A4). Likewise, national news provides many issues related to African Americans, Native Americans, Latinos, Asian Americans, Jewish people, and people from the Middle East who live in America.

Encouraging students to relate themes, conflicts, and characterizations in books to current national and international news helps them apply their learning to current problems. It also leads to the development of higher cognitive skills as they learn to read, discuss, criticize, and evaluate what they read and hear.

REFERENCES

Ackerman, Arlene. Quoted in "Report Calls for 'A Writing Revolution.'" *Reading Today* 20 (July 2003): 4.

Adler, Mortimer J., and Charles Van Doren. *How to Read a Book: The Classic Guide to Intelligent Reading.* New York: Simon & Schuster, 1972.

Altick, Richard D., and John J. Fenstermaker. *The Art of Literary Research,* 4th ed. New York: Norton, 1993.

Arnold, Renea, and Nell Colburn. "Habla Ingles?" *School Library Journal* 53 (May 2007): 33.

Aronson, Marc. "Getting to Know You: There's More to History Than Facts and Dates." *School Library Journal* 53 (May 2007): 31.

Ballinger, Franchot. "A Matter of Emphasis: Teaching the 'Literature' in Native American Literature Courses." *American Indian Culture and Research Journal* 8 (1984): 1–12.

Barack, Lauren. "Islam in the Classroom." *School Library Journal* 56 (October 2010): 34–37.

Barrionuevo, Alexei. "With Life Skills and Leadership, Trapped Miners Forge a Refuge." *New York Times* (September 1, 2010): A1.

_____. "Plan for Hydroelectric Dam in Patagonia Outrages Chileans." *New York Times* (June 17, 2011): A4.

Broder, John M. "Immigration Issues Play Out in Arizona Education Fight." *New York Times* (February 3, 2006): A16.

Bronner, Ethan. "Israel Warns of Using Force if New Flotilla Heads to Gaza." *New York Times* (June 17, 2011): A4.

Carter, Forrest. *The Education of Little Tree.* Albuquerque: University of New Mexico Press, 1991, 2001.

DeNicolo, Christina P., and Maria E. Franquiz. "'Do I Have To Say It?' Critical Encounters with Multicultural Children's Literature." *Language Arts* 84 (November 2006): 157–170.

Dillon, Sam. "Test Shows Drop in Science Achievement for 12th Graders." *New York Times* (May 25, 2006): A18.

_____. "U.S. Data Show Rapid Minority Growth in School Rolls." *New York Times* (June 1, 2007): A21.

Fackler, Martin. "Japanese City's Desperate Cry Resonates Around the World." *New York Times* (April 7, 2011): A1, 10.

Gettleman, Jeffrey. "U.N. Officials Warn of a Growing 'Panic' in Central Sudan as Violence Spreads." *New York Times* (June 16, 2011): A5.

Golden, Daniel. "Aiming for Diversity, Textbooks Overshoot." *The Wall Street Journal* (August 19–20, 2006): A1.

Grice M., and C. Vaughn. "Third Graders Respond to Literature for and about Afro-Americans." *The Urban Review* 24 (1992): 149–164.

Hearne, Betsy. "Cite the Source: Reducing Cultural Chaos in Picture Books, Part One." *School Library Journal* (July 1993a): 22–26.

_____. "Respect the Source: Reducing Cultural Chaos in Picture Books, Part Two." *School Library Journal* (August 1993b): 33–37.

Herszenhorn, David M., and Susan Saulny. "As Far as Teachers and Students Are Concerned, Scores Rose on Hard Work, Period." *New York Times* (June 12, 2005): 30–31.

Hibbing, Anne Nielsen, and Joan L. Rankin-Erickson. "A Picture Is Worth a Thousand Words: Using Visual Images to Improve Comprehension for Middle School Struggling Readers." *The Reading Teacher* 56 (May 2003): 758–770.

Johnson, Kirk. "Message of Survival Won Denver Race for Mayor." *New York Times* (June 9, 2011): A15.

Johnston, Bill, Andrea Juhasz, James Marken, and Beverly Rolfs Ruiz. "The ESL Teacher as Moral Agent." *Research in the Teaching of English* 32 (May 1998): 161–181.

Lewin, Tamar. "Summer Reading Programs Gain Momentum for Students About to Enter College." *New York Times* (August 8, 2007): C13.

Lewis, Rena, and Donald Doorlag. *Teaching Special Students in the Mainstream,* 4th ed. Upper Saddle River, N.J.: Merrill/Prentice Hall, 1995.

Liaw, M. "Looking into the Mirror: Chinese Children's Responses to Chinese Children's Books." *Reading Horizons* 35 (1995): 185–198.

MacFarquhar, Neil. "Social Media Help Keep the Door Open to Sustained Dissent Inside Saudi Arabia." *New York Times* (June 16, 2011): A5.

Medina, Jennifer. "Blending of Cultures Visible in the Food Trucks." *New York Times* (April 8, 2011): A15.

National Commission on Writing in America's Schools and Colleges. "The Neglected 'R': The Need for a Writing Revolution." http://www.writingcommission.org.

Norton, Donna E. "The Development, Dissemination, and Evaluation of a Multi-Ethnic Curricular Model for Preservice Teachers, Inservice Teachers, and Elementary Children." New Orleans: International Reading Association, National Conference, April 1981.

_____. "Changing Attitudes Toward Minorities: Children's Literature Shapes Attitudes." *Review Journal of Philosophy and Social Science* 9 (1984): 97–113.

_____. "Teaching Multicultural Literature." *The Reading Teacher* 44 (1990): 28–40.

_____. *Through the Eyes of a Child: An Introduction to Children's Literature,* 7th ed. Upper Saddle River, N.J.: Merrill/Prentice Hall, 2007.

Parker-Pope, Tara. "Web of Popularity, Achieved by Bullying." *New York Times* (February 15, 2011): D1, 6.

Richtel, Matt. "Outdoors and Out of Reach, Studying the Brain." *New York Times* (August 16, 2010): A1.

Rochman, Hazel. *Against Borders: Promoting Books for a Multicultural World.* Chicago: American Library Association, 1993.

Tavernise, Sabrina. "Numbers of Children of Whites Falling Fast." *New York Times* (April 6, 2011): A14.

"Teachers' Choices: Great Books for Curriculum Use." *Reading Today* 24 (October/November 2006): 34.

Van Natta, Jr., Don, "Latinos Rise In Numbers, Not Influence." *New York Times* (April 8, 2011): A15.

Chapter 2
African American Literature

Our journey through the study of African American literature includes both the literature from Africa and the literature from the Americas. African American traditional literature, for example, cannot be understood and appreciated without also studying the literature that provides the foundations for it; namely, African folklore. In this chapter, we discuss how the literature has evolved over time as we consider changing issues related to the literature. We discuss historical and contemporary literature and analyze the contributions of outstanding authors and illustrators who create quality works and who write and illustrate with sensitivity and understanding. One of the ways to begin our journey is to consider the changing issues that have developed around the literature.

Issues Related to African American Literature

An analysis of the various studies and issues surrounding African American literature provides insights into the changing scholarship and attitudes toward the literature that have occurred over time. Studies conducted in the 1970s and 1980s focused on issues related to stereotypes and images found in African American children's literature published in the past. Dorothy May Broderick (1971), for example, analyzed U.S. children's literature published between 1827 and 1967. She reports that the personal characteristics of African American people portrayed in these books suggested that they (1) are not physically attractive, (2) are musical, (3) combine religious fervor with superstitious beliefs, (4) are required to select life goals that benefit African American people, and (5) are dependent on white people for whatever good things they could hope to acquire. Broderick concluded that in the 140-year period she studied, African American children would find little in literature to enhance pride in their heritage and that if these books were children's only contacts with African American people, white children would develop a sense of superiority. Likewise, Beryle Banfield (1985) discovered numerous negative stereotypes found in pre–Civil War literature. In 1985, author Eloise Greenfield presented a harsh evaluation of authors who still perpetuate racism and stereotypes in literature.

One of the issues frequently discussed by literature scholars is the changing attitudes toward the writings of Mark Twain (Samuel Clemens), especially *The Adventures of Huckleberry Finn*. In the 1800s, Twain was accused of going too far in advancing the cause of human equality and justice. In the 1980s and 1990s, *The Adventures of Huckleberry Finn* was attacked and frequently censored from school libraries or English reading lists for being racially inflammatory or degrading.

African American Timeline

Late 1400s	Beginning of slave trade, which causes forced movement of slaves to the Americas
Early 1800s	Beginnings of the Underground Railroad (organized in 1838), which helps many slaves to escape to freedom in the North
1850	Passage of Fugitive Slave Act, which made it illegal to help runaway slaves
1852	*Uncle Tom's Cabin* published in book form
1861–1865	Civil War years
1863	Emancipation Proclamation, which abolishes slavery in the South
1882	First known collection of African tales published for European audiences
1932	Langston Hughes's *The Dream Keeper*
1933	Newbery Honor: Hildegarde Swift's *The Railroad to Freedom: A Story of the Civil War*
1948	Newbery Honor: Harold Courlander's *The Cow-Tail Switch, and Other West African Stories*
1949	Newbery Honor: Arna Bontemps's *Story of the Negro*
1951	Newbery: Elizabeth Yates's *Amos Fortune, Free Man*
1960s	Civil rights movement
1965	Nancy Larrick's article "The All-White World of Children's Books," which emphasizes lack of books about minorities
1969	Newbery Honor: Julius Lester's *To Be a Slave*
1970	Beginning of Coretta Scott King Award, which is given to writers and illustrators who make inspiring contributions to African American literature
1970	Newbery: William H. Armstrong's *Sounder*
1970s	Several Caldecott Honors books about African and African American subjects: Illustrators Tom Feelings, Ezra Jack Keats, Gerald McDermott
1970s	Studies related to stereotypes in African American literature
1971	Caldecott: Gail E. Haley's *A Story—A Story: An African Tale*
1974	Newbery: Paula Fox's *The Slave Dancer*
1975	Newbery: Virginia Hamilton's *M. C. Higgins, the Great*
1976	Caldecott: to artists Leo and Diane Dillon for *Why Mosquitoes Buzz in People's Ears*
1976	Newbery Honor: Sharon Bell Mathis's *The Hundred Penny Box*
1977	Caldecott: to artists Leo and Diane Dillon for *Ashanti to Zulu: African Traditions*
1977	Newbery: Mildred D. Taylor's *Roll of Thunder, Hear My Cry*
1980s and 1990s	*The Adventures of Huckleberry Finn* attacked and frequently censored
1983	Caldecott: to artist Marcia Brown for *Shadow*
1985	Newbery Honor: Bruce Brooks's *The Moves Make the Man*
1987	Caldecott Honor: Ann Grifalconi's *The Village of Round and Square Houses*
1988	Caldecott Honor: John Steptoe's *Mufaro's Beautiful Daughters: An African Tale*
1992	Hans Christian Andersen Medal: Virginia Hamilton
1990s	Caldecott Honors: to artists Carole Byard (*Working Cotton*), Jerry Pinkney (*The Talking Eggs*), Brian Pinkney (*The Faithful Friend* and *Duke Ellington*), Faith Ringgold (*Tar Beach*), and Christopher Myers (*Harlem*)
1990s	Newbery Honors: Patricia McKissack (*The Dark-Thirty*), Walter Dean Myers (*Somewhere in the Darkness*), Carol Fenner (*Yolonda's Genius*), Christopher Paul Curtis (*The Watsons Go to Birmingham—1963*), and Nancy Farmer (*A Girl Named Disaster*)
2000	Newbery and Coretta Scott King Awards: Christopher Paul Curtis's *Bud, Not Buddy*
2000	Carnegie Medal: Beverley Naidoo's *The Other Side of Truth*
2006	Coretta Scott King Award: Julius Lester's *Day of Tears: A Novel in Dialogue*
2007	National Book Award: M. T. Anderson's *The Astonishing Life of Octavian Nothing: Traitor to the Nation*
2008	Scott O'Dell Award: Laurie Halse Anderson's *Chains*
2010	Coretta Scott King Award: Langston Hughes's *My People*
2011	Newbery Honor: Rita Williams-Garcia's *One Crazy Summer*

Robert Scott Kellner (1982), a recognized Twain scholar, believes, however, that a "close examination of Twain's writing reveals an element of satire in his seemingly racist language, a satire directed at the reader who would choose to agree with the stereotyped image" (p. 1D).

The debate over the writings of Mark Twain is a continuing issue. You may want to read Twain's writings and search for his viewpoint. You might consider whether it reflects a belief in the inequality of human beings or whether it suggests that people of all races share a common humanity.

Censorship of contemporary writing is still a controversial issue. For example, in 2006 a school board member in a Chicago suburb wanted to ban Tony Morrison's *Beloved* and Walter Dean Myers's *Fallen Angels* on the charges of sexual images, graphic violence, and vulgar language. Following hours of debate, the school board voted to retain the books.

Books written for younger children have also been the subject of controversy. For example, in the 1960s, Garth Williams's *The Rabbits' Wedding* was criticized because the illustrations showed the marriage of a black rabbit and a white rabbit. The criticism at the time focused on a belief that there should not be marriages between black and white people.

In contrast, the issues around Helen Bannerman's *Little Black Sambo,* published in 1899, illustrate the changing sensitivities of Americans toward certain social issues. Although the book was popular for many years, eventually many people considered the crudely drawn features of the characters and the story line to be offensive, and the book was taken off many library shelves.

The concerns about a shortage of books about African Americans, negative stereotypes found in many books, and fewer positive images, especially in textbooks, resulted in ratios for minority populations depicted in textbooks. For example, Daniel Golden (2006) reports that textbook companies aiming for diversity may be altering history. He reports that according to some guidelines, African Americans should be shown in positions of power and not be portrayed in crowded tenements. To overcome the stereotype of poverty, African village children were photographed wearing shoes and not barefoot. To balance the depiction of historical characters, one publisher profiled Bessie Coleman as the first African American woman pilot but left out a discussion of the contributions of Wilbur and Orville Wright. These are the kinds of concerns that can be answered through the use of numerous selections of children's literature that develop a balanced and authentic view of history and that show African American people in all walks of life.

Marc Aronson (2007) questions the accuracy of some of the stories written about the Underground Railroad. Consequently, some of the aspects of the experience are being questioned. For example, were there "freedom quilts" that contained coded maps that showed African American slaves the way to freedom? Or, were the freedom quilts a plot device created by a children's literature author? Aronson also identifies new studies that challenge the authenticity of the ballad *Follow the Drinking Gourd.* Was it sung by Harriet Tubman as she helped slaves escape or was it published in 1928, years after the Underground Railroad? After reporting these studies, Aronson concludes:

> I don't think the existing books about the Underground Railroad need to be pruned from library shelves nationwide. But I do think parents, librarians, and teachers need to tell young readers that exciting new studies have added to and, in some cases, radically changed our understanding of this important topic. (p. 34)

He maintains that it is up to the next generation of scholars to answer these questions. This next generation of scholars might be in today's classrooms.

As you read these books and ones like them and the various articles about the issues associated with the books, you may decide if you agree or disagree with the various conclusions.

As you evaluate picture books, consider which books might be controversial and the reasons for the controversy. Does controversy change with the times? What subjects might have caused controversy in picture books published in the 1950s, 1960s, 1970s, 1980s, 1990s, or 2000s? Are those subjects still controversial? Are any new areas of controversy developing today? This chapter discusses numerous selections of excellent African American literature that try to avoid stereotypes from the past.

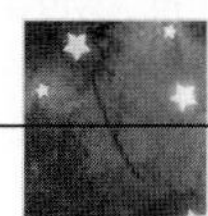

Changing Availability of Quality Literature

There have been considerable changes in the availability of and the quality of multicultural literature since Nancy Larrick's article, "The All-White World of Children's Books" (1965). This article had considerable impact because Larrick's research disclosed that there was a lack of books about minorities and that stereotypes were found in the few available books. Many changes in U.S. social life and literature have occurred since then. This is especially true when evaluating the current availability and quality of African American literature.

Currently, there are numerous high-quality books on African American literature. For example, in 2010 more than twenty-five books received starred reviews in *School Library Journal.* This is a greater annual number than for any of the other cultures discussed in this text. Quality nonfiction is also reflected in the "Best Books 2010" recommendations from the *School Library Journal.* This list includes David A. Adlers's *Frederick Douglass: A Noble Life,* Marc Aronson and Marina Budhos's *Sugar Changed the World: A Story of Magic, Spice, Slavery, Freedom, and Science,* and Charles R. Smith, Jr.'s *Black Jack: The Ballad of Jack Johnson.* Books for adult research such as *Virginia Hamilton: Speeches, Essays, & Conservations* edited by Arnold Adoff and Kacy Cook (2010) are also available.

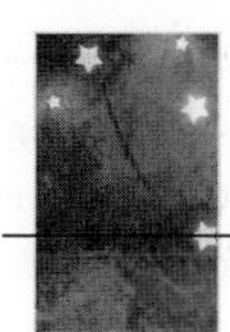

Authors Who Write and Illustrate African American Literature

In the 1920s, authors and illustrators were inspired by the Harlem Renaissance. Elizabeth Schafer (1998) identifies the works of African American authors such as Jesse Jackson and Lorenz Graham who wrote about strong African American characters in the 1940s and 1950s. By the 1960s and the 1970s, authors such as Mildred Taylor, Virginia Hamilton, Walter Dean Myers, and Rosa Guy wrote African American children's literature. In the 1990s, Schafer identifies African Americans Eleanora E. Tate, Valerie Wilson Wesley, and Jacqueline Woodson as authors whose works represent modern African American voices and values. In 2006, Jacqueline Woodson was given the Edwards Award for her lifetime contributions to literature.

A sampling of award-winning books in recent years shows the availability of quality literature. For example, the 1997 Newbery Honor Awards include Nancy Farmer's *A Girl Named Disaster*. The 1996 Newbery Honor Awards include Christopher Paul Curtis's *The Watsons Go to Birmingham—1963* and Carol Fenner's *Yolonda's Genius*. The 1993 Newbery Honor Awards include Patricia McKissack's *The Dark-Thirty: Southern Tales of the Supernatural* and Walter Dean Myers's *Somewhere in the Darkness*. The 1989 Newbery Honor Awards include Virginia Hamilton's *In the Beginning: Creation Stories from Around the World* (the text includes stories from Africa) and Walter Dean Myers's *Scorpions*. The 2000 Newbery Award book was Christopher Paul Curtis's *Bud, Not Buddy*. A 2011 Newbery Honor was Rita Williams-Garcia's *One Crazy Summer*.

A sampling of the previous few years for the Caldecott Medal and Honor Awards includes 1998 Caldecott Honors for Christopher Myers's illustrations for Walter Dean Myers's *Harlem;*

1995 Caldecott Honors for Jerry Pinkney's illustrations for Julius Lester's *John Henry;* 1993 Caldecott Honors for Carol Byard's illustrations for Sherley Anne Williams's *Working Cotton;* 1990 Caldecott Honors for Jerry Pinkney's illustrations for Robert D. San Souci's *The Talking Eggs;* and 1989 Caldecott Honors for Jerry Pinkney's illustrations for Patricia McKissack's *Mirandy and Brother Wind.* The 2011 Caldecott Honors includes Laban Carrick Hill's *Dave the Potter: Artist, Poet, Slave,* illustrated by Bryan Collier.

Since 1970, students may choose to read books that have won the Coretta Scott King Award. The award is made to one African American author and one African American illustrator for outstandingly inspirational contributions to children's literature. Recent Coretta Scott King Awards include Julius Lester's *Day of Tears: A Novel in Dialogue* and Langston Hughes's *My People.*

Biographies and informational books have made strong impacts. Newbery Award author Russell Freedman adds a powerful biography with *The Voice That Challenged a Nation: Marian Anderson and the Struggle for Equal Rights.* A 2006 Orbis Pictus Recommended Book, Tonya Bolden's *Maritcha: A Nineteenth-Century American Girl,* is a pictorial biography of an African American girl who was born free in New York during the time of slavery. Nikki Giovanni's *Rosa* was awarded the Coretta Scott King Award for an African American illustrator, Bryan Collier. Diane McWhorter, winner of the 2002 Pulitzer Prize for her adult nonfiction *Carry Me Home,* used her considerable knowledge and scholarship to write a book for younger audiences, *A Dream of Freedom: The Civil Rights Movement from 1954 to 1968.* The 2007 National Book Award Winner M. T. Anderson's *The Astonishing Life of Octavian Nothing: Traitor to the Nation* is a powerful historical novel about slavery during the Revolutionary War. Laurie Halse Anderson's powerful historical fiction novel *Chains* won the Scott O'Dell Award and is a National Book Award finalist. Rita Williams-Garcia's *One Crazy Summer* is a 2011 Newbery Honor Award and a National Book Award finalist.

Traditional Literature

The traditional literature collected from the African continent and from the southern parts of the United States form the basis for many popular books. Some of these books provide highly illustrated versions of one tale; others are anthologies in which authors retell numerous stories. In this section, we consider the history of the recording of African folklore in writing, the types of stories that might be found in specific regions, the literary characteristics of the stories, and examples of folklore collected from African and African American sources.

History of Recording of African Folklore

Africa has a long and rich history of oral literature. In 1828, the first known collection of African tales was published for European audiences. This collection, *Fables Sénégalaises Recueillies de l'Oulof,* was translated into French by le Bon Roger, the French commandant of Senegal. More collections appeared as administrators, traders, and missionaries gathered and recorded traditional African stories for various purposes. A brief review of these purposes shows how important an understanding of folklore is for understanding people. Daniel Crowley (1979) states: "Linguists collected tales as samples of language usage, teachers as a means of inculcating local languages, missionaries to study local values and beliefs, African elites in pursuit of vindication against colonialism, diffusionists in the search of distribution patterns on which to base migration theories, litterateurs and journalists looking for 'authentic' themes" (p. 11).

Roger D. Abrahams (1983) warns, however, that early collections may not have been totally accurate: "There are well over a thousand major collections, most of these made by missionaries and colonial officials around the turn of the century. They often reflect the bias of such reporters,

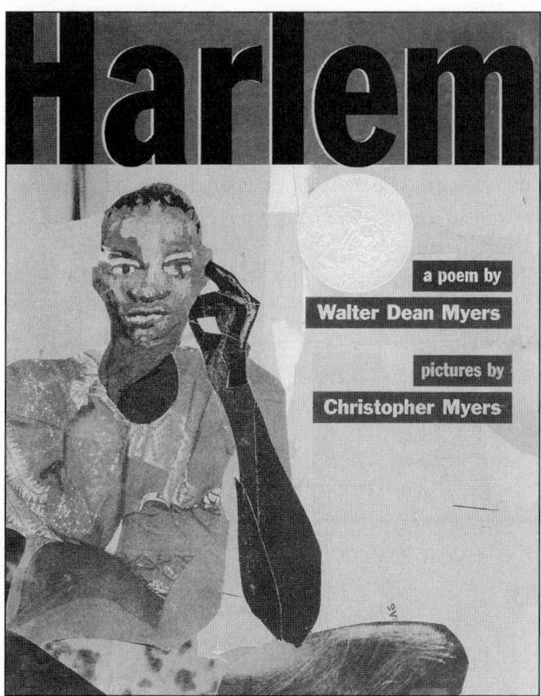

This book is a poem about growing up in Harlem.

Illustration © 1997 by Christopher Myers from *Harlem: A Poem* by Walter Dean Myers. Scholastic Inc./Scholastic Press. Reprinted by permission.

but recently, more 'objective' tellings have become available through the reports of anthropologists and folklorists" (p. xiv).

The collection of authentic folklore and artistic representations by ancient peoples is considered so important that Leo Frobenius and Douglas Fox (1983) state in the introduction to *African Genesis:* "Every fact, object, and belief which can help us to understand the growth of human culture should be recorded and indexed for use. . . . We will find that there are peoples of whom we do not know enough, and so it will be necessary to send out expeditions to find and gather the material we lack" (p. 16). There are currently expeditions whose objective is to gather the oral stories and traditions of specific groups. For example, Kioi wa Mbugua's *Inkishu: Myths and Legends of the Maasai* (1994) is a result of an expedition with a team from OXFAM International who work with the Masai people of the Narok district (the Masai live in Kenya and Tanzania).

Knowledge about the original sources or means of collecting the stories is important to readers, especially useful for students of literature. When writing for adults, many collectors of the African folklore explain how they collected their stories, reveal their original sources, discuss problems they encountered in regard to translations, and provide reasons for any editing or changes made within the stories. Unfortunately, many retellers of African folktales for children do not provide this information. As we discuss the folklore collections and the highly illustrated individual stories, we will highlight the retellers' notes or any other information that allows readers to analyze and evaluate the authenticity of the retellings.

Types of Stories from Specific Regions

Africa is a huge continent with folklore that reflects not only the geography but the religions of the various peoples who live on the continent. As you read the stories from various African countries and their people you may look for some of the following types of stories. For example, if you are reading the tales from the various countries of West Africa, you may discover Hausa tales that reveal a Muslim influence; Yoruba tales that develop a rich mythology; and Ashanti tales that tell about the great trickster, Anansi the Spider. The Hausas tell about Spider or Jackal, and the Yoruba have Ajapa the Tortoise. The tales of southern Africa include marvels or Marchen. The human or animal tricksters may be called "Little Weasel" or "Little Hare." The Hottentots tell about Jackal.

The stories from Central Africa include tales about animals, stories about hunting and adventures in the bush. These stories may tell about greedy adults and unfaithful wives. Tshikashi Tsikulu is an old woman with strange powers who lives in the forest. The tricksters of Central Africa include Hare and Tortoise. Many of the stories from East Africa reflect Muslim influence, especially the Swahili tales. Here are animal and trickster stories about Hare and Spider. There are also tales that show the influence of folktales from the Middle East and Europe.

Stories from the West Indies demonstrate the merging of European and African folklore. The story characters include trickster characters that are similar to the African Hare and the African Anansi. Stories collected from the United States show the interaction of the Plantation South and African culture. There are many animal stories and trickster tales. Sometimes Spider,

ISSUE Selecting and Evaluating African American Literature

In her article "Writing for Children—A Joy and a Responsibility," African American author Eloise Greenfield (1985) provides an excellent introduction to the selection and evaluation of African American literature. Greenfield emphasizes the need for both literary merit and cultural authenticity when she states:

> The books that reach children should: authentically depict and interpret their lives and their history; build self-respect and encourage the development of positive values; make children aware of their strength and leave them with a sense of hope and direction; teach them the skills necessary for the maintenance of health and for economic survival; broaden their knowledge of the world, past and present, and offer some insight into the future. These books will not be pap—the total range of human problems, struggles and accomplishments can be told in this context with no sacrifice of literary merit. (p. 21)

Authors who make powerful statements communicate their ideas through the artistic and skillful use of language. Accuracy and authenticity are emphasized as important selection criteria by the authors of *Multicultural Literature for Children and Young Adults* (Kruse, Horning, and Schliesman, 1997), a volume published by the Cooperative Children's Book Center of the University of Wisconsin. They state:

> We carefully considered books that were written or illustrated by people of color; we also looked carefully at books written or illustrated by individuals whose racial backgrounds are outside those of the experiences depicted in their books. We paid careful attention to issues of accuracy and authenticity, often seeking the opinions of content specialists when we were unsure about a certain historical or cultural matter, as well as listening to colleagues who pointed out significant features or cultural values that we, as outsiders, would otherwise have missed. (p. 2)

Johnson and Smith (1993) emphasize the importance of considering both the literary quality and the values and perspectives conveyed by the books. They believe questions of literary quality should be "examined with a particular focus on the importance of authenticity in multicultural fiction" (p. 47). Consequently, when selecting books, they ask questions such as these: Does the book succeed in arousing my emotions? Is the book well written? Is the book meaningful? and Have we examined the impact of stereotypes, if any, on the readers?

In addition to these questions concerning literary quality and personal responses, you may wish to consider the following criteria when evaluating the illustrations in picture books:

1. Are the illustrations authentic for both the time period and the geographical locations? Are the settings authentic so readers can recognize the settings as rural, suburban, or urban?
2. Do the characters look natural?
3. Are the characters shown as individual people with characteristics in their own right?
4. Do the illustrations perpetuate stereotypes?
5. Do the illustrations across the books in a collection help the reader visualize the variety of socioeconomic backgrounds, educational levels, and occupations that are possible for African American characters?

The following provide additional evaluative criteria you may consider when evaluating the text in African American literature:

1. If dialect is used, does the dialect have a legitimate purpose and does it ring true?
2. Are social issues and problems depicted frankly, accurately, and without oversimplification?
3. Are the factual and historical details accurate? Does the book appear to be authentic for the culture?
4. Does the author accurately describe any contemporary settings and conflicts?
5. Does the author avoid offensive vocabulary?
6. Does the book reflect an awareness of the changing status of females within African American culture?

These evaluative criteria will be useful through the study of all of the genres of literature: traditional literature, historical fiction and nonfiction, contemporary realistic fiction, biography and autobiography, and poetry.

Tortoise, or Hare merges into the cunning Brer Rabbit. There are also human trickster characters like the slave John who outwits Old Massa. Another character is John Henry, who characterizes the strength and beliefs of the African people. Many stories from the U.S. South reveal the slaves' passion to be free; consequently, there are stories that tell about "flying" to freedom.

Many of the African tales tell how the natural or tribal worlds began. These tales are explanatory tales that include both myths and *pourquoi* ("why") tales. Such tales reflect a deep interest in both the natural and supernatural. They tell how life began, how various tribes came to be, and how animals acquired certain characteristics. Most of the stories reveal various values, beliefs, and cultural patterns. Some of the stories focus on societal problems and suggest solutions. Dilemma tales are very popular for helping listeners reach solutions that reflect both acceptable moral and social behaviors.

Literary Characteristics of the Folklore

The art of storytelling, the role of the storyteller, and the participation of the audience are very important in African folklore and influence the literary characteristics of the tales. The original traditional settings in which the stories were told involved singing, acting, using a variety of voices, and audience participation in a way in which the audience and the speaker were intimately intertwined.

In forewords and authors' notes, many retellers of African folklore emphasize the importance of singing, acting, and audience participation as part of the stories that they are retelling. For example, Michael Rosen (1992) states that in Uganda "myths were told in song and dance by the elders as the tribe gathered around a fire" (p. 47). In the foreword of Geraldine Elliott's *The Long Grass Whispers* (1939), we learn that "at night the people gather round the flickering fire, within the dark circle of the hut, to hear the grandmother, as she leans against the hut pole, telling how the animals live and talk. Her imagination and her personality illuminate the ancient stories with her own turns and phrases. The story is the same, but its telling is ever changing" (p. vii).

In *Tales from the Story Hat,* Verna Aardema (1960) states that in addition to the old women of the tribes who have told stories to children, "there have been professional storytellers who have gone from place to place telling their tales and gathering new ones. They were the first historians and the first literary members of the tribe, and it was they who preserved and handed down the traditions" (p. 7).

Many of the African folktales include formulaic openings and closings. According to Jack Berry (1961), when a group in West Africa prepares for storytelling each storyteller begins a tale with an opening formula that serves to announce a tale is about to be told, and the audience follows with a response. Such a story opener and audience response is presented by Philip Noss (1972), who relates the following common story starter from *Cameroon:*

> Storyteller: Listen to a tale! Listen to a tale!
> Audience: A tale for fun, for fun. Your throat is a gong, your body a locust; bring it here for me to roast!
> Storyteller: Children, listen to a tale, a tale for fun, for fun.

Rute Larungu's *Myths and Legends from Ghana* (1992) includes examples of both story openings and closing formulas. Nelson Mandela (2002) identifies the words with which Ashanti storytellers begin their stories: "We do not really mean, we do not really mean, that what we are going to say is true" (p. 7).

The closing of the story includes:

> This is my story, which I have told you, if it be sweet, or if it be not sweet take some with you and let some come back to me. (p. 61)

Just as African folklore may include specific types of openings and endings, the tales include other interesting linguistic styles. As might be expected from the oral tradition of the tales, the tales have a storytelling style that can be characterized as a lively mixture of mimicking dialogue, body action, audience participation, and rhythm. Storytellers mimic the sounds of animals, change their voices to characterize both animal and human characters, imitate dialogue between characters, and encourage their listeners to interact with the story. Consequently, the most effective stories have strong oral language patterns.

By studying the various stories in Aardema's *Misoso: Once upon a Time Tales from Africa,* readers can discover many of the linguistic styles that are characteristic of the folklore. Many of the stories use repetitive words that are used to imitate sounds in nature. For example, the antelope coughs "kaa, kaa, kaa," the animals laugh "gug, gug, gug," the leopard binds the fly "kpong, kpong, kpong," and the banana hurries off "tuk-pik, tuk-pik, tuk-pik." Repetitive refrains are also found in many of the tales. These repetitive and sometimes cumulative refrains give the listeners ample opportunities to participate in the storytelling experience.

Notice how Ashley Bryan's introduction to "Ma Sheep Thunder and Son Ram Lightning," found in his retelling of Nigerian tales in *The Story of Lightning and Thunder,* reflects the oral storytelling style and a rich language tradition: "A long time ago, I mean a long, long time ago, if you wanted to pat Lightning or chat with Thunder, you could do it. Uh-huh, you could."

By reading or listening to the language in the folklore, students of children's literature discover one of the important values reflected in the folklore: language and oral storytelling are important. As you read various examples of the folklore, select some of your favorite tales for oral retellings and practice them so the stories sound authentic.

Examples of African Folklore

The examples in this section include folktales, legends, and myths. As we discuss the folklore, we consider the motifs found in the tales, the values and beliefs reflected in the tales, and the literary characteristics of the tales. In addition, we consider the importance of variant and incorporated tales that reflect the impact of other cultures on the content of the tales.

Folktales The introduction to Kioi wa Mbugua's *Inkishu: Myths and Legends of the Maasai* (1994) emphasizes the importance of folktales in the cultural heritage of the people: "Traditionally, Maasai children are taught community customs, social values and history through stories. Like the fairy tales of Europe, the characters of giants, greedy animals and fierce warriors in Maasai literature serve to warn, prepare, and amuse children for their adult life to come" (Foreword).

African folktales frequently explore societal problems and provide possible solutions to these problems. The stories may include a moral or a human truth that is taught through the story. The moral and social values reflected in the tales are emphasized by Mabel H. Ross and Barbara K. Walker (1979): "The measure of a narrator's skill is indicated in the degree to which he can leave with the listener a valid key to acceptable moral and social behavior, a guide to the making of a responsible choice, within the framework of his own culture" (p. 236). For example, Verna Aardema's *Bringing the Rain to Kapiti Plain: A Nandi Tale* shows that individuals have obligations for the betterment of the people, the environment, and the animals that provide their welfare. Ashley Bryan's "The Husband Who Counted the Spoonfuls," found in *Beat the Story-Drum, Pum-Pum,* develops the theme of stability in marital relationships.

Ann Grifalconi's *The Village of Round and Square Houses* reveals how a social custom began. In this case, a volcanic eruption in the distant past leaves only two houses within the village: one round and one square. To meet the needs of the village, the women and children move into the round house and the men stay in the square house. According to the tale, the custom continues today because people "live together peacefully here—Because each one has a place to be apart, and a time to be together" (unnumbered).

As you read collections of African folktales for children, notice how most of the values and beliefs identified by Ross and Walker in their adult collection are also found in folktales published for children: the importance of maintaining friendship, a need for family loyalty, the desirability of genuine hospitality, a strict code for ownership and borrowing, gratitude for help rendered, high risk in excessive pride, care for the feelings of those in authority, respect for individuality, appropriate awe of the supernatural, and the use of wit and trickery in the face of unequal relationships.

One of the ways that the folktales show the importance of the values and beliefs is through reward and punishment. Individuals who adhere to the values and beliefs of the culture are frequently rewarded, whereas individuals who reject the values and beliefs are usually punished.

An Ethiopian woman learns a strong lesson in how to treat others in Nancy Raines Day's *The Lion's Whiskers: An Ethiopian Folktale*. When a stepmother is met by the rejection of her stepson, she seeks advice from the medicine man. When he tells her that the magic potion she desires requires three whiskers from a lion, she gradually tames the lion and eventually acquires the whiskers. Now the medicine man tells her she does not need the magic potion because she should "Approach your stepson as you did the lion, and you will win his love." The advice succeeds and there is a happy ending for a stepmother story.

Nelson Mandela (2002) identifies the following characters and symbols found in African folktales: a cunning animal, a trickster, a lion as ruler, a snake that creates fear, and magic spells.

African folktales are filled with stories of trickster characters. In many of these stories, wit and trickery are acceptable responses when the relationships among animals or people are unequal. For example, Verna Aardema's *Who's in Rabbit's House?* is a humorous Masai tale about tricky animals. This tale, written in play form and performed by villagers for the townsfolk, explains how Caterpillar, who is smaller, slower, and weaker than any of the other animals (including Rabbit, Jackal, Leopard, Elephant, and Rhinoceros), must use wit and trickery to correct the imbalance. Repetition of words is part of the vivid descriptive language. The descriptions and dialogues among the animals suggest the richness of the African language. The jackal trots off "kpata, kpata," the leopard jumps "pa, pa, pa," and the frog laughs "dgung, dgung, dgung."

A small rabbit also wins the prize when larger animals fail in John Kilaka's *The Amazing Tree*. In this tale from Tanzania, the animals must learn the name of the magic tree so they can eat the fruit during a time of drought. The animals seek advice from the wise tortoise, but it is the tiny rabbit who learns the name of the tree and saves the people during the drought. Stories of a wily tortoise and an arrogant girl who is humbled are found in Ifeoma Onyefulu's *The Girl Who Married a Ghost and Other Tales from Nigeria*. The familiar tale of a lion who captures a rodent, releases him, and later is rewarded for his kindness is found in Jerry Pinkney's *The Lion & the Mouse*. Pinkney's illustrations place the tale on the African Serengeti.

Wit and trickery are also appropriate actions in Gerald McDermott's retelling of *Zomo the Rabbit: A Trickster Tale from West Africa*. McDermott describes Zomo as not big or strong, but very clever. In this tale, Zomo approaches Sky God because he wants more than cleverness—he wants wisdom. To acquire wisdom, however, he must earn it by bringing Sky God three items: the scales of Big Fish, the milk of Wild Cow, and the tooth of Leopard. Zomo is able to acquire these items through his wit and trickery. Consequently, Sky God tells him that courage, good sense, and caution are worth having. Unfortunately, the Rabbit lacks caution. This is an example of a folktale in which the advice given by Sky God reflects the beliefs and values of the people. It is also an example of a tale in which a ruler gives an impossible request; consequently, wit and trickery are the only means for succeeding. The Sky God and Anansi the Spider are together in Aardema's trickster tale *Anansi Does the Impossible: An Ashanti Tale*.

Another type of tale that is very common in African folklore is the *pourquoi* or "why" tale. *Pourquoi* tales answer a question or explain why animals, plants, or humans have certain characteristics. For example, two tales in Ashley Bryan's *Beat the Story-Drum, Pum-Pum* explain animal characteristics. "How Animals Got Their Tails" reveals not only how animals received their individual tails but also why there is animosity between rabbits and foxes. "Why Bush

Cow and Elephant Are Bad Friends" reveals why animals fight in the bush. Verna Aardema's *Why Mosquitoes Buzz in People's Ears* explains why mosquitoes are noisy. The conclusion of *pourquoi* stories frequently depicts both a why explanation and a moral.

In addition to animal characteristics, African *pourquoi* tales may explain natural phenomena or the origin of human characteristics. Aaron Shepard's *Master Man: A Tall Tale of Nigeria* reveals both why there is thunder in the sky and the foolish consequences that result from bragging: "Two fools fighting forever to see which one is Master Man." David Wisniewski's collage illustrations add power to this tale. In addition, a useful "Author's Note" provides information about the Hausa people and identifies the sources used for retelling.

Symbolism is important in both the text and illustrations in many African folktales. Baba Wague Diakite provides interpretations for the symbolism found in the illustrations in *The Magic Gourd,* a tale from the Bamana people of Mali, West Africa. Diakite lists page-by-page interpretations, such as "The Sickle Blade" and "Calabash Flower," which signify hard work and happy family, and the "Crooked Road Walker," which signifies dishonest actions.

As you read the folktales from Africa, develop your own list of important themes and values found in the tales.

Legends By reading legends, we discover the heroes of a culture and the characteristics that are considered important in leaders. Legends, although they may be exaggerated, are usually written about people who really lived in the historic past. David Wisniewski's *Sundiata: Lion King of Mali* is such a legend, telling the story of a ruler who lived in the late 1200s. The tale begins in this fashion: "Listen to me, children of the Bright Country, and hear the great deeds of ages past. The words I speak are those of my father and his father before him, pure and full of truth" (p. 1, unnumbered). Sundiata's courage and leadership are especially valued in this tale. In addition, when he is returned to the throne, he tells his people that from that time on, no one shall interfere with another's destiny.

In endnotes, Wisniewski (1992) provides information about the source of this tale. Wisniewski presents enough source information that a reader could obtain the original source and compare the two versions.

Myths Virginia Hamilton's *In the Beginning: Creation Stories from Around the World* includes several myths from Africa. In each of the myths, Hamilton provides information on places the myths were told and gives interpretations that improve readers' understanding. For example, in "Man Copies God: Nyambi the Creator" Hamilton informs readers that the myth is from the Lozi people of Zambia. She classifies the myth as a Divine Myth because in this type of myth, god is simply there and creates earth and all that is human. This tale is also an explanatory story that reveals such concerns as why god is separated from man. Spider plays an important role in the myth as it is through his web, or thread to the sky, that the god Nyambi is able to live away from humans and find peace in the sky.

The importance of Spider as part of mythology is also developed by Hamilton in "Spider Ananse Finds Something: Wulbari the Creator." In this tale, Spider Ananse is the captain of God Wulbari's court. He is also the boastful trickster character of folktale fame. The tale is an explanatory tale as it reveals how sun, moon, and darkness came to the earth and explains how blindness came to some humans.

Virginia Hamilton's *In the Beginning: Creation Stories from Around the World* includes a bibliography of mythology books. Several of these sources are from African mythology. For example, Hamilton recommends sources such as D. Arnott's *African Myths and Legends Retold* (1962), Ulli Beier's *The Origin of Life and Death: African Creation Myths* (1966), Susan Feldman's *African Myths and Tales* (1963), Geoffrey Parrinder's *African Mythology: Library of the World's Myths and Legends* (1986), and Paul Radin's *African Folktales* (1952).

Neil Philip's *Mythology of the World* includes a section on African mythology. According to the creation myth from the ancient west African kingdom of Dahomey, the world and the first man and woman were created by the god Mawu-Lisa. In this myth, Mawu-Lisa was carried everywhere by another deity, Aido-Hwedo, the rainbow serpent. Consequently, the earth curves because it is shaped by the movement of the serpent whose coils now support the world. This is also a "why" myth. When the earth rubs against the serpent, the deity shifts and earthquakes result.

Many more examples of African folklore could be added to this discussion. In summary, we have discovered that there are both commonalities and differences among folktales from different regions of Africa. The folktales are characterized by an oral storytelling style that encourages interactions with the audience. Stylistic elements in the folktales include story openings and story closings, as well as repetitive language. Many of the folktales, legends, and myths develop strong moral values and suggest the cultural values of the people.

African American Folklore

African American folklore includes many similarities to the folklore collected from Africa. For example, there are similar storytelling styles, values and beliefs, characters, and motifs. There are also differences, however, as the stories take on the characteristics of the new settings and situations. Virginia Hamilton (1985) highlights the relationships between the African folklore and the African American experience: "Out of the contacts the plantation slaves made in their new world, combined with memories and habits from the old world of Africa, came a body of folk expression about the slaves and their experiences. The slaves created tales in which various animals . . . took on characteristics of the people found in the new environment of the plantation" (p. x).

For example, the favorite Brer Rabbit was small and apparently helpless when compared with the more powerful bear and fox. However, he was smart, tricky, and clever, and usually won out over larger and stronger animals. The slaves, who identified with the rabbit, told many tales about his exploits.

Hamilton's collection of tales *The People Could Fly: American Black Folktales,* is divided into four parts: (1) animal tales, (2) extravagant and fanciful experiences, (3) supernatural tales, and (4) slave tales of freedom. The collection provides sources for listening, discussing, and comparing. For example, readers can compare the folklore elements, plot, and themes in Hamilton's "The Beautiful Girl of the Moon Tower," a folktale from the Cape Verde Islands, and elements and motifs found in European folktales.

Hamilton's *When Birds Could Talk and Bats Could Sing: The Adventures of Brush Sparrow, Sis Wren, and Their Friends* is a collection of retellings of eight folktales from the southern United States. The tales are written in the form of fables, with each fable ending with a moral. Like the African folktales, these tales are filled with rhyming and singing. Barry Moser's watercolors provide vivid visual characterizations of the animals. In *Her Stories: African American Folktales, Fairy Tales, and True Tales,* Hamilton retells nineteen tales about African American females. As in her other books, Hamilton provides notes on the stories that tell readers where the stories came from, how they traveled to new locations, and how they changed. The acrylic illustrations painted by Leo and Diane Dillon enhance the emotional impact of the tales.

The most famous collection of African American folktales originating in the southern United States are the stories originally collected and retold by Joel Chandler Harris's "Uncle Remus" in the late nineteenth century. Again, that "monstrous clever beast," Brer Rabbit, always survives by using his cunning against stronger enemies. William J. Faulkner's *The Days When the Animals Talked* (1977) presents background information on African American folktales about animals. Faulkner tells how the tales were created and what their significance is in American history.

Two authors, Van Dyke Parks and Julius Lester, have adapted highly acclaimed versions of the Uncle Remus stories originally written down by Joel Chandler Harris. Parks's text and Barry Moser's illustrations for *Jump! The Adventures of Brer Rabbit* and *Jump Again! More Adventures of Brer Rabbit* combine to provide a satisfying reading and visual experience. It is interesting to analyze the animal characters, to consider the social impact of slavery as depicted in the stories, to identify values that are similar to those found in African tales, to compare similar tales found in other cultures or various versions of the Uncle Remus stories, and to consider the impact of the authors' style.

For example, Brer Rabbit is considered a character who can use his head, outdo and outwit all other creatures, and rely on trickery if necessary. In this role, Brer Rabbit uses trickery if he is in conflict with bigger and more powerful characters, but Brer Rabbit also represents what happens when folks are full of conceit and pride. They "are going to get it taken out of them. Brer, Rabbit did get caught up with once, and it cooled him right off" (*Jump!*, p. 19). Notice that both of these values are also found in African folklore. In addition, the tales reflect changes caused by the new environment, where the storytellers are influenced by slavery and European colonization and the need to protect their families and the tendency to develop friendships that are tempered with distrust.

Symbolism, onomatopoeia, and personification are essential aspects of Parks's storytelling style. For example, Parks uses symbolic meaning to contrast the length of night and day in *Jump!*: "When the nights were long and days were short, with plenty of wood on the fire and sweet potatoes in the embers, Brer Rabbit could outdo all the other creatures" (p. 3). Onomatopoeia is used to imitate sounds. Brer Rabbit relies on his "lippity-clip and his blickety-blick" (p. 3). Personification is found in descriptions of nature: "Way back yonder when the moon was lots bigger than he is now" (p. 3).

By analyzing the various Brer Rabbit stories, you may make comparisons within and across cultures. For example, you might compare the stories retold in Parks's version with stories retold in Lester's *The Tales of Uncle Remus: The Adventures of Brer Rabbit,* and stories in earlier versions retold by Joel Chandler Harris. Make cross-cultural comparisons by analyzing "Brer Rabbit Finds His Match" (*Jump!*) and the Aesop fable "The Tortoise and the Hare."

Stories such as these Brer Rabbit tales are filled with symbolism and suggested meanings. For example, in *The Adventures of High John the Conqueror,* Steve Sanfield states that when the slaves told and heard the stories, they understood "the only way to defeat all that power and brute force was to be just a little bit more clever" (p. 5). Alice McGill's retelling of *Way Up and Over Everything* symbolizes the slave's desire for freedom.

Clever female animal characters outsmart males in Robert D. San Souci's *Sister Tricksters: Rollicking Tales of Clever Females*. In one tale, Miz Goose convinces Mistah Bear that a pile of pumpkins are really eggs and that if he sits on them they will hatch and he will have a family. Searching for fools who are greater than the ones left behind forms the plot for Zora Neal Hurston's *The Six Fools*. The oil paintings give the story a folk-art style set in the 1920s.

There are distinct oral storytelling styles in African American folktales. Current retellers of these tales frequently mention the influence of storytellers in their own youth. For example, Patricia McKissack introduces *Flossie and the Fox* by telling readers: "Here is a story from my youth, retold in the same rich and colorful language that was my grandfather's. He began all his yarns with questions. 'Did I ever tell you 'bout the time lil' Flossie Finley come out the Piney Woods heeling a fox?' I'd snuggle up beside him in the big porch swing, then he'd begin his tale" (author's note, unnumbered). As you read various African American tales, look for, compare, and analyze the influence of the storyteller's style in the selections.

Robert D. San Souci's *The Talking Eggs* is adapted from a Creole folktale collected in Louisiana. The tale shows that kindness is a respected value, and greed is not rewarded. William H. Hooks's *The Ballad of Belle Dorcas* is a tale set in the tidewater section of the Carolinas during the time of slavery. The protagonists are a freeborn woman and a slave who fall in love, but they are threatened with separation when the master wishes to sell the slave. In addition to showing the consequences of social injustice, the tale reveals the power of love and belief in the magical ability of the spells created by conjurers. San Souci's *Sukey and the Mermaid,* collected from the Sea Islands off South Carolina's coast, is a melding of the story elements from West Africa and the Caribbean.

San Souci's *The Hired Hand* is a folktale in which the following values and beliefs are clearly indicated: the value of hard work and the consequences of laziness; the need to show respect for one's fellow human; the consequences of greed, dishonesty, and wastefulness; the power of forgiveness. Notice how the son's plea for forgiveness states the story's primary themes: "Don't be lazy an' greedy an' wood-headed. 'Specially don' act high-handed and biggity with no one, 'cause if I didn't act that way to a man who's standin' in this here crowd, I'd be back at the saw-mill, 'stead of headin' to a jail cell" (unnumbered).

John Henry, a real person and the great hero of African American folklore, is characterized as a "steel-drivin' man." Julius Lester's *John Henry* begins with the child's unusual birth when "[t]he bears and panthers and moose and deer and rabbits and squirrels and even a unicorn came out of the woods to see him. And instead of the sun tending to his business and going to bed, it was peeping out from behind the moon's skirts trying to get a glimpse of the new baby" (p. 2, unnumbered). The major focus of the text and illustrations is on John Henry's contest with the steam drill. Lester's language is filled with personification and poetic similes. For example, the sun yawns, washes its face, flosses and brushes its teeth, and hurries over the horizon; the wind is out of breath trying to keep up with John Henry. Jerry Pinkney's illustrations enhance the impact of the legendary tall tale. The introduction to the tale provides background information on the legend and lists the sources Lester used in his retelling.

Stories of another folk hero are retold by Steve Sanfield in *The Adventures of High John the Conqueror*. High John is similar to Brer Rabbit because he uses cleverness to outwit his more powerful adversary, the Old Master. The themes in these stories show that people's spirit cannot be taken away even if they are living in the worst conditions. Sanfield's text includes factual information to help readers understand and interpret the tales.

Spirituals provide another source for understanding the values in the African American folktales. Spirituals provide the text to accompany Ashley Bryan's colorful illustrations in John Langstaff's *What a Morning! The Christmas Story in Black Spirituals*. The format of the book includes a colorful illustration and appropriate biblical text followed by the words and music for the accompanying spiritual.

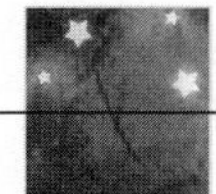

Historical Nonfiction and Fiction

Most of the historical literature, which includes nonfiction informational books, autobiographies and biographies, and historical fiction, focuses on a harsh time in U.S. history during which African Americans experienced slavery or discrimination. The philosophies, values, and beliefs depicted in the folklore also appear in the historical literature. Here, however, pain and the consequences of prejudice frequently overshadow other concerns.

Authors who write about this period in the early centuries of American history emphasize a time when white slave traders brought hundreds of thousands of black Africans to this continent in chains and sold them on auction blocks as field workers, house servants, and skilled craftspeople.

Many authors of historical literature focus their attention on conflicts. Authors who produce realistic biographies and create credible plots in historical fiction consider not only the historical events but also the conflicting social attitudes of the times. The themes developed in historical literature reflect a need for personal freedom, ponder the right of one person to own another, and consider the tragedies of both war and slavery. As we discuss the informational books, the biographies, and the historical fiction associated with this time period, we will also

Authenticating an Example of African Folklore

If enough information is provided, both the text and pictures of highly illustrated versions of folktales may be authenticated. For example, John Steptoe provides source notes that identify the original source, the culture, and the geographical location for *Mufaro's Beautiful Daughters: An African Tale.* He states:

> *Mufaro's Beautiful Daughters* was inspired by a story collected by G. M. Theal and published in 1895 in his book *Kaffir Folktales.* The tale was collected from people living near the Zimbabwe ruins, a site that archaeologists now consider to have been a magnificent trade city built and occupied by indigenous Africans. Details in the illustrations for *Mufaro's Beautiful Daughters* are based on the architecture of the ruins and on the flora and fauna of the Zimbabwe region. (unnumbered back cover)

In addition, the author provides information about the names of the characters and scholars who provided assistance:

> The names of the characters are from the Shona language: Mufaro (moo-FAR-oh) means "happy man"; Nyasha (nee-AH-sha) means "mercy"; Manyara (mahn-YAR-ah) means "ashamed"; and Nyoka (nee-YO-kah) means "snake." The author wishes to thank Niamani Mutima and Ona Kwanele, of the Afro-American Institute, and Jill Penfold, of the Zimbabwe Mission, for their helpful assistance in the research of this book. (unnumbered dedication page)

Although Steptoe does not state whether or not he changed the text in his adaptation, he does provide enough information for literature students to authenticate the text by comparing it with the original source and to authenticate the illustrations by searching for sources that describe or illustrate the place and the time in which the story is set. This authentication task was completed by my student Diana Vrooman (1993).

A search for Theal's original source in *Kaffir Folklore* (1886/1970) provides both important background information for understanding the values, the customs, and the beliefs of the people, as well as the text of the original source, "The Story of Five Heads." Theal provides the following background information that may also be used to authenticate Steptoe's version and to identify if any important differences are found in values, customs, and beliefs between the original story and Steptoe's adaptation. This background information may also be used to help authenticate the illustrations.

Theal states that each tribe was presided over by a chief, descendants of the ruling house had aristocratic rank, chiefs might have many wives, leopard skins were reserved for chiefs, people lived in villages in hemispherical huts thatched with reeds or grass, people were skilled potters, people lived in an agricultural society in which horned cattle and millet were important, men cared for cattle and women cultivated the ground, a taboo stated that women were not permitted to touch the milksack, people believed that spirits can and do influence their affairs, snakes were highly respected, fathers usually arranged marriages, and bridal processions were formed to escort brides to their new homes.

Comparisons between Theal's "The Story of Five Heads" and Steptoe's *Mufaro's Beautiful Daughters* illustrate both differences and similarities. One of the most obvious differences is in the names of the girls. Theal's Mpunzikazi is changed to Steptoe's Manyara; Theal's Mpunzanyana is changed to Nyasha. Steptoe expands the plot of the story to include Nyasha's tender interactions with the small snake. This addition allows Steptoe to develop the caring, loving nature of Nyasha, as well as show a kinder, gentler personality for the transformed king.

When characterizations are compared, however, both stories suggest it is the arrogant, impatient sister who disregards customs and beliefs who is eventually punished (death in Theal, servitude in Steptoe). In contrast, it is the sister who honors the ways of her people and abides by tradition who is rewarded. Both Mpunzikazi and Manyara show disrespect for their elders and for the supernatural.

Theal's original version places more emphasis on traditions and taboos. The wedding party seems more important in Theal because the girl who enters the village of the chief without her family is chastised for coming alone. The girl in Theal's version touches a milksack, which goes against women's roles in the society, and she is dishonored because she cannot grind millet properly. Grinding millet is also one of the major roles of women in the culture.

Steptoe's adaptation places more emphasis on the personal characteristics of the protagonist and antagonist. Steptoe expands the characterizations of the two sisters by emphasizing the consequences of such undesirable characteristics as greed and such desirable characteristics as kindness and generosity. In both stories, it is despised traits found in the two female characters that justify their downfalls. These downfalls are also different. Although both characters are either punished or rewarded, the punishment in Theal's version is harsher. The monstrous snake kills the girl; in Steptoe's version she becomes the servant to her sister, the Queen.

These changes in personal characteristics and plot create different moods for the two folktales. Theal's harsher consequences produce a stronger feeling for the importance of cultural traditions and taboos. Steptoe's gentler version with the kind snake and the transformation of this small snake into the king, creates a "happier-ever-after" mood that is similar to a Cinderella story. Steptoe is writing for American audiences who are accustomed to magical folktales and who might not understand the harsher realities of the original version.

The source notes in Steptoe's *Mufaro's Beautiful Daughters* provide enough information to evaluate the authenticity of the illustrations. Because Steptoe identifies Zimbabwe as the location of the folktale, many sources may be used to authenticate the illustrations. It is interesting to note that photographs taken of architectural sites in this region show almost identical characteristics to those found in the illustrations drawn by Steptoe. Ruins of an actual city in the region, Great Zimbabwe, are shown in photographs accompanying a *National Geographic* article titled "Rhodesia, A House Divided" by Allan C. Fisher (1975). The clay pots illustrated by Steptoe on page 2 (unnumbered) are similar to those shown in photographs in G. C. Thompson's *The Zimbabwe Culture: Ruins and Reactions* (1971). The huts illustrated on page 20 (unnumbered) are similar to the illustrations of mud huts with thatched roofs shown in Patricia Barnes-Svarney's *Places and People of the World: Zimbabwe* (1989). A chevron pattern on the great wall illustrated by Steptoe on page 20 is similar to one found in a photograph in Wilfrid Mallows's *The Mystery of the Great Zimbabwe* (1984). The soapstone birds illustrated by Steptoe on the throne of the king on page 22 (unnumbered) are shown in photographs in Patricia Cheney's *The Land and People of Zimbabwe* (1990). The conical tower shown by Steptoe on page 27 (unnumbered) is shown in a photograph in Richard Worth's *Robert Mugabe of Zimbabwe* (1990) and in a *National Geographic* article "After Rhodesia, A Nation Named Zimbabwe" (1981).

Many additional examples supporting the authenticity of the illustrations are available. Although Steptoe's text has been changed from the original, his illustrations are extremely authentic.

discover many of the same values and beliefs identified in the African and African American folklore. As you read historical literature, consider both the literary merit of the works and the authenticity of their content.

Informational Books That Develop Historical Perspectives

Some authors who chronicle the African American experience write nonfiction informational books about the forced passage of Africans from Africa to America or focus attention on the experiences of slaves. Informational books such as Milton Meltzer's *The Black Americans: A History in Their Own Words, 1619–1983* help students understand this time period. It includes firsthand accounts from African Americans of the past. This is also an excellent book to read before reading historical fiction such as Paula Fox's *The Slave Dancer*. The excerpt from Meltzer's text, which is titled "I Saw a Slave Ship," describes a slave ship. As you read historical fiction by authors such as Fox, notice how closely descriptions in them match nonfiction descriptions like this one from Meltzer's text. "The shrieks of the women, and the groans of the dying, rendered the whole a scene of horror almost inconceivable" (p. 8).

Marc Aronson and Marina Budhos's *Sugar Changed the World: A Story of Magic, Spice, Slavery, Freedom, and Science* presents an interesting perspective on slavery. The authors show how the harvesting demands for the cultivation and production of sugarcane led to the need for many workers and brought about the brutal treatment of slaves. The authors cover a 200-year period that includes both the slave trade and abolition. They discuss the impact of revolutions as well as the Louisiana Purchase. Maps and photographs add to the authenticity of the text. The chapter "How We Researched and Wrote This Book" should prove very helpful to students who are conducting their own research.

Marjorie Gann and Janet Willen's *Five Thousand Years of Slavery* focuses on a global history of slavery from the times of ancient Greece through the transatlantic slave trade that brought millions of slaves from Africa to the Americas and finally to current instances of slavery. The authors recommend global enforcement of antislavery laws and purchasing slave-free products. They include a timeline of important moments in slavery, photographs, and helpful websites.

Slavery in America, edited by Dorothy and Carl J. Schneider, is an extensive reference text (554 pages) that includes chapters beginning with "The West Coast of Africa: 1441–1866" and proceeding to "The Argument Over Slavery: 1637–1877." The chapters include time lines, eyewitness testimonies, newspaper reports, and court records. The text is supported with charts, maps, bibliography, glossary, and index. It is a valuable source for older students who are authenticating biographies and informational books, as well as those preparing reports on slavery.

The Underground Railroad played an important role in freedom as African American slaves risked many hardships on the journey north. Both the text and the illustrations in Carole Boston Weatherford's *Moses: When Harriet Tubman Led Her People to Freedom* depict the harsh life of slavery and the faith and resilience of the woman who has been called the Moses of her people. Weatherford's poetic style, in which Tubman communicates with God as she escapes to Philadelphia and later guides other slaves to freedom, develops a character who has both strong religious faith and a longing for freedom.

Biographies and Autobiographies about the Slavery Period

Many authors of nonfiction books choose to tell about this historical period through the biographies of slaves who sought freedom or of abolitionists who too fought hard for individual freedoms. The literature frequently stresses that many people in both the North and the South believed slavery was immoral; therefore, unable to pass laws against it, they assisted slaves in their flight toward Canada and freedom.

In *Minty: A Story of Young Harriet Tubman,* Alan Schroeder develops a fictionalized account of Harriet Tubman's childhood on a Maryland plantation. The account of her childhood emphasizes the cruel experiences in slavery that caused her to become a leader in the Underground Railroad. Readers may become motivated to research Tubman's life and decide if the fictionalized account is close to the reality of Tubman's life. Jerry Pinkney's watercolors depict the harshness of Tubman's situation. An author's note provides historical background information. Many of the authors who write biographies about the slave experiences highlight conflict and difficulties as they describe the dangers related to helping runaway slaves, especially after the passage of the Fugitive Slave Act in 1850 made it a crime to assist in the escape of a slave.

Ann Petry's *Harriet Tubman: Conductor on the Underground Railroad* is an interesting biography to analyze because it contains many of the values and beliefs identified in the traditional literature as well as authentic historical information about the time period. For example, readers see exemplified in the book traditional values and customs such as storytelling, singing, respect for elders, integrity in family obligations, and family loyalty. Notice in the following quote how Petry develops both the importance of storytelling and the use of oral stories to pass down to children the more terrifying experiences on the slave ships:

> The mumbling old voice evoked the clank of chains, the horror of thirst, the black smell of death, below deck in the hold of a slave ship. (p. 13)

Notice that this quote also reinforces a vivid language style that encourages listeners to hear, see, and feel the storyteller's experience. One of the motifs found in some of the folklore from the Plantation South is the longing to fly in order to escape slavery and to acquire freedom. This motif is also found in Petry's biography.

When analyzing Petry's biography for literary merit, you will discover four types of conflict—all consistent with the time period and the African American experience. For example, person-against-self conflict occurs when Tubman faces the inner problems of whether she should attempt an escape without her husband. Person-against-person conflict occurs when Tubman interacts with slave owners and with her own husband when she discovers he is willing to betray her if she attempts to escape. Person against nature is indicated when Petry describes the icy rivers, the thick underbrush, and the harsh conditions Tubman overcomes as she escapes. The overwhelming conflict, however, is the person-against-society conflict she faces as she struggles to change society's attitudes toward slavery.

Biographies of personages on the Underground Railroad may be compared with Shane W. Evans's highly illustrated *Underground: Finding the Light to Freedom*. Evans's text is narrated by a group of slaves. As you read this book, notice how the illustrations change from darker colors as they are escaping, to brighter colors as they reach their goal of freedom. You may also consider how the changes in tone reflect the title of the book.

Several biographies for juvenile audiences portray the life of nineteenth-century freedom fighter Frederick Douglass. For example, Douglas Miller's *Frederick Douglass and the Fight for Freedom,* which covers similar events, is interesting for comparative study. Miller, a professor of American history, includes a valuable list of additional readings and discusses some of the problems with previous biographies.

Some biographers use Douglass's own writings and speeches to portray his life. For example, Michael McCurdy's *Escape from Slavery: The Boyhood of Frederick Douglass in His Own Words,* preserves Douglass's original writings. Milton Meltzer's *Frederick Douglass: In His Own Words,* a book for older readers, presents primary-source materials that portray Douglass's beliefs. The text is divided into three chronological sections: Before the War, The War Years, and After the War. Meltzer introduces each of the speeches or writings with a commentary that provides information about the occasion. It is interesting for readers to analyze the emotional impact of Douglass's language and to evaluate his oratorical skills.

Virginia Hamilton's *Anthony Burns: The Defeat and Triumph of a Fugitive Slave* covers the life of a slave who is less well known than Frederick Douglass. However, the escape of Burns to Boston, his arrest, and trial had much impact on the abolitionists and advanced the antislavery movement. Because of the lack of documentation, Hamilton draws from supporting materials to recreate the early life of Burns.

Hamilton uses an interesting technique to help readers understand the early life of Burns. After Burns is captured as a fugitive slave, he goes within himself and remembers his happier childhood days. In a later chapter, Hamilton returns to the current world as the innocent child of five slips away and Burns's more painful memories and experiences come to the fore. When Hamilton suggests the character is having a vision or a dream, she gives credibility to her invented dialogues and happenings. Dreams and visions do not always reflect the exact happenings in a person's life.

Several authors provide shorter accounts of the people who were involved in the fight for freedom from slavery. Virginia Hamilton's *Many Thousand Gone: African Americans from Slavery to Freedom* provides short accounts of people who were involved in this fight. The book is divided into three parts: Slavery in America, Running-Away, and Exodus to Freedom, and it includes a bibliography and an index. Michele Steptoe's *Our Song, Our Toil: The Story of American Slavery As Told by Slaves* is another book that provides short biographies of specific people.

Authors who write biographies of earlier personages may have difficulty locating supporting evidence for all the thoughts and actions of their characters. Tonya Bolden addresses this problem in her biography *Maritcha: A Nineteenth-Century American Girl.* In this tale of a free African American girl, Bolden uses a style that allows readers to identify where she is filling in missing information that she cannot verify. In the following quote, notice how she uses vocabulary such as "only wonder," "it is likely," and "may have included": "One can only wonder about her day-to-day activities . . . it is likely that Maritcha was helping with housekeeping. . . . Her chores may have included" (p. 7). When Bolden can verify thoughts and actions, she uses terms such as "recalled," "took pride in," and "treasured" a memory.

The lives of white abolitionists are also popular subjects for biographers. For example, Jean Fritz's *Harriet Beecher Stowe and the Beecher Preachers* tells about the life of an important abolitionist who also is the author of one of the most influential novels of the time period, *Uncle Tom's Cabin: or, Life Among the Lowly*. Fritz's biography presents a character who fights for both women's rights and the rights of slaves. The biographer describes Stowe's determined personality and unique personal abilities, as well as the challenges she faced. It also highlights her strong desire to provide changes in the laws governing slavery. Readers may follow Stowe's development as an author and her strong need to write a book that would influence the world. Fritz concludes her biography with the importance of Stowe's novel: "Yet in almost any list today of ten books that have changed the world, *Uncle Tom's Cabin* will appear. Harriet Beecher Stowe was a towering figure in her time, and although Lymann Beecher might not have admitted it, she was the best preacher of them all" (p. 131). Fritz includes notes on the text, a bibliography of primary and secondary sources, and an index.

Students of literature may read *Uncle Tom's Cabin* and decide for themselves why the book was so influential. The story first appeared as a serial that ran from June 1851 to April 1852 in *The National Era*, an abolitionist weekly publication. It was published in book form in 1852 by John P. Jewett of Boston. The book became so popular that it was translated into nearly forty languages.

Two highly illustrated biographies for younger readers focus on the exceptional talents of a slave and a former slave. Laban Carrick Hill's *Dave the Potter: Artist, Poet, Slave* is set in rural nineteenth-century South Carolina. The illustrations and text reveal the strength of Dave's hands and his talent as he creates his art and the strength of his intellect as he creates his poetry. The illustrations in watercolors and collage reinforce these talents. An author's note provides additional information about Dave's life and includes several of his short poems. Emily Arnold McCully's *Wonder Horse: The True Story of the World's Smartest Horse* focuses on the life of Bill "Doc" Key, who was born a slave with special abilities to work with and understand animals. Following the Emancipation Proclamation, he uses his talents with animals to first create a liniment, the sale of which makes him wealthy. He uses some of his money to buy a racehorse and then train her foal. Although the foal is born with a deformity that prevents racing, Key uses his talent with animals to train the horse to do unusual tasks. He trains him to count and to pick out letters and colors. The author's theme reflects one of Key's major beliefs: It is important to be kind to all creatures.

Historical Fiction about the Slavery Period

The settings and conflicts for M. T. Anderson's *Octavian Nothing: Traitor to the Nation* are based on the Revolutionary War, as the main character tries to overcome his life of slavery as well as being placed in the drama of the war. Laurie Halse Anderson uses a similar setting and conflict in her *Chains* and *Forge*. (See the survival strategies developed by the author that are discussed later in this chapter.)

In *Chains*, the winner of the Scott O'Dell Award for Historical Fiction, the author uses several techniques that make authentic literature. For example, Anderson introduces each chapter with an appropriate quote from a newspaper or a letter from the time period. These quotes foreshadow the plot in the chapter. The themes are appropriate for the time period and for literature set during the Revolutionary War. For example, "freedom is worth fighting for" and "strong beliefs require strong commitments" are found in numerous pieces of literature set in this time period (Norton, 2011). Through the characters' actions and beliefs, Anderson develops the themes that there is power in freedom and that people will fight for freedom. Throughout *Chains* the characters express their need to seek freedom and to do whatever is necessary to set themselves free. As in other slave literature there is also the prejudice of racism. For example, there is a refusal to accept the fact that Isabel can read because slaves cannot read, there is an attitude expressed that slaves are not people, slaves are described as invisible because people talk in front of them, and characters express that freedom and liberty are only possible for nonslaves.

These themes and conflicts are expanded in Anderson's sequel, *Forge*. By placing Curzon, another escaped slave from *Chains,* into the terrible winter at Valley Forge the book shows both the slave's continual search for freedom and the racism that he experiences. As an example of racism, one of the soldiers spits at Curzon's feet, accuses him of stealing, and makes crude and foul comments about his parents. This book may be read as an introduction to the atrocities of the Revolutionary War as well as the experience of an escaped slave. After Isabel, the main character from *Chains,* and Curzon, her friend and the main character from *Forge,* are recaptured and escape again, the author provides foreshadowing in the form of a notice for two runaway slaves, Isabel Bellingham and Curzon Bellingham (the surname of their owner). The notice states: "Will Be Continued in the Forthcoming Volume *Ashes*." (Also see the "Featured Book for Young Adults" later in this chapter. *The Astonishing Life of Octavian Nothing: Traitor to the Nation* is a powerful and disturbing book for older readers.)

Characters such as the slave in Gary Paulsen's *Nightjohn* show both the ordeals experienced by the slaves and the hope and perseverance that allowed them to survive. Even though he is cruelly treated, Nightjohn brings his gifts of teaching reading and writing to the young slave children. Notice in the following quote how the author reveals both Nightjohn's suffering and personal values as they see the tracks showing his missing toes: "we see his tracks with the middle toe missing on the left foot and the middle toe missing on the right and we know . . . it be Nightjohn and he bringing us the way to know" (p. 92).

Both the biographies and the historical fiction set during times of slavery have strong themes about the importance of freedom. When evaluating the literature, we need to decide if both the settings and conflicts are authentic for the time period. If the story is a biography, the authors have responsibilities for both factual accuracy and telling stories with literary merit. Accurate characterization is especially important for real-life people who lived during these historical time periods. As you read the literature discussed in this section, compare the various authors' abilities to illuminate the time period and to express the emotions that accompanied the conflicts.

African American Poetry

African American poetry provides a bridge between historical and contemporary literature. Poetry is available that reflects both the historical and contemporary searching for freedom and questing for individual dreams. *Masterpieces of African-American Literature,* edited by Frank N. Magill (1992), provides both a listing of the works of notable African American poets and a discussion of their works. The text includes the following poets, whose writings will be of interest to students studying the works of African American poets: Amiri Baraka, Gwendolyn Brooks, Sterling Brown, Lucille Clifton, Countee Cullen, Owen Dodson, Rita Dove, Paul Laurence Dunbar, Nikki Giovanni, Michael S. Harper, Robert Hawden, George Moses Horton, Langston Hughes, June Jordan, Etheridge Knight, Audre Lorde, Claude McKay, Haki R. Madhubuti, Carolyn M. Rodgers, Sonia Sanchez, Melvin B. Tolson, Alice Walker, Phillis Wheatley, and Jay Wright.

As you read this list of poets, you will notice that several of the poets such as Gwendolyn Brooks, Lucille Clifton, and Nikki Giovanni write for both children and adult audiences. The poetry of other poets such as Langston Hughes is frequently included in children's anthologies of poetry.

Read a selection of the poetry by both adult and children's poets. What subjects and themes are developed in the poetry? Are there differences in the subjects between adult and children's poetry? Are there differences in the poetry between poets who wrote in the 1800s and those who are considered contemporary poets? How would you account for these differences?

The poetry of Langston Hughes is among the most famous of American poetry. Although Hughes is not considered primarily a children's poet, his poetry explores feelings, asks difficult questions, and expresses hopes and desires that are meaningful to readers of any age. Some of his poems—such as "Merry-Go-Round"—can be used to help children understand and identify with the feelings and experiences of African Americans in earlier eras of U.S. history. In another poem, Hughes vividly describes what life would be like without dreams.

DREAMS

Hold fast to dreams
For if dreams die
Life is a broken-winged bird
That cannot fly.
Hold fast to dreams
For when dreams go
Life is a barren field
Frozen with snow.

Langston Hughes
The Dream Keeper, 1932

Many of Langston Hughes's poems are published in single-volume texts illustrated by award-winning illustrators. For example, E. B. Lewis is a winner of the 2010 Coretta Scott King Award for *The Negro Speaks of Rivers.* Full-page watercolor illustrations show how rivers have influenced the people's history. There are illustrations showing people bathing in the Euphrates, living in huts adjacent to the Congo, and listening to the sounds of the Mississippi. The poem ends as Hughes compares the depth of his soul to the depth of the rivers. Charles R. Smith, Jr., uses photographs to illustrate Hughes's poem *My People.* The resulting book portrays a varied people who are all beautiful. Again, Hughes ends his poem with a tribute to the beauty of the soul.

Poetry written by another famous African American author of adult texts adds a source for poetry appropriate for older children and young adults. Marilyn Nelson's poetry combines both African American history and poetic style. Her *Fortune's Bones: The Manumission Requiem,* a Coretta Scott King Honor book, is an account of a slave named Fortune who died in 1798. The bones in the title refer to the fact that a doctor preserved Fortune's bones for anatomy studies. Each page of verse faces a page containing text and archival graphics that reveal facts about Fortune's history. *Carver: A Life in Poems,* a Newbery Honor book and a Coretta Scott King Honor Award, is an account of the life of George Washington Carver, born a slave around 1864. Nelson's free-verse poems are told from the different perspectives of those who knew Carver at different times in his very productive life as a botanist, naturalist, herbalist, inventor, painter, musician, and poet.

"Dreams" from *The Collected Works of Langston Hughes* by Langston Hughes, edited by Arnold Ramersad with David Roessel, Associate Editor. Copyright © 1994 by the Estate of Langston Hughes. Used by permission of Alfred A. Knopf, a division of Random House, Inc.

Nelson's *A Wreath for Emmett Till,* winner of both the 2006 Coretta Scott King Honor Award and the 2006 Printz Honor Award for Young Adult Literature, is a memorial to a more recent tragedy in African American history. The book includes 15 sonnets about the kidnapping and lynching of a fourteen-year-old African American boy in Mississippi in 1955. This incident helped spark the civil rights movement of the 1950s and 1960s. Consequently, the book makes an excellent accompaniment for the civil rights books discussed later in this chapter.

Poetry written for younger children frequently emphasizes the universal feelings and desires of children. For example, Nikki Grimes's *Oh, Brother!* is a collection of poems that show that it is possible to grow to like a stepbrother. The titles of many of the poems reflect the changes in feelings as attitudes go from dislike to a realization that the two boys are actually brothers. The poems include "Trouble," "Imitation Brother," "Showdown," "The Name Game," and finally "Pact." Joyce Carol Thomas's *The Blacker the Berry* explores feelings toward different colors, especially different shades of black. Jan Spivey Gilchrist's *My America* is a highly illustrated book that reflects both the diversity and beauty of America. A minimal text is printed on Ashley Bryan's full-page illustrations that reflect the diversity of skies, water, land, birds, water creatures, beasts, and people.

Poetry frequently has close relationships with music. Toyomi Igus's *I See the Rhythm* encourages readers to explore poetry, music, art, and history. Each section in this book traces the history of a different type of African American music. The book gives information on the origin of traditional African griots, as well as on contemporary rap and hip-hop. Each section includes poetic verses about the type of music, lyrics from a representative song, an appropriate painting to depict the era associated with music, and a historical time line for that period. The rhythm of the poetry can be used to teach poetic elements and the time line places the music into a historic perspective. Walter Dean Myers's *Jazz* and Jonah Winter's *Dizzy* also explore music. Ntozake Shange's *Ellington Was Not A Street* is a memory of both Duke Ellington and others who influenced African American history. Arnold Adoff's *Roots and Blues: A Celebration* celebrates the history of blues and its performers.

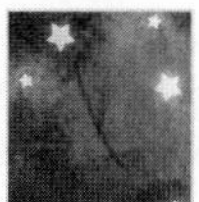

Contemporary African and African American Literature

Picture Books

Picture books with African and African American themes and content include concept books, biographies, and fictional stories. Books such as Kelly Cunnane's *For You Are a Kenyan Child* develop themes about family responsibility and curiosity that are common to all children's books.

Several concept books, although they focus on teaching the alphabet and counting, provide information about culture as well. In addition, some alphabet and number books are specifically designed to provide information to older students rather than to teach letter/sound relationships and numbers to younger ones. For example, two award-winning books present information about African life: Margaret Musgrove's *Ashanti to Zulu: African Traditions,* vividly illustrated by Leo and Diane Dillon, depicts the customs of twenty-six African peoples; *Jambo Means Hello: Swahili Alphabet Book,* by Muriel Feelings, introduces Swahili words and customs. Another book by Muriel Feelings, *Moja Means One: Swahili Counting Book,* with illustrations by Tom Feelings, depicts the East African culture. Each two-page spread provides a numeral from one to ten, the Swahili word for the number, a detailed illustration that depicts animal or village life in Africa, and a sentence describing the contents of the illustration. Ifeoma Onyefulu uses colorful photographs to depict both numbers and scenes from Nigeria in *Emeka's Gift: An African Counting Story.* In addition to numbers, Onyefulu provides information on what is depicted in the photographs. The beautiful books just described can encourage children of all cultural backgrounds to learn more about African people.

Picture book biographies about sports figures and musicians are popular subjects. Many of the sports biographies emphasize the difficulties that African American athletes face as they enter what had been an all-white world of sports. For example, Matt Tavares's *Henry Aaron's Dream* stresses Aaron's determination to play in the major leagues at a time when "Whites Only" signs are common. This biography follows Aaron's career as he progresses from playing in the Negro League in the 1940s to his triumph in 1954 when he joins the Milwaukee Braves.

Charles R. Smith's *Black Jack: The Ballad of Jack Johnson* is the biography of the first African American heavyweight champion. In addition to determination, the author stresses the importance of reading biographies as inspiration. Audrey Vernick's *She Loved Baseball: The Effa Manley Story* tells of the life of a person who fights both sexism and racism. As the first woman to be inducted into the Baseball Hall of Fame she overcomes both racial and sexual injustice. All of these picture biographies illustrate the difficulties experienced by both male and female athletes as they face and overcome racial prejudices.

The world of jazz is the focus of both picture biographies of individual musicians and of jazz as a musical form. Robert Andrew Parker's *Piano Starts Here: The Young Art Tatum* provides an inspiration not only to jazz pianists but also to those who must overcome failing eyesight. Parker's illustrations for the text add to the impact of Tatum's impaired vision. As the biography progresses, the illustrations symbolize his blurred vision. The author includes a bibliography of related literature. Roxane Orgill's *Skit-Scat Raggedy Cat: Ella Fitzgerald* progresses from Fitzgerald as a child who loves music to her joining the Chick Webb Band in Harlem. The biography includes her experiences in an orphanage where she is abused. The biographer, however, emphasizes Fitzgerald's love of jazz by including language that suggests her vocal style. The author includes resources for learning more about Fitzgerald through listening, reading, and exploring websites. Three excellent sources allow readers to gain more information about jazz and the people involved: Leo and Diane Dillon's *Jazz on a Saturday Night,* Johnny Hannah's *Hot Jazz Special* and Laban Carrick Hill's *Harlem Stomp! A Cultural History of the Harlem Renaissance.*

Many of the picture storybooks written for younger children depict children facing situations and problems that are common to all young children: overcoming jealousy, adjusting to a new baby, expressing a need for attention, experiencing rivalry with siblings, developing personal relationships, and overcoming family problems.

Books for younger children frequently depict warm relationships between children and their mothers or positive interracial experiences. Irene Smalls-Hector's *Jonathan and His Mommy* depicts a mother and her son walking in the neighborhood. On this walk, they try various movements, such as zigzag walking and itsy-bitsy baby steps. Michael Hays's illustrations show the city neighborhood and the people who live there. The actions and the illustrations suggest warm interpersonal relationships.

Imagination and desire to win a cakewalk combine to make a girl try to capture the wind as her dancing partner in Patricia McKissack's *Mirandy and Brother Wind.* The background of the story may seem so realistic because the author was influenced by a picture of her grandparents after they won a cakewalk. Imagination also plays a role in Faith Ringgold's *Tar Beach.* The illustrations show a girl lying on the rooftop of her apartment building and flying over Harlem in the late 1930s. Margaree King Mitchell's *Uncle Jed's Barbershop* is set in the 1920s South. The author develops the themes that it is important to make dreams come true and great value in perseverance even when the going becomes difficult. Another type of imagination plays tricks on Patricia C. McKissack and Onawumi Jean Moss's *Precious and the Boo Hag* when a young girl stays home alone. She discovers that a victory song saves the day.

An older brother's prank sets off the captors in Chris Van Allsburg's humorous *Probuditi!* The plot of this story follows the consequences resulting when children are home alone. Even though Trudy's older brother practices hypnosis on her, causing her to believe that she is a dog, there is a satisfying ending as she has the final laugh.

Fiction for Middle-Elementary Grades

Many African American stories written for children in the middle-elementary grades are written by authors—black and white—who are sensitive to the African American experience. Some themes—such as the discovery of oneself, the need to give and receive love, the problems experienced when children realize the parents they love are getting a divorce, and the fears associated with nonachievement in school—are universal and suggest all children have similar needs, fears, and problems. Other themes, such as searching for one's roots in the African past, speak of a special need by African American children to know about their ancestry.

Virginia Hamilton's *Zeely* is a warm, sensitive story about an imaginative girl named Geeder who makes an important discovery about herself and others when she and her brother spend the summer on their Uncle Ross's farm. After seeing Zeely, her uncle's tall, stately neighbor who resembles a photograph of a Watusi queen, Geeder is convinced Zeely has royal blood. Geeder is swept up in this fantasy and shares her beliefs with the village children. Her greatest discoveries occur, however, when she realizes dreaming is fine, but being yourself is even better and that Zeely is indeed a queen, but not like the ones in books, with their servants, kingdoms, and wealth. Zeely is a queen because she understands herself and always does her work better than anybody else.

Another book that explores a character's personal discovery and strength of character is *Sister,* by Eloise Greenfield. Sister, whose real name is Doretha, keeps a journal in which she records the hard times—and the good times that "rainbowed" their way through those harder times. Doretha's memory book helps her realize "I'm me." The words of the school song sung in *Sister* are characteristic of the themes found in this and other books by Greenfield. Notice the importance of words such as "strong brothers and sisters," "working in unity," and "building our community" (p. 69). Greenfield's *The Great Migration: Journey to the North* is a story in verse about the migration of African Americans from the rural South in the early 1900s. The poetry is divided into five subjects. "The News," "Goodbye," "The Trip," "Questions," and "Up North." This book is a good choice for oral reading as well as making discoveries about African American history.

The power of love to overcome difficulties is the theme in a cross-cultural story by Jenny Lombard. The main characters in *Drita, My Homegirl* are Maxie, a precocious African American girl who is often in trouble at school, and Drita, a refugee from Kosova, who is having difficulty adjusting to a new culture. The protagonists are strong, intelligent females who use determination to solve their problems.

Fiction for Older Children

Outstanding realistic fiction written for older children incorporates both strong characters and strong themes. The themes in these stories include searching for freedom and dignity, learning to live together, tackling problems personally rather than waiting for someone else to do so, survival of the body and the spirit, and the more humorous problems involved in living through a first crush. Contemporary realistic fiction for older readers frequently focuses on the destructive forces of prejudice.

Christopher Paul Curtis's *The Watsons Go to Birmingham—1963,* a 1996 Newbery Honor book, provides an excellent source for both literary analysis and examination of historic authenticity of a text. It is a book that changes mood at about the halfway point in the story. At the beginning of the book, the author describes a typical African American family, who happen to live and work in Flint, Michigan. The problems of the various characters are typical of those of many families. When they decide to travel to Alabama, the tone of the book changes. Because it is a time of racial tension, person-against-society conflict is the most prominent. The racial conflict is developed early in the story when the mother wants to go from Flint to Birmingham because life is slower in Alabama and the people are friendlier. Dad responds, "Oh yeah, they're a laugh a minute down there. Let's see, where was that 'Coloreds Only' bathroom downtown"

(p. 5). The culmination of this person-against-society conflict occurs toward the end of the book when a church is bombed and several African American children are killed.

Curtis develops parallels between the person-against-society and person-against-self conflicts. As a ten-year-old, Kenny tries to understand the hatred that could cause such deaths. In addition, he, with the help of his older brother, reaches a point where he releases his personal feelings and begins to cry. At a moment of complete self-understanding, Kenny admits to his brother that he is no longer afraid in the aftermath of the bombing incident; instead; he is ashamed of himself because he ran from the church rather than try to find his sister, who he believed was still inside. His older brother helps him clarify the situation and makes him realize he has no reason for embarrassment.

The themes in the book also relate to the person-against-society conflict. Through the actions of the various characters, we learn that prejudice and hatred are harmful. The harmful nature of prejudice is revealed when Kenny's brother, Byron, tries to explain the actions of the bombers to Kenny: "I don't think they're sick at all, I think they just let hate eat them up and turn them into monsters" (p. 200). By the end of the story, the boys conclude that the world is not necessarily fair, but they just need to keep going. This ending also relates to an earlier theme developed by the boys' father: growing up is not easy; we all must work to accomplish this task.

In *Bud, Not Buddy,* Curtis wins both the 2000 Newbery Award and the Coretta Scott King Award. Curtis places his ten-year-old protagonist in the setting of the Great Depression of the 1930s. By developing his main character as a mistreated orphan boy, Curtis describes a very dark side of the Depression as Bud experiences waiting in line for food at missions and living with other homeless people in "Hooverville," shantytowns made of cardboard and wood. There is also a very positive side to the story as Bud, clutching the few possessions left to him by his mother, searches for the man he believes is his father. This search takes Bud into the world of a famous jazz band. Throughout the book, Curtis used Bud's "Rules and Things for Having a Funnier Life" to explore Bud's character and to add humor to the story. It is interesting to learn in the author's afterword that Curtis modeled two of his characters after his own grandfathers: one a redcap for the railroad and the other a bandleader for several musical groups including "Herman E. Curtis and the Dusky Devastators of the Depression."

In *Scorpions,* Walter Dean Myers's characters face person-against-society conflicts related to the contemporary world of drug dealers and gangs. They also face person-against-self conflicts created by inner fears and consequences related to owning a gun. The characters of Mama and her younger son, Jamal, are especially strong. Myers develops Mama's character through numerous contrasts. For example, when Mama thinks about her older son, who is in jail for robbery, she remembers looking at him as a baby and feeling great expectations. Later, Mama is torn between her need to help this older son and to protect her younger children. Myers develops Mama's inner conflict as she discusses her problems with her minister.

In Jamal, the younger son, Myers develops a character who is tortured by his feelings of being weak and small. At the beginning of the story, Jamal thinks about all of the people who make him feel this way, such as the big kids who laugh at him, the teachers who make him stand in class, and the shop owners who yell at his mama. Later, Myers contrasts Jamal's earlier fears with his changing feelings after obtaining a gun.

In a tragic ending, Jamal discovers the consequences of having the gun and makes an even greater personal discovery. There was "the part of him, a part that was small and afraid, that still wanted that gun" (p. 214). This poignant story reveals the complex problems facing two generations of people who are fighting for personal and family survival in a dangerous world. Myers's *Shooter* develops a similar theme as a story about troubled teenagers that ends with a school shooting.

In *Lockdown,* Myers again writes about the world in a juvenile detention facility. This is the world in which Reese, a teenage boy, has a chance to redeem himself when he is chosen to participate in a work program at a senior citizens' home. The final chapter in the book, "One Year Later," reveals not only the lessons Resse learned but also how hard and dangerous it is to live the life he wants to live in the outside world. The book concludes on a hopeful note as Reese knows what he needs to do and hopes that his life will now reflect the good parts.

Carol Fenner, the author of another of the 1996 Newbery Honor books, *Yolonda's Genius,* uses several techniques to develop the characteristics of two African American children: bright fifth-grader Yolonda and her slower, younger brother, Andrew. For example, the author reveals both Yolonda's intelligence and her ability to use this intelligence after she is teased about her size. During this incident, Yolonda responds to being called a whale by letting her fellow bus rider and the readers of the book know she is very knowledgeable. Yolonda states, "Whales are the most remarkable mammals in the ocean—all five oceans" (p. 16). She then provides information about whales. We learn later that Yolonda goes to the library each week to learn new facts.

Yolonda's positive attitudes and Andrew's possible musical genius are developed as Yolonda reviews what Andrew can do and not what he cannot do. Later, Yolonda's actions show both her respect for Andrew's talents and her dislike for those who torment her younger brother because he is a slower learner in school and gains his enjoyment primarily out of playing his harmonica. Yolonda takes vengeance on the three boys who destroy Andrew's harmonica. She does this while Andrew is watching because she wants it to be Andrew's vengeance as well as her own.

The author shows characterization through the symbolism of music. Andrew makes discoveries about people through sounds, he learns the alphabet after a teacher relates the alphabet to the instruments, and Andrew eventually plays his harmonica to celebrate Yolanda's character. Students may analyze how the author describes Yolonda through Andrew's music. This book, like any good book of literature, shows the importance of carefully developed characters and the importance of developing self-esteem.

Developing and expressing racial pride through working for change, creating unity of ideas, and believing in equality for all are themes developed by Rita Williams-Garcia in her 2011 Newbery Honor book, *One Crazy Summer.* The crazy summer is 1968 and the location is Oakland, California, during the time of the Black Panther Party. The main characters are eleven-year-old Delphine and her two younger sisters, who leave Brooklyn to spend the summer with the mother who abandoned them when they were very young. The author develops a strong feeling for place and African American beliefs and racial conflicts of the time period as the children attend a summer camp sponsored by the Black Panthers. Readers will discover beliefs, issues, and conflicts of the time period as the girls try to understand this quite different setting. The author uses both comparisons and symbolism to help readers understand the characters and the issues. For example, to show differences in characterization she compares saying good-bye between Big Ma (the loving grandmother) and Cecile (the often-distant mother). There is symbolism in the poetry that often reveals characterizations and in the broken stool and the moveable type that reflects Cecile's poetry. The author also reveals the characters' search for cultural self-esteem as they wish for more television shows featuring African American characters and long to hear more of the poets who reflect their values.

An In-Depth View of an African Contemporary Fiction Story *The Other Side of Truth* by Beverley Naidoo is the winner of the Carnegie Medal for Children's Literature. The novel is a contemporary survival story set in Nigeria and in London following the escape of the major characters from an oppressive regime. As we evaluate this book we consider three criteria: (1) how the author develops the political setting for this book; (2) how the author develops the themes that indicate justice and freedom are essential for personal happiness and survival; and (3) how the author uses an effective literary style to support the themes, characterizations, and conflicts.

The political settings for this book create the background and the conflict for the story. The foreword places the story in the politically oppressive climate of Nigeria in which a family (twelve-year-old Sade, her younger brother, and her journalist father) must flee from the threat of murder. The Author's Note identifies the political setting as the time in 1995 when the Nigerian writer Ken Saro-Wiwa was executed for his writing. This information, along with the fact that the author herself was imprisoned for her views and forced into exile, add considerable authenticity to the story.

The author develops a vivid political setting by providing quotes from the journalist's articles that result in his wife's murder and his need to flee the country in secret. This oppressive political setting is reinforced by describing the police roadblocks that are everyday occurrences. A description of the trial and hanging of the journalist Ken Saro-Wiwa for writing the truth convinces readers that Sade's father, if captured, will receive a similar treatment. The political setting extends to London where the father is placed in custody until the British authorities decide if the family should be given political asylum. Readers will be interested in the process that Sade and her younger brother Femi use to save their father from being returned to Nigeria, where he faces probable imprisonment and possible death.

The themes developed by the author relate to the political setting as the author shows through various characters and actions that justice and freedom are essential and truth can make you free. The actions and views of the father develop many of these themes, and so do the experiences of Sade as she combats prejudice among her classmates in London and fights for her father's release. By interacting with bullies in school, Sade discovers she must stand up for herself because "There is no medicine to cure hatred . . . but even children have to stand up to bullies. If they don't those bullies put on even bigger boots" (p. 137).

The author's style supports the characterizations, themes, and political settings in the book. For example, the author uses similes to reveal the children's feelings after their mother is shot: grief burst like a pierced boil, or breath wrung out like a snake squeezing her throat.

The author uses numerous flashbacks to compare Sade's current experiences with experiences in Nigeria. Some of these flashbacks allow her to remember unhappy experiences. For example, a run-in with the London police causes her to flash back to the Nigerian police. Some flashbacks, however, are pleasant as a friendly arm around her reminds her of an emotionally warm experience with her mother.

The author uses allusions to African folklore to make a point. In several places she alludes to a tale about Tortoise or Leopard to reveal a truth or a theme. For example, Papa writes a letter to the children in which he tells them the tale of "Leopard and Tortoise." He concludes the story with the importance of stories, because "Words are mightier than swords" (p. 213).

As you read, notice how the author relates the political setting, the themes, and the literary style to develop a compelling book about survival. You will also discover that the author uses her own African heritage to reveal important values and beliefs.

Nonfiction

Many authors of nonfiction books create biographies about individuals who were or are active in the civil rights movement or who are leaders in such areas as the arts and the theater. Other authors develop historical perspectives about the fight for freedom.

Biographies about civil rights leaders encourage readers to examine historical, political, and social perspectives of the movement. For example, there are several biographies of Martin Luther King, Jr., that may be used for comparative studies and analysis. Lillie Patterson's *Martin Luther King, Jr. and the Freedom Movement* begins with an account of the 1955–1956 Montgomery, Alabama, bus boycott and King's involvement in the boycott. Patterson then explores King's earlier background and discovers some of the influences that caused King to become a leader in the boycott and the civil rights movement. James Haskins's *The Life and Death of Martin Luther King, Jr.* presents a stirring account of King's triumphs and tragedies. Haskins's *I Have a Dream: The Life and Words of Martin Luther*

King, Jr. focuses on King's involvement with the civil rights movement. You may wish to compare these biographies of Martin Luther King, Jr., with the revised edition of *My Life with Martin Luther King, Jr.* by Coretta Scott King.

Interesting comparisons may be made between two highly illustrated biographies of Martin Luther King, Jr.: one by Faith Ringgold and the other by Rosemary L. Bray. Ringgold's *My Dream of Martin Luther King* develops the biography of the civil rights leader through a dream sequence. The text and illustrations present various stages in King's vision for a better world, tracing events in King's life such as joining demonstrations, being arrested, listening to his father's sermons, being influenced by the teachings of Mahatma Gandhi, becoming an adult minister, and finally dying from an assassin's bullet. The text and dream sequence ends as people in a crowd scene trade bags filled with prejudice, hate, ignorance, violence, and fear for Martin Luther King's dream for the promised land. The text includes a chronology of important dates in King's life.

Bray's biography, *Martin Luther King,* is illustrated with folk-art paintings by Malcah Zeldis. Bray's biography includes more details about King's life than the one by Ringgold. It also includes a chronology of dates. Neither book includes source notes. Students of children's literature can compare the impact of the illustrations and the depiction of King's life in these two highly illustrated biographies written to appeal to younger readers.

Several biographies reflect the contributions of African Americans to the fine arts. James Weldon Johnson's *Lift Every Voice and Sing* is often referred to as the African American national anthem. This book combines the song with linocut prints that Elizabeth Catlett originally created in the 1940s. Andrea Davis Pinkney's *Duke Ellington* provides an introduction to the life and music of the jazz artist. Brian Pinkney's illustrations create the mood of the Jazz Era as well as support the theme that creating music and art is an important human endeavor.

Jonny Hannah's *Hot Jazz Special* is a highly illustrated picture book that depicts jazz artists and a feeling for the mood of the music. Wynton Marsalis's *Jazz ABZ: An A to Z Collection of Jazz Portraits* includes personages from Louis Armstrong to Dizzy Gillespie. The stylized art makes an interesting comparison to *Hot Jazz Special.*

Russell Freedman's biography, *The Voice That Challenged a Nation: Marian Anderson and the Struggle for Equal Rights* is appropriate for the study of the civil rights movement and of great musicians. This winner of the 2005 Newbery Honor and the Robert F. Sibert International Award presents a chronological account of Anderson's life from her childhood in Philadelphia through her American and European concert tours in the 1920s and 1930s. In addition to her history as a singer, Freedman develops Anderson's struggle for equal rights. A feeling of authenticity is enhanced by the photographs from the time period and copies of programs of her performances. Many of these photographs show the racism Anderson faced, especially when the Daughters of the American Revolution (DAR) banned her from singing at the Constitution Hall in Washington, D.C. The importance of this experience is shown when Eleanor Roosevelt resigned from the DAR in protest of Anderson's treatment.

The study of outstanding African American artists and writers would be enhanced through several books. For example, John Duggleby's *Story Painter: The Life of Jacob Lawrence* presents an interesting combination of biography and art. The text is illustrated with reproductions of Lawrence's paintings. Wade Hudson and Cheryl Willis Hudson compile profiles of African American authors and artists in *In Praise of Our Fathers and Our Mothers: A Black Family Treasury by Outstanding Authors and Artists.* This collection includes stories, poetry, interviews, and illustrations contributed by more than forty African American authors and illustrators. Steven Otfinoski's *Great Black Writers* provides brief profiles of ten authors including Phillis Wheatley, James Weldon Johnson, and Langston Hughes. These books may also provide motivation for future authors and illustrators.

There are several highly illustrated biographies of sports figures that develop the contributions of African American athletes. Lesa Cline-Ransome's *Major Taylor: Champion Cyclist* is a biography of the bicyclist who won the 1899 World Championship. Sharon Robinson's *Promises to Keep: How Jackie Robinson Changed the World* is a biography of the legendary Brooklyn Dodger. In *The Champ: The Story of Muhammad Ali,* Tonya Bolden uses a lyrical style to present the life of the heavyweight boxing champion. Carole Weatherford's *Jesse Owens: Fastest Man Alive* is a biography of the 1936 Olympic gold medal winner. The author also covers topics such as segregation and Hitler's failed goal of demonstrating Aryan superiority. Many students enjoy reading about someone who has mastered a favorite sport.

Excellent books develop the history of and the personages involved in the struggle for civil rights for African Americans. For example, Diane McWhorter's *A Dream of Freedom: The Civil Rights Movement from 1954 to 1968* explores the sacrifices and triumphs of African Americans in their pursuit of social and political equality. The author profiles the accomplishments of major personages such as Rosa Parks and Martin Luther King, Jr. (Compare this coverage with biographies such as Nikki Giovanni's *Rosa* and the various biographies about King.) McWhorter uses a chronological organization that highlights the major incidents in the movement.

Toni Morrison's *Remember: The Journey to School Integration* uses photographs and text to present the history and the impact of the 1954 Supreme Court decision, *Brown v. Board of Education.* The text concludes with a chronological order of events beginning with the 1896 Supreme Court ruling that legalizes separate but equal facilities up through the 1992 *Brown v. Board of Education.* The author includes "Photo Notes" that also provide a documented history. You may compare these books on civil rights with Russell Freedman's *Freedom Walkers: The Story of the Montgomery Bus Boycott,* Ann Bausum's *Freedom Riders: John Lewis and Jim Zwerg on the Front Lines of the Civil Rights Movement,* and Elizabeth Partridge's *Marching for Freedom.* What information is covered by each author? How would you describe the point of view of each author? What are the major themes developed by the texts? How does each author document the text?

Older students might compare the experiences of African Americans during the civil rights movements and the slavery experiences with Hanna Jansen's *Over a Thousand Hills I Walk With You.* This book is set during the genocide in Rwanda in 1994. Students could consider how and why authors use journeys in their titles by comparing Jansen's text with Judith Bloom Fradin and Dennis Brindell Fradin's *5,000 Miles to Freedom: Ellen and William Craft's Flight from Slavery.*

Biographies and other nonfiction works have broad appeal for children and juvenile audiences. Comparisons between the historical biographies and the contemporary ones are especially interesting. They can lead to examining questions such as these: What are the values and beliefs expressed by the biographical characters from the earlier Civil War period and from the later civil rights movement? If there are similarities, what do you believe accounts for the similarities?

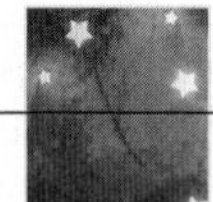

Survival

Many African American books include characters who face some of the most severe and brutal conflicts in their quests for personal survival. These books range from historical fiction texts that depict person-versus-society conflicts as authors focus on the years of slavery and later school desegregation or more contemporary person-versus-person problems associated with racism.

Laurie Halse Anderson's careful depiction of authentic setting, characterizations, and conflict in *Chains* won the book a Scott O'Dell Award for Historical Fiction. The author develops a strong undercurrent for survival as she places the main character, Isabel, in the turbulent setting of New York during the Revolutionary War. Now Isabel must face and try to overcome both the problems associated with slavery and the increasing conflicts caused by Loyalists versus Patriots. The author introduces readers to Isabel's growing realization that if she wants to be free she must have a plan, a map for her life. The author stresses Isabel's dreams for freedom by describing her actions. She secretly reads favorite books such as *Robinson Crusoe,* plants the seeds her mother saved in hopes of having a new garden, and discovers that to be free she must cross her own River Jordan. The author creates a turning-point-incident after Isabel is branded as a traitor. Readers know she has overcome a person-versus-self conflict when she realizes that the scar is not a symbol of shame but a sign of strength that signifies her personal survival. The title of the book may be the author's strongest revelation of Isabel's survival as she realizes that her body may be in chains caused by slavery, but no one can chain her soul without her permission. The author includes two helpful additions to the text: An "Appendix" that includes questions and answers related to the subject and time period and a "Reading Group Guide" that includes discussion questions.

Forge, the sequel to *Chains,* focuses on Isabel's friend and fellow slave, Curzon. As the title suggests, Anderson sets this historical fiction novel at Valley Forge as the soldiers suffer cold, hunger, and lack of supplies. Curzon now faces two battles for survival: he joins his countrymen in the war against the English, but he must also hide the fact that he is an escaped slave. When both Curzon and Isabel are recaptured they must again strive for freedom. Their past experiences have taught them that running without thinking and planning is foolish. They must have a well-developed plan. Unfortunately, Isabel has a new constraint. Her owner has forged an iron collar that he locks around her neck. The only key is worn around his neck. The importance of friendship and people who can be trusted is developed as Curzon and Isabel join forces in their fight for freedom.

Anderson uses Curzon's reactions to Greek mythology that is told by one of the soldiers to show the strength of Curzon's commitment to his fight for freedom. For example, when he remembers the story of a god who is chained to a rock only to have an eagle peck out his revived liver each night, he realizes that to retain his own freedom he would fight the eagle and the chains that bind him to the mountain. He would do this as long as he had breath. Anderson uses such stories to help readers understand the depth of Curzon's fight for freedom and personal survival.

Two other excellent books are also about this time period and the issues related to slavery during the Revolutionary War. M. T. Anderson's *The Astonishing Life of Octavian Nothing: Traitor to the Nation, Volume 1: The Pox Party* is the focus for "A Featured Book for Young Adults" in this text. To this book you may add Anderson's sequel *The Astonishing Life of Octavian Nothing: Traitor to the Nation, Volume II: The Kingdom of the Waves.* It is interesting that both of these books and *Chains* and *Forge* include many of the same strategies for personal survival: retaining a dream for freedom; gaining satisfaction from books or stories (Octavian adds satisfaction from playing music); keeping memories of family alive; and searching for emancipation from whichever side, Patriot or Loyalist, will provide freedom for the slaves.

A Coretta Scott King Award winner, Julius Lester's *Day of Tears: A Novel in Dialogue,* is also about slavery. The setting is a plantation in Georgia. According to the "Author's Note" the text is based on factual information about the largest auction of slaves in American history, a sale in 1859 known as "The Weeping Time." As the characters share their experiences they also reveal their survival strategies: listening to music and stories such as High John, Brer Rabbit, and Bible stories; knowing what the white folks are thinking and doing what the white folks tell you; retaining dreams of freedom and hoping they will eventually find lost family members; needing someone to talk to, someone who listens, and someone who understands; wanting to learn to read and write even under dangerous circumstances; and knowing that the only people who can be trusted are those with a heart.

Survival during a more contemporary form of racism is found in Sharon M. Draper's *Fire from the Rock,* a fictional story based on the true incidents in 1957 when nine African American students are selected to be the first to integrate Central High School in Little Rock, Arkansas. The author tells the story through the viewpoint of Sylvia Faye and her family who experience much

A Featured Book for Young Adults

The Astonishing Life of Octavian Nothing: Traitor to the Nation by M. T. Anderson is a National Book Award winner and has appeared on several recommended lists of reading for young adults, especially those in advanced placement classes. This book has also been on the *New York Times* "Children's Best Sellers" list, where it was recommended for ages 14 and above (April 15, 2007, p. 20).

The book, however, requires careful reading and discussions, as highlighted by the following review from *Kirkus Review*: "A historical novel of prodigious scope, power, and insight. . . . This is the Revolutionary War seen at its intersection with slavery through a disturbingly original lens." *Booklist* identifies the book as highly accomplished and demanding rereading.

What is it that makes it both powerful and possibly requiring rereading for understanding? The book is historical fiction set in the United States during the Revolutionary War. It requires some understanding of the issues, the conflicts, and the setting as well as the role of slavery during the eighteenth century. In addition, the characters and the conflict develop a paradox in which beliefs expressed and actions demonstrated by the Sons of Liberty, who fight for equality and freedom from English rule, are inconsistent with and contradictory to their beliefs in freedom. They consider slaves to be their property and may treat them cruelly.

When critically evaluating this book, you may find it worthwhile to begin with the "Author's Note" in which he states that while the book is historical fiction it is founded on fact. For example, the educational experiments in the book are based on actions in the late seventeenth century, in which researchers sought to answer questions of equality between African slaves and white Europeans. To test equality, the researchers tested to see if non-Europeans could absorb the classics and other traditional European disciplines such as languages, mathematics, and music. The author further discusses his purpose for writing the book and his attitude toward the Revolutionary War.

The book is divided into sections. The first section describes the educational experiments conducted on Octavian, an African slave who was a prince in his homeland. Again, there is the paradox of his current situation when compared with his royal status in Africa. Now, when he displeases the master, he is whipped and eventually evicted from the setting that encourages and tests Octavian's ability to learn.

The second section describes the changing conflict when a new investor in the educational experiments is interested in proving the inequality of slaves and believes that educational pursuits should fit a slave who must labor with his hands. The contrasts between early experiences and later experiences are especially insightful when a fellow slave describes what masters expect from slaves: They want us empty, to have nothing inside but our ability to follow orders. Now, instead of anticipating his lessons in music, literature, and reading his books, Octavian's lessons in hard labor bring him only the wrath of the master through the whip or the birch rod.

The third section focuses on the war, Boston under the King's army, and Octavian's experiences as a runaway slave and his fighting alongside free soldiers. This section includes numerous examples of person-versus-self and person-versus-society conflict as Octavian tries to understand his changing circumstances, especially the meaning of personal freedom.

In the fourth section, the author describes the punishment when Octavian, the runaway slave, is recaptured. The section begins as the author describes the most extreme paradox in Octavian's life: "They gave me a tongue, and then stopped it up, so they would not have to hear it crying" (p. 309). This section includes numerous flashbacks as Octavian thinks about his earlier experiences. He considers the irony of the term *liberty*: both slaves and free whites fight for liberty, but his own search for liberty ends in shackles and a face mask. The author states Octavian's point of view when Octavian thinks about how the slaves risked their lives for the liberty of their masters without having any assurance that the slaves would have liberty. In one case, Octavian realizes that a slave killed in the fighting at last has liberty.

The final chapter includes dialogue in which some characters argue against freeing the slaves, state their beliefs about the inferiority of the African race, and use God as a determiner to the "Great Chain of Being." Other characters, however, argue for the values of kindness and equality and discuss the hypocrisy of liberty for some but not for slaves. Through these dialogues, the author develops many of the issues related to the time period. The text concludes with a biblical allusion about hiding a Prince in the bulrushes, a foreshadow that uses the term "a brimful of promise," and a suggestion that the second volume of *Octavian Nothing* will continue the protagonist's search for the meaning of freedom.

Although this book requires careful reading, analysis, and investigating background information for comprehension, it does lend itself to the type of activities recommended by advocates of more challenging work in schools, especially in college-preparatory English and history classes. As reported by Karen W. Arenson (2007), only 26% of high school graduates who take college preparatory classes are ready for college work, and 14% of those who do not take the courses are ready for college work. One way to help solve this problem, according to Kati Haycock, director of the English Trust, is to offer challenging work, especially analysis of what is read.

of the hatred and racism. The author develops the survival techniques through two different generational sources. There are the viewpoints and beliefs of Sylvia's mother (a teacher) and father (a pastor). In contrast are the survival strategies of Sylvia, her older brother, and their peers.

Through various characters actions and dialogue the author reveals the conflicting attitudes that will hopefully lead to survival and equality. For example, Sylvia's mother stresses the benefits gained from being very proper, wearing white gloves, and a hat. She believes that tolerance and understanding will eventually lead to equality. Sylvia's father believes that it will be the young people who eventually change the world. During a sermon he tells the Bible story of Gideon to stress that it is now time to step out on faith. The author brings in the title of the book as in the story, the Lord makes fire explode from a rock to support Gideon's actions. This is a change in attitude for the father who did not originally believe in desegregation. He believed that African American schools teach children to have pride in their heritage, history, and culture.

Sylvia and her older brother, Gary, express two different strategies for survival. Gary believes that African American survival requires fighting back and that the people should never stop fighting for what is right The author again brings in the fire in the title when she describes Gary as having the fire needed for the battle but not the gentle breeze to control it. In contrast, teachers describe Sylvia as someone who is steady, dependable, and capable of handling the social and emotional difficulties she will face. The author describes Sylvia as someone who believes that her dream of going to college gives her a plan that will help her survive. Sylvia shows her determination for college by preferring demanding teachers who prepare students to make it in a rough world. Many of Sylvia's dreams are reinforced through her diary entries and her poetry. The author concludes her book with an "Author's Note" that reveals what happened in Little Rock, Arkansas, and Central High School.

While *Fire from the Rock* focuses on survival during school desegregation, several biographies focus on survival as characters fight to overcome segregation on buses. *Rosa* by Nikki Giovanni is a highly illustrated book about Rosa Parks and her arrest in 1955 in Montgomery, Alabama, when she refuses to give up her seat on the bus. The author develops Park's nonviolent survival techniques as she decides not to give in to that which is wrong. She cites the 1954 *Brown v. Board of Education* decision, realizes that she is tired of living in a world where people are separate but not equal, and remembers the strength of her ancestors. The author portrays the other women who stand under the umbrella of courage and would rather walk than ride a bus, until 1956 when the Supreme Court rules that segregation on buses is wrong.

Claudette Colvin: Twice Toward Justice by Phillip Hoose is another biography about a person involved in the Montgomery, Alabama, bus boycott. As you read the books, do you notice any similarities or differences between Claudette Colvin and Rose Parks? The author describes Claudette as a person with a mission for herself; she is going to be like Harriet Tubman and liberate her people. She is tired of hoping for justice; instead she decides that when her time comes she will be ready. When she is arrested for not giving up her seat on the bus, she recites the Lord's Prayer and Psalm 23. She feels proud because she has challenged the white bus law and stood up for her people's rights. Some people congratulate her for her courage, self-respect, and integrity. Others, however, criticize her and blame her for the violence that follows. As she grows older, she discovers that caution is a habit that allows her to survive. Many years later, her advice to students reveals her beliefs and values: Do not give up, keep struggling, and take education seriously.

A more violent struggle for survival is developed in Ishmael Beah's autobiography *A Long Way Gone: A Memoir of a Boy Soldier.* Beah's dedication, "to all the children of Sierra Leone who were robbed of their childhood," also reveals the focus for the book. The book begins in a New York City high school in 1993 as a student remembers his childhood from the age of twelve until he is rehabilitated and arrives in the United States. This childhood includes violent and emotional experiences as he escapes from rebels, sees the consequences of the rebels' killings, and is forced to take up weapons to fight against the rebels. His survival strategies change with the increasing conflict. As a young boy he listens to rap music and remembers pleasant memories from his childhood to drive away the terrible images of destroyed villages and slaughtered people. As Ishmael becomes more involved with the war his goal is to survive one day at a time. He now realizes that his innocence has been replaced by fear and a reliance on drugs. To survive as a boy soldier he considers the gun his provider and protector as his new rule is kill or be killed. His life and prospect for survival change when he is taken away by UNICEF representatives and sent to a rehabilitation center. Here he gradually learns to forgive himself, to regain his humanity, and to heal. He eventually moves to the United States where he finishes high school and later graduates from Oberlin College. As a consequence of his experiences, he is a member of the Human Rights Watch Children's Division Advisory Committee. He is a frequent member of panels on children affected by war.

The book concludes with a "Chronology" of happenings in Sierra Leone. Beginning in 1462 with the landing of Portuguese explorers and concluding with a peace-building mandate in 2005 and the incarceration of Charles Taylor in a UN jail in 2006 where he is awaiting trial on eleven counts of war crimes.

Oakland, California during the summer of 1968 is the setting for Rita Williams-Garcia's *One Crazy Summer,* a 2011 Newbery Honor and a finalist for a National Book Award. Three children leave New York City to spend the summer with their mother who abandoned them when they were very young. The girls find themselves attending a summer camp that is sponsored by Black Panther revolutionaries. This setting allows the author to develop the racial attitudes of the time period as well as the history of the Black Panthers.

The setting also provides many opportunities for readers to search for survival strategies used by the three children as they live in a very different environment than the members and followers of the Black Panther movement. For example, Delphine, the oldest sister who feels responsible for her siblings, survives the summer by spinning stories that make her younger sisters believe that everything is all right, by reading *Peter Pan* to her sisters and reading *Island of the Blue Dolphins* for her own escape, and by discovering that it is sometimes necessary to forgive.

Through the teachings at the summer camp and listening to Black Panther sympathizers, the children learn the survival strategies stressed by the African American characters. For example, believing that it is necessary to express racial pride; understanding that revolution requires constant turning and making things change; knowing that surviving requires unity and standing together; and realizing that information is power because keeping the people informed keeps them empowered.

To expand an understanding of these survival strategies, we will search for the survival strategies developed in a nonfiction novel written for adults: John Carlin's *Invictus: Nelson Mandela and the Game That Made a Nation* (2009). This book describes Mandela's campaign to reconcile the black and white citizens of South Africa and to unify the nation. Carlin begins with the dream that sustained Mandela during his twenty-seven years in prison: His hope that people in his country will eventually be judged by their character and not by the color of their skin. Carlin suggests that Mandela uses the following strategies to gain his dream: using negotiations to overcome apartheid, realizing that persuading is better than violence, sharing his belief in equality, understanding that the Rugby World Cup is an event that can bring people together and result in national pride, and appealing to what binds people together rather than emphasizing their differences. After reading this book, you may agree with Carlin's theme that sports may have the power to change the world.

As you read books about different time periods in African American history, notice the similarity in survival strategies developed by the authors. Authors who set their stories during times of slavery and in times of desegregation emphasize the retaining of a dream for freedom or equality and developing a careful plan for reaching that dream. Stories and friends and family who support the dream are important in both periods. All of the authors develop strong characters who believe in their goals and retain pride in their history, heritage, and culture.

Summary

The investigation of African and African American traditional literature indicates the strong values, beliefs, and themes of the cultures. Love, life, family commitment, respect for elders, cooperation, gratitude for help rendered, maintenance of friendships, respect for individuality, respect for heritage, respect for storytelling, community responsibilities, courage, hope, honesty, use of wit and trickery in unequal relationships, hard work, singing, and a respect for nature are values and beliefs that strongly link the traditional literature with more contemporary literature.

In the context of these broader conflicts, values, and beliefs, the themes developed in African American picture storybooks written for younger readers also reflect strong themes. We learn that life is precious, we are responsible for helping others overcome adversity, living involves changes, love is eternal, the past can be relived through memories in the form of stories, black is wonderful and powerful, honesty brings rewards, the dreams of our elders are passed on to us, nature/God sometimes intervenes in the affairs of people, and knowing one's past gives one's present meaning.

This chapter has discussed historical fiction and nonfiction as well as contemporary literature and poetry. The emergence of outstanding authors who write about the African and African American experience with sensitivity and honesty has provided many excellent books. Many more books are available than can be discussed in one chapter. Add new books to this discussion as you discover them in your own research and reading.

Suggested Activities for Developing Understanding of African American Literature

1. Read an article that uses African American literature as a research tool, such as Wanda Brooks's "Reading Representations of Themselves: Urban Youth Use Culture and African American Textual Features to Develop Literary Understandings" (July/August/September 2006). Read one of the books she used (*Scorpions, Roll of Thunder, Hear My Cry,* and *The House of Dies Drear*). Search for the following examples of recurring themes identified by students in the study: forging family and friend relationships, confronting and overcoming racism, and surviving city life. Why do you believe that these themes developed responses among the students? Were there any other themes that were important in your reading? What were those themes? Why were they important?

2. Read an article such as Ilene Cooper's "The African American Experience in Picture Books" (1992). According to the author,

   > Thirty years ago there were almost no picture books featuring African American children. Happily, this is no longer the case—throughout children's literature, there are now stories (and nonfiction) that examine the black experience, from both a particular and a universal perspective. This is especially true of picture books, where each publishing season seems to bring more titles featuring African American children. (p. 1036)

   Test Cooper's points by analyzing the copyright dates of African American picture books in a public, university, or school library. What changes do you find in the last thirty years?

3. John Carlin's *Invictus* states that in 2007 a bronze statue of Nelson Mandela was unveiled in London's Parliament Square along side of Abraham Lincoln and Winston Churchill. This

honor was given to world leaders and to Mandela as "the president of humanity." Research the lives of these three world leaders and compare their beliefs and values. Where might they agree and disagree about world politics, conflicts, and issues of humanity?

4. With a group of your peers, create an oral storytelling experience using African and African American folklore. Try to use authentic openings, closings, and storytelling style.

5. Choose a well-known author of African American literature such as Virginia Hamilton or Walter Dean Myers. Read several books by the author. What makes the plots and characters memorable? What are the themes in the writer's work? Is there a common theme throughout the writing? What changes, if any, have occurred between the earliest books and those with later copyrights?

6. Read the works of several African American poets such as those discussed in this chapter. Analyze the themes, subjects, and poetic styles developed by the poets. Are there differences depending on time periods and audiences? If there are differences, how do you account for the differences?

7. With a group of your peers, read Joyce Adams Burner's "Stomping Grounds: Focus on the Harlem Renaissance" (November 2006). Analyze the list of recommended books. Select and read several of the books. Discuss how you would use these books to add interest to a study of African American history and culture.

8. Read an article about or an interview with an African American author such as Deborah Taylor's "Jacqueline Woodson" (June 2006). Discuss how the author's favorite reading choices might have influenced her writing. Woodson identifies her favorite authors as James Baldwin, Toni Morrison, and Alice Walker. Read one of these favorite authors and consider how the authors might have influenced Woodson.

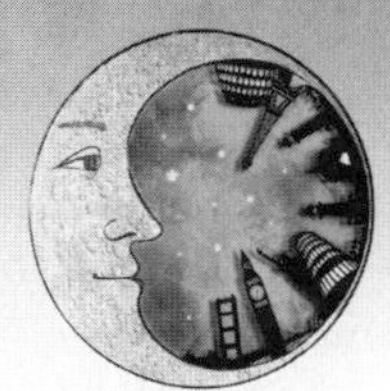

Involving Children with African American Literature

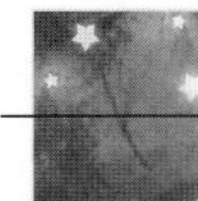

Phase One: Traditional Literature

As we have discovered, the oral tradition was very important in transmitting the folktales, myths, and legends from Africa. Rhonda D. Goolsby (2004) reinforces the value of the oral tradition in Africa: "Regardless of the type of tale, each will bring to light something of importance to the natives of Africa. Through oral storytelling traditions of these tales, people were taught important ways of life. The beliefs, religions, and social and moral viewpoints meander through the tales of tricksters, hero tales, and tales that answer the why question. Looking beyond the words and diving into the meaning of the tale shines a light on the African people" (p. 16). To help students understand and appreciate the importance of oral language in transmitting cultural information, begin with a study of African folklore. Emphasize the role of oral storytellers in keeping alive the cultural past. Storytellers chanted and sang, interacted with the audience, and acted out story elements. The art of storytelling was so highly valued that storytelling competitions were held to encourage the most vivid and entertaining stories. Tell the students that they will be listening to oral storytellers, identifying oral storytelling styles, and creating their own storytelling experiences.

Discovering Oral Storytelling Styles from Africa

Examples of African folklore suitable for storytelling include Gail Haley's *A Story, A Story: An African Tale,* a folktale that reveals how Anansi, the spider man, outwitted various animals and brought stories from the Sky God down to the people; Verna Aardema's *Anansi Does the Impossible: An Ashanti Tale,* a folktale about how Anansi and his wife outwit the Sky God to obtain stories; Aardema's *Who's in Rabbit's House?,* a folktale in play form that features players wearing masks to represent the various animals in the story; Aardema's *Why Mosquitoes Buzz in People's Ears,* a cumulative tale that reveals why mosquitoes make their specific noise; and Ashley Bryan's *Beat the Story-Drum, Pum-Pum* and *The Ox of the Wonderful Horns and Other African Folktales,* collections of folktales that are developed on strong oral language traditions.

After you have told several stories to the class, discuss possible advantages of telling a story rather than reading a story. Share information with the students about how traditional folktales were handed down from one generation to the next by oral storytellers. Tell the students that the art of traditional storytelling, cultivated in every culture by people from every level of society, reflects the culture, the nature of the land, the social relationships, and the traditional values of the people. African folktales, for example, arise out of a highly developed oral tradition. The influence of this oral language is shown in the repetitive language and the interaction between the audience and the storyteller.

Ask the students to identify the ways in which a storyteller may begin a story. (Most children and young adults will probably identify "Once upon a time.") If they cannot identify any common story openers, share several examples from folktales. Explain that many cultures used a beginning that introduced their listeners to an earlier time. African storytellers might begin a story with the examples discussed in this chapter. Read introductions to various folktales aloud and discuss what each one means. Explore the similarities between the introductions and identify the traditional values found in the African folktales.

As students read the various folktales recommended earlier, ask them to search the folktales to discover how interpreters and translators of traditional folklore introduced their stories. Are there differences in the type of tale or the people who told the stories? For example, they can find these story openers in Bryan's *The Ox of the Wonderful Horns and Other African Folktales:*

> We do not mean, we do not really mean, that what we are going to say is true.
> Listen, let me tell the story of . . .
> I never tire of telling the tale of . . .
> Listen, brothers and sisters, to the story of . . .

You may develop a comparative chart showing the locations of the stories and include examples of the story openers.

Ask the students to identify any endings that storytellers may use. Explain that African storytellers also used certain types of endings. For example, if the story was dramatic it might end with one of the following:

> Hausa Suza zona ("they remained")
> Mahezu ("finished")

An exaggerated story might end in the following way:

> Chase the rooster and catch the hen.
> I'll never tell a lie like that again.

If the story was humorous it might end in this way:

> They lived in peace, they died in peace
> And they were buried in a pot of candle grease.

Read the endings aloud and discuss what they mean. You may discuss which endings might be appropriate for a dramatic tale, an exaggerated tale, or a humorous tale. Ask the students to explore endings they find in the various African folktales.

To prepare students to develop their own storytelling, model a storytelling experience for them. Tell an African folktale with a traditional introduction and ending. Allow students to select African folktales and develop their own stories to share with a group. They may enjoy using musical instruments to accompany their stories.

Additional Activities to Enhance Phase One

There are numerous oral language, writing, art, and library research projects that enhance students' understandings of the various phases. Some are listed in these Additional Activities sections, one of which follows each of the phases. The activities are ones for children or young adult students to do. For example, you might help students do any of the following activities for Phase One:

1. Read aloud and analyze the storytelling style in Verna Aardema's *The Lonely Lioness and the Ostrich Chicks.* Discuss the power of the repetitive language.
2. Prepare and present Verna Aardema's *Who's in Rabbit's House?* as a play.
3. Prepare and present folktales from Ashley Bryan's *Beat the Story-Drum, Pum-Pum* as a readers' theater.

Phase Two: Folklore of the American South

Webbing Traditional Values

Identifying and webbing the traditional values of folklore from the American South helps students identify similarities and differences between the African and the African American folklore. They will also discover the role of slavery in the adaptations of many of the tales that were brought across the ocean. Some of the stories such as the tales of a trickster rabbit are similar to those found in Africa. Other stories such as those found in Virginia Hamilton's *The People Could Fly: American Black Folktales* reflect the experiences of the people and their dreams for freedom.

Select a group of folktales from the American South such as Virginia Hamilton's *Her Stories: African American Folktales, Fairy Tales, and True Tales, The People Could Fly: American Black Folktales* and *When Birds Could Talk and Bats Could Sing;* Van Dyke Parks's adaptations of Joel Chandler Harris's *Jump! The Adventures of Brer Rabbit* and *Jump Again! More Adventures of Brer Rabbit;* Julius Lester's *John Henry,* and his adaptations of Joel Chandler Harris, *The Tales of Uncle Remus: The Adventures of Brer Rabbit,* and *More Tales of Uncle Remus: Further Adventures of Brer Rabbit, His Friends, Enemies, and Others;* Patricia McKissack's *Flossie and the Fox;* Steve Sanfield's *The Adventures of High John the Conqueror;* Robert D. San Souci's *The Faithful Friend* and *The Hired Hand;* and Janet Stevens's *Tops and Bottoms.*

Select several of the African American folktales to read and discuss as a group. Ask students to identify and discuss the traditional values found in the stories as they are placed on the web. Following the analysis and discussion of several folktales as a group, they can continue the activity in small groups or individually. The web in Figure 2.1 shows a partially completed web. The folktales used were the ones previously listed.

Discussing African American Folktales That Show European Influences

Numerous African American tales reflect European influences. Students can read and discuss these influences using books such as Robert D. San Souci's *Cendrillon, The Faithful Friend,* and *The Talking Eggs;* "Catskinells" in Virginia Hamilton's *Her Stories: African American Folktales, Fairy Tales, and True Tales* and "The Beautiful Girl of the Moon Tower" in *The People Could Fly: American Black Folktales.*

There is interesting information in the various authors' notes in these books that may be used for discussion and additional research. For example, the author's note in *Cendrillon* states,

> This story is loosely based on the French Creole tale "Cendrillon," in Turiault's nineteenth-century *Creole Grammar.* That version follows the basic outline of Perrault's "Cinderella," while incorporating elements of West Indian culture and costume. I have expanded the tale considerably, drawing on details of life on the island of Martinique, culled from such sources as Lafcadio Hearn's *Two Years in the French West Indies* (New York and London: Harper & Brothers Publishers, 1890) and Patrick Chamoiseau's *Creole Folktales* (New York: The New Press, 1994), translated from the French by Linda Coverdale. (author's note)

Students may use this information to compare various versions of the text, identify elements that would make the story seem French or West Indian, and evaluate any changes made by the author. They may also evaluate the illustrations in search of Caribbean characteristics. (I have used this type of activity to help students compare and authenticate texts with students ranging from the third grade up through university students.)

FIGURE 2.1 African American Traditional Values Web for Selected Folktales

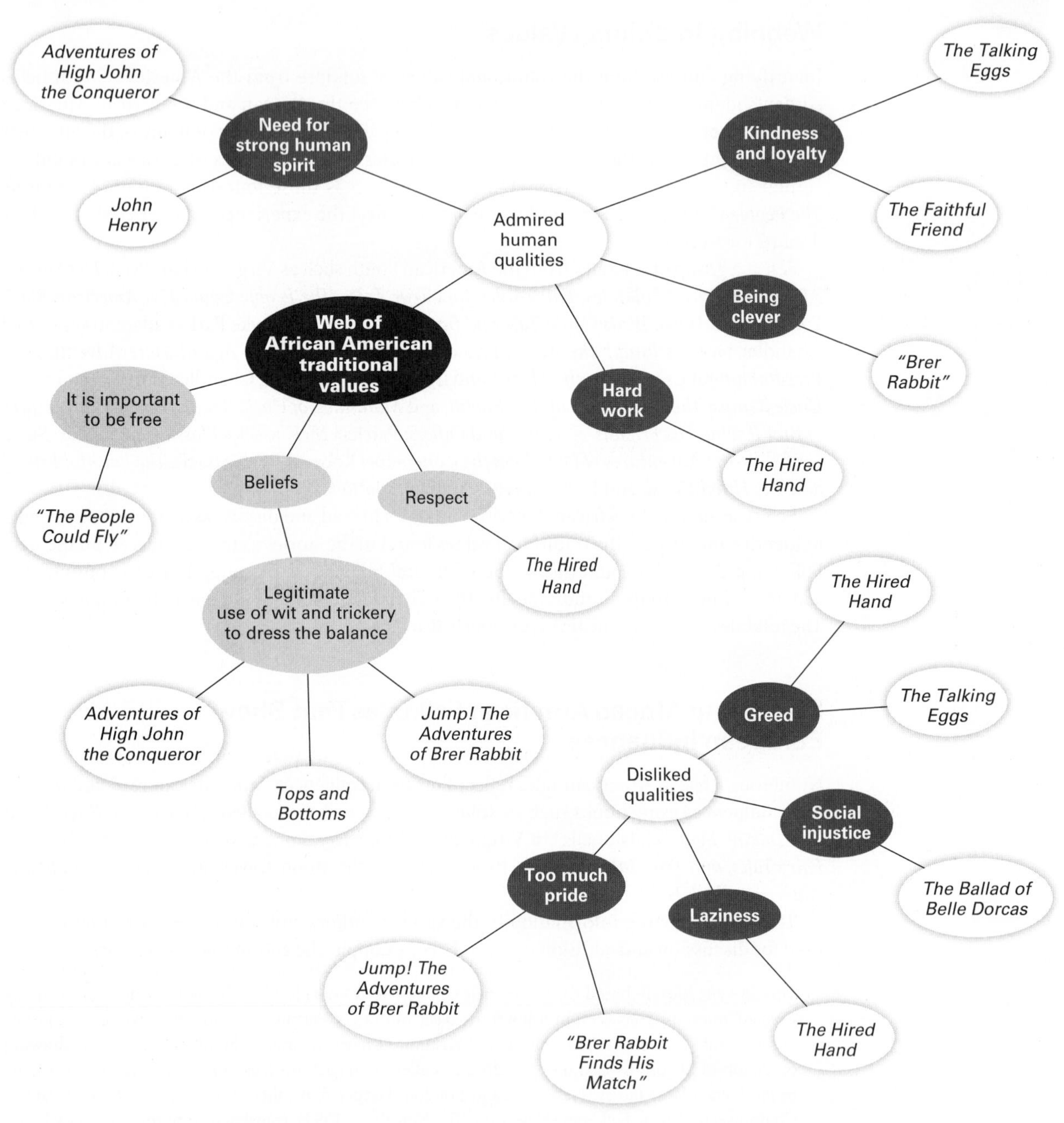

Additional Activities to Enhance Phase Two

Here are some activities for children or young adult students related to this phase:

1. Compare the characteristics of African folktales with the characteristics of African American folktales. What are the similarities and what are the differences? How would you account for these similarities and differences?

2. Compare the oral storytelling style of African folktales with the oral storytelling style in African American folktales.
3. Prepare one of the folktales as a choral reading or readers' theater.
4. Write a literary folktale using the characteristics of African American folklore. Walter Dean Myers used a similar approach when writing his literary African tale *The Story of the Three Kingdoms.*

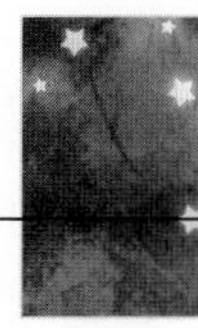

Phase Three: Historical Nonfiction and Phase Four: Historical Fiction

Developing understanding of historical nonfiction and historical fiction may be enhanced through units that encourage students to compare the literature and to authenticate the fictional literature through the use of nonfiction materials.

Developing a Multicultural Study of African American Historical Fiction and Biography

Units using historical fiction and biography are a popular method for increasing students' understandings. The following unit is based on one developed in Donna E. Norton's *The Impact of Literature-Based Reading* (1992). The unit has been used with students in the upper-elementary and middle-school grades. The unit was also used with student teachers as a model to develop their own units.

Unit Objectives

1. To analyze the role of African traditional values in historical fiction and biography.
2. To evaluate the settings, conflicts, characterizations, themes, and authors' style in historical fiction.
3. To authenticate historical fiction and biography by referring to historical events in informational books.
4. To provide a personal response to the characters and the situations developed in historical fiction, biographies, and informational literature.

Two time periods are reflected in the bulk of African American historical fiction and biographies. Powerful historical fiction and biographies have been written about overcoming problems associated with slavery and about the fight for civil rights in the 1990s. Teachers can use both periods or focus on one. For example, if choosing the topic of slavery, teachers could choose Carole Boston Weatherford's *Moses: When Harriet Tubman Led Her People to Freedom;* Jeri Ferris's *Go Free or Die: A Story About Harriet Tubman* (biography), Tubman's experiences during slavery and the Underground Railroad; and Meltzer's *The Black Americans: A History in Their Own Words, 1619–1983* (informational), a collection of writings of many people from different times. Additional historical fiction books about slavery include Paula Fox's *The Slave Dancer,* Belinda Hurmance's *A Girl Called Boy* (although there is a time-warp segment in this book, it presents a vivid picture of slavery), N. Monjo's *The Drinking Gourd,* and Gary Paulsen's *Nightjohn.*

Additional biographies about slavery include Virginia Hamilton's *Anthony Burns: The Defeat and Triumph of a Fugitive Slave* and Elizabeth Yates's *Amos Fortune, Free Man.* Additional informational books about slavery include Judith Bloom Fradin and Dennis Brindell

CHART 2.1 Chart for Analyzing Historical Biography and Autobiography

Analyzing Historical Biography and Autobiography			
Literature	Evidence of Philosophy, Values, Beliefs, and Language from Phases One and Two	Sources of Conflict	Historical Happenings and Evaluations

Fradin's *5,000 Miles to Freedom: Ellen and William Craft's Flight from Slavery* and Dorothy and Thomas Hoobler's *The African American Family Album.*

Historical fiction books about later periods in African American history include Mildred Taylor's *Roll of Thunder, Hear My Cry; Let the Circle Be Unbroken;* and *The Gold Cadillac.*

Prepare the school environment by collecting pictures that show the various stages in African American history from freedom in Africa to slavery in earlier America to the contributions of contemporary politicians, authors, and musicians. Ask the students to bring to class any examples of music, writing, and art that reflects African American culture.

Introduce one of the historical fiction books. Explain to older students that authors who write about slavery face special problems. How accurately should historical fiction reflect the attitudes and circumstances of the times? Should authors use terms of the period that are considered insensitive and offensive today? For example, you could read the authors' note in *Jump Ship to Freedom* in which James and Christopher Collier consider the use of some of the terminology. After students have read the book, ask them if they think the authors were successful in depicting conflict, characters, and changes in attitude. After students have read the book, ask them to debate the issue of using controversial words in historical fiction.

Use the same discussion and analysis structure as that shown for evaluating historical fiction about Native Americans in Chapter 3, "Involving Children with Native American Literature, Phase Three." Ask students to identify and discuss examples of setting, conflicts, characterizations, theme, and authors' style. You may follow a similar discussion procedure as the one described for Native American historical fiction.

After the students have read, responded to, and discussed several historical fiction selections, introduce the biographies. You may tell them that as they read each biography they will be searching for evidence of the values and beliefs found in traditional folklore, themes that are similar to those found in traditional folklore and historical fiction, and sources of conflict that might relate to the traditional values and the historical fiction. Finally, they will use nonfiction informational books to try to identify the historical events and evaluate the authenticity of the biographies. Place a shell of a chart on the board or on a transparency to guide the reading and discussions. See Chart 2.1 for an example of a shell to use.

For example, when using this chart to analyze Ferris's *Go Free or Die: A Story about Harriet Tubman,* students will find the following evidence of values and beliefs found in both traditional folklore and in the two examples of historical fiction:

1. The themes developed by the author show that freedom is worth risking one's life for and we must help others obtain freedom.
2. The values illustrated by the characters and their actions show that obligations to family and others are important, wit and trickery might be needed to influence the balance of power, responsibility is important, and expressing gratitude is essential.

Students will discover that the sources of conflict are person against society as Harriet fights to free the slaves and combat injustice. When they look to various nonfiction informational sources to identify the historical events, they will discover the following:

1. The setting is in the United States from the mid-1800s to the end of the Civil War.
2. The story is based on facts about slavery, the Underground Railroad, the 1850 Fugitive Slave Act, and the 1863 Emancipation Proclamation.
3. They will discover that Tubman freed more than 300 slaves in ten years.

Either in groups or individually, ask students to read and analyze additional biographies. After students have read biographies about those who were active during the antislavery movement, have them read biographies about contemporary people, and ask them to consider any similarities between the themes, values, and conflicts. Ask students to think about why these themes, values, and person-against-society conflicts might be important in the lives of people today.

The following projects and other activities could be used with this multicultural unit:

1. *Creative dramatizations and role playing:* Ask students to choose a scene from one of the books and dramatize the scene or choose an issue and role-play the various responses that pe ople might have as they try to decide the issue.
2. *Library research:* Ask students to choose one of the African countries from which slaves were sent to America. Compare the country during the time of slavery with the country today.
3. *Personal responses through writing and art:* Ask students to keep a writing journal and to respond to what happens to the characters in the historical fiction or biographical stories. For example, in Hurmance's *A Girl Called Boy,* they can respond to both the beliefs of the contemporary girl and what happens to her when she experiences slavery. They can create a collage that expresses their feelings as a historical character faces and overcomes conflict.
4. *Personal responses through writing and music:* Ask students to read Deborah Hopkinson's *A Band of Angels: A Story Inspired by the Jubilee Singers.* This is a story about how the daughter of a slave forms a gospel singing group and goes on tour to raise money in support of Fisk University. Ask students to consider how they would react in similar circumstances. They may also conduct research into the music performed by the singers such as "Swing Low, Sweet Chariot," "Many Thousand Gone," and "Go Down, Moses."

Additional Activities to Enhance Phases Three and Four

Here are some activities for children or young adult students related to these phases:

1. Interview several African American families and develop a history similar to that developed by Dorothy and Thomas Hoobler in *The African American Family Album.*
2. Research the historical role of African Americans in your community, county, or state.
3. Create a challenge by asking students to research Marc Aronson's (2007) questions about the accuracy of several artifacts and stories associated with the Underground Railroad. What is the accuracy of the freedom quilts? What is the evidence that they were or were not used as part of the quest for freedom? What is the accuracy of the song "Follow the Drinking Gourd"? What is the evidence that it was or was not sung by Harriet Tubman? When was the ballad composed? Was it part of the oral tradition or was it first published in 1928? This activity could be developed as a debate.

CHART 2.2 Examples of Authors and the African American Books They Chose

Author	Chosen Book	Why It Could Motivate
Russell Freedman	Virginia Hamilton's *Anthony Burns: The Defeat and Triumph of a Fugitive Slave*	
Nikki Grimes	Julius Lester's *To Be a Slave*	
Angela Johnson	Virginia Hamilton's *Sweet Whispers, Brother Rush*	
Pat Mora	Virginia Hamilton's *The People Could Fly*	
Jim Murphy	Wynton Marsalis's *Jazz ABZ*	
Andrea Pinkney	Patricia C. McKissack's *The Dark Thirty: Southern Tales of the Supernatural*	
Jerry Pinkney	Julius Lester's *To Be a Slave*	
Lewell Parker Rhodes	Langston Hughes's *The Dream Keeper*	
Anita Silvey	Rita Williams-Garcia's *One Crazy Summer*	
Carole Boston Weatherford	Jacqueline Woodson's *Coming on Home Soon*	

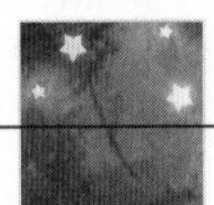

Phase Five: Contemporary Literature

Reading and Comparing African American Literature Chosen by Children's Book Authors

In celebration of Black History Month editors at the *School Library Journal* (Margolis, 2011) asked twenty authors of children's literature to "choose their favorite children's book about the black experience. . . . The only requirement? It had to be a book that they truly loved—and, of course, it couldn't be one of their own" (p. 34). Many of these authors stress how the books motivated them and often inspired them to reach new creative heights in their own writings.

Ask the students to select an author and a book. They should read the book and decide what it is about the book that would encourage a well-known writer to select the book. They may also read a book written by the author and try to discover if there are any similarities between the chosen book and the writings of the author. Chart 2.2 includes a few of the authors and their selections. The article includes additional authors. Chart 2.2 could be completed by the students.

After the students have read their selections. Ask them to complete the chart by first speculating about why the authors identified these books as ones that can motivate. Then have them consider what it was in the books (the themes, the characters, the plots, and the language or author's style) that made the books appealing. Students may choose passages from the books to read orally. They may also select their own books that have power to motivate or inform them about African American history.

Research and Writing Connections

Music and peaceful negotiations are frequently suggested as ways to make connections among people and to resolve some of their differences. In this section we will consider some of the ways that you may use a study of music and a study of the techniques used by an African political leader to improve both research and writing skills.

Using Music to Develop an Understanding of Civil Rights

A study of music is an excellent way to help students respond to African American culture. For example, students could be introduced to a history of the civil rights movement by listening to "Songs on the Road to Freedom" recorded by the Chicago Children's Choir and included in *Freedom Songs, Young Voices and the Struggle for Civil Rights* by Mary C. Turck. The book includes "A Message from the Chicago Children's Choir" in which they state, "It is important for our young singers and those they touch to understand our country's struggle for civil rights and apply those lessons to solving current social tensions and injustices for all people. Our belief is that this understanding will help Reverend Moore's dream of a peacefully integrated society become a reality" (p. 44).

Ask the students to conduct their own research into the music of the civil rights movement and to investigate how the music and the words of the various songs have been used to bind people together. Students might write letters to the Chicago Children's Choir and tell them how their music helped them develop an understanding of the civil rights movement.

How Might Nelson Mandela's Philosophies Help Other African Countries?

Older students may conduct research into contemporary issues in Africa and consider how Nelson Mandela might overcome the problems using the skills and beliefs he expressed in his biography and other writings. According to David Patrikarakos in the *New Statesman* (2010): "The Democratic Republic of Congo is one of the most tragic nations on earth. It has been ravaged by war for nearly two decades" (p. 25). The journalist states that as many as five million people have died in this war. He also reports that this is one of the wealthiest countries (diamonds, gold, cassiterite, coltan, timber, and rubber) in one of the world's toughest neighborhoods.

Ask students to conduct research into the problems in the Democratic Republic of Congo and any peace initiatives that have been tried. Ask them to identify the major issues that must be overcome to produce peace and to list any positive measures that might be used to ensure peace.

After the students have read a biography or other writings about Nelson Mandela or watched the movie *Invictus* (PG-13), directed by Clint Eastwood, ask them to write a report about how Mandela might solve the problems in the Democratic Republic of Congo. What strategies might he use to bring about peaceful negotiations? How might the wealth of the country be used to bring about peace rather than war? Do they believe that a sports activity could have the power to change the world as it did in South Africa? Have them support their conclusions with evidence from Mandela's successful experiences in South Africa.

Additional Activities to Enhance Phase Five

Here are some activities for children or young adult students related to this phase:

1. *Personal responses through dialogue:* Choose an incident in the life of a contemporary worker for civil rights such as Martin Luther King, Jr. Pretend you can have a conversation with the person: What would you talk about? What questions would you ask? What advice might you give the person?

2. *Library research:* After reading a biography about an African American athlete such as Kathleen Krull's *Wilma Unlimited: How Wilma Rudolph Became the World's Fastest Woman,* an illustrated biography of Wilma Rudolph, research and discuss records set by the athlete.
3. *Literary and artistic expansion:* Read several works by an African American author or carefully examine the works of an African American illustrator. Analyze the types of stories the chosen people write or illustrate, consider how these authors or illustrators develop a cultural perspective in their works, and respond personally to their works. Wade Hudson and Cheryl Willis Hudson's *In Praise of Our Fathers and Our Mothers: A Black Family Treasury by Outstanding Authors and Artists* will help you select authors or artists.

REFERENCES

Aardema, Verna. *Tales from the Story Hat.* New York: Coward, McCann & Geoghegan, 1960.

_____. *Misoso: Once upon a Time Tales from Africa.* New York: Knopf, 1994.

Abrahams, Roger D. *African Folktales.* New York: Pantheon, 1983.

Adoff, Arnold, and Cook, Kacy, eds. *Virginia Hamilton: Speeches, Essays, & Conversations.* New York: Scholastic, 2010.

Arenson, Karen W. "Study Finds College-Prep Courses in High School Leave Many Students Lagging." *New York Times* (May 16, 2007): A21.

Arnott, D. *African Myths and Legends Retold.* London: Oxford University Press, 1962.

Aronson, Marc. "History That Never Happened." *School Library Journal* 53 (April 2007): 34.

Banfield, Beryle. "Racism in Children's Books: An Afro-American Perspective." In *The Black American in Books for Children: Readings in Racism,* 2nd ed., edited by Donnarae MacCann and Gloria Woodard. Metuchen, N.J.: Scarecrow Press, 1985, 23–38.

Barnes-Svarney, Patricia. *Places and Peoples of the World: Zimbabwe.* New York: Chelsea House, 1989.

Beier, Ulli. *The Origin of Life and Death: African Creation Myths.* London: Heineman, 1966.

Berry, Jack, collector. *West African Folk Tales.* Chicago: Northwestern University Press, 1961.

Broderick, Dorothy May. *The Image of the Black in Popular and Recommended American Juvenile Fiction, 1827–1967.* New York: Columbia University, 1971. University Microfilm No. 71-4090.

Brooks, Wanda. "Reading Representations of Themselves: Urban Youth Use Culture and African American Textual Features to Develop Literary Understandings." *Reading Research Quarterly* 41 (July/August/September 2006): 372–392.

Burner, Joyce Adams. "Stomping Grounds: Focus on the Harlem Renaissance." *School Library Journal* 52 (November 2006): 49–54.

Carlin, John. *Invictus: Nelson Mandela and the Game That Made a Nation.* New York: Penguin, 2009.

Cheney, Patricia. *The Land and People of Zimbabwe.* New York: Lippincott, 1990.

Cobb, Charles E., Jr. "After Rhodesia, A Nation Named Zimbabwe." *National Geographic* (November 1981): 616–651.

Cooper, Ilene. "The African American Experience in Picture Books." *Booklist* 88 (February 1, 1992): 1036–1037.

Crowley, Daniel. Foreword to *"On Another Day . . .": Tales Told among the Nkundo of Zaire,* collectors Mabel Ross and Barbara Walker. Hamden, Conn.: Archon, 1979.

Elliott, Geraldine. *The Long Grass Whispers.* London: Routledge & Kegan Paul, 1939.

Faulkner, William J. *The Days When the Animals Talked.* Chicago: Follett, 1977.

Feldman, Susan, ed. *African Myths and Tales.* New York: Dell, 1963.

Fisher, Allan C. "Rhodesia, A House Divided." *National Geographic* (May 1975): 641–671.

Frobenius, Leo, and Douglas Fox. *African Genesis.* Berkeley, Calif.: Turtle Island for the Netzahualcoyal Historical Society, 1983.

Goolsby, Rhonda D. "African & African American Literature: A Study of Literature and Culture." Paper presented at Texas A&M University. College Station, Texas (Spring 2004).

Golden, Daniel. "Aiming for Diversity, Textbooks Overshoot." *The Wall Street Journal* (August 19–20, 2006): A1.

Greenfield, Eloise. "Writing for Children: A Joy and a Responsibility." In *The Black American in Books for Children: Readings in Racism,* 2nd ed., edited by Donnarae MacCann and Gloria Woodard. Metuchen, N.J.: Scarecrow Press, 1985, 19–22.

Hamilton, Virginia. *The People Could Fly: American Black Folktales.* New York: Knopf, 1985.

Johnson, Lauri, and Sally Smith. *Dealing with Diversity through Multicultural Fiction: Library-Classroom Partnerships.* Chicago: American Library Association, 1993.

Kellner, Robert Scott. "Defending Mark Twain." *The Eagle.* Bryan-College Station, Texas (April 11, 1982): 1D.

Kruse, Ginny Moore, Kathleen T. Horning, and Megan Schliesman. *Multicultural Literature for Children and Young Adults.* Madison, Wis.: Cooperative Children's Book Center, 1997.

Larrick, Nancy. "The All-White World of Children's Books." *Saturday Review* 48 (September 11, 1965): 63.

Larungu, Rute. *Myths and Legends from Ghana.* Akron, Ohio: Telcraft, 1992.

Magill, Frank N. *Masterpieces of African-American Literature.* New York: HarperCollins, 1992.

Mallows, Wilfrid. *The Mystery of the Great Zimbabwe.* New York: Norton, 1984.

Margolis, Rick. "Places in the Heart." *School Library Journal* (February 2011): 34–37.

Mbugua, Kioi wa. *Inkishu: Myths and Legends of the Maasai.* Nairobi, Kenya: Jacaranda Designs, 1994.

Norton, Donna E. *The Impact of Literature-Based Reading.* New York: Merrill/Macmillan, 1992

Noss, Philip. "Descriptions in Gbaya Literary Art." In *African Folklore,* edited by Richard Dorse. Bloomington: Indiana University Press, 1972.

Parrinder, Geoffrey. *African Mythology: Library of the World's Myths and Legends.* New York: Bedrick, 1986.

Patrikarakos, David. "Deliver Us from Evil." *New Statesman* (November 29, 2010): 24–27.

Radin, Paul, ed. *African Folktales.* Princeton, N.J.: Bollingen Series, Princeton University Press, 1952.

Rosen, Michael. *How the Animals Got Their Colors.* San Diego: Harcourt Brace Jovanovich, 1992.

Ross, Mabel H., and Barbara K. Walker. *"On Another Day . . ."; Tales Told among the Nkundo of Zaire.* Hamden, Conn.: Archon, 1979.

Schafer, Elizabeth. " 'I'm Gonna Glory in Learnin': Academic Aspirations of African American Characters in Children's Literature." *African American Review* 32 (Spring 1998): 57–67.

Taylor, Deborah. "Jacqueline Woodson." *School Library Journal* 52 (June 2006): 42–45.

Theal, George McCall. *Kaffir Folk-lore.* New York: Negro Universities Press, 1970 (first printing 1886).

Thompson, G. C. *The Zimbabwe Culture: Ruins and Reactions.* London: Frank Cass, 1971.

Vrooman, Diana. Authenticating *Mufaro's Beautiful Daughters: An African Tale.* Unpublished paper. College Station: Texas A&M University, 1993.

Wisniewski, David. *Sundiata: Lion King of Mali.* New York: Clarion, 1992.

Worth, Richard. *Robert Mugabe of Zimbabwe.* New York: Messner, 1990.

CHILDREN'S AND YOUNG ADULT LITERATURE REFERENCES

Aardema, Verna. *Anansi Does the Impossible: An Ashanti Tale.* Illustrated by Lisa Desimini. Simon & Schuster, 1997 (I: 4–8 R: 4). Anansi brings stories to the people.

_____. *Bringing the Rain to Kapiti Plain: A Nandi Tale.* Illustrated by Beatriz Vidal. Dial, 1981 (I: 5–8). This is a cumulative tale.

_____. *Misoso: Once Upon a Time Tales from Africa.* Knopf, 1994 (I: 5–8). A collection of tales.

_____. *Who's in Rabbit's House?* Illustrated by Leo and Diane Dillon. Dial, 1977 (I: 71 R: 3). A Masai folktale is illustrated as a play.

_____. *Why Mosquitoes Buzz in People's Ears.* Illustrated by Leo and Diane Dillon. Dial, 1975 (I: 5–9 R: 6). An African folktale explains why mosquitoes buzz.

Aardema, V., and Y. Heo. *Lonely Lioness and the Ostrich Chicks.* Random House Children's Books, 1996.

Adler, David A. *Frederick Douglass: A Noble Life.* Holiday, 2010 (1: 12+ R: 5). A biography of the African American leader.

_____. *A Picture Book of George Washington Carver.* Illustrated by Dan Brown. Holiday, 1999 (I: 71 R: 4). This is a heavily illustrated biography.

I = Interest age range
R = Readability by grade level

Adoff, Arnold. *Roots and Blues: A Celebration.* Illustrated by R. Gregory Christie. Clarion, 2011 (1: 9–YA). This collection of poems is about blues music.

Anderson, Laurie Halse. *Chains.* Atheneum, 2008 (I: 10–YA). A story of slavery set during the Revolutionary War.

_____. *Forge.* Atheneum, 2010 (I: 10–YA). A sequel to *Chains.*

Anderson, M. T. *The Astonishing Life of Octavian Nothing: Traitor to the Nation.* Candlewick, 2006 (I: 12–YA R: 7). The story of a slave during the Revolutionary War.

_____. *The Astonishing Life of Octavian Nothing: Traitor to the Nation, Volume II: The Kingdom of the Waves.* Candlewick, 2008 (I: 12+ R:7). This is a story of slavery during the Revolutionary War.

Armstrong, William H. *Sounder.* Harper, 1969 (I: 101 R: 6). Winner of the 1970 Newbery.

Aronson, Marc, and Marina Budhos. *Sugar Changed the World: A Story of Magic, Spice, Slavery, Freedom, and Science.* Clarion, 2010 (I: 12+ R: 6). The authors cover a 200-year period of history.

Bang, Molly. *Ten, Nine, Eight.* Greenwillow, 1983 (I: 3–6). A number game counts backward.

Bannerman, Helen. *Little Black Sambo.* Lippincott, 1899. A once popular book that is now considered politically incorrect.

Bausum, Ann. *Freedom Riders: John Lewis and Jim Zwerg on the Front Lines of the Civil Rights Movement.* National Geographic, 2006 (I: 101 R: 6). The experiences of an African American and a white man are described.

Beah, Ishmael. *A Long Way Gone: A Memoir of a Boy Soldier.* Macmillan, 2007 (I: YA R: 6). A 13-year-old boy from Sierra Leone remembers his experiences.

Bolden, Tonya. *The Champ: The Story of Muhammad Ali.* Illustrated by Gregory Christie. Knopf, 2004 (I: 6–10 R: 5). A picture book biography of the boxer.

_____. *Maritcha: A Nineteenth-Century American Girl.* Abrams, 2005 (I: 81 R: 5). Photographs, documents, and paintings add to the biography based on an unpublished memoir.

Bontemps, Arna. *Story of the Negro.* Knopf, 1948. Winner of the 1949 Newbery Honor.

Bray, Rosemary L. *Martin Luther King.* Illustrated by Malcah Zeldis. Greenwillow, 1995 (I: 7–10 R: 5). The biography is illustrated with folk-art paintings.

Brooks, Bruce. *The Moves Make the Man.* Harper, 1984 (I: 101 R: 6). Winner of the 1985 Newbery.

Bryan, Ashley. *Beat the Story-Drum, Pum-Pum.* Atheneum, 1980 (I: 61 R: 5). This is a collection of tales.

_____. *The Ox of the Wonderful Horns and Other African Folktales.* Atheneum, 1971 (I: 61 R: 5). A collection of tales.

_____. *The Story of Lightning and Thunder.* Atheneum, 1993 (I: 61 R: 5). A Nigerian folktale.

Cline-Ransome, Lesa. *Major Taylor: Champion Cyclist.* Illustrated by James E. Ransome. Atheneum, 2004 (I: 6–10 R: 4). In 1899 an African American youth won the World Championship.

Collier, James, and Christopher Collier. *Jump Ship to Freedom.* Delacorte, 1981 (I: 101 R: 7). A slave acquires his freedom.

Courlander, Harold. *The Cow-Tail Switch and Other West African Stories.* Holt, 1947 (I: all). Winner of the 1947 Newbery Honor.

Cunnane, Kelly. *For You Are a Kenyan Child.* Illustrated by Ana Juan. Simon & Schuster, 2006 (I: 4–8 R: 4). A gentle picture book that presents one day in the life of an African boy.

Curtis, Christopher Paul. *Bud, Not Buddy.* Delacorte, 1999 (I: 101 R: 6). The story is set during the Depression.

_____. *The Watsons Go to Birmingham—1963.* Delacorte, 1995 (I: 101 R: 6). A family experiences racial tensions and a church bombing.

Day, Nancy Raines, reteller. *The Lion's Whiskers: An Ethiopian Folktale.* Illustrated by Ann Grifalconi. Scholastic, 1995 (I: 5–8 R: 5). A stepmother makes friends with her stepson.

Diakite, Baba Wague. *The Magic Gourd.* Scholastic, 2003 (I: 6–9 R: 5). A folktale from West Africa.

Dillon, Leo, and Diane Dillon. *Jazz on a Saturday Night.* Scholastic, 2007 (I: all). A highly illustrated book shows many of the jazz greats.

Draper, Sharon M. *Fire from the Rock.* Dutton, 2007 (I: 12+ R: 5). This is a story about high school integration.

Duggleby, John. *Story Painter: The Life of Jacob Lawrence.* Chronicle, 1998 (I: all). A biography set during the Harlem Renaissance.

Evans, Shane W. *Underground: Finding the Light to Freedom.* Roaring Brook, 2011 (I: 5–8). The story is told from the viewpoint of fugitive slaves.

Farmer, Nancy. *A Girl Named Disaster.* Jackson/Orchard, 1996 (I: 101 R: 6). Winner of the 1997 Newbery Honor.

Feelings, Muriel. *Jambo Means Hello: Swahili Alphabet Book.* Dial, 1974 (I: all). A beautiful book that uses the Swahili alphabet.

_____. *Moja Means One: Swahili Counting Book.* Illustrated by Tom Feelings. Dial, 1971 (I: all). The book uses Swahili numbers.

Fenner, Carol. *Yolonda's Genius.* McElderry, 1995 (I: 101 R: 6). A fiction book about a bright fifth-grade girl and her younger brother, who has a special musical talent.

Ferris, Jeri. *Go Free or Die: A Story about Harriet Tubman.* Carolrhoda, 1988 (I: 71 R: 4). The biography describes Tubman's experiences during slavery and the Underground Railroad.

Fox, Paula. *The Slave Dancer.* Illustrated by Eros Keith. Bradbury, 1973 (I: 121 R: 7). A fife player experiences the slave trade.

Fradin, Judith Bloom, and Dennis Brindell Fradin. *5,000 Miles to Freedom: Ellen and William Craft's Flight from Slavery*. National Geographic, 2006 (I: 101 R: 6). The authors use many primary sources such as diaries and newspapers.

Freedman, Russell. *Freedom Walkers: The Story of the Montgomery Bus Boycott.* Holiday, 2006 (I: 91 R: 5). This informational book discusses the bus boycott.

_____. *The Voice That Challenged a Nation: Marian Anderson and the Struggle for Equal Rights*. Clarion, 2004 (I: 101 R: 6). A biography about one of the great African American singers.

Fritz, Jean. *Harriet Beecher Stowe and the Beecher Preachers.* Putnam, 1994 (I: 81 R: 4). This is a biography of the abolitionist and author of *Uncle Tom's Cabin.*

Gann, Marjorie, and Janet Willen. *Five Thousand Years of Slavery.* Tundra, 2011 (I: 10–YA R: 7). This is a global history of slavery.

Gilchrist, Jan Spivey. *My America*. Illustrated by Ashley Bryan and Jan Spivey Gilchrist. HarperCollins, 2007 (I: all). The poetry and illustrations depict the diversity in America.

Giovanni, Nikki. *Rosa*. Illustrated by Bryan Collier. Henry Holt, 2005 (I: all R: 4). A biography about the woman who instigated the Montgomery bus boycott.

Greenfield, Eloise. *The Great Migration: Journey to the North.* Illustrated by Jan Spivey Gilchrist HarperCollins, 2010 (I: all). Using poetic form, the author presents the history of African Americans going north in search of jobs.

_____. *Honey, I Love and Other Love Poems.* Illustrated by Jan Gilchrist. HarperCollins, 1995 (I: 3–6). A highly illustrated poem.

_____. *Sister.* Illustrated by Moneta Barnett. Crowell, 1974 (I: 8–12 R: 5). A thirteen-year-old reviews memories.

_____. *The Village of Round and Square Houses.* Little, Brown, 1985 (I: 4–9 R: 6). A *pourquoi* tale explains why women live in round houses and men live in square houses.

Grimes, Nikki. *Bronx Masquerade.* Dial, 2002 (I: 91). A group of students study the Harlem Renaissance and write their own poetry.

Haley, Gail E. *A Story, A Story: An African Tale.* Atheneum, 1970 (I: 6–10 R: 6). An African tale tells about a spider man's bargain with Sky God.

Hamilton, Virginia. *Anthony Burns: The Defeat and Triumph of a Fugitive Slave.* Knopf, 1988 (I: 101 R: 6). This is a biography of the escaped slave whose trial caused riots in Boston.

_____. *Her Stories: African American Folktales. Fairy Tales, and True Tales.* Illustrated by Leo and Diane Dillon. Scholastic, 1995 (I: 101 R: 6). This collection includes nineteen tales about women.

_____. *The House of Dies Drear.* Illustrated by Eros Keith. Macmillan, 1968 (I: 111 R: 4). A suspenseful story about a family who is living in a home that was a station on the Underground Railroad.

_____. *In the Beginning: Creation Stories from Around the World.* Illustrated by Barry Moser. Harcourt Brace Jovanovich, 1988 (I: all R: 5). Creation stories come from many cultures.

_____. *Many Thousand Gone: African Americans from Slavery to Freedom.* Illustrated by Leo and Diane Dillon. Knopf, 1993 (I: 81 R: 5). Short stories tell about people who were involved in fighting for freedom.

_____. *M. C. Higgins, the Great.* Macmillan, 1974 (I: 121 R: 4) M. C. dreams of fleeing from the danger of a strip mining spoil heap.

_____. *The People Could Fly: The Picture Book.* Illustrated by Leo and Diane Dillon. Knopf, 2004 (I: all). One of Hamilton's tales in a highly illustrated text.

_____, reteller. *The People Could Fly: American Black Folktales.* Illustrated by Leo and Diane Dillon. Knopf, 1985 (I: 91 R: 6). A collection of tales told by or adapted by African Americans.

_____. *When Birds Could Talk and Bats Could Sing: The Adventures of Bush Sparrow, Sis Wren, and Their Friends.* Illustrated by Barry Moser. Scholastic, 1996 (I: 101 R: 4). This collection includes eight tales from the southern part of the United States.

_____. *Zeely.* Illustrated by Symeon Shimin. Macmillan, 1967 (I: 8–12 R: 4). Geeder believes her stately neighbor is a Watusi queen.

Hannah, Jonny. *Hot Jazz Special.* Candlewick, 2005 (I: all). A highly illustrated book that depicts images about jazz musicians.

Harris, Joel Chandler. *Jump! The Adventures of Brer Rabbit.* Adapted by Van Dyke Parks. Illustrated by Barry Moser. Harcourt Brace Jovanovich, 1986 (I: all R: 4). Five Brer Rabbit stories.

_____. *Jump Again! More Adventures of Brer Rabbit.* Adapted by Van Dyke Parks. Illustrated by Barry Moser. Harcourt Brace Jovanovich, 1987 (I: all R: 4). Five additional tales.

_____. *More Tales of Uncle Remus: Further Adventures of Brer Rabbit. His Friends, Enemies, and Others.* Retold by Julius Lester. Dial, 1988 (I: all R: 4). A collection of tales from the South.

_____. *The Tales of Uncle Remus: The Adventures of Brer Rabbit.* Retold by Julius Lester. Illustrated by Jerry Pinkney. Dial, 1987 (I: all R: 4). This book contains forty-eight Brer Rabbit tales.

Haskins, James. *I Have a Dream: The Life and Words of Martin Luther King, Jr.* Millbrook, 1993 (I: 101 R: 7). This biography focuses on the civil rights movement.

_____. *The Life and Death of Martin Luther King. Jr.* Lothrop, Lee & Shepard, 1977 (I: 101 R: 7). This biography covers the life of the civil rights leader.

Hill, Laban Carrick. *Dave the Potter: Artist, Poet, Slave.* Illustrated by Bryan Collier. Little, Brown, 2010 (I: all). The life of a poet and artist who was a slave in South Carolina.

_____. *Harlem Stomp! A Cultural History of the Harlem Renaissance.* Little, Brown, 2003 (I: 8+ R: 5). Photographs add to this history.

Hoobler, Dorothy, and Thomas Hoobler. *The African American Family Album.* Oxford University Press, 1995 (I: 101 R: 5). Photographs, reproductions, a list of further reading, and an index are included in this pictorial history.

Hooks, William H. *The Ballad of Belle Dorcas.* Illustrated by Brian Pinkney. Knopf, 1990 (I: 71 R: 4). An African American folklore.

Hoose, Phillip. *Claudette Colvin: Twice Toward Justice.* Farrar, Straus & Giroux, 2009 (I: 10+ R: 5). An African American girl refuses to give up her seat on the bus.

Hopkinson, Deborah. *A Band of Angels: A Story Inspired by the Jubilee Singers.* Illustrated by Raul Colon. Atheneum, 1999 (I: all). This fictional story is based on real events.

Hudson, Wade, and Cheryl Willis Hudson, compilers. *In Praise of Our Fathers and Our Mothers: A Black Family Treasury by Outstanding Authors and Artists.* Just Us Books, 1997 (I: 101). A collection of writings and art.

Hughes, Langston. *The Dream Keeper and Other Poems.* Illustrated by Brian Pinkney. Knopf, 1994 (I: all). This is a revision of a text first published in 1932.

_____. *My People.* Photographs by Charles R. Smith, Jr. Atheneum, 2009 (I: all). An illustrated poem.

_____. *The Negro Speaks of Rivers.* Illustrated by E. B. Lewis, Disney, 2009 (I: all). The poems focus on rivers in many locations.

Hurmance, Belinda. *A Girl Called Boy.* Houghton Mifflin, 1982 (I: 101 R: 6). A contemporary girl experiences slavery.

Hurston, Zora Neal. *The Six Fools.* Adapted by Joyce Carol Thomas. Illustrated by Ann Tanksley. HarperCollins, 2006 (I: 6–10 R: 5). A man searches for greater fools than found in his fiancée's family.

Igus, Toyomi. *I See the Rhythm.* Illustrated by Michele Wood. Children's Press, 1998 (I: 71). The text explores both poetry and music.

Jansen, Hanna. *Over a Thousand Hills I Walk with You.* Translated by Elizabeth D. Crawford. Carolrhoda, 2006 (I: YA R: 8). The book is set in Rwanda in 1994.

Johnson, James Weldon. *Lift Every Voice and Sing.* Illustrated by Elizabeth Catlett. Walker, 1993 (I: all). Linocut prints accompany the song.

Kilaka, John. *The Amazing Tree.* Northsouth, 2011 (I: 5–8 R: 4). In a tale from Tanzania, a small rabbit saves the people.

_____. *Why the Crab Has No Head.* Carolrhoda, 1987 (I: all R: 4). This is a *pourquoi* tale from Zaire.

Krull, Kathleen. *Wilma Unlimited: How Wilma Rudolph Became the World's Fastest Woman*. Illustrated by David Diaz. Harcourt Brace, 1996 (I: 81 R: 5). This biography is about the track-and-field star.

Langstaff, John. *What a Morning! The Christmas Story in Black Spirituals*. Illustrated by Ashley Bryan. McElderry, 1987 (I: all). Five spirituals focus on the Christmas story.

Lester, Julius. *Day of Tears: A Novel in Dialogue*. Hyperion, 2005 (I: 8+ R: 5). This novel about slavery is written in dialogue.

______. *John Henry*. Illustrated by Jerry Pinkney. Dial, 1994 (I: all R: 5). This is an illustrated version of the legend.

______. *The Last Tales of Uncle Remus*. Illustrated by Jerry Pinkney. Dial, 1994 (I: all R: 4). The text includes thirty-nine stories.

Lewin, Hugh. *To Be a Slave*. Dial, 1968 (I: 101 R: 6). Winner of the 1969 Newbery Honor.

Lombard, Jenny. *Drita, My Homegirl*. Putnam, 2006 (I: 8–10 R: 4). A bond is forged between two fourth-grade girls.

McCully, Emily Arnold. *Wonder Horse: The True Story of the World's Smartest Horse*. Holt, 2010 (I: 5–8 R: 4). A former slave uses his skills to train horses.

McCurdy, Michael, ed. *Escape from Slavery: The Boyhood of Frederick Douglass in His Own Words*. Knopf, 1994 (I: 91). This autobiography presents Douglass's original language.

McDermott, Gerald. *Anansi the Spider: A Tale from the Ashanti*. Holt, Rinehart & Winston, 1972 (I: 7–9). This is a folktale about the trickster.

______. *Zomo the Rabbit: A Trickster Tale from West Africa*. Harcourt Brace, 1992 (I: 4–8 R: 4). This tale shows the importance of courage, sense, and caution.

McGill, Alice. *Way Up and Over Everything*. Illustrated by Jude Daly. Houghton Mifflin, 2008 (I: 5–8 R: 4). An African American tale symbolizes slaves' dreams for freedom.

McKissack, Patricia. *The Dark-Thirty: Southern Tales of the Supernatural*. Illustrated by Brian Pinkney. Knopf, 1992 (I: 81 R: 5). This is a collection of ghost stories.

______. *Flossie and the Fox*. Illustrated by Rachel Isadora. Dial, 1986 (I: 3–8 R: 3). This is a tale of the rural South.

______. *Mirandy and Brother Wind*. Illustrated by Jerry Pinkney. Knopf, 1988 (I: 4–9 R: 5). A girl enters a cakewalk contest.

McKissack, Patricia C., and Onawumi Jean Moss. *Precious and the Boo Hag*. Illustrated by Kyrsten Brooker. Simon & Schuster, 2005 (I: 5–8 R: 4). A humorous story about being home alone with your imagination.

McWhorter, Diane. *A Dream of Freedom: The Civil Rights Movement from 1954 to 1968*. Scholastic, 2004 (I: 10–YA R: 6). The book follows a chronological order of the civil rights movement.

Mandela, Nelson. *Nelson Mandela's Favorite African Folktales*. Norton, 2002 (I: 10–YA R: 6). A large collection of folktales.

Marsalis, Wynton. *Jazz ABZ: An A to Z Collection of Jazz Portraits*. Illustrated by Paul Rogers. Candlewick, 2005 (I: 121 R: 6). Includes short biographical selections of musicians.

Mathis, Sharon Bell. *The Hundred Penny Box*. Illustrated by Leo and Diane Dillon. Viking, 1975 (I: 6–9 R: 3). An elderly relative tells her story through the pennies in her box.

Mbugua, Kioi wa. *Inkishu: Myths and Legends of the Maasai*. Jacaranda Designs, 1994 (I: 81 R: 5). A collection of folktales from Kenya and Tanzania.

Meltzer, Milton. *The Black Americans: A History in Their Own Words, 1619–1983*. Crowell, 1984 (I: 101 R: 6). Short writings provide a political and social history.

______, ed. *Frederick Douglass: In His Own Words*. Illustrated by Stephen Alcorn. Harcourt Brace, 1995 (I: 121). Each of Douglass's speeches or writings is introduced with a commentary.

Miller, Douglas. *Frederick Douglass and the Fight for Freedom*. Facts on File, 1988 (I: 101 R: 6). A biography of the leader who escaped slavery.

Mitchell, Margaree King. *Uncle Jed's Barbershop*. Illustrated by James Ransome. Simon & Schuster, 1993 (I: 5–9 R: 3). A man retains his dreams.

Monjo, N. *The Drinking Gourd*. Illustrated by Fred Brenner. Harper & Row, 1970 (I: 7–9 R: 2). This is a history of the Underground Railroad for beginning readers.

Morrison, Toni. *Remember: The Journey to School Integration*. Houghton Mifflin, 2004 (I: all). Numerous photographs depict this history.

Musgrove, Margaret. *Ashanti to Zulu: African Traditions*. Illustrated by Leo and Diane Dillon. Dial, 1976 (I: 7–12). Traditions of twenty-six African peoples are presented.

Myers, Walter Dean. *Fallen Angels.* New York: Scholastic, 1988 (I: YA R: 6). A young soldier from the mean streets.

_____. *Harlem.* Illustrated by Christopher Myers. Scholastic, 1997 (I: all). This is a book of poetry.

_____. *Jazz.* Illustrated by Christopher Myers. Holiday, 2006 (I: 101). This poetry explores different types of jazz forms.

_____. *Lockdown.* HarperCollins, 2010 (I: YA R: 5). A teenage boy learns lessons while in detention.

_____. *Scorpions.* Harper & Row, 1988 (I: 111 R: 5). A boy faces problems with a gang.

_____. *Shooter.* HarperCollins, 2004 (I: 12–YA R: 5). A story of troubled teens ends in a school shooting.

_____. *Somewhere in the Darkness.* Scholastic, 1992 (I: 101 R: 5). Winner of the 1993 Newbery Honor.

_____. *The Story of the Three Kingdoms.* Illustrated by Ashley Bryan. New York: HarperCollins, 1995 (I: 71 R: 4). This is an original tale that uses a folkloric style.

Naidoo, Beverley. *The Other Side of Truth.* HarperCollins, 2000 (I: 101 R: 5). A twelve-year-old Nigerian girl is smuggled to England after her journalist father writes against the current political environment.

Nelson, Marilyn. *Carver: A Life in Poems.* Front Street, 2001 (I: 101). This biography of George Washington Carver is written through poetry.

_____. *Fortune's Bones: The Manumission Requiem.* Front Street, 2004 (I: 101). Poetry develops the life of a slave who died in 1798.

_____. *Snook Alone.* Illustrated by Timothy Basil Ering. Candlewick, 2010 (I: all). A story of a dog and a monk told in free verse.

_____. *A Wreath for Emmett Till.* Illustrated by Philippe Lardy. Houghton Mifflin, 2005 (I: 101). The poem is a memorial to a lynched African American fourteen-year-old.

Onyefulu, Ifeoma. *Emeka's Gift: An African Counting Story.* Cobblehill, 1995 (I: 4–8). Photographs from a southern Nigeria market show counting from 1 to 10.

_____. *The Girl Who Married a Ghost and Other Tales from Nigeria.* Illustrated by Julia Cairus. Lincoln, 2010 (I: 8–12 R: 4). Ten tales from Nigeria.

Orgill, Roxane. *Skit-Scat Raggedy Cat: Ella Fitzgerald.* Illustrated by Sean Qualls. Candlewick, 2010 (I: 8–12 R: 5). This is a jazz biography.

Otfinoski, Steven. *Great Black Writers.* Facts on File, 1994 (I: 121). The text includes examples of subjects writings as well as information about their careers.

Parker, Robert Andrew. *Piano Starts Here: The Young Art Tatum.* Schwartz, 2008 (I: 5–9 R: 5). The biography of the jazz pianist.

Partridge, Elizabeth. *Marching for Freedom.* Viking, 2009 (I: 6–9 R: 6). Photographs accompany this nonfiction book.

Patterson, Lillie. *Martin Luther King. Jr. and the Freedom Movement.* Facts on File, 1989 (I: 101 R: 6). This book chronicles King's nonviolent struggles against segregation.

Paulsen, Gary. *Nightjohn.* Delacorte, 1993 (I: 101 R: 4). A slave teaches children to read.

Petry, Ann. *Harriet Tubman: Conductor on the Underground Railroad.* Crowell, 1955 (I: 101 R: 6). This is a biography of a woman who led over 300 slaves to freedom.

Philip, Neil. *Mythology of the World.* Illustrated by Nicki Palin. Kingfisher, 2004 (I: 121 R: 7). The collection includes a section on African mythology.

Pinkney, Andrea Davis. *Duke Ellington.* Illustrated by Brian Pinkney. Hyperion, 1998 (I: all). A highly illustrated biography.

Pinkney, Jerry. *The Lion & the Mouse.* Little, Brown, 2009 (I: all). Saving a lion is rewarded.

Ringgold, Faith. *My Dream of Martin Luther King.* Crown, 1995 (I: 5–9 R: 4). This is a highly illustrated biography that develops as the author tells about King's life through a dream sequence.

_____. *Tar Beach.* Crown, 1991 (I: 4–7 R: 4). A girl imagines she can fly over the city.

Robinson, Sharon. *Promises to Keep: How Jackie Robinson Changed America.* Scholastic, 2004 (I: 81 R: 5). A biography of a great baseball player.

Sanfield, Steve. *The Adventures of High John the Conqueror.* Illustrated by John Ward. Watts, 1989 (I: 81 R: 4). The text includes sixteen southern folktales.

San Souci, Robert D. *Cendrillon.* Illustrated by Brian Pinkney. Simon & Schuster, 1998 (I: 5–10 R: 5). This is a Cinderella variant.

_____. *The Faithful Friend.* Illustrated by Brian Pinkney. Simon & Schuster, 1995 (I: 5–10 R: 5). A folktale from the West Indies.

_____. *The Hired Hand.* Illustrated by Jerry Pinkney. Dial, 1997 (I: 5–10 R: 5). This folktale is set in Virginia.

_____, retold by. *Sister Tricksters: Rollicking Tales of Clever Females.* Illustrated by Daniel San Souci. August House, 2006 (I: 8–12 R: 5). Characters such as Miz Goose outwit Mistah Bear.

_____. *Sukey and the Mermaid.* Illustrated by Brian Pinkney. Four Winds, 1992 (I: 5–10 R: 5). A folktale that has elements from West Africa, the Caribbean, and the Sea Islands of South Carolina.

_____. *The Talking Eggs.* Illustrated by Jerry Pinkney. Dial, 1989 (I: all). A folktale from the American South.

Schneider, Dorothy, and Carl J. Schneider, eds. *Slavery in America.* Facts on File, 2007 (I: 121). An extensive coverage of topics related to slavery.

Schroeder, Alan. *Minty: A Story of Young Harriet Tubman.* Illustrated by Jerry Pinkney. Puffin, 1996 (I: 8–11 R: 41). An illustrated story about the African American.

Shange, Ntozake. *Ellington Was Not a Street.* Illustrated by Kadir Nelson. Simon & Schuster, 2004 (I: all). A highly illustrated poem about the many men who influenced African American history and culture.

Shepard, Aaron. *Master Man: A Tall Tale of Nigeria.* Illustrated by David Wisniewski. HarperCollins, 2001 (I: all). The tale reveals foolish consequences of bragging.

Smalls-Hector, Irene. *Jonathan and His Mommy.* Illustrated by Michael Hays. Little, Brown, 1992 (I: 3–8). A boy and his mother take a walk in the neighborhood.

Smith, Charles R., Jr. *Black Jack: The Ballad of Jack Johnson.* Illustrated by Shane W. Evans. Roaring Brook, 2010 (I: 8–10 R: 5). A biography of the first African American heavyweight champion.

Steptoe, John. *Mufaro's Beautiful Daughters: An African Tale.* Lothrop, Lee & Shepard, 1987 (I: all R: 4). An African folktale with some Cinderella elements.

Steptoe, Michele, ed. *Our Song, Our Toil: The Story of American Slavery As Told by Slaves.* Millbrook, 1994 (I: 81). Text is developed around short biographies of slaves.

Stevens, Janet. *Tops and Bottoms.* Harcourt Brace, 1995 (I: 4–7). A folktale from the Plantation South.

Swift, Hildegarde. *The Railroad to Freedom: A Story of the Civil War.* Harcourt Brace Jovanovich, 1932 (I: 101 R: 6). This book won the 1933 Newbery Honor.

Tavare, Matt. *Henry Aaron's Dream.* Candlewick, 2010 (I: 8–10 R: 5). Aaron's dream is to play for the major leagues.

Taylor, Mildred. *The Gold Cadillac.* Illustrated by Michael Hays. Dial, 1987 (I: 8–10 R: 3). An African American family experiences racial prejudice during a drive into the segregated South.

_____. *Let the Circle Be Unbroken.* Dial, 1981 (I: 101 R: 6). This is a sequel to *Role of Thunder, Hear My Cry.*

_____. *Roll of Thunder, Hear My Cry.* Dial, 1976 (I: 101 R: 6). An African American family in Mississippi experiences humiliating and frightening situations in 1933.

Thomas, Joyce Carol. *The Blacker the Berry.* Illustrated by Floyd Cooper. HarperCollins, 2008 (I: all). The poetry tells about feelings associated with colors.

Turck, Mary C. *Freedom Song: Young Voices and the Struggle for Civil Rights.* Chicago Review Press, 2009 (I: 10+ R: 5). A history of the civil rights movement and a CD of "Songs on the Road to Freedom."

Van Allsburg, Chris. *Probuditi!* Houghton, 2006 (I: 4–8 R: 5). A sister has the last laugh after her brother plays a prank on her.

Vernick, Audrey. *She Loved Baseball: The Effa Manley Story.* Illustrated by Don Tate. HarperCollins, 2010 (I: 7–9 R: 4). The story of the first woman to be inducted into the Baseball Hall of Fame.

Weatherford, Carole Boston. *Moses: When Harriet Tubman Led Her People to Freedom.* Illustrated by Kadir Nelson. Hyperion, 2006 (I: 7–10). Tells the story of Tubman and the Underground Railroad.

Williams, Garth. *The Rabbits' Wedding.* HarperCollins, 1958 (I: all). A book that became controversial.

Williams, Sherley Anne. *Working Cotton.* Illustrated by Carole Byard. Harcourt Brace, 1992 (I: all). The memories of a migrant family working in California.

Williams-Garcia, Rita. *One Crazy Summer.* HarperCollins, 2010 (I: 9+ R: 5). In 1968, sisters interact with the Black Panthers.

Winter, Jonah. *Dizzy.* Illustrated by Sean Qualls. Scholastic, 2006 (I: 8–12). Poetry develops the life of Dizzy Gillespie.

Wisniewski, David. *Sundiata: Lion King of Mali.* Clarion, 1992 (I: all). This is a highly illustrated legend.

Woodson, Jacqueline. *Coming On Home Soon.* Illustrated by E. B. Lewis. Putnam, 2004 (I: 5–8 R: 4). Set during World War II; a grandmother takes care of her granddaughter while her mother works away from home.

Yates, Elizabeth. *Amos Fortune, Free Man.* Illustrated by Nora S. Unwin. Dutton, 1950, 1989 (I: 101 R: 6). A slave becomes a free man in Boston.

Chapter 3

Native American Literature

In our study of Native American literature, we will discover both traditional and contemporary literature that reflects many different groups. We begin our study with a historical perspective, extend the study to folklore, discuss the historical nonfiction and fiction, and conclude with contemporary literature, both fiction and nonfiction.

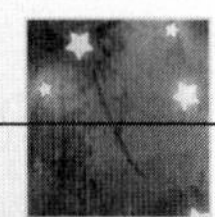

Historical Perspective

The history of Native American literature extends thousands of years into the past. According to Ron Querry (1995),

> [W]hile the writings of the seventeenth century English colonists have traditionally been considered—and are taught—as the first works of American literature, the continent of North America already had a 28,000-year history of storytelling when John Smith and Anne Bradstreet first sat down to write of their experiences in the "new" world. The texts of that long Indian history were oral and communal. Because of that fact, it is often assumed that Indians had no literature or, at the very least, that its oral quality made that literature inferior. Early on, however, their oral traditions gave Indian people a rich literary heritage. (p. 1)

In addition to the importance of literature in the Native American culture, Native American languages are also important. Michelle Nijhuis (2003), in her article "Tribal Talk," discusses why immersion schools are being developed that help revive and preserve Native American languages. She states, "What is at stake is more than words. Filled with nuance and references to Blackfeet history and traditions, the language embodies a culture. The language allows kids to unravel the mysteries of their heritage" (p. 36). This is important according to Nijhuis because "The Blackfoot language, also known as Piegan, has been in danger of disappearing for nearly a century. From the late 1800s through the 1960s, the Bureau of Indian Affairs forced tens of thousands of Native Americans into English-only government boarding schools. Taken hundreds of miles from the reservations, the children were often beaten for speaking native languages and sent home ashamed of them. As adults, they cautioned their own children to speak English only" (p. 36). Nijhuis describes a movement among various Native American cultures that encourages students to learn and use their own languages at schools that teach subject matter and culture using language immersion techniques. Rand Valentine and Barbara Juhas Walsh (2010) emphasize the need to include courses in the Ojibwe language in a university curriculum.

Native American Timeline

50,000 BCE	Shamanic religion and core Earth-Diver creation myths and trickster myths brought to North America by Native Americans
1823	*Poor Sarah . . .* by Elias Boudinot (Cherokee), a fictionalized conversion story, possibly the first Native American fiction
1827	David Cusick's (Tuscarora) *Ancient History of the Six Nations* published; cited as first historical work by Native American
1829	William Apes's (Pequot) *A Son of the Forest* published; cited as the first autobiography written by a Native American
1831–1832	Sovereignty of Native American tribes affirmed by the Supreme Court
1832	The first "as-told-to" autobiography, from Black Hawk (Sauk), published
1837	Beginning of enforcement of the Indian Removal Act of 1830 by President Andrew Jackson, driving southern tribes on the Trail of Tears
1839	Two volumes of Chippewa tales published by Schoolcraft
1868	John Rollin Ridge's (Cherokee) *Poems*; first volume of poetry published by a Native American
1871	Refusal of Congress to recognize tribes as independent nations
1876	Custer defeated at Little Bighorn
1890	Massacre of Ghost Dancers at Wounded Knee, South Dakota
1902	Charles Eastman's (Yankton Sioux) *Indian Boyhood* published
Early 1900s	Importance of Native American myths and folktales recognized
1924	Indian Voting Rights Act stressed by anthropologist Franz Boas
1929	Types and motifs of tales identified by Stith Thompson in *Tales of the North American Indians*
1942	Newbery Honor: Lois Lenski's *Indian Captive: The Story of Mary Jemison*
1952	Newbery Honor: Elizabeth Baity's *Americans Before Columbus*
1966	Canadian Book of the Year: Farley Mowat's *Lost in the Barrens*
1969	Pulitzer Prize: N. Scott Momaday's (Kiowa) *House Made of Dawn*
1970s	Several Caldecott Honor Awards to artists of books about Native Americans: Tom Bahti, Peter Parnall
1970s	Several Newbery Honor Awards to books about Native American subjects: Scott O'Dell (*Sing Down the Moon*), Miska Miles (*Annie and the Old One*), Jamake Highwater (*Anpao: An American Indian Odyssey*)
1973	Newbery: Jean Craighead George's *Julie of the Wolves*
1974	James Welch's (Blackfoot/Gros Ventre) *Winter in the Blood* identified in *New York Times* as "best first novel of the season"
1975	Caldecott: Gerald McDermott's *Arrow to the Sun*
1977	Leslie Silko (Laguana) published *Ceremony*; later awarded MacArthur Foundation Fellowship (1981) for her achievement
1979	Caldecott: Paul Goble's *The Girl Who Loved Wild Horses*
1982	Caldecott Honor: Artist Stephen Gammell's *Where the Buffaloes Begin*
1980s	Newbery Honor Awards: Elizabeth George Speare (*The Sign of the Beaver*) and Gary Paulsen (*Dogsong*)
1984	Canadian Book of the Year: Jan Hudson's *Sweetgrass*
1994	Caldecott Honor: Gerald McDermott's *Raven: A Trickster Tale from the Pacific Northwest*
1995	Newbery: Sharon Creech's *Walk Two Moons*
1999	National Book Award finalist: Louise Erdrich's *The Birchbark House*
2005	Woodcraft Circle of Native Writers named Deborah L. Duvall Children's Writer of the Year (*Rabbit and the Bears*)
2006	American Indian Library Association winner *Beaver Steals Fire: A Salish Coyote Story* by Salish and Kootenai tribes
2007	National Book Award for Young People's Literature: *The Absolutely True Diary of a Part-Time Indian* by Sherman Alexie
2009	Pen/Faulkner Award for Sherman Alexie's *War Dances*

Stereotypes in Literature from the Past

What is a stereotype? Catherine Verrall and Patricia McDowell (1990) in a publication by the Canadian Alliance in Solidarity with the Native Peoples present a definition of stereotypes:

> A stereotype is a fixed image, idea, trait, convention, lacking in originality or individuality, most often negative. Noble savage, stoic warrior in noble defeat, drunken savage, heathen, lazy Indians, children of the forest, Indian princess, whore, dead and dying saints . . . how many others can you identify? Stereotypes rob individuals and their cultures of human qualities, and promote no real understanding of social realities. (p. 7)

Books about Native Americans written for juvenile audiences and published prior to the mid-1970s are frequently filled with such negative stereotypes. Researchers who analyze the images of Native Americans in these books have been especially critical of the common stereotypes. Laura Herbst (1977) found the most common stereotypes characterize Native Americans as savage, depraved, and cruel; noble, proud, silent, and close to nature; or inferior, childlike, and helpless. Terms and comparisons suggesting negative and derogatory images often reinforce such stereotypes. She also identified the stereotypical ways in which Native American culture has been portrayed in children's literature as inferior to the white culture; valueless, and not worthy of respect; and quaint or superficial, without depth or warmth. In the cultural stereotypes, the suggestion is made that life will improve if the Native Americans abandon their culture. Stereotypes of the Native American culture as valueless and not worthy of respect usually ignore the rich diversity of Native American cultures, spiritual beliefs and ceremonies, moral values, artistic skills, and lifestyles in favor of the attitude that violence is the chief Native American value.

The changing attitudes toward stereotypes in Native American literature are apparent in the literary criticism of award-winning books. For example, in 1941, Robert Lawson's *They Were Strong and Good* won the Caldecott Medal. The book has since been criticized for having a stereotypical text and illustrations. Similarly, although *The Matchlock Gun* by Walter Edmonds won the 1942 Newbery Medal, the book has been criticized in later years for its stereotypical views of Native Americans. As you read these books and books like them, consider your own responses and the stereotypes they develop.

Any of the stereotypical portrayals described in this section is offensive. More current books, however, especially those written by Native American authors or other authorities on Native American culture, are usually sensitive to the heritage and individuality of the native peoples of North America.

Authors Who Write and Illustrate Native American Literature

According to Ron Querry (1995), many of the Native American authors

> trace their identities back to the voices of the continent's earliest storytellers. Unlike most of their ancestors, these contemporary Indian authors tell their stories in writing, but they continue an ancient tradition nonetheless. Like their ancestors, they tell distinctive stories about times and places that have shaped the identities of those who inhabit them. Like their ancestors, these modern storytellers provide challenging discoveries of America by showing what has happened here. (p. 1)

Querry traces the emergence of high-quality novels written for adult audiences to the 1968 publication of N. Scott Momaday's Pulitzer Prize–winning novel *House Made of Dawn*. Querry states that following this publication there have been more than one hundred novels written by Native American writers.

The same increase in Native American literature is apparent in the juvenile market. Books by both Native American authors and authors who write with a Native American perspective are available in picture books, traditional literature, and contemporary titles. A review of Caldecott Medal and Honor books for the 1990s, 1980s, and 1970s indicates the number of books relating to Native Americans is increasing from earlier periods and shows they are receiving recognition for their literary quality: *Raven: A Trickster Tale from the Pacific Northwest* by Gerald McDermott (1994 Caldecott Honor); Olaf Baker's *Where the Buffaloes Begin* (1982 Caldecott Honor, illustrated by Stephen Gammell); Paul Goble's *The Girl Who Loved Wild Horses* (1979 Caldecott); Byrd Baylor's *Hawk, I'm Your Brother* (1977 Caldecott Honor, illustrated by Peter Parnall); Byrd Baylor's *The Desert Is Theirs* (1976 Caldecott Honor, illustrated by Peter Parnall); Gerald McDermott's *Arrow to the Sun* (1975 Caldecott); and Byrd Baylor's *When Clay Sings* (1973 Caldecott Honor, illustrated by Tom Bahti).

The Newbery Medal and Honor books include Sharon Creech's *Walk Two Moons* (1995 Newbery); Virginia Hamilton's *In the Beginning: Creation Stories from Around the World* (this 1989 Newbery Honor book includes several Native American myths); Gary Paulsen's *Dogsong* (1986 Newbery Honor); Elizabeth George Speare's *The Sign of the Beaver* (1984 Newbery Honor); Jamake Highwater's *Anpao: An American Indian Odyssey* (1978 Newbery Honor); Jean Craighead George's *Julie of the Wolves* (1973 Newbery); Miska Miles's *Annie and the Old One* (1972 Newbery Honor); and Scott O'Dell's *Sing Down the Moon* (1971 Newbery Honor).

Many other authors are either Native American or write with a Native American perspective. For example, John Bierhorst, Joseph Bruchac, Deborah L. Duvall, and Maurice Metayer retell Native American folklore. Michael Dorris and Jan Hudson write historical fiction. Dorothy Nafus Morrison and Jean Fritz write biographies. Virginia Driving Hawk Sneve and White Deer of Autumn are known for contemporary literature. Louise Erdrich is an Ojibwa author.

The works of Native American artists are beginning to be found in the illustrated texts. For example, Navajo artist Shonto Begay's illustrations are found in *Navajo: Visions and Voices Across the Mesa*. Cherokee artist Murv Jacob's works illustrate Joseph Bruchac's *The Boy Who Lived with the Bears and Other Iroquois Stories*. Cayuga/Tuscarora artists' works are found in Chief Jake Swamp's *Giving Thanks: A Native American Good Morning Message*. Cherokee artist Christopher Canyon's works illustrate Sandra DeCoteau Orie's *Did You Hear Wind Sing Your Name? An Oneida Song of Spring*. Cree artist George Littlechild's illustrations are found in *This Land Is My Land*. The paintings of Chief Lelooska from the Northwest Coast are found in *Echoes of the Elders: The Stories and Paintings of Chief Lelooska*. Ojibwa artist Leo Yerxa's paintings are found in *Ancient Thunder*. Throughout this chapter, we will discover many excellent books and illustrated texts written and illustrated by both Native Americans and non–Native Americans.

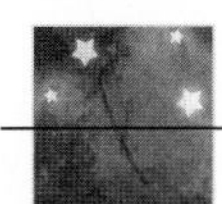

Issues Related to Native American Literature

There are numerous influences on the interpretation, writing, and acceptance of Native American literature. A review of these influences and the associated issues includes the following major areas of concern (Norton, 1996): (1) authenticity of text and illustrations; (2) conflicts over sovereignty related to who may write, adapt, or interpret the stories and culture; (3) disputes over translations of poetry, folklore, and biography/autobiography; and (4) disagreements over literal versus metaphorical interpretations.

Authenticity of Text and Illustrations

There are numerous issues related to authenticity of both the text and illustrations. For example, Jon C. Stott (1990) contrasts two versions of the Sedna tale, an Inuit myth. After

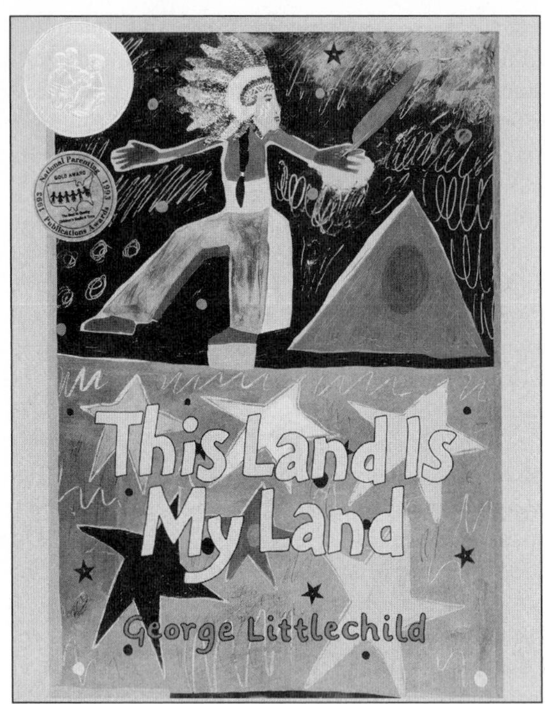

In *This Land Is My Land*, the author, a Plains Cree Indian from Canada, describes his experiences.

Cover of *This Land Is My Land*, by George Littlechild. Children's Book Press, 1993. Reprinted by permission of George Littlechild.

his analysis of Robert and Daniel San Souci's *Song of Sedna*, he says that the text is "so altered as to be virtually worthless as a reflection on Inuit culture" (p. 199). Stott declares that throughout the book, the illustrations are inaccurate, the visual depictions of the setting are inappropriate, and the illustrations counteract the Inuit values found in the original story. Stott describes the illustrations as appropriate for the Native Indians of southern Alaska and northern British Columbia rather than the Inuit peoples. Stott concludes, "The effect of these inaccuracies is to rob the accompanying story of its cultural background. More important, it implicitly reflects the attitude that cultural accuracy in portraying a story of these people is unimportant" (p. 200).

In contrast, Stott finds that Beverly Brodsky McDermott, the reteller and illustrator of *Sedna: An Eskimo Myth*, "combines art and text in a way that presents and amplifies the traditional meanings of the myth" (p. 199). Stott concludes his analysis of McDermott's text by stating, "McDermott clearly respects the culture and the story, as well as the young audience for whom it is adapted. Not only has she closely followed the outline of the Inuit myth, but also she has embodied the cultural dualities that are one of its essential aspects" (p. 201). The types of errors identified in *Song of Sedna* or the accuracy in *Sedna: An Eskimo Myth* also show the importance of identifying authentic nonfiction informational books that allow readers to evaluate the authenticity of illustrations and settings.

Authenticity in text and illustrations is a major issue in books such as Susan Jeffers's *Brother Eagle, Sister Sky: A Message from Chief Seattle*. Critics are now questioning the authorship of the text. Was the text really written by the Suquamish Indian chief who lived in the Washington Territory in 1854 or was the text written by a playwright in much more recent times? Are the illustrations accurate for a tale supposedly about the people who lived in the Washington Territory?

Debbie Reese (2007), a Pueblo Indian from Nambe Pueblo, is very critical of the retellings of many Zuni folktales. She compares original Zuni versions of "Turkey Girl" and "Dragon's Tale" with retellings in picture book format and concludes that the retellings should not be used in classrooms to teach children about the Zuni people. She states, "Stories matter to the people who tell them, and they should matter to all of us, whether we are Zuni Indians or not" (p. 255).

Conflicts over Sovereignty of the Stories

Conflicts over sovereignty raise significant issues related to writing, publishing, and reading Native American literature. The major question is, Who should write or retell stories about Native American people and their culture? People who adhere to one viewpoint argue that the Native American people should have total sovereignty over their traditions, their culture, their past, and their present circumstances. Advocates of this viewpoint believe Native American literature should be protected against the desecration committed by the imposition of alien cultures and American/European standards of literacy. In this viewpoint, only Native Americans can translate their traditions or write about their history and culture with an accurate perspective. The contrasting viewpoint encourages writing by knowledgeable and sensitive authors who are able to write with a Native American perspective even though they are not themselves Native American.

Selecting and Evaluating Native American Literature

Since the late 1960s, the numbers of literature selections identified as Native American have increased dramatically. Some of these books are of high literary and cultural quality; others, however, are filled with stereotypes or inaccurate information about people, their culture, their beliefs, and their values.

Criteria for Evaluating Native American Literature

Criteria for evaluating Native American literature include both generic criteria related to Native American literature and criteria that apply to specific genres of literature. In addition, the literature should be evaluated for literary quality. You may use the following generic criteria when evaluating the literature.

1. Are the Native American characters portrayed as individuals with their own thoughts, emotions, and philosophies? The characters should not conform to stereotypes.
2. Do the Native American characters belong to a specific tribe, or are they grouped together under one category referred to as "Indian"?
3. Does the author recognize the diversity of Native American cultures? Are the customs and ceremonies authentic for the Native American tribes?
4. Does the author respect Native American culture?
5. Does the author use offensive and degrading vocabulary?
6. Are the illustrations realistic and authentic?
7. If the story has a contemporary setting, does the author accurately describe the life and situation of Native Americans today?

Beverly Slapin, Doris Seal, and Rosemary Gonzales (1989) emphasize the need to evaluate for stereotypes; to consider loaded words with insulting overtones, as well as racist adjectives; to look for distortions of history; to evaluate the lifestyles and culture to make sure the culture, religions, and traditions are described accurately; to evaluate the dialogue to make sure it represents the skill of those who come from an oral tradition; to consider the role of women, who should be portrayed as an integral and respected part of society; to analyze the role of elders, who should be considered as valued custodians of the people's history, culture, and lifeways; to consider the effects of the story on children's self-images; and to analyze authors' or illustrators' backgrounds to ascertain if they have the background and skills that qualify them to write or illustrate books about Native Americans.

Analyzing, evaluating, and selecting Native American literature is a complex task. Several authors emphasize this complexity and problems associated with selection. For example, in a bulletin published by the National Council for the Social Studies, Karen D. Harvey, Lisa D. Harjo, and Jane K. Jackson (1990) identify the following facts that everyone should consider when evaluating and selecting materials about Native Americans. First, Native American cultures span twenty or more millennia, from before written history to today. Second, most of the Native American history is tentative, speculative, and written by European or Anglo-American explorers or scholars, and much of the oral history of the Native Americans was lost. Third, widely diverse physical environments influenced the development of ancient and contemporary Native American cultures, including Arctic tundra, woodlands, deserts, Mesoamerican jungles, prairies, plateaus, plains, swamps, and mountains. Fourth, linguists believe that at least 200 languages were spoken in North America before European contact, and scholars estimate that seventy-three language families existed in North America at the time of European contact. Fifth, currently, there are about 500 federally recognized tribes and about 300 federal reservations. Sixth, no one federal or tribal definition establishes a person's identity as an Indian. Consequently, Harvey et al. conclude, "the subject is vast, complicated, diverse, and difficult" (p. 2).

Jon C. Stott (1992) focuses on another problem faced by people seeking literature written by Native American authors. He states, "Works by native authors generally appear on the lists of smaller regional publishers, and, unfortunately, seldom reach a wide audience" (p. 374). Consequently some Native American literature is not easily available. Thankfully, as we analyze the literature, we will discover a considerable collection of newer quality literature that is available.

The debate in journals and among scholars has not as yet been resolved. Questions such as the following are frequently debated in journals, by publishers, and at scholarly meetings: Should anyone but a member of that specific Native American group write about the group? Who should be the intended audience for Native American literature? Must Native American writers be spokespersons for that group, or may they write about any subject?

Disputes over Literary Styles and Translations

The issues related to disputes over literary styles and translation frequently focus on the desirability or undesirability of changing literature so it is more accessible to, and able to be more easily understood by, a broader audience. Should the literature retain its total context within the Native American culture, or should it be changed to meet the standards and literary style of literature written from an American/European perspective?

Jamake Highwater (1981) emphasizes the communication differences between Anglo/European and Native American languages and literary styles that may interfere with translations and understandings. For example, in the Anglo/European cultures, words convey explanations and the question is "What does it mean?" In contrast, in Native American cultures, literature conveys a picture of an object or situation into the mind of the listener. The Native American perspective embraces all senses.

Differences in style affect the retellings of many types of literature. Changes in language and style are frequently found in the translations of folklore, poetry, chants, and autobiographies, especially the literature written for younger audiences. Native American scholars such as Michael Dorris (1979) argue against diluting the literature so it can be understood by a broader audience; Dorris maintains that scholars and readers need to develop an understanding of Native American literature by taking part in a study that progresses from an awareness of the language and philosophy of creation stories; proceeds through reading myth cycles; continues to historical sagas; proceeds to reading riddles, songs, and religious chants; continues to treaties, diaries, and autobiographies; and concludes with modern authors from the culture. Donna Norton (1990) modifies Dorris's approach to identify appropriate Native American literature and suggests a sequence of study that helps children and adolescents understand Native American culture and literature. In this type of study, students need to read and have access to a wide variety of literature. This is also the sequence developed throughout this textbook.

Translations of early Native American autobiographies are also of concern when choosing Native American literature. The authenticity of these translations may be questioned. What is the influence of interpreters on the content of the autobiography? What is the consequence if editors add information to place the narrative in a context that will be better understood by their audiences? Is a book really an autobiography if it has been translated and rewritten? We explore this issue in greater detail when we discuss biographies.

Disagreements over Literal versus Metaphorical Interpretations

Native American literature frequently includes visions such as those described by Black Elk in the autobiography *Black Elk Speaks: Being the Life Story of a Holy Man of the Oglala Sioux* (1932, 1979) and by Plenty-Coups in *Plenty-Coups: Chief of the Crows* (1962). Are these visions to be interpreted as literal experiences or should they be analyzed for their metaphorical meanings? The Native American authors of both books state their strong beliefs in the literal interpretations of their medicine dreams. They maintain that these dreams controlled their actions. Literary critics, however, debate these interpretations. Some critics maintain that seeking meaning subverts the integrity of the literature. Others believe that the images bear no real connection to the meaning of the experience. Still others argue that certain traditions make sense only in a metaphorical, not in a historical or literal, way. Finally, some believe a literal interpretation should be used to limit misinterpretation and to encourage fundamental understanding of the Native American experience. These questions are debated, especially in children's and adolescent literature. As students of multicultural literature, we need to decide for ourselves. How do you believe visions should be interpreted?

Guidelines for Librarians

Barbara Juhas Walsh (2010) states that it is important for librarians to address indigenous information issues in the library collection. She cites guidelines for Native American literature identified by representatives of fifteen Native American, First Nation, and Aboriginal communities. These protocols emphasize consulting with tribal communities, understanding Native American values and perspectives, recognizing and providing special treatment for culturally sensitive materials, providing culturally responsive content, respecting intellectual and cultural property rights, and raising awareness of issues within the library profession.

This group of Native Americans added that the library collection should reflect key perspectives on Native American issues. It is important that the collection includes materials created by Native Americans, and not only materials about Native Americans. This collection needs to include materials that use culturally specific terminology as well as provide detailed identification of Native American people, places, and events. Walsh states: "Librarians and archivists should be aware that each Native American tribe, band, and community is unique" (p. 11). As we proceed through this chapter on Native American literature, we will try to adhere to the protocols and guidelines identified by this group.

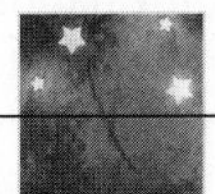

Traditional Literature

Ron Querry (1995) defines traditional Native American literature as "that which was composed in an Indian language for an Indian audience at a time when tribal cultures were intact and contact with whites was minimal. It was literature made up of sacred stories, myths, legends, and songs" (p. 2).

Native American tales show that the North American continent had traditional tales centuries old before the European settlers arrived. Traditional Native American tales make up a heritage that all North Americans should take pride in and pass on to future generations.

An authentic folklore collection is one of the most important elements in any Native American literature collection. This is especially true for myths, or narratives about gods, superhuman beings, animals, plants, and creation that are truths to the people who believe in them and give the people spiritual strength and guidance. Critics and reviewers of multicultural literature emphasize the need for authenticity in texts and in illustrations. For example, Betsy Hearne (1993) emphasizes that not only should the reteller provide information about the original source for the tale but also a text adapted from folklore should be judged for its balance of two traditions: the one from which it is drawn and the one that it is entering. Consequently, both texts and illustrations should ring true for the culture from which they are adapted and be meaningful to the culture that is reading them. In an evaluation of children's literature about Native Americans, Clifford E. Trafzer (1992), the director of Native American Studies at the University of California, Riverside, emphasizes the need for citing tribal sources and creating works that are culturally authentic for the tribe.

For example, the Artist's Note that introduces Deborah L. Duvall's *The Opossum's Tale* (2006) includes information about the Native American tribal association, the written origins of the tale, and the changes made by the reteller. This introduction states: "This story, popularly told among Cherokees both in the southeast and in Indian Territory (now Oklahoma), was probably first written down in the late 1800s by ethnologist James Mooney. Several variants explain why the opossum's tail is hairless. . . . Our new version includes an original ending by Duvall wherein Si-qua the Opossum learns to make useful the tail he once saw as strictly ornamental" (unnumbered).

In this section, we consider the history of the collection of Native American folklore in written form, discuss the importance of folklore in developing understanding of Native American cultures, and evaluate and discuss specific examples of Native American traditional literature. We will discover numerous examples of folklore. In fact, in a review of Native American literature, Debbie Reese (1998) states: "Most of the good books about Native Americans are folktales" (p. 638).

Author and storyteller Tim Tingle (2006), a member of the Choctaw Nation of Oklahoma, emphasizes the importance of Native American folklore when he invites readers to read a collection of tales told by contemporary Native American storytellers. Notice how he informs readers that characteristics of the traditional tales are very important, even with current Native American storytellers: "trickster is still alive and well, strong women and warriors still populate Indian Country, and courage, faith in the Creator, and humility are still the common trademarks" (p. 22).

History of European Recording of North American Folklore in Written Form

The Native American folklore we now read or hear was told through generations of oral storytellers before it was collected in written form. As early as the 1600s, Jesuit missionaries recorded a few myths they collected in the regions east of the Great Lakes.

John Bierhorst, in *The Mythology of North America* (1985), provides specific information about the collection of the stories. He identifies the role of explorers and Indian agents. He credits the recordings to the work of Henry Rowe Schoolcraft, who in a July 31, 1822, diary entry describes these mythologies as a source "which lifts up indeed a curtain, as it were, upon the Indian mind and exhibits it in an entirely new character" (p. 3). The two volumes of Chippewa tales published by Schoolcraft in 1839 titled *Algic Researches* were compared with the collections of German folklore by Jacob and Wilhelm Grimm published in 1812–1815.

In the early 1900s, anthropologist Franz Boas recognized Native American myths and folktales as a source for deciphering Indian languages and learning about the Native American culture. Collections from such cultures and tribes as Navajo, Hopi, Caddo, and Kwakiutl were then published by scholarly presses. During this time, Boas described the basic tale types and motifs. In 1929, folklorist Stith Thompson analyzed Native American traditional literature. His *Tales of the North American Indians* (1929) analyzed the stories by types and motifs to identify common plots and incidents. Both Boas and Thompson looked at common types of motifs among all Native American tribes rather than characteristics of the folklore of one group.

By 1935, there was a changing attitude among anthropologists, who began viewing myths as a means of analyzing a single cultural group such as the Cherokee or the Zuni. At that time, folklore was not considered generic. It was believed to belong to a particular people who had particular livelihoods, social organizations, and religions.

In the 1950s, the emphasis shifted to a cultural and personality approach to anthropology. At that time, collectors noted how characteristics such as sex, age, or psychology of the teller affected the story. By the 1960s, performance ethnographers and some collectors of mythology emphasized the narrator's art, which included such characteristics as tone of voice and comments made by listeners.

Currently, there is considerable interest in the publications of myths and other traditional narratives by Native American groups. Many groups are publishing their own traditional tales to retain their culture, their stories, and their histories. Groups such as the Wordcraft Circle of Native Writers give awards for Children's Writer of the Year. The American Indian Library Association (AILA) gives awards for Native American books in the three categories of picture books, middle school, and young adult literature. This award, according to the AILA (2006), "was created as a way to identify and honor the very best writing and illustrations by and about

American Indians. Books selected to receive the award present Native Americans in the fullness of their humanity in the present and past contexts" (p. 9).

Importance of Native American Folklore

Joseph Campbell (1988) provides compelling reasons for including mythology in the literature when he identifies four functions of myth. First, a mythical function allows people to realize and experience the wonder of the awe in the universe. Second, a cosmological dimension shows people the shape of the universe. Third, a sociological role supports and validates a certain order. Fourth, a pedagogical function teaches people how to live under any circumstances.

Clifford E. Trafzer (1992) emphasizes the importance of myths, legends, and folktales in transmitting the beliefs and values of the Native Americans. He states, "The words of the old stories are not myths and fairy tales. They are a communion with the dead—the Animal, Plant, and Earth Surface Peoples who once inhabited the world and whose spirits continue to influence the course of Native American history" (p. 381). Trafzer also emphasizes the importance of these stories for children, saying, "There is something sacred in the old texts, the ancient literature of America. . . . The accounts provide children with a better understanding of this land and its first people" (p. 393).

The importance of the oral tales is reinforced through the contemporary writings of many Native American authors. For example, Ray A. Young Bear, when writing his own autobiography, *Black Eagle Child: The Facepaint Narratives* (1992), includes creation myths and tales that depict his cultural history and influence his life.

Native American traditional literature is an excellent source for identifying and understanding tribal traditional values and beliefs. Eldrena Douma (2006), a Tewa Hopi and Laguna storyteller, emphasizes the importance of the traditional values and beliefs in her own life and her storytelling. She states: "No matter how far I go, what has kept me grounded are the teaching words of all the people that God has put in my path. Many are gone now, but their memories remain. Every now and then I'll catch their laughter and teaching words" (p. 25).

Tim Tingle, a Choctaw storyteller, comments, "Throughout the body of Choctaw stories, whether they are traditional or contemporary, the quality of heart is of supreme importance. Truthfulness and generosity are valued far above bravery and even cunning. One other character trait shines through the collective Choctaw narrative, that of respect. Those who show respect for their elders and heed their teachings overcome powerful supernatural enemies. Conversely, those who don't meet terrible fates through their callous lack of respect" (2003, p. 2).

Stephen Dow Beckham, in his introduction to Christine Normandin's *Echoes of the Elders: The Stories and Paintings of Chief Lelooska*, explains, "The stories were the primary means of passing on the tribal memory. They recounted how the world had come to be, why things were named as they were, and how humans should act. They speak through time to listeners and readers today" (1997, p. 5).

A review of these sources indicates that many of the traditional values, such as living in harmony with nature, viewing religion as a natural phenomenon closely related to nature, showing respect for wisdom gained through age and experience, acquiring patience, and emphasizing group and extended needs rather than individual needs, are also dominant themes in the traditional tales from various tribal regions. As you read various Native American traditional tales, see if you can identify these important values.

For example, living in harmony with nature is a dominant theme in Tomie dePaola's retelling of the Comanche tale, *The Legend of the Bluebonnet*. In the legend, selfishly taking from the land is punished by drought, whereas unselfishly giving of a prized possession is rewarded with bluebonnets and rain. The name change in the main character as she goes from She-Who-Is-Alone to One-Who-Dearly-Loved-Her-People supports the emphasis on extended family rather than the individual.

The interactions between buffalo and Great Plains Indians are developed in Olaf Baker's *Where the Buffaloes Begin* and Paul Goble's *Buffalo Woman* and *The Legend of the White Buffalo Woman.* In *Where the Buffaloes Begin,* Stephen Gammell's marvelous black-and-white drawings capture the buffaloes surging out of a mythical lake after their birth, rampaging across the prairie, and eventually saving Little Wolf's people from their enemies. In traditional tales from the Great Plains, the buffalo people frequently save those who understand and respect them. Goble's *Buffalo Woman* ends with a statement of why the relationship between the Great Plains Indians and the buffaloes is so important. Because a brave young man who loved his wife and child became a buffalo, "In return the Buffalo People have given their flesh so that little children, and babies still unborn, will always have meat to eat. It is the Creator's wish" (unnumbered). *The Legend of the White Buffalo Woman* shows another close spiritual relationship as the Buffalo Woman gives the Sacred Calf Pipe to the Lakota so that the people can pray and commune with the Great Spirit.

Showing respect for animals, keeping one's word, and listening to elders are interrelated themes in Frank Cushing's "The Poor Turkey Girl," found in *Zuni Folk Tales.* In this Cinderella-type tale, a Zuni maiden who cares for the turkeys is helped to go to a festival by the turkeys. When the girl does not heed old Gobble's admonition and return on time to feed the turkeys, she loses everything.

Traditional tales of legendary heroes reflect many important values and beliefs of the people. The legendary heroes may have many of the same characteristics found in heroic tales from other cultures. For example, like Beowulf in the Norse legend, an Inuit hero shows bravery, honor, and a willingness to avenge wrongs. In the introduction to one of the tales included in *Stories from the Canadian North,* Muriel Whitaker states:

> In order to understand fully the ending of "The Blind Boy and the Loon," one must realize that the Eskimo hero was predominantly an avenger. Just as the spirits of weather, thunder, lightning, and the sea took vengeance on those who mistreated them, so too was the mortal hero expected to have the will and the power to exact retribution for evil. (p. 20)

Native American peoples developed a rich heritage of traditional myths and legends. John Bierhorst (1976) identifies the following four categories found in Native American folklore: (1) creation myths that emphasize "setting the world in order," in which the world is created out of the chaos of nature, or in which physical or social order is brought to the tribal world; (2) tales that deal with "family or tribal drama" by centering on conflicts and affinities rising out of the kinship unit; (3) "fair and foul" trickster tales such as the trickster cycle tales, in which the hero progresses from being a character of utter worthlessness to one that displays a gradual understanding of social virtue; and (4) "crossing the threshold" tales that reflect major changes such as the passage from unconsciousness to consciousness, the ordeal of puberty, the passage into and out of the animal world, the passage into and out of death, and the transition from nature to culture. In a book for adults, *The Red Swan: Myths and Tales of the American Indians* (1976), Bierhorst presents and discusses examples of these various categories of myths. Bierhorst's categories are similar to those used in other anthologies that include tales passed down in Native American cultures across the North American continent. Consequently, we use Bierhorst's categories when discussing Native American folklore.

Setting-the-World-in-Order Tales Creation myths that emphasize setting the world in order usually tell about the creation of the earth and animal and plant life. Earth creation myths are frequently "Earth-Diver" tales such as "Turtle Dives to the Bottom of the Sea: Earth Starter the Creator," a Maidu tale from California, and "The Woman Who Fell from the Sky: Divine Woman the Creator," a Huron myth from northeastern United States. Both of these stories are found in Virginia Hamilton's *In the Beginning: Creation Stories from Around the World.*

Creation stories from several tribes are found in Michael J. Caduto and Joseph Bruchac's *Keepers of the Earth: Native American Stories and Environmental Activities for Children*. "The Earth on Turtle's Back," an Onondaga tale from the northeastern woodlands, tells how Great

Turtle gives his shell to hold Earth and the seeds brought to Earth by the Great Chief's wife. In "Four Worlds: The Dine Story of Creation," the Holy People move from the first world to the fourth world by way of a female reed. This tale is an excellent example of tales that depict the disastrous consequences of not taking care of Earth. The warning associated with Earth is characteristic of many of the setting-the-world-in-order tales: "Fourth World was destined to be destroyed when the people do not live the right way. That is what the Dine say to this day" (p. 34). A Cherokee myth, "The Coming of Earth," is found in Caduto's *Earth Tales from Around the World*.

"The Great Flood" is one of the creation stories found in *The Serpent's Tongue: Prose, Poetry, and Art of the New Mexico Pueblos*, edited by Nancy Wood. In this Zia tale, the people and animals leave their underworld as Spider Sussistinnako places a huge reed on the top of the mesa and the people pass through this reed until they reach Earth. The creation stories in this volume develop the strong relationship between the people and the spirit world because "This connection, this belief in the spirit world, was all the Pueblo Indians needed to survive. Tribes do not accept the idea that their ancestors crossed the Bering Strait land bridge and moved southward during the Ice Age. We have always been here, they insist. Our world came with us" (p. xii).

Native American tales, such as Barbara Juster Esbensen's *The Star Maiden,* account for the creation of plant life. In this lyrical rendition of an Ojibwa tale, Star Maiden and her sisters leave their home in the sky and become the beautiful star-shaped water lilies.

Several of the tales in George Bird Grinnell's adult texts *Blackfeet Indian Stories* (1993/1913) and *Blackfoot Lodge Tales: The Story of a Prairie People* (1962) are creation stories. For example, "The Blackfeet Creation" is an Earth-Diver type of story. The origin of the medicine lodge is told in "Scarface: Origin of the Medicine Lodge." The section of "Stories of Ancient Times" also includes the origin of the medicine pipe.

Family Drama Tales Family drama tales focus on various family needs and conflicts, such as learning from elders, providing protection, obtaining food, and overcoming problems, including rivalry and aggression. The family in these stories may be the smaller tribal unit or the greater cosmos. If the tale deals with the greater world family, the storyteller may refer to Earth as mother, Sky as father, and humans as children. Many of these stories reveal tribal standards.

The importance of tribal stories in providing instructions for life is emphasized in several Native American folklore collections. For example, consider Tewa Vickie Downey's comments in *The Serpent's Tongue,* edited by Nancy Wood:

> Now people call our Instructions legends because they were given as stories. But to the Indian people, that was like a reality at some point in history. . . . The Instructions during that time, at the beginning, were to love and respect one another even with all the differences—different cultures, different languages. We were told we were all from the same source. We were coming from the same mother, same parents. . . .We were told if the Instructions were lost, then harm would come to the people. (p. 55)

The need for leading a balanced life is the theme created in *The Magic of Spider Woman* retold by Lois Duncan. When Wandering Girl is given the secret of weaving by Spider Woman, she is given both the name change of Weaving Woman and advice for herself and her people. Spider Woman tells her: "The Navajo People must walk the Middle Way, which means that they must respect boundaries and try to keep their lives in balance" (unnumbered). Unfortunately, when Weaving Woman becomes totally engrossed in weaving a beautiful blanket she forgets the warning and her spirit becomes trapped within the blanket. A shaman holds a Blessing Way during which he chants a prayer asking that Weaving Woman be restored. Spirit Woman hears the prayer and creates a spirit pathway through the border of the blanket. Now Weaving Woman has learned her lesson as she cries out to Spirit Being: "Never again will I weave for too long at a sitting, and never again will I doubt the wisdom of my creators" (unnumbered).

The story concludes with the information that since then every Navajo blanket is woven with a pathway so the spirit of the weaver will not be imprisoned by its beauty.

Overcoming problems through the use of one's wit is the focus of Lois Ehlert's *Mole's Hill: A Woodland Tale.* This Seneca tale reveals how Mole saves her home by creating a hill that is too big to move and then uses her tunneling skills to solve the animals' problem. The medium of collage with abstract geometric designs used to illustrate text adds to the pleasure of the story. The depth of Mole's tunnels are suggested by two double-page spreads in which both the text and illustrations are turned sideways.

Trickster Tales Trickster tales are among the most common folklore throughout the world, and trickster characters are found throughout North America. Trickster tales reveal both good and bad conduct; they allow the narrator an opportunity to tell about immoral or antisocial temptations in humorous ways. On the northwestern coast of the Pacific Ocean, the trickster is called Raven. When evaluating the role of Raven, Bierhorst (1993) states,

> Raven is tough. Whatever is ascribed to him, he can survive it. . . . One of the old Tsimshian narrators used to say that after each scrape Raven doggedly "journeys on." Or as another of the old texts once phrased it, the trickster simply "put on his raven garment and flew away."

Raven the trickster is the central character in Gerald McDermott's *Raven: A Trickster Tale from the Pacific Northwest.* In this tale, to bring light from Sky Chief, Raven changes himself into a pine needle that is in a drinking cup of Sky Chief's daughter. After swallowing the needle, the daughter eventually gives birth to a child that is really Raven in human form. Thus Raven is able to acquire the sun, which is in a set of nested boxes found in the sky lodge, and bring light to the earth.

Iktomi is the Sioux name for trickster. In *Iktomi and the Boulder: A Plains Indian Story,* Paul Goble describes the fair and foul side of Iktomi: "People say that what seem to be the 'mistakes' and 'irrational' aspects of Creation, such as earthquakes, floods, disease, flies, and mosquitoes, were surely made by Iktomi" (introduction).

In Goble's version of the Sioux tale, conceited Iktomi first gives his blanket to a boulder and then deceitfully takes the blanket back when he needs it for protection. Iktomi uses trickery to save himself from the angry boulder. Even though Iktomi eventually wins the confrontation, he is frightened and momentarily humbled by his experience. Goble's *Iktomi and the Berries* provides another humbling experience for the trickster character.

Another trickster character is Coyote, who may be a creator or a trickster in folklore. Native American author Simon Ortiz (1990) states that trickster characters are extremely important in Native American literature, both past and present. He discusses various trickster characters and concludes,

> Coyote, or Perruh, is a part of a tradition of literature of resistance, of struggling against what will overcome you, that is, Western colonialism. . . . In some stories Perruh is a figure who represents Indian people in their struggle against the Spanish soudarrhu, or the soldier, the Spanish troops who came among the people aggressively, destroying. Perruh is the spokesperson; he outthinks, outsmarts, the foolish soldiers; in that case he is a survivor. (p. 106)

In *Coyote Steals the Blanket: A Ute Tale,* a tale retold by Janet Stevens, Coyote repeatedly declares, "I go where I want, I do what I want, and I take what I want." Consequently, when Hummingbird warns him not to touch the blankets that cover the rocks, he does it anyway. When Coyote brags and disobeys, he is humbled.

In Gerald McDermott's introduction to *Coyote: A Trickster Tale from the American Southwest*, the author describes Coyote's image in the Southwest as a troublesome trickster who is portrayed as a devious, gluttonous fool who is a victim of his own inquisitiveness. His desires to imitate others, to intrude on their lives makes him seem both very foolish and very human.

McDermott emphasizes that the Pueblo of Zuni associate Coyote with the West and the color blue. Consequently, McDermott's illustrations picture Coyote as blue. The theme of the story stresses that human vanity and misbehavior result in misfortune. In addition to being a trickster tale, this is also an explanatory tale as it reveals why Coyote is the color of dust, has a tail with a black tip, and finds trouble by following his nose.

The Opossum's Tale retold by Deborah L. Duvall is a trickster tale, a why tale, and a tale that reveals both disliked and admired characteristics. As a trickster tale, Ji-Stu the rabbit and Cricket play a trick on Si-Qua the Opossum who is always bragging about his beautiful tail. As a why tale, the story reveals why Opossum now has a long, hairless tail that allows him to hang from trees. As a tale that reveals values, we discover that boasting and bragging will be punished. This is what happens when the animals become tired of hearing Opossum sing and dance while he brags about his magnificent tail, covered with glistening fur. The ending of the tale also suggests admired qualities. After Opossum uses his newly hairless coiled tail to hang on to a tree root and save Ji-Stu from drowning in a rushing river, Opossum is rewarded with songs of the hero because: "Do you see how you have changed? Once you sang songs about yourself, but now your friends sing songs about you. Even Cricket!" (unnumbered)

Trickster: Native American Tales: A Graphic Collection is a large collection of tales edited by Matt Dembicki. The tales are from various Native American peoples across North America. This collection allows readers to compare the role of trickster among various tribes and locations. A few examples of Native American contributors include John Active, a Yup'ik Eskimo; Roy Boney, a Cherokee; Joseph Bruchac of Abenaki ancestry; J. Chris Campbell, a Cherokee; Sunny Dooley, a Navajo; Dayton Edmonds from the Caddo Nation; Jack Gladstone, a Blackfoot; Dan Jones, an Ojibwe; and Dimi Macheras, a Chickaloon Village tribal member. The contributions in this edited text exemplify various storytelling styles and art. These trickster tales also allow students of children's literature an opportunity to authenticate the tales. Although the tales include the name of the contributor and the location of the tribal connection, they do not include an original source or any information about if and how the tales might have been changed. As students of children's literature, you may wish to search for original sources and compare the sources with these retellings.

Threshold Tales Threshold tales in Native American folklore depict many different types of thresholds: These include transformations that allow characters to go into and out of the animal world, to pass the threshold from childhood to adulthood, or to go into the spirit world. Paul Goble's *Buffalo Woman* presents transformations from the human to the animal world, but also illustrates the bond between Native Americans and the buffalo that were so important to the people of the Great Plains.

In *Beyond the Ridge,* Goble's main character goes from the land of the living to the spirit world. An elderly Plains Indian experiences the afterlife as believed by her people. On her way, she discovers Owl Maker. The spirits of individuals who have led good lives pass Owl Maker to the right, toward Wanagiyata, Land of Many Tipis. However, Owl Maker pushes the spirits of those who have led bad lives to the left, along a short path where they fall off, landing back on Earth to wander for a time as ghosts.

In Laura Simms's retelling of *The Bone Man: A Native American Modoc Tale*, the main character, Nulwee, goes from a frightened boy to a warrior whose strength comes from compassion. Along the way, he discovers the importance of both tradition and courage, confronts his fears, and transforms the evil monster into something that helps his people. According to the Author's Note, the story was recorded by Jeremiah Curtin around 1900.

Paul Owen Lewis's *Storm Boy* is an original story that uses Native American elements. This is a hero epic that develops the three rites of passage: separation, initiation, and return. The Author's Note provides information about each of these Northwest Coast motifs. For example, separation occurs when the boy in the story wanders too far from the village. This invites supernatural encounters and the boy finds a mysterious entrance to the spirit world, which allows him to enter the realm of the killer whales. Initiation occurs when the boy encounters animals in human form and there is an exchange of gifts and cultural information. Return occurs when the boy is given a dancing staff shaped like a dorsal fin and instructions on how to return to his own realm (the boy closes his eyes and visualizes his home). The return motif includes a time disparity between the two realms: for every day spent in the spirit world, a year passes in the earth realm. The return concludes with a reunion celebration in which the boy recounts his mysterious adventure and displays the killer whale staff and demonstrates the dance shown him in the other realm. Because he has been adopted by the Killer Whale People, he can now claim the killer whale crest. The illustrations for the text depict the art of the Haida and Tlingit people of the Northwest Coast.

Combination Tales Many of the traditional tales combine several of the folklore types. For example, in *Keepers of the Animals: Native American Stories and Wildlife Activities for Children,* Michael J. Caduto and Joseph Bruchac discuss the various circles found in "Salmon Boy," a Haida tale from the Pacific Northwest. They state, "'Salmon Boy' is an allegory of great importance, revealing a series of interlocking circles which, as the story proceeds, run progressively deeper into the life ways of the Haida. . . . There is an important, independent relationship here: The salmon give people food and the people show their appreciation through prayer and reverence" (p. 97).

Caduto and Bruchac identify the first circle as the great circle of life and death and as the reality of the spirit world. Another circle is transformation, depicted when Salmon Boy returns to his people as a healer and a teacher to instruct them in the ways of the Salmon People and to help them when they are sick. The circle shows the sense of interconnectedness between this world and the spirit world, and between animals and people. Finally, Salmon Boy's body is placed in the river, where it circles four times, a sacred number, and returns to the Salmon People. Notice how this tale includes a combination of the types of tales identified by Bierhorst.

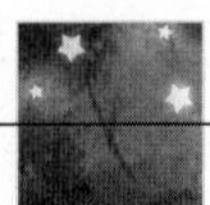

Historical Nonfiction and Fiction

Ron Querry (1995) identifies much of the historical nonfiction as transitional literature that is "generally represented by translations of the great Indian orators of the nineteenth century and by memoirs of the Indian experience as it related to white dominance" (p. 2). In this section, we consider biographies written about earlier Native American peoples, informational literature that is about the earlier cultures, and historical fiction.

Biography about Early Peoples

Biographies and autobiographies of the earlier Native American figures are important for developing understanding of various Native American cultures. These texts provide a source for researchers, whether adult or children, who are investigating the early history of United States or the impact of an alien culture on native peoples. Books written for a juvenile audience, however, are frequently criticized for their lack of accuracy or their nonrealistic depiction of their Native American subjects. Autobiographies of Native Americans, biographies of Native Americans written for adults, and historical documents provide sources for comparisons with juvenile texts and sources to use when authenticating children's biographies.

My own research (Norton, 1987) investigated the authenticity of the conflicts described in Native American biographies intended for children and young adults by comparing information in juvenile biographies with information found in Native American biographies, autobi-

Application of Knowledge about Native American Folklore

Barbara Juster Esbensen's *The Great Buffalo Race: How the Buffalo Got Its Hump* provides an excellent source for authentication. In the Author's Note, Esbensen identifies the source for the original tale as the Seneca people who were part of the Iroquois Nation. The source for the tale is identified as "The Buffalo's Hump and the Brown Birds" retold by Arthur C. Parker in his collection *Skunny Wundy: Seneca Indian Tales* (1926). Esbensen identifies the home of the Seneca people as New York State, although they fought campaigns that took them to the Mississippi River and beyond. She states, "The patterns and costumes found in the illustrations were inspired by traditional beadwork and clothing found in books on the Iroquois as well as the American Museum of Natural History and the American Indian Museum, Heye Foundation, both in New York" (note to the reader, unnumbered).

A search for the original source provides both Arthur C. Parker's background and information about the Seneca people. Parker, whose Seneca name is Gawaso Wanneh, was an anthropologist as well as a member of the Seneca tribe. His career in anthropology included experience at the American Museum of Natural History, the Peabody Museum, and the Rochester Museum of Arts and Sciences. His studies focused on the Iroquois and the League of the Iroquois, a confederation of five tribes or nations: the Mohawks, Oneidas, Onondagas, Cayugas, and Senecas who lived in what is now New York state.

The introduction to Parker's *Skunny Wundy: Seneca Indian Tales* provides additional information that may be used to authenticate tales about the Seneca. For example, the lands where they lived were in a region of forest and lakes in what is now New York state; the people lived on close terms with the animals; clan names, rituals, symbols, and stories reflect the importance of these animals; different creatures have special traits including the cleverness of the fox and raccoon, the easy duping of the rabbit, the bravery of the bear, the villainous nature of the wolf, and the special place for the turtle from whose back grew the Tree of Life with Sun at its top; the people lived in houses built of posts covered with elm bark; and the people not only hunted, but raised vast fields of corn, beans, squash, melons, and tobacco.

A textual comparison of the original "The Buffalo's Hump and the Brown Birds" and the retelling found in Esbensen's *The Great Buffalo Race: How the Buffalo Got Its Hump* shows a close similarity in characters, plot, and theme, although the language of the texts is different. In both versions, the major conflict is between Old Buffalo and Young Buffalo as they vie for leadership of the buffalo herd. The members of the buffalo herd are called followers in the original version and tribesmen in the adaptation. The spiritual being is called "The Masterful One" in the original and "Haweniyo, the Great Spirit" in the retelling. Both versions identify trickery as inappropriate behavior in the eyes of the spiritual being. In both versions, Old Buffalo and Young Buffalo are punished because of their foolish actions when they ignore the rights of the small animals of the fields as the competing herds race westward toward what they believe is rain and green grazing grounds. In both versions, it is Brown Buffalo, son of Old Buffalo, who is rewarded because he had the wisdom to stay in the original grazing area and wait for the lush green grasses to return with the rain. Both versions explain why buffaloes have shoulder humps and heavy heads that almost touch the ground: it is so they will remember the actions of the two herds that were punished and will remember to be careful in their dealings with the smaller animals who live or nest on the ground. This care for the smaller animals of the field reflects the close relationship between the Seneca Indians and the animals in their environment.

Additional authentication may focus on the location of the buffalo, the setting in the illustrations, the name of the great spirit, and the patterns and costumes found in the illustrations. In the area in which the buffalo lived, the question arises, Would buffalo be common in the land of the Seneca, which is the eastern United States? A map showing the range of the buffalo, or bison, found in Bryan Hodgson's article "Buffalo: Back Home on the Range," published in *National Geographic* (1994), identifies the bison, circa 1500, as ranging east into what is now the southern portion of New York state. In addition, the Seneca traveled long distances on their war and hunting trips and may have seen buffalo herds grazing on the prairies. This speculation is especially important for authenticity because Helen K. Davies's illustrations for *The Great Buffalo Race: How the Buffalo Got Its Hump* reflect the prairies with their vast stretches of grass—and not the forests and trees of the Seneca homeland.

Instead of the original "The Masterful One," Esbensen's name for the spiritual being is "Haweniyo, the Great Spirit." According to Sam D. Gill and Irene F. Sullivan in *Dictionary of Native American Mythology* (1992), Hawenniyo (Gill and

(continued)

Sullivan have a different spelling for the name) is the main character in the Seneca origin story of the False Faces and also a Seneca term that later came to be used to refer to the Christian God.

The designs on the costumes in the illustrations in Esbensen's book are similar to designs in beadwork and porcupine-quill-embroidered buckskin in pictures of Seneca artifacts found in nonfiction texts such as Peter T. Furst and Jill L. Furst's *North American Indian Art* (1982) that show artifacts from earlier time periods in the Seneca culture.

You may choose to authenticate texts such as Kristina Rodanas's *Dance of the Sacred Circle: A Native American Tale* in which the author identifies the original source as Robert Vaughn's *Then and Now. Or Thirty-Six Years in the Rockies* (1900).

ographies, and other historical documents written for adults. You may choose to complete a similar type of research in which you search for answers to questions such as these: Are the types of conflicts similar in adult and juvenile biographies? Are the depictions of cultural details similar for biographies of Native Americans from the same tribal areas? Are there differences in the Native American responses to an intrusion of an alien culture in biographies written for adults and those written for children?

First, a search of historical documents revealed two types of conflicts in historical studies about Native Americans who lived in the eighteenth and nineteenth centuries, during the period of European expansion and settlement in the United States: (1) conflicts over land and (2) conflicts resulting from cultural confrontation, which included differences in beliefs, values, customs, and religion. The historical documents also showed that the Native Americans responded to the intrusion of the Europeans in various ways that included the following: (1) retreatism, in which the reservation and the traditional way of life served as a sanctuary; (2) rebellion, in which Native Americans fought rather than accommodated to the white culture; (3) ritualism, in which the Native Americans rejected white values and sought refuge in Native American rituals, religious beliefs, and cultural values; (4) innovation, in which the Native Americans retained some Native American identities and values while accepting some of the Anglo/European values, customs, and religion; and (5) conformity, in which the Native Americans rejected Native American beliefs, values, customs, and religions while totally accepting the alien culture.

In an analysis of adult biographies and autobiographies of Native Americans from the Great Plains, the Great Basin, and the Southwest, conflicts over land were found in all three areas. For example, 61% of the literature from the Great Plains emphasized the displacement of the people, 77% stressed the impoverishment of the people, and 38% told of the emergence of leaders because of these conflicts. The literature from the Great Basin showed 100% of the books emphasized the displacement and the impoverishment of the people; 50% of the literature developed the emergence of leaders. The literature from the Southwest did not emphasize as many conflicts over land. Fifty percent of the texts emphasized displacement of the people. Twenty-five percent stressed impoverishment and 38% developed emergence of leaders because of conflicts over land.

A majority of the adult texts written about Great Plains and Great Basin Indians emphasized conflicts over land, which resulted in both the trauma associated with displacement and the impoverishment resulting from greed and dishonesty. Comparisons between life before and after interaction with Anglo Europeans and visions depicting the consequences of interaction are common in autobiographies such as *Black Elk Speaks: Being the Life Story of a Holy Man of the Oglala Sioux* (1932, 1979), who compares his memories of an earlier idyllic summer with the actuality of his later life on the reservation.

Two types of leaders emerge in the adult texts as the Native Americans faced conflicts over land. There were Native American patriots such as Chief Joseph (1879), leaders who were considered good and brave by their people and who fought for their freedom, their right of conscience, or their personal security. The second type of leader was less hostile toward, or even friendly to, the settlers. Many of the Native Americans of this type tried peaceful solutions because they recognized the consequences of European expansion and wanted security for their people. For example, Sioux Charles Eastman's (1916) leadership emphasizes cooperation.

It is apparent from the literature that the closer the interaction with European settlers, with missionaries, and with the U.S. government, the harsher the resulting personal conflict between Native American beliefs, values, customs, and religions and those of the Europeans. Historian Gerard Reed (1984) highlights the importance of cultural interaction during the period of European expansion. This interaction was favorable to the Europeans and disastrous to the native populations. Reed states, "No economic development rivals the prosperity enjoyed by Europeans as a consequence of their conquest and its attendant technological development. No social devastation equals the destruction suffered by indigenous cultures in conquered lands where European invaders imposed their own customs and civilizations" (p. 4). We could assume that conflicts over customs and beliefs would be developed in biographies and autobiographies.

The resulting analysis of the adult texts showed that 46% of the Native American subjects from the Great Plains revealed conflicts over beliefs, 50% from the Great Basin showed these conflicts, and 50% from the Southwest described conflicts over beliefs. Conflicts over values were reflected in 85% of the Native American subjects from the Great Plains, 50% from the Great Basin, and 75% from the Southwest. Conflicts over customs were reflected in 54% from the Great Plains, 50% from the Great Basin, and 50% from the Southwest. Religion caused conflicts in 85% of the literature from the Great Plains, 0% from the Great Basin, and 63% from the Southwest.

In all of the texts, the autobiographers or biography writers emphasize and describe in detail responses to some type of cultural conflict. Conflicts over beliefs frequently center on beliefs over ownership of the land, characteristics of the earth, and visions that rule one's life. A Great Plains Indian, Lame Deer, in *Lame Deer: Seeker of Visions* (1972), states this conflict: "because deep down with us lingers a feeling that land, water, air, the earth, and what lies beneath its surface cannot be owned as someone's private property" (p. 46). Black Elk (1932, 1979) describes his conflict when he is forced to live in square wooden houses when his people believed in the power of the circular tipis. Another Great Plains Indian, Edward Goodbird (1914), emphasizes the power of the medicine man when he states, "If our beliefs seem strange to white men, theirs seemed just as strange to us" (p. 33).

Conflicts over values caused the greatest concern for Native Americans in the Great Plains and the Southwest. Lame Deer (1972) describes his discomfort as the Native Americans' chasing the vision versus the white man's chasing the dollar. Carl Sweezy (1966), an Arapaho, discusses differences in attitudes toward time: "We enjoy time; they measure it" (p. 17). Charles Eastman (1916) describes his conflicts in values: "From childhood I was consciously trained to be a man; that was after all the basic thing; but after this I was trained to be a hunter and not to care for money or possessions, but to be in the broader sense a public servant . . . to harmonize myself with nature" (p. 1). Later, Eastman acknowledges experiencing considerable conflict when his honor was questioned because his tribe "valued nothing except honor: that cannot be purchased!" (p. 47).

Conflicts over religion are apparently the most traumatic for Great Plains Indians and to a slightly lesser extent for Southwest Indians. Two different attitudes emerge as Native Americans either accept or reject the teachings of the missionaries. Most Native Americans, however, even if they finally accept Christianity, express considerable conflict. Charles Eastman (1916) expresses shock when he first hears prayers in school because he had been taught that the Supreme Being can be communed with only in the solitude of the wilderness. Carl Sweezy (1966), states that for the Indian this conflict arises because everything they do or own is connected with religion. An Apache, Jim Whitewolf (1969), describes major conflicts because the Indian people interpreted the missionaries' Christianity through the various Indian religions. Belief in the Ghost Dance and the Peyote Cult and the conflicts with missionaries are emphasized.

Many Native American autobiographers express concern because they were expected to respect and understand the white people's God but the respect and understanding were not returned. Edward Goodbird (1914) expresses this bewilderment: "Worshipping as we did many gods, we Indians did not think it strange that white men prayed to another God; and when missionaries came, we did not think it wrong that they taught us to pray to their God, but that they said we should not pray to our own gods. 'Why,' we asked, 'do the missionaries hate our gods?'" (p. 33).

The autobiographical writers and subjects of biographies responded in different ways to the conflicts with alien cultures. For example, rebellion was a common method of responding to this alien culture. The causes of rebellion are closely related to conflicts over land. Chief Joseph (1879) states this position: "This land has always belonged to my people. It came unclouded to them from our fathers, and we will defend this land as long as a drop of Indian blood warms the hearts of men" (p. 418).

Ritualism was a response primarily used by holy men such as Sioux Lame Deer, Black Elk, and Crow Plenty-Coups. Black Elk (1932, 1979) states that he must use his power and his visions to bring the "people back into the sacred hoop, that they might again walk the red road in a sacred manner pleasing to the Powers of the Universe that are One Power" (p. 238).

The degree to which some Native Americans accepted European values is illustrated in responses characterized as either innovation or conformity. Innovation in the study sample is more common than conformity. Althea Bass, the recorder of Carl Sweezy's autobiography (1966), expresses the role of innovation:

> Unlike many of the Indians, Carl Sweezy never lost his way: he saw good along both roads and accepted something of both. The old Arapaho virtues, courtesy, and hospitality, and loyalty, and deep religious feelings, he found to be virtues among the best of the white people too; it was only the methods by which they practiced that differed. So he could sing Mennonite hymns with the missionaries and chants with the Sun Dance participants. (p. viii)

The greatest conformity with the new culture is reflected in the autobiography of Charles Eastman (1916), *From the Deep Woods to Civilization: Chapters in the Autobiography of an Indian*. Eastman chronicles his experiences in 1876: "I renounced finally my bow and arrows for the spade and the pen; I took off my soft moccasins and put on the heavy and clumsy but durable shoes. Every day of my life I put into use every English word that I knew, and for the first time permitted myself to think and act as a white man" (p. 58). This conformity, however, was not easy and it does include some retention of Indian values as Eastman concludes his autobiography: "I am an Indian; and while I have learned much from civilization, for which I am grateful, I have never lost my Indian sense of right and justice. I am for development and progress along social and spiritual lines, rather than those of commerce, nationalism, or material efficiency. Nevertheless, so long as I live, I am an American" (p. 195).

Finally, this study analyzed differences in texts written for adult and juvenile audiences. Table 3.1 shows the differences found in the extent and type of conflict between adult and juvenile texts with settings in the Great Plains.

As seen in Table 3.1, for some of the categories, readers of texts for adults and for juveniles would find different and often contradictory profiles for Native Americans who lived in the Great Plains. The profile developed through adult autobiographies and biographies suggests that the Native Americans were alienated and impoverished because of their physical displacement, and they suffered even greater conflicts because of cultural confrontation. Major conflicts resulted from conflicts with Christianity and alien value systems, customs,

TABLE 3.1 Comparisons between Adult and Juvenile Biographies with Settings in the Great Plains

Conflicts Over Land			
	People Displaced (%)	People Impoverished (%)	Leaders Emerge (%)
Adult	61	77	38
Juvenile	78	44	56

Cultural Confrontation				
	Beliefs (%)	Values (%)	Customs (%)	Religion (%)
Adult	46	85	54	85
Juvenile	22	22	33	0

Acculturation Continuum					
	Retreatism (%)	Rebellion (%)	Ritualism (%)	Innovation (%)	Conformity (%)
Adult	0	30	30	34	6
Juvenile	0	33	1	33	33

and beliefs. The Native Americans in the adult texts rarely responded through complete conformity to the alien culture, but they were more apt to rebel, to reject European values and to practice traditional religion and ritualism, or to retain group identities while accepting some European values. The consequences of intrusion of an alien culture were both physically and psychologically detrimental.

In contrast, the profile developed through juvenile texts suggests that displacement of people caused the greatest conflict. Cultural conflicts between two value systems were viewed as of minimal significance. In addition, the majority of biographical subjects and autobiography writers either conformed to the alien culture or combined aspects of the two cultures. Only biographies of the great war chiefs suggest rebellion. Retaining Native American religious practices was not a significant factor in the juvenile biographies. The consequences of intrusion of an alien culture are seen as detrimental because of loss of land, but they could be inferred as beneficial because of the acceptance of superior value and belief systems.

As we discuss biographies written for younger audiences, we consider these conflicts and the responses of Native Americans who are their subjects. How closely do the biographies written for younger people reflect some of the same concerns as those developed by Native Americans who write about their own experiences? Unlike adult autobiographies and biographies, few juvenile biographies develop conflicts over both land and culture. Biographies of Crazy Horse and Red Cloud tend to emphasize conflicts over land. Dorothy M. Johnson's *Warrior for a Lost Nation: A Biography of Sitting Bull* is an exception to this trend. Johnson presents a profile of a leader who not only fought for his land but also experienced personal conflicts because of alien beliefs and customs. In general, conflicts in juvenile biographies are simplified, and cultural conflicts experienced by many Native Americans are absent.

There are also discrepancies between the information presented in the adult texts and the juvenile biographies. The consequences of forced education and the practice of hiding children so they could not be educated are frequently emphasized in adult texts. If the descriptions in adult autobiographies are representative, the seeking for white people's learning is incorrect for many Native Americans of this time period. Native Americans are frequently shown as seeking education in white schools in juvenile biographies. In a more accurate depiction, Johnson's juvenile biography of Sitting Bull chronicles his final battle with the U.S. government to retain Sioux customs and his arguments with the educational system that repudiated the values of his people. After Sitting Bull reluctantly accepts the reservation for his people, he remains suspicious about the motives of educators. He tells a congressional mission that his people needed a medicine woman. He wanted her to teach them to read, but he did not want her to try to convert them to her religion. This depiction seems more accurate when comparisons are made with the attitudes in adult texts.

Many of the juvenile biographies are less candid than the adult sources and imply different consequences for the Native Americans who interacted with the European settlers. The reasons for these differences between adult and juvenile texts may reflect a belief that children are not able to understand the more complex issues associated with cultural confrontation. In the evaluation of the literature written for the two groups, however, several questions emerge that you may want to consider: By ignoring confrontation with values, are biographers lying to children or are they only focusing on content that children can understand? By placing less emphasis on cultural conflict, are biographers implying that Native Americans living in the eighteenth and nineteenth centuries did not have a culture worthy of preservation? By emphasizing conformity and innovation as the two most frequent responses to intrusion, are biographers again lying to children, or are they only presenting content that is necessary if children are to develop a respect for governmental authority and a belief in the heroic deeds of all U.S. leaders from the past? There are educators and other individuals who will argue on different sides of these issues. It may happen that biographers and historians will eventually write juvenile biographies that present a truthful profile of this turbulent period in U.S. history.

Several juvenile biographies are exceptions and provide historically accurate depictions of the time period and the people. For example, Dorothy Nafus Morrison's *Chief Sarah: Sarah Winnemucca's Fight for Indian Rights* is one of the strongest biographies as the author develops the numerous conflicts the biographical character faces as the character tries to gain rights for her people and preserve their culture. Morrison develops conflicts through contrasts when she describes Sarah's confusion: "The whites killed—but they had made her well. They took the Indians' meadows—but gave them horses and presents. They burned stores of food—but they gave food, too" (p. 31). Throughout the biography, Morrison shows Sarah's battle for retention of the Paiute culture.

As you read various juvenile biographies of Native Americans, you may use the findings from adult autobiographies and biographies to compare the types of conflicts depicted in the literature.

Several juvenile biographies look at famous Native Americans who interacted with white settlers of the continent. For example, *Sacajawea, Wilderness Guide*, by Kate Jassem, is the biography of the Shoshone woman who guided the Lewis and Clark expedition across the Rocky Mountains to the Pacific Ocean.

Conflicts between worlds provide numerous opportunities for character and plot development in Jean Fritz's *The Double Life of Pocahontas*. Fritz effectively develops a character who is torn between loyalty to her father's tribe and to her new friends in the Jamestown colony. As in her other biographies, Fritz documents her historical interpretations. Notes, a bibliography, an index, and a map add to the authenticity.

Brandon Marie Miller's *Buffalo Gals: Women of the Old West* includes a chapter on "Clash of Cultures" that focuses on the lives of Native American women. Instead of providing biographical information on specific women, the author focuses on the role of women in Native American cultures and changes caused by white settlement. For example, notice in the following quote how Miller describes both the culture and the role of women within the culture. Also notice that unlike many of the biographies, this author stresses the role of religion within the culture: "Prayers asked for food and good health for the tribe. In some tribes, women, as well as men, hoped for a vision or special dream to show them the road to a good life" (p. 71).

Laurie Lawlor's *Shadow Catcher: The Life and Work of Edward S. Curtis* documents the life and work of the man who photographed and researched the cultures of Native Americans. The biography is illustrated with photographs that exemplify the thirty years of Curtis's work. Both the photographs and the text provide insights into the lives of Native Americans. Each photograph is labeled and accompanied by interpretive text. For example, a photograph of a clam digger includes the following information: "Clams, an important food source for Northwest Coast tribes, are gathered using a wooden digger called a dibbler. Many of Curtis's earliest Native American photos were of clam diggers from the nearby Tulahip Reservation in Washington State" (p. 26). The text includes a listing of the twenty volumes of Curtis's works, the sources of the photographs, an index, and a bibliography of books for children. This biography is divided into three parts: Books About Indians, Books by and About Edward S. Curtis, and Books About Photography.

Informational Books about Earlier Time Periods

Nonfiction books about early Native American cultures provide information about the various groups. They can serve to authenticate literature about Native Americans. Books, both adult and juvenile sources, with authentic paintings and illustrations, may be used to authenticate the art in picture storybooks. Books with detailed descriptions of settings, cultures, and conflicts are valuable for authenticating historical fiction and biographical settings.

The symbolism in Native American folklore, biography, fiction, and poetry may be difficult to understand without some background information. One excellent informational source for this interpretative purpose is the *Dictionary of Native American Mythology* (1992) by Sam D. Gill and Irene F. Sullivan. Each entry in this adult reference source includes an entry title, a tribal or cultural area association, a definition of the entry, cross-references that provide related information, and bibliographic references. The dictionary also includes maps of tribal or cultural areas, a bibliography, and an index by Native American group.

Sources that depict the Americas prior to Columbus or detail the lives and cultures of people who lived in North America at that time are valuable parts of Native American literature. Some of these sources encourage readers to compare life and culture on different continents during the fifteenth century. For example, *The World in 1492,* written by Jean Fritz, Katherine Paterson, Patricia and Frederick McKissack, Margaret Mahy, and Jamake Highwater, includes information on the history, customs, beliefs, and accomplishments of people living in Europe, Asia, Africa, Australia and Oceania, and the Americas. Photographs and illustrations add to the readers' understandings. A bibliography of sources divided according to these areas adds references for further research. The adult text *Circa 1492: Art in the Age of Exploration* (1991), edited by Jay A. Levenson and published by the National Gallery of Art in Washington, D.C., includes detailed commentaries and photographs of art and other cultural sites. There is a large section titled "The Americas."

Books that chronicle the lives of Native Americans prior to the Age of Exploration are popular subjects for young audiences. In *People of the Breaking Day,* Marcia Sewall takes readers back to the Wampanoag nation of southeastern Massachusetts before the English settlers arrived. The text, which is divided into sections, presents information about the tribe, the belief in the Great Spirit, the celebrations, the role of warriors and other members of the tribe, and the family.

Two nonfiction books written for upper elementary and older readers provide information about the history of Native Americans. Neil Philip's *The Great Circle: A History of the First Nations* includes a discussion about the clash between European settlers and Native American tribes. The author explores the conflicting beliefs of the two groups and how each group viewed the earth and nature. The text provides an excellent source for the study of history, culture, and religious beliefs of tribes including the Seminole, the Modoc, and the Lakota. The text also describes how these tribes are currently working to reclaim their cultures. Dorothy Hinshaw Patent's *The Buffalo and the Indians: A Shared Destiny* relates both the history of the Native Americans before the arrival of the Europeans and the importance of the buffalo to the physical and spiritual survival of the Plains Indians. Patent ties mythology to this history by introducing each chapter with an appropriate Native American myth.

"America, Found & Lost" by Charles C. Mann (2007) is an adult source that discusses the legacy of Jamestown. This *National Geographic* article includes drawings of an Indian village and a landscape before and after the arrival of English settlers. Copies of early drawings are labeled as "Eyewitness to a way of life that soon would vanish."

John M. Dunn's *The Relocation of the North American Indian,* a book for older readers, discusses the various efforts by the U.S. government to remove the Native Americans from their lands. An annotated bibliography makes the book a very useful source for research. Two additional histories of relocation include Lydia Bjornlund's *The Trail of Tears: The Relocation of the Cherokee Nation* and Kevin and Laurie Hillstrom's *American Indian Removal and the Trail to Wounded Knee*. The Hillstroms' text includes biographies of personages such as Sitting Bull and Red Cloud.

The experience of relocation is made very painful and vivid by Greg Rodgers's (2006) retelling of an experience retold from his Choctaw ancestry. His story relates a family's experience from the Trail of Tears. As you read Rodgers's comments, notice why he believes it is important to remember this history: "This story lives in the historic conscience of the Choctaws, not as a reminder of the horrors and hardships of the Trail, but to remind us of the triumph and perseverance of the Choctaw spirit. All over the Choctaw Nation there are thousands of family stories that tell of hardship, tragedy, survival, and miracles. But together, they tell one greater story—the story of the Oklahoma Choctaws" (p. 41).

The preservation of a culture because of hardships and fights for survival is also a strong theme in Lawrence W. Cheek's *The Navajo Long Walk*, a book for older readers. This book tells about the forcible removal of the Navajo from their homeland in east-central New Mexico during the mid-1800s. Cheek develops this preservation theme when he states: "The irony—no, the lesson—of the Long Walk is that it preserved Navajo identity instead of destroying it. The Navajos returned to their land with a new and deeper bond to it, and the stories tightened the fiber that held the culture together. The tribe today numbers more than 200,000 members, and the Navajo Nation is the largest reservation in the United States" (p. 57). Historic and contemporary photographs, recommended readings, and places to visit in Navajo country add to the text.

Paul Goble's *Death of the Iron Horse* and Russell Freedman's *Buffalo Hunt* and *An Indian Winter* also provide historical perspectives. Goble uses an actual incident in 1867, when a Union Pacific train was derailed by the Cheyenne. In this fictionalized story, Goble shows that the Cheyenne fought the encroaching white culture by attacking the railroad. In *Buffalo Hunt*, Freedman shows the importance of buffaloes to the Native Americans living on the Great Plains. His text includes descriptions of the hunts, attitudes of the Indians toward the buffaloes, and the consequences to the Indians when the white culture all but eliminated the buffaloes. The text is illustrated with reproductions of paintings by such artists as George Catlin and Karl Bodmer, who actually saw the buffalo hunts. The titled and dated illustrations add interest to the text. Freedman uses a similar approach in *An Indian Winter*, accompanying his description of traditional Mandan life in the 1800s with paintings and drawings created by Karl Bodmer, a young Swiss artist who traveled through the Missouri River Valley in 1832. Many authors of informational books rely on reproductions of paintings completed during earlier times in Native American history to add a sense of authenticity to their texts.

Historical Fiction

Themes and conflicts in historical fiction about Native Americans often emphasize survival—either of the body or of the spirit. Some authors emphasize periods in history in which contact with white settlers or cavalry resulted in catastrophic changes. Others emphasize growing interpersonal relationships between Native American and white characters. Four award-winning books provide examples for these two types of historical fiction.

Scott O'Dell's Newbery Honor book, *Sing Down the Moon*, focuses on the mid-1860s, when the U.S. Cavalry forced the Navajo to make the 300-mile Long Walk from their beautiful home in Canyon de Chelly to stark Fort Sumner. O'Dell effectively develops the resulting conflict through descriptions of the contrasting settings. He provides detailed descriptions of Canyon de Chelly, a place of miracles. This idealistic setting does not last. It is followed by horror when Colonel Kit Carson's soldiers first destroy the crops and livestock in the canyon and then force the Navajo to walk through desolate country to a setting that is inconducive to physical or spiritual survival. Fifteen hundred Navajo die, and many others lose their will to live. O'Dell's protagonist, a Navajo woman named Bright Morning, retains an inner strength based on hope for the future. While she is a captive, she hoards food and plans for the day when she and her husband will return to their canyon. You may compare this book with Cheek's *The Navajo Long Walk*.

Jan Hudson's *Sweetgrass*, a winner of the Canadian Library Association's Book of the Year Award, develops the harmful influences of an expanding white population. Hudson focuses on the struggle for maturity of a young Blackfoot girl as she faces a life-and-death battle in 1837. Smallpox, the "white-man's sickness," results in hunger and death. The themes in *Sweetgrass* are that it is important to honor moral obligations toward others and retain one's dreams.

Hudson employs figurative language involving signs and omens that are meaningful to the characters and reinforce themes related to retaining one's identity and meeting obligations toward family members. For example, the main character considers the importance of her name. She believes it is appropriate because sweetgrass is "ordinary to look at but it's fragrant as the spring" (p. 12). Later, her grandmother tells her that sweetgrass has the power of memories. As Sweetgrass considers her future, readers discover that she is joyfully approaching womanhood. She says, "I felt mightier than a brave. . . . I felt I was holding the future like summer berries in my hands" (p. 26). Instead of allowing the signs and omens to control her life, Sweetgrass uses them to overcome taboos and to help her family in a time of great trouble.

A Canadian Library Association Book of the Year, Farley Mowat's *Lost in the Barrens* takes place in the twentieth century in a remote, arctic wilderness, hundreds of miles from the nearest town. The main characters are Awasin, a Woodland Cree, and Jamie, a white Canadian orphan who moves north to live with his uncle. The setting becomes hostile to both boys when they accompany the Crees on a hunting expedition and then become separated from the hunters. Mowat vividly describes the boys' searching for food and preparing for the rapidly approaching winter. Through long periods of isolation, the boys develop a close relationship and an understanding of each other.

A Newbery Honor book, Elizabeth George Speare's *The Sign of the Beaver* focuses on the friendship between a Native American boy and a white boy in the Maine wilderness of the 1700s. Themes of friendship, faith, moral obligation, working together, and love for the land are developed in this book—in which the wilderness can be either an antagonist or a friend. Matt, the thirteen-year-old main character, faces a life-and-death struggle when his father leaves him alone to guard his family's frontier cabin through the winter. Without food or a gun, Matt confronts a harsh natural environment, fear of the local Indians, and the possibility that he may never see his parents again. In spite of conflicts about the ways in which white settlers are changing their land, a Penobscot boy befriends Matt and teaches him how to survive. For the Penobscot tribe, the wilderness is a friend rather than an antagonist.

In his last book, *Thunder Rolling in the Mountains,* Scott O'Dell, with the assistance of his wife Elizabeth Hall, again develops a story based on the removal of Indian peoples from their land. This time, the narrator is Chief Joseph's daughter, who tells, from her point of view, the story of the forced removal of the Nez Percé tribe from their homeland in 1877. In the foreword to the book. Hall describes O'Dell's fascination with this subject: "At the time of his death, Scott O'Dell was immersed in the story of Chief Joseph and his people. Their courage and determination in the face of cruelty, betrayal, and bureaucratic ignorance moved him deeply. So deeply that he continued to work on the manuscript in the hospital until two days before he died" (p. ix). Readers will also experience O'Dell's fascination with this time period and the plight of these brave people.

The 500th anniversary of Columbus's voyage resulted in the publication of several books written from the viewpoint of the native peoples. Jane Yolen's picture storybook *Encounter* develops the hypothetical interaction between a Taino Indian boy and Columbus and his men on the island of San Salvador in 1492. The text is based on the premise that dreams forewarn the boy about the disastrous consequences of interacting with the explorers, whom the people believe have flown down from the sky. Yolen includes descriptions of the Taino people and their beliefs, details about the loss of culture and human life that resulted because of the exploration and colonization by the Spanish, and details describing trade between the explorers and the Taino people. Information provided in the author's notes indicate how disastrous this encounter was for the Taino people, who went from a population of 300,000 at the time of Columbus's landing to 500 people only fifty years later. Yolen's book develops a common theme found in contemporary books: interaction with people who do not respect your culture can have terrible consequences for the native people. The final illustration by David Shannon depicts a much older Taino Indian, whose body is literally disappearing just as his culture disappeared. As a result of this encounter, the Taino people lost their language, religion, and culture.

In *Morning Girl,* Native American author Michael Dorris sets his story on a Bahamian island at the time of Columbus's landing. The unique quality of this book is the alternating points of view the author develops as he describes the day-to-day activities of Morning Star and Star Boy, two Taino children. Through this approach, Dorris encourages readers to understand the nature of the Taino people and to realize they had individual identities and a culture worth preserving. Unlike Yolen, Dorris concludes his book at the time the first Spanish sailors were sighted. Dorris includes an epilogue that quotes Columbus's journal on October 11, 1492, the day he first encounters the Taino people. You may also find it interesting to compare *Encounter* and *Morning Girl.*

In *Sees Behind Trees,* Dorris sets his historical fiction novel in sixteenth-century America. Dorris's choice of Walnut, a Powhatan boy who has a physical handicap, allows the author to stress the importance of "seeing" with senses other than just sight. Throughout the book, the author develops Walnut's character as the boy learns to use his other senses and receives the honor of a new name, Sees Behind Trees. The boy's special abilities allow the author to depict the setting through senses such as smelling and hearing. Notice in the following quote how these senses are used to depict the setting: "the hush of a brook just behind me and . . . the rush of a river. The buzz of a beehive on a tree not far over to my right" (p. 6). Throughout the book, Dorris encourages readers to hear the various activities of the village such as the stacking of firewood, the approaching hunters, and the peeling of bark from saplings and to smell the environment through descriptions of stewing venison, pemmican scent of berries mixed with dried meat, and smoke from the campfire. Sees Behind Trees develops his unique capabilities as he learns to believe in himself and discovers the importance of looking within himself and respecting the dreams of others. In addition to setting, readers will discover many values and beliefs associated with the Powhatan tribe. This book provides an excellent source for discovering the symbolic and cultural meanings associated with name changes, especially the tests that are given prior to the name change and the differences in expected behaviors that follow the name change.

One of the best newer historical fiction books about Native American culture is Louise Erdrich's *The Birchbark House,* a National Book Award finalist. The book is set on an island in Lake Superior in 1847 and describes an Ojibwa girl's life as she experiences four seasons of the year. See "Involving Students in Native American Literature" for a detailed authentication project with *The Birchbark House* that considers both Erdrich's development of Native American values, specifically Ojibwa, and her ability to create credible historical fiction for the time period. *The Game of Silence* is Erdrich's sequel to this book.

Through all of these stories, readers can experience Native American characters who have personal thoughts and emotions and who live within a family as well as within a tribal group. In addition, children will begin to understand the impact of white people on the Native American way of life. Interesting comparisons may also be made between the themes, settings, and conflicts in biographies and historical fiction.

Characteristics of Contemporary Native American Authors

According to Paula Gunn Allen (1994), tradition remains important in Native American fiction:

> [C]eremonial texts provide a major source of the symbols, allusions, and philosophical assumptions that inform our world and thus our work. It is a mistake to believe that ceremonial texts are "dated" and thus irrelevant to the work of modern writers. . . . They interact, as wings of a bird in flight interact. They give shape to our experience. They signify. (p. 7)

Some contemporary Native American authors have described the characteristics of Native American writing and its distinguishing features. Many also emphasize the need to read and analyze Native American literature in ways that are quite different from mainstreamed American literature. In this section, we discuss some of these characteristics identified by Native American authors and then search for these characteristics in poetry and contemporary writing.

Laura Coltelli in her introduction to *Winged Words: American Indian Writers Speak* (1990), a collection of interviews with contemporary Native American authors, contends that the Native American author's voice of protest, of resistance, of literary creativity has only begun to receive attention from readers and literary critics. She maintains that memory, language, and storytelling tradition—so closely intertwined—are crucial to Native American authors. Throughout the subsequent interviews conducted by Coltelli, the Native American authors emphasize important characteristics of, and influences on, their writing. Of recurring emphasis is the importance of the oral tradition, geographic locations, and tribal backgrounds. Most authors maintain that the oral tradition is central to all forms of Native American expression. For example, N. Scott Momaday (1968), of Kiowa and Cherokee descent and the author of the Pulitzer Prize–winning *House Made of Dawn,* discusses the importance of the oral tradition and the sense of place within the oral tradition. Momaday states, "The understanding of the landscape is one of the most important aspects of Indian oral tradition" (p. 90). Momaday places special emphasis on prose poetry because he claims it is very close to the Native American oral tradition.

The importance of place in the oral tradition and the Native American heritage is also emphasized by Simon Ortiz (1990), who is of Acoma Pueblo descent. He maintains that the spirit of place informs his writing. Ortiz qualifies the spirit of place, "Place is more than just a physical or geographical place, but obviously a spiritual place, a place with the whole scheme of life, the universe, the whole scheme and power of creation. Place is the source of who you are in terms of your identity, the language that you are born into and that you come to use" (p. 105). Ortiz, like many other Native American authors, emphasizes the link among historical stories, recent historical stories, and older stories from the oral tradition. He maintains that these older stories and profiles are used in his writing because "they often refer to certain values that Indian people hold precious and dear. Whether the stories are tragic or happy, they are examples of values Indian people should follow, or see in reflections" (p. 108).

Native American authors may emphasize the role of struggle and conflict in their writing. Paula Gunn Allen discusses the problems associated with keeping a sense of self as she moves from one world to another. Simon Ortiz (1990) maintains that struggle is hopeful and optimistic because "As long people do not stop struggling, they do not become cynical; they may get pessimistic sometimes, but not cynical or hopeless" (p. 112).

By reading a collection of adult literature such as those found in *Voice of the Turtle: American Indian Literature, 1900–1970*, edited by Paula Gunn Allen (1994), you will discover many of the symbols, allusions, and philosophical assumptions of the authors. For example, in "The Great Vision," Black Elk and John G. Neihardt focus on the importance of sacred herbs and colors. Zitkala-Sa in "The Widespread Enigma Concerning Blue-Star Woman" emphasizes the cultural values associated with the old teachings and the importance of visions. John Joseph Mathews in "Sundown" decries the spiritual poverty brought on by Western values. Don C. Talayesva in "School off the Reservation" includes a soul traveling to the House of the Dead, belief in a Guardian Spirit, learning lessons from the Guardian Spirit, and the symbol of the eagle prayer feather. N. Scott Momaday in "Feast Day" emphasizes supernatural power.

Louis Owens's *The Sharpest Sight* (1992) provides many examples of characteristics of contemporary writing. For example, he includes belief in visions, dreams, spirit walking, ancient tribal memories, the panther or soul-eater, the medicine pouch, and unbroken circles. The author uses traditional stories to develop values and stress history. Contemporary conflicts include racism, comparing historic and contemporary feelings, and the need to stay on a straight path and know who you are. Notice how many of these contemporary Native American authors discuss the values and beliefs found in the traditional literature discussed earlier in this chapter. As you read contemporary Native American literature written for children, you may search for these characteristics, values, and beliefs, which are emphasized by outstanding Native American authors.

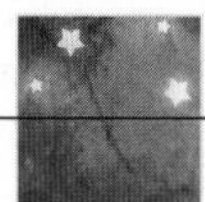

Native American Poetry

In this section and the next sections on contemporary fiction, we analyze the contemporary Native American literature written for children by both Native American authors and non-Native American authors. In these sections, we search for the previously identified characteristics, values, and beliefs.

Rob D. Walker's *Mama Says: A Book of Love for Mothers and Sons* reflects the universal nature of love. The book is a collection of poems written in English and translated into other languages depending on the cultures. The book includes poems written in Cherokee and Inuktitut. Leo and Diane Dillon's illustrations depict each cultural group and show the love felt between mother and child.

In Helen Frost's *Diamond Willow*, twelve-year-old Willow, a dog musher who helps her father with sled dogs when not in school, longs to spend more time with her Athabascan grandparents. Diamond-shaped poems that express her thoughts and feelings alternate with prose sections that take on the point of view of the spirits of her ancestors who live in the wild animals of the Alaskan wilderness she encounters. As with Paul Goble's *All Our Relatives: Traditional Native American Thoughts About Nature*, there is an acknowledgment that there is a strong connection between humans and animals.

Songs, chants, and poems are very important in the various Native American cultures. Many of the poems express reverence for creation, nature, and beauty. Native Americans created poetry for a purpose; they believed there was power in the word. Songs were often part of ceremonial rituals, with their symbolism portrayed through dance. The Author's Note in Edward Field's *Magic*

Words, poems inspired by traditional Inuit stories, contains a definition of poetry that relates the words in poems to songs: "Songs are thoughts, sung out on the breath, when people are moved by great feelings, and ordinary speech is no longer enough" (Note About the Poems). In this section, we consider both historical and contemporary poetry. Also notice as you read the poetry discussed in this section, that many of the poems have a close relationship to the values and beliefs found in the traditional literature.

The beauty of both ancient Native American poetry and contemporary poetry about Native American experiences can be shared with children. An interesting resource book that shares the music of Native Americans with children of many cultures is John Bierhorst's *A Cry from the Earth: Music of the North American Indians.* According to Bierhorst, people throughout North America shared a belief in the supernatural power of music to cure disease, bring rain, win a lover, or defeat an enemy.

Many Native Americans today sing the songs for pleasure and to express pride in their heritage. Bierhorst's book contains words and music for many songs, including songs of prayer, magic, and dreams, songs to control the weather, and music to accompany various dances. There are greeting songs, love songs, a Hopi flute song, a Hopi sleep song, a Cherokee lullaby, and a Kwakiutl cradlesong. Music, words, and dance steps are included so children can recreate, experience, and respect this musical heritage. The text includes extensive commentaries on the sources and meanings of the selections. Each selection is also identified according to tribal origin.

In "Law of the Great Peace," adapted from the Iroquois Book of the Great Law, John Bierhorst presents a poem that reflects the values of the original League of Five Nations, which included the Mohawk, Oneida, Onondaga, Cayuga, and Seneca. The poem expresses a strong desire for unity among all peoples because the "Great Creator has made us of one blood, and of the same soil."

The importance of the oral tradition, geographic locations, and tribal backgrounds are especially meaningful in poetry collections such as *Spirit Walker* by Nancy Wood. Wood's poetry reflects the values of the Taos Indians, especially their interconnections with nature and spirituality. The oral tradition is exemplified in poems such as "Generations" in which she retells the story of creation and emphasizes the importance of Grandfather, who created the people; Grandmother, who issued the stars and moon; Father, who is the Living Sun; and Mother, who is the Enduring Earth.

Both the poems and the paintings in Shonto Begay's *Navajo: Visions and Voices Across the Mesa* explore the beliefs, values, struggles, and settings of the Navajo world. Through the poetry, Begay presents the "constant struggle for balance—balance in living between the 'New World' and the ancient world of my people, the Navajo. And ever present, there are the voices of my elders—warning us to guard and protect our mother the earth" (p. 7). Poems such as "Echoes" and "Creation" tell about the ancient spirits, the arrival of beings into the Fourth World, and the power of First Man and First Woman. Poems such as "Mother's Lace," "Reflections After the Rain," and "Early Spring" reflect the beauty of the earth. Poems such as "Into the New World," "Storm Pattern," and "Down Highway 163" express the modern struggle of the Navajo people. This collection represents an excellent view of traditional beliefs and shows how traditional beliefs and values are still important even in a world that includes struggle.

Inuit traditional beliefs are reflected in the poems in Edward Field's *Magic Words.* Poems such as "The Earth and the People," "Magic Words," and "Day and Night: How They Came to Be" reflect traditional stories told in poetic form.

The roles of struggle and conflict are current themes in contemporary poetry written by Native American poets for older audiences. Many of these poets develop themes related to inner conflicts as the poets try to retain their Native American values in a white culture. Poetry collections such as *Songs from This Earth on Turtle's Back: Contemporary American Indian Poetry,* edited by Joseph Bruchac, allow readers and researchers to understand these present-day conflicts. For example, poems by Maurice Kenny (Mohawk) develop the poet's strong love for nature. Poems by Simon Ortiz (Acoma), Carrol Arnett/Gogisgi (Cherokee), and Karoniaktatie (Turtle Clan) explore contemporary conflicts with society. As you read the poetry discussed in this section, try to identify both the traditional values and the contemporary conflicts expressed by the poets. Ask this question: Do the poems reflect characteristics of Native American literature contemporary Native American authors identified?

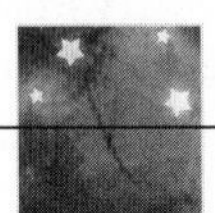

Contemporary Realistic Fiction

Contemporary realistic fiction about Native Americans develops many of the same themes and conflicts found in the poetry and the Native American literature previously discussed in this chapter. In books for younger children, Native American characters frequently explore nature or develop close ties with their traditional roots. Native American characters often express conflict between the old ways and the new ones. Characters must frequently decide whether to preserve their heritage or abandon it. Many of the stories allow Native Americans to honor the old ways but also live with the new ones. Some stories show life on modern reservations; others depict families who have left the reservation to live in cities.

Picture Story Books

Chief Jake Swamp, a member of the Mohawk Nation, praises the natural world in *Giving Thanks: A Native American Good Morning Message*. This is a tribute to Mother Earth, to the life-sustaining foods and to the animals, to the Four Winds that bring clean air, to Grandfather Thunder Beings for bringing rain, to Elder Brother Sun for light and warmth, to Grandmother Moon for lighting the darkness, to Spirit Protectors of past and present, and to the Great Spirit for giving all of these wonderful gifts.

Jean Craighead George's *The Buffalo Are Back* is a combination of fiction and nonfiction. The author goes back to the earlier relationship between the buffalo and the Native Americans, then continues into the near extinction of the buffalo, and finally to the resurgence of the herds and the land that supports them. Wendell Minor's watercolor illustrations provide an appropriate prairie setting.

An unusual alphabet book exploring Native American contributions to the English language, Linda Boyden's *Giveaways: An ABC Book of Loanwords from the Americas* uses the ABC format to categorize words where the original sources are the names of plants, objects, and animals that have Native American roots. The author expands the ABC format by including several paragraphs with each letter where she relates the history of the subject. The author also includes Internet sources.

In *The Seasons and Someone,* Virginia Kroll uses a question-and-answer format to allow readers to accompany a young Inuit girl as she explores what happens during each of the seasons in the Arctic. For example, she asks in the spring, "What will happen when Wind's roars change to whispers and icicles grow thin?" (unnumbered).* The text and illustrations indicate how lichen dapples rocks, ground squirrels scurry from burrows, and people laugh at the sight of buds. The text develops both descriptions of the environment and the importance of family life.

In *This Land Is My Land,* Cree author and artist George Littlechild presents a historical preview of his people and his own experiences. The importance of both nature and the ancestors are found in his introduction when he describes how he is inspired by the night sky, which for him is a doorway to the Spirit World, and by the ancestors who had courage and survived.

*Excerpt from *The Seasons and Someone,* copyright © 1994 by Virginia Kroll, reprinted by permission of Harcourt, Inc.

Littlechild then provides brief histories that develop a chronology of his people and his own life. Through the dedication in which Littlechild pictures his own ancestors, readers receive a very personal message from the author.

Like other contemporary realistic fiction written for younger children, stories about Native Americans frequently develop themes related to love and family relationships. In *Mama, Do You Love Me?* by Barbara M. Joosse, a young child tests her mother's love. Through satisfactory responses, the girl discovers that her mama loves her. Each of the questions and responses relates to the culture.

A loving relationship between a Navajo girl and her grandmother provides the foundation in Miska Miles's *Annie and the Old One.* The conflict in the story develops because Annie does not want to accept the natural order of aging and death. In an effort to hold back time, Annie tries to prevent her grandmother from completing the rug she is weaving because her grandmother has said, "My children, when the new rug is taken from the loom, I will go to Mother Earth" (p. 15). The author emphasizes the way that Annie's inner conflict ends, and the theme that we are all part of nature emerges when Annie finally realizes, "The cactus did not bloom forever. Petals dried and fell to earth. She knew that she was a part of the earth and the things on it. She would always be part of the earth, just as her grandmother had always been, just as her grandmother would always be, always and forever. And Annie was breathless with the wonder of it" (p. 41).* Annie's actions show that she has accepted nature's inevitable role. Annie picks up the weaving stick and begins to help her grandmother complete the rug. These stories reflect a respect for older people as well as a respect for the natural order.

Two picture books for younger readers develop the Native Americans' strong relationships with animals. Jim Arnosky's *Grandfather Buffalo* develops the protective bond between an old buffalo and a mother buffalo and her young calf who cannot keep up with the herd. The illustrations depict the harshness of the environment as well as the powerful relationship among the animals. Leo Yerxa's *Ancient Thunder* is a visual tribute to the wild horses that wander freely across the Great Plains. The artist and author describes how the book reflects his love of horses from the time he was born on the Little Eagle Reserve in northern Ontario. The illustrations show horses running through the tall grass, chasing buffalo and antelope, soaring like the eagles, and sleeping in the moonlight until they wake again and race across the prairies on hooves of ancient thunder.

Books for Older Readers

In *Walk Two Moons,* Sharon Creech's heroine, thirteen-year-old Sal, is proud of her mother's Native American heritage. Now she faces conflicts because her mother has left her. The author develops two parallel stories as the heroine tells the story of her best friend, Phoebe, and her experiences when Phoebe's mother left.

Sal makes discoveries about her own life and learns to accept her own mother through a series of mysterious messages. The answers to the messages allow the author to show characters' actions and motivation as Sal and her grandparents trace the route of her mother's disappearance. For example, the first message is, "Don't judge a man until you have walked two moons in his moccasins" (p. 51). The text continues with a series of messages that reveal characterization through actions and interpretations until the final message, which is the same as the first message.

Journeys that allow Native American characters to search for their ancient traditions and cultural heritages are important themes in much of the Native American literature for children and adolescents. In Jean Craighead George's *Water Sky,* a boy from Massachusetts journeys to Barrow, Alaska, in search of his uncle and his Inuit heritage. During his quest, he lives in a whal-

---

*Excerpt from *Annie and the Old One* by Patricia Miles Martin and Peter Parnall. Reprinted by permission of Little, Brown and Company.

ing camp, where he learns to respect his Inuit heritage and discovers Inuit values and beliefs. In Gary Paulsen's *Dogsong,* a contemporary Inuit boy leaves the modern world to discover the ways and beliefs from the days of dogsleds. The protagonist discovers his traditional heritage through his interactions with an elderly Inuit and by journeying alone on a 1,400-mile dogsled trek across the isolated ice and tundra. The author uses many traditional references through dreams and visions that allow the boy to travel back to earlier times.

In Scott O'Dell's *Black Star, Bright Dawn,* an Inuit girl drives a dogsled team in the Iditarod Trail Sled Race from Anchorage to Nome. Through her experiences, the girl learns to depend on her dogs and herself. In addition, she discovers the strength in her Inuit heritage, values, and beliefs.

Conflicts involving settings are often used to develop the plots in contemporary realistic fiction written for older readers. The conflict frequently occurs when a protagonist leaves the reservation and lives in urban environments. The protagonist in Robert Lipsyte's *The Brave* leaves the reservation and the support of his people to try to become a boxer in Manhattan. In the city, he experiences the harsh underworld of violence, drugs, gangs, and prison. It is his heritage, however, and the teachings of his uncle about the Running Braves that make it possible for him to face his problems and control his life. Knowing oneself and relying on traditional teachings and cultural heritage are frequently shown as sources for personal strength.

Symbolism, traditional values, tribal customs, and conflict with contemporary society are common elements in Native American books written for older readers. For example, Jamake Highwater's Ghost Horse Cycle, which includes *Legend Days, The Ceremony of Innocence,* and *I Wear the Morning Star,* is a series of three books that follow three generations of a Northern Plains Indian family as they progress from a proud and powerful people to a people who are alienated from both their roots and the encroaching white culture. The cycle focuses on the life of Amana, a woman of power, courage, and tragedy, who symbolizes the fate of her people.

The importance of believing in the traditional ways of one's people is an important theme in *Legend Days.* This theme is developed through the "legend days" motif used throughout the book. Omens, powers, visions, and close relationships with animals and nature are important in both the plot and Amana's characterization. That alienation will result if one loses his or her identity is a strong theme developed in both *The Ceremony of Innocence* and *I Wear the Morning Star.* This theme is developed as Amana finds herself alienated from both her tribal ancestors and her half-French, half-Indian daughter. As she confronts her daughter, she reveals the importance of her tribal heritage and the depth of her alienation. The theme of the destructive force of alienation is reinforced through the unhappiness of two of Amana's children. When the characters try to deny their Native American heritage and struggle to become part of the white culture, they do not know their own identities. It is only Amana and her son, Sitko, who eventually obtain acceptance of self and peace of mind. Amana succeeds by escaping into her earlier visions and reuniting with Grandfather Fox through death. Sitko learns the myths of his grandmother and recaptures her visions through art.

The historical perspective of Highwater's *Legend Days* is based on accounts of life in the Northern Plains as found in the oral history of the Blackfoot Confederacy. The book is grounded in mythological foundations typical of the mythology of the Great Plains. The social context of Highwater's *The Ceremony of Innocence* and *I Wear the Morning Star* is similar to the context of Native American authors writing for adult audiences. For example, N. Scott Momaday (Kiowa) in *House Made of Dawn* (1968) focuses on the alienation of a returning Native American soldier as he feels separated from both urban society and tribal ways. Many of the short stories of Simon J. Ortiz (Acoma Pueblo) and his poems, such as "From Sand Creek" in *Songs from This Earth on Turtle's Back: Contemporary American Indian Poetry,* reveal how difficult it is to face stereotypical attitudes and be accepted as an individual. Louis Owens (Choctaw/Cherokee/Irish) uses visions and belief in traditional values and mythology to allow his protagonist to discover who he is in *The Sharpest Sight* (1992). The themes by these Native Americans writing for adult audiences are quite similar to the themes in contemporary realistic fiction written for juvenile audiences.

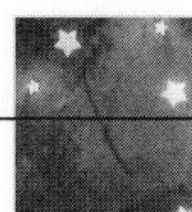

Nonfiction Informational Books

Native American author Paula Gunn Allen (Coltelli, 1990) expresses concern that many people do not realize Native Americans are active participants in not only the history, but also the culture and arts of contemporary America. To overcome this problem the Native American informational literature should include sources that describe the lives, contributions, and problems of contemporary Native Americans.

The juvenile sources in this area tend to portray both the promises and the conflicts faced by Native Americans as they live in two worlds. Arlene Hirschfelder's *Happily May I Walk: American Indians and Alaska Natives Today* is a comprehensive text, discussing such contemporary topics as tribal governments, education, economic life, and organizations. The text includes photographs, further reading lists, and an index. A map of Native American lands and communities helps readers find locations identified in the text. It is interesting to compare this map with the maps showing the historic tribal lands of the 1600s.

Tricia Brown's *Children of the Midnight Sun: Young Native Voices of Alaska* provides a unique perspective by focusing on the lives of eight children who each represent a different culture: Eskimo—Yuk'ik and Inupiat; Aleut; and Indian—Athabascan, Tlingit, Tsimshian, and Haida. Through their stories, readers understand how these young people meld the contemporary world with the traditional cultural values and beliefs. Roy Corral's photographs add considerable interest. The text includes a glossary and a list of recommended readings.

Normee Ekoomiak's *Arctic Memories,* written in both English and Inuktitut, the Inuit language illustrates and discusses the Inuit artist's own memories of life in the Arctic. The illustrations by the Inuk artist also provide information about the culture, including the igloo, ice fishing, traveling, games, and ancestral hunters. Carol Finley's *Art of the Far North: Inuit Sculpture, Drawing, and Printmaking* shows the art of contemporary Inuit people and discusses how it relates to the environment and the culture.

Highly illustrated informational books for young readers follow the lives of children growing up in the culture or provide insights into characteristics of the culture. For example, Marcia Keegan's *Pueblo Boy: Growing Up in Two Worlds* is a photographic essay that accompanies a boy as he engages in activities in his pueblo and in his school. The contrasting environments of ceremonial dances in the pueblo and computers in the school are shown through the photographs. Diane Hoyt-Goldsmith's *Arctic Hunter* is a photographic essay that follows the activities of a contemporary Inupiat boy in Kotzebue, Alaska.

Through text and photographs, Diane Hoyt-Goldsmith's *Buffalo Days* covers not only the history of the buffalo (bison), but also focuses on the celebration of the Crow Fair and Rodeo, which is held during the third week of August on the Crow Reservation in Montana. Lawrence Migdale's photographs add to the cultural understanding. Jacqueline Left Hand Bull and Suzanne Haldane's photo essay *Lakota Hoop Dancer* follows the activities of Kevin Locke, a Hankpapa Indian and member of the Lakota Nation, as he prepares for and performs the traditional dance. Both text and photographs emphasize the importance of retaining the Lakota culture. The text includes a glossary and a list of recommended readings.

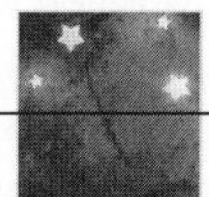

Survival

There is a close relationship between the values and beliefs expressed in Native American survival strategies and the values and beliefs found in Native American folklore, especially tales categorized as setting the world in order or family drama tales. For example, as you read the traditional tales you probably noticed elements the people consider important for personal and tribal survival such as respect for elders; close relationships between humans, Earth, and animals; willingness to sacrifice loved objects to save the tribe; importance of keeping vows; honoring a name change that reflects respected actions; and paying close attention to messages revealed through dreams, spirit beings, and traditional storytelling.

The survival strategies expressed in Louise Erdrich's historical fiction trilogy *The Birchbark House*, *The Game of Silence*, and *The Porcupine Year* are excellent examples showing survival strategies that reflect the values found in Native American folklore. As shown in the "Authentication of *The Birchbark House*" section found later in this chapter, the main character, Omakayas, is taught by her grandmother to listen to and to learn from nature and the stories that reflect the values of the people living around the Great Lakes. These lessons allow her to successfully nurse her family during a smallpox epidemic. Many of the lessons that allow her to survive are revealed through dreams and voices she hears in nature.

Survival strategies continue in *The Game of Silence* and *The Porcupine Year*. Now survival becomes more precarious as the Ojibwa tribe prepares for a forced removal from their beloved island because the U.S. government wants to move them farther west to make room for white settlers. The author illustrates differences in survival strategies between the white man who survives through written words and the Ojibwa who survive through the oral traditions of memorized stories, songs, and the value of spoken words. As the people face this new conflict over land they listen to the advice of the old ones, especially as they gather food and belongings for what may be a long and dangerous journey. As Omakayas matures and faces new dangers, the author stresses her survival because of advice gained from dreams and personal spirit beings.

Strategies for survival in nature become especially important in *The Porcupine Year* as the author develops the setting as both an antagonist and a protagonist. The setting is antagonist as the children use all of their skills to canoe through dangerous rapids, survive a forest fire, and gather food during a brutal winter. But it is protagonist as they listen to nature and rely on their ability to understand animals and the seasons to survive. In this book the author develops the strongest importance of believing that a name change reflects the true nature of a person. Omakayas's younger brother, Pinch, becomes Quill because he spares a baby porcupine; the porcupine then becomes his helping spirit, his medicine animal.

Omakayas's name change shows the importance or courage for personal and tribal survival; she calls down an eagle and becomes Leading Thunderbird Woman. The author's use of symbolism in nature also reveals how the people survive by listening to nature. For example, when the people are covered by a blanket of yellow butterflies, the butterflies are considered a good sign from the Great Spirit and a smile from the Creator. Songs, stories, and beneficial animals help the people survive their frequently dangerous journey, including a raid during which their life-saving provisions are stolen. They finally reach the beautiful Lac Du Bois (Lake of the Woods) and find a land that members of their own tribe settled. They know that they will never forget their original island in Lake Superior, but they also know that they can make a new home for themselves.

Believing in visions of the future that tell of happenings and searching for lost lands that are part of tribal memories are important survival strategies in both historical fiction such as Erdrich's trilogy and in legends handed down through generations of storytellers such as the protagonist in E. Pauline Johnson's *The Lost Island*. This legend is considered a classic in Canadian children's and native literature. Johnson, the daughter of a Mohawk chief is known for her poetry and retellings of folklore. *The Lost Island* describes the visions that allow a great medicine man to look across 100 years into the future and see how the city of Vancouver and its inhabitants will take away the lands and traditions of his people. In an effort to regain the courage, confidence, bravery, and traditions of his people that are now hidden on this island, there is a continuous search for the island that has been lost. None of the people have been able to find the island or their lost survival strategies. Atanas Matsoureff's illustrations show the grandeur of British Columbia and the land lost by the people. The illustrations also depict the close relationships between animals and humans, especially moose, bears, and wolves. The illustrations suggest that these relationships are essential if people are to survive.

Survival strategies of tribal members or whole groups of people frequently emphasize developing, protecting, or restoring close relationships between humans, animals, and Earth. Some animals such as the buffalo are essential for food, clothing, and housing. Other animals such as wolves are considered important spirit animals. Two quite different attitudes are found about wolf survival. Attitudes range from ranchers who consider the animal an evil predator that should be exterminated, to groups that consider the wolf a symbol of the nobility of nature and whose survival is essential for reestablishing natural ecosystems.

The attitudes of Native Americans toward wolves is expressed by Peter Steinhart (1996) when he quotes ethnographic studies that describe the high regard of Native Americans, especially the Plains Indians, toward the wolf. He describes how the Native peoples celebrated the high degree of similarities between humans and wolves through wolf-clan totems, wolf-warrior societies, and hunting techniques that imitated wolf behavior. Steinhart's *The Company of Wolves* details the history of human interactions with wolves. His chapter "Looking for Spirit" describes many tribal viewpoints toward wolves and why people need to help the wolf survive.

One of the contemporary Cree Indians interviewed for Steinhart's chapter explains why respecting wolves is so important for preserving the Cree's culture. He describes the wolf as his father's spirit brother and explains why listening to the wolf is important because the wolf's wisdom helps his people. Without the survival of the wolf, the people lose their sense of being part of the land, part of nature, and part of the circle of life.

Scott Ian Barry's *Wolf Empire: An Intimate Portrait of a Species* is a heavily illustrated book showing photographs of wolves that express Barry's belief: "Perhaps the reason that wolves have managed to survive over the millennia is they don't pass through nature, they become part of it" (p. 12). While the text is appropriate for older readers, the photographs may be used to provide information about wolves for any age group. Many of the books discussed in this Native American chapter include references to wolves. Consequently, these photographs may help readers, especially those living in cities, have a better understanding of this often elusive animal.

Biographies of Native American leaders are excellent sources for identifying cultural values and beliefs and analyzing survival strategies. S. D. Nelson's *Black Elk's Vision: A Lakota Story* is a heavily illustrated biography of the Lakota-Oglala medicine man who lived from 1865 until 1950. The author, a member of the Standing Rock Sioux tribe of the Dakotas, describes the visions that Black Elk sees as he first hears and sees the spirit voices calling to him. When he is nine years old he experiences his great vision. The author shows in both illustrations and in text what Black Elk sees and hears as he is drawn into the world of the Six Grandfathers, the ancient ones. While in the company of the Grandfathers he is given advice for the survival of both his people and others living on Earth. When he is given a cup filled with water the ancients tell him that the water is the power of life. When he is presented with a red stick he is told that it is the tree of life; he should take the tree back to his people and teach them to care for the tree. If all people share the same vision, the tree will flower. Black Elk shares his vision with his people and relates the importance of the Native American belief in honoring the Circle of Life. According to the Author's Note Black Elk used the belief in his vision to teach people that: "We are part of the landscape and everything in it. With this awareness comes humility and the gift of harmony" (p. 42).

Stories set in times of war may reflect the greatest need for survival strategies. Retaining and respecting language and culture are major survival strategies in Joseph Bruchac's *Code Talker*, discussed in "A Featured Book for Young Adults." There is irony in this story based on true incidents. In earlier times the U.S. government tried to suppress and even eradicate the Navajo language by forcing children to learn and speak only English. But during WWII, speakers of the Navajo language used their language skills to send coded messages that could not be read by the Japanese. We can infer that knowledge of the Navajo language helped all Americans survive. Bruchac's main character reflects on the importance of his language as he feels at peace because his language is respected; he realizes that keeping the Navajo Way helped him survive.

Sherman Alexie's *The Absolutely True Diary of a Part-Time Indian* won a National Book Award for Young Adult Literature, a Boston Globe Award, and is on the *New York Times* Best Sellers list. This is a contemporary story about a Native American boy who leaves the reservation to attend an all-white high school. Consequently, his survival strategies relate to two environments: surviving with his people and family on the reservation as the people battle poverty, bone-crushing reality, low levels of education, unemployment, and alcoholism; and surviving in the all-white school and town where there is suspicion of Native Americans and attitudes of racism but there are students who have hope for the future, positive role models, and expectations for college educations.

To survive on the reservation, Arnold draws cartoons to illustrate his experiences and feelings because words are too unpredictable and too limited. These cartoons are important to him because he feels like his world is a series of floods and his cartoons act like lifeboats. On the reservation he knows that to survive families must stick together and he must sometimes be brave like a warrior.

As he leaves the reservation school to attend the all-white school, he believes that it is important to search for hope; hope will only come as he walks farther and farther away from the reservation. As he attends this new school and interacts with people outside the reservation, he discovers new sets of survival strategies. Now it is important for him to pay respect to the "alpha dog" in the high school. He feels honorable when he raises money for the poor and discovers that he is smarter than 99% of the kids in the high school. His desire for learning is

A Featured Book for Young Adults

In *Code Talker* Joseph Bruchac, whose own tribal heritage is western Abenaki, combines traditional Navajo cultural heritage and values, a history of the Navajo people, and a conflict set in the Pacific during World War II. Bruchac bases his fictional story on the experiences of Ned Begay, who was one of the Navajo marines who used his native language to develop an unbreakable code that helped defeat the Japanese. Bruchac's major theme is that it is important to respect other languages and cultures. The evidence for this theme is found throughout the book. It is especially important when Begay realizes that the Navajo language, which the government tried to wipe out through forced education in the Indian schools, was used during World War II as a means to send coded messages that helped the United States win the war against Japan.

Bruchac uses an interesting author's style that allows him to explain various aspects of Navajo history and culture. For example, throughout the book when readers need to have additional information about the Navajo he speaks to the readers through language such as "Yes, grandchildren. I am sure you want to know" (p. 106). He uses this technique to explain the importance of various cultural beliefs and ceremonies, the impact of Fort Defiance as part of the Long Walk in 1863, and contrasting differences between Navajo and white cultures. He also uses Navajo myths to explain reasons for actions and beliefs.

This book may also be read as a history of World War II in the Pacific. Bruchac describes the attack on Pearl Harbor, includes experiences during boot camp, uses military vocabulary, and provides descriptions of places such as the Solomon Islands, the battle of Iwo Jima and the raising of the American flag on Mount Suribachi, Okinawa, and the bombing of Hiroshima and Nagasaki. To provide additional authenticity, the marines sing songs of the time period, describe seeing John F. Kennedy's PT boat experience, and quote broadcasts using Japanese propaganda. Throughout the book, the author includes the importance of the Navajo culture in helping these marines keep their balance and retain their love of country. The author includes an extensive Author's Note that provides additional history of the Navajo culture and peopleand a description of the Code Talkers. He alsoincludes a bibliography of books about the Navajos, books about Code Talkers, and books about World War II.

Many of these themes may be found in Lori Carlson's collection of stories, *Moccasin Thunder: American Indian Stories for Today*. This collection, written by ten different authors, depicts contemporary issues and concerns. As you read these stories, identify the themes and values that are shared by contemporary Native authors. What are the issues that are reflected in contemporary stories?

reinforced through his new classes. By working with the class genius, he learns how to read a book (three times to really understand and evaluate the contents); discovers the joyous feeling of accomplishment when he finishes a task; and realizes that he must continue searching for a dream. In both environments, he discovers the importance of being tolerant and that both laughter and crying are sometimes important during human interactions.

To discover the importance of Sherman Alexie's survival strategies as developed by the protagonist in *The Absolutely True Diary of a Part-Time Indian* you may compare the strategies with those developed in Alexie's adult text *War Dances* (2009). *War Dances*, winner of the Pen/Faulkner Award, is a collection of short stories and poems. The selections reveal survival strategies developed by the various protagonists, cultural beliefs, and themes that suggest values to live by. As you read the following strategies, beliefs, and themes, decide whether there are any similarities between Alexie's fiction written for young adults and fiction written for an adult audience.

For example, when searching for survival strategies expressed by various characters, readers discover that writing poetry is a lifesaver, a predictable moral code helps one through compromised situations, anger should not be carried in the heart, it is important to learn to work under pressure, and laughter helps characters survive many situations.

Cultural beliefs include faith in healing songs and close relationships with nature. The author uses animal symbolism such as "I was the weak antelope in the herd" (p. 55) and "We all slept curled around one another like sled dogs in a snow storm" (p. 45). Several themes emerge in the stories that reveal different values. For example, "We must be taught to choose goodness and to become good," "Each citizen of the world is ultimately responsible for his own actions," and "It is better to be forgotten than to be inaccurately remembered."

What, if any, are the similarities in survival strategies, cultural beliefs, and themes expressed in the two books? If you found similarities, why do you believe that similarities exist? If the survival strategies, beliefs, and themes are different, why do you believe that they are different?

An excellent conclusion for Native American survival strategies is found in Tim Tingle's biographical remembrances of his grandmother in *Saltypie: A Choctaw Journey from Darkness into Light*. This is a story about a loving family and the stories that unite them; the family shares stories about Grandmother's troubles and Choctaw troubles as they wait for their blind grandmother to receive an eye transplant. Tingle shares his grandmother's survival strategies when he states that everywhere we go we all leave footfalls and change the people we meet. Consequently, "If we learn to listen to the quiet and secret music, as my Mawmaw did, we will leave happy footfalls behind us in our going" (unnumbered).

Summary

Through the study of Native American literature, we discover a continuum that begins with the traditional literature and extends through the contemporary literature. The traditional literature is of vital importance because it reflects the values and beliefs of the people that are still important in the contemporary literature. For example, a review of traditional literature of the Northern Plains Indians indicates that traditional values include living in harmony with nature, showing respect for wisdom gained through age and experience, viewing religion as a natural phenomenon closely related to nature, acquiring patience, and emphasizing group and extended needs rather than individuals' needs.

Themes and conflicts in historical fiction about Native Americans often emphasize survival during periods in history in which contact with settlers or cavalry resulted in catastrophic changes. Another theme emphasized is growing interpersonal relationships between Native American and white characters.

Many of the contemporary works discussed in the chapter indicate that oral tradition remains important in Native American fiction. Native American authors may emphasize the role of struggle and conflict in their writing. Some authors use traditional stories to develop values and recall history. The importance of the spoken word is reflected in both ancient and contemporary Native American poetry.

Native American literature is a complex subject. An understanding of the literature requires an in-depth study of both the history and the contemporary role of the people.

Suggested Activities for Developing Understanding of Native American Literature

1. Compile a bibliography of illustrated books that develop a Native American perspective. Emphasize the strengths in both the text and the illustrations.
2. Using the evaluation criteria identified in this text, evaluate a selection of Native American literature available in a university, public, or school library. What conclusions do you reach about the quality of the books available? Or, choose two time periods and use your evaluation criteria to compare the quality of the books.
3. Consult recent journal articles that deal with issues related to Native American literature. What are the current opinions about authenticity, sovereignty, translations, and literal versus metaphorical interpretations? With a group of your peers, choose one of the topics and conduct a debate on the subject.
4. Read "The Beaver and the Porcupine Woman" in Michael Dorris's "Native American Literature in an Ethnohistorical Context," *College English* 41 (October 1979): 147–162. Try to interpret the example of Athapaskan folklore given in the article before you read Dorris's background information or the interpretation. How does your interpretation of the tale change after you have this background information? What message did you gain about the importance of background information when interpreting or comprehending Native American folklore?
5. Choose a highly illustrated version of Native American folklore you can authenticate through other sources. Authenticate both the text and the illustrations.
6. Choose a Native American tribal or cultural area. Compile a list of the values and beliefs that are developed in the folklore of that area. Use examples of folklore to prove your points.
7. Read an adult biography or autobiography of a Native American subject and read a children's biography written about the same figure. Compare the two texts, using some of the same characteristics as discussed in this text.
8. Using the characteristics of contemporary Native American authors discussed in this text, do a literary analysis of a contemporary realistic fiction book or a collection of poetry by a Native American author. Use quotes from the literature to identify and support any of the characteristics discussed.
9. Choose a Native American tribal or cultural area. Develop an annotated bibliography of nonfiction informational sources that can be used to add understanding of that tribal group.

10. Authenticate Joseph Bruchac's *Code Talker* for the two settings developed in the book: The history of the Navajo and the World War II settings. Analyze the techniques Bruchac uses to encourage readers to understand and visualize the conflicts developed for each setting. How does Bruchac include a culture of Navajo beliefs and values in the development of each setting?

11. Read the 2007 National Book Award winner for young people's literature, *The Absolutely True Diary of a Part-Time Indian* by Sherman Alexie. Identify how the author develops the themes: families are important, it is important to be tolerant, and drinking is harmful. Why do you believe that these themes would be important to the author who spent his childhood on the Spokane Reservation in Washington?

Involving Children with Native American Literature

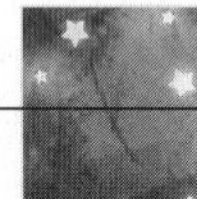

Phase One: Traditional Literature

Before beginning a study of traditional Native American literature and culture, students need to understand the diversity of locations for Native American peoples. John Bierhorst's *The Mythology of North America* (1985) includes a map of North American mythological regions. A map is also located in Michael J. Caduto and Joseph Bruchac's *Keepers of the Animals: Native American Stories and Wildlife Activities for Children* (1991). According to the authors, this map indicates the cultural areas and tribal locations of Native North Americans as they appeared around 1600. Students could begin their study of Native American folklore with an investigation of the oral language as reflected in storytelling.

Developing Oral Storytelling Styles

You could begin the study of storytelling by explaining to students that Native American storytellers developed styles of telling stories over centuries of oral tradition. Storytelling was an important part of earlier Native American life, and stories were carefully passed down from one generation to the next. It was quite common for Native Americans to gather around a fire or sit in their homes and listen to stories. Each tribe member told a story, and storytelling sessions frequently continued for long periods. Several collectors of tales and observers of storytellers have identified opening sentences, storytelling styles, and endings that characterize the storytelling of various tribes. Copying and implementing the techniques may be used to make the storytelling experience more authentic for students of literature.

For example, Navajo storytellers frequently opened their stories with one of these openings:

> In the beginning, when the world was new . . .
> At the time when men and animals were all the same and spoke the same language . . .

White Mountain Apache frequently opened their stories with

> Long, long ago, they say . . .

Discuss the meanings of each introduction and consider how the introduction relates to traditional Native American values.

Now you may select a collection of Native American folklore suitable for storytelling. The following texts provide a few suggestions: Joseph Bruchac's *Tell Me a Tale: A Book About Storytelling* includes tales from various tribal areas as well as suggestions for telling the stories; Chief Lelooska's *Echoes of the Elders: The Stories and Paintings of Chief Lelooska* includes tales from the Northwest Coast; Nancy Wood's *The Serpent's Tongue: Prose, Poetry, and Art of the New Mexico Pueblos* includes stories divided according to such categories as creation, childhood, a lasting way of life, hunting, and ceremony. You may also select examples of individual stories that are appropriate for storytelling such as Barbara Juster Esbensen's *The Star Maiden*, which is an Ojibwa tale about the creation of water lilies; Paul Goble's *Iktomi and the Berries* and *Iktomi and the Boulder: A Plains Indian Story*, which are trickster tales from the Lakota Sioux; and

Laura Simms's *The Bone Man: A Native American Modoc Tale,* which explores the values of courage, wisdom, and compassion.

Students may use these folktales to discover how interpreters and translators of traditional folklore introduce their stories. They can ask, "Are there differences according to tribe or region?" For example, students can find the following examples in Chief Lelooska's *Echoes of the Elders* (Northwest Coast):

> Many generations ago, there lived . . .
> Our ancestors believed there were . . .

These examples of story openers are in Nancy Wood's *The Serpent's Tongue* (from the nineteen Pueblos of New Mexico):

> Many, many years ago, all things came to be.
> In the beginning, long, long ago, there was but one being in the lower world.
> It seems—so the words of the grandfathers say . . .

You may share with the students information about various Native American storytelling styles. For example, storytellers from the Northwest used a terse, staccato, and rapid style to tell their stories. Coeur d'Alene storytellers used gestures to increase the drama of their tales. Hopi children responded to the story by repeating the last word of the sentence, and Crow children responded with "E!" (yes) following every few sentences. Jicarilla Apache storytellers gave kernels of corn to children during story time. (It was believed that if children ate corn during the storytelling, they would remember the content and the importance of the stories.) Kiowa Indians did not tell trickster tales during daylight hours because when trickster was about ready to leave our world, he told the people never to tell stories about him in the daytime.

Choctaw storyteller Tim Tingle (2003) describes a style of performing employed by many Choctaw storytellers in which the storyteller tells the tale in a semitrance state that "encourages listeners to tune out their surroundings. Both the performer and the audience appear to experience the narrative rather than observe it from a distant perspective" (p. 8). This storytelling may be followed by a period of silence. The length of the silence appears to be related to the level of seriousness of the story. For example, "a lighter tale would soon be followed by soft laughter and conversation, while a tragedy seemed to require a respectful and lengthy silence" (p. 8).

To help students develop an understanding of story endings, you may discuss the following examples:

> Clackama storytellers ended many of their stories with words that meant "myth, myth" or "story, story."
>
> The Kiowa ended many of their stories with "That's the way it was—and is—down to this day."

Students may now want to search Native American folklore to discover how interpreters and translators ended their stories. For example, the following are from Nancy Wood's *The Serpent's Tongue:*

> . . . the People shall continue.
>
> I will pass here again, with other stories. Go home to your parents and sleep well. Songe-de-ho, goodbye!

They may discuss the meaning of each ending and consider how the ending might relate to Native American traditional values.

You may divide the students into groups according to a Native American tribe or a region of the country. Ask them to develop appropriate storytelling techniques for that tribe and ask them to practice and present their stories to the rest of the group. In *Tell Me a Tale,* Bruchac stresses the importance of introducing folktales by telling information about the story. Students could provide background about the tribe, when and why the story was told, and any other background information that could increase understanding and enjoyment. Bruchac also recommends using objects that help storytellers remember the stories. He identifies devices such as wampum belts and storytelling bags that were used by Native Americans in the Northeast. These mnemonic devices add interest as well as provide help remembering the story. Wampum belts have patterns that symbolize important events. Bruchac describes how he uses a wampum belt to tell stories based on the designs depicted in the belt. The storytelling bags contain objects related to various stories. These bags could be held out to the audience. Someone would reach into the bag and pull out an object; the storyteller would relate a story associated with the object.

Identifying Types of Tales Found in Native American Folklore

You may want to collect as many examples of Native American folklore as possible. Ask the students to categorize the tales according to John Bierhorst's (1985) story types discussed earlier in this chapter and repeated here. The following are a few tales that exemplify these types:

- **Setting the world in order.** The creation stories in Michael J. Caduto and Joseph Bruchac's *Keepers of the Earth: Native American Stories and Environmental Activities for Children,* Nancy Wood's *The Serpent's Tongue,* and Barbara Juster Esbensen's *The Star Maiden.*
- **Family drama tales.** Tribal stories that provide instruction in Nancy Wood's *The Serpent's Tongue,* Michael Rosen's *Crow and Hawk: A Traditional Pueblo Indian Story,* Lois Duncan's *The Magic of Spider Woman,* and Jennifer Berry Jones's *Heetunka's Harvest: A Tale of the Plains Indians.*
- **Trickster tales.** Gerald McDermott's *Raven: A Trickster Tale from the Pacific Northwest* and *Coyote: A Trickster Tale from the American Southwest,* Paul Goble's *Iktomi and the Boulder: A Plains Indian Story* and *Iktomi and the Berries,* and Deborah L. Duvall's *The Opossum's Tale: A Grandmother's Story.*
- **Threshold tales.** Paul Goble's *Buffalo Woman* and *Beyond the Ridge,* and Laura Simms's *The Bone Man: A Native American Modoc Tale.*

Have students discuss the various types of tales found in North American folklore. Before leaving Phase One, students can summarize generalizations about Native American folklore and review discoveries about oral storytelling.

Additional Activities to Enhance Phase One

Here are some activities for children or young adult students related to this phase:

1. Collect trickster tales from as many tribes as possible. What are the characteristics of the various tricksters? Why do you believe a trickster character is associated with that tribe?
2. On a map of North America, label the locations of various tribal regions. Compare the tribal regions today with the tribal regions identified by Bierhorst or Caduto and Bruchac. How have the regions changed? What might account for these changes?

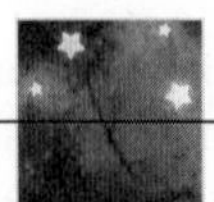

Phase Two: Folklore from Specific Peoples

During this second phase, the emphasis is narrowed to the study of the folklore of one or two Native American peoples or tribal regions, and students do an in-depth study of the folklore of that region. Colleen Wilson (1996), a teacher on the Blackfoot Indian Reservation in Browning, Montana, uses a literature-based approach in which she has students examine Native American literature from various regions of the United States. She states,

> We examine literature for the cultural significance of beliefs, traditions, history, and geography of other Native tribes, past and present. For example, I developed a sequence of lessons designed to improve literacy skills as well as increase students' interest in their own culture. We also worked to develop an appreciation for and social awareness of the lifestyles of other Native peoples across North America, helping students to connect these tribal characteristics to locations in North America. (p. 20)

For these extensive learning experiences, Wilson uses folklore, historical fiction and nonfiction, informational books, biographies, and contemporary literature. She also includes books by Native authors such as Joseph Bruchac and Simon Ortiz as well as non-Native authors such as Paul Goble and Scott O'Dell "who have made the effort to immerse themselves in Native sources and write sensitively about them" (p. 21). (At the conclusion of this chapter, see a list of books from different genres you could use to develop such a study about various regions.)

There are numerous folklore collections and individual stories retold from the Plains Indians, from the Southwest Pueblo peoples, and from Indians of the Pacific Northwest. Ask the students to search for examples of the story types found in Phase One and analyze the literature for values and beliefs of the specific people. Ask them to consider the importance of variants in the story types and search for cultural and geographical reasons for these variants. For example, students might choose literature from the Great Plains tribal areas such as "How the Spider Symbol Came to the People" (Osage—Plains), "The First Flute" (Sioux), "How the Fawn Got Its Spots" (Sioux), and "The Passing of the Buffalo" (Kiowa—Plains) in Michael J. Caduto and Joseph Bruchac's *Keepers of the Animals: Native American Stories and Wildlife Activities for Children;* "Tunka-Shila, Grandfather Rock" (Lakota), "How Turtle Flew South for the Winter" (Sioux), and "The White Buffalo Calf Woman and the Sacred Pipe" (Sioux) from Caduto and Bruchac's *Keepers of the Earth: Native American Stories and Environmental Activities for Children;* George Bird Grinnell's *Blackfeet Indian Stories* and *Blackfoot Lodge Tales: The Story of a Prairie People;* Paul Goble's *Buffalo Woman, The Legend of the White Buffalo Woman* (Lakota) and *The Gift of the Sacred Dog;* and Kristina Rodanas's *Dance of the Sacred Circle: A Native American Tale* (Blackfoot). There are many additional sources from various tribal regions identified in the beginning of this chapter and in the list at the conclusion of the chapter.

Students should summarize the values, beliefs, and themes found in the traditional literature of a specific people and compare the types of stories found in Phases One and Two. You may also use the activities described in detail below: locating traditional values in folktales, comparing variant versions of a story, and webbing to discover additional information about the Native Americans (see Figure 2.1 for an example done for African American literature).

Identifying Traditional Values in Native American Folklore

Native American folklore can be used to develop an appreciation of a cultural heritage that places importance on oral tradition; respect for nature; understanding between animals and humans; knowledge of elderly people; and passing on cultural and tribal beliefs. An examination of folklore shows the rich diversity of Native American folktales, cultures, and customs.

You may introduce the same questions as were used to identify and compare traditional values in African folktales:

1. What reward or rewards are desired?
2. What actions are rewarded or admired?

TABLE 3.2 Chart with Values Identified in Native American Folklore

Questions for Values	*The Legend of the Bluebonnet* (Comanche)	*Star Boy* (Blackfoot)
What reward is desired?	To end the drought and famine To save the land and the people	To remove a scar To marry the chief's daughter
What actions are rewarded or admired?	Sacrifice of a loved object to save the tribe	Courage Obedience to the Creator
What actions are punished or despised?	Selfishness Taking from the earth without giving back	Disobedience (cast out of Sky World; son's face marked with scar)
What rewards are given to heroes, heroines, or great people?	Bluebonnets, beautiful flowers A sign of forgiveness Rain Honored name change	Scar removed Married chief's daughter Life in Sky World after death
What are the personal characteristics of heroes, heroines, or great people?	Unselfishly loved her people Willing to give her most prized possession	Poor Courageous Respect for wisdom of animals Wisdom, purity, honoring Creator

3. What actions are punished or despised?
4. What rewards are given to the heroes, the heroines, or the great people in the stories?
5. What are the personal characteristics of the heroes, the heroines, or the great people in the stories?

You may develop a chart with the questions, listing books that include various values. (Using the same chart with different cultures helps students compare the traditional values across cultures.)

Table 3.2 shows how these values might appear when analyzing Tomie dePaola's *The Legend of the Bluebonnet,* a Comanche tale that shows how unselfish actions are rewarded, and Paul Goble's *Star Boy,* a Blackfoot tale that reveals the importance of courageous and wise actions. (These books are both from the Great Plains.) You may ask students to listen for answers to the questions printed in the table.

You may discuss any similarities and differences identified in the values. You may use additional Native American folklore and compare the values in various Native American groups living on the Great Plains, the Southwest, the Northwest Coast, and the Arctic regions.

Comparing Variants of the Cinderella Story

Students enjoy comparing stories that include elements with which they are familiar. Frank Hamilton Cushing's *Zuni Folk Tales* (1901, 1986) includes a Cinderella variant, "Poor Turkey Girl." Penny Pollock uses Cushing's retelling in her variant *The Turkey Girl: A Zuni Cinderella Story*. Consequently, these two versions provide interesting examples for comparisons, for searching for Cinderella elements, for analyzing Native American elements, and for identifying references to time and place. For example, the following details are found from an analysis of Cushing's "Poor Turkey Girl."

The Cinderella elements include the following:

1. A humble girl wears old clothing and works very hard.
2. A girl longs for kindness.
3. A dance or festival is announced.
4. A girl is not allowed to attend the dance.
5. A girl is helped to attend the dance.
6. A promise is demanded.
7. Fine clothes change back to rags at a given time.

Native American elements in Cushing's tale:

1. Zuni Indians
2. Belief in Middle World
3. Dance of the Sacred Bird
4. Respect for elders
5. Importance of keeping a vow
6. Close relationships between humans and animals
7. Reference to Maiden Mother
8. Theme: God disposes of people according to how the people are fitted; and if the poor be poor in heart and spirit as well as appearance, how will they be anything but poor to the end of their days?
9. Birds that sing are using their orenda, or magical power.
10. Birds with magical power will give favors if they are honored.
11. The tale accounts for phenomena in nature.
12. The Turkey Girl is a favorite character in Pueblo tales.

References to time and place in Cushing's tale:

1. Matsaki or Salt City
2. Southwest, North America
3. Thunder Mountain and mesas beyond
4. Plains
5. Canon Mesa
6. Time of the ancients
7. Zuni Mountains
8. Land where turkeys are plentiful

Now students may analyze Penny Pollock's text and Ed Young's illustrations for *The Turkey Girl: A Zuni Cinderella Story*. Identify the Cinderella elements, the Native American elements, and references to time and place. Students should focus on these questions: What are the similarities and differences between Cushing's tale and Pollock's retelling? How would you compare the two stories?

Students may be warned that Debbie Reese (2007) made comparisons between Pollock's text and Cushing's original tale and concluded that Pollock's retelling has been "romanticized and Disneyfied" (p. 350). She maintains that the retelling is not factually, historically, and culturally accurate. As a consequence of this warning, students may wish to focus on any differences in content that relate to Zuni culture.

FIGURE 3.1 Literary Web for *The Magic of Spider Woman*

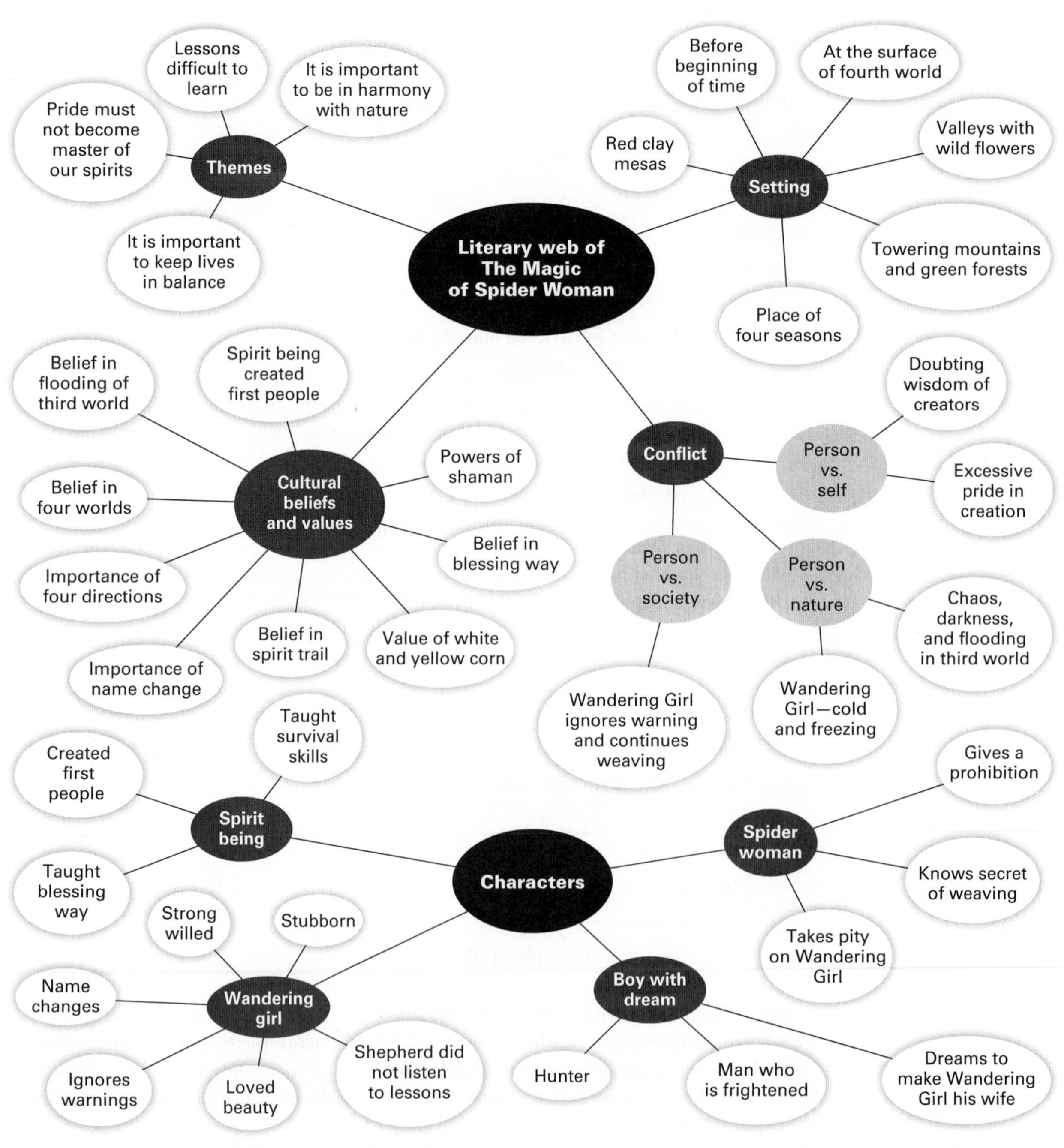

Webbing the Literary and Cultural Elements in Native American Folklore

There are numerous versions of folklore that may be used for a webbing activity. For example, you may read Lois Duncan's *The Magic of Spider Woman* and ask students to identify the elements that would be included under setting, characters, conflict, theme, and cultural beliefs and values. For this activity, draw a web with *The Magic of Spider Woman* placed in the center. Now on arms extending from the center draw the following categories: setting, characters, conflict, theme, and cultural beliefs and values.

You may approach this activity in several ways. You may read the tale and ask students to fill in all of the parts. Alternatively, you may assign specific categories to certain students: those students are only responsible for identifying setting, or one of the other categories.

If students are responsible for certain categories, after they have filled in their category, ask them to share their responses with each other before you lead a whole-group discussion. This early sharing helps them develop more in-depth analysis of the book. After they have shared their responses, lead a whole-group discussion in which you develop a detailed web on the board or on overhead transparencies. Students may use both the text and illustrations in the text to develop their webs. When students discuss their listings on their webs, they should refer back to the text and illustrations to provide evidence for why they included specific details on the web. Figure 3.1 is a partially completed web following a discussion of the book *The Magic of Spider Woman*.

After completing a web together as a group, students may develop individual webs to accompany other books and share them with the group. If the books are chosen from a specific tribal area, students will gain considerable information about that group.

Additional Activities to Enhance Phase Two

Here are some activities for children or young adult students related to this phase:

1. Summarize the major types of tales found in the folklore from each of the tribal regions of North America.
2. Compare the motifs in tales from the Northwest and the Southwest. How would you account for any similarities and differences?
3. Compare Rafe Martin's Cinderella variant *The Rough-Face Girl* with the two Cinderella variants discussed earlier. Locate Cinderella elements and elements that relate to a Native American culture.

Phase Three: Historical Nonfiction

Historical nonfiction includes biographies, autobiographies, and other informational books. Students may analyze biographies and autobiographies and search for evidence of philosophy, values, beliefs, and language discovered in Phases One and Two. They may identify the sources of conflict in the biographies and autobiographies and use other examples of nonfiction informational books to evaluate the authenticity of the historical happenings and sources of conflict. You may also use the information presented earlier in the chapter that analyzed biographies and autobiographies of Native Americans from the Great Plains, the Great Basin, and the Southwest to evaluate the probable authenticity of the conflict developed in the biographies.

Some of the biographies that you might use in Phase Three include Dorothy M. Johnson's *Warrior for a Lost Nation: A Biography of Sitting Bull,* Dorothy Nafus Morrison's *Chief Sarah: Sarah Winnemucca's Fight for Indian Rights,* James Rumford's *Sequoyah: The Cherokee Man Who Gave His People Writing,* and Kate Jassem's *Sacajawea, Wilderness Guide.*

Nonfiction sources such as Peter Aleshire's *Reaping the Whirlwind: The Apache Wars,* Paul Goble's *Death of the Iron Horse,* Russell Freedman's *Buffalo Hunt* and *An Indian Winter,* Rayna Green's *Women in American Indian Society* and Lawrence W. Cheek's *The Navajo Long Walk* provide historical perspectives and sources for information about the conflicts and historical happenings.

Additional Activities to Enhance Phase Three

Here are some activities for children or young adult students related to this phase:

1. Using Phase Three literature, locate any of the references to folklore and folkloric themes and motifs that were found in Phases One and Two.
2. Compare Johnson's Biography of Sitting Bull with Judith St. George's *To See with the Heart: The Life of Sitting Bull.* Encourage students to speculate about the meaning of the title of St. George's biography.
3. On a Native American tribal map of North America, place the locations of the various tribal leaders read about in the biographies.
4. Select a book reviewed in Lucinda Snyder Whitehurst's "Jamestown, 400 Years of History" (2007). What is the impact of the Native Americans discussed in the book?

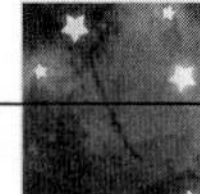

Phase Four: Historical Fiction

Several historical fiction books about Native Americans have won Newbery Awards or Canadian book awards: Jan Hudson's *Sweetgrass* and Farley Mowat's *Lost in the Barrens* have won the Canadian Library Association's Book of the Year; Scott O'Dell's *Sing Down the Moon* and Elizabeth George Speare's *The Sign of the Beaver* have won as Newbery Honor books. Consequently, these books provide excellent sources for evaluating historical fiction and identifying authors' techniques that result in believable and accurate historical fiction. The books also develop themes, values, and beliefs that may be compared with those found in the traditional literature depicting a similar group of Native Americans.

Evaluating Historical Fiction about Native Americans

You may explain to the students they will be reading historical fiction set during the time when many Native Americans experienced great changes in their lives. They will be evaluating the books for each author's ability to produce believable historical fiction and to create authentic depictions of Native Americans living during that time period. You may use the following criteria for evaluating historical fiction found in Norton's *Through the Eyes of a Child: An Introduction to Children's Literature* (2003):

1. The setting must be authentic and encourage readers to understand time, place, and conflict.

2. The conflict must accurately reflect times and attitudes of the people.
3. The characters' actions, beliefs, and values must be true to the time period without depending on stereotypes.
4. The theme should be worthwhile, as relevant today as in the historical time.
5. The Native American culture, values, and beliefs should be respected.
6. The language should be authentic for the time.
7. The style should vividly depict setting, characters, and culture.

Ask students as they read the historical fiction either in a group or individually to identify examples from the books they believe are either good or poor examples of the author's ability to develop believable historical fiction. When this activity was completed with a group of fifth- and sixth-grade students, they identified and discussed some of the following examples: For setting, Farley Mowat in *Lost in the Barrens* developed a believable person-against-nature conflict by describing foaming rapids, searching for food, and preparing for winter. Scott O'Dell in *Sing Down the Moon* developed settings by contrasting the beautiful and peaceful Canyon de Chelly with the harsh, dry Fort Sumner.

For conflict, Jan Hudson in *Sweetgrass* developed a believable conflict by describing how Sweetgrass fought to save her family from the smallpox epidemic of 1837. This epidemic really happened. Elizabeth George Speare in *The Sign of the Beaver* developed conflict with nature by describing the setting that is an enemy of the inexperienced white boy and a friend to the Penobscot Indians. A believable person-against-society conflict develops because the Indians must move west to get away from the settlers.

For characterization, Jan Hudson in *Sweetgrass* describes Sweetgrass's emotions and concerns about growing up. The girl's actions show that she respects the traditions of her people and believes in their values. For theme, Farley Mowat in *Lost in the Barrens* showed that working together is important for survival. This is developed by a believable theme as a white boy and a Cree both struggle to survive in the wilderness. In *Sing Down the Moon,* Scott O'Dell suggests that the loss of spiritual hope might be the greatest tragedy, that hatred and prejudice are destructive. These themes are developed as the Navajo try to survive the march to Fort Sumner. In *Sweetgrass,* Jan Hudson develops the theme that it is important to have moral obligations toward others. It is also important to keep one's dreams and to respect one's family and one's tribe. In the area of language, the author of *Sweetgrass* uses figurative language and prairie symbolism to describe Sweetgrass—when picking strawberries. "Her little hands pulled at them as daintily as a deer plucking grass in a meadow."

As each example is identified and discussed, ask the students to consider why this is a good (or bad) example to be used in a book reflecting the Native American culture. After they have completed their analysis of the literary elements in historical fiction, ask them to look carefully at the conflicts developed in the books. Have students answer the following questions: Do you think these conflicts were authentic for the time period? Why or why not? How could we find out? Do you think the settings and the characterizations were accurate for the time period? Why or why not? How could we find out?

You may ask the students to remember the beliefs and values they learned about when they read the Native American folklore. They may consider whether the beliefs and values are also shown in the historical fiction. They may speculate about what might happen to them if they experienced conflict between their own culture and one that is imposed on them from outside. They may discuss the characterizations, conflicts, and values identified earlier, and whether the themes developed in historical fiction relate to the traditional beliefs and values found in Native American literature. They may place themselves in the position of a character who is in conflict with a strong belief or value. Ask them to consider how they would respond in that situation. Ask the students to do additional research to authenticate the historical fiction.

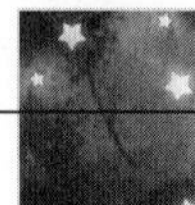

Authentication of *The Birchbark House*

Analysis of *The Birchbark House*

The Birchbark House (1999) by Louise Erdrich is a National Book Award Finalist. Set on an island in Lake Superior in 1847, the book describes an Ojibwa girl's life as she experiences the four seasons of the year. Consequently, we must consider both the author's development of Native American values, specifically Ojibwa, and the ability of the author to create credible historical fiction for the time period.

First, the author creates credibility for the story by identifying herself as a member of the Turtle Mountain Band of Ojibwa and stating that she became interested in writing the book while researching her own family history. In her acknowledgments Erdrich states, "My mother, Rita Gourneau Erdrich, and my sister Lise Erdrich, researched our family life and found ancestors on both sides who lived on Madeline Island during the time in which the book is set. One of them was Gatay Manomin, or Old Wild Rice. I'd like to thank him and all of his descendants, my extended family. . . . This book and those that will follow are an attempt to retrace my own family's history" (unnumbered acknowledgments).

Two of the evaluative criteria for Native American literature are (1) the Native American characters belong to a specific identified tribe and are not grouped together under one category referred to as "Indian," and (2) the customs, values, and beliefs for the specific tribe are authentic and respected. In *The Birchbark House,* the development of Ojibwa values is especially meaningful. For example, the author conveys the value of nature as the girl is taught by her grandmother to listen to and to learn from nature. The importance of her lessons are reinforced as she nurses her family during a smallpox epidemic. The author reinforces Ojibwa values and beliefs through traditional stories told by the girl's father and grandmother. One of the stories told by the grandmother is "Nanabozho and Muskrat Make an Earth." Grandmother uses the stories to teach lessons to her granddaughter. When you read the folklore from various Native American tribes, you will discover that the oral stories were used to pass on various beliefs and to educate the members of the tribe. In addition, the "Earth-Diver" story as told by the grandmother is one of the oldest and most common creation stories told among various North American Indian tribes, including those living around the Great Lakes. You will be able to locate examples of these myths that reflect the values of the people.

Another Native American value and belief is developed as the author explores the importance of messages revealed in dreams and voices heard in nature. Notice in this quote how the grandmother reveals the importance of the fact that her granddaughter, Omakayas, can hear the voices: "Nokomis understood the meaning of what had happened, understood why the voices had spoken, understood what it meant for Omakayas's future and was proud and glad to have a granddaughter who was chosen to be a healer" (p. 206). When you read many of the autobiographies of early Native American leaders, such as Black Elk, a member of the Oglala Sioux, you will learn that showing respect for and relying on messages revealed in dreams and listening to voices found in nature are of considerable value within the culture. Consequently, only people of great stature within the tribe are given this special ability.

When analyzing the book for historical accuracy for settings and conflicts, you will discover that the author provides detailed descriptions of the island during each of the four seasons. This information can be authenticated through comparisons with nonfictional sources. A map of the general region of the island and Lake Superior and a detailed map of the Ojibwa village are included in the book, which you can compare with other nonfictional sources. The major conflict the village must overcome is the smallpox epidemic of 1847 during which eighteen Ojibwa died. You can evaluate this kind of information as you consider the authenticity of both the settings for the island and the major health problems of this period.

Preparing Students to Read and Authenticate *The Birchbark House*

Read the author's "Thanks and Acknowledgments" in the text. Ask the students to speculate about what they believe will be in the text. Direct them to look at the maps inside the front and back covers of the book. You may show them current maps of Lake Superior and the land around it. Have them consider what type of setting this would have been in the mid–nineteenth century and think about why the place names on the maps may be different. After looking at the map and reviewing what they know about a northern setting on an island in Lake Superior, students might hypothesize about the meaning of the title of the book. Read the "Analysis of *The Birchbark House*" to the students. Ask them to listen carefully for any areas they could evaluate for the truthfulness of setting, values, beliefs, and the culture of the Ojibwa people. Explain the process of authentication, emphasizing the importance of discovering if the information about Native Americans is accurate for the setting, the time period, the issues, the lifestyles, the values and beliefs, and the plot of the story.

Authentication Project with *The Birchbark House*

In addition to increasing higher thought process and discussion skills, you may use this activity to practice expository writing. This authentication project is an excellent way to help students discover both the importance and enjoyment associated with searching for clues related to the authenticity of a text. Authentication also increases students' abilities to search for pertinent information, to summarize that information, to compare and evaluate information, and to draw conclusions about the reliability and truthfulness of a literary text. The categories for authentication are placed in question format to help students with the process.

For a group activity in authentication and expository writing, divide students into groups of five and have each group conduct research into one of the questions. They should search for support for the topics and compare the information found in the text with other nonfictional sources. They may also use information found on reliable websites to authenticate the text. If preferred, this authentication project, in which each group presents the findings to the class, may be reported orally. The search for folklore that supports the values is especially enjoyable when students combine an oral activity with a writing activity.

Let's begin by evaluating the author's source notes and deciding if information in these notes will help during the authentication. Read the author's source notes and ask students to identify information that would help them in an authentication project. For example, the author identifies herself as a member of the Turtle Mountain Band of Ojibwa and the main character as a young Ojibwa girl living on an island in Lake Superior in 1847. Ask the students to respond to the level of information discovered in the Author's Note. How could it help them begin their research? What will they still need to know in order to conduct research on the story?

Now introduce each of the questions: Following each question is a summary of the type of information students may find to authenticate the book.

1. *What are the geographical and social settings for the book, and are they authentic?* Students should use nonfictional sources to evaluate this area. According to the book the story is set on an island in Lake Superior near the village of La Pointe. The author includes a map of Lake Superior that includes an island and La Pointe. Information books such as Helen Hornbeck Tanner's *The Ojibwa* (1992) confirm that the Ojibwa lived in this area. Maps show an island called Madeline Island and a major mission called La Pointe. William W. Warren's *History of the Ojibwa People* (1984) includes a chapter on the town of La Pointe and describes the interactions of the people. Using such sources, students may analyze the lifestyles of the people, their living conditions, including types of homes in summer and in winter, and the descriptions of the geographical locations, and compare these with descriptions found in *The Birchbark House*. Erdrich's drawings include illustrations of peeling the birchbark, a birchbark house, a winter cabin, and maps that may be used for comparisons and authentication.

2. *What are the values and beliefs of the people in the book, and are they authentic?* As noted earlier, two of the evaluative criteria for Native American literature are that the Native American characters belong to a specific identified tribe and not be grouped together under one category referred to as "Indian," and that the customs, values, and beliefs for the specific tribe are authentic and respected.

In this book the Ojibwa tribe is identified and Ojibwa values are especially meaningful. The author reinforces Ojibwa values and beliefs through traditional stories told by the girl's father and grandmother. One of the stories told by the grandmother is "Nanabozho and Muskrat Make an Earth." The text develops the importance of using oral stories to pass on various beliefs and to educate the members of the tribe. In addition, the Earth-Diver story as told by Grandmother is one of the oldest and most common creation stories told among North American tribes living around the Great Lakes. Students may authenticate this part of the story by searching for examples of an Earth-Diver type story such as "The Earth on Turtle's Back" found in Michael J. Caduto and Joseph Bruchac's *Keepers of the Earth* (1989).

3. *What are the major events that make up the plot of the story?* Many of the major events that can be authenticated follow the seasons and the associated tasks performed by the Ojibwa people: for example, building the birchbark house to live in during the warmer seasons when the people peel the birchbark from the trees, create a frame from wood saplings, and cover the frame with sheets of birchbark. This process can be authenticated by reading Eileen Lucas's *The Ojibwa: People of the Northern Forests* (1994) and Tanner's *The Ojibwa* (1992). Another major event includes collecting the sap from maple sugar groves and boiling the sap into maple sugar. *The Ojibwa* describes this process. The collection of wild rice is also described in *The Birchbark House*. The interactions with the fur traders and missionary schools are important events as is overcoming the smallpox epidemic. These events can be authenticated.

4. *What are the major conflicts in the book, and are they authentic for the time period?* The major challenge the village must overcome is the smallpox epidemic of 1847. During this time, eighteen of the villagers died from the disease. This overcoming of a smallpox epidemic is also a big issue in Jan Hudson's *Sweetgrass* (1989). Another major conflict results because of the European intrusion through trading posts and mission schools. Sources such as *The Ojibwa: People of the Northern Forests* and *History of the Ojibwa People* describe the impact of the British and French fur traders.

5. *What are the major themes, and are they found in other literature written about the time period or the people?* Several themes developed in *The Birchbark House* are common in other Native American literature. For example, important messages are revealed in dreams and through voices heard in nature. This ability is revealed as "Nokomis understood the meaning of what had happened, understood why the voices had spoken, understood what it meant for Omakaya's future and was proud and glad to have a granddaughter chosen to be a healer" (p. 209). Many autobiographies and biographies of early Native American leaders such as *Black Elk Speaks: Being the Life Story of a Holy Man of the Ogala Sioux* (1932/1979) show respect for and rely on messages revealed in dreams and listening to voices found in nature. Consequently, this information confirms that only people of great stature within a tribe are given this special ability. It also suggests that the grandmother is correct to be proud about her granddaughter's future.

Another theme shows that being responsible for one's family is important. Students may compare this theme in *The Birchbark House* with Jan Hudson's *Sweetgrass* (1989), a story about a young Blackfoot girl who grows up during the winter of a smallpox epidemic in 1837. Students may also search for similar themes in Erdrich's *The Game of Silence*, sequel to *The Birchbark House*.

Analytical Reading of Jan Hudson's *Sweetgrass*

The following series of lessons uses Adler and Van Doren's (1972) stages in analytical reading and applies those stages to the Canadian Book of the Year for Children, Jan Hudson's *Sweetgrass*. This guide includes stages and rules that readers can use when outlining a book and later when applying informed criticism, either written or oral, to the book. The following example provides an in-depth analysis of how to discuss, analyze, and criticize this book.

1. *Classify the book according to kind and subject matter.* Let's begin this activity by reading and discussing the Author's Note. According to the author, "The people in this story are not historical personages, but fictional creations. The events, however, are based on written records of the Blackfoot Indians during the winter of 1837 to 1838. The Blackfoot, also known as Siksika, occupied the territory that is now northern Montana and southern and south central Albert, Canada" (unnumbered page). Ask the students to consider what type of historical fiction would be developed by Hudson and what they already know about the Plains Indians. Ask them to look at Hudson's bibliography and to consider what sources Hudson may have used for her research.
2. *Briefly state what the book is about.* (This book uses considerable amounts of symbolism, metaphors, and similes to develop the story. Consequently, we focus on the author's use of technique related to figurative language in parts of our discussion.)

To prepare to read a book that includes considerable symbolism, explain to the students that authors of books frequently tell us about the characters by using symbolism to extend our understanding of the character and how the character feels about himself or herself and how the character changes over the course of the story. Authors may compare the characters' actions and personalities with items found in nature to let us know more about the character and the setting. This is especially true in Native American literature, in which the people are frequently depicted as close to nature. Jan Hudson uses all of these techniques to develop her main character, a Blackfoot Indian girl who lives on the Canadian prairies in the 1800s. As we read *Sweetgrass*, we identify the symbolism in the book and discuss how it is used to develop the setting, the values of the Blackfoot people, the conflict in the story, and the various themes. As you consider the appropriateness or inappropriateness of the symbolism, ask yourself, What is the author telling us about the character? How does the author's choice of comparisons increase our understanding of Sweetgrass and the Blackfoot people? How does

Sweetgrass change in the course of the story? Are these changes authentic for the type of conflict she is facing? Why or why not?

3. *List and outline the major parts of the book.* The following incidents are taken in chronological order from the book. Ask the students to discuss and consider the appropriateness of the various forms of figurative language as Hudson's language relates to the Blackfoot people, to the main character, to the Blackfoot culture, to the conflicts in the story, and to the setting of the book:

p. 10: The author compares the lives of the Blackfoot people to a beaded design or to the roundness of a folktale told on a winter night.

p. 10: Sweetgrass's hands as they pick strawberries are compared to the dainty actions of a deer as it plucks grass in a meadow.

p. 12: The author develops the symbolic title as it relates to the heroine's characterization: "Sweetgrass. It's ordinary to look at but it's fragrant as the spring." (What is she saying about herself?)

p. 15: Sweetgrass would make her father do what she wanted. She would search for the signs and the power to control her own life.

p. 23: Sweetgrass has the power of memories.

p. 26: Sweetgrass describes herself as feeling mightier than a brave on the warpath.

p. 37: Foreshadow of plot: The reeds, the silence, and the mist seem threatening.

p. 39: When Sweetgrass returns safely to the circle of tipis, she feels like a calf who is safe in its own herd of buffalo.

p. 86: Sweetgrass reflects on the power of dreams and the conflict in male and female roles within her tribe.

p. 93: Smallpox, the white-man's sickness, is followed by hunger and death.

p. 110: Sweetgrass describes the omen of decay caused by the dead. She wraps and buries the dead members of her family so that she can protect the living people.

p. 115: Sweetgrass deals with death by fighting for survival, even though it is sometimes without hope.

p. 133: Sweetgrass breaks a Blackfoot taboo by catching, cooking, and serving a certain type of fish to her starving family. She knows she should not break the taboo, but there is no other food available. Father is proud of her actions and ability and tells her that she is now a woman.

4. *Define the problems the author has tried to solve.* The quotes just cited develop both Sweetgrass's personal and tribal conflicts as she faces the death and the taboos placed on her by her culture. Discuss the significance of the language with the students. Did the language reflect the settings, values, conflicts, and characterizations developed in the story? Why or why not? Ask the students to consider their favorite image in the book. Do they agree this book should be an award winner? You may share with the students that Jan Hudson wrote this book when she was in high school. This information is very motivational for students who would like to become authors. They may write their responses to the conflicts, plots, and values in *Sweetgrass.*

5. *Identify and interpret the author's key words (vocabulary).* Ask students to identify their favorite use of figurative language in the story. Which symbols, metaphors, and similes were the most vivid for them? (Ask students to describe what they visualize when they identify their favorite use of figurative language.)

6. *Understand the author's leading propositions by identifying and discussing the author's most important sentences.* Ask students to trace the changes in the book by identifying sentences in the beginning of the book, the middle of the book, and the close of the book. Contrasts are especially vivid between quotes from the beginning of the book where Sweetgrass is trying to identify her place in the world and the final quote when Father replies with pride that she may not be a warrior, but she is a woman.

7. *Know the author's arguments by identifying them in the text.* Again, it is the use of symbolism and the comparisons through figurative language that depict the author's arguments. Ask students to find quotes and occurrences that depict Sweetgrass's arguments with herself and her people. What is the author saying about the impact of the "White-Man's Death" on the Blackfoot tribe?

8. *Determine which of the problems the author has solved and which are not solved.* Students may discuss how the author developed the problems related to the interaction of the Blackfoot and white people. Did the author solve these problems? Why or why not? Did the author solve the coming-of-age problems identified by Sweetgrass? Why or why not? How did the students' understanding of history make a difference in the way Hudson solved the problems related to the interaction of the Blackfoot and white people? How did students' understanding of human development influence their response to how Hudson solved the problems related to coming of age?

9. *Do not begin criticizing the book until you have completed your interpretation.* What do you still need to know before you can give your judgment?

10. *What areas of the book cause you to disagree with the author?* What are your reasons?

11. *Give your reasons for your critical judgments of the text and the author's techniques.* Because this book is filled with symbolism and figurative language, you may choose to develop critical judgments by discussing the impact of the author's use of language. How much additional information about the Blackfoot Indians living on the prairies in the nineteenth century do you need to know in order to develop your own critical judgment of the author and the book?

Additional Activities to Enhance Phase Four

Here are some activities for children or young adult students related to this phase:

1. Choose an informational book that covers the same time period and setting as a historical fiction text. Use the informational book to authenticate the historical fiction.

2. Investigate the life and writings of one of the award-winning authors of historical fiction about Native Americans. Try to discover why the author chose to write about the subject and time period.

3. Compare the authors' development of setting, characterization, and themes in Mowat's *Lost in the Barrens*, O'Dell's *Sing Down the Moon*, Hudson's *Sweetgrass*, and Speare's *The Sign of the Beaver* with the development of the same literary elements in Dorris's *Sees Behind Trees*. What are the similarities and the differences? How do you account for either the similarities or the differences in these historical fiction novels? How do the differences in locations and time periods influence the development of the literary elements and the lives of the Native American people?

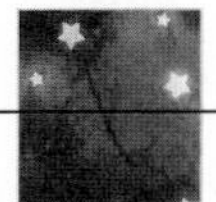

Phase Five: Contemporary Literature

How Would Charles Eastman, Chief Joseph, or Lame Deer Respond to Current Issues Related to the Spirituality of Native Lands?

One issue that allows students to conduct research and to speculate about how historical personages might solve contemporary problems is the recurring disagreement between

Native American tribes and developers who wish to use tribal lands. One such battle is reported by Marc Lacey (2011) in the following article "Majestic Views, Ancient Cultures, and a Profit Fight."

This article describes the contest between a Las Vegas developer and the Hualapai tribe in Arizona. The legal battle is over profits gained from the Skywalk that was built over the Grand Canyon's edge in Hualapai territory. The Skywalk allows tourists to walk out over the canyon and look down thousands of feet through a floor of glass. On one side of the controversy is the developer, David Jin, who claims that in exchange for the $30 million dollars he spent to build the Skywalk, he has the right to receive a portion of the profits over twenty-five years and to receive cut-rate prices for the tourists he brings to the site from all over Asia. In contrast, the Hualapai accuse him of not fulfilling his end of the bargain by not finishing the project. When the project started, Hualapai traditionalists were saddened by construction that for them threatened the spiritual significance of the land. Later, however, the tribe benefited financially by tourism that included tickets to the Skywalk, helicopter and horseback tours of the Grand Canyon, profits from gift shops, entrance fees to a faux Indian village, and performances by Hualapai elders and storytellers. Tourist dollars have brought prosperity to many tribal members. Ask students to conduct research that explores the outcome of this battle and to identify other places in which Native tribes have fought for their sacred lands or debated the profit motive that many believe influences changes in sacred lands such as the carving of Mount Rushmore in the Black Hills.

Another issue related to sacred lands is identified by Tim Vanderpool (2008) in an article titled "Threatened Vistas." Vanderpool reports that some Navajo and Hopi Indians are fighting the Desert Rock power plant. He begins the article with a quote from Enei Begaye: "Navajo people respect these sacred areas—they are part of our history" (p. 30). The problem is that pollution caused by coal-fired power plants in the Four Corners region will jeopardize Mesa Verde and Chaco Canyon as well as several other national parks in the area that are sacred to tribal members. The article presents two sides of the issue. The Navajo and Hopi people who are fighting the power plants maintain that acids from the coal-based pollution may damage the natural and cultural resources as well as damage the quality of air for all of the residents. On the other side of the conflict are the Sithe Global Power Company and tribal members who hope to use expanded power plants to boost employment and income for the reservations where unemployment approaches 50% and the yearly household income averages $8,000. This is a conflict that could lead to interesting debates and hopeful solutions.

Going back to the biographies of Native American leaders discussed in this text, students can speculate about how Charles Eastman, who emphasized cooperation; Chief Joseph, who fought for freedom, the right of conscience, and personal security; or Lame Deer, who described his discomfort because the Native Americans chase the vision, while the white man chases the dollar, would respond to these issues. Students may speculate about how each personage would describe the gains and losses to the tribe through nontribal intervention. What solutions might each personage present? What happens to sacred lands when tourism is involved or when power companies want to use the sacred lands? Students could also conduct interesting court trials as each side argues their points. The students should use beliefs of the historic personages to make their points.

Additional Activities to Enhance Phase Five

Here are some activities related to this phase for children or young adult students:

1. Compare the themes of living in harmony with nature and the importance of ancestral beliefs in the contemporary story by White Deer of Autumn, *Ceremony—In the Circle of Life,* with the themes found in traditional literature.
2. The importance of nature and the close relationships between a Native American boy and a hawk may be analyzed in Byrd Baylor's contemporary story from the Southwest, *Hawk,*

I'm Your Brother. Discuss the importance of point of view in literature. Rewrite the story from the point of view of the hawk.

3. Search for the evidence of continuity in the themes in Native American literature in the writings of Virginia Driving Hawk Sneve and Jamake Highwater. For example, search for any of the themes, values, and conflicts found in Phases One through Four in Jamake Highwater's *Legend Days, The Ceremony of Innocence* and *I Wear the Morning Star*. Highwater's books contain many examples of symbolism, traditional values, tribal customs, and conflict with contemporary society.
4. Trace the emergence of conflict, characterization, and theme in Sharon Creech's *Walk Two Moons* as the character receives mysterious messages and searches for the answers to the messages, thus allowing the author to relate characters' actions and motivation to the developing plot and resolution.
5. Choose a book such as Tricia Brown's *Children of the Midnight Sun: Young Native Voices of Alaska*, and ask children to compare their own lives with the children profiled in the book. What are the similarities? What are the differences? Why are there similarities and differences? Then use this book as a model to interview students in your own school or people in your neighborhoods.

At the conclusion to Phase Five, have students do the following: Summarize the findings and the threads discovered across the ages of literature. Review examples of continuity and evidences of change. Analyze how what they know about the literature of Native Americans will make a difference in their lives. Have them review their tribal maps and summarize what they know about specific tribes. Ask them to list areas of interest or questions that they would like to use for continued study.

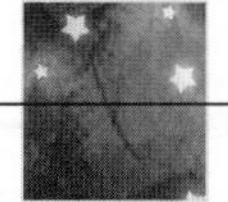

Visualizing Native American Culture

Numerous highly illustrated books present the various arts and artifacts related to Native Americans who lived during earlier times and provide excellent sources for authenticating and visualizing these cultural artifacts as described in books. For example, Penny's *Art of the American Indian Frontier: The Chandler-Pohrt Collection* (1993) provides very useful sections on nineteenth-century dress. Information such as the following are very important when authenticating and visualizing aspects of Native American cultures:

> Throughout the nineteenth century, Native American women of the Woodlands, Prairie, and Plains persisted in a long-standing tradition that required them to produce the clothing for their families. . . . Men of some Plains tribes, such as the Pawnee and Oglala Sioux, made shirts of particular significance although often further embellished with quill or glass bead embroidery by women. Men also contributed to the design of their garments, and their expressive meaning, by painting on them images related to their war record or visionary experiences. (p. 28)

Large colored photographs are of special value when authenticating illustrations or descriptions in books about Native Americans. Hassrick's *The George Catlin Book of American Indians* (1977) is an extremely useful source for Native American art. The paintings included in the text were completed by Catlin as he traveled throughout the West beginning in 1830. The photographs of Catlin's art reproduced in this text are from the originals found in the National Collection of Fine Arts, Washington, D.C. Each of the paintings is labeled by date and tribal affiliation.

According to Jamake Highwater in *Arts of the Indian Americas* (1983), "Art is a way of seeing, and what we see in art helps to define what we understand by the word 'reality'" (p. 74). Highwater discusses an aesthetic view of Native American art in which there is a close relationship between artists and nature and their belief that dreams and intuition are all important aspects of reality. Highwater presents various Native American art forms and discusses the arts as revealed in basketry, textiles, skinwork and beadwork, pottery, carving, metalwork, architecture, and painting.

The Native American books illustrated by Paul Goble are among the most popular and accessible for students. As a visualization activity, collect as many of his books as possible. Ask students to analyze the illustrations and to describe their reactions to the illustrations and to Goble's ability to depict the Native American culture of the early Plains Indians. The following books by Paul Goble may be used for this activity: *Beyond the Ridge, Buffalo Woman, Death of the Iron Horse, The Dream Wolf, The Gift of the Sacred Dog, The Girl Who Loved Wild Horses, Iktomi and the Berries,* and *Iktomi and the Boulder: A Plains Indian Story.* In the introduction to *Ancient Thunder*, artist Leo Yerxa states "These magnificent creatures, combined with the traditional clothing of the native people of the plains, were the inspiration for this book" (unnumbered).

REFERENCES

Adler, Mortimer J., and Charles Van Doren. *How to Read a Book*. New York: Simon & Schuster, 1972.

"AILA Literature Awards." *Curriculum Connections* 2 (Fall 2006): 9.

Alexie, Sherman. *War Dances.* New York: Grove Press, 2009.

Allen, Paula Gunn, ed. *Voice of the Turtle: American Indian Literature, 1900–1970.* New York: Ballantine, 1994.

Barry, Scott Ian. *Wolf Empire: An Intimate Portrait of a Species.* Guilford, Conn.: Lyons, 2007.

Bierhorst, John. *The Red Swan: Myths and Tales of the American Indians.* New York: Farrar, Straus & Giroux, 1976.

_____. *The Mythology of North America.* New York: Morrow, 1985.

_____. "Children's Books." *New York Times Book Review* (May 23, 1993).

Black Elk, as told through John G. Neihardt. *Black Elk Speaks: Being the Life Story of a Holy Man of the Oglala Sioux.* New York: Morrow, 1932; Lincoln: University of Nebraska Press, 1979.

Campbell, Joseph. *The Power of Myth.* New York: Doubleday, 1988.

Coltelli, Laura. *Winged Words: American Indian Writers Speak.* Lincoln: University of Nebraska Press, 1990.

Cushing, Frank Hamilton. *Zuni Folk Tales.* Tucson: University of Arizona Press, 1986 (first printing 1901).

Dorris, Michael. "Native American Literature in an Ethnohistorical Context." *College English* 41 (October 1979): 147–162.

Douma, Eldrena. "The Call of an Eagle." *Storytelling Magazine* 18 (November/December 2006): 24–25.

Duvall, Deborah L. *The Opossum's Tale.* Albuquerque: University of New Mexico Press, 2005.

Eastman, Charles. *From the Deep Woods to Civilization: Chapters in the Autobiography of an Indian.* Boston: Little, Brown, 1916.

Edmonds, Walter. *The Matchlock Gun.* New York: Dodd, Mead, 1941.

Furst, Peter T., and Jill L. Furst. *North American Indian Art.* New York: Rizzoli, 1982.

Gill, Sam D., and Irene F. Sullivan. *Dictionary of Native American Mythology.* New York: Oxford University Press, 1992.

Goodbird, Edward, retold to Gilbert L. Wilson. *Goodbird the Indian: His Story.* New York: Fleming H. Revell, 1914.

Grinnell, George Bird. *Blackfeet Indian Stories.* New York: Scribner's, 1993 (first printing 1913).

_____. *Blackfoot Lodge Tales: The Story of a Prairie People.* Lincoln: University of Nebraska Press, 1962.

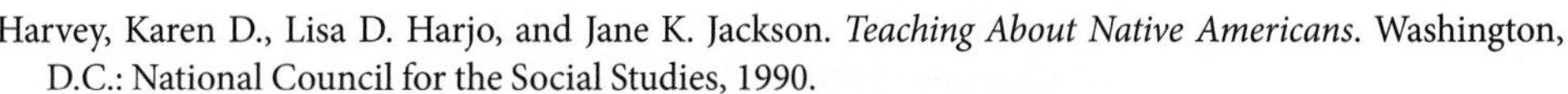

Harvey, Karen D., Lisa D. Harjo, and Jane K. Jackson. *Teaching About Native Americans*. Washington, D.C.: National Council for the Social Studies, 1990.

Hassrick, Royal B. *The George Catlin Book of American Indians*. Secaucus, N.J.: Castle, 1977.

Hearne, Betsy. "Cite the Source: Reducing Cultural Chaos in Picture Books, Part One." *School Library Journal* 39 (July 1993): 22–27.

Herbst, Laura. "That's One Good Indian: Unacceptable Images in Children's Novels." In *Cultural Conformity in Books for Children*, edited by Donnarae MacCann and Gloria Woodard. Metuchen, N.J.: Scarecrow, 1977.

Highwater, Jamake. *Arts of the Indian Americas*. New York: Harper & Row, 1983.

_____. *The Primal Mind: Vision and Reality in Indian America*. New York: Harper, 1981.

Hodgson, Bryan. "Buffalo: Back Home on the Range." *National Geographic* (November 1994): 64–89.

Chief Joseph, edited by Allen Thornkike Rice. "An Indian's View of Indian Affairs." *The North American Review* (1879): 412–433.

Lacey, Marc. "Majestic Views, Ancient Culture, and Profit Fight." *New York Times* (April 24, 2011): 14, 19.

Lame Deer, J. Fire, and E. Richard. *Lame Deer: Seeker of Visions*. New York: Simon & Schuster, 1972.

Lawson, Robert. *They Were Strong and Good*. New York: Viking, 1940.

Levenson, Jay A., ed. *Circa 1492: Art in the Age of Exploration*. Washington, D.C.: National Gallery of Art, 1991.

Lucas, Eileen. *The Ojibwa: People of the Northern Forests*. Brookfield, Conn.: Millbrook Press, 1994.

Mann, Charles C. "America, Found & Lost." *National Geographic* 211 (May 2007): 32–55.

Momaday, N. Scott. *House Made of Dawn*. New York: Harper & Row, 1968.

Nijhuis, Michelle. "Tribal Talk." *Smithsonian* 14 (November 2003): 36, 38.

Norton, Donna E. "The Intrusion of an Alien Culture: The Impact and Reactions as Seen Through Biographies and Autobiographies of Native Americans." *Vitae Scholasticae* 6 (Spring 1987): 59–75.

_____. "Teaching Multicultural Literature in the Reading Curriculum." *The Reading Teacher* 44 (September 1990): 28–40. Reprinted in *Literacy Instruction for Culturally and Linguistically Diverse Students*, edited by Michael F. Opitz, pp. 213–228. Newark: International Reading Association.

_____. "Dimensions of Native American Literature for the Library Collection." *Encyclopedia of Library and Information Science* 57 (Supplement 20, 1996): 123–154.

_____. *Through the Eyes of a Child: An Introduction to Children's Literature*, 6th ed. Upper Saddle River, N.J.: Merrill/Prentice Hall, 2003.

Ortiz, Simon J., in *Winged Words: American Indian Writers Speak*, edited by Laura Coltelli. Lincoln: University of Nebraska Press, 1990.

Owens, Louis. *The Sharpest Sight*. Norman: University of Oklahoma Press, 1992.

Parker, Arthur C. *Skunny Wundy: Seneca Indian Tales*. Chicago: Whitman, 1926.

Penny, David W. *Art of the American Indian Frontier: The Chandler-Pohrt Collection*. Detroit, Mich.: Detroit Institute of Arts and University of Washington Press, 1993.

Plenty-Coups, edited by Frank B. Linderman. *Plenty-Coups: Chief of the Crows*. Lincoln: University of Nebraska Press, 1962.

Querry, Ron. "Discovery of America: Stories Told by Indian Voices." In *American Diversity, American Identity: The Lives and Works of 145 Writers Who Define the American Experience*, edited by John K. Roth. New York: Holt, 1995.

Reed, Gerald. "The Significance of the Indian in American History." *American Indian Culture Research Journal* 8 (1984): 1–21.

Reese, Debbie. "'Mom, Look! It's George, and He's a TV Indian!'" *The Horn Book Magazine* (September/October 1998): 636–643.

_____. "Proceed with Caution: Using Native American Folktales in the Classroom." *Language Arts* 84 (January 2007): 245–256.

Rodgers, Greg. "Harriet's Burden." *Storytelling Magazine* 18 (November/December 2006): 39–41.

Slapin, Beverly, Doris Seal, and Rosemary Gonzales. *How to Tell the Difference: A Checklist for Evaluating Native American Children's Books*. Berkeley, Calif.: Oyate, 1989.

Steinhart, Peter. *The Company of Wolves*. New York: Vintage, 1996.

Stott, Jon C. "In Search of Sedna: Children's Versions of a Major Inuit Myth." *Children's Literature Quarterly* 15 (Winter 1990): 199–201.

_____. "Native Tales and Traditions in Books for Children." *The American Indian Quarterly* 16 (Summer 1992): 373–380.

Sweezy, Carl, told to Althea Bass. *The Arapaho Way: A Memoir of an Indian Boyhood.* New York: Clarkson N. Potter, 1966.

Talayesva, Don C., edited by Leo W. Simmons. *Sun Chief: The Autobiography of a Hopi Indian.* New Haven, Conn.: University Press, 1942.

Tanner, Helen Hornbeck. *The Ojibwa.* New York: Chelsea House, 1992.

Thompson, Stith. *Tales of the North American Indians.* Bloomington: Indiana University Press, 1929.

Tingle, Tim. "Indian Offerings." *Storytelling Magazine* 18 (November/December 2006): 22.

_____. *Walking the Choctaw Road.* El Paso: Cinco Puntos Press, 2003.

Trafzer, Clifford E. "The Word Is Sacred to a Child: American Indians and Children's Literature." *The American Indian Quarterly* 16 (1992): 381–395.

Vanderpool, Tim. "Threatened Vistas." *National Parks* (Winter 2008): 30–35.

Vaughn, Robert. *Then and Now: Or Thirty-Six Years in the Rockies.* Minneapolis: Tribune Printing, 1900.

Verrall, Catherine, and Patricia McDowell. *Resource Reading List 1990.* Quebec, Canada: Canadian Alliance in Solidarity with the Native Peoples, Kahnawake Mohawk Territory, 1990.

Walsh, Barbara Juhas. "Serving Many Communities." *Friends of the Libraries Magazine,* 50 (2010): 6–9.

Warren, William W. *History of the Ojibwa People.* St. Paul: Minnesota Historical Press, 1984.

Whitehurst, Lucinda Snyder. "Jamestown: 400 Years of History." *School Library Journal* 53 (January 2007): 52–55.

Whitewolf, Jim, edited by Charles S. Bryant. *The Life of a Kiowa Apache Indian.* New York: Dover, 1969.

Wilson, Colleen. "Exploring the United States with Native American Literature." *Primary Voices K–6* 4 (August 1996): 19–30.

Young Bear, Ray A. *Black Eagle Child: The Facepaint Narratives.* Iowa City: University of Iowa Press, 1992.

CHILDREN'S AND YOUNG ADULT LITERATURE REFERENCES

Aleshire, Peter. *Reaping the Whirlwind: The Apache Wars.* Facts on File, 1998 (I: 12 + R: 8). This informational book focuses on wars between the government and the Apache people.

Alexie, Sherman. *The Absolutely True Diary of a Part-Time Indian.* Little, Brown, 2007 (I: 14–18 R: 6). The author grew up on the Spokane Reservation in Washington.

Arnosky, Jim. *Grandfather Buffalo.* Putnam, 2006 (I: 5–8 R: 4). The author develops a protective bond between a young and older buffalo.

Baity, Elizabeth. *Americans Before Columbus.* Viking, 1951 (I: 8+). A 1952 Newbery Honor book.

Baker, Olaf. *Where the Buffaloes Begin.* Illustrated by Stephen Gammell. Warne, 1981 (I: all R: 6). The story tells about the lake where the buffaloes were created.

Barry, Scott Ian. *Wolf Empire: An Intimate Portrait of a Species.* Lyons, 2007 (I: YA R: 7). Numerous photographs may be used with any age group.

Baylor, Byrd. *The Desert Is Theirs.* Illustrated by Peter Parnall. Scribner's, 1975 (I: all). The life of the Papago people is captured in illustrations and text.

_____. *Hawk, I'm Your Brother.* Illustrated by Peter Parnall. Scribner's, 1976 (I: all). A boy would like to glide like a hawk.

Begay, Shonto. *Navajo: Visions and Voices Across the Mesa.* Scholastic, 1995 (I: all). Navajo philosophy is reflected in poetry and illustrations.

I = Interest age range
R = Readability by grade level

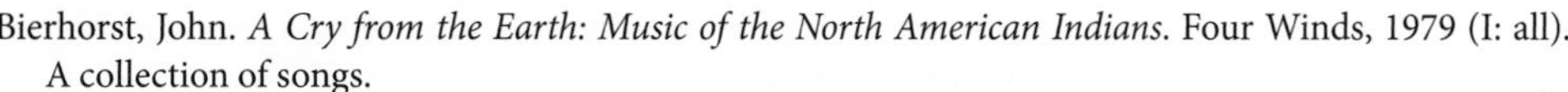

Bierhorst, John. *A Cry from the Earth: Music of the North American Indians.* Four Winds, 1979 (I: all). A collection of songs.

Bjornlund, Lydia. *The Trail of Tears: The Relocation of the Cherokee Nation.* Gale/Lucent, 2010 (I: 10–YA R: 6). The history of how the Cherokee people were forced from their lands.

Boyden, Linda. *Giveaways: An ABC Book of Loanwords from the Americas.* University of New Mexico, 2010 (I: all). The basis for the book is a collection of animals, plants, and objects whose names come from Native American words.

Brown, Tricia. *Children of the Midnight Sun: Young Native Voices of Alaska.* Photographs by Roy Corral. Graphic Arts Center, Alaska Northwest, 1998 (I: 8+ R: 6). The author focuses on the daily lives of children.

Bruchac, Joseph, reteller. *The Boy Who Lived with the Bears and Other Iroquois Stories.* Illustrated by Murv Jacob. HarperCollins, 1995 (I: 81 R: 6). Six Iroquois tales.

_____. *Code Talker.* Dial, 2005 (I: 10–YA R: 6). A novel about the Navajo marines in World War II.

_____, adapter. "Law of the Great Peace" in *The Book of Peace*, edited by Ann Durell and Marilyn Sachs. Dutton, 1990 (I: all). This poem reflects the values of the Iroquois.

_____, ed. *Songs from This Earth on Turtle's Back: Contemporary American Indian Poetry.* Greenfield, 1983 (I: 101). A collection from many poets.

_____. *Tell Me a Tale: A Book About Storytelling.* Harcourt Brace, 1997 (I: all). The author discusses the components of storytelling.

Caduto, Michael J. *Earth Tales from Around the World.* Illustrated by Adelaide Murphy Tyrol. Fulcrum, 1997 (I: 101 R: 6). The text includes several Native American tales.

_____, and Joseph Bruchac. *Keepers of the Animals: Native American Stories and Wildlife Activities for Children.* Illustrated by John Kahionhes Fadden. Fulcrum, 1991 (I: all). The text includes folklore and activities.

_____, and Joseph Bruchac. *Keepers of the Earth: Native American Stories and Environmental Activities for Children.* Illustrated by John Kahionhes Fadden and Carol Wood. Fulcrum, 1989 (I: all). Folklore and activities about the earth.

Cheek, Lawrence W. *The Navajo Long Walk.* Rio Nuevo, 2004 (I: 12–YA R: 7). Photographs illustrate the location of the forced walk in the 1800s.

Creech, Sharon. *Walk Two Moons.* HarperCollins, 1994 (I: 10+ R: 6). A thirteen-year-old girl makes discoveries about herself and her Native American mother.

Cushing, Frank Hamilton. *Zuni Folk Tales.* University of Arizona Press, 1901/1986. An adult source that contains many tales that may be retold to or read by older students.

Dembicki, Matt, edited by. *Trickster: Native American Tales: A Graphic Collection.* Fulcrum, 2010. (I: 10–YA R: 5). This is a collection of over forty tales.

dePaola, Tomie. *The Legend of the Bluebonnet.* Putnam, 1983 (I: all R: 6). Unselfish actions are rewarded.

Dorris, Michael. *Morning Girl.* Hyperion, 1992 (I: 8+ R: 5). This historical fiction book is set in the Bahamas in 1492.

_____. *Sees Behind Trees.* Hyperion, 1996 (I: 8+ R: 5). A partially sighted boy earns his name through his senses.

Duncan, Lois. *The Magic of Spider Woman.* Illustrated by Shonto Begay. Scholastic, 1996 (I: all R: 5). This is a Navajo myth.

Dunn, John M. *The Relocation of the North American Indian.* Gale (I: 12–YA R: 8). This is part of the World History Series.

Duvall, Deborah L. *The Opossum's Tale: A Grandmother Story.* Illustrated by Murv Jacob. University of New Mexico Press, 2005 (I: all). A Cherokee folktale about why the opossum has a hairless tail.

Ehlert, Lois. *Mole's Hill: A Woodland Tale.* Harcourt Brace, 1994 (I: 5–8 R: 4). A Seneca tale in which Mole uses her wits.

Ekoomiak, Normee. *Arctic Memories.* Holt, 1990 (I: all). The text is written in both English and Inukitut, the Inuit language.

Erdrich, Louise. *The Birchbark House.* Hyperion, 1999 (I: 8+ R: 6). A seven-year-old Ojibwa girl survives the winter in 1847 overlooking Lake Superior.

_____. *The Game of Silence.* HarperCollins, 2005 (I: 81 R: 6). This is a sequel to *The Birchbark House.*

_____.U.S. *The Porcupine Year*. HarperCollins, 2008 (I: 8+ R: 6). This is a sequel to *The Birchbark House* and *The Game of Silence*.

Esbensen, Barbara Juster, reteller. *The Great Buffalo Race: How the Buffalo Got Its Hump*. Illustrated by Helen K. Davie. Little, Brown, 1994 (I: all). A Seneca tale reveals a characteristic.

_____. *The Star Maiden*. Illustrated by Helen K. Davie. Little, Brown, 1988 (I: all). Tells about the creation of water lilies.

Field, Edward. *Magic Words*. Illustrated by Stefano Vitale. Harcourt Brace, 1998 (I: all). These poems are based on Inuit folklore.

Finley, Carol. *Art of the Far North: Inuit Sculpture, Drawing, and Printmaking*. Lerner, 1998 (I: 8+ R: 5). The text includes art of contemporary Inuit people.

Freedman, Russell. *Buffalo Hunt*. Holiday, 1988 (I: 81 R: 6). Text shows the importance of the buffalo.

_____. *An Indian Winter*. Illustrated by Karl Bodmer. Holiday, 1992 (I: 81 R: 6). A detailed description of the Mandan and Hidasta tribes.

Fritz, Jean. *The Double Life of Pocahontas*. Illustrated by Ed Young. Putnam, 1983 (I: 8–10 R: 7). A biography of Pocahontas.

_____, Katherine Paterson, Patricia McKissack, Fredrick McKissack, Margaret Mahy, and Jamake Highwater. *The World in 1492*. Illustrated by Stefano Vitale. Holt, 1992 (I: 8+). The section "The Americas in 1492" is written by Jamake Highwater.

Frost, Helen. *Diamond Willow*. Farrar, Straus & Giroux, 2008 (I: 10+). Set in Alaska, a novel in verse form.

George, Jean Craighead. *The Buffalo Are Back*. Illustrated by Wendell Minor. Dutton, 2010 (I: 7–10 R: 4). The author presents a history of the near demise and comeback of the buffalo.

_____, *Julie of the Wolves*. Illustrated by John Schoenherr. Harper & Row, 1972 (I: 10+ R: 7). An Inuit girl survives with the help of wolves.

_____. *Water Sky*. Harper & Row, 1987 (I: 101 R: 6). A boy discovers his Inuit heritage.

Goble, Paul. *All Our Relatives: Traditional Native American Thoughts about Nature*. World Wisdom, 2005 (I: 8+ R: 5). The theme of the book is that people, animals, and plants are all related, all things share in the creation.

_____. *Beyond the Ridge*. Bradbury, 1989 (I: all R: 5). An elderly Native American woman experiences death and goes to the afterlife.

_____. *Buffalo Woman*. Bradbury, 1984 (I: all R: 6). A bond is developed between animals and humans.

_____. *Death of the Iron Horse*. Bradbury, 1987 (I: 81 R: 5). This story is based on an incident in 1867 between the Union Pacific Railroad and the Cheyenne people.

_____. *The Dream Wolf*. Bradbury, 1990 (I: all R: 6). This tale from the Plains tells how a wolf saves two children.

_____. *The Gift of the Sacred Dog*. Bradbury, 1980 (I: all R: 6). This Sioux tale tells how the horse was given to the people.

_____. *The Girl Who Loved Wild Horses*. Bradbury, 1978 (I: 6–10 R: 5). A Native American girl's attachment to horses is described.

_____. *Iktomi and the Berries*. Watts, 1989 (I: 4–10 R: 4). Iktomi is a trickster from the Lakota Sioux.

_____. *Iktomi and the Boulder: A Plains Indian Story*. Orchard, 1988 (I: 4–10 R: 4). Iktomi learns a lesson.

_____. *The Legend of the White Buffalo Woman*. National Geographic, 1998 (I: 81 R: 4). A sacred legend of the Lakota Indians.

_____. *Star Boy*. Bradbury, 1983. (I: 6–10 R: 5). A Blackfoot Indian returns to the sky world.

Green, Rayna. *Women in American Indian Society*. Chelsea, 1992 (I: 12+ R: 7). The text presents the history of Native American women.

Hamilton, Virginia. *In the Beginning: Creation Stories from Around the World*. Illustrated by Barry Moser. Harcourt Brace Jovanovich, 1988 (I: all R: 5). This collection includes several Native American myths.

Highwater, Jamake. *Anpao: An American Indian Odyssey*. Illustrated by Fritz Scholder. Lippincott, 1977 (I: 12+ R: 5). Anpao journeys across the history of North American traditional tales.

_____. *The Ceremony of Innocence*. Harper & Row, 1985 (I: 12+ R: 6). This is part two of the Ghost Horse Cycle.

_____. *I Wear the Morning Star*. Harper & Row, 1986 (I: 121 R: 6). This is part three of the cycle.

_____. *Legend Days*. Harper & Row, 1984 (I: 12+ R: 6). This is the first part of the Ghost Horse Cycle.

Hirschfelder, Arlene. *Happily May I Walk: American Indians and Alaska Natives Today*. Scribner's, 1986 (I: 101 R: 6). This informational book is about contemporary life.

Hoyt-Goldsmith, Diane. *Arctic Hunter*. Photographs by Lawrence Migdale. Holiday, 1992 (I: 8+ R: 5). A photographic essay follows the life of an Inuit boy and his family.

Hudson, Jan. *Sweetgrass*. Philomel, 1989/Tree Frog, 1984 (I: 10+ R: 4). A Blackfoot girl grows up during the winter of a smallpox epidemic in 1837.

Jassem, Kate. *Sacajawea, Wilderness Guide*. Illustrated by Jan Palmer. Troll Associates, 1979 (I: 6–9 R: 2). This is an illustrated biography of the Shoshone woman who guided the Lewis and Clark expedition.

Jeffers, Susan. *Brother Eagle, Sister Sky: A Message from Chief Seattle*. Dial, 1991 (I: all). A poetic retelling of the message.

Johnson, Dorothy M. *Warrior for a Lost Nation: A Biography of Sitting Bull*. Westminster, 1969 (I: 10+). A biography of the Native American leader.

Johnson, E. Pauline. *The Lost Island*. Illustrated by Atanas Matsoureff. Simply Read Books, 2010 (I: all R: 4). A legend from *Legends of Vancouver*.

Jones, Jennifer Berry. *Heetunka's Harvest: A Tale of the Plains Indians*. Illustrated by Shannon Keegan. Roberts Rinehart, 1994 (I: 6–9 R: 5). The tale develops the theme of the need to share with others.

Joosse, Barbara M. *Mama, Do You Love Me?* Illustrated by Barbara Lavalle. Chronicle, 1991 (I: 3–7). A young child tests her mother's love.

Keegan, Marcia. *Pueblo Boy: Growing Up in Two Worlds*. Cobblehill, 1991 (I: 6–10 R: 5). A photographic essay depicts the life of a contemporary boy.

Kroll, Virginia. *The Seasons and Someone*. Illustrated by Tatsuro Kiuchi. Harcourt Brace, 1994 (I: 4–8). A young Inuit girl witnesses the changes in the seasons.

Lawlor, Laurie. *Shadow Catcher: The Life and Work of Edward S. Curtis*. Walker, 1994 (I: 12+ R: 7). This biography is illustrated by photographs of Native Americans taken by Curtis.

Left Hand Bull, Jacqueline, and Suzanne Haldane. *Lakota Hoop Dancer*. Dutton, 1999 (I: all). The book follows the activities of the dancer.

Lelooska, Chief. *Echoes of the Elders: The Stories and Paintings of Chief Lelooska*. Edited by Christine Normandin. Callaway, 1997 (I: all). The stories and paintings focus on the Northwest Coast.

Lenski, Lois. *Indian Captive: The Story of Mary Jemison*. Lippincott, 1941 (I: 101 R: 5). A 1942 Newbery Honor book.

Lewis, Paul Owen. *Storm Boy*. Beyond Words, 1995 (I: 8+ R: 5). The tale includes Northwest Coast motifs.

Lipsyte, Robert. *The Brave*. HarperCollins, 1991 (I: 12+ R: 6). A young Native American man desires to become a boxer.

Littlechild, George. *This Land Is My Land*. Children's Book Press, 1993 (I: 81 R: 5). The text presents a historical viewpoint of Native Americans.

McDermott, Beverly Brodsky. *Sedna: An Eskimo Myth*. Viking, 1975 (I: 8+ R: 5). This is a tale from the Eskimo people.

McDermott, Gerald. *Arrow to the Sun*. Viking, 1974 (I: 3–9 R: 2). Strong shapes and colors complement a Native American tale.

_____. *Coyote: A Trickster Tale from the American Southwest*. Harcourt Brace, 1994 (I: all). Coyote's vanity brings him misfortune.

_____. *Raven: A Trickster Tale from the Pacific Northwest*. Harcourt Brace & Jovanovich, 1993 (I: all). This trickster tale tells how light was brought to the people.

_____. *The Rough-Face Girl*. Illustrated by David Shannon. Putnam, 1992. (I: All R: 5). An Algonquin Indian Cinderella tale.

Miles, Miska. *Annie and the Old One*. Illustrated by Peter Parnall. Little, Brown, 1971 (I: 6–8 R: 3). Annie's love for her Navajo grandmother causes her to prevent the completion of a rug, which would signal her grandmother's death.

Miller, Brandon Marie. *Buffalo Gals: Women of the Old West*. Lerner, 1995 (I: 10+ R: 6). The text includes a section on Native American women.

Morrison, Dorothy Nafus. *Chief Sarah: Sarah Winnemucca's Fight for Indian Rights*. Atheneum, 1980 (I: 10+ R: 6). Sarah was a leader of the Paiute people.

Mowat, Farley. *Lost in the Barrens*. Illustrated by Charles Geer. McClelland & Stewart, 1996, 1984 (I: 91 R: 6). A Cree boy and his friend are lost in northern Canada.

Nelson, S. D. *Black Elk's Vision: A Lakota Story*. Abrams, 2010 (I: 8–10 R: 5). Photographs and illustrations support this biography.

Normandin, Christine, ed. *Echoes of the Elders: The Stories and Paintings of Chief Lalooska*. DK, 1997 (I: all). A collection of tales and paintings reflect the Northwest Coast Indians.

O'Dell, Scott. *Black Star, Bright Dawn*. Houghton Mifflin, 1988 (I: 8+ R: 6). An Inuit girl enters the Iditarod Trail dogsled race.

_____. *Sing Down the Moon*. Houghton Mifflin, 1970 (I: 101 R: 6). A young Navajo girl tells of the forced march of her people in 1864.

_____, and Elizabeth Hall. *Thunder Rolling in the Mountain*. Houghton Mifflin, 1992 (I: 10+ R: 6). This historical novel is told from the point of view of Chief Joseph's daughter.

Orie, Sandra DeCoteau. *Did You Hear Wind Sing Your Name? An Oneida Song of Spring*. Illustrated by Christopher Canyon. Walker, 1995 (I: 4–8). The text and illustrations present the Oneida view of the cycle of spring.

Patent, Dorothy Hinshaw. *The Buffalo and the Indians: A Shared Destiny*. Illustrated by William Munoz. Clarion, 2006 (I: 10+ R: 6). The text develops the importance of the buffalo to the Plains Indians.

Paulsen, Gary. *Dogsong*. Bradbury, 1985 (I: 10+ R: 6). An Inuit boy journeys 1,400 miles on dogsled.

Philip, Neil. *The Great Circle: A History of the First Nations*. Clarion, 2006 (I: 12–YA R: 6). The text covers Native American history, culture, and religions of several tribes.

Pollock, Penny. *The Turkey Girl: A Zuni Cinderella Story*. Illustrated by Ed Young. Little, Brown, 1996 (I: 5–10 R: 5). A story first retold by Frank Hamilton Cushing.

Rodanas, Kristina. *Dance of the Sacred Circle: A Native American Tale*. Little, Brown, 1994 (I: all R: 5). A Blackfoot tale about the first horse.

Rosen, Michael. *Crow and Hawk: A Traditional Pueblo Indian Story*. Illustrated by John Clemenston. Harcourt Brace, 1995 (I: 5–9 R: 5). A family drama tale that depicts the consequences of not caring for one's young.

Rumford, James. *Sequoyah: The Cherokee Man Who Gave His People Writing*, translated by Anna Sixkiller Huckaby. Houghton Mifflin, 2004 (I: all). The text is written in both Cherokee and English.

San Souci, Robert D., and Daniel San Souci. *Song of Sedna*. Doubleday, 1981 (I: 10+ R: 6). This may be used for comparisons with other Sedna tales from the Inuit.

Sewall, Marcia. *People of the Breaking Day*. Atheneum, 1990 (I: 8+ R: 5). This is a nonfiction description of the Wampanoag nation of southeastern Massachusetts.

Simms, Laura. *The Bone Man: A Native American Modoc Tale*. Illustrated by Michael McCurdy. Hyperion, 1997 (I: 6–8 R: 4). The author includes information to help authenticate the tale.

Speare, Elizabeth George. *The Sign of the Beaver*. Houghton Mifflin, 1983 (I: 8–12 R: 5). A white boy survives through the help of a Native American friend.

Stevens, Janet. *Coyote Steals the Blanket: A Ute Tale*. Holiday, 1993 (I: all). This tale is from the Southwest.

St. George, Judith. *To See with the Heart: The Life of Sitting Bull*. Putnam, 1996 (I: 10+ R: 6). A biography of the Sioux Chief.

Swamp, Chief Jake. *Giving Thanks: A Native American Morning Message*. Illustrated by Erwin Printup, Jr. Lee & Low, 1995 (I: 5–8). An ancient message of peace and appreciation for Mother Earth.

Tingle, Tim. *Saltypie: A Choctaw Journey from Darkness into Light*. Illustrated by Karen Clarkson. Cinco Puntos, 2010 (I: 6–10 R: 4). The author tells a story from his youth.

_____. *Walking the Choctaw Road*. Cinco Puntos Press, 2003 (I: 12–YA R: 6). The text covers tales about the Trail of Tears.

Walker, Rob D. *Mama Says: A Book of Love for Mothers and Sons*. Illustrated by Leo and Diane Dillon. Scholastic, 2009 (I: all). The poems represent twelve different cultures.

Whitaker, Muriel, ed. *Stories from the Canadian North*. Illustrated by Vlasta Vankampen. Hurtig, 1980 (I: 12+ R: 7). This is a collection of short stories.

Wood, Nancy, ed. *The Serpent's Tongue: Prose, Poetry, and Art of the New Mexico Pueblos*. Dutton, 1997 (I: 8+). A large collection of tales.

_____. *Spirit Walker*. Illustrated by Frank Howell. Doubleday, 1993 (I: all). Native American poetry.

Yerxa, Leo. *Ancient Thunder*. House of Anansi Press, 2006 (I: 4–8). An Ojibwa author and artist creates a book celebrating the world of horses.

Yolen, Jane. *Encounter*. Illustrated by David Shannon. Harcourt Brace, 1992 (I: 6–10 R: 5). This is a hypothetical story of a Taino boy who tells about the landing of Columbus.

Chapter 4

Latino Literature

A statistical survey of the nation's schools (Dillon, 2007) reports: "The most pronounced development in school demographics has been in Hispanic growth. Hispanic students accounted for just 6% of public school enrollment in 1972, but by 2005 their numbers had grown to 20%" (p. A21). The percentage of Hispanic students is even greater in the western United States. The survey reported that 37% are Hispanic in the western states.

In this chapter, we discover the rich and varied literature of peoples whose ancestry originates in such diverse areas as Mexico, Puerto Rico, Cuba, and other Latin American and South American countries. As might be expected, there is no clear preference for names to be applied to this literature. Terms such as *Hispanic, Latino,* and *Chicano* are used frequently. Authorities argue for the use of each of these terms. In a *New York Times* article, David Gonzalez (1992) points out that the U.S. Census Bureau uses the term *Hispanics.* He argues, however, that "the term of choice is often Mexican, Puerto Rican, or something that specific" (p. 6). In the same article, author Sandra Cisneros states that she prefers being called Latino. She maintains, "To say Latino is to say you come to my culture in a manner of respect. . . . To say Hispanic means you're so colonized you don't even know for yourself or someone who named you never bothered to ask what you call yourself" (p. 6E). The National Association of Hispanic and Latino Studies (2000) uses both terms to identify the organization. In this chapter, we try, whenever possible, to identify the literature with the specific area of the setting and the people.

The literature discussed in this chapter also includes stories set both in the United States and in other countries. Hazel Rochman (1993) states that Latino literature lists should include both because "[p]eople don't come to America blank: their memories and stories and poetry stay with them and enrich us all, even as new experience changes them, and they change us. And many Latinos go back often to the places and peoples they came from, and that returning and leaving is part of their story" (p. 207).

In addition to crossing contemporary borders, the literature includes influences from numerous cultures. When discussing folklore, Jose Griego y Maestas and Rudolfo A. Anaya (1980) emphasize the importance of cultural infusion on Latino literature:

> The stories reflect a history of thirteen centuries of cultural infusing and blending in the Hispano mestizaje, from the Moors and Jews in Spain, to the Orientals in the Philippines, Africans in the Caribbean, and the Indians in America—be they Aztec, Apache or Pueblo. . . . The Native American influences create ambients of folk healers and other levels of reality that are not often dealt with by Western man. The popular legends about Death, kings and queens, and country rogues come to us directly from the Middle Ages—and the Spanish Golden Age that spread its influence as far away as New Mexico" (p. 4).

Latino Timeline

1400 BCE	Probable beginning of Mesoamerican culture
1400 BCE to 1000 CE	Flourishing of Mayan civilization in southeastern Mexico and Central America (200–800 CE, classic Mayan Period)
1150 BCE to 500 CE	Flourishing of Olmec culture
200 BCE to 1200 CE	Rise of Toltec cultures in the central valley of Mexico
1000	Beginning of Inca culture in South America
1200	Aztecs arrive at central plateau of Mexico
1400s	Height of Aztec imperial conquest and construction of great temple and pyramid to God of War
1492	Columbus arrives at San Salvador
1519	Cortes takes Montezuma prisoner
1531	Apparition of Our Lady of Guadalupe to Juan Diego
1560s	Recording of Aztec oral literature by Fra Bernardino de Sahagun
16th century	Early Aztec and Mayan folklore recorded for Europeans by Spaniards
1947	Caldecott Honor: Leo Politi for *Pedro, the Angel of Olvera Street*
1950	Caldecott Medal: Leo Politi for *Song of the Swallows*
1953	Newbery Medal: Ann Nolan Clark's *Secret of the Andes*
1954	Newbery Medal: Joseph Krumgold's *. . . And Now Miguel*
1959	Newbery Honor: Francis Kalnay's *Chucaro: Wild Pony of the Pampa*
1960	Caldecott Medal: Marie Hall Ets and Aurora Labastida for *Nine Days to Christmas—A Story of Mexico*
1961	Newbery Honor: Jack Schaefer's *Old Ramon*
1965	Newbery Medal: Maia Wojciechowska's *Shadow of a Bull*
1966	Newbery Medal: Elizabeth Borton de Trevino's *I, Juan de Pareja*
1967	Newbery Honor: Scott O'Dell's *The King's Fifth*
1968	Hans Christian Andersen International Medal: Jose Maria Sanchez-Silva (Spain)
1982	Hans Christian Andersen International Medal: Lygia Bojunga Nunes (Brazil)
1992	Nobel Prize to Mexican poet and essayist Octavio Paz, who becomes Mexico's first Nobel laureate for literature
1999	Américas Award given by the Consortium of Latin American Studies Programs to books published in 1998 that portray Latin America, the Caribbean, or Latinos in the United States, with winners including George Ancona's *Barrio: José's Neighborhood* and Amelia Lau Carling's *Mama and Papa Have a Store*
2003	Newbery Honor and National Book Award: Nancy Farmer's *The House of the Scorpion*
2006	Pura Belpré Award for Viola Canales's *The Tequila Worm*
2008	Margarita Engle's *The Surrender Tree*
2009	Francisco Jiménez's *Reaching Out*
2011	Pura Belpré Award for Pam Muñoz Ryan's *The Dreamer*

As we read and discuss the literature, we locate examples of this cultural infusion. Morales (2002) reinforces this cultural diversity within Latino literature when he concludes, "The market is fragmented in its cultural diversity and language preferences. Latin American immigrants come from more than 20 different countries and are split down the middle when it comes to choosing their information in English or Spanish" (p. 20). Morales also believes the latest immigration pattern of Latino populations is spreading across the United States rather than moving to more traditional locations. He claims this pattern will "most likely ensure their commitment to hold on to their language and culture" (p. 20).

Even though the number of Latino students is growing rapidly, there are fewer children's books about Latinos than there are books about either African Americans or Native Americans. When discussing the total publication of multicultural books, Kathleen Horning, Merri Lindgren, Hollis Rudiger, and Megan Schliesman (2005) state that multicultural literature makes up about 10% of thetotal number of books published in 2004. They state, "Of the nearly 2,800 titles we received at the CCBC (Cooperative Children's Book Center), we documented the following with regard to books about people of color. . . . 61 were on Latino themes and topics, 37 were created by Latino authors and/or artists" (p. 18).

In addition to the fewer numbers of books published, the books tend to go out of print faster than books about the other cultures. This phenomenon is readily seen between the third edition of Norton's *Through the Eyes of a Child: An Introduction to Children's Literature* (1991) and the fourth edition of the same text (Norton, 1995). A search of *Books in Print* disclosed that the following percentage of books from the 1991 text were no longer in print in 1995: 14% of African American, 25% of Asian American, 35% of Native American, and more than 50% of Latino books.

Sally Lodge (1997) identifies another concern that may contribute to the shortage of books, especially those published in English and Spanish. Lodge states, "Finding good translators is one of the major hurdles publishers of Spanish language translations face. Many publishers admitted to scrapping one or more translations they had commissioned because of unacceptable quality, a dilemma that is both costly and time-consuming" (p. 549). Lodge is hopeful for the future of books that focus on Latino populations and Spanish-language texts. She indicates, however, that publishers must encourage authors if there is to be an increase in high-quality books.

Most children's books about Latinos depict people of Mexican or Puerto Rican heritage, although the U.S. population contains numerous other groups such as Cuban Americans and the many new Americans from Central American countries. There is also an imbalance in the types of stories available. Many award-winning novels are about a small segment of the American population, the sheep herders of Spanish Basque heritage, whose ancestors emigrated to parts of North America before those parts came under U.S. control. Although collections of folktales and poetry are available for adults, a shortage of children's literature exists. In addition, there is a lack of balance in the settings for the literature. For example, the majority of books about Puerto Ricans overuse a New York City ghetto setting.

In this chapter, we investigate historical perspectives including stereotypes in literature from the past, discuss Latino values identified by researchers, consider criteria for evaluating the literature, and discuss examples of the literature from various Spanish-speaking countries and literature that reflects a Latino perspective in the United States. The chapter includes the following: the ancient literature of the Aztecs and Maya; the more recent folklore that reflects interaction with other cultures; historical nonfiction that helps readers understand the ancient people and their cultures; the historical fiction; and the contemporary literature including biography, informational books, realistic fiction, and poetry.

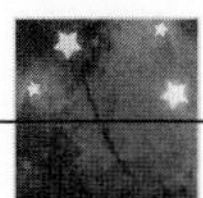

Historical Perspectives

Latino educators are particularly critical of the previous educational systems in the United States that tended to ignore their heritage and identity. For example, Rosalinda B. Barrera (1999) comments,

> I think our own professional development is a topic that we need to address as Latino teachers and teacher educators. So many of us are in need of healing from the culturalectomies that we endured as children in U.S. schools. There are many scars left from this process. For example, many currently practicing Latino educators in the U.S. Southwest, in particular those of Mexican American heritage, never saw their culture, language, and history reflected in the school curriculum as they moved through the elementary and secondary grades. In fact, some faced school biases related to both English and Spanish language learning. . . . Consider what something like this does to identify formation and self-concept. (p. 217)

If we add to these concerns the issues related to stereotypes in the literature from the past, we begin to understand the historical conflicts faced by Latinos who did not read books that valued their cultures. We also begin to understand the reasons for carefully evaluating the literature we present to children.

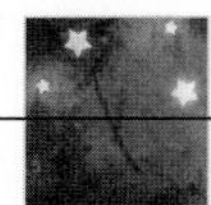

Authors Who Write and Illustrate Latino Literature

A search of the books winning Caldecott and Newbery awards again points to the shortage of books with Latino characters and about Latino cultures. For example, the Caldecott book winners with Latino characters and cultures are older titles such as Marie Hall Ets and Aurora Labastida's *Nine Days to Christmas,* a winner in 1960, and Leo Politi's *Song of the Swallows,* a winner in 1950.

A list of the Newbery Award and Honor books includes the following: Walter Dean Myers's *Scorpions* (this 1986 award includes a Puerto Rican character—the story is set in Harlem); Scott O'Dell's *The Black Pearl* (1968 award, set in Baja, California); Scott O'Dell's *The King's Fifth* (1967 award, set in the Southwest); Elizabeth Borton de Trevino's *I, Juan de Pareja* (1966 award, set in Spain): Maia Wojciechowska's *Shadow of a Bull* (1965 award, set in Spain); Margarita Engle's *The Surrender Tree* (2009 Newbery Honor, set in Cuba); Jack Schaefer's *Old Ramon* (1961 award, set in the Southwest); Francis Kalnay's *Chucaro: Wild Pony of the Pampa* (1959 award, set in South America); Joseph Krumgold's *. . . And Now Miguel* (1954 award, set in New Mexico); Ann Nolan Clark's *Secret of the Andes* (1953 award, set in South America) and Nancy Farmer's *The House of the Scorpion* (2003 Newbery Honor). As you will notice from the titles, the majority of the books are historical fiction. In addition, several of the books reflect settings in Spain.

University students have selected some of their favorite authors and illustrators whose works they believe enhance an understanding of various cultures. In addition to the already listed books, the students identified the following favorite illustrated books: Barbara Cooney's illustrations for John Bierhorst's *Spirit Child: A Story of the Nativity* and for Margot C. Griego's *Tortillitas para Mama and Other Spanish Nursery Rhymes*; Peter Sis's illustrations for Pam Muñoz Ryan's *The Dreamer*; Tomie dePaola's *The Lady of Guadalupe*; Scott Taylor's photographs for June Behrens' *Fiesta!*; photographs in Milton Meltzer's *The Hispanic Americans*; and photographs in Carolyn Meyer and Charles Gallenkamp's *The Mystery of the Ancient Maya.* (Unfortunately, some of these books are no longer in print.)

ISSUE Stereotypes in Latino Literature from the Past

The examples of stereotypes in this discussion are related to Mexican Americans but the general issues may apply to all Latino groups.

The Council on Interracial Books for Children (1977) has been especially critical of the depictions of Mexican Americans in children's literature of the past. After analyzing 200 books, the council concluded that little in the stories would enable children to recognize a culture, a history, or a set of life circumstances. The council criticized the theme of poverty that recurs as if it is a "natural facet of the Chicano condition" (p. 57) and the tendency for Mexican American problems to be solved by the intervention of Anglo Americans. The council also maintained that Mexican Americans' problems had been treated superficially in the books it studied. For example, many books suggest that if children learn English, all of their problems will be solved.

Isabel Schon (1981) is critical of the literature of the recent past because the "overwhelming majority of books incessantly repeat the same stereotypes, misconceptions, and insensibilities that were prevalent in the books published in the 1960s and the early 1970s" (p. 79). Schon supports this contention by reviewing books published in 1980 and 1981 that develop the stereotypes of poverty, embarrassment of children about their backgrounds, distorted and negative narratives about pre-Columbian history, and simplistic discussions of serious Latin American problems.

In a recent review of the images depicted by the media of Mexican immigrants and Latinos living in the United States, Lucila Vargas and Bruce De Pyssler (1998) conclude that the stereotypes of Mexican immigrants are overwhelmingly negative and "U.S. Latinos are regularly presented as uneducated immigrants who are unable or unwilling to help or speak for themselves" (p. 408). They found the following media stereotypes: "(1) dark lady, (2) Latin lover, (3) female clown, (4) male buffoon, (5) half-breed harlot, and (6) bandit" (p. 410). This evaluation of the media is of particular concern because "Research suggests that teen attitudes toward current affairs derive more from the mass media than from teachers, parents, or peers" (p. 410).

Vargas and De Pyssler recommend that teachers counter these negative images through activities that explore and discuss the biases that might be operating in the media stories. They conclude, "Using a media literacy approach, the social studies teacher has a unique opportunity to guide students to a rich appreciation of immigration generally, and Mexican immigration specifically. With this approach, the social studies teacher can help future citizens in our democracy make well-informed, objective, and morally sound decisions" (p. 411).

As you read the literature, try to identify these stereotypes found in both older books and more recent media and consider the possible influences of stereotypes on juvenile or adult audiences. You may try the suggestions presented by Vargas and De Pyssler to guide students to a better understanding of Latino literature and culture.

The students also identified some of their favorite Latino authors: Rudolfo A. Anaya, Pura Belpré, Sandra Cisneros, Nicloa DeMessieres, Francisco Hinojosa, Jose Griego y Maestas, Nicholasa Mohr, and Gary Soto.

The Américas Award provides a source for literature. These books are identified as outstanding books by the Consortium of Latin American Studies Program. The books are chosen from selections "in English or Spanish that authentically and engagingly portray Latin America, the Caribbean, or Latinos in the United States. . . . The award winners and commended titles are selected for their (1) distinctive literary quality; (2) cultural contextualization; (3) exceptional integration of text, illustration, and design; and (4) potential use" (Américas Award, 1999, p. 38).

The Pura Belpré Award celebrates authors and illustrators whose works best embody the Latino cultural experience. It is given each year to outstanding authors and illustrators of books for children and youth. The 2011 Author Award winner was Pam Muñoz Ryan for *The Dreamer*. The Illustrator Award winner was Eric Velasquez for *Grandma's Gift*. The 2011 Author Honor award books were George Ancona's *Ole! Flamenco*, Margarita Engle's *The Firefly Letters: A Suffragette's Journey to Cuba*, and Enrique Flores-Galbis's *90 Miles to Havana*. The 2011 Illustrator Honor books were Carmen Tafolla's *Fiesta Babies*, illustrated by Amy Cordova; Amy Novesky's *Me, Frida*, illustrated by David Diaz; and Duncan Tonatiuh's *Dear Primo:*

A Letter to My Cousin, illustrated by the author. Past award winners include 2010 Author Award for Julia Alvarez's *Return to Sender* and Illustrator Award for Pat Mora's *Book Fiesta,* illustrated by Rafael Lopez. The 2009 Author's Award went to *The Surrender Tree: Poems of Cuba's Struggle for Freedom* by Margarita Engle (a Newbery Honor Award) and the Illustrator Award went to Yuyi Morales's *Just in Case.*

Searching for starred reviews of Latino books in major literary journals produces examples of books that are well worth reading and have been analyzed for authors' and illustrators' techniques. For example, Pam Muñoz Ryan's *The Dreamer,* illustrated by Peter Sis, received starred reviews from *Booklist*, *The Horn Book*, *Kirkus Review*, *Publishers Weekly*, and *School Library Journal*. The reviewers used terms such as "rewarding and eminently readable," "recreates Neruda's spirit and sensibility," "rich, resonant and enchanting," "immaculately crafted," and "the perfect marriage of text and art." As you read the book, write your own review.

As you read the various books discussed in this chapter, try to develop your own list of favorites and the reasons you believe the books or illustrations enhance an understanding of the cultures and the people.

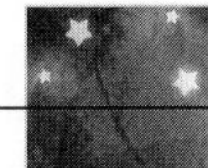

Values in Latino Culture

How important is it that we not reinforce the stereotypes in Latino literature discussed earlier? How important is it that we identify books that develop values and beliefs authentic for the culture and then use those books with children?

One way to answer the question of the importance of using positive Latino literature with children is to identify the percentage of people who are members of the Hispanic/Latino cultural groups in the United States. For example, David E. Rosenbaum (2000) identifies the percentage of Hispanic people (the *New York Times* uses the term *Hispanic*) in various states. California has one of the highest percentages of Hispanic people with 31%; New York has 14.4%; Massachusetts has 6.1%. Although not identified in Rosenbaum's article, Texas, Arizona, and Florida also have large percentages of Hispanic populations. Don Van Natta, Jr., writing about Latinos in Florida uses the headline, "Latinos Rise in Numbers, Not Influence" (2011, p. A15). These estimates highlight the need for not using literature that projects stereotypes and for selecting literature that highlights cultural values.

Denise Ann Finazzo (1997) is emphatic about the issue of stereotypes in children's literature when she states,

> It is important in multicultural children's selections that the characters not be depicted in stereotypical fashion. Stereotypical, flat characters are those cast in images that are commonplace and predictable. The danger in character development is to portray certain groups of people in certain ways—for example, strong males and weak females; athletic and rhythmic African-Americans: intellectual Asians; lazy and unpunctual Latinos; hot-tempered Italians; savage Native Americans; frugal Jews; inactive, failing elderly people. It is crucial for readers to examine characters for well-roundedness and to recognize the limited extent to which the author has developed certain characters. (p. 123)

In addition to stereotyping characters, authors of Latino literature frequently emphasize superficial cultural aspects such as holidays, food, and dances rather than the rich body of oral tales available throughout Mexico, Central America, and South America.

Kathryn H. Au (1993) identifies four values in using multicultural literature that benefit all students. First, when students from diverse backgrounds read literature that highlights the experiences of their cultural group, they learn to feel pride in their identity and heritage. This literature may give students the inspiration and confidence to write about and to value their own experiences. Second, all students learn about the diversity and complexity of U.S. society.

ISSUE Evaluating Latino Literature

Both the shortage of books on Latinos and Latino culture and the possible stereotypes found in the literature make the evaluation of Latino literature especially important. You may want to use the following criteria when evaluating the literature (Norton, 2003):

1. Does the book suggest that poverty is a condition for *all* the people? This is a negative stereotype suggested in some literature.
2. Are problems handled individually, allowing the main characters to use their efforts to solve their problems? Or are all problems solved through the intervention of Anglo Americans?
3. Are problems handled realistically or superficially? Is a character's major problem solved by learning to speak English?
4. Is the cultural information accurate? Are Mexican American, Mexican, Cuban, Puerto Rican, or other Latin American and South American cultures realistically pictured? Is the culture treated with respect?
5. Do the illustrations depict individuals, not stereotypes?
6. Is the language free from derogatory terms?
7. If the author portrays dialects, are they a natural part of the story and not used to suggest a stereotype?
8. If the author uses Spanish language, are the words spelled and used correctly?

They potentially will develop tolerance and appreciation for other cultural groups. Third, students gain a more balanced view of the historical forces that shaped U.S. society. Fourth, students can explore issues of social justice.

As we read the literature in this chapter, we will discover some of the values and beliefs identified in the literature. For example, there is a strong integration of religious beliefs developed throughout daily life; consequently, religion is important. There is strong respect for both the immediate family and the extended family. As part of the extended family, godparents are extremely important. The family is of primary importance throughout much of the literature. Within the family and the culture, there is respect for elderly members of the family. Mutual cooperation is important within the family as each family member contributes to the family's welfare. This cooperation is especially important in the definition of behavioral expectations for children. Within this close family, children are expected to be polite, cooperative, and respectful.

In addition to strong family ties, there are also traditional cultural values related to personal characteristics. For example, when analyzing the literature, we find a great value on cleverness, and wasting time is punished. Both cleverness and sharing are rewarded; greed and evil actions are punished.

As we read the literature, we will discover strong cultural values that are very different from the stereotypical characters in many of the early books.

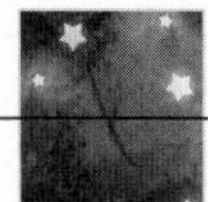

Folklore

The wide cultural areas for Latino folklore encompass Mexico, South and Central America, Cuba, and the American Southwest. The folklore incorporates the ancient tales of the Aztecs, Maya, and Incas. The Spaniards colonized the areas, and many different groups, such as the Apache and Pueblo Indians, interacted with the Spanish and other groups in the Spanish colonies. As in other cultures, there are myths that explain (*ejemplo*), as well as folktales and fairy tales (collectively called *cuento*). Jose Griego y Maestas and Rudolfo A. Anaya (1980) emphasize that we need to understand the traditional literature to understand the culture because the tales "are a great part of the soul of our culture, and they reflect the values of our forefathers" (p. 4), as well as the cultural infusion that occurred over thirteen centuries as different cultural groups influenced both different peoples and their folklore.

Maria Perez-Stable (1997) emphasizes the importance of Latino folklore in helping children learn about the people. She contends that although folklore should not replace nonfiction books, the traditional tales "provide readers with unique insights into cultures, attitudes, and national mores" (p. 30). Perez-Stable identifies the following categories found in Latino folklore: (1) creation and religious stories, (2) magical tales based on historical events, (3) folktales about animals, (4) *pourquoi* tales, (5) stories that present moral lessons, and (6) trickster and noodle-head stories. Notice how these categories are very similar to those identified in other cultures. As we discuss the various forms of folklore, try to identify both the categories of the tales and the cultural values and beliefs found in the literature.

Ancient Mayan, Aztec, and Inca Folklore

The ancient roots of the early cultures and their folklore are emphasized by Roberta H. Markman and Peter T. Markman (1992):

> The Aztec culture confronted by the Spanish was a very late-flowering and relatively short-lived development of the tradition of which it was an integral part; the Aztec myths and gods are but the very tip of the iceberg that is the mythological tradition of Mesoamerica, the high culture area comprising the southern two-thirds of today's Mexico, all of Belize and Guatemala, and portions of Honduras and El Salvador, a culture reaching back at least to 1400 B.C. in its history of urban civilizations, with the earliest village-culture roots of those civilizations going back at least another thousand years. (p. 4)

Within these thousands of years prior to Spanish conquest are such cultures as the Olmec, the Toltec, and the Maya.

Markman and Markman (1992) discuss problems related to the collection and translation of the tales associated with these early people. For example, there are mythic images carved in stone, formed in ceramic, and painted on books made of bark paper or skin called *codices* from each of the cultures. Markman and Markman state, "Unfortunately, very few of the narrative myths that recounted the exploits of these flayed gods, feathered serpents, were-jaguars [animals similar to European werewolves], obsidian butterflies, and snake women have survived, and those that do remain are almost all from one area—the Basin of Mexico—and in the form in which they were recorded after the conquest" (p. 25). Unfortunately, at the time of the conquest, some Christian priests burned many of these codices, which they believed were the "books of the devil."

Fortunately for current scholars, some of the early Aztec and Mayan tales were recorded for European audiences by Spaniards in the sixteenth century. For example, Bernardino de Sahagún, a Franciscan priest, recorded Aztec history and folklore in *La historia general de las cosas de Nueva España,* which was a twelve-book collection of stories and history he collected from the Aztec people. Other tales and histories were written down by Aztecs who learned to read and write in the Texcoco Seminary. These early collections by both Spaniards and Aztecs provide many of the sources used by current folklorists and retellers of the tales. Other adult sources such as John Bierhorst's translation of *History and Mythology of the Aztecs: The Codex Chimalpopoca* (1998) provide sources for early tales, which may be told to children or used for comparative purposes.

Mayan Folklore During the classic period from 200 to 800 CE, the Maya in southeastern Mexico and Guatemala perfected the arts of painting, sculpture, and architecture, and developed a system of writing. According to Neil Philip (2004), "The civilization of the Maya developed slowly over the first millennium B.C. and reached its classical peak in the A.D. 200s. Theirs was a culture based on dynastic rule in city-states, with phonetic writing and a complex calendar with a number of different ways of telling time" (p. 114). They also told myths that explained the creation of the earth, humans, and animals.

The mythology includes references to the early gods such as the Lord of the Hills and the Valleys, also called Lord of the Thirteen Hills. The Rain God, Chac, has a frog orchestra because frogs when they croak are believed to be calling for rain. A major deity, known as Hackakyum, made the sun, but his elder brother, Sukunkyum, carries it through the sky each day. At night, Sukunkyum goes to his house in the underworld, feeds the sun, and spends time with his wife until the sun is again brought up to the sky. Kisin (Death Maker) lives permanently in the underworld. Later myths identify Death Maker with the devil of Christianity. The underworld ruler of the dead is a traditional Mayan concept, illustrated in paintings that are more than a thousand years old.

Roberta H. Markman and Peter T. Markman's adult source *The Flayed God: The Mythology of Mesoamerica* (1992) includes several Mayan creation myths: "The Birth of the Uinal" (the awakening of the world); "The Birth of All of Heaven and Earth"; "The Creation of Animals"; "The Human Made of Earth and Mud"; "The Human Carved of Wood"; "The Creation of Humanity"; and "The Creation of the Sun and Moon." To assist the researcher, the authors include the sources for each of the translations. The text includes both examples of stories appropriate for storytelling and background information about the stories. My students use this book as the basis for oral storytelling with both children and adults.

Virginia Hamilton's *In the Beginning: Creation Stories from Around the World* includes a creation story from the Popol Vuh, the sacred history and ancient Book of Wisdom of the Quiche Maya of the highlands of Guatemala. Hamilton states that the earliest authors for the story, "Four Creations to Make Man: Maker and Feathered Serpent the Creators," were "ancient Mesoamericans who lived in Central America in 950–1500 A.D." (p. 99). This Mayan creation story proceeds through four creations until humans are finally created in their final form.

One of the better sources for juvenile folklore is John Bierhorst's *The Monkey's Haircut and Other Stories Told by the Maya,* collected from the Maya in Guatemala and southeastern Mexico. Bierhorst's collection includes "Notes on Sources and Variants" and a bibliography. Both of these sections are useful for readers who wish to conduct their own research. The tales indicate many of the traditional Mayan values and cultural characteristics. For example, tales such as "Rabbit and Coyote" and "Tup and the Ants" depict champion riddlers who place great value on cleverness. In "Rabbit and Coyote," a double meaning allows Rabbit to dupe Coyote and escape from his cage. In "Tup and the Ants," the plot hinges on a pun when the old man says, "Cut trees," which Tup interprets to mean "clear the forest." His foolish brothers waste time cutting into the trees trying to hollow them out.

Numerous cultural characteristics are also emphasized in Bierhorst's retelling of the tales. For example, husbands must pay a "bride service" extending from several weeks to a year or two. During this time, husbands live with their wife's families and work for their fathers-in-law. Later the couple lives with his parents until they can build a house of their own. In "The Mole Catcher," the main character works for his father-in-law, the Death Maker. Another cultural characteristic is the importance of corn, which is considered the flesh and blood of mankind, and may be called "divine grace" or "Our Lord's sunbeams."

Although David Wisniewski's *Rain Player* is an original story created by the author rather than a tale retold from an oral source, the author uses Mayan history and legend to develop his characters and the plot. Wisniewski's extensive author's note provides considerable background about the Mayan culture. The themes in the story are very similar to those found in other folklore—for example, the belief that the future was divinely decreed. The stunning cut-paper illustrations artistically and colorfully depict the early culture.

Following your reading of Mayan folklore, develop a list of the characteristics you discover. For example, a summary of the books included in this discussion indicates the Mayan people had a well-developed mythology that accounted for the creation of the earth and the people. *The Popol Vuh* is a mythological history of the world that tells about the creation of the earth, the animals, and the first people. It also reveals the adventures of the Maya Hero Twins,

Hunahpu and Xbalanque. According to the myth, the twins successfully defeated the lords of death by winning a game of tlachtli, a Mayan ritual ball game, and by surviving considerable torture. The Mayans expressed strong beliefs in their gods and deities including the Lord of the Thirteen Hills and Chac, the Rain God. Death Maker, the underworld ruler of the dead, was also a strong personage. The belief in their deities led to a belief that the future was divinely decreed. In addition to the deities, the characters in the folklore include demons, monsters, and witches. The folklore also reveals additional values of the people. For example, cleverness was valued, and wasting time was not. Corn was considered so important that it was believed to be the flesh and blood of humankind. The folklore also reveals the importance of such cultural practices as paying a bride price through service to the bride's father.

As you read additional Mayan folklore, add to your lists of values and beliefs. You may also use your study of Mayan folklore to authenticate an illustrated version of a tale or to compare values and beliefs across cultures.

Aztec and Other Mexican Folklore Harriet Rohmer and Mary Anchondo's *How We Came to the Fifth World* is a retelling of a creation story that develops the theme that deities will destroy a world that is faulty, especially when the people become greedy and selfish. In this Aztec tale, the worlds are destroyed by elements of nature including water, air, and fire. In the fifth world, the people experience peace and happiness, but destruction is always possible if humans have evils in their hearts. (Compare this tale with a Native American creation tale from the Southwest.)

The author's note in Gerald McDermott's *Musicians of the Sun* states that the tale is a fragment from the mythological tradition of the Aztecs. The text, according to McDermott, survived in a 1543 French translation. The tale reveals how Tezcatlipoca, Lord of the Night, commands Wind to fly to the house of the Sun and free the four musicians who are held prisoner: Red, Yellow, Blue, and Green. This becomes a creation myth as Wind overcomes Sun's power, frees the musicians, and brings color and music to Earth. The importance of the four directions is emphasized as each color faces a different direction. The myth concludes as the world is now filled with color and happy people: "All gave thanks to Lord of the Night, King of the Gods, Soul of the World" (unnumbered).*

Two retold and illustrated versions of the Cinderella story provide interesting sources for comparisons. Joe Hayes's *Estrellita de oro/Little Gold Star: A Cinderella Cuento* is based on the Hispanic tradition of the Southwest. Hayes uses a bilingual retelling in which the wicked stepsisters encounter a magical hawk. Hayes's Author's Note includes information related to his sources. Robert San Souci's *Little Gold Star: A Spanish Cinderella Tale* includes a heroine who is mistreated by her cruel stepsisters. She is rescued by her fairy godmother, who appears in the form of the Virgin Mary. The gold star refers to the reward for actions given the girl by a magical fish.

As you conclude your study of Aztec and other Mexican folklore, you will discover that the mythology details the creation of the world and the people. There is a belief in spirits and gods such as Ometecutli, Lord of Duality, and Quetzalcoatl, the Plumed Serpent. These gods are jealous and must be appeased. In the agricultural society, corn is of great value. The people, however, are responsible for caring for the land and the plants. Cleverness and sharing are rewarded, but greed and evil actions are not. It appears that the people enjoyed frightening stories about fearful monsters as well as the stories of the great gods.

Inca and Other South American Folklore Legends, myths, and riddles from South America are found in collections by John Bierhorst. Bierhorst's *The Mythology of South America* provides scholarly background and selections that reflect the creation of the world and the

*Excerpt reprinted with the permission of Simon & Schuster Books for Young Readers, an imprint of Simon & Schuster Children's Publishing Division, from *Musicians of the Sun* by Gerald McDermott. Text copyright © 1997 Gerald McDermott.

origins of civilization, as well as the conflicts between people. Bierhorst divides the stories and the discussions according to Greater Brazil, Guiana, Brazilian Highlands, Gran Chaco, Far South, Northwest, and Central Andes. Extensive notes on sources and references add to the value of the text. Bierhorst's *Lightning Inside You and Other Native American Riddles* includes 150 riddles from several North and South American cultural regions, including southern Mexico and western South America. An annotated list of sources is helpful for students of children's literature.

Ten Little Puppies/Diez perritos by Alma Flor Ada and F. Isabel Campoy is a popular counting rhyme that can be sung or spoken in either English or Spanish.

Lois Ehlert's *Moon Rope* is adapted from a Peruvian tale called "The Fox and the Mole," in which Fox convinces Mole that they should try to climb to the moon on a rope woven of grass. The story ends as a *pourquoi* tale because, after falling off the rope, Mole prefers to stay in the earth and come out only at night, avoiding other animals and never having to listen to Fox. Fox, however, may have made it to the moon because "[t]he birds say that on a clear night they can see him in the full moon, looking down on earth. Mole says he hasn't seen him. Have you?" (unnumbered).* The text, written in both English and Spanish, is illustrated with pictures inspired by ancient Peruvian textiles, jewelry, ceramics, sculpture, and architectural detail.

The Pemones Indian community in Venezuela is the setting for Irania Macias Patterson's bilingual telling of *Wings and Dreams: The Legend of Angel Falls*. One of the beliefs stressed in the tale is the belief in visions and dreams. After the tribe's land was invaded, young Takupi goes in search of a wonderful land he envisioned in a dream. Along the way he meets many challenges until finally he reaches his destination. The author also provides information about the setting for Angel Falls, the tallest waterfall in the world, and how a U.S. pilot eventually discovered the falls.

Tales from the Rain Forest is a collection of stories from the Amazonian Indians of Brazil, retold by Mercedes Dorson and Jeanne Wilmot. The theme developed in many of these myths is the need to respect the jungle. These creation stories reveal the beginnings of night, fire, rain, thunder, and plants. Each of the tales concludes with a comment that helps readers interpret the tales and place them into the culture.

Two highly illustrated books written by Nancy Van Laan and Pleasant DeSpain present Brazilian folktales for younger readers. Van Laan's *So Say the Little Monkeys* uses a rhyming text that incorporates the sounds of the mischievous and active monkeys with the sounds of the jungle. DeSpain's *The Dancing Turtle: A Folktale from Brazil* develops the theme that survival requires courage and wit.

Barbara Knutson's *Love and Roast Chicken: A Trickster Tale from the Andes Mountains* is a humorous tale that pits Cuy, a small guinea pig who uses his brains instead of force, against the larger Tio Antonio, a fox who is trying to eat the guinea pig. The author includes a glossary of Spanish words, their pronunciations, and meanings as well as an Author's Note that discusses the meaning of the tale.

Folklore That Reflects Interaction with Other Cultures

Numerous folktales from Mexico, South and Central America, and the southwestern part of the United States reflect a blending of cultures. Many of the values, beliefs, and characteristics of ancient literature are found in more recent traditional literature. F. Isabel Campoy and Alma Flor Ada (2006) state that many of the folktales originated in Spain, "a land that has been a cultural crossroad throughout history" (p. 1). Historically, Spain served as a bridge between Europe and Africa. Consequently, the tales show influences from such diverse cultures as the Roman Empire, the Arabs from North Africa and their desire to spread the Muslim faith, and

*Excerpt from *Moon Rope: A Peruvian Folktale,* copyright © 1992 by Lois Ehlert, reprinted by permission of Harcourt, Inc.

the Christians and Jews who added their folklore and their religious and cultural beliefs. The most dramatic additional factor affecting traditional literature coincides with the arrival of Cortes and the Spanish. A large body of folklore reflects the interactions between the ancient peoples and Christianity or the Spanish culture or African cultures. Some tales show the clash of cultural values; others are examples of stories that changed because of a different setting.

For example, "The Man Who Knew the Language of the Animals," a folktale in Jose Griego y Maestas and Rudolfo A. Anaya's *Cuentos: Tales from the Hispanic Southwest* (1980), is based on a Moorish tale from "A Thousand and One Nights." The tale is also similar to Verna Aardema's African tale *What's So Funny, Ketu?* Differences between the African and Hispanic tales reflect cultural values. The main character in the Hispanic tale portrays a stronger masculine role than is developed in the African tale. From your reading of the folklore, can you account for these differences?

"Dear Deer! Said the Turtle" found in F. Isabel Campoy and Alma Flor Ada's *Tales Our Abuelitas Told: A Hispanic Collection* is a version of a tale about a race between a swift animal and a slower animal who uses his wits. According to the authors it is a Cuban tale with African elements. (You may compare the tale with "The Tortoise and the Hare.")

John Bierhorst's *Doctor Coyote: A Native American Aesop's Fables*, a retelling, also indicates cultural infusion. Bierhorst identifies the text as Mexican in origin and shows the strong Spanish-Aztec connection. The fables were adapted in the 1500s by Indian retellers, who used a Spanish collection of fables. Several of the fables reflect the Spanish obsession with gold. Resulting morals about gold include conclusions such as if you have gold, you had better keep it hidden. The message appears to be that it is not good to be obsessed with gold. In contrast, hard work is a better way of obtaining true riches.

Pat Mora's *The Race of Toad and Deer* is a Guatemalan variant of the tortoise and the hare. It is interesting to compare these fables with Aesop's fables and with coyote trickster tales. Comparisons may also be made between stories that contain trickster rabbit characters. Stories similar to "The Tar Baby" are believed to be imported from Spain or Africa.

Bierhorst's *Spirit Child: A Story of the Nativity* shows the infusion of Christian and Aztec beliefs. The text describes and Barbara Cooney's illustrations depict an Aztec setting for the birth of the Christ child. Extensive Aztec beliefs are infused within the Christian story. For example, after reading this book and analyzing the pictures, readers will discover a belief in the supernatural and in the devil who plots our deaths, a belief that gods can take human form and that people are servants of all gods and must do their bidding, and a knowledge that Jesus does not demand human sacrifice and blood. Now even though the devil plots deaths, the people are saved because Jesus is the redeemer of humans who have faith.

Likewise, various versions of the story of the Virgin of Guadalupe represent the merger of Spanish-Catholic and Aztec heritages. Tomie dePaola's *The Lady of Guadalupe*, a retelling of a Mexican story, develops the connection between the people and their religious faith. The tale develops such values as a belief in God, trust and faith in the Lady of Guadalupe, respect for people in authority, and the need to do God's bidding. According to legend, the Lady of Guadalupe, now the patron saint of Mexico, appeared to a poor Mexican Indian on a December morning in 1531. Juan Diego, "He-who-speaks-like-an-eagle," was walking toward the Church of Santiago when he saw a hill covered with a brilliant white cloud. Out of the cloud came a gentle voice calling Juan's name and telling him that a church should be built on that site so the Virgin Mary could show her love for Juan's people, the Indians of Mexico. On Juan's third visit to the bishop to ask for the church to be built, Juan's story is finally believed because he brought with him a visual sign from the Lady of Guadalupe: his rough cape had a painting of the lady on it. The church was built on the location, and the cape with its miraculous change was placed inside the structure. The author, dePaola, says that he has had a lifelong interest in the legend of the Lady of Guadalupe. His drawings, based on careful research, depict the dress and architecture of sixteenth-century Mexico.

Several of the tales in Bierhorst's *The Monkey's Haircut and Other Stories Told by the Maya* are adaptations that reflect cultural infusion. For example, "How the Christ Child Was Warmed" and "How Christ Was Chased" reflect the influences of Christianity on the Mayan culture. "The Lost Children" is a Hansel and Gretel variant that reflects the influence of European folklore. A variant of "The Gingerbread Boy" is found in James Luna's bilingual text, *The Runaway Piggy.* In this version the runaway cookie is a pig and the setting shows a city with a flower shop, a thrift store, and a coffee shop. The young girl who captures the cookie gives it to her teacher.

Two traditional tales originate with the Miskito people of Nicaragua. *The Invisible Hunters,* adapted by Harriet Rohmer, Octavio Chow, and Morris Vidaure, reflects the impact of European cultures on the Miskito people. Three hunters are punished when they break their promise and forsake their people. European traders influence the hunters' actions, playing on their greed. The theme developed in the story shows that a trader culture threatens the values and beliefs respected by the villagers. *Mother Scorpion Country,* adapted by Harriet Rohmer and Dorminster Wilson, is a tale of love. In this tale, a husband tries to accompany his wife into the land of the dead.

Both of Rohmer's texts include information about the author's research. For example, Rohmer began her research for *The Invisible Hunters* in anthropological archives, visited the Miskito communities in the company of an Afro-Indian Catholic priest, learned more details of the story from an elder Miskito Catholic deacon, and finally met a Miskito bishop of the Moravian Church who provided many additional details. During this final contact, Rohmer was told, "According to the stories I heard as a child the Dar has a voice. I can take you to people who say they have heard that voice" (p. 31). In *Mother Scorpion Country,* Rohmer traces the story to the endeavors of a young Moravian minister who recorded the stories and customs of the Miskito Indians in the early 1900s.

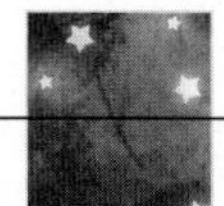

Historical Nonfiction and Fiction

High-quality informational books about Latino peoples for adults and children include books on history, geography, culture, and people from various places. There are also numerous adult sources that provide illustrations and background information that can be used to authenticate juvenile literature. The historical fiction often depicts the early Spanish presence in the Americas.

Informational Books That Develop Historical Perspectives

Articles in the science sections of newspapers and adult nonfiction sources focus on discoveries of the art works and the earliest writing in the Western Hemisphere. For example, John Noble Wilford (May 16, 2006) reports that discoveries in Guatemala including art masterpieces and the earliest Maya writing "are overturning old ideas of the Preclassic period" (p. D1). Yale Mayanist, Michael Coe (2006), states that the new discoveries mean that the great age of Maya archaeology is only beginning. In another science article, Wilford (September 15, 2006) states, "A stone slab bearing 3,000-year-old writing previously unknown to scholars has been found in the Mexican state of Veracruz," and "archaeologists say it is an example of the oldest script ever discovered in the Western Hemisphere" (p. A8). This date compares with Mesopotamian written texts dating to 3200 BC and Egyptian pictorial hieroglyphics dating from 3200 to 3000 BC.

Two articles in the *National Geographic* special section (2007) "Maya: How a Great Culture Rose and Fell" are of particular interest. Guy Gugliotta's "The Maya Glory and Ruin: Saga of a Civilization in Three Parts: The Rise, the Monumental Splendor, and the Collapse" discusses the rise of the kingmaker or warlord, the marking of a new era, and the consequences of foreign influence and the collapse due to fatal rivalries. Simon Norfolk's "Built to Awe: Mesoamerica's Grand Monuments" features photographs of the ruins of the temples. These articles provide considerable history of the Maya and photographs that may be used to support the settings in literature.

Several books appropriate for young people discuss accomplishments of the ancient native cultures of the Western Hemisphere. In *The World in 1492,* Jean Fritz, Katherine Paterson, Patricia and Fredrick McKissack, Margaret Mahy, and Jamake Highwater discuss the history of various parts of the world at the time of Columbus. The section titled "The Americas in 1492" is written by Jamake Highwater. This chapter includes information on the Aztecs, the Incas, and other native peoples. Readers will discover information about social classes and religious ceremonies and festivals. Maps show the Aztec and Inca empires, and illustrations show art from the time period. Lila Perl's *The Ancient Maya* and Liz Sonneborn's *The Ancient Aztecs* present the history of the early culture through discussions about rulers, priests, and artisans. Albert Prago's *Strangers in Their Own Land: A History of Mexican-Americans* traces the history of Mexican Americans and explores reasons for difficulties that Mexican Americans face today.

Johan Reinhard's *Discovering the Inca Ice Maiden: My Adventures on Ampato* provides a fascinating glimpse into the search for Inca antiquities by describing the true experiences of the author as he discovers a 500-year-old Peruvian mummy. The photographic essay provides knowledge about the ancient culture, as well as the people who still live in the area. Readers will also gain an understanding of the scientific method as they follow how the discovery is handled at both the original site and later in the laboratory.

Information on the history and contributions of Puerto Ricans, Mexican Americans, and Cubans is discussed in Milton Meltzer's *The Hispanic Americans.* Meltzer explores Spanish influences resulting from exploration and colonization. Then he considers the development of the political, economic, and cultural status of Hispanic Americans.

The Gods and Symbols of Ancient Mexico and the Maya: An Illustrated Dictionary of Mesoamerican Religion by Mary Miller and Karl Taube (1993) provides an illustrated source for information about the gods and symbols of the Olmecs, Zapotecs, Maya, Teotihuacanos, Mixtecs, Toltecs, and Aztecs. The text includes almost 300 entries.

The Incas and Their Ancestors—The Archeology of Peru by Michael E. Moseley (1992) traces the Incas from the first settlement in Peru over 10,000 years ago to the Spanish conquest. The text includes 225 illustrations. Another adult source, *Maya Cosmos: Three Thousand Years on the Shaman's Path* by David Freidel, Linda Schele, and Joy Parker (1993), provides extensive information about religious beliefs of the Maya. The book includes drawings, photographs, detailed chapter notes, and references.

Circa 1492: Art in the Age of Exploration, edited by Jay A. Levenson (1991), is an adult source that includes topics similar to those found in Fritz's juvenile text, *The World in 1492.* This large adult text includes sections on both Spain and the Americas. The sections on the Americas include reproductions of art from the Aztec and Inka (text spelling) empires. This extensive book also provides a source for comparative study.

Historical Fiction

Historical fiction includes several books that deal with the Spanish conquest. An understanding of history is important for readers to analyze historical fiction about this time period. Some of the previously mentioned informational books provide useful background information.

Award-winning authors Elizabeth Borton de Trevino and Scott O'Dell have written historical fiction novels set in either seventeenth-century Spain or in the Americas at the time of the Spanish conquest. For example, de Trevino's *I, Juan de Pareja* is set in Spain in the 1600s. The story focuses on two quite different people: the court painter, Diego Rodriguez de Silva y Velázquez, and his slave, Juan de Pareja. The author's Afterword provides interesting information for students of children's literature who are interested in the techniques an author uses to gather information and to write a historical novel about personages who really lived.

The author, de Trevino, states that her book is fictional because "Whenever one tells a story about personages who actually lived, it becomes necessary to hang many invented incidents, characters, and events upon the thin thread of truth which has come down to us. The threads of the lives of Velázquez and Pareja are weak and broken; very little, for certain, is known about them" (p. 177). Next, de Trevino states that only one direct quote can be authenticated. But, notice how much character information can be inferred from this quote: "I would rather be first in painting something ugly than second in painting beauty" (p. 178). The writer also reveals that she relied heavily on portraits Velázquez painted.

This book develops both views of the Spanish culture and the human interactions between a caring master and the slave who becomes his friend. Students of children's literature will gain insights into the culture of the time, as well as discover ways that authors develop historical novels from threads of the past.

Person-against-self and person-against-society conflicts, settings that depict Mayan and Aztec cultures, as well as themes that illustrate the consequences of greed, are found in O'Dell's novels based on the Spanish conquest of Mexico in the early 1500s. *The Captive, The Feathered Serpent,* and *The Amethyst Ring* focus not so much on the events of the time as on the moral dilemmas that a young priest faces in the New World. The books are told through the point of view of a young idealistic Jesuit seminarian, Julian Escobar, who leaves his secure home in Spain and joins an expedition to Central America, inspired by the prospect of saving the souls of native peoples in New Spain.

Through the three books, O'Dell creates both Escobar's character and his changing conflicts: Escobar is shown as a scholar interested in Mayan history and restoring their city, a Christian who is open to other cultural beliefs, and a man who experiences great conflicts as he is taken for a Mayan god. O'Dell explores changes in Julian by stressing the changing conflicts in Julian's life: Should he take on the role of the mythical Kukulcan to save his life and make his views palatable to people with their own ancient beliefs? Should he advise attacking a neighboring city before his own Mayan city is attacked? How should he respond to the Mayan rites of sun worship? Why does God permit both good and evil? Julian's defense of his inability to change the Maya and of his own eventual grasping for power demonstrate changes in his character. Much of the conflict is person against society and person against self as Escobar struggles with differences between Mayan and Spanish beliefs and then struggles with his own desires to convert the Indians to Christianity.

O'Dell's series of books are rich in cultural information, including values, beliefs, and customs. Students of children's literature will discover in O'Dell's books many beliefs and values that are similar to those found in the traditional literature of the Mayan people. For example, there are beliefs in the legend of Quetzalcoatl's return and in the importance of the ancient gods and the accompanying religious ceremonies. The people value an honorable life and expect to pay the consequences if they do not live such lives. Detailed settings provide extensive cultural information. O'Dell's themes also reflect the time period. For example, there are themes that greed is a powerful force that can ruin lives and people have moral obligations that must be met.

O'Dell's descriptions of Mayan and Aztec cities and temples and other aspects of the cultures encourage readers to understand that an advanced civilization inhabited the Americas long before European exploration and settlement. Readers may also ponder the right of one culture to destroy another culture whose people worship different gods and possess riches desired by a foreign power.

In *The King's Fifth,* O'Dell sets his story in the American Southwest. As in the previous books, O'Dell's characters reflect the conflicts of the time period. There is Esteban de Sandoval, an adventurous cartographer who accompanies Coronado and the conquistadors on their search for the cities of gold. There is arrogant and ambitious Captain Mendoza, who is drawn to the

Focus on Sid Fleischman's *Bandit's Moon*

Bandit's Moon is especially good for exploring changes in characters that reveal developing understanding between people of two cultural groups. Fleischman accomplishes this task by placing his characters in the days of the California Gold Rush, a time in the 1850s that is often characterized by lawlessness and in which people are shown as motivated by greed and even racial hatred.

The two major characters are Annyrose, a newly orphaned girl who finds herself on this lawless frontier and Joaquin Murieta, a Mexican bandit who some believe to be notoriously cruel while others believe to be a Robin Hood type of character whose major role is to right the wrongs against the Mexican settlers.

Fleischman first develops the character of Annyrose by describing her reactions to the villainous O. O. Mary. Fleischman compares O. O. Mary to a black widow spider and describes Annyrose's reactions to the loss of her violin and classical music when they are taken by the thieving woman. Through these descriptions, readers get a clear understanding of Annyrose's values and beliefs and learn about the frequent instances of greed and cruelty that are part of the setting. It is into this environment that Fleischman places Joaquin as he first saves Annyrose from O. O. Mary by taking Annyrose with him as part of his group of bandits. It is Annyrose's request to accompany the bandits that provides a foreshadowing of the relationships that may develop.

Through the interactions between Annyrose and Joaquin readers obtain a vicarious experience that allows them to understand the differences between the two individuals and then to accompany them on their road to understanding. For example, notice their attitudes toward each other as Fleischman develops this early dialogue between the two characters.

> "You are not frightened?" he asked. "Don't you believe the stories about me?"
>
> "Some of them," I said "But no man could be that heartless and cruel." (p. 11)

They continue the dialogue as they debate the role of gringos and Yankees.

From this early beginning that introduces the conflict among the various groups, Fleischman develops understanding as the characters become friends, help each other obtain some of their goals, and even rescue each other from dangerous circumstances.

The degree of their changing attitudes toward each other is especially revealing at the close of the book when Fleischman describes Annyrose's heartbroken reaction when she believes Joaquin has been killed and then expresses her relief when she discovers it is an impostor and not Joaquin who has been captured and killed. Readers can feel her relief as she takes a deep breath and realizes that Joaquin is probably someplace in California and that an oak tree is still waiting as well as a hangman. By the end of the book, she understands that Joaquin will probably still be hunted by the law. But she also knows her actions had nothing to do with the possible capture of her friend.

Southwest because of his greed for treasure. There is also Father Francisco, who goes on the journey in the hopes of saving souls. As would be expected from this cast of characters, there are both person-against-society and person-against-self conflicts as the various characters try to achieve their goals. O'Dell's themes suggest that strong beliefs require strong commitments, people have moral obligations that must be met, and greed is a powerful and dangerous force. Notice how all four of O'Dell's books about the Spanish conquest develop very similar themes. Students of children's literature can speculate about why these themes are so important for this time period.

Two other books by O'Dell are set in later times. *Carlota* is set in Spanish California in the mid-1800s. O'Dell explores the conflicts that occur between people who expect females to play a traditional female role and others who encourage a different type of behavior. Carlota is the strong and independent daughter of Don Saturnino, a native Californian whose ancestors came from Spain. Her father supports her brave and adventurous inclinations.

O'Dell's *The Black Pearl* is set in La Paz, a small mountainous town in Baja California. The characters include Ramon, a boy who tries to please his father and also dreams of finding the magnificent Pearl of Heaven; Manta Diablo, the fearsome, giant sea monster that is bigger than a ship; Blas Salazar, the strong proud pearl diver who is ashamed of his son's lack of size; Sevillano, the finest diver in the fleet who is a troublemaker and an antagonist; and Soto Luzon, the old, wise Native American who teaches the old ways of pearl diving.

By analyzing this book, students of children's literature will discover value systems that reflect the interaction of the old traditions and the newer Christian traditions. For example, there are both strong superstitions and suggestions that God favors those who are generous. O'Dell develops themes that are similar to his books set in an earlier time period. For example, people have moral obligations to themselves, to their community, and to the spirits and to God; greed and wrong doings will be punished; and honorable actions result in a clear conscience.

As you conclude your reading of historical fiction, notice how many of the values and beliefs are similar to those expressed in the earlier folklore. Also notice how the authors of historical fiction develop many of their plots and conflicts by showing person-against-society and person-against-self conflicts. Also notice how the authors of historical fiction develop settings, plots, conflicts, and themes that reflect the major happenings of the time periods.

Contemporary Realistic Fiction and Nonfiction

Both historical texts and contemporary realistic fiction frequently develop conflicts caused by immigration, either legal or illegal, from Mexico to the United States. Katherine Fennelly (2007) traces the historical origins of Mexican immigration. She states, "The origin of the contemporary chant, 'We didn't cross the border, the border crossed us' can be found in the terms of the 1848 Treaty of Guadalupe Hidalgo after the Mexican-American War. The treaty gave the northern half of Mexico to the United States and stipulated that all inhabitants in the ceded area who did not announce their intention to remain Mexican citizens or leave the territory in one year would automatically become U.S. citizens. Those who did not, de facto, became 'illegal aliens'" (p. 5).

Fennelly then provides a history of Mexican immigration that follows cycles of recruitment in times of labor shortages. As we progress into the study of contemporary literature, we discover that conflicts related to immigration and clashes of cultures are still found in the texts.

Contemporary Latino literature includes picture books for young children that reflect many of the feelings and desires expressed by all children. Poetry reflects traditional beliefs and values and contemporary concerns. Realistic fiction for older children frequently presents problems related to growing up and to racial tensions. Many of the nonfiction titles are photographic essays that follow the lives of various families or groups or describe the geography of a region or festivals. The biographies reflect the lives of people who have made contributions to the Latino culture.

Poetry

Listening to and saying rhymes from various cultures encourage children to interact with language, as well as to discover the joy in language and in word play. *Ten Little Fingers and Other Play Rhymes and Action Songs from Latin America* selected by Jose-Luis Orozco includes musical accompaniment as well as lyrics in both Spanish and English. Nancy Van Laan's *So Say the Little Monkeys* is written in poetic form. The tale is based on folklore from the Brazilian rain forest. The repetitive language is especially appealing to young children.

Alice Schertle's *Pio Peep! Traditional Spanish Nursery Rhymes* includes nursery rhymes written in English and Spanish. The rhymes focus on many everyday experiences and are rich in rhythms that make them enjoyable to read orally. Tish Hinojosa's *Cada niño/Every Child: A Bilingual Songbook for Kids* includes bilingual lyrics and explanations for each of the eleven songs. One of the songs, "Hasta los Muertos Satan a Bailar/Even the Dead Are Rising Up to Dance," commemorates the Day of the Dead.

Ana Maria Fernandez's *Amar y otros verbos/To Love and Other Verbs* uses actions as a source for poetry. Poetry accompanies such verbs as to eat, to love, and to dance. The poetry uses metaphors and similes to depict each of the actions. Xose Cobas's watercolors convey the meanings of the poems.

The Pot That Juan Built by Nancy Andrews-Goebel is a combination of cumulative rhyme and biography that tells the story of Juan Quezada, one of the best-known potters in Mexico. The author focuses on how the potter transformed the village of Mata Ortiz from an impoverished village into a prosperous community of artists. One page is told as a cumulative rhyme in the style of "This Is the House That Jack Built." The rhyme outlines the process of making a pot. The facing page is written in prose and tells the story of the potter's life. This life reveals how the artist discovered pottery created by artisans of an ancient culture, experimented to recreate the lost art, and taught villagers and family members to create the pottery by using this lost art.

Red Hot Salsa: Bilingual Poems on Being Young and Latino in the United States, an anthology edited by Lori Marie Carlson, is written in both English and Spanish. There are poems by well-known authors such as Gary Soto and Luis J. Rodrequez as well as poems written by students of the New York schools. These poems reflect many of the problems faced by young adults.

Poet Margareta Engle has won both a Pura Belpré and Newbery Honor awards. Her poetry combines biographical data as well as poetic and cultural elements. For example, the biographical and historical source is revealed through the subtitle for her book *The Firefly Letters: A Suffragette's Journey to Cuba.* The "Survival" section in this chapter considers the survival strategies used by the three characters in her poems: a Swedish novelist, a slave from Africa, and the daughter of a wealthy Cuban slave owner. In this section we will consider Engle's use of poetic and literary elements.

As you read the poetry in this book, search for the poet's use of symbolism; you may find that it is one of the strongest poetic elements in the poetry. For example, the reference to the firefly in the title suggests a possible symbolic meaning. An early poem titled "Fredrika" reinforces this connection as the poet uses the light from fireflies to write in her journal, draw her sketches, and present her observations about the rights of women and slaves. Later, the fireflies are associated with the plight of slaves as some people capture and enslave the fireflies until they starve, while others search for and release the fireflies so that they can be free. The poet uses fireflies to reveal considerable characterization as she describes Fredrika and the slave Cecilia's reactions to captured fireflies; they feel like heroines in a story because they buy captive fireflies and set them free. The character of the wealthy landlord's daughter, Elena, is revealed as she longs to be out with the two women as they release the fireflies. As you read the poems, notice how she uses characteristics of fireflies to describe slavery. Do you believe that her use of fireflies is an effective symbol for both slavery and women's rights?

Picture Books

Several of the contemporary picture books written for young children present the text in both English and Spanish. The purpose for many of these books is to provide language instruction. For example, a series of picture dictionaries by Rebecca Emberley provide illustrated vocabularies in the two languages. *Let's Go: A Book in Two Languages* introduces words associated with topics such as animals at the zoo, camping, going to the beach, and going to the circus. *My Day: A Book in Two Languages* pictures activities that a child might do during the day. The book begins with clocks showing different times and proceeds through vocabularies associated with activities such as getting dressed, eating breakfast, walking to school, and attending various classes. *My House: A Book in Two Languages* includes captioned illustrations showing items found inside and outside the house. The book begins with labeled colors and proceeds from the inside of the house, to the family members, to various rooms in the house, to objects and activities associated with the outside of the house. *Taking a Walk: A Book in Two Languages* presents labeled illustrations showing objects a child might see while taking a walk. The book begins with labeled shapes. It includes many items a child might see, such as the neighbor's house, the school, the playground, and the library.

My First Book of Proverbs by Ralfka Gonzalez and Ana Ruiz is also written in both English and Spanish. The text includes simple proverbs such as "A good listener needs few words." Each of the proverbs is illustrated with a colorful picture that has the flavor of folk art. An analysis of the proverbs also indicates some of the traditional values that are important in the Mexican culture such as the importance of experience, love, and singing.

Pat Mora's book *Fiesta!* is both a bilingual picture book and a Pura Belpré Award winner. The text, along with Rafael Lopez's illustrations, provides an exuberant celebration for Children's Day/ Book Day. This colorful book suggests many of the adventures that children may have through books. The author includes suggestions for celebrating this special day on April 30 each year.

Two books use nature as a framework for the story. Taro Gomi's *Spring Is Here/Llego la Primavera* follows a calf as it experiences nature from the melting snows, to the blooming flowers, and finally to the return of winter. By now the calf is a full-grown cow. In *So Happy!* Kevin Henkes builds a story on the planting of a seed, a flooding stream, a wandering rabbit who becomes separated from his family on the wrong side of the stream, and a small boy who is looking for something to do. The story follows nature through the falling rain, the buried seed, and the blooming plant that becomes a flower. In a gentle story, the boy masters the flooding stream caused by the falling rain by building a bridge from branches, stretching the bridge across the stream, and saving the rabbit who is now able to return home. Anita Lobel's illustrations place the story in a rural Mexican or a southwestern setting. In a satisfying ending, the boy gives the flower to his mother, the lost rabbit is asleep with its family, and the boy's father gives the boy a book about building bridges.

Values related to the importance of family are central to Latino literature. These values are reflected in Benjamin Alire Saenz's *A Gift from Papa Diego*. This story, written in both English and Spanish, highlights the importance of family relationships through the story of a young boy who wishes to spend his birthday with his grandfather who lives far away. The story has a happy ending and reinforces the importance of family values.

Happy family values are also in Tony Johnston's *My Abuelita*. Yuyi Morales's colorful illustrations accompany a book that shows a grandmother and a child in a loving relationship. The text shows the importance of storytelling as the child decides that she wants to be like her abuelita and entertain boys and girls with her stories. Duncan Tonatiuh's *Dear Primo: A Letter to My Cousin* shows both a relationship between relatives and contrasting lifestyles as two boys write letters. One of the boys lives on a farm in Mexico and the other lives in a city in the United States. The text and illustrations show differences in the boys' lives such as riding to school on a bike or taking the subway, enjoying favorite foods after school, playing games, shopping, and celebrating traditions and holidays. The text and illustrations include Spanish words, which are defined in the book's glossary.

The importance of family bonds and family gatherings are major values in Diane Gonzales Bertrand's *Uncle Chente's Picnic/El Picnic de Tio Chente*. In this bilingual story about a happy family gathering, the family prepares for a Fourth of July celebration to honor a visiting uncle. A rainstorm and the loss of electricity does not ruin the picnic because Uncle Chente tells stories and shows the children how to make shadow animals with a flashlight and Ernesto plays the guitar for singing and dancing. The time spent together makes a special day that the rain cannot ruin.

Richard Keep's *Clatter Bash! A Day of the Dead Celebration* is a highly illustrated book with minimal text written in combinations of English and Spanish. The cut-paper montage illustrations provide considerable sources for discussions about this celebration. As the author states, it is not a time to be sad or to fear death, but a time for families to share their memories and the joy of being alive.

A house filled with family is the setting for Lulu Delacre's *Salsa Stories*. The New Year's Day setting is enhanced when Carmen Teresa is given a blank notebook. Family members tell her stories about other holidays and traditions that they believe would make good entries for the empty notebook. Because the stories are all about food, Carmen Teresa decides she will fill her notebook with family recipes. This book could be used to motivate a similar activity with students.

Another book that uses food as a focus is Pat Mora's bilingual text, *The Bakery Lady*. This book describes close family relationships. In this story, which highlights the Feast of the Three Kings (January 6), a young girl helps her grandparents in their bakery and hopes to find the doll representing the Christ child. As the girl observes the preparations, her grandmother explains that the work is shared. The text and illustrations are filled with holiday symbols such as piñata invitations, King's Rings, and special lemon cookies as well as frijoles and tamales.

The importance of friendship between an older man and a boy are important themes in Avelino Hernandez's bilingual story, *That Boy and That Old Man*. When the boy watches the man going fishing each day without catching any fish, he solves the fishing problem by tossing leftover food into the water to attract the fish before the man arrives. Now the man catches fish, and a friendship results between the man and the boy. The collage illustrations that include seeds and dried flowers add to the visual enjoyment of the story.

Leo Politi has written and illustrated a number of award-winning picture storybooks about Mexican American children living in Southern California. His *Song of the Swallows* tells the story of a young boy whose dear friend is the gardener and bell ringer at the mission of San Juan Capistrano. Politi shares Mexican American history with readers as the gardener tells Juan the story of the mission and of *las golondrinas*, the swallows who always return to the mission in the spring, on Saint Joseph's Day, and remain there until late summer. Politi's illustrations recreate the Spanish architecture of the mission and demonstrate a young boy's love for plants and birds.

Song of the Swallows is a good source for searching for values and themes that may be similar to those found in traditional literature and historical fiction. For example, you will discover that Politi develops values such as respect for elders, love of history and nature, responsibility for care of the earth, and a belief in God. The themes developed in the book show the importance of living in harmony with nature, respecting the past because history provides many lessons, and respecting people who have this knowledge of the past.

Marie Hall Ets and Aurora Labastida's *Nine Days to Christmas: A Story of Mexico* tells of a kindergartener who is excited because she is going to have her own special Christmas party, complete with a piñata. In the midst of numerous other everyday activities, Ceci chooses her piñata at the market, fills it with toys and candy, and joins the La Posada procession. After Ceci sees her beautiful piñata being broken at the party, she is unhappy until she sees a star in the sky that resembles her piñata. Children relate to the girl's feelings and learn about the Mexican celebration of Christmas when they read this book. This story depicts a middle-class family that lives in an attractive city home. Children can see that poverty is not the condition of all people with a Spanish heritage.

Fiction for Middle-Elementary Grades

The fiction written for students in the middle-elementary grades deals with problems such as gaining feelings of self-worth and solving problems that are common for children of that age. Some of the stories that have inner-city settings develop tensions related to racial issues. Maia Wojciechowska's Newbery Award winner set in Spain, *Shadow of a Bull,* develops two important themes: it is important to be true to oneself, and facing death is not the only way to demonstrate courage. In this realistic book, the son of a famous and supposedly fearless bullfighter learns that a male does not have to prove his manliness through acts of physical daring or violence. Manolo's village expects him to follow in his dead father's footsteps. As the men of the village begin training him in the art of bullfighting, Manolo believes that he is a coward because he has no interest in being a bullfighter. Manolo eventually learns that to be truly brave, he must be true to himself and not attempt to satisfy others' expectations. Wojciechowska effectively resolves Manolo's person-against-self conflict when Manolo tells the waiting crowd in the bullring that he prefers medicine to bullfighting.

Another Newbery Award book, Joseph Krumgold's . . . *And Now Miguel,* also has ties to Spain. This book, based on a full-length documentary film feature, is the story of the Chavez family, which has been raising sheep in New Mexico since before their region became part of the United States. Their ancestors raised sheep in Spain. Krumgold tells the story from the viewpoint of the middle child, Miguel, who unlike his older brother, is too young to get everything he wants and, who unlike his younger brother, is too old to be happy with everything he has. Miguel has a secret wish to accompany the older family members when they herd the sheep to the summer grazing land in the Sangre de Cristo Mountains. With the help of San Ysidro, the patron saint of farmers, Miguel strives to make everyone see he is ready for this responsibility. When he is allowed to accompany his elders on the drive and reaches the summer camp, he feels pride in his family's traditions and in his own accomplishments.

Pam Muñoz Ryan's *The Dreamer* is identified as a fictional biography about the Nobel Prize–winning poet Pablo Neruda (1904–1973). This Chilean poet is one of the most widely read poets in the world. Ryan's biography explores Neruda's boyhood experiences and suggests influences that led to his adult role as an outstanding poet. In addition to the biography, Ryan includes excerpts from Neruda's poetry and sources for additional reading.

In this section, we will consider some of the literary elements that make this an outstanding book. In the "Survival" section, we will explore the poet's characteristics and strategies that make it possible for him to endure and flourish during a time of authoritarian suppression under both his father and his country's rulers.

Ryan uses an interesting writing style that encourages readers to become involved with the book, to answer questions, and to speculate about content that may be in the following section. For example, on pages 236–237 the author asks: "Where will the waves take the debris abandoned in the freckled sand?" The words drawn in the sand are words that his father called him such as idiot, daydreamer, fanatic, amount-to-nothing, absent-minded, worthless, and dim-witted. On the following page is a drawing by Peter Sis that shows a lone traveler walking down a winding road through trees, hills, and ponds. The drawing flies through the air on the back of the poet's pen. On the same page is a poem that surrounds the dreamer, captures his spirit, and becomes the poet's only road.

Other questions such a "Is fire born of word? Or are words born of fire?" (p. 310) emphasize the poet's strong commitment to the power of words and suggest the conflicts that led to much of Neruda's poetry. Ryan's inclusion of people who are Neruda's heroes also suggests this strong commitment to the power of words and his beliefs. For example, his heroes write about fairness and justice and use words that stir people's thoughts. They write about changing the world. They are champions of free speech even when their words cause them to be imprisoned.

The inclusion of the arrest of poets allows the author to emphasize the person versus society conflicts that surround writers during this period of Chilean history. Through Neruda's thoughts the author explores his concerns such as "Why does the government arrest people for writing what is true?" and "Why is it treasonous to present another viewpoint?" Readers gain an understanding of Neruda's beliefs as he considers why it is better to present several viewpoints and allow readers to make up their own minds.

The author reveals the importance of poetry in Neruda's life through conclusions such as, "Poetry had laid down its path, and he had no choice but to follow" (p. 343). Ryan develops a character who follows this path and writes no matter what his circumstances. He writes with conviction and determination even when his writing causes him, after a military coup, to be considered an enemy of the country. Ryan includes an Author's Note that provides additional information about Neruda's love for poetry and about General Pinochet's military regime that killed and imprisoned thousands of Chileans.

Pam Muñoz Ryan allows her main characters to make discoveries about themselves and their Mexican families or heritage by sending American-born heroines to visit their families in Mexico. In *Becoming Naomi León*, Ryan develops considerable cultural information as Naomi, her younger brother, and her grandmother go to Mexico for the Christmas holidays, experience Las Posadas, and take part in the carvings associated with the Night of the Radishes. These carvings, especially those created by Naomi, provide a vehicle, enabling Naomi to discover her true self. In Julia Alvarez's *Return to Sender*, a family of Mexican workers moves to a large Vermont dairy farm to help the owner, who has been injured. The author explores the conflicts the Mexican family faces as they make adjustments to their new life, and also that they need to hide in fear of being sent back to Mexico. It is also a story of friendship as the Vermont family gains respect for their Mexican workers. The author uses letters written by the oldest daughter to her mother, who disappeared, revealing her feelings, conflicts, and experiences. These letters also explain a considerable amount of American and Mexican history as Mari tells about her experiences and her emotions. The author includes A Reader's Guide that has questions for discussion and a conversation with the author.

Fiction Written for Older Readers

Many of the conflicts developed in books for older readers express a harsher and even a dangerous world. Some of the stories express conflicts as main characters try to cross borders or survive in the streets of major cities. Authors who set their stories in other countries may place their protagonists in conflicts against governments. Now the protagonists must escape or lose their lives.

Nicholasa Mohr's *Going Home* provides additional adventures for Felita, who is twelve years old. Now Felita finds she must face and overcome new person-against-self and person-against-society conflicts. During a trip to visit relatives in Puerto Rico, Felita finds she is the object of attack because she is the gringa and not accepted by some of the Puerto Rican girls.

It is interesting to compare the setting in *Going Home* with the setting in *Danza!* by Lynn Hall. Hall's story takes place on a farm in Puerto Rico and emphasizes the interaction between Paulo, a Puerto Rican boy, and Danza, a Paso Fino stallion. Hall develops characters with believable emotions and actions.

Gary Soto has several contemporary books that appeal to readers. *Taking Sides* is a realistic fiction story about a boy who moves from the barrio to the suburbs. The protagonist, who is a basketball player, must decide how he will respond when his new team plays his old team in a league game. Soto develops themes related to loyalty and friendship. In *Pacific Crossing,* the boys from the barrio participate in an exchange program in Japan.

The harsher, brutal realities of a border-town existence are developed in two books for older readers written by Gary Paulsen. In *The Crossing,* the protagonist, Manny, dreams of crossing the border to live in America. In this story of a teenage boy who must use his wits to stay alive, Paulsen develops harsher themes such as you may need to lie as well as use your wits to survive in the streets; life is not always fair, but you should keep up the struggle; and one person can make a difference. *Sisters/Hermanas* also deals with the realities of a harsh border town including prostitution, prejudice, and explicit language. By telling the story of a young illegal immigrant and an Anglo girl from a wealthier family, Paulson develops a person-against-society struggle that reflects some of the inequalities of life. Even through these conflicts, Paulsen's characters develop positive values such as striving for success, believing in dreams, and working hard. Paulsen's books may be compared with Ann Jaramillo's *La Linea* and Will Hobbs's *Crossing the Wire*. Both of these books develop the harsh and dangerous settings as teenagers try to cross the border from Mexico into the United States.

Sandra Cisneros's *The House on Mango Street* is another book that reflects the complexities of a neighborhood and a family and the conflicting feelings that may be found within a character. Through Esperanza's experiences, readers discover that the same place may be loving and cruel, safe and dangerous, and liked and hated. All of these emotions about a place are expressed as Esperanza struggles with life and the problems associated with growing up. Through the Latino girl's struggles, Cisneros develops strong themes such as dreams and goals are always important; family ties are important; and be proud of your culture, your family history, and your success.

A girl and her Mexican American family prepare for the traditional celebration marking a girl's fifteenth birthday in Diane Gonzales Bertrand's *Sweet Fifteen*. The novel shows both strong family values and the conflicts that occur within the family. This book was selected as a commended title for the 1995 Américas Award for Children's and Young Adult Literature. Music and baseball provide the mix in John H. Ritter's *Under the Baseball Moon*. The story, set in San Diego's Ocean Beach neighborhood, includes considerable references to a type of Latin jazz called "Fu Char Skool."

Stories that take place in foreign settings frequently show the protagonists engaged in dangerous conflicts. For example, Ben Mikaelsen's *Sparrow Hawk Red* is a story of survival in the streets and drug trafficking milieu of Mexico. Thirteen-year-old Ricky Diaz discovers that his mother was murdered by drug smugglers because of his father's work for the Drug Enforcement Agency. In an effort to avenge his mother, Ricky disguises himself as a Mexican street urchin. With the help of Soledad, another street urchin, he enters the smugglers' compound, steals a plane, and narrowly escapes. Through his adventures, Ricky discovers the importance of his heritage.

Surviving in the dangerous world of political turmoil is another popular plot device found in books written for older readers. James Watson's *Talking in Whispers*, a 1983 British Carnegie Honor book for older children, is a political thriller and a survival story in which the main character is hunted by the security forces of a South American government that denies basic human rights. The book develops a strong statement about what humans will do to retain their rights and their freedom.

A similar plot is developed in Anilú Bernardo's *Jumping Off to Freedom* when a Cuban father and son must escape from the political rulers of the dictatorship. This book develops both person-against-society and person-against-nature conflicts as the protagonists first escape from the authorities and then face the stormy ocean as they try to reach the Florida coast on a raft. This is another survival story that suggests humans will face great obstacles to retain their freedom. The author is a Cuban American who now lives in Florida after her family escaped from the communist government.

Grab Hands and Run by Frances Temple is another survival story set in El Salvador. The plot follows a family who tries to leave El Salvador after the father disappears.

To authenticate the nature of the harsher settings and conflicts described by the authors in some of these survival stories, search current newspapers for stories that might clarify the conflicts. For example, Larry Rohter's article in the *New York Times* "Driven by Fear, Colombians Leave in Droves" (2000) describes civil conflict and political violence that caused 800,000 people to leave Colombia in a period of four years.

Joan Abelove, the author of *Go and Come Back*, is a cultural anthropologist who placed her fictional work for older readers in a Peruvian jungle village. By telling the story from the viewpoint of a villager who is interacting with an anthropologist, the author encourages readers to understand cultural conflicts and respect differences. Through conversations and various experiences, the author shows clashing cultural values, differing views about the roles of men and women, contrasting attitudes about sex and babies, and opposing views about healing and medicine. As you read this book, consider Betsy Hearne's (1998) evaluation of the book:

> The viewing of the norm through an outsider's eyes is a perennially appealing device that should draw teens right in as well as give them some food for cultural thought. Reading this novel is like feeling wind rush through a stuffy room. We are taken by surprise. We breath deeper for the freshness of observing our own culture from the outside, for seeing two characters so like and unlike ourselves begin to expand, and for experiencing new possibilities of vision. (p. 272)

Nancy Farmer's *The House of the Scorpion* won both the Newbery Honor for 2003 and the 2002 National Book Award. Farmer's science fiction book develops a hypothetical land between Mexico and the United States. The science fiction characteristics include cloning to create human replacement parts, the development of eejits who work as slave laborers, and the identification of social conflicts that need to be resolved. The book includes many Latino references such as the Virgin of Guadalupe and descriptions of Cinco de Mayo and celebrations of the Day of the Dead. Issues connected with illegal immigration are covered through descriptions of a coyote: a man who takes people over the border and the flight of illegal immigrants.

This book has been well received by my Latino students and their parents. One father and brother said it was the best book they had ever read. They indicated that the issues were realistic and the culture was authentic. There is an in-depth description of how this book can be used in a classroom setting in the "Involving Children with Latino Literature" section in this chapter.

Contemporary Nonfiction

Informational books for young children are frequently highly illustrated books that depict various holidays or are photographic essays about families or people. For example, Cinco de Mayo, the commemoration of the Mexican army's defeat of the French army on May 5, 1862, is a major holiday for Mexican Americans. June Behrens's *Fiesta!* is an informational book describing the modern-day celebration of this holiday. Photographs show a Mexican American festival in which music is played by a mariachi band, costumed dancers perform traditional Mexican dances, and young and old enjoy the celebration.

Several nonfiction books provide information about children and families. Tricia Brown's *Hello, Amigos!* is a photo essay for younger children. It chronicles a special day in the life of six-year-old Frankie Valdez, a Mexican American boy whose family lives in San Francisco's Mission District. Fran Ortiz's photographs show the boy as he goes to school, attends classes, plays with friends, reacts to a classroom birthday cake, goes to the Boys' Club, and shares his birthday celebration with his family.

The lives of migrant children are depicted in several books. Beth Atkin's *Voices from the Fields: Children of Migrant Farmworkers Tell Their Stories* presents insights into the lives of children of migrant laborers. Atkin uses interviews to recount the stories of the children, who tell about their dreams and the joys of family relationships, as well as their hardships. In *Calling the Doves,* Juan Felipe Herrera tells a story about his childhood as a migrant farmworker. The story reflects a strong relationship between the family and the land, as well as depicting the grueling nature of farm labor.

Biographies of Latino figures provide interesting sources for analysis and comparisons. This is especially true if biographies are available about the same person but written for different age levels. For example, students of children's literature can compare the coverage, characterizations, and conflicts developed in three biographies about the artist Diego Rivera. Jeanette Winter's *Diego* is written for younger children. James Cockcroft's *Diego Rivera* is written for adolescent audiences, and Cynthia Newman Helms's *Diego Rivera: A Retrospective* (1986) is an adult biography.

By studying all three biographies, readers may find characterizations, values, and beliefs similar to those found in other genres of Latino literature: for example, the importance of fiestas, the role of women in sustaining religion, a belief in healers, a belief in the supernatural, a belief that people should be good and work hard, and a pride in one's heritage.

Each of the books, however, has a slightly different point of view about Rivera. Winter's biography, written for younger readers, portrays Rivera as a hero of the people whose mural paintings were influenced by the cultural events around him and the economic depression in Mexico. There is a strong theme in the book that one must be proud of one's heritage. Cockcroft's biography, written for adolescent audiences, includes more information about Rivera's personality, his character flaws, and his political affiliations. As in the biography written for younger readers, there is a strong theme about being proud of one's heritage. The adult biography explains the inspirations of Rivera's artistic works. This biography presents a chronology of his art and life, as well as discusses Rivera's influences on other artists. The text includes reproductions of Rivera's murals and gives explanations about his artwork. All of the biographies emphasize that Rivera was considered an artistic genius.

Another highly illustrated biography presents insights into Rivera's life and his influence on other artists. Robyn Montana Turner's *Frida Kahlo: Portraits of Women Artists for Children* presents the life and work of another great Mexican artist—Frida Kahlo. The text tells how Kahlo was influenced by Diego Rivera and eventually became his wife. Many of the large colored reproductions of her paintings "symbolize Kahlo's strong sense of being rooted in the land and culture of Mexico" (p. 27). As you look at Kahlo's paintings, try to identify the influence of the Mexican culture. It is interesting to compare Kahlo's artwork with that of other great artists from Mexico.

Jonah Winter's *Frida* is a highly illustrated biography about the artist. Winter stresses how art helps Frida Kahlo through especially painful times of her life: drawing keeps her from being sad when she is stricken with polio and confined to bed and when she is recovering from a terrible bus accident. In the Author's Note, Winter discusses the importance of Kahlo's marriage to Diego Rivera.

Two biographies about poets are written for different age groups. Both texts, however, develop the importance of literature and writing poetry in the lives of the biographical characters. Monica Brown's *My Name Is Gabriel: The Life of Gabriela Mistral* is a biography about the Chilean Nobel Prize winner written for younger children. The text is written in both English and Spanish. Younger children will enjoy listening to the text as well as viewing and discussing the illustrations. A much harsher reality is developed in Margarita Engle's *The Poet Slave of Cuba: A Biography of Juan Francisco Manzano*. In this biography, which is appropriate for young adults, Engle introduces the poet who was born into slavery in Cuba in 1797. The author develops both the poet's extraordinary abilities and the harsh realities of his suffering. Like Frida Kahlo's use of painting to save her in times of stress, Manzano's poetry saves him when he is faced with beatings and confinement.

César Chávez: The Struggle for Justice by Richard Griswold del Castillo is a bilingual biography about a Mexican American leader who worked to improve the lives of poor farmworkers through the United Farm Workers Union. The heavily illustrated biography traces Chavez's life from a small farm near Yuma, Arizona, through the Depression when the family lost their farm and became migrant farmworkers in California, to his reading of the writings of Mahatma Gandhi, who won independence for his people through nonviolent means, to his work as an organizer who helped poor families register to vote. The biography emphasizes Chavez's political work to help farm laborers through nonviolent means such as boycotts and strikes. The text concludes with a timeline of the important incidents in Chavez's life.

A Featured Book for Young Adults

Red Hot Salsa: Bilingual Poems on Being Young and Latino in the United States, an anthology edited by Lori Marie Carlson, presents poems in both Spanish and English by poets such as Gary Soto, Martin Espada, Trinidad Sanchez, Jr., and Luis Rodriguez. Carlson also includes a few poems written by young adults.

The poems in the anthology are especially good for meeting three of the evaluation criteria for poetry identified by Donna Norton (2007). First, the most effective poems allow readers to interpret, to feel, and to put themselves into the poems. The poems encourage readers to extend comparisons, images, and findings. The poems selected by Carlson are divided into five topics that are meaningful to Latino readers. For example, "Language, Identity" includes Gary Soto's "Spanish" in which the poet describes what it means to speak Spanish. This experience extends from a baby behind the bars of a crib to experiences growing up. The poems in "Neighborhoods" include poems such as "Life in el Barrio" by Kizzilie Bonilla that focuses on visual and auditory experiences associated with living in the neighborhood. The section titled "Amor" includes "Love" by Gwylym Cano in which the poet states that there should be one hundred words for love, including both positive and negative experiences. Another poem in this section expresses the varied feelings expressed in "Prom Poem for Jorge Barroso" by Sandra M. Castillo.

The poems in "Family Moments, Memories" speak to many students. Experiences vary from visiting relatives in Michele Serros's "Dead Pig's Revenge" to "Saturdays Set Within Memory" by Isaac Goldemberg. The poems in the final section, "Victory," depict the Latino struggle such as Luis S. Rodriguez's "Piece by Piece," in which the poet asks Latinos not to be perpetual victims but to use their given talents to go against those who would conquer them. "The Journey That We Are" by Luis Alberto Ambroggio states that victory comes with being strong like the wind and having fire in the heart.

The second important criterion states that the subjects of the poems should delight readers, say something to them, enhance their egos, strike happy recollections, tickle their funny bones, or encourage them to explore. Imagery is one of the primary elements in poems that encourage readers to see, hear, feel, taste, smell, and touch the worlds created by the poet. In "Love," Gwylym Cano uses metaphors, implied comparisons between things that have something in common. In her poem, metaphors highlight certain similar qualities in love and snow to encourage readers to see them in new ways. Cano compares love to snow because both can be cold, slushy, mushy, and difficult to walk in. Like love snow falls silently and mysteriously. Both warm the cold city streets, but they invariably melt. While no two snowflakes are alike, love like the snow comes back again.

In contrast to the comparisons between love and various qualities in snow, David Hernandez in "Martin and My Father" describes anger as "ice-blue hot" and then uses the imagery of drowning in a lake to describe the act of throwing away a gun and a knife after he pulls a knife on his father and feels like an assassin. His feelings are strengthened when he learns that his friend Martin has been shot.

The third criterion suggests that poems should be good enough to stand under repeated readings. Many of these poems written in both English and Spanish meet the requirements of Pulitzer Prize–winning author Oscar Hijuellos who states in his "Introduction" to the text: "The poets' intense feelings about survival and 'becoming' are palpable on the page. And the Spanish/English verses of their poetry are equally beautiful, stirring, and worthy of our humanity" (p. xix). The poems written by young adults such as Kizzilier Bonilla, Robert B. Feliciano, and Amiris Ramirez, who are students in New York City public schools, may be used to motivate other students to write.

The author includes a Glossary of Spanish terms and Biographical Notes about the poets in the collection. These notes include additional publications by the poets. These references may be helpful for students who wish to read additional poetry by a favorite poet.

Survival

In this section on survival we will identify survival strategies found in a variety of genres. Beginning with folklore, we discover survival strategies related to the values and beliefs of the people. We find it is important to be strong and good, to respect the advice of older family members, and to use a love of music even when isolated in a tower. For example, the main character in *Martina the Beautiful Cockroach: A Cuban Tale*, retold by Carmen Agra Deedy, listens to her grandmother's advice when it is time to choose a husband. To find the right husband, her grandmother recommends "The Coffee Test" to discover a suitor's disposition. Readers discover unlikable qualities as the various suitors respond with anger as the coffee is spilled on their shoes. To survive in a happy marriage suitors should not be too cocky, too boorish, or too cold-blooded. Characteristics of the final suitor suggest the following survival techniques for a happy marriage: humor, matching personal characteristics, and best of all, a wise Cuban grandmother.

A love of music is a powerful survival strategy for the character in Patricia Storace's *Sugar Cane: A Caribbean Rapunzel*. In this variant, Madam Fate, a sorceress, places a fisherman's child named Sugar Cane in a tower as punishment for her father who took sugarcane from her garden. While in the tower, Sugar Cane learns music from her spirit beings who are called to the tower: an angel teaches her to sing, a gypsy from Spain teaches her to play the guitar, and a jazz master from New Orleans teaches her to play the piano. She learns poetry from a Greek poet and storytelling from an African griot. When Sugar Cane matures into a young woman it is her music that attracts the King to the tower. After Sugar Cane escapes from the tower, her singing allows the King to find her again. When they marry, music permeates the ceremony as guests dance the rumba, the bolero, the samba, and the mambo. Many of Raúl Colon's illustrations also suggest the magic of music for happiness and survival.

Francisco Jimenez's writings have won a Boston Globe–Horn Book Award and an Américas Award for Children's and Young Adult Literature. His book *Reaching Out*, a sequel to *Breaking Out* and *The Circuit*, is an autobiography of his survival as he goes from a migrant community of dilapidated housing in a family struggling to get out of poverty, to a well-educated individual who is now a university professor.

His survival strategies correspond with many of the strategies used by minority characters who succeed academically. Hard work and a strong work ethic are survival strategies, whether he is working three part-time jobs to bring money to the family, or doing academic work to have an opportunity to attend college. The need for goals is developed throughout the book. To help him obtain his goals he emphasizes his role models and his sense of personal responsibility. His autobiography emphasizes his hope, his faith, and his dreams. He constantly discusses his faith and his hope for a better life.

As many minorities do, he expresses the importance of pride in heritage and personal dignity. As in many Latino books, the author stresses values such as the importance of family and his father's need for respect. Even in poverty, Francisco maintains that personal dignity cannot be taken from anyone without his or her consent. This book also has a religious emphasis as Francisco maintains that trust in God is necessary for personal survival.

Pam Muñoz Ryan's *The Dreamer* allows readers to identify the survival strategies a Nobel Prize–winning poet used during a time when his father is totally against his son's chosen profession and rulers of the country consider poets and journalists treasonous when they write about freedom of choice and individual thoughts.

Ryan begins her fictional biography with the life of a young boy who is an incessant daydreamer. This survival strategy is developed throughout the novel as he forgets himself in the pages of books he reads. His imagination allows him the greatest escape from reality as evidenced by instances when he touches or sees treasured objects, imagines himself journeying to the stars with a found pine cone, or wonders what wisdom an eagle whispers to a baby chick who is learning to fly. His imagination allows him to daydream and survive unhappy experiences. After his father forces the boy and his sister to swim in the ocean, he imagines himself as a flamingo at the edge of the salt marsh or as a swan whose body glides across the water. It is at this point that he wonders where the waves will take the debris of hateful words his father uses.

Determination is a survival strategy that influences his career choice. The more his father insists that he become a doctor or a dentist, the more he knows that he wants to be a poet. At this point, a librarian tells him that there is always a way to do what you truly love. To survive after his father angrily burns his notebooks and stories, his uncle's newspaper office is burned, and a poet is arrested, the boy knows that he must protect himself. He decides to write under an alias and chooses the name Pablo Neruda, a name that he feels fits him like a suit of fine clothing. He also knows that to survive he must move to a place of culture, a place with more like-minded people, a place where being a student and a poet is not discouraged.

Ryan concludes that Neruda uses the rhythms of his childhood to influence his words, his fury to choose words and emotions in his essays, and his convictions and determination to frame his poetry and develop creative freedom. Neruda's poetry chosen for the conclusion of the novel reinforces these survival strategies. In a poem he becomes the raging bird in a quiet storm, searches for objects carelessly abandoned by the sea, or presses himself against a wall and, like a shadow, slips away.

Another novel about people who actually lived is Elizabeth Borton de Trevino's 1966 Newbery Award winner *I, Juan de Pareja*. The author uses history, legend, and interpretations of paintings to develop the details in this fictional biography about the relationship between sixteenth-century Spanish painter Valazquez and his slave, friend, and assistant, Juan de Pareja. The novelist seeks answers to one of the great survival questions: How did "those two, who began in youth as master and slave, continued as companions in their maturity, and ended as equals and as friends" (p. 180) accomplish this transition? As readers we will search for characteristics, values, and beliefs that made this survival possible.

As a young slave, Juan learns not to be surprised at the actions of his mistress who might cuff or cuddle him, but also teaches him his letters so that he can read and write. After her death he is inherited by her nephew in Madrid, the artist Don Diego Rodriguez de Silva y Valazquez. There he learns that it is important for him to remain trustworthy and to be careful as he works in his master's studio. Here he learns to grind the colors, clean the brushes, and stretch the canvas to the frames. Readers discover that for artists to survive, it is important to keep professional secrets pertaining to their art, never writing them down. Consequently, to survive as an artist's assistant, Juan trains his memory so that he can perform various tasks. Through conversations with the artist, Juan learns to carefully observe; he discovers that art must be true, otherwise it is worthless. He discovers that the most important setting for the artist is the quality of the light—nothing else matters. The greatest survival strategies that Juan learns from his master are to never take art for granted, to respect art, and to try to learn more to improve the art.

Juan's desire to study painting is so strong that he sells his mother's gold earring to purchase art supplies even though it is against the law in Spain for slaves to study art. He believes it is wrong to go against the law, but he decides to continue copying art secretly to practice. He also learns about art by observing his master and copying his techniques. A person-against-self conflict emerges as his paintings cause him to feel guilt because he is a religious person. As he considers his problem he realizes that he is not a sinner because the law is an injustice. After a friend helps him solve his problems about art and painting, Juan paints with the friend and feels "that life could offer me no further joys" (p. 128).

Juan's master pays him the highest tribute and summarizes Juan's survival strategies when he states that Juan is loyal, resourceful, proud, dignified, and good. These characteristics are rewarded when Velazquez gives Juan his freedom, names him as his assistant, and states that Juan will always be his friend.

While Juan survives in a setting of sixteenth-century Spanish slavery, the characters in Gary Soto's young adult fiction books face survival in contemporary American settings. For example, his protagonist in *Buried Onions* is a Mexican American youth who must survive in a setting in which many of his friends and relatives are victims of violence. The title of the book reveals one of the survival strategies as characters symbolically bury their onions to cry out their sadness. The protagonist in *Buried Onions* is nineteen-year-old Eddie who finished high school but dropped out of college. He lives in a setting where revenge is expected and many youths may wind up in jail, in hospitals, or in the morgue. Soto, however, creates a story in which Eddie does not want to live under those conditions. Instead, Eddie knows that to survive the gangs in

Suggested Activities for Developing Understanding of Latino Literature and Culture

1. Select one of the books that received an Author's or Illustrator's Award for the Pura Belpré Award. Analyze the book to identify why you believe it was chosen as a book that embodies the Latino cultural experience. Share your results with your class.
2. Find the qualifications for the Pura Belpré Award and for the Newbery Award. Read Margarita Engle's *The Surrender Tree: Poems of Cuba's Struggle for Freedom*. Analyze why you believe that the book was honored for both awards.
3. Choose several selections of folklore that show the impact of Spanish culture on the earlier traditional beliefs of the people. Analyze the tales for evidence of the infusion of the alien culture.
4. Compare Jose Griego y Maestas and Rudolfo A. Anaya's "The Man Who Knew the Language of the Animals" in *Cuentos: Tales from the Hispanic Southwest*, with Verna Aardema's *What's So Funny, Ketu?*, which is based on an African tale. Identify the similarities and differences and note ways in which the differences reflect cultural differences.
5. Choose an outstanding author of historical fiction such as Scott O'Dell, and read several books by that author. What makes the plot and the characters memorable? What are the themes in the writer's work? Is there a common theme throughout the writing?
6. Many stories, such as Sandra Cisneros's *The House on Mango Street*, express the pain and fear of characters who struggle to find themselves in a world that is often alien. In books such as Nicholasa Mohr's *Going Home*, analyze the forces that cause an American girl from Puerto Rican ancestry to not be accepted by Puerto Rican girls.
7. Develop a timeline showing the chronology of famous Latinos or historical happenings that reflect the culture. Identify literature that may be used with the timeline.
8. Choose an illustrated book from the area of Latino literature and authenticate both the text and the illustrations. Provide sources for your authentication activity.

Involving Children with Latino Literature

Phase One: Ancient Aztec and Mayan Folklore

Before exploring Latino literature and the culture, students should understand that Latino culture is very complex. This complexity results from the infusion of numerous influences. Also, the literature covers a wide time span. The literature extends from the ancient Aztecs and Maya to the recent poetry and fiction set in the contemporary world.

Show the students the locations of the Aztec and Mayan peoples on a map of Mexico and Central America. *Atlas of Ancient America* (Coe et al., 1986) and *The Maya* (Coe, 1992) include useful maps and information about the cultures of these peoples. Neil Philip's *Mythology of the World* (2004) includes a map of North and South America (p. 102) that identifies the locations of various mythological characters such as "The Maya Hero Twins." For additional background information, share and discuss Deborah Lattimore's *The Flame of Peace: A Tale of the Aztecs*, the introduction titled "Welcome" in F. Isabel Campoy and Alma Flor Ada's *Tales Our Abuelitas Told: A Hispanic Folktale Collection*, and "Maya: How a Great Culture Rose and Fell" (*National Geographic*, August 2007). This background information could also be shown on a map.

Read and discuss several selections of Aztec folklore such as those found in C. Shana Greger's *The Fifth and Final Sun: An Ancient Aztec Myth of the Sun's Origin* and Gerald McDermott's *Musicians of the Sun*. Discuss the values and beliefs reflected in the stories. After reading and discussing these tales, ask students to look again at the illustrations and text in Lattimore's *The Flame of Peace: A Tale of the Aztecs*. Ask students to answer this question: What, if any, are the similarities between the folklore and the plot, characters, and illustrations in *The Flame of Peace: A Tale of the Aztecs?*

Next, share and discuss several sources of Mayan folklore. Explain to the students that John Bierhorst in *The Monkey's Haircut and Other Stories Told by the Maya* identifies several characteristics of Mayan folklore that reflect the group's values. As the students listen to or read these stories, ask them to identify those characteristics. Bierhorst identifies the following recurring characteristics: (1) cleverness, as shown by stories that include riddles, puns, double meanings, and tricksters; (2) culture and customs, such as paying a bride service and being godparents; and (3) corn and farming practices. Students should also listen for and identify additional traditional values in the stories. Either share or have students read independently tales such as Francisco Hinojosa's *The Old Lady Who Ate People*, Geraldine McCaughrean's "The Monster with Emerald Teeth" in *The Bronze Cauldron*, Harriet Rohmer and Dorminster Wilson's *Mother Scorpion Country*, and Vivien Blackmore's *Why Corn Is Golden: Stories about Plants*.

Have students develop and discuss webs of the Aztec and Mayan folklore. Figure 4.1 illustrates a web developed around the cultural values discovered in Mayan folklore. Ask students to compare the values found in Aztec and Mayan folklore and to summarize the cultural values discovered from reading the literature.

Additional Activities to Enhance Phase One

Here are some activities for children or young adult students related to this phase:

1. Research the early Aztec or Mayan cultures or one of the cultures that influenced the Aztec or Mayan cultures. If you choose one of the cultures that influenced the people, emphasize the time that the culture had the greatest influence and detail the influence.

FIGURE 4.1 Web Showing Traditional Mayan Values Found in Folklore

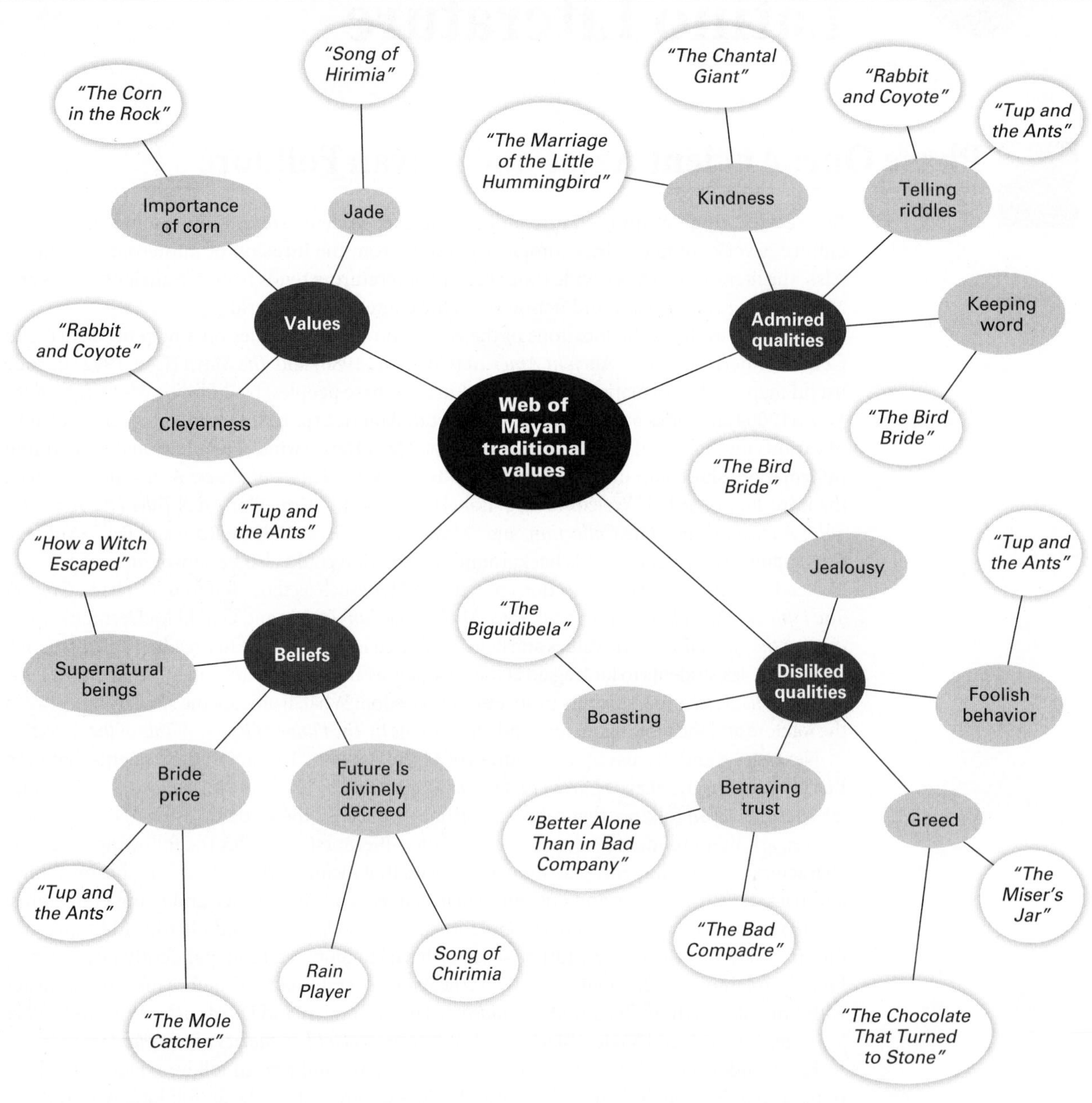

2. Read *Tales from the Rain Forest: Myths and Legends from the Amazonian Indians of Brazil* by Mercedes Dorson and Jeanne Wilmot. Carefully consider the authors' comments at the end of each of the tales. These stories and comments could be used in a study of geography and science. Try to answer these questions: How do the myths and legends about plants and animals compare with the geography of the Amazon? How does the theme, the need to respect the jungle, found in many of the tales correspond with geography and science? How and why were the people prepared to take care of nature and to live in close relationship to both plants and animals?

3. Do an artistic investigation. Choose a folklore text with illustrations that reflect strong Mexican influences. Some of the texts such as Francisco Hinojosa's *The Old Lady Who Ate People,* illustrated by Leonel Maciel, and Vivien Blackmore's *Why Corn Is Golden: Stories about Plants,* illustrated by Susana Martinez-Ostos, are illustrated by well-known Mexican artists. Investigate other works by these artists.
4. Choose a story with few illustrations such as Mary Grace Ketner's "Sinukuan: A Filipino Folk Tale" (2007). Ask students to illustrate this *pourquoi* tale about why mosquitoes bite people. The animal characters include Bird, Frog, Turtle, Firefly, and Mosquito.

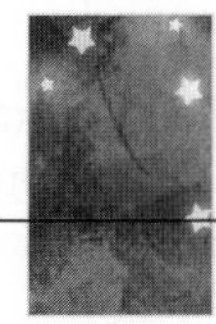

Phase Two: Stories That Reflect Interaction with Other Cultures

Many of the folktales from the Southwest, Mexico, and South and Central America reflect a blending of cultures. There are numerous folktales that reflect interactions with other cultures and show the clash of cultural values.

Analyzing Folklore That Reflects Interactions with Other Cultures

Introduce a series of folktales that reflect interactions with other cultures and show the clash of cultural values. Ask the students to consider at what point in history they would expect the greatest changes. Encourage the students to identify the arrival of Cortes and the Spanish as one of the greatest influences on the cultures and folklore. Ask them to think about how this occurrence changed the lives of the people and might have influenced their folktales, fables, myths, and legends.

Choose tales such as Verna Aardema's *The Riddle of the Drum: A Tale from Tizapan, Mexico*; John Bierhorst's *Doctor Coyote: A Native American Aesop's Fables* (this tale is retold from an Aztec manuscript) and *Spirit Child: A Story of the Nativity*; Harriet Rohmer, Octavio Chow, and Morris Vidaure's *The Invisible Hunters*; Tomie dePaola's *The Lady of Guadalupe*; and Jose Griego y Maestas and Rudolfo A. Anaya's *Cuentos: Tales from the Hispanic Southwest.* As students read the tales, ask them to identify both the cultural values and the influences that are incorporated in the tales. For example, both *The Riddle of the Drum: A Tale from Tizapan, Mexico* and *Doctor Coyote: A Native American Aesop's Fables* are easily analyzed according to the influences of physical setting and architecture. "'Dear Deer!' Said the Turtle" in Campoy and Ada's *Tales Our Abuelitas Told: A Hispanic Folktale Collection* includes African and African American elements. Their "The Castle of Chuchurumbe" is a cumulative tale that is similar to the nursery rhyme "The House that Jack Built." The retellers identify a Russian Jewish source for "The Little Horse of Seven Colors" and suggest this influence as the story traveled to Spain among the Sephardic Jews, to Latin America, and to the American Southwest. They identify Muslim influences for the tale "The Happy Man's Tunic." Comparisons can also be made showing the influence of Spanish folktales and Aesop's fables.

Students can share and discuss what happens when cultures clash in *The Invisible Hunters* and the interactions of the people and Christianity in *The Lady of Guadalupe and Spirit Child: A Story of the Nativity*. These books also develop strong cultural patterns through their illustrations.

Folktales in Jose Griego y Maestas and Rudolfo A. Anaya's *Cuentos: Tales from the Hispanic Southwest* are especially good for identifying cultural values and the influence of other cultures. For example, share "The Man Who Knew the Language of the Animals," and ask students to identify the plot of the story. Next, ask the students to identify the values and beliefs stressed in the folktale and then compare it with a similar African folktale, Verna Aardema's *What's*

So Funny, Ketu? Ask the students to draw a plot structure of the African tale and identify the emphasized values and beliefs. Next, ask them to identify the similarities and differences between the two tales, Ask, "What do the similarities tell us about human values? How might the differences reflect cultural differences between the Hispanic and African peoples?"

Additional Activities to Enhance Phase Two

Here are some activities for children or young adult students related to this phase:

1. For a creative writing activity, choose one of the Aesop's fables or another European folktale. Pretend that you heard this story from one of the early Spaniards who came to your country. Retell and adapt the story to reflect the southwestern setting, culture, and beliefs.
2. Create a museum that shows important artifacts from the cultural groups that influenced the literature. The museum can have drawings of art, clothing, and architecture. Develop an introduction to their museum and create a multicultural festival including such activities as storytelling, musical features, slide shows, and guest experts.
3. Choose a source like Jeannine Pasini Beekman's "Telling and Crafting Stories for Young Listeners" from the May–June 2003 issue of *Storytelling Magazine*. Use the suggestions to develop a Latino story.

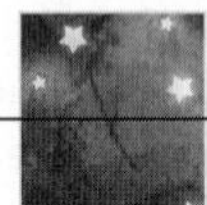

Phase Three: Historical Nonfiction

Choose books for discussion that will help students understand the ancient cultures and the changes that occurred because of interactions with other cultures. These can include books such as Albert Marrin's *Aztecs and Spaniards: Cortes and the Conquest of Mexico,* Albert Prago's *Strangers in Their Own Land: A History of Mexican-Americans,* Lila Perl's *The Ancient Maya,* and Liz Sonneborn's *The Ancient Aztecs.* Ask the students to compare their knowledge of the cultures gained from the nonfiction books with their knowledge gained from the folklore. What are the similarities and differences?

Encourage students to read nonfiction books that describe contemporary explorations and discoveries that authenticate the lives of earlier peoples such as Johan Reinhard's *Discovering the Inca Ice Maiden: My Adventures on Ampato.* Ask students to answer this question: What did you learn about the earlier periods from reading this book? Reinhard's text includes a timeline of history beginning with the Inca civilization in 1200–1438 CE and extending to the landing of the Pilgrims in 1620. Ask students to identify nonfiction books that could be used to add information about the various cultures of South, Central, and North America.

Additional Activities to Enhance Phase Three

Here are some activities for children or young adult students related to this phase:

1. On maps of North America, Central America, and South America, show the locations where the various people lived. Tell how their lives were influenced by other cultures.
2. Create a collage depicting some of the mysteries of the ancient Maya, Aztec, or Inca.
3. Develop a timeline for a famous Latino historical figure or for a specific movement. In *The Surrender Tree,* Margarita Engle provides a timeline for early independence movements in Cuba.

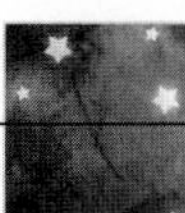

Phase Four: Historical Fiction

Searching for Cultural Beliefs and Historical Happenings in the Writings of Scott O'Dell

Scott O'Dell's historical novels *The Captive, The Feathered Serpent,* and *The Amethyst Ring* provide many opportunities for students to search for cultural values and beliefs, customs, Mayan history, and consequences of Spanish intervention. For example, they will discover the belief in the legend of Quetzalcoatl's return and the importance of the ancient gods and the accompanying religious ceremonies. They will also find evidence that the people valued an honorable life and expected to pay the consequences if they did not live such lives. Through reading other history texts, they can authenticate the historical happenings described by O'Dell.

O'Dell provides descriptions of Mayan and Aztec cities and temples and other aspects of the culture. These descriptions may be used to motivate students to illustrate sections of his books. They can search for photographs and drawings in informational books to help them with their illustrations. For example, Freidel et al.'s adult source *Maya Cosmos: Three Thousand Years on the Shaman's Path* (1993) includes drawings and photographs.

Modeling Comprehension of Characterization with Fleischman's *Bandit's Moon*

Before developing a modeling activity, review the background for modeling presented in Chapter 6, Involving Children with Jewish Literature, Phase Four, pages 269–272. Review with the students the requirements needed for effective reasoning related to characterization, the objectives for modeling, and the sequence that will be used in a lesson. The following modeling example has been used with middle- and upper-elementary students.

Objectives: To be involved in a modeling activity designed to show students how to analyze evidence from the text and to speculate about the characters. To understand the requirements for effective reasoning. To appreciate and understand the author's use of implication when developing characterization. To respond to the themes developed in the book.

Source Materials: Sid Fleischman's *Bandit's Moon.* Background material for the time period about the Gold Rush. Sources of criticism about the book including *School Library Journal* (September 1998) and *Publishers Weekly* (August 3, 1998).

Procedures: First, identify and review the requirements for effective reasoning. Second, review characterization by asking students to identify how authors develop three-dimensional, believable characters. Share examples of each type of characterization as part of this review. Third, explain to the students that in this modeling activity, they will listen to you read a selection, ask a question, answer the question, provide evidence from the story that supports the answer, and share the reasoning process used to reach the answer. Tell the students that after they have listened to you proceed through the sequence, they will use the same process to answer questions, identify evidence, and explore their own reasoning processes. As part of this introduction, discuss the meanings of evidence and reasoning. Encourage the students to identify evidence about characters in literature and to share how they would use this evidence.

Develop an introduction to the story *Bandit's Moon,* which has a setting in California during the Gold Rush of the 1850s. Show the students a map of California and help them locate the region associated with the Gold Rush. Provide background information about the Gold Rush. To help students understand that part of this book is based on factual information and on a real character, read and discuss the Author's Note on pages 133–136. To provide background information related to some of the themes in the book, read the reviews found in *Publishers Weekly* (1998) and *School Library Journal* (1998). You may discuss such comments as "he expertly crafts a fictionalized tale that takes a clear-eyed look at bigotry and racism" (p. 86, *Publishers Weekly*) and "Fleischman makes Joaquin a sympathetic central character as he shows the injustice suffered by minorities during this time of greed and lawlessness. This is classic Sid Fleischman; a quick read, with lots of twists, wonderful phrasing, historical integrity, and a bit of the tall tale thrown in" (p. 203, *School Library Journal*).

Provide the first modeling example. Read orally the first paragraph of the book, which is told from the viewpoint of Annyrose, one of the novel's main characters: "I had hardly got three miles down the road when O. O. Mary herself caught me running away and locked me up in the harness room off the barn" (p. 1).

Ask: "What do you know about Annyrose's character and Mary's character from this introductory paragraph?" My answer: "Annyrose is probably very frightened and living in dangerous circumstances. She is an independent character even though she is frightened about being in an environment inhabited by black widow spiders. O. O. Mary is a very nasty, mean, and dangerous character." Provide the evidence from the text: "Annyrose ran away from her environment and is now being forced to live in a locked-up space with insects she hates. O. O. Mary is compared to something that Annyrose fears. The author develops a description in which the setting is filled with both darkness and spiders." Provide the reasoning you used to reach your answer: "I believe Annyrose is an independent character because she ran away even though she probably realized that she would be punished. She is also living in a region that is not familiar to her. The way the author describes the setting as dark and filled with spiders allows me to envision a very frightening and even dangerous environment. I can feel Annyrose's fear and dislike for the location. I would be afraid if I were in a similar setting. Annyrose compares the black widow spiders to O. O. Mary. I know that a black widow spider is very poisonous and a bite could be extremely dangerous. This would be especially true if I lived a long way away from doctors. Consequently, I think that O. O. Mary has many of the characteristics that Annyrose dislikes and fears. Also the thought of O. O. Mary does not allow Annyrose to forget her circumstances. I believe that these thoughts must be very bad if they are not pleasant enough to take her mind off of O. O. Mary. I wonder what O. O. Mary must be like to be compared to a black widow spider."

Provide the second modeling example. At this point verify that the students understand the process, let them join the discussion by providing an answer, the evidence, and the reasoning. It is advisable to allow students to jot down brief answers to the questions, evidence, and reasoning. These notes increase the quality of the discussion that follows each question.

The next logical discussion point comes in the middle of page 4 after "She'd sold my New Orleans petticoats and dresses months ago. She had me walking around in some boy's castoffs, shirt and pants, and brown boots as curled up as a dead fish" (p. 4). Ask a question such as "What additional characteristics are being implied about O. O. Mary? What characteristics does O. O. Mary suggest about the bandits? What might Annyrose's behavior suggest about the bandits?" Ask the students to answer the questions, provide their evidence for the answer, and discuss their reasoning.

Chapter 1 includes many additional places that lend themselves to discussion centering on inferring characterizations. For example, read through page 7 to discuss additional characteristics about Annyrose and O. O. Mary. Students will discover that Annyrose comes from an educated background because of her reactions to the loss of her violin and music by Mozart and Schubert. Additional characteristics of O. O. Mary are also discovered by her actions when she takes letters, horses, and even Annyrose's hair.

The characteristics of Joaquin, the bandit, are introduced through the author's physical descriptions on pages 8 and 9, his reactions to a Yankee on page 11, his reactions to Annyrose's request to accompany him on pages 13 and 14, and his request that Annyrose teaches him how to read. At the close of Chapter 1, students should summarize what they now understand about the characters of Annyrose, O. O. Mary, and Joaquin. They could also consider what they believe will happen in the remainder of the story.

Longer stories, such as *Bandit's Moon,* lend themselves to discussions by chapters. Students can read and discuss several chapters each day. After each session, ask the students to summarize what they know about Annyrose, O. O. Mary, and Joaquin.

The following is a list of a few of the logical places in *Bandit's Moon* to ask questions about implied characterization, and some questions that might be asked and answered. Remember to have students provide evidence for their answers and explore their reasoning.

End of page 16: "What do Annyrose's actions reveal about herself, O. O. Mary, and Joaquin?"

Close of Chapter 2: "What do Joaquin's actions with the stolen horses reveal about him?"

Chapter 3: "Compare what you discovered about both the bandits and Annyrose through their actions and responses related to survival."

Close of Chapter 4: Ask questions about and discuss Joaquin's desires to learn to read and his responses to the reward poster that asks for $1,000 and his increasing the amount to $10,000.

Continue discussing characterization as revealed by the author's use of descriptions, characters' actions, characters' thoughts, and dialogue. By the end of the book, summarize Annyrose's changing responses to Joaquin. This book also includes several important themes that students could discuss. For example, "Injustice and greed are dangerous actions," "There is no honor in mistreating others," and "Revenge is a harmful human motivation."

A comparative study could also be accomplished after the completion of this book. A newspaper headline identifies Joaquin as "The Robin Hood of the Mountains."Students could compare Joaquin's character with that of the British legendary character Robin Hood. Ask students to examine these questions: How are they alike? How are they different? What might have motivated each character to take on his respective role?

Additional Activities to Enhance Phase Four

Here are some activities for children or young adult students related to this phase:

1. Search additional historical fiction stories to identify any references to traditional folklore, values, and beliefs of the culture. What influences do these traditional beliefs have on the characters and conflicts in the historical fiction?
2. As a creative writing activity, choose a character who might have lived during earlier periods of Latino history. Create a fictional story about the character. Refer to the informational books to create believable setting, characterization, and conflict.
3. Using a "You Are There" format, choose an incident from one of Scott O'Dell's books and recreate it as a drama.

Phase Five: Contemporary Literature

How Would Francisco Jimenez or Pablo Neruda Respond to Lack of Latino Influence or Underrepresentation?

An autobiography by Francisco Jimenez and a novel about Pablo Neruda are discussed in the "Survival" section of this text. In his autobiography, Jimenez shows survival strategies that allow him to break out of poverty, become educated, and be a leader in both the academic and social communities. Neruda's survival strategies, such as determination and imagination, allow him to overcome obstacles created by both his father and the political regime that considers him a traitor. Both of these characters display survival strategies that might be useful in facing and solving contemporary problems.

Ask the students to search newspapers and magazines to locate articles about specific problems facing the Latino populations and to consider how Jimenez or Neruda might respond to the problems. What advice would they give? What survival strategies might be the most beneficial for a current problem? For example, they might read Don Van Natta's "Latinos Rise in Numbers, Not Influence" (*New York Times*, April 8, 2011). The author points out that the percentage of Hispanic residents in Orange County, Florida, has jumped 84% in the last decade but their representation on influential political boards has not kept pace with these population numbers. One of the Latino community leaders states: "How do you ignore one-third of the entire population? It's not right" (p. A15). Another Latino resident responded to the lack of Latinos on the redistricting board in the following way: "That's just absolutely atrocious in my mind. It's almost like they are making an effort to suppress the Hispanic representation" (p. A15).

Ask the students to consider how either Jimenez or Neruda would respond to this issue of underrepresentation. Using evidence from the books, ask the students to defend their positions. It might be helpful if they know that Jimenez is the director of an ethnic studies program at a university and Ryan, the author of *The Dreamer,* has won the NEA's Human and Civil Rights Award.

Responding to Courage in Literature

Numerous multicultural literature books develop themes related to the importance of individual courage. These books provide excellent springboards for students to develop a carefully detailed argument and develop a written or oral position about the meaning of courage. This type of activity is designed to help students define, for themselves and the class, the elements of courage. As a consequence of reading a book and debating the subject, they will write a paper that documents what they believe courage is. They will share their ideas and write a group paper that defines courage. Begin the activity by brainstorming the following questions with students: What is courage? When do we know that a person has courage? What are the characteristics we would look for? Write a list of attributes related to courage on the board or on a transparency on an overhead projector.

Select a book to share with students in which courage is an important element; for example, Maia Wojciechowska's *Shadow of a Bull,* which is set in Spain. The book develops a person-against-self conflict as a boy struggles with his own feelings when the men of the village begin training him to become a bullfighter like his father. The boy, however, prefers to be a doctor, but does not know if he has the courage to go against the wishes of the townspeople.

Tell the students that they will be reading or listening to a book about a boy who has a special problem. As they read the book or listen to the book, they will explore these questions: What is courage? Does the boy demonstrate courage? Introduce the book so that students become interested in the subject. For example, you might say the following to students:

> Imagine that you live in Spain. Your father was a famous and fearless bullfighter and the whole town expects you to be just like your father. What would you feel if you were afraid of bulls and if you thought that you were a coward? How would you work it out if you had a dream for a career that was different from that of your father? How would you convince people that it was all right for you to follow your own dream? This is the problem that you will read about in *Shadow of a Bull.* As you read this book, place yourself in Manolo's position. You have your own preferences, but everyone believes you will follow in your dead father's footsteps. Try to imagine Manolo's inner conflicts as he learns to be true to himself. What do you think Manolo learns about himself? What do you think the people in his town discover about Manolo? When you finish this book, try to decide what courage is. Do you believe Manolo is courageous? Why or why not?

As the students read or listen to the book, ask them to be thinking about the question, "What is courage?" For example, is it courageous or cowardly to admit fear of the bull? Is it more courageous to face the bull in the bullring or to face the crowd and to tell them that you prefer being a doctor? After students have finished the book, ask them to write a paragraph on the question "What is courage?" They should decide if they believe Manolo is courageous or cowardly. They should document their answers by providing support from the text.

After students have finished their paragraphs, divide them into writing groups and ask them to share their paragraphs with their peer group. Ask someone in the group to list the various definitions of courage and to list the pros and cons of Manolo's actions that make him either courageous or cowardly. After the group has shared and recorded all of their thoughts, ask them to write a joint paragraph that develops the beliefs of the majority of the students. Make sure they carefully develop their arguments with evidence from the book. After these group papers are completed, share each of the group papers with the total class.

Students may extend this activity into an oral debate as they discuss the various definitions of and attributes related to courage. Again, they should support their arguments with details and evidence. Another extension activity would be to ask students to identify other real-life or literary characters who the students believe demonstrate the characteristics of courage and meet their definitions of what courage is. They can develop a cross-cultural study by identifying and analyzing the theme of the importance of courage in stories from different cultures. For example, courage is important in Gary Paulsen's Native American story *Dogsong,* in Laurence Yep's Chinese American story *Dragon's Gate,* and in Karen Cushman's novel set in early England *The Midwife's Apprentice.*

Analytical Reading of Nancy Farmer's *The House of the Scorpion*

The following series of lessons uses Adler and Van Doren's (1972) stages in analytical reading and applies those stages to the 2003 Newbery Honor recipient and 2002 National Book Award winner, Nancy Farmer's *The House of the Scorpion*. As described in Chapter 1, this is an approach that may be used with the more complex books designed for middle- and upper-elementary grades and into middle school. This guide includes stages and rules that readers can use when outlining a book and later when applying informed criticism of the book. The approach provides excellent guidelines for teachers when they are leading critical discussions with their students. The following example provides an in-depth analysis of how to discuss, analyze, and criticize a book.

Let's now use these stages of analytical reading to discuss, analyze, and criticize a book.

1. Identify and discuss the kind of literature and subject matter in *The House of the Scorpion*. This book is science fiction. Writers of science fiction develop plots around hypothesized scientific advancements and technology. To develop believable stories, authors must provide detailed descriptions of the technology, develop characters who believe in the technology, and create worlds where science interacts with society. We must decide whether or not Farmer has developed a credible science fiction world.
2. Briefly describe the book. Farmer's book develops a hypothetical land between Mexico and the United States. The science fiction characteristics include cloning to create human replacement parts, the development of eejits who work as slave laborers, and the identification of social conflicts that need to be resolved. Matt, a young boy, is a clone who tries to overcome the conflicts resulting from greed, slave labor, and his own treatment by society because he is a clone.

3. List the major parts of the book in order. We can use major incidents in the development of plot and conflict to identify and outline the order of the major events. Such an outline might include the following parts:

    p. 4: There is a foreshadowing of the types of conflict in the book.

    p. 11: Celia's belief reflects danger.

    p. 60: Matt is so frightened when he interacts with people that he cannot talk.

    p. 87: Matt finds the secret passage that plays an important part in the story.

    p. 122: Matt discovers a clone whose brain has been altered and he worries he will also be altered.

    p. 127: The author describes Matt's discoveries through his use of the secret passage.

    p. 138: Tam Lin, the man who cares for Matt, treats him as an equal, causing Matt to change his beliefs about himself.

    p. 149: Tam Lin leaves a chest at the oasis for Matt. The contents of the chest foreshadow the possible trouble to come.

    p. 150: A book in the chest gives Matt needed information about the history of the country and the drug traffic.

    p. 246: Matt escapes and begins his quest to find his friend.

    p. 263: Matt is captured and forced into labor.

    p. 368: After many frightening experiences, Matt goes back to El Patron's estate and discovers he is now the new El Patron.
    p. 380: Matt realizes that with help he can break down the empire of opium and free the slave laborers.

4. Define the problem. As seen from the outline of the conflict and plot, the author has tried to describe problems associated with cloning to replace human parts, controlling slave labor through inserts in the brain, illegal immigration, and the drug trade.
5. Identify and interpret key words. Some of the words students could identify and interpret include *clones, eejits, illegal immigrants,* and *slave labor*.
6. Identify and discuss the most important sentences in the text:

    p. 26: Sentences that identify society's attitudes toward clones.

    p. 145: Sentences describing how people who crossed the borders are turned into eejits.

    p. 147: Sentences that describe the before and after operation that allows people to become eejits.
    p. 191: Find the sentences that foreshadow the plot and conflict.

7. Know the author's arguments by finding them and constructing them out of a sequence of sentences. One of the best ways to discover Farmer's arguments is to identify and discuss the themes in the book. Many of these themes are developed through the beliefs and values expressed by Tam Lin, a close friend and protector of Matt. For example (these are all paraphrased):

    p. 70: When you are small you can choose which way to grow. If you're kind and decent, you grow into a kind and decent person. If you are greedy and evil, you will grow up to be like El Patron.
    p. 139: Matt discovers he needs someone to believe in him. This theme is later displayed through Tam Lin, Celia, and Maria's actions and their trust in Matt.

8. Determine which of the problems the author has solved. The problems in this book cover major issues in society. Students can decide which of the problems may be solved after Matt takes over as El Patron. Will he be able to solve such problems as those related to slave labor, cloning for use of human parts, the use of illegal immigrants, and even the hoarding of wealth?

9–11. Criticism: Before students develop critical judgments of this book, they should conduct their own research into questions like these:

   a. Did Farmer develop a believable description of cloning and the societal issues related to cloning for the use of human part replacements? Why or why not?
   b. Is slave labor a problem along the border? What happens to illegal immigrants and the people who try to influence and control them?
   c. Ask students to review the author's themes. Why or why not do they believe the author supported those themes?

Additional Activities to Enhance Phase Five

Here are some activities for children or young adult students related to this phase:

1. Read a book such as Carmen Lomas Garza's *Family Pictures*. Create your own book that develops the ideas of family pictures. Tell a story about growing up in your family.

2. Read, analyze, and discuss several of the books listed in "Américas Award," *School Library Journal*, August 1999. Consider why the committee might have chosen the books and how they meet the following criteria: distinctive contextualization; exceptional integration of text, illustration, and design; and potential for classroom use.

3. Investigate the background of and the literature written by Gary Soto, one of the prolific authors of Latino literature. What are the recurring themes in the literature?

4. Complete a project similar to one of the ones in Judy Cozzen's *Kids Explore America's Hispanic Heritage*.

5. Perform a play found in Joe Rosenburg's *¡Aplauso!* (the book includes plays for preschool, elementary, and young adult audiences for you to perform). There are plays in English and Spanish. The plays are from a variety of genres. Each play includes background information and guides for staging the plays.

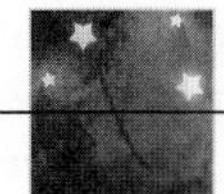

Visualizing Latino Culture

Background Information for Latino Literature

The following texts, many of which are adult references, provide highly illustrated background information about various cultural components and artists.

Robyn Montana Turner's *Georgia O'Keeffe* is a highly illustrated children's biography of a prominent American artist whose paintings feature Southwestern desert scenes.

Charles C. Eldredge's *Georgia O'Keeffe* (1991) is an adult source that includes reproductions of the subjects O'Keeffe painted. The paintings were taken from real life and related to places where she lived. There are scenes from the Southwest such as the Purple Hills and Ghost Ranch in New Mexico.

Robyn Montana Turner's *Frida Kahlo* is a highly illustrated children's biography about the artist, born near Mexico City in 1907. Many of her paintings include Mexican motifs and relate to Mexican folklore. Compare the illustrations with Jonah Winter's *Frida*.

There are numerous adult sources that provide examples of Kahlo's paintings and insights about her life. For example, Elizabeth Carpenter's *Frida Kahlo* (2007) includes sections such as "Mexican Modernist," "Photographic Memory: A Life (And Death) in Pictures," and "Legacy: The Poetics of Self." Andrea Kettenmann's *Kahlo, 1907–1954: Pain and Passion* (2007) is a biography of her life and includes reproductions of her paintings. Helga Prignitz-Poda's *Frida Kahlo: The Painter and Her Work* (2003) is divided into sections according to "Childhood 1907–1925" which discusses Frida's beginnings as a painter; "Frida and Diego's Marriage," which discusses Frida's symbolic language and surrealism; "Crazy Love (1941–1946)," which discusses her public recognition and her inner frailty; and "After 1946," which includes her escape into Buddhism and Stalinism. All of these sources include plates of her paintings and photographs associated with her life.

Two adult sources provide broader presentations of Latin American artists and a history of art. Joseph J. Rishel's *The Arts in Latin America: 1492–1820* (2006) includes sections on decorative arts, textiles, Hispanic silver, Brazilian silver, sculpture, paintings, and furniture. The text includes short biographies of the artists. Edward J. Sullivan's *Latin American Art in the Twentieth Century* (2006) focuses on the works of major contemporary artists from Latin American countries. These two books provide an excellent history of art in Latin America.

Laura Emilia Pacheco Romo's *Mexican Lifestyles* (2002) is an adult source that includes numerous photographs showing subjects such as the people engaged in different activities, handicrafts, typical dress, and museums. These photographs may be especially helpful for authenticating the illustrations in children's books.

Texts for Student Visualization

Numerous books, especially those that are not illustrated, may be read so students visualize and describe what they see in their minds. If desired, students may draw what they visualize. The following books have detailed descriptions of settings.

In Nancy Farmer's *The House of the Scorpion* (Newbery Honor and National Book Award), these pages suggest a few of the possibilities:

p. 79: Tam Lin takes Matt to see the secret oasis.

p. 140: El Patron's storeroom of gifts that is like King Tutankhamun's tomb.

pp. 349–350: Descriptions of celebration of The Day of the Dead. This could be compared with Luis San Vincente's *The Festival of the Bones*.

Joseph Krumgold's . . . *And Now Miguel* (Newbery Award) is based on a full-length documentary film about a boy who wants to accompany his family of sheepherders to the Sangre de Cristo Mountains in New Mexico. Ask each student to select one of the chapters and to draw or describe how they believe the chapter would be depicted in film. They might pretend to be Joseph Krumgold and describe the decisions they would need to make when they are filming this true story.

For a comparative visualization activity, choose an illustrated book and read the text orally to the students without showing them the illustrations. As you read the book, stop and ask students to describe what they see in their minds. Pat Mora's *Tomas and the Library Lady* describes a number of emotional scenes that are good for visualization. For example, Tomas is tired and sad when he leaves his home to follow his family who are migrant workers, he is happy when playing ball with his brother, he is thrilled when he listens to his grandfather telling stories, and he shows his creativity when he visualizes the adventures he reads in the books at the library. Students could also describe what happens to them when, like Tomas, they place themselves into a story. After completing the visualization, they may reread the book and compare Raul Colon's illustrations with the ones they visualized.

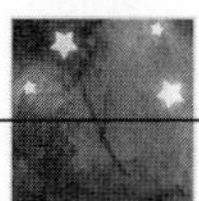

Writing Connections with Latino Literature

During the study of Latino literature and culture, you may choose writing activities that encourage students to utilize cultural information and expand their knowledge of Latino values and beliefs. Numerous activities relate to written composition. For example, rewriting a folktale from a European culture to reflect southwestern settings, cultures, and beliefs in Phase Two; developing a timeline for a famous Latino historical figure and writing a biography about the figure in Phase Three; creating a fictional story about a character from Latino history by using informational books to create believable settings and characterizations or recreating a drama in a "You Are There" format in Phase Four, using information following an analytical reading activity to write a critical evaluation of the book as it might appear in a newspaper in Phase Five.

Ina Cumpiano's *Quinto's Neighborhood/El Vecindario de Quinto* could be used as a model for writing a similar text. In Cumpiano's text a child introduces his family and the people in his community to the readers. This book is written in both English and Spanish; consequently, it could be a model for writing in two languages.

Censorship is frequently mentioned in writing books for children and young adults. Students may have opinions about the subject that could create interesting writing activities. For example, older students may respond to this comment by Diane Ravitch (2003) in *The Language Police: How Pressure Groups Restrict What Students Learn:* "In 2001 Houghton Mifflin (a major publisher of textbooks used in schools) added new criteria for selecting multicultural literature. . . . When choosing stories about Latinos, they must limit those that feature migrant workers and avoid those that are about illegal immigration and religious holidays. Editors are directed to seek out selections by authors who are the same ethnic group that they are describing" (p. 47). Ask students to first discuss this topic orally to gather different responses. They may also choose to create an oral debate in which one either agrees or disagrees with the limiting of Latino literature to certain topics and authors who are Latino. They may respond to this topic in writing by taking a pro or con position on the publishing of Latino literature that will be either read in their school or selected to be included in textbooks. What role do they believe a publisher should take in the selection of stories included in a text or published in novel form?

REFERENCES

Adler, Mortimer J., and Charles Van Doren. *How to Read a Book*. New York: Simon & Schuster, 1972.

"Américas Award" by The Consortium of Latin American Studies Programs. *School Library Journal* 45 (August 1999): 38–39.

Au, Kathryn H. *Literacy Instruction in Multicultural Settings*. San Diego: Harcourt Brace, 1993.

Barrera, Rosalinda B. "Latina and Latino Researchers Interact on Issues Related to Literacy Learning: Conversations." *Reading Research Quarterly* 34 (April/May/June 1999): 217–230.

Beekman, Jeannine Pasini. "Telling and Crafting Stories for Young Listeners." *Storytelling Magazine* 15 (May/June 2003): 27–35.

Bierhorst, John. *The Mythology of Mexico and Central America*. New York: Morrow, 1990.

_____, trans. *History and Mythology of the Aztecs: The Codex Chimalpopoca*. Tucson: University of Arizona Press, 1998.

Coe, Michael. *The Maya*. New York: Thames and Hudson, 1992.

_____, Dean Snow, and Elizabeth Benson. *Atlas of Ancient America*. New York: Facts on File, 1986.

Council on Interracial Books for Children. "Chicano Culture in Children's Literature: Stereotypes, Distortions and Omissions." In *Cultural Conformity in Books for Children,* edited by Donnarae MacCann and Gloria Woodard. Metuchen, N.J.: Scarecrow, 1977.

Dillon, Sam. "U.S. Data Show Rapid Growth in School Rolls." *New York Times* (June 1, 2007): A21.

Fennelly, Katherine. "U.S. Immigration: A Historical Perspective." *The National Voter* 56 (February 2007): 4–7.

Finazzo, Denise Ann. *All for the Children: Multicultural Essentials of Literature*. Albany, N.Y.: Delmar, 1997.

Freidel, David, Linda Schele, and Joy Parker. *Maya Cosmos: Three Thousand Years on the Shaman's Path*. New York: Morrow, 1993.

Gonzalez, David. "What's the Problem with 'Hispanic'? Just Ask a 'Latino.'" *New York Times* (Sunday, November 15, 1992): 6E.

Griego y Maestas, Jose, and Rudolfo A. Anaya. *Cuentos: Tales from the Hispanic Southwest*. Santa Fe: The Museum of New Mexico Press, 1980.

Gugliotta, Guy: "The Maya Glory and Ruin: Saga of a Civilization in Three Parts: The Rise, the Monumental Splendor, and the Collapse." Photographs by Kenneth Garrett, Art by Vania Zouravliov. *National Geographic* 212 (August 2007): 68–85.

Hearne, Betsy. "The Big Picture." *The Bulletin* 51 (April 1998): 271–272.

Helms, Cynthia Newman, ed. *Diego Rivera: A Retrospective*. Founders Society, Detroit, Mich.: Detroit Institute of Arts, 1986.

Horning, Kathleen T., Merri V. Lindgren, Hollis Rudiger, and Megan Schliesman. *CCBC Choices 2005*. Madison: University of Wisconsin, 2005.

Ketner, Mary Grace, reteller. "Sinukuan: A Filipino Folk Tale." *Storytelling Magazine* 19 (March/April 2007): 10.

Levenson, Jay A., ed. *Circa 1492: Art in the Age of Exploration*. New Haven: Yale University Press and Washington, D.C.: National Gallery of Art, 1991.

Lodge, Sally. "Spanish-Language Publishing for Kids in the U.S. Picks Up Speed." *Publishers Weekly* (August 25, 1997): 48–49.

Marek, Nancy Carolyn. "Authenticating *Song of Chirimia—A Guatemalan Folktale*." Paper presented at Texas A&M University, 1994.

Markman, Roberta H., and Peter T. Markman. *The Flayed God: The Mythology of Mesoamerica*. New York: HarperCollins, 1992.

Meyer, Carolyn, and Charles Gallenkamp. *The Mystery of the Ancient Maya*. New York: Atheneum, 1985.

Miller, Mary, and Karl Taube. *The Gods and Symbols of Ancient Mexico and the Maya: An Illustrated Dictionary of Mesoamerican Religion*. New York: Thames and Hudson, 1993.

Morales, Ed. "Who's Buying Books in Spanish & Where Do They Find Them? Meet the Readers." *Criticas: School Library Journal* 2 (November/December 2002): 19–23.

Moseley, Michael E. *The Incas and Their Ancestors: The Archaeology of Peru*. New York: Thames and Hudson, 1992.

National Association of Hispanic and Latino Studies. National Conference. February 21–26, 2000, Houston, Texas.

Norfolk, Simon. "Built to Awe: Mesoamerica's Grand Monuments." *National Geographic* 212 (August 2007): 86–95.

Norton, Donna E. *The Effective Teaching of Language Arts,* 6th ed. Upper Saddle River, N.J.: Merrill/Prentice Hall, 2003.

Norton, Donna E., and Saundra Norton. *Through the Eyes of a Child: An Introduction to Children's Literature,* 3rd ed. Upper Saddle River, N.J.: Merrill/Prentice Hall, 1991, 1995.

Perez-Stable, Maria. "Keys to Exploring Latino Cultures: Folktales for Children." *The Social Studies* 88 (January/February 1997): 29–34.

Philip, Neil. *Mythology of the World*. Boston: Kingfisher, 2004.

Publishers Weekly. "Review of Sid Fleischman's *Bandit's Moon*." (August 3, 1998): 86.

Ravitch, Diane. *The Language Police: How Pressure Groups Restrict What Students Learn*. New York: Knopf, 2003.

Rochman, Hazel. *Against Borders: Promoting Books for a Multicultural World*. Chicago: American Library Association, 1993.

Rohter, Larry. "Driven by Fear, Colombians Leave in Droves." *New York Times* (International, March 5, 2000): 8.

Rosenbaum, David E. "Coast to Coast: Troves of Delegates at Stake on Tuesday." *New York Times* (March 5, 2000): 22.

Schon, Isabel. "Recent Detrimental and Distinguished Books about Hispanic People and Cultures." *Top of the News* 38 (Fall 1981): 79–85.

School Library Journal. "Review of Sid Fleischman's *Bandit's Moon*." (August 3, 1998): 86.

Van Natta, Jr., Don. "Latinos Rise in Numbers, Not Influence." *New York Times* (April 8, 2011): A15.

Vargas, Lucila, and Bruce De Pyssler. "Using Media Literacy to Explore Stereotypes of Mexican Immigrants." *Social Education* 62 (November/December 1998): 407–412.

CHILDREN'S AND YOUNG ADULT LITERATURE REFERENCES

Aardema, Verna. *The Riddle of the Drum: A Tale from Tizapan, Mexico*. Illustrated by Tony Chen. Four Winds, 1979 (I: 6–10 R: 5). o.p.* The man to marry the king's daughter must guess the kind of leather in a drum.

_____. *What's So Funny, Ketu?* Dial Press, 1982 (I: 6–10 R: 5).

Abelove, Joan. *Go and Come Back*. DK, 1998 (I: 14+ R: 6). Set in a Peruvian jungle, the story is told by a cultural anthropologist.

Ada, Alma Flor, and F. Isabel Campoy. *Ten Little Puppies/Diez perritos*. Translated by Rosalma Zubizarreta. Illustrated by Ulises Wensell. HarperCollins, 2011 (I: 3–5). A popular counting rhyme.

Alvarez, Julia. *Return to Sender*. Knopf, 2009 (I: 9–12 R: 5). A family of Mexican workers moves to Vermont.

Ancona, George. *Barrio: José's Neighborhood*. Harcourt Brace, 1998 (I: 6+ R: 4). Photographs enhance a story set in the Mission District of San Francisco.

_____. *¡Ole! Flamenco*. Lee & Low, 2010 (I: 8–10 R: 5). Photographs accompany a photo essay about the history and techniques of flamenco dancing.

Andrews-Goebel, Nancy. *The Pot That Juan Built*. Illustrated by David Diaz. Lee & Low, 2002 (I: all). A cumulative poem about Juan Quezanda.

Atkin, S. Beth, ed. *Voices from the Fields: Children of Migrant Farmworkers Tell Their Stories*. Little, Brown, 1993 (I: 10+). The text includes interviews with nine children.

Behrens, June. *Fiesta!* Photographs by Scott Taylor. Children's Press, 1978 (I: 5–8 R: 4). This book contains photographs of the Cinco de Mayo fiesta.

Bernardo, Anilú. *Jumping Off to Freedom*. Pinata, 1996 (I: 10+ R: 5). A boy and his father flee from Cuba on a raft.

Bertrand, Diane Gonzales. *Sweet Fifteen*. Pinata, 1995 (I: 11+ R: 6). A family prepares for Stephanie's fifteenth birthday.

_____. *Uncle Chente's Picnic/El Picnic de Tio Chente*. Illustrated by Pauline Rodriguez Howard. Pinata Books, 2001 (I: 7+).

Bierhorst, John, ed. *Black Rainbow: Legends of the Incas and Myths of Ancient Peru*. Farrar, Straus & Giroux, 1976 (I: 10+ R: 7). The text includes twenty traditional tales.

_____. *Doctor Coyote: A Native American Aesop's Fables*. Illustrated by Wendy Watson. Macmillan, 1987 (I: all). This fable is from Native Americans in Mexico.

_____, ed. *Lightning Inside You and Other Native American Riddles*. Illustrated by Louise Brierley. Morrow, 1992 (I: 8+). Text includes riddles from southern Mexico and western South America.

_____, ed. *The Monkey's Haircut and Other Stories Told by the Maya*. Illustrated by Robert Andrew Parker. Morrow, 1986 (I: 8+ R: 6). o.p.* This book contains twenty-two tales.

_____. *The Mythology of South America*. Morrow, 1988 (I: 12+ R: 7). o.p.* This is a good resource for information.

_____, trans. *Spirit Child: A Story of the Nativity*. Illustrated by Barbara Cooney. Morrow, 1984 (I: 8–12 R: 6). Pre-Columbian illustrations accompany an Aztec story.

Blackmore, Vivien. *Why Corn Is Golden: Stories about Plants*. Illustrated by Susana Martinez-Ostos. Little, Brown, 1984 (I: all R: 5). This book contains folklore about corn.

Brown, Monica. *My Name Is Gabriela/Me llamo Gabriela: The Life of Gabriela Mistral/la vida de Gabriela Mistral*. Illustrated by John Parra. Luna Rising, 2005 (I: 5–8 R: 4). This poetic text is a biography of a Chilean author.

I = Interest age range
R = Readability by grade level
*o.p. = Books out of print but too good to eliminate

Brown, Tricia. *Hello, Amigos!* Photographs by Fran Ortiz. Holt, Rinehart & Winston, 1986 (I: 3–8 R: 3). Photographs tell the story of a boy on his sixth birthday.

Campoy, F. Isabel, and Alma Flor Ada. *Tales Our Abuelitas Told: A Hispanic Folktale Collection.* Illustrated by Felipe Davalos, Viri Escriva, Susan Guevara, and Leyla Torres. Atheneum, 2006 (I: all). Each story includes notes about the tale.

Canales, Viola. *The Tequila Worm.* Wendy Lamb Books, 2005 (I: YA R: 6). A fourteen-year-old girl discovers the American dream.

Carling, Amelia Lau. *Mama and Papa Have a Store.* Dial, 1998 (I: 3–8 R: 4). A Chinese family have a store in Guatemala City.

Carlson, Lori Marie, ed. *Sol a Sol.* Holt, 1998 (I: all). A collection of bilingual poems.

_____. ed. *Red Hot Salsa: Bilingual Poems on Being Young and Latino in the United States.* Henry Holt, 2005 (I: YA). A collection of poems by authors such as Gary Soto that are written in both English and Spanish.

Carpenter, Elizabeth, ed. *Frida Kahlo.* Minneapolis, Minn.: Walker Art Center, 2007 (I: YA).

Cisneros, Sandra. *The House on Mango Street.* Arte Publico, 1983 (I: 12+ R: 7). A girl records her feelings about her world.

Clark, Ann Nolan. *Secret of the Andes.* Illustrated by Jean Charlot. Viking, 1952, 1980 (I: 8+ R: 5). A boy learns about the traditions of his Inca ancestors.

Cockcroft, James. *Diego Rivera.* Chelsea House, 1991 (I: 10+ R: 6). A biography of the artist written for adolescent readers.

Cozzen, Judy, ed. *Kids Explore America's Hispanic Heritage.* John Muir, 1992 (I: all). This is a report of a school project.

Cumpiano, Ina. *Quinto's Neighborhood/El Vecindario de Quinto.* Illustrated by Jose Ramirez. Children's Book Press, 2005 (I: 4–8 R: 4). Written in English and Spanish, a child introduces his family and the people in his community.

Cushman, K. *The Midwife's Apprentice.* HarperTrophy, 1996 (I: 12+ R: 8).

Deedy, Carmen Agra. *Martina the Beautiful Cockroach: A Cuban Tale.* Illustrated by Michael Austin. Peachtree, 2007 (I: 5–9 R: 4). A cockroach interviews her suitors.

Delacre, Lulu. *Arroz con Leche: Popular Songs and Rhymes from Latin America.* Scholastic, 1989 (I: all). This text includes a variety of songs and poems.

_____. *Salsa Stories.* Scholastic, 2000 (I: all).

dePaola, Tomie. *The Lady of Guadalupe.* Holiday House, 1980 (I: 8+ R: 6). This is a traditional Mexican tale.

DeSpain, Pleasant. *The Dancing Turtle: A Folktale from Brazil.* Illustrated by David Boston. August House, 1998 (I: 5–8 R: 4). An animal uses its wits.

de Trevino, Elizabeth Borton. *I, Juan de Pareja.* Farrar, Straus & Giroux, 1965 (I: 10+ R: 6). The story is set in Spain in the seventeenth century.

Dorson, Mercedes, and Jeanne Wilmot. *Tales from the Rain Forest: Myths and Legends from the Amazonian Indians of Brazil.* Ecco, 1997 (I: 8+ R: 7). A collection of folktales.

Ehlert, Lois. *Moon Rope.* Harcourt Brace, 1992 (I: all). This Peruvian tale is about two animals that try to reach the moon.

Eldredge, Charles C. *Georgia O'Keeffe.* New York: Abrams, 1991.

Emberley, Rebecca. *Let's Go: A Book in Two Languages.* Little, Brown, 1993 (I: 4–8). A picture dictionary of concepts related to places children might go.

_____. *My Day: A Book in Two Languages.* Little, Brown, 1993 (I: 4–8). A picture dictionary of concepts related to daytime activities.

_____. *My House: A Book in Two Languages.* Little, Brown, 1990 (I: 4–8). A picture dictionary shows captioned illustrations of things found in the house.

_____. *Taking a Walk: A Book in Two Languages.* Little, Brown, 1990 (I: 4–8). A picture dictionary showing items a child sees while on a walk.

Engle, Margarita *The Firefly Letters: A Suffragette's Journey to Cuba.* Holt, 2010 (I: YA) A suffragette's journey to Cuba is depicted through poetry.

_____. *The Poet Slave of Cuba: A Biography of Juan Francisco Manzano.* Illustrated by Sean Qualls. Holt, 2006 (I: 12–YA R: 6). This biography is about a poet born into slavery in Cuba in 1797.

_____. *The Surrender Tree: Poems of Cuba's Struggle for Freedom.* Henry Holt, 2008 (I: 10–YA). The poems present the history of the people.

Ets, Marie Hall, and Aurora Labastida. *Nine Days to Christmas: A Story of Mexico*. Illustrated by Marie Hall Ets. Viking, 1959 (I: 5–8 R: 3). Ceci is going to have her first Posada with her own piñata.

Farmer, Nancy. *The House of the Scorpion*. Simon & Schuster/Atheneum, 2002 (I: 10+ R: 6).

Fernandez, Ana Maria. *Amar y otros verbos/To Love and Other Verbs*. Illustrated by Xose Cobas. Everest, 2002 (I: all).

Fleischman, Sid. *Bandit's Moon*. Illustrated by Jos. A. Smith. Greenwillow, 1998 (I: 8+ R: 5). Historical fiction set in the time of the California Gold Rush.

Fritz, Jean, Katherine Paterson, Patricia McKissack, Fredrick McKissack, Margaret Mahy, and Jamake Highwater. *The World in 1492*. Illustrated by Stefano Vitale. Holt, 1992 (I: 8+). The section "The Americas in 1492," written by Jamake Highwater, includes information about the Aztecs and the Incas.

Garza, Carmen Lomas. *Family Pictures*. Children's Book, 1990 (I: 4–8). The illustrations and text in English and Spanish show family scenes.

Gomi, Taro. *Spring Is Here/Llego la Primavera*. Chronicle, 2006 (I: 3–6). The picture book and text follow a calf through the course of a year.

Gonzalez, Ralfka, and Ana Ruiz. *My First Book of Proverbs*. Children's Book, 1995 (I: all). A collection of sayings in English and Spanish.

Greger, C. Shana. *The Fifth and Final Sun: An Ancient Aztec Myth of the Sun's Origin*. Houghton Mifflin, 1994 (I: 8+ R: 5). A myth about the creation of the sun.

Griego y Maestas, Jose, and Rudolfo A. Anaya. *Cuentos: Tales from the Hispanic Southwest*. Illustrated by Jaime Valdez. Museum of New Mexico, 1980 (I: 9+ R: 5). This is a collection of tales.

Griego, Margot C. *Tortillitas para Mama and Other Spanish Nursery Rhymes*. Illustrated by Barbara Cooney. Holt, Rinehart & Winston, 1981 (I: 3–7). Nursery rhymes appear in Spanish and English.

Griswold del Castillo, Richard. *Cesar Chavez: The Struggle for Justice*. Illustrated by Anthony Accardo. Pinata Books, 2002 (I: 9+ R: 5).

Hall, Lynn. *Danza!* Scribner's, 1981 (I: 10+ R: 6). A boy and his horse share life on a farm in Puerto Rico.

Hamilton, Virginia. *In the Beginning: Creation Stories from Around the World*. Illustrated by Barry Moser. Harcourt Brace, 1988 (I: all R: 5). The text includes a creation story from the Mayan people of Guatemala.

Hayes, Joe. *Estrellita de oro/Little Gold Star: A Cinderella Cuento*. Illustrated by Gloria Osuna Perez and Lucia Angela Perez. Cinco Puntos Press, 2000 (I: 8+).

Henkes, Kevin. *So Happy!* Illustrated by Anita Lobel. Greenwillow, 2005 (I: 4–8 R: 4). A highly illustrated book about a boy, a seed, and a rabbit.

Hernandez, Avelino. *That Boy and That Old Man*. Illustrated by Federico Delicado. Kalandraka, 2002 (I: 8+).

Herrera, Juan Felipe. *Calling the Doves*. Illustrated by Elly Simmons. Children's Press, 1995 (I: all R: 5). The story of an immigrant family.

Hinojosa, Francisco, adapter. *The Old Lady Who Ate People*. Illustrated by Leonel Maciel. Little, Brown, 1984 (I: all R: 6). o.p.* These four frightening folktales are from Mexico.

Hinojosa, Tish. *Cada niño/Every Child: A Bilingual Songbook for Kids*. Illustrated by Lucia Angela Perez. Cinco Puntos Press, 2002 (I: all).

Hobbs, Will. *Crossing the Wire*. HarperCollins, 2006 (I: 10–YA R: 6). The author describes the dangerous trip north from Mexico.

Jaramillo, Ann. *La linea*. Roaring Brook, 2006 (I: 10–YA R: 6). The author describes the harsh realities of crossing the border.

Jimenez, Francisco. *Reaching Out*. Houghton Mifflin, 2008 (I: YA R: 7). This autobiography tells the story of a young Hispanic man whose dreams for a better life bring considerable success.

Kalnay, Francis. *Chucaro: Wild Pony of the Pampa*. Harcourt, Brace, 1958 (I: 8+). Winner of the 1959 Newbery Honor.

Keep, Richard. *Clatter Bash!: A Day of the Dead Celebration*. Peach Tree, 2004 (I: all). A highly illustrated book about the celebration.

Kettlenmann, Andrea. *Kahlo, 1907–1954: Pain and Passion*. Los Angeles: Taschen, 2007 (I: YA).

Knutson, Barbara. *Love and Roast Chicken: A Trickster Tale from the Andes Mountains*. Carolrhoda, 2004 (I: 6–10 R: 4). A clever guinea pig outsmarts a fox.

Krumgold, Joseph. *. . . And Now Miguel*. Illustrated by Jean Charlot. Crowell, 1953 (I: 10+ R: 3). Miguel Chavez is a member of a proud sheep-raising family.

Lattimore, Deborah. *The Flame of Peace: A Tale of the Aztecs*. Harper & Row, 1987 (I: all R: 6). This story is based on Aztec mythology.

Luna, James. *The Runaway Piggy/El cochiniyo fugitivo*. Translated by Carolina Villarroel. Illustrated by Laura Lacarrara. Arte Publico, 2010 (I: 5–8 R: 4). This folktale is similar to "The Gingerbread Boy."

Marrin, Albert. *Aztecs and Spaniards: Cortes and the Conquest of Mexico*. Atheneum, 1986 (I: 12+ R: 7). This book is a history of the Aztecs and tells about the influence of Cortes.

McCaughrean, Geraldine. *The Bronze Cauldron: Myths and Legends of the World*. Illustrated by Bee Willey. Margaret K. McElderry, 1998 (I: 8+ R: 4). Includes a Mayan myth.

McDermott, Gerald. *Musicians of the Sun*. Simon & Schuster, 1997 (I: all). An Aztec myth.

Meltzer, Milton. *The Hispanic Americans*. Photographs by Morrie Camhi and Catherine Noren. Crowell, 1982 (I: 9–12 R: 6). Puerto Ricans, Chicanos, and Cubans have influenced the United States.

Meyer, Carolyn, and Charles Gallenkamp. *The Mystery of the Ancient Maya*. Atheneum, 1985 (I: 10+ R: 8). This book tells about early explorers and discoveries.

Mikaelsen, Ben. *Sparrow Hawk Red*. Hyperion/Little, Brown, 1993 (I: 10+ R: 6). A thirteen-year-old boy tries to avenge his mother's murder by drug smugglers.

Mohr, Nicholasa. *Going Home*. Dial, 1986 (I: 10+ R: 6). Twelve-year-old Felita spends the summer with relatives in Puerto Rico.

Mora, Pat. *The Bakery Lady*. Illustrated by Pablo Torrecilla. Pinata Books, 2001 (I: 7+ R: 4).

_____. *The Race of Toad and Deer*. Orchard, 1995. (I: all) An adaptation of a fable.

_____. *Tomas and the Library Lady*. Illustrated by Raul Colon. Knopf, 1997 (I: 7+ R: 4).

Myers, Walter Dean. *Scorpions*. Harper & Row, 1998. (I: 11+ R: 5). A boy has difficulties with a gang.

O'Dell, Scott. *The Amethyst Ring*. Houghton Mifflin, 1983 (I: 10+ R: 6). This is the final story of Julian Escobar.

_____. *The Black Pearl*. Illustrated by Milton Johnson. Houghton Mifflin, 1967 (I: 10+ R: 6). A boy dreams of finding a wonderful pearl while pearl diving.

_____. *The Captive*. Houghton Mifflin, 1979 (I: 10+ R: 6). A young Spanish seminarian named Julian Escobar witnesses the exploitation of the Maya during the 1500s.

_____. *Carlota*. Houghton Mifflin, 1981 (I: 10+ R: 6). A high-spirited Spanish American girl fights beside her father during the days of the Mexican War in early California.

_____. *The Feathered Serpent*. Houghton Mifflin, 1981 (I: 10+ R: 6). This book is the sequel to *The Captive*.

_____. *The King's Fifth*. Houghton Mifflin, 1966 (I: 10+ R: 6). Esteban de Sandoval accompanies Coronado's army in search of the cities of gold.

Orozco, Jose-Luis. *Ten Little Fingers and Other Play Rhymes and Action Songs from Latin America*. Illustrated by Elisa Kleven. Dutton, 1997 (I: 4+). Music and words in Spanish and English.

Paulsen, Gary. *The Crossing*. Doubleday, 1987 (I: 12+ R: 6). The harsh realities of a border town are developed as a boy longs to cross into the United States.

_____. *Dogsong*. Simon Pulse, 1999.

_____. *Sisters/Hermanas*. Harcourt Brace, 1993 (I: 12+ R: 6). Two girls, one Mexican and one Anglo, discover they have many similarities.

Perl, Lila. *The Ancient Maya*. Watts, 2005 (I: 10+ R: 5). This nonfiction presents a history of the early culture through discussions about rulers, priests, and artisans.

Politi, Leo. *Pedro, the Angel of Olvera Street*. Scribner's, 1946 (I: 5–8 R: 4). Winner of the 1947 Newbery Honor.

_____. *Song of the Swallows*. Scribner's, 1949 (I: 5–8 R: 4). Juan lives in Capistrano, California.

Prago, Albert. *Strangers in Their Own Land: A History of Mexican-Americans*. Four Winds, 1973 (I: 10+ R: 7). This book traces both the history and the difficulties of Mexican Americans.

Prignitz-Poda, Helga. *Frida Kahlo: The Painter and Her Work*. Schirmer/Mosel, 2003.

Reinhard, Johan. *Discovering the Inca Ice Maiden: My Adventures on Ampato*. National Geographic, 1998 (I: 8+ R: 4). Photographs show the discovery.

Rishel, Joseph J., organized by. *The Arts in Latin America: 1492–1820*. New Haven: Yale University Press, 2006 (I: YA).

Ritter, John H. *Under the Baseball Moon*. Philomel, 2006 (I: 12–YA R: 6). A teenager who plays the trumpet has a friendship with a girl who is a softball pitcher.

Rohmer, Harriet, and Mary Anchondo. *How We Came to the Fifth World*. Children's Book Press, 1988 (I: all R: 5). This is an Aztec version of creation.

_____, Octavio Chow, and Morris Viduare. *The Invisible Hunters.* Illustrated by Joe Sam. Children's Press, 1987 (I: all R: 5). The tale reflects the impact of European traders.

_____, and Dorminster Wilson. *Mother Scorpion Country.* Illustrated by Virginia Steams. Children's Press, 1987 (I: all R: 4). A Central American tale is written in both English and Spanish.

Romo, Laura Emilia Pacheco. *Mexican Lifestyles.* Mexico: Atrium Group, 2002.

Rosenberg, Joe. *¡Aplauso!.* Pinata, 1995 (I: all). Hispanic children's plays.

Ryan, Pam Muñoz. *Becoming Naomi León.* Scholastic, 2004 (I: 10+ R: 4). A girl discovers her Mexican heritage.

_____. *The Dreamer.* Illustrated by Peter Sis. Scholastic, 2010 (I: 9–YA R: 6). A novel about the Chilean poet Pablo Neruda, a Nobel Prize winner.

Saenz, Benjamin Alire. *A Gift from Papa Diego.* Illustrated by Geronimo Garcia. Cinco Puntos, 1998 (I: 7+). A story in English and Spanish about a boy's love for his grandfather.

San Souci, Robert D. *Little Gold Star: A Spanish American Cinderella.* Illustrated by Sergio Martinez. HarperCollins, 2000 (I: 7+ R: 5).

San Vincente, Luis. *The Festival of the Bones.* Translated by John Williams and Bobby Byrd. Cinco Puntos, 2002 (I: all).

Schaefer, Jack. *Old Ramon.* Houghton Mifflin, 1960 (I: 8+ R: 5). Winner of the 1961 Newbery Honor.

Schertle, Alice, trans. *Pio Peep! Traditional Spanish Nursery Rhymes.* Illustrated by Vivi Esciva. HarperCollins, 2003 (I: all).

Sonneborn, Liz. *The Ancient Aztecs.* Watts, 2005 (I: 10+ R: 5). This nonfiction presents a history of the early culture through discussions about rulers, priests, and artisans.

Soto, Gary. *Buried Onions.* Harcourt Brace, 1997 (I: YA R: 6). A young Mexican American lives in Fresno, Calif.

_____. *Pacific Crossing.* Harcourt Brace Jovanovich, 1992 (I: 10+ R: 6). In a sequel to *Taking Sides,* boys from the barrio in San Francisco participate in an exchange program in Japan.

_____. *Taking Sides.* Harcourt Brace Jovanovich, 1991 (I: 10+ R: 6). A boy faces problems of loyalty as his new basketball team meets the old team from the barrio.

Storace, Patricia. *Sugar Cane: A Caribbean Rapunzel.* Illustrated by Raúl Colón. Hyperion, 2007 (I: 5–9 R: 4). A variant on the tale.

Sullivan, Edward J., ed. *Latin American Art in the Twentieth Century.* London: Phaidon Press, 2006.

Temple, Frances. *Grab Hands and Run.* Orchard, 1993 (I: 10+ R: 6). Twelve-year-old Felipe tells about his family's attempts to leave El Salvador after the disappearance of his father.

Tonatiuh, Duncan. *Dear Primo: A Letter to My Cousin.* Abrams, 2010 (I: 6–8 R: 4). Letters contrast life in Mexico and the United States.

Turner, Robyn Montana. *Frida Kahlo: Portraits of Women Artists for Children.* Boston: Little, Brown, 1993 (I: all). A biography of a great Mexican artist.

_____. *Georgia O'Keefe: Portraits of Women Artists for Children.* Boston: Little, Brown, 1991(I: 9+ R: 5).

Van Laan, Nancy. *So Say the Little Monkeys.* Illustrated by Yumi Heo. Atheneum, 1998 (I: all). A rhythmic text set in Brazil.

Volkmer, Jane Anne, reteller. *Song of Chirimia: A Guatemalan Folktale.* Carolrhoda Books, 1990 (I: 6–10 R: 5). A Mayan folktale in English and Spanish tells how a man tries to win the hand of a Mayan princess.

Watson, James. *Talking in Whispers.* Victor Gollancz, 1983 (I: 12+ R: 7). In a political thriller, a boy survives against an oppressive military government.

Wilford, John Noble. "Stones Said to Contain Earliest Writing in Western Hemisphere." *New York Times* (September 15, 2006): A8.

Winter, Jeanette. *Diego.* Scholastic. 1991 (I: 8+ R: 5). A biography of the artist written for younger readers.

Winter, Jonah. *Frida.* Illustrated by Ana Juan. Scholastic, 2002 (I: 6+ R: 4). A highly illustrated biography of the Mexican artist Frida Kahlo.

Wisniewski, David. *Rain Player.* Clarion, 1991 (I: 5–8 R: 5). Paper constructions enhance this Mayan tale.

Wojciechowska, Maia. *Shadow of a Bull.* Illustrated by Alvin Smith. Atheneum, 1964 (I: 10+ R: 5). Manolo discovers that true bravery is not always in the bullring.

Yep, L. *Dragon's Gate.* HarperTrophy, 1995 (I: 10+ R: 6).

Chapter 5
Asian Literature

Asian literature encompasses the rich and diverse cultural and ethnic heritage found in such countries as China, India, Japan, Vietnam, and Korea. Asian American literature also shows the impact of immigrating to a new country, with the Asian characters trying to retain their previous culture and adjust to new situations.

In this chapter, we consider cultures that have long histories and considerable influences. For example, according to Michael Kampen O'Riley (2006) the traditional name of China, Zhongquo (Middle Kingdom) may date back to the Xia dynasty (c 2205–1700 BCE). O'Riley states: The Middle Kingdom "envisions China as the hub of the world, the place through which all power flows. The emperors, sons of heaven, mediated between the hub of the world, humankind, and the heavens. The modern name, China, comes from Qin, the name of the first imperial dynasty, established in 221 BCE" (p. 100). As we study literature from India, we discover the worldwide influence of ancient religions such as Buddhism and Hinduism and the influence of Buddhists who strive for enlightenment and inner peace.

The early Japanese literature and culture reflect influences from China and Korea. During the ninth century, the Japanese felt the need to separate themselves from foreign influences and close their borders to the outside world. Consequently, they devised new Japanese forms of Buddhism, courtly styles of art, and a new social order. O'Riley states that through this process, the "emperors eventually lost most of their political powers to the shoguns, secular leaders who stood at the apex of a complex feudal society" (p. 152).

Asian literature provides readers with opportunities to explore various cultures through a wide variety of literary genres. For example, the folklore of India includes the Jataka tales, which are fables associated with Gautama Buddha. The folklore collected from Chinese Americans indicates how the people brought their beliefs, values, and stories with them when they came to a new land. Informational books about China take readers back to the time of the Silk and Spice routes and encourage them to understand how the routes supported the movement of ideas, industry, and religious beliefs. Historical fiction set in feudal Japan or in early China encourages readers to grasp such important themes as the need for people to overcome racial and cultural conflicts if they are to gain self-respect. Historical fiction set in an earlier United States develops the importance of the Chinese Americans as they worked on the transcontinental railroad or shows how people acculturate to a new land while maintaining their ethnic identities. Through contemporary literature, readers discover how characters develop cross-cultural understanding, as well as face and overcome conflicts in their own lives.

In addition to reading the Asian American literature for pleasure and appreciation, students need to develop an understanding of the literature and the cultures. The increasing numbers of Asian immigrants to the United States—and high numbers of Asian Americans in the overall population—make an understanding of Asian culture and the literature very important.

Asian Timeline

3000–1500 BCE	Development of many of the great Hindu stories found in the Mahabharata
563–483 BCE	Period in which Gautama Buddha lived and taught in India
100 BCE to 1500 CE	Silk Route main trade link between East and West
Circa 2,000 years ago	Jataka tales, or stories of Buddha's former birth, with teachings, beliefs, and values associated with the Buddhist religion
681	Order by Emperor Temmu to place Japanese traditions into writing
Circa 800	Tuan Ch'eng Shih's *Yu Yang Tsa Tsy,* early Chinese "Cinderella"
1100–1350	Many Japanese tales collected
1160	Birth of Mongol leader, Ghengis Khan, who conquered Persia and China
Late 1600s	Tales of the supernatural collected in Shandong (Shantung) province (*The Beggar's Magic*)
Late 1800s	2,000 tales collected, translated, and published by Indian scholars, civil servants, and foreign missionaries
1926	Newbery: Arthur Bowie Chrisman's *Shen of the Sea*
1933	Newbery: Elizabeth Forman Lewis's *Young Fu of the Upper Yangtze*
1935	Newbery Honor: Elizabeth Seeger's *Pageant of Chinese History*
1939	Caldecott: Thomas Handforth's *Mei Li*
1941	Bombing of Pearl Harbor and start of World War II for the United States
1951	Newbery Honor: Jeanette Eaton's *Gandhi, Fighter Without a Sword*
1956	Caldecott Honor: Taro Yashi ma's *Crow Boy*
1973	Caldecott: Artist Blair Lent's *The Funny Little Woman*
1976	Newbery Honor and Children's Book Award: Laurence Yep's *Dragonwings*
1980	Hans Christian Andersen International Medal: Illustrator Suekichi Akaba (Japan)
1983	Mildred L. Batchelder Award: Toshi Maruki's *Hiroshima No Pika*
1984	Hans Christian Andersen International Medal: Illustrator Mitsumasa Anno (Japan)
1986	Newbery Honor: Rhoda Blumberg's *Commodore Perry in the Land of the Shogun*
1989	Nobel Peace Prize awarded to the Dalai Lama
1989	Caldecott Honor: Artist Allen Say's *The Boy of the Three-Year Nap*
1994	Caldecott: Allen Say's *Grandfather's Journey*
1994	Newbery Honor: Laurence Yep's *Dragon's Gate*
1994	Hans Christian Andersen International Medal: Illustrator Michio Mado (Japan)
1997	Mildred L. Batchelder Award: Peter Sis's *Tibet: Through the Red Box*
2000	National Book Award: Gloria Whelan's *Homeless Bird*
2001	Newbery Award: Linda Sue Park's *A Single Shard*
2005	Newbery Award: Cynthia Kadohata's *Kira-Kira*
2006	Charlotte Zolotow Honor Award: Jon J. Muth's *Zen Shorts*
2010	Newbery Honor: Grace Lin's *Where the Mountain Meets the Moon*
2011	Newbery Honor: Margi Preus's *Heart of a Samurai*

In this chapter, we investigate values that are part of the cultures, discuss stereotypes in literature from the past, consider criteria for evaluating Asian and Asian American literature, and discuss examples of the literature from various Asian countries, as well as literature that reflects an Asian American perspective.

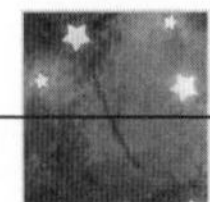

Values That Are Part of the Cultures

Before we consider the inappropriateness of stereotypes of Asian literature from the past or evaluate and discuss the literature from various Asian cultures, it is helpful to identify some of the values from those cultures. Scholars who investigate traditional values provide us with important information for analyzing the values and beliefs embedded in folklore and historical literature. Those who analyze the values in contemporary Asian cultures provide helpful sources for analyzing contemporary literature, as well as more traditional stories.

Donald Holzman (1998) provides a very useful analysis of the importance of filial piety in China since the earliest times and as part of the Confucian canon. Holzman traces the importance of this respect for ancestors and the utmost regard for parents when he states, "That a son should love his parents is fate—you cannot erase this from his heart—to serve your parents and be content to follow them anywhere—this is the perfection of filial piety" (p. 190). Filial piety was so important in the early stories that extreme cases of filial piety provoked supernatural intervention in favor of such children, as well as rewards for this behavior. In addition to filial piety, Holzman identifies the values of reaching the gods through one's ancestors; punishing unfilial conduct; and respecting and developing the virtues of righteousness, love, goodness, and truth.

In an interview with Leonard Marcus (2000) in *Publishers Weekly,* Laurence Yep discusses his difficulty in his writing when he tries to bridge two cultures. He states,

> Now, though, I am not so sure that it is possible to blend two cultures together. Asia cultures are family- and cooperation-oriented. American culture on the other hand emphasizes the individual and competition. The two cultures pull in opposite directions. So I see myself now as someone who will always be on the border between two cultures. That works to my benefit as a writer because not quite fitting in helps me be a better observer. (p. 101)

Holland Cotter (2002) analyzes ancient Chinese art to suggest that the images from nature express ethical dilemmas for the people, provide ethical guidance for the early Chinese, and suggest important values in the culture. For example, the bamboo and the flowering plum symbolize resilience and embattled survival because the bamboo weathers devastating storms by relying on resilience and the flowering plum blooms even in the snow and is a forerunner of spring. Cotter believes the spirit of patience in adversity is an important theme in Chinese art and suggests the following Chinese values: patience is a virtue, haste makes waste, and we are responsible for nature. This responsibility toward nature is why "China imbued mountains and flowers with moral consciousness" (p. B27). In the visualization section later in this chapter, we search for some of these values in art. We also search for these values in poetry.

Robert Beer (2003) identifies and discusses the importance of the "Five Buddhas" or the "Five Enlightened Families." He states, "Essentially the Five Buddhas represent the transmutation of the five delusions or poisons (ignorance, desire, jealousy, and pride) into the five transcendent windows (all-pervading, discriminating, mirror-like, all-accomplishing, and equanimous)" (p. 234). His illustrations and examples showing symbolism, themes, and motives depicted in Buddhist literature and art are helpful for the analysis of the literature and the identification of important values of the culture.

Additional contemporary values are identified by Gail M. Hickey (1998) and Nancy K. Freeman (1998). Hickey identifies the following cultural values as exemplified by recent Southeast Asian immigrants to the United States: respect for parents, family, and elders and emphasis on children's academic success as a way to elevate personal and family status. Freeman stresses that Eastern cultures emphasize community, cooperation, and interrelatedness. She compares these values with Western cultural values that are apt to foster individualism, competition, and personal possessions. She believes such differences in cultural values may result in cultural conflicts.

As we proceed with the analysis of literature from various Asian cultures, try to identify the importance of these cultural values. Which are found in traditional literature? Which are found in more contemporary literature? Which values may be found in both traditional and contemporary literature? How do the values reflect the various Asian cultures? Are there differences in the values depicted in some of the earlier children's books about Asian cultures and more recent editions?

Concerns over Stereotypes in Literature from the Past

Fortunately today there are many more excellent books written from an Asian or Asian American perspective than there were in the past. In 1976, the Asian American Children's Book Project (Council on Interracial Books for Children, 1977) identified sixty-six books with Asian American central characters, and most of these books were about Chinese Americans. The members of the project concluded that with only a few exceptions the books were grossly misleading. They presented stereotypes suggesting that all Asian Americans look alike, choose to live in "quaint" communities in the midst of large cities, and cling to "outworn, alien" customs. The project also criticized the books because they tended to measure success by the extent to which Asian Americans have assimilated white middle-class values and because they implied that hard work, learning to speak English, and keeping a low profile would enable Asian Americans to overcome adversity and be successful.

The stereotypes in earlier books were undoubtedly influenced by the Chinese Exclusion Act, passed by Congress in 1882. Katherine Fennelly (2007) states that this legislation "forever changed American's relationship to immigration by endorsing definitions of race and class as criteria to define particular groups as 'undesirable aliens'" (p. 5). Additional information about this act is reported by Lee (2002).

It is interesting to compare the older books and the stereotypes with the image of Asians and Asian Americans in the more recent books. As you read contemporary books about Asian Americans, you may consider the impact of Asian Americans on the U.S. educational system and their potential for influencing all aspects of U.S. life.

One of the reasons for this change of attitude toward Asian cultures is highlighted by Natasha Degen (2006) when she describes the increase in the non-Asian students who attend Chinese American International Schools in America. She states, "School officials attribute the changes largely to a growing awareness of China as a global economic force, and to a strong sense among parents that learning Chinese could help their children professionally" (p. C19). She reports that schools that teach Chinese language and culture are increasingly attracting non-Asian students. Several states including Kentucky, Minnesota, Washington, Ohio, Kansas, and West Virginia are developing Chinese language and cultural curriculums for public schools.

The new stereotype of Asia Americans is one of high achievement as revealed by Timothy Egan (2007) in his report about the percentage of Asian American students who are enrolled in American universities. For example, 46% of freshmen at Berkeley are Asian. Other universities with high percentages of Asian students include Stanford (24%), Harvard (18%), MIT (27%), and Carnegie Mellon (24%). These percentages are considered high because Asians make up 5% of the U.S. population.

Asian Folklore

Folklore collected from Asian cultures, like other folklore, portrays the feelings, struggles, and aspirations of common people; depicts the lives of the well-to-do; and reflects the moral values, superstitions, social customs, and humor of the times and societies in which they originated. Like medieval Europe, ancient Asia contained societies in which royalty and nobles led lives quite different from those of peasants. Females had less freedom and social influence than did males. Asian tales tell about the rich and the poor, the wise and the foolish, mythical quests, lovers, animals, and supernatural beings and powers, common to all folklore, but they also reflect the customs and beliefs of specific cultures. In this section on Asian folklore, we explore in depth the folklore from China, India, and Japan. We also review some of the folklore from other Asian countries.

Folklore from China

Chinese folktales are of ancient origin. For example, Maria Leach (1972) maintains that complete versions of many of the Marchenforscher (folktales) were published in China hundreds of years before they were published in Europe. "Thus Des Perrier's story of Pernette in Nouvelles Récréations, 1558, the first European version of one of the complete Cinderellas, was anticipated in China by 700 years in Tuan Ch'eng Shih's *Yu Yang Tsa Tsy,* published in the middle of the T'ang Dynasty" (p. 228).

Difficulties Associated with the Study of Chinese Folklore Long before published versions appeared, the folklore of China had stratified into the lore of the aristocrats and the lore of the populace. During the centuries, Chinese folklore had been modified by the rise of various philosophical schools, the migration of religious systems, and changes in politics. The influences of philosophical schools, religious systems, and politics all cause difficulties for those who are studying the folklore. Leach (1972) identifies the following causes for some of the difficulties associated with the study of Chinese folklore:

1. Chinese folklore extends over a long period of time and was collected from vast territories without clearly defined boundaries.
2. The Chinese nation includes a mixture of many cultures.
3. Stories were borrowed and adapted among many cultures.
4. The scholarly class had great power and prestige and consequently influenced the collection, telling, and publishing of the tales.
5. The Chinese written language is considered the property of the scholars, and thus the written materials may be distorted. The priestly class reworked and rationalized the folklore.
6. Extensive collections were gathered by missionaries who were eager to demonstrate the evil effects of the superstitions of others or by ethnographers attempting to impose European standards on Chinese data; consequently, some of the stories are incomplete and fail to demonstrate the variations of custom and belief in the various parts of China.

As we read and interpret the folklore, we must remember the possible influences of each of these factors.

Early Beliefs That Influence the Folklore As in any other folklore, an understanding of the early beliefs and customs of the Chinese people is necessary before we try to analyze and

ISSUE Evaluating Asian Literature

Following their study in the stereotypes found in the earlier Asian American literature, the Council on Interracial Books for Children (1977) recommended the following criteria for evaluating Asian American literature:

1. The book should reflect the realities and way of life of Asian American people. Is the story accurate for the historical period and cultural context? Are the characters from a variety of social and economic levels? Does the plot exaggerate the exoticism or mysticism of the customs and festivals of the Asian American culture? Are festivals in the perspective of everyday activities?
2. The book should transcend stereotypes. Do the Asian American characters handle their own problems, or do they require benevolent intervention from a white person? Do the characters have to make a definite choice between two cultures, or is there an alternative in which the two cultures can mingle? Do the characters portray a range of human emotions, or are they docile and uncomplaining? Are there obvious occupational stereotypes—do all Asian Americans work in laundries or restaurants?
3. The literature should seek to rectify historical distortions and omissions.
4. The characters in the book should avoid the model minority and super minority syndromes. Are the characters respected for themselves, or must they display outstanding abilities to gain approval?
5. The literature should reflect an awareness of the changing status of women in society. Does the author provide role models for girls other than subservient females?
6. The illustrations should reflect the racial diversity of Asian Americans. Are the characters all look-alikes, with the same skin tone and exaggerated features, such as slanted eyes? Are clothing and settings appropriate to the culture depicted?

Some researchers maintain that many of the older stereotypical books should be placed in an historical collection rather than used with children. They provide guidelines for evaluating the literature that are very similar to those just listed.

In a study of the images of Chinese and Chinese Americans found in seventy-three picture storybooks, Cai (1994) concluded,

> Most of the picture books that have been subjected to scrutiny in this survey present quite positive images of Chinese and Chinese Americans and give the reader a sense of the Chinese culture. A number of authors and illustrators have turned out many artistically commendable and culturally authentic works. While biased stereotypical portraits have not been eliminated, cultural inauthenticity is the main flaw of many books exhibited in both the content of the texts and the details of the illustrations. To transmit accurate information and to maintain the integrity of the culture, authors and illustrators are obligated to undertake earnest research in that culture. Imagination alone cannot help them to cross cultural gaps. Inexact scholarship will inevitably lead to ridiculous misrepresentation. (p. 188)

As you conduct your own research in Asian literature and read and evaluate the literature, be aware of the necessity of evaluating the literature for both stereotypes and for authenticity of text and illustrations.

understand the folklore. For example, "yin-yang" is a basic concept in early Chinese cultures. The yin-yang provides a balance among positive and negative forces of the universe such as male-female and heaven-earth.

During early periods in the history of China, the priests and cults formed powerful influences. A belief in the use of oracle bones to tell the future was part of the aristocratic cult in the Shang dynasty (1766–1122 BCE). The wu priests were part of the Shang culture; they operated in both the aristocratic and the popular cults. The priest kings had their own cults involving heaven, earth, soil, grain, and ancestor worship. Ancestor worship was highly developed in the earliest records.

Beliefs about the soul influenced the early culture. The cults maintained that humans had two souls: an animal soul, p'o, which is created at the moment of conception, and the spirit soul, hun, which enters the body at birth. P'o follows the dead body to its tomb and is nourished by the sacrifices of descendants, and it is dissipated as the body disintegrates. In the early historic times in China, the soul of the aristocrat was followed by the sacrifice of his wives and retainers. In later times, papier-mâché figures were burned at the grave. It is not only human souls, however, that deserve homage. Homage is also paid to the spirits of rivers and mountains.

Several philosophies also influenced Chinese folklore. For example, during the Chou dynasty, the philosophers, historians, and theologians preserved and reinterpreted the ancient beliefs and customs. Confucianists maintained that the Chinese must return to the practices of the wise rulers of earlier times. Tales that illustrate the Confucian philosophies frequently reflect the superior orders of emperor, father, and husband. In contrast, the Taoist philosophers were social critics who opposed the Confucians. Their populist view found their way into many of the tales. Moss states that one of the purposes for Taoist literature was to publicize the crimes of the mighty and the injustices suffered by the ordinary people including children and women—and even injustices suffered by animals. The Taoists had a central leader and thousands of priests and nuns who devoted their lives to the attainment of The Way. As you read the folklore, try to identify the philosophy that is being developed through the story.

Types of Tales and General Elements in Chinese Folklore The important plots and themes in these Chinese tales include transformations of humans into beasts and beasts into humans; trials involving perilous encounters with humans or supernatural creatures; dragon lore that features human involvement in the family feuds of dragon clans; revelations of what is in store for humans in the future and dream phenomena; and supernatural, fantastic elements. According to Kao (1985), these tales are especially important because they influenced later fiction and served as a source of allusions for poetry and often provided the plots for the dramas of the Yuan and Ming dynasties.

Gia-Zhen Wang (2006) maintains that "In Chinese folklore, there exists a traditional theme of animals and plants that, having lived on Earth for thousands of years, have absorbed the essence of Heaven, Earth, Sun, and Moon and thus develop the ability to transform themselves into human forms. The bad spirits in such animals and plants would exploit their morphing powers to prey on humans. The good spirits would long to become part of human society and would try hard to blend in" (p. 42 "Notes on the Stories").

Certain elements and motifs may be found in much of the Chinese folklore. For example, the universe is governed by Shang Ti, thought to be the Supreme Ruler of Heaven, or Yu Huang, the Jade Emperor, the highest of all things, physical or spiritual. Gods such as the Gods of the Cities and Villages control life. The Kitchen God controls life in the home and reports once a year on the behavior of each family. These deities are very important. Temples of the Gods of Place or Locality are scattered throughout the fields and are believed to allow the peasants to have a direct approach to Heaven. Heaven decrees the moment of death, when the soul is judged according to the Book of Destiny, which contains a record of all the acts of an individual. Following a family member's death, the disposition, repose, and happy journey of the soul are matters of great importance to the family.

Demons, spirits, and ghosts are important in the folklore. The two souls of a person may mingle with the throng of demons, spirits, and ghosts. During sleep, the superior soul leaves the body and goes about its own affairs—which become the substance of dreams. The souls of humans, animals, and things enjoy the pleasures and vices enjoyed by living human beings.

Fortune-telling, oracle bones, and astrology are considered complex sciences. The results of these sciences influence lives. In addition, there are strong beliefs related to locations of various dwellings. Houses, tombs, and palaces should face toward the south and be located near the veins of strength so they may absorb the yang (male) influences, which produce strength. They should be protected at the back by high mounds of trees, which screen off the yin (female) influences from the north. The importance of the male is also found in the family because the line is carried through the male, and the head of the house performs as priest during the ceremonies for the ancestors of the group. Consequently, male offspring are essential.

Additional elements include the role of scholarship in obtaining life goals and the family in arranging marriages. Scholarship is highly valued in the Chinese culture and considered the means for success. Much of the folklore illustrates respect for knowledge and learning. Marriage brokers make arrangements between the families of two young people. This is a common practice found in the literature. An understanding of the importance of these elements is useful in the analysis of folklore. The same elements may be found in historical fiction and poetry.

Examples of Chinese Folklore Many of the adapters of Chinese folklore identify Buddhist sources for their tales. For example, *What the Rat Told Me: A Legend of the Chinese Zodiac*, retold by Marie Sellier, Catherine Louis, and Wang Fei, is adapted from a Chinese Buddhist legend from the Han dynasty (206 BCE–220 CE). This *pourquoi* tale reveals why the cat is not part of the twelve signs of the Chinese zodiac and explains why the cat and the rat are no longer friends. The text and illustrations present the story of each of the twelve animals and identify their characteristics. In addition, the authors include a calendar that shows the dates associated with each sign so that readers can identify their own birth sign.

Chinese New Year traditions, rewarding the poor, and punishing the greedy are all motifs found in Ying Chang Compestine's *The Runaway Wok: A Chinese New Year Tale*. Ming's family is at first distressed when he trades their food for an old, rusty wok. After polishing the wok, however, they discover that it has a magical power of singing. The wok also tricks members of a greedy family into filling the wok with food and money that the poor family shares with their neighbors. In addition to reading a pleasant story, readers will gain knowledge about Chinese New Year traditions and foods associated with the holiday.

Traditional Chinese sayings frequently suggest Chinese values and express philosophical viewpoints found in Chinese folktales over the centuries. For example, "A teacher can open the door, but the pupil must go through it alone" and "The home that includes an old grandparent contains a precious jewel." These sayings suggest the value of scholarship and respect for older people. The importance of sayings and proverbs are reflected in Ed Young's *The Lost Horse*. Young based his story on a Chinese proverb: it teaches trust in ever-changing fortune and the belief that things are not always as bad or as good as they seem. These two themes provide the key for developing harmony between father and son.

Paintings of horses may also inspire the imagination as found in Chen Jiang Hong's *The Magic Horse of Han Gan*. This tale is based on the life of a Tang Dynasty artist. The magic occurs when the artist throws his drawing of a war horse into the fire because he believes that he cannot produce a living creature that is as great as the real thing. A transformation occurs, the war horse leaps from the painting and is ridden into battle by the warrior who commissioned the painting. In an equally magical conclusion, the transformed war horse discovers that real war is terrible; consequently, he escapes and returns to the artist's house and lives again on the face of the canvas.

As you read the following descriptions and analysis of some of the Chinese folktales, try to identify some of the early beliefs that might have influenced the tales and the common elements that may be found in the tales. Can you identify any possible philosophies that might have influenced the tales?

The conflict between nobility and commoners is a popular topic in Chinese tales. A dislike for imperial authority is evident in several Chinese equivalents to the cottage tales of medieval European peasants. In these tales, the dragon, the symbol of imperial authority, is usually evil and is overcome by a peasant's wit.

It is interesting to search through Chinese folktales to discover if the dragon is evil or good. The dragon is frequently a symbol of imperial authority. Consequently, if the dragon is evil the story probably reflects a dislike for imperial authority. If the dragon is kind and benevolent, however, the dragon also suggests a benevolent ruler. A benevolent dragon is found in "Green Dragon Pond" in Neil Philip's *The Spring of Butterflies and Other Chinese Folktales*. According to this tale, the dragon only does good deeds. This is a tale of transformation in which the dragon changes himself into a man and plays chess with an old monk who lives in the temple by the pond. (We will discover later that in ancient Chinese art the dragon frequently symbolizes imperial authority and is considered a good character.)

Marilee Heyer's *The Weaving of a Dream: A Chinese Folktale* reveals rewarded behavior: bravery, unselfish love, understanding, respect for one's mother, faithfulness, and kindness. In contrast, disrespect for one's mother and selfishness are punished. This tale also shows the power of a dream and the perseverance that may be required to gain the dream. Ed Young's *Lon Po Po: A Red-Riding Hood Story from China* shows the cleverness of the eldest daughter, and the cooperation of the three sisters are powerful enough to outwit the intentions of the evil wolf.

The Cricket's Cage retold by Stefan Czernecki reveals how a wise cricket helps his owner design a tower for the Forbidden City and gain respect and recognition from the emperor. The close relationship between humans and nature is a frequent element in Chinese folklore. The importance of really seeing what is around us in nature is developed in Ed Young's *Mouse Match*. The tale is presented to resemble a Chinese scroll and is written with Chinese text on the reverse side.

In *Auntie Tigress and Other Favorite Chinese Folktales,* Gia-Zhen Wang develops three tales that reveal Chinese motifs and values and provide sources for comparisons. The first tale, "Auntie Tigress," is an example of a traditional motif in which an animal, an old tigress, transforms herself into an old lady. Auntie Tigress is also an example of an animal with bad spirits who seeks human prey. The second tale, "The Fisherman and the Tycoon," shows how a generous fisherman outwits a greedy tycoon. "The Greatest Treasure" develops the theme that the greatest treasure is love and devotion. The change in the human character reveals both disliked and admired human characteristics. As a result of love and devotion he is no longer snobbish and greedy. Instead, he helps the poor, takes delight in simple pleasures, and lives happily with his family. The "Notes on the Stories" provide details about both the content of some of the stories and the meanings of artistic details related to Chinese culture.

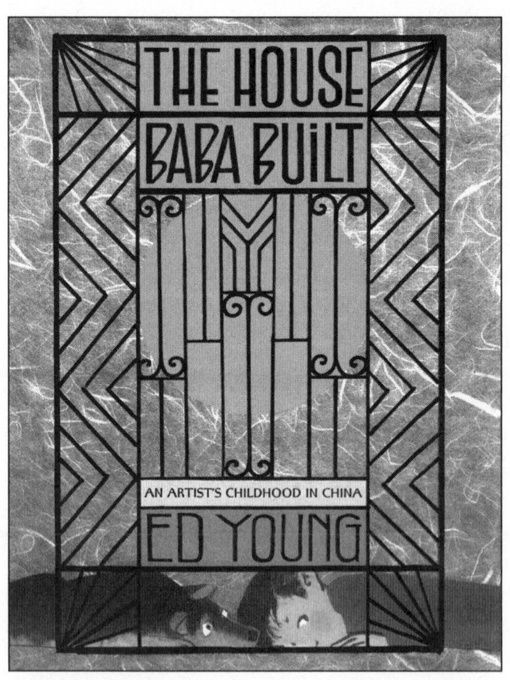

The House Baba Built: An Artist's Childhood in China, by Ed Young. Little, Brown Books for Young Readers, 2011.

The "Author's Note" in Grace Lin's *Where the Mountain Meets the Moon* indicates the importance of Chinese folktales in her writing. She classifies her book as "a fantasy inspired by the Chinese folktales that enchanted me in my youth and the land and culture that fascinates me in my adulthood" (p. 281). Lin includes a bibliography of folktale sources so that readers can locate the folktales that are included in her text such as tales about the jade dragon, the Old Man in the Moon, a string of destiny, and the dragon's pearl. This book is discussed in more detail in the "Survival" section of this chapter.

The Chinese American experience is emphasized in folktales collected by Laurence Yep. *The Rainbow People* is a collection of twenty Chinese folktales from Chinese Americans in the United States. The text is divided according to tales about tricksters, fools, virtues and vices, Chinese America, and love. Yep has included introductory comments for each of the sections. Many of the values and vices found in folklore from China are also found in these tales. Notice how a sampling of these values and vices could be used to summarize many of the values and vices discussed previously. For example, values highlighted in the stories include the importance of loyalty and wits and punishment for treachery found in "Natural Enemies," the importance of luck as found in "The Professor of Smells," the value of learning in "The Butterfly Man," the value of kindness to animals in "We Are All One" and "The Superior Pet," the punishment for impatience and the value for patience in "Snake-Spoke," the value of faithful service in "The Old Jar," the punishment for greed in "The Boasting Contest," and the virtue of obedience in "Dream Flier."

Folklore from India

Like China, India is a huge country with diverse people, languages, and religions. It is also an ancient country with folklore that goes back to ancient civilizations. An early record of Indian mythology is contained in the *Rig-Veda,* or "Hymn Veda." These myths along with the *Yajur-Veda* (Formula Veda), the *Atharva-Veda* (Veda of the Atharvan priests), and the Brahmanas, or explanatory prose texts attached to them, date from the first and second millennium before Christ.

Much of the folklore from India is influenced by two great religions: Hindu and Buddhist. Many of the great Hindu stories are found in the Mahabharata, which dates anywhere from 3000 BCE to about 1500 BCE Donald A. Mackenzie (1987) reinforces the importance of myths and legends for the Hindus when he states,

> In no other country have the national poets given fuller and finer expression to the beliefs and ideals and traditions of a people, or achieved as a result a wider and more enduring fame. At the present day over two hundred million Hindus are familiar in varying degrees with the legendary themes and traditional beliefs which the ancient forest sages and poets of India invested with much beautiful symbolism, and used as mediums for speculative thought and profound spiritual teachings. The sacred books of India are to the Hindus what the Bible is to Christians. Those who read them, or hear them read, are believed to be assured of prosperity in this world and of salvation in the next. (pp. iii–iv)

One of the oldest and most important collections of folktales from India are Jataka tales, or stories of the Buddha's former births. These stories were first told more than 2,000 years ago and reveal many of the teachings, beliefs, and values associated with the Buddhist religion.

In the late nineteenth century there was a major thrust toward collecting and publishing the folktales from India. According to A. K. Ramanujan (1991), "some of the finest folktale collections were compiled then, and published in journals like *The Indian Antiquary, The Journal of the Royal Asiatic Society of Bengal,* and *North Indian Notes and Queries*" (unnumbered preface). During this time, about 2,000 tales were collected, translated, and published by Indian scholars, civil servants, and foreign missionaries. Many of the tales found in the various religious sources and in other collections such as the Pañcatantra.

Types of Tales As we would expect from our discussion about the role of religion in Indian folklore, there are many tales about the gods, goddesses, and legendary heroes. Felix Guirand (1987) in the *New Larousse Encyclopedia of Mythology* identifies the following as subjects of myths in Indian folklore: royalty and the priestly caste, gods and goddesses, Brahmanas (the most ancient texts of Hindu sacred literature), heroes, and Buddha.

A. K. Ramanujan (1991) categorizes folktales into the following seven types: male-centered tales, in which a hero searches for adventure; women-centered tales, in which women may solve riddles that men cannot answer and thus rescue the men; tales about families that emphasize various types of family relationships; tales about fate, gods, and demons; humorous tales about rogues, jesters, and fools; and animal tales, especially those from the Jatakas and the Pañcatantra, which are often didactic fables.

Examples of Folklore from India Numerous myths and legends from India are found in two books published for adults. These texts provide background information as well as examples of tales. Sister Nivendita and Ananda K. Coomaraswamy's *Myths and Legends Series: Hindus and Buddhists* (1987) includes chapters on the mythology of the Indo-Aryan races, the Ramayana, the Mahabharata, Krishna, Buddha, Shiva, and additional stories from the Puranas, epics, and Vedas. Donald A. Mackenzie's *India: Myths and Legends Series* (1987) includes many tales about the deities. The following section describes some books for children and young adults.

Aaron Shepard's *Savitri: A Tale of Ancient India* is a Hindu myth that appears in the Mahabharata. This epic tale tells about a king with many wives but no children. For eighteen years he prays for children until a god hears his prayers and grants him a daughter. This tale includes a righteous hero who is rich in virtue and intelligence. The plot includes the importance of both prayers and fasting and female loyalty and wit. The tale has a characteristic ending, "They lived long and happily, blessed with many children. So they had no fear or tears when Yama came again to carry them to his kingdom" (p. 33, unnumbered).

Debjani Chatterjee, an Indian-born storyteller and poet, retells several of the Hindu myths in *The Elephant-Headed God and Other Hindu Tales*. Notice in the following introduction to "The Elephant-Headed God" how the oral storyteller's style provides interest in the character.

> Just look at the picture opposite this page. Take a good long look. You cannot help smiling, can you? (p. 10)

Hanuman, the tale of the monkey-hero found in an ancient text called *Ramayana* (The Path of Rama), is retold by Erik Jendresen and Joshua M. Greene. According to the Authors' Note, the original text was written thousands of years ago in Sanskrit. The story follows Prince Rama's childhood, his marriage, his exile, his wife's abduction by the demon king, and Rama's final victory. The retelling employs an interesting storytelling style as revealed through this opening: "Listen now while I tell you a tale of a time long past when the world was menaced by a ten-headed beast whom the gods could not control. He was called Ravana: He who makes the universe scream" (p. 1, unnumbered). As you read the book, try to identify the characteristics of a hero as revealed in this tale from India.

The Jataka tales, which were passed down orally, are among the most important for revealing stories about Buddhist beliefs and values. The tales are attributed to Gautama Buddha, who lived and taught in northeast India between 563 and 483 BCE Many of these tales develop the importance of cooperation, understanding, creativity, and wisdom—uniquely human potentials—as the key to life. The tales demonstrate the benefits derived from cooperation, friendship, respect, independent thought, responsible behavior, courage, humility, and education. They also reveal the problems caused by greed, ambition, foolishness, bad company, environmental damage, and disrespectful language.

Demi's *Buddha Stories* includes twelve of the tales that reveal moral values. These moral values are strengthened because Demi concludes each of the tales with a moral such as "When one person tells a falsehood, one hundred repeat it as true," "Treat others with kindness and your deeds will be rewarded," "It is easier to make a promise than to keep it," and "Pride leads to a fall, but humility is rewarded in the end." As you read the tales and the accompanying morals, what values do you discover related in the Buddhist tales?

Selfless generosity and actions are also the powerful force of goodness that opens hearts in *The Rabbit in the Moon: A Jataka Tale* also by the Dharma Publishing Staff. In this tale, a great being in the form of a rabbit possesses such a pure heart that even the greedy learn to share, the sly do not steal, and the mischievous forget to tease. Not only does the ending of the tale present the theme, but it also reveals why there is the shape of a rabbit in the moon: "Then in order to remind the world of the power of selflessness, he placed the rabbit in the moon, where he has dwelt from that day forward (p. 20, unnumbered). In Judith Ernst's retelling of *The Golden Goose King: A Tale Told by the Buddha,* the storyteller uses another tale told by the Buddha to reveal how a king and queen should rule wisely. Another source for Buddha tales is *The Wisdom of the Crows and Other Buddhist Tales,* retold by Sherab Chodzin and Alexandra Kohn.

Gerald McDermott's *Monkey: A Trickster Tale from India* is also a Buddhist tale that sets Monkey and Crocodile as antagonists. It is Monkey's cleverness that allows him to outsmart his enemy and gain his favorite food, mangoes. McDermott's author's note presents both a history of the tale and an explanation of the artwork.

K. T. Hao's *Little Stone Buddha* is a highly illustrated tale that depicts the Buddha's close relationship with animals and nature. In this tale, the stone Buddha searches for people who need help. In a *pourquoi*-type tale, the storyteller reveals why foxes are revered and not hunted.

Ed Young's retelling of the moral fable "The Blind Men and the Elephant" in *Seven Blind Mice* concludes with an important moral; "Knowing in part may make a fine tale, but wisdom comes from seeing the whole" (unnumbered).

As you read the folklore of India, notice the importance of the Hindu and Buddhist religions. Also try to discover the types of folktales—especially the male-centered tales, the women-centered tales, the family relationship tales, the tales about gods and demons, the humorous tales, and the animal tales. The folklore we have discussed develops values such as devotion to truth, integrity, friendship, and selfless actions.

Robert Beer's *The Handbook of Tibetan Buddhist Symbols* (2003) is helpful when conducting in-depth analysis of the folk literature. The sections "Animals and Mythical Creatures," "Cosmological Symbols," and "Plant Attributes" are especially helpful. Beer's "Glossary" is also helpful when identifying and defining terms.

Folklore from Japan

The folklore of Japan presents a complex subject because the early Japanese were influenced by the peoples of China, Korea, and other countries of the Asiatic continent. The myths were preserved by oral tradition through the Katari-be, a group of reciters whose function was to recite the ancient myths and legends during the Shinto festivals. The Katari-be were believed to be closely linked with the priests and priestesses who related ancient tales about the gods or the tribe during religious services.

In 681, Emperor Temmu ordered a committee to place the old traditions into writing. At the beginning of the eighth century, Japanese folklore was used as a source to compile the old histories of Japan. In 711, the Empress Gemmyo ordered the collection of old legends. This work was completed in 712 under the title of *Kojki*. In 720, *Jindaiki* was presented to the Emperor.

Royal Tyler (1987) states that many of the tales in his large collection of folklore titled *Japanese Tales* were gathered beginning in the early 700s, although most of the tales were collected between 1100 and 1350 CE. Many of the tales in this collection tell about events that happened between 850 and 1050, a classic period in Japanese civilization.

Like the folklore of India, the folklore of Japan is influenced by religion. Medieval Japan was as steeped in religion as medieval Europe. Buddhism was dominant, but other religions or magical traditions were important, too. Buddhism emphasized honoring of nature—mountains, valleys, and rivers play a great part in enlightenment. The treatment of the dead is also influenced by Buddhism. Buddhist rites had to be performed daily for the first seven days after death, then every seventh day thereafter until the forty-ninth day. Without this care, spirits were miserable and could easily linger on as harmful or unhappy ghosts.

The folktales of Japan also include supernatural monsters and beasts such as demons, tengu, foxes, badgers, dragons, turtles, snakes, and boar. The greatest trickster in Japanese folklore is the fox. Foxes are famous in Japanese folklore for masquerading as beautiful women. Dragons and snakes are closely associated in Japanese folklore with the water. The dragon may be associated with the energy of the water cycle: rain, river, sea, vapor, and rain. Dragon symbols are common in both folklore and in East Asian painting.

Examples of Japanese Folklore Japanese folklore is influenced by the folklore of India and China. The importance of the teachings of the Buddha illustrates the impact of this religion on Japanese culture. Two of the tales in Royal Tyler's *Japanese Tales* provide sources for understanding the importance of meditation, contemplation, and nature. For example, in the tale "Paradise in the Palm of the Hand," the hero discovers he must contemplate the Buddha's countenance and the beauty of paradise if he is to enter paradise. In "Among the Flowers," a monk discovers the beauty and religion found in nature when he finds a man who lives in reverence in a field of flowers.

The Buddha plays an important role in Fiona French's *Little Inchkin*. After bravely protecting Prince Sanjo's daughter from two fiery demons, the small hero is rewarded by Lord Buddha, who grants his dearest wish: to be as tall as other men. The story ends with a moral that emphasizes both the importance of his brave actions and the honoring of the samurai warriors because, small or large, he becomes "the most honored samurai swordsman in the land" (unnumbered).

Yuri Yasuda's *A Treasury of Japanese Folktales* is a bilingual version of Japanese folktales that includes twelve tales such as "The Peach Boy," "The One-Inch Boy," and "The Kachi Kachi Mountain." This last tale tells how a kindhearted rabbit tricks a mean badger. This book is a retelling of a text that was originally published in 1953 as *Old Tales of Japan*.

Merrily Baird (2001) identifies important Japanese symbols and their comparisons or analogies that liken one object or phenomenon to another. This is especially important in comparisons among humans and animals in which human traits are ascribed to animals and positive traits of animals are ascribed to people associated with them. For example, a tiger is said to be courageous and compassionate; likewise, certain humans may take on those traits. Plants may also symbolize human traits and emotions. For example, pampas grass may symbolize the loneliness and desolation of autumn, while fallen cherry blossoms could refer to a warrior who dies at a young age. Many of these symbols are also found in the illustrations that accompany traditional literature.

Chinese culture influenced Japanese culture, and many Japanese tales are similar to Chinese tales. Dragons, for example, are common in tales from both countries. The tiger, usually considered a symbol of power, is a creature often found in Japanese tales. The cat is important in Arthur Levine's *The Boy Who Drew Cats: A Japanese Folktale*. When a boy paints cats on screens after he is trapped in an abandoned temple, the cats come alive to save him from a giant rat.

Japanese folktales reflecting respected values and disliked human qualities include Katherine Paterson's *The Tale of the Mandarin Ducks*. Paterson develops strong messages, such as kindness will be rewarded, creatures cannot survive when held captive, honor is important, and sharing helps people through trouble. These respected values are developed when two servants help a coveted mandarin duck that has been captured by a greedy lord. When the kitchen maid releases the duck against the lord's command, she and another servant are sentenced to death. The grateful drake and his mate, however, outwit the lord and reward the kindness of the servants. In Yoshiko Uchida's *The Magic Purse*, a courageous act brings rewards.

Frequently cranes are important in Japanese folktales. Anne Laurin's *The Perfect Crane* suggests the desirability of friendship between humans and supernatural creatures. In this story, a lonely magician develops a strong friendship with a crane that he creates from rice paper. Molly Bang's *The Paper Crane* has a similar theme. A hungry man rewards a restaurant owner with a paper crane that can be brought to life by clapping hands, and this attraction creates many customers for the business. A sadder outcome is developed in Odds Bodkin's *The Crane Wife* when the husband makes selfish demands on his wife, who is a crane transformed into a woman.

Dianne Snyder's *The Boy of the Three-Year Nap* has a strong female protagonist who outwits her lazy son. The tale is a humorous match of wits. The lazy son tries to trick a wealthy merchant into letting him marry the merchant's daughter. The mother, however, shows that she is the equal of the son. She not only convinces the merchant to repair and enlarge her house, but also tricks her son into getting a job. Other strong female protagonists are found in *Three Strong Women*, retold by Claus Stamm and in Robert D. San Souci's *The Samurai's Daughter: A Japanese Legend*. A strong female protagonist in Judy Sierra's *Tasty Baby Belly Buttons* battles the terrible oni.

Respecting the wisdom of older people is an important value in Japanese folklore, as it was in other Asian traditional literature. Yoshiko Uchida's *The Wise Old Woman* is set in medieval Japan. A cruel lord declares that people over the age of seventy should be abandoned in the mountains. The value of older people is established, however, when a young farmer with the help of his mother is able to arrive at the solutions to meet three seemingly impossible tasks. The story develops the strong theme that wisdom comes with age.

Other Asian Folklore

Laurence Yep's *The Khan's Daughter: A Mongolian Folktale* develops both a quest motif and a change in character as Mongke, a shepherd boy, accomplishes three trials to win the khan's daughter. Two of the trials are imposed by the girl's mother: he must demonstrate proof of strength and proof of bravery. The third trial is formulated by the khan's daughter. It is this third trial that shows both the character of the girl in determining her own destiny and the changes in Mongke as he goes from a rather foolish and boastful character to one who is both contrite and filled with considerable wisdom.

Naomi C. Rose's *Tibetan Tales from the Top of the World* is a collection of three tales. One of the tales, "Prince Jampa's Surprise," reflects the amazement the prince experiences when he attacks a kingdom that he believes to be composed of savages, only to discover that the people are peaceful and they welcome his invaders. Another tale, "Tashi's Gold," teaches a lazy boy that true riches do not come from gold. All of the tales reflect the search for true wisdom.

Suzanne Crowder Han uses a format in which she writes the text of her tales in both Korean and English. *The Rabbit's Escape* is a tale in which a rabbit uses his wits to escape death, and a loyal turtle is rewarded for his fidelity with a ginseng cure for the king. Han's *The Rabbit's Judgment* is a Korean variant of "The Tiger, the Brahmin, and the Jackal."

The theme of Ed Young's *I, Doko: The Tale of a Basket*, a tale from Nepal, stresses the importance of caring for and respecting an elderly father. The tale is told from the basket's viewpoint, which has been used by three generations of a family as they carry grain, transport a child, and bring wood for the fire. The moral develops as the son decides to use the basket to carry and leave his elderly father on the temple steps so that the priests will care for him. The moral is stated when the grandson tells his father to bring back the basket because he will need the basket when it is his turn to leave his elderly father on the steps. At this point, the son realizes his mistake and takes his elderly father back to his home.

Eastern folktales contain such universal motifs as reward for unselfishness, assistance from magical objects, cruel adversaries, and punishment for dishonesty. The tales also emphasize the traditional values of the specific people: homage is paid to ancestors, knowledge and cleverness are rewarded, and greed and miserly behavior are punished. The in-depth view of the folktales from the various cultures shows us how important are the traditional values of that culture as reflected in the folklore.

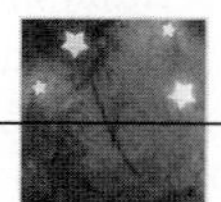

Early History of the People and the Culture

Informational books, biographies, and historical fiction present information about the early history and cultures of the people from China, India, Japan, and other Asian countries.

Informational Books That Depict Asian History

The Silk and Spice routes that ran from China to European cities from about 100 BCE to 1500 CE are popular subjects for informational books. These books illustrate the importance of the routes for transferring not only goods but also knowledge. The routes promoted culture exchange and exchange of religious beliefs as well.

The focus of John S. Major's *The Silk Route: 7,000 Miles of History*, as well as Stephen Fieser's illustrations accompanying the text, are the cities along the way and explanations about the importance of the cities to the caravan's progress. Readers receive a feeling of the different cultures as the author discusses topics such as religion, industry, and daily life of people who lived along the route. Readers may authenticate the impact of the trade routes on the expansion of religious beliefs by reading Reza's "Pilgrimage to China's Buddhist Caves" (1996). This article in *National Geographic* shows the impact of Buddhism's influences on the cave paintings dating from 400 to 700 CE along China's Silk Route.

As sea travel became more common, the traders began to use the oceans rather than the land. In 1853, Commodore Matthew Perry traveled to Japan in an attempt to open Japan to U.S. trade. Rhoda Blumberg's *Commodore Perry in the Land of the Shogun* depicts the attempts of the American naval officer Matthew Perry to open Japanese harbors to U.S. trade. This book, an excellent choice for multicultural studies, strongly emphasizes the dramatic interactions between Perry and the Japanese. Reproductions of the original drawings that recorded the expedition, contemporaneous Japanese scrolls and handbills, and photographs from the period enhance children's understanding of the setting and Japanese culture.

The author includes several appendixes, including some with firsthand sources. There is a letter from the president of the United States, Millard Fillmore, to the emperor of Japan; a translation of the answer to the president's letter, signed by Yenosuke, the chief interpreter; a list of some of the American presents for the Japanese; a list of some of the Japanese presents for the Americans; and the text of the Treaty of Kanagawa, a treaty designed for "a perfect, permanent, and universal peace, and a sincere and cordial amity between the United States of America, and on the one part, and the Empire of Japan on the other" (p. 131). The text also includes author's notes, a bibliography, and an index.

In *Ancient India*, Virginia Schomp provides a study of the early culture by describing rulers, priests, and artisans. Colleen Sexton's *Japan* and Walter Simmons's *Vietnam* are part of the "Exploring Countries Series." Both books include maps, photographs, further readings, and websites. The books are useful for elementary students who are beginning to conduct research on various Asian countries.

Biographies about Figures from Early Culture

Many biographies of early personages are about the Buddha. For example, Susan L. Roth's *Buddha* presents the early life of Prince Siddhartha. Readers discover that before the prince's birth, a wise man predicts that the child to be born will become a very holy man. Readers discover that, during the prince's early years, he learns to read, write, ride, and shoot, but he cannot learn to kill. The author focuses on experiences that led Prince Siddhartha to become a holy man and try to find a way to end the suffering in the world. The author's Afterword discusses information about Siddhartha's life. It covers the time after he renounces his earthly possessions, living in the forest studying and meditating. Near the city of Benares, India, he delivers his Deer Park sermon, one of the most sacred events in the history of Buddhism. During this period, he presents his Noble Eightfold Path and Doctrine of the Four Truths, all of which emphasize gentleness, kindness, and love. It is interesting that 2,500 years later Buddhism is one of the world's major religions with more than 250 million followers. A biography of Buddha may be read in association with the various Jataka tales that are related to the early teachings of the Buddha.

Russell Freedman's biography, *Confucius: The Golden Rule*, begins with the following quote from "The Analects of Confucius": "Do you know what knowledge is? When you know something, recognize that you know it, and when you don't know something, recognize that you don't know it. That's knowledge" (unnumbered). This quest for knowledge is also the theme of the book as Freedman recounts the life of the scholar who lived more than 2,500 years ago.

Of additional value to readers is Freedman's "In Search of Confucius: A Note on Sources and Suggestions for Further Reading" that Freedman used in his own search for information about Confucius's life and teachings. Frederic Clement's illustrations and quotations from "The Analects of Confucius" add to the feeling of authenticity for the text.

Historical Fiction about Asian Cultures

Fascinating historical fiction books about ancient Asian cultures are available about time periods such as feudal Japan and early China. In this section, we progress on an historical timeline from books set in the earlier time periods to later time periods. We conclude with the historical fiction books about Asian cultures that are set in the United States.

Jean Merrill's *The Girl Who Loved Caterpillars* is one of the most interesting picture storybooks: it is set in twelfth-century Japan. According to the author's note, the story is adapted from an anonymous Japanese story found on a scroll. The author also provides sources for three English translations that were used as the basis for the adaptation. The story presents a strong, clever female character, Izumi, who resists social and family pressures as she develops her own interests. The author contrasts Izumi's interests with those of a noblewoman called "The Lady Who Loved Butterflies," who was considered "The Perfect Lady" because "she dressed exquisitely, wrote poetry in a delicate script, and played with skill on the lute and the sho" (unnumbered). In contrast, Izumi loves caterpillars and other living creatures that most people dislike to touch. In addition, Izumi does not blacken her teeth or trim her bushy eyebrows. The story ends with a mystery because, according to Merrill, the original scroll inferred this was part of a longer story that would be found in the second chapter. Unfortunately, the second chapter has been lost. Interesting speculations could be made, however, as readers consider what might have happened to this wise woman who was so interested in nature. Would she become a scientist, a philosopher, or did she become alienated from her family and society, or have some other fate?

Linda Sue Park's Newbery Award book, *A Single Shard*, is set in twelfth-century Korea. When writing about how she developed the idea for the book (Johnson and Giorgis, 2002) she states that she "happened upon information about how 11th- and 12th-century Korea produced the finest pottery in the world" (p. 396). This information fascinated her so much that she created a story about an orphan boy and how he learned the art of pottery making by watching a master potter create celadon pottery. Additional information about the creation of this book is found on her website (http://www.lindasuepark.com). An analytical reading activity later in this chapter focuses on using *A Single Shard* in the classroom.

Erik Christian Haugaard's *The Boy and the Samurai* is set in feudal Japan during the period of civil wars in the late 1400s and 1500s. As do the authors of many other stories with wartime settings, Haugaard emphasizes the search for peace and the painful realities resulting from war. Haugaard's settings and characters allow readers to visualize the world of street orphans, warlords, samurai, and priests.

Haugaard uses several techniques to help involve his readers and make the story seem more immediate. For example, in the preface, Haugaard introduces the book in the first person, as if he is telling his own autobiography: "As I wrote the tale of my youth, I relived it with each stroke of the brush" (p. xxi).

Another technique used by Haugaard is the inclusion of cultural traditions and beliefs throughout the text. For example, as the young boy thinks to himself, he also reveals his belief in the god, Oinari-sama. He tells readers about the god and the roles of the foxes, the Badger, and the Crane who serve the god of rice.

As you read Haugaard's book, you might try to locate examples of important symbols and beliefs such as the following: the symbol of the monkey (p. 42), the belief in signs of luck (p. 45), belief in ill omens (p. 49), the importance of being able to compose poetry (p. 136), the belief that writing poetry is the noblest of the arts (p. 137), the belief in benefits of honor and disadvantages for greed (p. 162), and the importance of bravery (p. 168). *The Boy and the Samurai* provides an interesting historical fiction text to use as the basis for searching for beliefs and values that are also depicted in the traditional folklore and in the art of ancient Japan.

Five young warrior monks, known in legend as The Five Ancestors, form the quest begun in Jeff Stone's *The Five Ancestors: Tiger.* Stone uses both their training in the martial arts and their belief in a peaceful philosophy of life to create adventures set in Henan Province, China in the Year of the Tiger, AD 1650. This is the first of a series of stories about these young warrior monks who are the only survivors following the destruction of Cangzhen Temple. Each of the warriors is named after an animal (tiger, monkey, snake, crane, and dragon) and is taught by the grandmaster of the temple to use the animal's fighting style. Before the grandmaster dies, he instructs the young warriors to search for the secrets of their past and to find the scrolls that were stolen from the temple. This is the first of a series of stories as Fu, a master of the tiger arts, begins this quest.

Joanna Cole's *Ms. Frizzle's Adventures: Imperial China* also takes readers back to AD 1000. In this highly illustrated book, the teacher and the students visit places such as the Great Wall of China and a New Years festival.

The year is 1841. The setting is Japan at a time when they are extremely isolated, consider foreigners to be devils and barbarians, and live by a strict social class system. This is the setting for Margi Preus's *Heart of a Samurai,* which places a fourteen-year-old fisherman who dreams of becoming a samurai in a position that would seem impossible because of his lowly birth. The "Historical Note" reveals that the book is based on a real character, Manjiro Nakahama, and real events when he and four fellow fishermen are shipwrecked by a violent storm, forced to live on a deserted island, and eventually saved by barbarians on an American whaling ship. The author states that the fictional part of the story allows her to add characters and incidents to enhance the conflict and acknowledge the prejudice against Japanese that Manjiro experiences while on the ship and later when he accompanies the captain to America.

The book is enhanced through the author's style, which allows her to develop the sources of conflict and the beliefs of the Japanese characters. For example, to develop Manjiro's dreams of becoming a samurai and to suggest characterizations he must strive for, Preus provides quotes from the Samurai Creed and relates the creed to the content and theme of the accompanying section. She uses frequent flashbacks that reveal facts about the Japanese culture and allow her to make comparisons between Western and Eastern cultures.

Readers will discover cultural beliefs that were prevalent in Eastern and Western cultures during that time period. For example, the Japanese respect for the Samurai culture, a belief in a social order that does not allow a person to advance from his or her level at birth, a respect for older people, and reference to Buddhist beliefs. Many of the Western beliefs are developed through Manjiro's person-versus-self and -society conflicts. For example, the captain tells him not to bow to older people because it is not done in America, this causes Manjiro great concern because he has always been taught that bowing is the way to show respect. Through Manjiro's training on the ship and later in school in America, he discovers that his learning and considerable ambitions will allow him to obtain his dreams without being held back by his social class as he would have been in Japan. Survival strategies that are associated with both Manjiro's character and the cultural beliefs are discussed later in this chapter in the "Survival" section.

Authors of historical fiction books with Chinese American heroes and heroines frequently develop themes about the difficulty of acculturation. In these books, the main characters frequently assimilate the mainstream culture while retaining their Chinese identity and value systems.

Several award-winning historical fiction books with Chinese protagonists are set in the United States. Both Laurence Yep's *Dragon's Gate* and *Dragonwings* were awarded the Newbery Honor Book award. Yep's characters do not reflect the stereotypes associated with literature about Asian Americans, and his stories integrate information about Chinese cultural heritage into the stories of everyday lives of his characters.

Yep's *Dragon's Gate* is set in the Sierra Nevada mountains in 1867 when Chinese immigrants are working on the transcontinental railroad. Yep begins his story in China and provides a historical perspective that allows readers to understand the viewpoint of the Chinese and to understand some of the reasons that Chinese people might have wanted to emigrate to America. As the story progresses, Yep shows the economic need of the characters to learn English and to go to the United States.

Yep's *Dragonwings*, set in 1903 San Francisco, is based on a true incident in which a Chinese American built and flew an airplane. The characters are people who retain their values and respect for their heritage while adjusting to a new country. The "town of the Tang people" is eight-year-old Moon Shadow's destination when he leaves his mother in the Middle Kingdom (China). He is filled with conflicting emotions when he first meets his father in the country that some call the "Land of the Demons" and others call the "Land of the Golden Mountain."

As the story progresses, Moon Shadow learns that his stereotype of the white demons is not always accurate. When he and his father move away from the Tang men's protection, Moon Shadow meets and talks to his first demon. Instead of being ten feet tall, with blue skin and a face covered with warts, the "demon" is a petite woman who is very friendly and considerate. As Moon Shadow and his father get to know this Anglo-Saxon woman and her family, all learn to respect people of different backgrounds as individuals. And when they share what they have learned, the father concludes, "We see the same thing and yet find different truths."

Readers also discover that many stereotypes about Chinese Americans are incorrect. This book is especially strong in its coverage of Chinese traditions and beliefs. For example, readers learn about the great respect that Chinese Americans feel for the aged and the dead. Family obligations do not end when a family member has died. As Moon Shadow seeks to educate his non-Chinese friend about the nature of dragons, readers discover traditional Chinese tales about a benevolent and wise dragon who is king among reptiles and emperor of animals. Readers realize the value of honor as the doubting Tang men pull *Dragonwings* up the hill for its maiden voyage. They do not laugh even though they may doubt the plane's ability to fly. To laugh would be an insult to Moon Shadow's father. Children who read this story learn about the contributions and struggles of the Chinese Americans and the prejudice they still experience.

Stories about early immigrant experiences in the United States are popular subjects in children's books. Allen Say's *Grandfather's Journey* is an immigration story that includes two journeys: one to California and then, many years later, one back to visit the Japan of his youth. The story also covers the time of World War II, when Grandfather cannot return to California again, but he tells his grandson, Allen Say, stories about the United States. *Grandfather's Journey* is an excellent companion for Say's *Tree of Cranes*, which is set in Japan. The story shows the melding of two cultures. The boy's mother, who was born in the United States, prepares a Christmas celebration that combines the Japanese and U.S. cultures.

Paul Yee's *Tales from Gold Mountain: Stories of the Chinese in the New World* includes eight stories about Chinese immigrants in the United States and Canada. You may find it helpful to compare Yee's stories with those developed in Yep's *Dragonwings*.

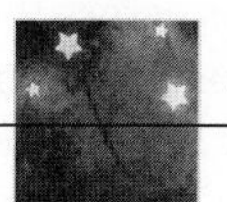

Poetry

Poetry forms a bridge between the older and more contemporary literature. Poetry by Asian and Asian American poets reflects the ancient values and beliefs as well as contemporary concerns. Many of the poems are found in both highly illustrated volumes for younger children and anthologies that may be enjoyed by all ages.

The universality of nursery rhymes is found by reading Demi's *Dragonkites and Dragonflies: A Collection of Chinese Nursery Rhymes*. The rhymes, many using rhythmic and rhyming language, focus on topics such as playing games, seeing dragon boats, beating the drums for a bride carried in a chair, and contemplating fireflies lighting up the sky. Demi's illustrations depict a colorful setting that makes the subjects of the nursery rhymes come to life. Japanese artist Satomi Ichikawa includes a Hindu and a Japanese prayer in *Here a Little Child I Stand: Poems of Prayer and Praise for Children*. The Hindu prayer glorifies God in fire, water, and plants. The Japanese prayer asks the Creator to help us love one another and bring peace to the world.

Haiku is a very old form of Japanese poetry. A traditional haiku has three unrhymed lines; the first line has five syllables, the second line has seven, and the final line has five. According to John Drury (1995), "the essential elements of haiku are brevity, immediacy, spontaneity, imagery, the natural world, a season, and sudden illumination" (p. 125). Celeste Davidson Mannis's collection of haiku, *One Leaf Rides the Wind: Counting in a Japanese Garden*, follows a young girl as she discovers delights in nature during her walk through a Japanese tranquility garden. Each haiku includes footnotes about Japanese religion and philosophy, such as the tea ceremony and the legend of the koi fish.

In *Wabi Sabi,* Mark Reibstein uses haiku alongside narration and Ed Young's collages to tell the story of a little cat's journey from Kyoto to discover the meaning of her name. Along the way, she is introduced to the Japanese philosophy of finding beauty in unexpected places. Haiku by Basho and Shiki, written in Japanese, appear decoratively on each page and are translated in an addendum.

Japan's most revered poet, Matsuo Basho, is considered the father of the haiku form. According to this seventeenth-century poet, the haiku was an exercise in reflection of the solitary self, and he made his living traveling around Japan teaching this art form. Dawnine Spivak's *Grass Sandals: The Travels of Basho* tells the story of Basho and people he met during his travels. Each page layout includes compressed excerpts from Basho's journals and an original haiku he composed during his walking journey across Japan.

In *Basho and the River Stones*, Tim Myers briefly describes the haiku form and includes an author's note about the poet, Basho. In his original trickster tale, Myers presents Basho as a character who considers the act of creating a haiku to be more valuable than gold. Basho's haiku humbles the fox and leads to their lasting friendship.

One of the most interesting introductions to both the eighteenth-century Japanese poet Issa and his haiku is Matthew Gollub's *Cool Melons—Turn to Frogs! The Life and Poems of Issa*. The text includes both a brief biography of the poet and haiku translations that highlight Issa's life; Kazuko G. Stone's illustrations add to the impact of the poetry. In addition, Japanese calligraphy lends visual appeal and conveys the feeling of the delicate brush strokes that were part of Issa's skill. As you read these poems, notice how they support Drury's essential elements of haiku. G. Bryan Karas's illustrations accompany selected poems by Issa in *Today and Today*. Haiku are arranged in the cycle of the seasons, while Karas's artwork depicts one family's life experiences—growth, celebration, and mourning—over the course of a year.

Poems in Naomi Shihab Nye's *This Same Sky: A Collection of Poems from Around the World* include ones from China, India, Japan, South Korea, and Vietnam. As students of children's literature, you may analyze and compare the content of these poems and search for underlying themes. As you make this search, try to discover both similarities and differences across the cultural groups. There are poems about dreams and desires such as "My Life Story," written by Lan Nguyen of Vietnam, in which the poet wishes she could do something for her people. There are poems about the beauties found in nature such as "House of Spring," written by Muso Soseki of Japan, in which the poet views hundreds of open flowers and the colors that appear in the garden. There are poems about creating a future such as "A Headstrong Boy," written by Gu Cheng from China, in which the poet wants to draw a future that has never been seen and paint out every sorrow. There are poems about the joys of reading such as "Companion," written by Manjush Dasgupta from India, in which the poet grows from a player with butterflies who does not read to a person whose constant companions are books. There are poems of longing for remembered scents and people associated with them such as "Jasmine" by Kyongjoo Hong Ryou of South Korea, in which the poet associates the fragrance of the scents with a mother who is now dead.

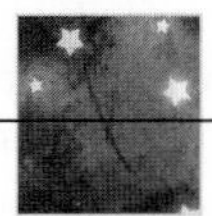

Contemporary Literature with Asian Roots

Nonfiction writing that focuses on various Asian cultures frequently presents both histories of, and contemporary practices associated with, religious beliefs. Other informational books present general information about Asian people, their countries, and their cultures. Several informational books describe the importance of Asian American culture. Biographies are about the important leaders and artists.

Informational Books

Many of the informational books on Asian cultures provide information about religious beliefs common in the cultures. For example, Catherine Hewitt's *Buddhism*, part of the World Religions Series, is an illustrated history that provides explanations of the beliefs and practices of Buddhism. The text begins with a discussion about the Four Noble Truths (there is suffering, the cause of suffering is wanting, suffering can end completely, and the Eightfold Path is the cure) and the importance of the Eightfold Path (right understanding, right thought, right speech, right action, right work, right effort, right mindfulness, and right meditation). The text includes considerable information about the background of Buddha and Buddhism and the importance of various Buddhist teachings. The text includes maps showing major locations of Buddhist populations. Color coding helps readers locate areas where Buddhism is the main religion and to identify countries where there are significant numbers of Buddhists. A glossary, a book list, and an index increase the usefulness of the book.

Hinduism is another major religion of Asian populations. Madhu Bazaz Wangu's *Hinduism: World Religions* informs readers that Hinduism is the third largest religion in the world, with more than 650 million Hindus throughout the world. The text and labeled photographs cover topics such as "The Modern Hindu World," "The Roots of Hinduism," "The Late Vedic Period," "The Gods and Devotion," "Political and Social Change," "The Hindu Temple," and "Social Duty and Rites of Passage."

Laura Buller's *A Faith Like Mine: A Celebration of the World's Religions Through the Eyes of Children* includes an overview of both Hinduism and Buddhism.

In addition to texts that focus mainly on religious beliefs, there are numerous informational sources that focus on general information about a country. For example, Anita Ganeri and Jonardon Ganeri's *India* is a source of general information about the country's geography, climate, weather, natural resources, population, daily life, rules and laws, food and farming, trade and industry, transportation, environment, and the future. Each section includes about four key facts that may be used as a rapid source for information. Some of the sections include maps and graphs.

Robert Arnett's *India Unveiled* is a beautifully illustrated book organized into six chapters that correspond with the major regions of India. The publication includes 272 photographs and seven maps. The book provides an introduction to cultural diversity, languages, religion, and geography.

> The diversity of Indian religions accounts for much of its cultural richness. Its ancient Hindu legacy intertwines with monuments from Jain, Buddhist, Mughal, Sikh, Christian and the British Raj period. There was even a Jewish presence in Kochi in South India, which probably dated back to

> the time of King Solomon's merchant fleets. Their descendants have intermarried with the Hindu population. . . . The reader should note that even within India's state boundaries, there are myriad ethnological differences, including languages, customs and foods. Because of such a diverse population, India has been referred to as a 'continent within a country.' (p. 7)

Readers of all ages will find this book (which won the Benjamin Franklin Award for the Best Travel Essay of the Year) allows them to explore the diversity of a large country.

Two authors have focused on the Ganges River. In *Sacred River*, Ted Lewin uses watercolors and text to introduce readers to the Ganges River as it passes through the holy city of Benares. This book, which presents most of its information through the illustrations, may be compared with David Cumming's *The Ganges*, in which the author provides a more comprehensive coverage of the topic. Cumming's text includes captioned color photographs, a glossary, a list of additional readings, addresses for additional information, and an index.

Informational books may explore the multicultural nature of United States and the Asian American cultures. Lauren Lee's *Korean Americans* focuses on the group's culture, family and community, religion and celebrations, various customs and expressions, and the contributions of Koreans to U.S. culture.

Biographies

The life of Indira Gandhi of India is the subject of several children's biographies as well as adult biographies. In addition, Gandhi wrote an autobiography. Consequently, these texts provide excellent sources for comparisons of biographical writing. You may choose to first read Indira Gandhi's autobiography, *My Truth* (1980). It provides information about her childhood and her feelings, how her personality was shaped, and how she came to govern one-sixth of the world's population. To broaden your understanding of the life of Indira Gandhi, her autobiography may be compared with an adult biography such as Paul Swaraji's *Indira Gandhi* (1985). The focus of Swaraji's biography is not on Gandhi's childhood, but on her political life after she becomes the prime minister. Swaraji explores the qualities that made Gandhi a dynamic leader including her understanding of people and politics and her worldwide vision. The biographer states, "Indira Gandhi's combination of coolness and poise under pressure contrasted sharply with the feebleness of many of her more senior colleagues" (p. 26). By examining both the autobiography and biography, readers can gain a clearer understanding of both her youth and her experiences as prime minister.

The information in several biographies of Indira Gandhi written for children may be compared with the information found in the adult texts. When Nandita Gurjar (1995), one of my graduate students from India, compared and authenticated the various biographies about Gandhi, she concluded that Shakuntala Masani's *The Story of Indira*, written for children, was authentic and written in an interesting style. When she analyzed Carol Greene's *Indira Nehru Gandhi: Ruler of India*, however, she concluded that the book written for younger children lacked authenticity. For example, Gurjar found differences in statements about the location of Gandhi's birth, inaccuracies in information about Gandhi's father, and inaccuracies in statements about relationships between Mohandas Gandhi and Indira Gandhi. There are no sources listed in Greene's text; consequently, readers cannot identify the primary sources the author may have used.

There are also numerous biographies of Mohandas Gandhi that may be used for comparison. For example, Victoria Sherrow's *Mohandas Gandhi: The Power of the Spirit* describes the life of the man who led a thirty-year struggle to free India from British rule. The author emphasizes the bitter conflicts among religious groups, including the conflict between Muslim Pakistan and Hindu India. The author presents a person whose deep moral sense gradually transforms him from an insecure young lawyer to a national leader whose influence transcended his time and place. Throughout the biography, readers discover a man who believed social and political goals could be won without violence—through peaceful resistance, marches, demonstrations, and strikes. The biography includes source notes for each chapter and a chronology of events in Mohandas Gandhi's life up until his assassination in 1948.

Glenn Alan Cheney's *Mohandas Gandhi* also emphasizes Gandhi's nonviolent crusade. In addition to providing information about Gandhi's life, Cheney relates Gandhi's beliefs to the civil rights movement in the United States. Doris and Harold Faber's *Mahatma Gandhi* is based on Gandhi's autobiography.

Demi's *The Dalai Lama: A Biography of the Tibetan Spiritual and Political Leader* is a biography of the Buddhist leader. Demi's highly illustrated text provides numerous insights into the search for the spiritual leader after the death of the thirteenth Dalai Lama in 1933. Through the description of this search, as well as descriptions of the Dalai Lama's later life, the biographer explores the values and beliefs associated with the man who received the Nobel Peace Prize in 1989. By quoting the words given by the Dalai Lama at this ceremony, notice how Demi reveals the important Buddhist values: "Because we all share this small planet earth, we have to learn to live in harmony and peace with each other and with nature. Live simply and love humanity. For as long as space endures and for as long as living beings remain, until then may I, too, abide to dispel the misery of the world" (unnumbered). Interesting insights may be revealed by reading *The Art of Happiness: A Handbook for Living* (Dalai Lama & Cutler, 1998).

Ken Mochizuki's *Passage to Freedom: The Sugihara Story* is a highly acclaimed biography of the Japanese consul to Lithuania who helped many Jewish refugees escape from the Holocaust. The biographer presents a strong character who continues to grant visas for refugees to pass through the Soviet Union to Japan, even though the Japanese government denied Sugihara's requests to issue visas. The biographer chose an interesting style by telling the story through the voice of Sugihara's five-year-old son. An Afterword by Sugihara's son places the heroic actions of his father into a contemporary context.

Historical Fiction with More Contemporary Settings Asian and Asian American literature set in more contemporary times frequently focuses on experiences during World War II, especially on those of Japanese Americans. For example, several books center their settings and plots on the internment of Japanese Americans. Many children are surprised to read stories about the treatment of Japanese Americans during World War II. See David Patneaude's *Thin Wood Walls* found under "Survival."

Laurence Yep's *Hiroshima* is set in Japan in 1945, during the time of the nuclear bombing of Hiroshima. Yep includes descriptions of both the crewmen on the *Enola Gay*, from which the atomic bomb was dropped, and the children in a Hiroshima classroom. Yep describes the various aspects of the bombing including the mushroom cloud and the destruction of the city. A section on the aftermath of the bombing, covering the arms race and the peace movement, should provide a springboard for interesting classroom discussions.

The setting for Graham Salisbury's *Under the Blood Red Sun* develops the historical time period associated with the Japanese bombing of Pearl Harbor on December 7, 1941. The following quote develops the sights and sounds of the actual bombing:

> Hundreds of planes circled the sky like black gnats, peeling off and dropping down to vanish into the boiling smoke, then reappearing, shooting skyward with engines groaning, circling back. (p. 106)

Throughout the book, Salisbury describes settings that allow readers an opportunity to experience vicariously the time period and the conflicts present during the war years.

The themes in children's historical fiction with settings during World War II resemble themes in books describing other times of great peril. The stories written about the Japanese American experience frequently develop themes related to the beliefs that prejudice and hatred are destructive forces and moral obligation and personal conscience are strong forces.

As students read these books about World War II, they may also consider the impact of changes in the history of World War II as reflected in current Japanese textbooks. According to two news articles by Norimitsu Onishi, Japanese educators are revising history textbooks to reflect changes in their interpretation of history. An April 2007 article reports that the Ministry of Education ordered publishers of high school textbooks to delete passages stating that the Imperial Army ordered civilians to commit suicide during the Battle of Okinawa. An April 2005 article reports changes in junior high school textbooks that downplay atrocities against China and South Korea.

Informational Books about World War II and Asian Experiences Several informational books focus on true experiences of Japanese during World War II. Tatsuharu Kodama's *Shin's Tricycle* focuses on experiences during the nuclear bombing of Hiroshima. This story is told by a teacher who survived the bombing but saw his child die. It tells about a boy who receives a longed-for tricycle for his fourth birthday, only to be riding the tricycle at the time of the bombing. When Shin dies during the bombing, his parents bury him with the tricycle. The tricycle has recently been recovered and is now found in the Peace Museum in Hiroshima. The impact of this book could be compared with Toshi Maruki's *Hiroshima No Pika*, which also depicts the consequences of the bombing.

Books that describe or depict nuclear war vary depending on the intended audiences and the messages to be related. Compare the highly visual and personalized descriptions in Maruki's *Hiroshima No Pika* with Carl B. Feldbaum and Ronald J. Bee's historical and scientific descriptions in *Looking the Tiger in the Eye: Confronting the Nuclear Threat.* Using a picture-storybook format, Maruki relates the experiences of seven-year-old Mii on August 6, 1945, as the child and her mother pass by fire, death, and destruction. Maruki, who actively campaigns for nuclear disarmament and world peace, concludes her book on a hopeful note: "It can't happen again if no one drops the bomb" (p. 43, unnumbered). Feldbaum and Bee's text includes the history of nuclear weapons and discusses decisions made by political, scientific, and military officials.

Jerry Stanley's *I Am an American: A True Story of Japanese Internment* describes the events that led up to the internment of Japanese Americans living on the West Coast and the effects this experience had on people. Ellen Levine's *A Fence Away from Freedom: Japanese Americans and World War II* includes personal narratives in which Japanese Americans describe their experiences. The text includes a bibliography, a glossary of terms, a chronology of major events, and a map of internment centers.

Books by Dorinda Makanaoalani Nicholson and Joanne Oppenheim are nonfictional presentations of World War II experiences. Nicholson's *Remember World War II: Kids Who Survived Tell Their Stories* includes the story of a Japanese American boy whose family was interned and a woman who survived the bombing of Tokyo. Oppenheim's *Dear Miss Breed: True Stories of the Japanese American Incarceration During World War II and a Librarian Who Made a Difference* includes letters written between a San Diego librarian and young people who are interned in camps. These books might be compared with historical fiction such as David Patneaude's *Thin Wood Walls.*

Contemporary Asian and Asian American Stories *Homeless Bird* by Gloria Whelan is the 2000 National Book Award winner. The book, set in modern India, is about Koly, a thirteen-year-old girl who overcomes difficulties associated with an arranged marriage. Whelan develops a heroine who must adhere to the cultural standards for women. Koly is forbidden to attend school and is criticized by her mother when her father decides to teach her to read. Instead, Koly's mother teaches her to embroider, a skill her mother considers more appropriate for females. Throughout the book Whelan emphasizes various cultural beliefs and values. For example, she describes Holi, the feast that celebrates the god Krishna's love for Radha; she stresses the importance of the poetry written by Rabindranath Tagore, one of India's greatest poets; and she describes the fate of many widows when they are deserted in Vrindavan, a city with many widows who beg for food.

The author uses the theme of the homeless bird throughout the book. Koly's changing attitudes about the homeless bird reflect her own development. Early in the book, Koly describes writing as caged birds that are caught forever; thinks of herself as a caged animal when contemplating her arranged marriage; and discovers her favorite poem is about a homeless bird that is always flying somewhere else. Finally, when Koly meets the young man she knows will make her happy, she feels like a homeless bird, but one that is flying home at last. Readers know she has resolved her person-against-self conflicts when she embroiders a quilt that includes all of the items that make her happy. She knows immediately that the border will include the homeless bird and items from Tagore's poems.

The widest range of Asian American experiences in current children's literature is found in the works of Laurence Yep, who writes with sensitivity about Chinese Americans who, like himself, have lived in San Francisco, California. His characters overcome the stereotypes sometimes found in literature about Asian Americans, and his stories integrate information about Chinese cultural heritage into the everyday lives of his characters. We have already discussed several of his historical fiction novels set in the United States and his collection of folklore collected from Chinese Americans.

In *Child of the Owl*, Yep develops the story of a heroine, twelve-year-old Casey, who discovers she knows more about her father's world of racehorses than about her own Chinese heritage. It is only after she is sent to live with Paw-Paw, her grandmother in San Francisco's Chinatown, that she makes discoveries about, and learns to understand, her Chinese heritage. The author uses a story about the Owl Spirit to help Casey make discoveries about her history.

Yep uses the owl as a symbol throughout the book. In an Afterword, Yep states that he presented the owl story, "which is based upon stories of filial devotion once popular among the Chinese and upon Chinese folklore concerning owls and other animals" (p. 217). In *Thief of Hearts*, the sequel to *Child of the Owl*, Yep has written another novel in which the main character, Casey, gains cross-cultural understanding. Yep's *Later, Gator* develops themes related to sibling rivalry, as well as insights into Chinese American and Caucasian attitudes.

Memory, seeds, and traditional beliefs are very important in Sherry Garland's *The Lotus Seed*, a book written for younger children. In this story, a Vietnamese family resettles in the United States. During happier days in Vietnam, the grandmother picks a seed from a lotus plant in the emperor's garden to remember a special occasion. Throughout her life, she looks at this seed during important moments in her life or when she feels sad. The seed is so important that she brings it to the United States when her family escapes the war. Years later, a grandson carelessly throws out the seed, which saddens his grandmother tremendously. Luckily, the seed is thrown where it eventually grows into a lotus plant. When the blossom fades, the grandmother gives a seed to each of her grandchildren. Garland develops a universal theme about how small things and the memories they evoke are important in our lives.

Adjusting to a new culture and developing understanding of oneself and others are problems faced by many new Americans. Lensey Namioka's *Yang the Youngest and His Terrible Ear* is a humorous, contemporary realistic fiction story that speaks to the needs of many readers. The author develops a protagonist, nine-year-old Yingtao, who is out of place in his musical family. Although he has a great eye, he has a terrible ear. Students of children's literature can analyze Yingtao's reactions to both learning English and trying to make his family understand he is not, and will never be, a talented musician. The author helps readers visualize the problems by relating them to Yingtao's Chinese background. In a satisfying ending, both the family of his American friend and Yingtao's own family realize the importance of honoring one's gifts. *Yang the Third and Her Impossible Family* is a humorous sequel in which Yingmei Yang, the family's third daughter, tries her best to learn to be an American.

Difficulties related to adjusting to a new country and retaining previous cultural values are important personal and social conflicts developed by Pegi Deitz Shea in *Tangled Threads: A Hmong Girl's Story*. In this story, a thirteen-year-old orphan, Mai Yang, from Laos travels with her grandmother to the United States. Readers will gain considerable information about Hmong values and culture. They will also discover some of the conflicts new immigrants faced as they follow Mai Yang's struggles to adapt to her new country.

Picture books written for younger children frequently focus on young Asian American children as they become familiar with various aspects of their culture. For example, in *Chin Chiang and the Dragon's Dance*, Ian Wallace creates a satisfactory conclusion for a person-against-self conflict. Young readers can understand Chin Chiang's conflict. He has practiced for and dreamed of dancing the dragon's dance on the first day of the Year of the Dragon. The time arrives, but he runs away because he fears he will not dance well enough to make his grandfather proud. With the help of a new friend, Chin Chiang discovers his dream can come true. Full-page watercolor paintings capture the beauty of the celebration and depict Asian influences on the city of Vancouver. Kate Waters and Madeline Slovenz-Low's *Lion Dancer: Ernie Wan's Chinese New Year* is a photographic essay that follows a boy as he prepares to take part in the very important lion dance. Readers can make interesting comparisons between these two books.

Books for younger children may explore emotions relating to adjusting to a new sibling or a relative who joins the family. Ed Young's *My Mei Mei* is based on the author's experiences related to two adopted daughters and their relationship with each other. Lenore Look's *Ruby Lu, Empress of Everything* deals with the various changing relationships between Ruby Lu and the arrival of a deaf cousin from China, Flying Duck. This is a chapter book illustrated with black-and-white cartoon drawings.

Numerous experiences in the life of a Vietnamese American are shown through a photographic essay in Diane Hoyt-Goldsmith's *Hoang Anh: A Vietnamese-American Boy*. Lawrence Migdale's photographs show the daily activities of Hoang Anh and his family in San Rafael, California, as they work on their fishing boat, live and play at home, prepare for the New Year, and experience the Tet Festival. Patricia McMahon's *Chi-Hoon: A Korean Girl* is a photographic essay that presents one week in the life of a girl.

Although Takaaki Nomura's picture storybook *Grandpa's Town* is set in Japan rather than North America, the themes of the story relate to the universality of loving relationships between grandfathers and grandsons, possible loneliness after the death of a loved one, and preferences for staying with old friends. This story, written in both Japanese and English, includes a great deal of cultural information. A young boy accompanies his grandfather around town, meets his grandfather's friends, and discovers his grandfather is not willing to leave these friends to move in with the boy and his mother. Changes resulting from urban development also cause the emotional difficulties in Allen Say's *Kamishibai Man*. In this highly illustrated book, an elderly Japanese storyteller travels a route he once followed with his bicycle as he told stories from a wood-and-paper theater. The urban changes are difficult for him.

The importance of even small cultural artifacts, such as eating utensils, stimulates a humorous plot in Ina R. Friedman's *How My Parents Learned to Eat*. Friedman suggests the solution to a problem on the first page of this picture storybook: "In our house, some days we eat with chopsticks and some days we eat with knives and forks. For me, it's natural" (p. 1, unnumbered).* The rest of the story tells how an American sailor courts a Japanese girl, and each secretly tries to learn the other's way of eating. The couple reaches a satisfactory compromise because each person still respects the other's culture.

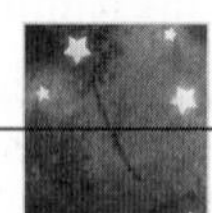

Survival

Many of the characters in stories discussed in this chapter express the traditional values found through family stories, folklore, and religious beliefs. First, let us consider what traditional values are expressed in some of the folklore and in the religious writings that may help characters

*Excerpt from *How My Parents Learned to Eat* by Ina R. Friedman. Text copyright © 1984 by Ina R. Friedman. Reprinted by permission of Houghton Mifflin Harcourt Publishing Company. All rights reserved.

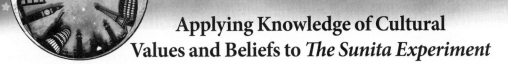

Applying Knowledge of Cultural Values and Beliefs to *The Sunita Experiment*

Mitall Perkins's *The Sunita Experiment* has been named on several lists for outstanding books including New York Public Library Books for the Teen Age Reader, 1994; ALA Recommended Books for Reluctant Readers, 1994, and IRA-CBC Notable Books in the Field of Social Studies. The book, about a family from India who now live in California, provides strong literary elements of character conflict, and theme, as well as examples of cultural beliefs. Consequently, the book provides a good source for identifying the values and beliefs that are implicit or explicit in the story and relating those values and beliefs to the plot and characterization.

The Sunita Experiment is a story about a thirteen-year-old girl whose life in California changes when her grandparents come for a visit from India. The text provides many insights into both Indian culture and Indian American culture. Three generations are represented in the story: the grandparents who have come to visit; the parents, who were originally from India but who have become quite "Westernized"; and their daughter, Sunita, who is totally "Westernized" and wants to remain that way. The clash of cultures is the main conflict of the story as Sunita struggles to understand her grandparent's culture.

As you read the following descriptions of Indian lifestyles, values, and beliefs found in the book, try to authenticate them with what you know or have learned about Indian culture. Also consider if and how these various beliefs might cause friction for an American teenager.

Husbands have authority over their wives.
Girls should not invite boys to their homes.
Teaching is a preferred profession for women.
Children stay with their parents until they are married.
Marriages are arranged by the families.
A woman's place is in the home.
The education of women is becoming more acceptable.
Respect for elders is important.

As you read the book, you may also trace the changes in Sunita as her character progresses from rejection of her cultural roots to acceptance of and appreciation for her cultural identify. For example, early in the book she experiences conflict in school because she does not want to identify her "roots" on a *National Geographic* map (p. 7) and then experiences additional feelings of person-versus-self conflict when most of the class identifies European ancestry. Only three students are not of European heritage: one identifies China, one identifies Africa, and Sunita reluctantly identifies India. After her grandparents arrive, Sunita is embarrassed by the differences between her home and the homes of her friends (pp. 12–14). Sunita resents the playing of Indian music in her home because the "twanging sitar music . . . grated on her nerves and made their house sound like a mecca for aging hippies. A grumpy neighbor had already complained three times since Sunita's grandparents had arrived" (p. 19). Sunita unfavorably contrasts her mother's normal tailored suits with the traditional saree she wears after her grandparents arrive (pp. 21–22). She is ashamed of her family's cultural differences (pp. 24–27). Sunita experiences embarrassment when her essay on arranged Indian marriages is read before the class (pp. 48–50). By the end of the book, however, Sunita shows that she respects her Indian heritage when she chooses to wear a saree on her own and feels like an Indian princess (pp. 177–179).

As you authenticate the lifestyles, values, and beliefs identified in the book, try to decide if the book is or is not authentic for the portrayal of Indian culture. As you read the book for portrayal of Sunita's characterization and conflict, decide if the author develops plausible characterization of, and conflict for, a girl living in two cultures.

in their quest for survival. *What the Rat Told Me: A Legend of the Chinese Zodiac,* adapted from a Chinese Buddhist legend by Marie Sellier, Catherine Louis, and Wang Fei, includes the valued strengths related to the animals that were selected by the Emperor of Heaven to represent the twelve signs of the zodiac. The following characteristics are represented by the animals: Rat—cunning; Ox—hard work, courage, and forcefulness; Tiger—courage and strength; Rabbit—supple and swift; Dragon—great heart; Snake—wisdom; Horse—spirit of adventure; Sheep—peace, love, and beauty; Monkey—crafty, charming, and amusing; Rooster—champion organizer; Dog—faithful guard and tireless protector; and Pig—good, humble, and sincere. As you read and evaluate the Asian literature, how many of these positive and admired values do you discover? Do the characters rely on any of these values in their quests for survival?

A Featured Book for Middle School and Young Adults

The setting for David Patneaude's *Thin Wood Walls* is the Tule Lake Relocation Camp during World War II. The protagonist is eleven-year-old Joe Hanada, whose Japanese American family is moved from the West Coast to the internment camp in interior California. The author develops both credibility for the time period and themes that relate to other historical fiction with similar settings. To develop credibility for the time period the author describes political actions such as President Roosevelt's speech after Pearl Harbor, cultural icons such as Captain Midnight comics, and military actions such as the Bataan Death March and D-Day beaches of Normandy. The author suggests themes such as prejudice and hatred are destructive forces by describing negative attitudes of neighbors. He develops themes related to other historical fiction such as moral obligations and personal conscience are strong forces by describing actions such as the oldest son joining the 442nd Reginal Combat team to show that Japanese Americans are loyal Americans. This book may be compared with Cynthia Kadohata's *Weedflower* in which the family is moved from a flower farm in Southern California to the Arizona desert. Readers may also compare the book to Amy Lee-Tai's *A Place Where Sunflowers Grow*. Lee-Tai's text is set at the Topaz Relocation Center in Utah.

Readers may receive additional verification about American internment camps by reading Amy Leinback Marquis's "The Other Prisoners of War" (2007). This article describes legislation that preserves the Japanese-American internment sites around the country. The article states that there are more than 70 sites around the United States related to World War II internment camps ranging from Honouliuli Internment Camp in Hawaii to Ellis Island in New York. There are ten relocation centers in isolated areas in Arizona, Arkansas, California, Colorado, Idaho, Utah, and Wyoming. These are the isolated locations that are frequently the settings for historical fiction.

The authors of *What the Rat Told Me* identify the source as a Chinese Buddhist legend from the Han dynasty (206 BCE–220 CE). *The Best Buddhist Writing: 2010,* edited by Melvin McLeod (2010), includes a chapter, "Answers to Children's Questions" written by Thich Nhat Hanh that may be used to further identify Buddhist values. For example, Hanh identifies the most important values as peace, loving-kindness, understanding, and the need to be mindful of what is happening in the present moment. This chapter answers questions that may be necessary for survival if characters express a Buddhist belief. These questions include "What is the best way to meditate?," "How do we overcome fear?," "How can we deal with anger?," and "How can I stop worrying?"

Demi's *The Dalai Lama* presents not only many Buddhist beliefs but also the biography of the current Tibetan spiritual and political leader. Demi develops the characterization of a man whose life reflects the Buddhist values and suggests what people must do to survive. For example, kindness and compassion lead to wisdom and people need to live in harmony and peace with each other and with nature. Quotes used by Demi indicate that the Dalai Lama strongly believes that war is not stopped by more war, but by peace and love. He states that the purpose of his life is to dispel the misery of the world. Demi's biography follows the Dalai Lama as the invading Chinese force him to leave Tibet and set up a government in exile in India. Demi concludes her biography with the Dalai Lama's philosophy of life: "Live simply and love humanity. For as long as space endures and for as long as living beings remain, until then may I, too, abide to dispel the misery of the world" (unnumbered).

Many of the beliefs expressed in Demi's biography of the Dalai Lama may be expanded upon and authenticated by reading Santideva's *A Guide to the Bodhisattva Way of Life* (1997). This guide, used by the Dalai Lama during a week-long workshop (Madison, WI, 2008), emphasizes values such as aspiring for Awakening, understanding that altruism and wisdom are the basis for a better life, and experiencing the power of thought and creativity. To increase Awakening, the Dalai Lama expressed his belief that a teacher must have vast knowledge and deep understanding to control one's mind. In addition, altruism brings lasting happiness. In contrast, evils that hinder Awakening include hatred, anger, and ignorance.

The writings of and descriptions of life lived by Confucius also are influential in some Asian literature. Russell Freedman's *Confucius: The Golden Rule* shows that Confucius had a strong belief in the value of education because "When people are educated, distinctions between classes disappear" (p. 15). His one requirement of his students was that they have a passion for learning. Confucius believed that the first task of a statesman was to speak the truth and to use words honestly. He also maintained that a person's worth depends on what he is and what he has done, not on what his family provided for him. To show his true worth, a person must display a compassionate love for humanity. Family obligations were also important to Confucius. He believed that young people should honor their parents and respect their elders. The Golden Rule Confucius followed was: "Do not impose on others what you do not wish for yourself" (p. 30).

Grace Lin's Newbery Honor winning *Where the Mountain Meets the Moon* is a fantasy that combines a quest for the answer to an important question that will save her people and their village, and legends and other stories that help the heroine as she proceeds on her quest. Because many of the stories rely on ancient legends about the Jade Dragon, the book is also discussed under Chinese folklore and fantasy.

The problem begins as Minli asks questions about why her valley and its people are dull, brown, and drought stricken. As she seeks ways of changing the fortunes of the land and the people, she is told that she may obtain her answers from the Old Man of the Mountain who lives on the Never Ending Mountain. As she proceeds on this dangerous quest, she reveals the important survival strategies that eventually help her succeed. For example, she remembers stories her father told each evening that kept her from becoming dull and brown like the rest of the village. She reveals a belief in the phrase "Nothing is impossible" as she discovers that even fates written in the "Book of Fortune" can be changed.

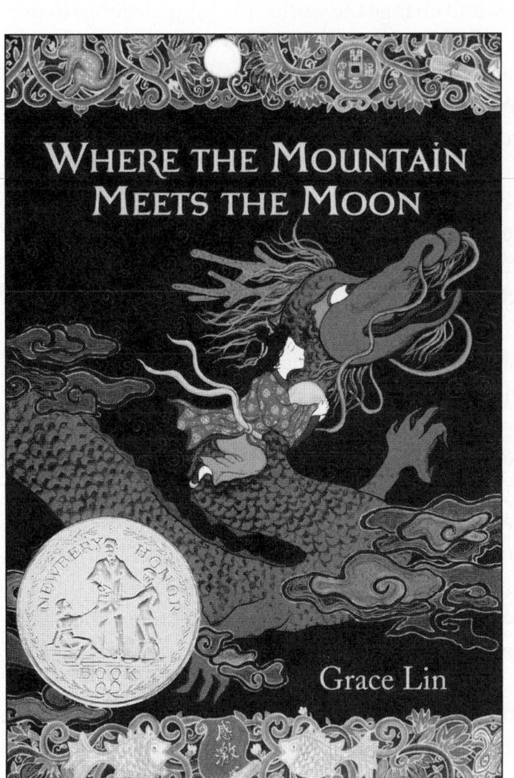

A girl goes on a quest to bring life to her mountain home.

Cover from *Where the Mountain Meets the Moon*, by Grace Lin. Little, Brown and Company, 2009. Reprinted by permission.

The personal characteristics that help her survive are curiosity and a belief in the power of happiness, wisdom, honor, love, kindness, and truth. She demonstrates which objects help her retain her happiness when she takes her favorite books of poetry and memories of the stories and songs she learned from her father on her quest.

Along the way she learns valuable lessons such as contentment and patience must be learned even if the lessons takes many years. Minli's adventures also reveal dishonored and honored values. She discovers that excessive pride is punished and good deeds and kindness are rewarded. As she interacts with both evil and good characters, readers discover what is considered evil and good in the culture. For example, the evil Green Tiger shows excessive anger as he attacks farm animals, not for his own food, but for the excitement of killing. His anger seems to add to his evil power. In contrast, Minli's kindness and wisdom allow the dragon to escape from bondage. He gratefully shows his thankfulness by bringing good fortune to Minli's village, making the land green and causing the people to become happy and contented.

These same survival strategies are found in more contemporary settings. For example, telling stories assists in times of need, determination helps survival, fighting may be required for equality, knowing that knowledge is power, needing to motivate yourself to work, and believing in oneself are all survival strategies developed by Adeline Yen Mah in *Chinese Cinderella and the Secret Dragon Society*. Like Cinderella, the main character, CC, begins life in a family of wealth and privilege but then falls under the power of a cruel stepmother. In this World War II historical fiction story, CC escapes by joining a secret dragon society and learning the martial arts from Grandma Wu.

These martial arts and her survival strategies become especially important during the Japanese invasion of China during the 1940s. Now CC helps to save a group of American pilots who were captured by the Japanese. Through the heroine's actions and courage, the author develops the theme that you can be anybody you want to be so long as you have faith in yourself and study hard to gain knowledge and power. In the historical note, Mah explains that the book is based on a true incident that took place in China. She also provides historical information about the conflict and setting.

It is interesting to compare the roles of dragons in *Where the Mountain Meets the Moon* with the dragon in the *Chinese Cinderella* and the dragon in *What the Rat Told Me: A Legend of the Chinese Zodiac*. All three dragons are considered positive symbols of good fortune. In *Where the Mountain Meets the Moon,* the dragon, freed out of bondage, provides the changes that bring happiness and prosperity to the people. In *Chinese Cinderella,* the sight of a dragon in a cloud formation is considered a good omen for the coming rescue. The dragon in *What the Rat Told Me* represents a creature with a great heart.

Forgiveness is also considered an important survival strategy in *Chinese Cinderella* and in *Where the Mountain Meets the Moon.* In *Chinese Cinderella* one of the rescued Americans tells CC that to survive she should not hate the Japanese, instead she should try to understand them and help them recover after they lose the war. The author concludes with a message of survival: "We are in China at this moment in history for a reason. We are here to make a difference. We are children of destiny who will unite East and West and change the world. The future belongs to us!" (p. 223).

Books with Japanese or Japanese American settings also develop strong survival strategies that reflect cultural values. Mark Reibstein's prose and haiku poetry and Ed Young's illustrations for *Wabi Sabi* reflect the beliefs found in Zen Buddhism. Wabi Sabi, according to the author, is a way of seeing the world that is at the heart of Japanese culture. This heart finds beauty and harmony in natural simplicity. Reibstein develops the meaning of Wabi Sabi through the story of an ordinary brown cat who searches for the meaning of her name. As she seeks this information, she learns to listen, to observe, and to feel. The cat discovers that the leaves in nature are beautiful, but they are both alive and dying. She survives her journey and returns home to her common straw mat in the warm kitchen. With contentment she understands the meaning of her name Wabi Sabi. Ed Young's collage illustrations add to the meaning of the word; they are beautiful, but are constructed from natural materials.

Another book illustrated by Ed Young also develops Buddhist philosophy. Kimiko Kajikawa's *Tsunami!* is adapted from Lafcadio Hearn's story, "A Living God" in *Gleanings in Buddha-Fields, 1897*. Notice how the characteristics of and the actions portrayed by Ojiisan, a wise, old farmer, reflect Buddhist values and lead to the survival of the people who live in a village by the sea. For example, although he is wealthy, he lives a simple life in a thatched cottage high on a mountain; to warn the people about a coming tsunami he sets fire to his own rice fields. Even though his wealth is gone, he saved 400 lives, and the people built a temple to honor the man who saved the people. Ed Young's collages depict the power of the huge wave and the devastation that happened to the village.

Margi Preus's 2011 Newbery Honor winning *Heart of a Samurai* is an example of a book in which the character's goals and the theme of the book all express survival strategies. This historical novel, set in the late 1800s, begins after a violent storm capsizes fourteen-year-old Manjiro and four of his Japanese fishing companions. The storm destroys their boat and strands them on a barren, deserted island. The book, based on the true story of Manjiro Nakahama, allows the author to develop an action-packed story that also reveals cultural conflicts after the characters are eventually rescued by an American whaling ship.

Survival and Manjiro's dreams are introduced early in the book when Preus tells readers that the idea of becoming a samurai kept Manjiro alive as he tries to survive on the island and later as he faces the American barbarians who rescue the fishermen and take them aboard the New England whaling vessel. Manjiro's character develops over the next few years on both the whaling ship and later in America. It is during these years that Manjiro discovers that not all Americans are barbarians and he develops his belief that to survive as nations and as cultures, both America and Japan must promote friendship and understanding between the two nations. Both must overcome deep-seated prejudices.

As you read *Heart of a Samurai,* search for evidence that the dream of becoming a samurai keeps Manjiro alive. Do you believe that his dream is fulfilled? For example, at the age of fourteen, Manjiro dreams of becoming a samurai even though his friends tell him that his lowly birth in the Japanese culture will not allow a fisherman to have such a high honor. As a reader you will discover numerous references to both his dream and the heroic qualities of a samurai. Notice that while on the deserted island Manjiro believes that the men can be their own rulers and he, Manjori, can be their samurai.

To further the samurai connection, the author uses quotes from books that reflect samurai creeds and beliefs such as those found in Yamamoto Tsunetomo's *Hagakure: The Book of the Samurai* (1979) to introduce each part of the book. These quotes suggest various survival strategies as well as themes and conflict developed in the section. For example, when experiencing difficult situations, rush forward to meet them with bravery and joy; when choosing the proper actions, be resolved, courageous, and devoid of doubt; when experiencing hardships and misfortune, know that these experiences will help you face misfortune in the future; and when striving for survival, have your heart set on a single purpose.

As you search for survival strategies in this book, you will discover many related personal characteristics that help Manjori survive. For example, to learn, he asks many questions; the answers to these questions that the American whaling captain and some of the crew members provided allow Manjori to survive both aboard the whaling vessel and later in America. Frequently, Manjori's imagination expands these answers and allows him to reach the right decisions. While in America, he is able to attend school for the first time and discovers the value of reading and writing. His ability to read shows him that he can learn to be a ship's navigator. His ability to observe, to write, and to draw allow him to realize that to survive, Japan needs to adopt the most important treasures he discovers while living in America: railroads, steamships, and square-rigged sailing ships.

In one of his final expressions for survival, Manjori maintains that the world is changing and he believes that good will come from this changing world. As you finish the book, do you believe that Manjori's dream of survival is realized? Has his heart finally become "the mighty heart of a samurai" (p. 274)?

The experiences of Japanese Americans in an internment camp during WWII create the plot and conflict in David Patneaude's *Thin Wood Walls.* It is a time when Japanese Americans living on the West Coast of the United States are being judged by the actions of the Japanese government after the bombing of Pearl Harbor and the actions of Japanese soldiers during the war. The author begins by describing the life of eleven-year-old Joe Hanada as he lives the normal life of a young boy before his family is moved to an internment camp. This comparison shows readers why living in the internment camp is extremely difficult for the family. The author describes the following survival strategies that help Joe through this difficult time: He likes to write haiku poems in his journal because they are a type of Japanese poetry that is frequently linked to nature; he finds satisfaction as his writings allow him to express his feelings; even when he is in the internment camp, he understands the importance of retaining his dreams and not giving up hope; and as a part of his writing, Joe remembers his father's advice to always observe, to think about what he sees, and to display patience. Patneaude develops a theme that suggests that family is important, especially in times of need. There is also a theme that education is very important. This theme is reinforced as Joe's older brother encourages him to study hard, go to college, and become a writer. By reading Joe's haiku, readers will discover not only Joe's survival strategies but also his personal feelings and the conflicts that he faces while he dreams of freedom.

The title of Cynthia Kadohata' Newbery award winning *Kira-Kira* means "glittering" in Japanese. The story follows a Japanese American family and their children as they move from Iowa to Georgia in the late 1950s. The author develops a strong friendship between the two sisters, Katie and Lynn, as they face the move. The greatest tests for survival occur after the older sister, Lynn, becomes terminally ill. After Lynn's death, Katie relies on several strategies for survival: she writes and gives a eulogy in which she remembers the wonderful things about her sister; she follows a Buddhist belief where, for forty-nine days, she cares for a box of Lynn's most beloved belongings; she remembers Lynn's belief that you can use simple things to prove that the world is amazing; and she starts to live by Lynn's certainty that you can make good things happen. Lynn's diary also becomes very important as Katie reads it and learns more about her sister. At this point, she remembers her sister's wishes that she improve her grades so that she will eventually be able to attend college. The book ends almost like it begins. Katie thinks about Lynn as she hears crows calling, "Kira-kira!" Now she realizes that her sister taught her to look at the world as a place that glitters.

The survival strategies in these examples of Asian literature written for children and young adults reflect many of the traditional values found in folklore and in Buddhist writings. There is a desire for peace, understanding of others, need for loving-kindness, and family unity. Even in times of great stress, such as internment during WWII, the characters gain strength from writing in journals, retaining dreams, and never giving up hope. Education and respect for knowledge and wisdom are expressed by many characters.

We may also authenticate these survival strategies by analyzing the strategies developed by well-known Asian authors who write for adult audiences. For example, *China: A Traveler's Literary Companion,* edited by Kirk A. Denton (2008), includes the writings of twelve Chinese authors. Lu Xun stresses the importance of asking Buddha for protection and remembering happy memories from childhood to recapture his homeland. Mao Dun believes in the importance of hard work and honesty as well as retaining hope to overcome poverty. Chu T'ien-hsin maintains that it is important to prepare for the unpredictable in life, and Xi Xi expresses the belief that history teaches lessons and that courage, willpower, and faith help people survive.

Summary

In this chapter, we have discussed the folklore of several Asian cultures including China, India, and Japan.

The discussion of Chinese folklore showed that Confucian and Taoist philosophies may influence tales from that culture. Popular elements in Chinese folklore include the importance of the emperor and gods that control life in the home. Scholarship is one of the highest values in the folklore, along with loyalty, patience, and obedience.

The discussion of folklore from India showed it is influenced by two great belief systems: Hindu and Buddhist. The Jakarta tales are among the most important for revealing Buddhist beliefs and values. These tales also highlight the importance of helping others and of living in harmony.

Folklore from Japan is also influenced by religion and belief systems, especially Buddhism. Folktales often include supernatural monsters and beasts. The fox is one of the greatest tricksters in Japanese folklore.

Numerous informational books about the early history and cultures of the Asian peoples are available. Books about trade routes are especially popular. There are historical fiction books that are set in early China or Japan. Historical fiction authors may place their characters in a setting in which Asian people immigrate to the United States.

Poetry with Asian or Asian American roots reflects ancient values and beliefs, as well as contemporary concerns. Literature reflecting more contemporary times may focus on various leaders, such as biographies of Indira Gandhi or Mohandas Gandhi. Contemporary authors of Asian American literature provide insights into conflicts faced by contemporary Asian Americans as many of the characters rediscover their Asian heritages and also live within the contemporary U.S. culture.

Suggested Activities for Developing Understanding of Asian Literature

1. Choose one of the cultural groups discussed in this chapter. Read a number of myths, legends, and folktales from that culture. Summarize the traditional beliefs and values. Provide quotations from the tales to show the beliefs and values. Try to identify those same beliefs and values in other genres of literature depicting the same culture. What conclusions can you reach about the importance of traditional literature?
2. After you have read a number of folktales from China, India, Japan, or another Asian country, identify the story openings, storytelling style, and story endings that are the most common for the culture.
3. Choose a religious belief such as one from the Buddhist or Hindu tradition and locate folklore that reflects that belief.
4. Folklore may be "rewritten" to emphasize the important beliefs of a political or a religious group. Choose a country in which the political or religious climate has changed over the years. Try to find evidence of these different beliefs in the folklore.
5. Choose an outstanding author of Asian or Asian American literature such as Laurence Yep or Allen Say, and read several books by that author. What makes the plots and the characters memorable? What are the themes in the writer's work? Is there a common theme throughout the writing?
6. Search a social studies or history curriculum and identify Asian Americans who have made contributions during the time periods or areas being studied. Identify literature selections that include additional information about those individuals and their contributions.
7. Compare an autobiography of an Asian or Asian American personage with biographies about the same person written for children or young adults.
8. Compare the themes and conflicts in poetry written by Asian Americans with the themes and conflicts in contemporary realistic fiction about Asian Americans.
9. Read an article in which the authors recommend Asian children's literature. What criteria do the authors use? Some examples might include Valerie Ooka Pang, et al., "Beyond Chopsticks and Dragons: Selecting Asian-American Literature for Children," and Charles Temple, "Reading Around the World."
10. Add to the "Survival" Section in this chapter. Locate and analyze a book that is not discussed in the section, or compare the survival strategies found in books featuring different Asian cultures. If you find differences, try to account for the differences.

Involving Children with Asian Literature

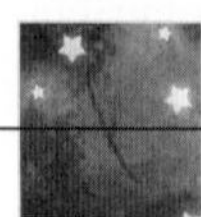

Phase One: Traditional Values in Folklore

Many of the examples provided in this section are from Chinese folklore. The techniques, however, may be used with folklore from any of the Asian countries.

Using a Web to Develop a Unit Around Chinese Folklore

As we have already discovered, students can learn a great deal about a country and its people by investigating a number of the traditional tales from that country. Such research also increases students' understanding of the multicultural heritage of the United States and develops understanding of, and positive attitudes toward, cultures other than one's own.

The web in Figure 5.1 (Norton, 2003) uses traditional tales from China to analyze personal values, important symbols, and disliked human qualities in the Chinese culture. It also looks at supernatural beings. Finally, it lists motivating introductions to the study of traditional tales, as well as stimulating activities to accompany the study.

This web was used as a structure for a successful study of folktales from China by the teacher of a fifth-grade class. Objects displayed throughout the classroom stimulated students' interest. A large red paper dragon met the students as they entered the room. Other objects included joss sticks (incense), lanterns. Chinese flutes, a tea service, fans, statues of mythical beasts, lacquered boxes and plates, silk, samples of Chinese writing, a blue willow plate, jade, and reproductions of Chinese paintings. Many Chinese folktales were displayed on the library table. Chinese music played in the background. The chalkboard contained a message, written in Chinese figures, welcoming the children to China. (Examples of useful reference books on Chinese art are included in the bibliography.)

The students looked at the displays, listened to the music, tried to decipher the message, and discussed what they saw and heard. They located China on a map and a globe. Then they listed questions they had about China—questions about the people, country, values, art, music, food, houses, animals, and climate.

The teacher shared several of her favorite Chinese folktales with the group. They included Marilee Heyer's *The Weaving of a Dream: A Chinese Folktale,* Margaret Mahy's *The Seven Chinese Brothers,* Demi's *The Empty Pot,* and tales found in Neil Phillip's *The Spring of Butterflies and Other Chinese Folktales,* as well as other collections of Chinese folktales. The teacher and students searched for values, symbols, and negative human qualities in these tales. The teacher also provided brief introductions to other tales to stimulate the children's interest in reading the tales. The children then chose tales to read independently. As they read, they considered their questions about China; when they discovered information about the culture and the people, they jotted it down so they could share it with the class.

After collecting their information, the children discussed ways of verifying whether or not the information was accurate. They compared the information with library reference materials and information in magazines such as *National Geographic.* They also invited to the classroom several visitors who were either Chinese or had visited China.

The students used their knowledge about the people, culture, and literature of China in their own art, creative drama, and writing. They drew travel posters as well as book jackets and illustrations for folktales. They also made mobiles of folk-literature objects.

FIGURE 5.1 Web of a Unit of Study on Chinese Folklore

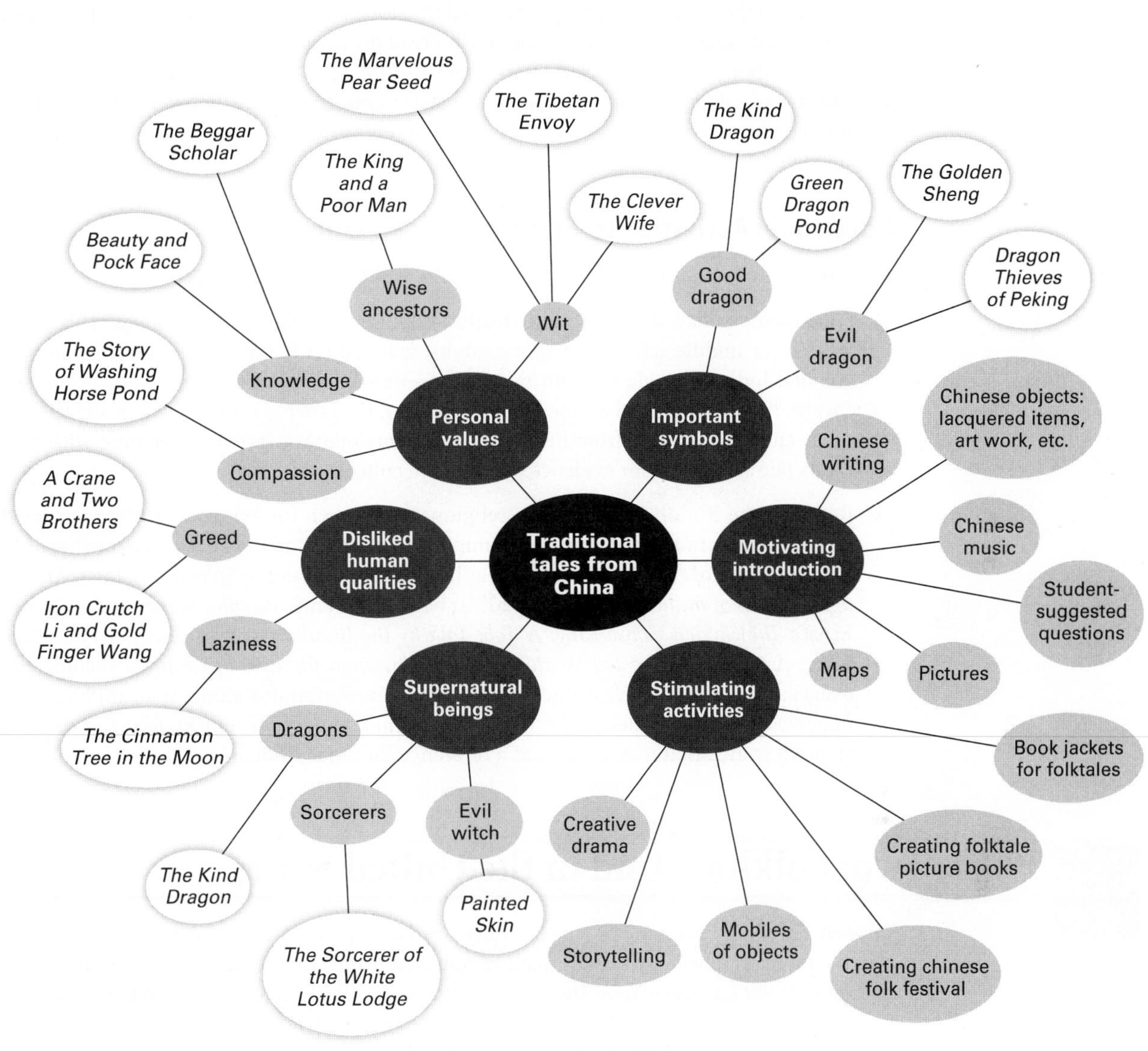

One artistic activity was to create picture storybooks from single folktales. The group chose a favorite tale not already in picture-book format, illustrated it with drawings, and bound the pages together. Because many of the published picture books contained information about the origins of their tales, the students included similar information inside their own front covers. Published book jackets often tell about the illustrator and the research to provide authentic pictures, and the students' books used this information. The students told about themselves and the ways in which they prepared for their drawing assignments. They described the mediums they used for their illustrations. Then they shared their books with one another and other classes and proudly displayed the books in the library.

The class also chose some stories for creative drama. The teacher divided the class into groups according to favorite folktales. Each group then chose a method for sharing the story with the rest of the class. Some groups recreated the stories as plays, others chose puppetry, and one group used pantomime with a narrator, who read the lines.

This unit about one country led to an interest in folktales from other countries. The students next read folktales from Japan and other Asian countries. They discovered the similarities among many Asian tales, especially in the symbolic animals found in both Chinese and Japanese tales.

Additional Activities to Enhance Phase One

Here are some activities for children or young adult students related to this phase:

1. Older readers may choose to read Heather Tomlinson's *Toads and Diamonds*. This story, written for middle school and young adults, is based on Perrault's tale but is set in precolonial India. The tale is about two sisters—one is beautiful and polite and when she speaks, flowers and jewels come from her mouth, the other is rude and when she speaks, toads and snakes come from her mouth. Students may compare this retelling with Perrault's tale and search for evidence of an Indian culture.

2. Research the Buddhist and Hindu religions and search for evidence of the associated cultural beliefs in the folklore. For example, search for Hindu beliefs in Aaron Shepard's *Savitri: A Tale of Ancient India* and Madhur Jaffrey's *Seasons of Splendour: Tales, Myths, and Legends of India*. Search for Buddhist beliefs in Demi's *Buddha Stories* and in Judith Ernst's *The Golden Goose King: A Tale Told by the Buddha*. Laura Buller's *A Faith Like Mine: A Celebration of the World's Religions Through the Eyes of Children* includes an overview of Hinduism and Buddhism and is appropriate for students in middle- and upper-elementary grades. Robert Beer's *The Handbook of Tibetan Buddhist Symbols* is an adult source that may be used as a reference for older students.

Phase Two: Folklore Told in the United States

You may develop a web similar to the one developed for Chinese traditional literature and compare the values and beliefs found in folklore collected from Chinese Americans. For this activity, you may use Laurence Yep's *The Rainbow People*, a collection of twenty folktales collected from Chinese Americans in the United States. The text is divided into tales about tricksters, fools, virtues and vices, Chinese America, and love.

Share and discuss with the students information from Yep's introductory comments. For example, folktales "are strategies for living. At the very least, the stories offered consolation and more often hope. But beyond that, the stories also expressed the loneliness, anger, fear, and love that were part of the Chinese-American experience" (p. x).

As part of this activity, students will discover in the trickster tales that keeping one's wits could save one's life, loyalty is important, and treachery is evil. In the tales about fools, readers discover that misinterpretations and bad luck can cause serious consequences. In the tales about virtues and vices, readers discover the positive worth of kindness and the negative worth of greed and impatience. In addition, one must be moderate in desires. Before students read the tales under "In Chinese America," share Yep's introduction to the section in which he describes the work of the Chinese in North America as they built railroad lines and worked in industry and agriculture. Ask the students to identify any examples or reflections of this work they find in the literature.

Students might also analyze the folklore components and the new cultural setting in Paul Yee's *Tales from Gold Mountain: Stories of the Chinese in the New World*. These are literary tales created by Yee that reflect both the traditional values and the conflict the Chinese faced as they overcame prejudice and adversity in North America.

Additional Activities to Enhance Phase Two

Here are some activities for children or young adult students related to this phase:

1. Add the folktales retold in the United States to the unit about China.
2. Interview someone living in the United States who originally came from an Asian country. Ask them to tell their favorite folktales.
3. Investigate the influence of the railroad in North America in the 1800s and early 1900s on Asian people.

Phase Three: Historical Nonfiction

Integrating Literature and Geography

Many of the multicultural books discussed in this text lend themselves to an analysis using five themes from geography. Geographers have developed a procedure that allows readers to inquire about places on the earth and to analyze their relationships to the people who live there. The following five fundamental themes in geography were developed by the Committee on Geographic Education (1983) and are also discussed in *GEO News* (1990):

1. *Location, including where and why:* Where does the story take place—as far as city, country, continent, longitude, latitude, and so forth? Why does the story take place in this location?
2. *Place, including physical and human characteristics:* What are the physical features and characteristics? What are the characteristics of the people, including distinctive cultural traditions?
3. *Relationships within places, including cultural and physical interactions and how relationships develop:* How do human-environmental relationships develop and what are the consequences? What is the primary use of land? How have the people altered the environment? Where do most people live?
4. *Movement, including people, ideas, and materials:* How are the movements of people, ideas, and materials influenced and accomplished? What are the consequences of such movements?
5. *Regions, including how they form and change:* What are the major languages? What are the vegetation regions? What are the country's political divisions? How do the regions change?

Introduce these five themes of geography and how the themes will be used to analyze books. Allow students to discuss information that would be included under each of the categories.

You may develop a chart for each of the books you will be using for the activity. On this chart, place the five themes of geography. As students read or listen to each book, ask them to identify and discuss the information that would be appropriate for each of the categories.

Begin this activity that focuses on the geography of the Silk Route by sharing information about how and why the cellist Yo-Yo Ma used the music from various cultures that made up the ancient trade route between China and Byzantium (Covington, 2002). You may choose to have students listen to Yo-Yo Ma's "The Silk Road," in which he uses authentic instruments to develop music that characterizes the route. Share the cellist's beliefs about why he developed the Silk Road Project:

> It seems that when connections flow, cultures thrive—such as that in Xi'an during the Tang Dynasty (618–907 CE), when Muslims, Christians, Jews and Persians all mingled. Whenever two cultures meet, it's the little things that made a difference. In music, you learn that different phrasing, timing, rhythms mean very specific things. In classical Azerbaijani music, the goal is to transport you to a different place. That was also Beethoven's goal. It's universal, but every culture will find its own way of achieving that goal. (p. 88)

The following activity is developed around John S. Major's *The Silk Route: 7,000 Miles of History*. Before students read this book, provide some historical background about the time period and the locations. For example, show and discuss the map at the beginning of the book on which the Silk Route is traced from Chang'an, China, to Byzantium during the Tang dynasty (618–907 CE). Discuss the geographical locations through which the Silk Route extends as well as the importance of trade routes during this time period. The following type of information may be placed on a chart. The listings show a few of the examples that were identified, discussed, and analyzed with a class of students using *The Silk Route: 7,000 Miles of History:*

Location: Chang'an, China, the largest city in the world in 700 CE. The Silk Route, or ancient trade route between China and Byzantium.
Oasis town of Dunhuang is an important trading and supply center.
The oasis city of Kashgar provides dried dates, raisins, and jade to bring back to China.
Pamirs are a range of mountains in eastern Afghanistan.
Market of Tashkent marks eastern edge of Persian cultural world.
Transoxiana is a wild area in which bandits attack caravans.
Herat is thriving city of artisans.
Baghdad is the greatest city of the Islamic world and a hub of trade.

Place: Network of caravan tracks cross the steppes and deserts of Central Asia.
Conditions on the caravan route include heat, hunger, thirst, and bandit raids.
Buddhist temples are seen in China.
Each different city specializes in goods that are made and traded.

Relationships within Places: Emperors of Tang dynasty brought China to a high point of power and culture.
The importance of silk to the ancient Western world brought trade with China.
In China, men grow grain; women produce silk.
Trade goods from China include porcelain, herbal medicines, and silk cloth desired by Islamic and Byzantine worlds.

Movement: The world of Islam expanded rapidly after its founding by Muhammad in 622.
Silk was used as money.
Materials brought to trade changed hands several times along the route.
Buddhist religion came to China from India along the Silk Route about 100 C.E.
In Heart, there are Muslim imams, Zoroastrian priests, Nestorian Christian priests, and Buddhist monks.

Regions: China includes farmland suitable for growing grains.
China has groves of mulberry trees whose leaves feed the silkworms.
Taklamakan, one of the world's driest deserts, has sand dunes, rocky flats, and dry riverbeds.
The Silk Route crosses the Pamirs, a range of high mountains in eastern Afghanistan.

As students identify and discuss these themes in geography, ask them to consider the importance of each of the themes to the development of the Silk Route and the movement of ideas across its 7,000 miles. They could compare the various categories found in this early time period and compare the contemporary routes and countries discussed in this book. Which categories would change? How would they change? Which categories would be similar to this earlier time period in history? Why would they be similar?

Many additional books may be used for a similar activity. The informational books discussed in the previous sections provide excellent sources for selecting appropriate literature.

Additional Activities to Enhance Phase Three

Here are some activities for children or young adult students related to this phase:

1. Many of the rare books about Asian cultures found in the University of Wisconsin Library or with collectors have been digitalized and are now available for study (McLimans, 2010). The following are cited in McLimans's article:

   UWDC East Asian Collection
   (http://digital.library.wisc.edu/1711.dl/East Asian.JapanRice)
   Sino-Japanese Conflict (1937–1945) and History of Buddhist Practices
   (http://digicoll.library.wisc.edu/EastAsian/)
   Diaries of Hayashi Kenzo
   (http://digicoll.library.wisc.edu/cgi-bin/EastAsian-idx?type=browse&scope=EastAsian.Hokkai)
   Ezo-shi by Arai Hakuseki
   (http://digital.library.wisc.edu/1711.dl/EastAsian.Ezoshi)

2. After investigating the history of one of the Asian countries, choose a time in the history of the country during which you would have liked to live. Write stories or journal entries that describe your life during that time period. Include your reasons for selecting the time period.

3. Reading biographies of Buddha and other religious figures is important to gain an understanding of Asian cultures. Research the connections between religious figures and art. How important is the art to the understanding of and the spread of the religion within the culture? For example, Michael Kampen O'Riley's *Art Beyond the West* (2006) includes sections on Buddhist art and the spread of Buddhist art, Hindu art, and Jain art. Numerous photographs of both art and architecture are included.

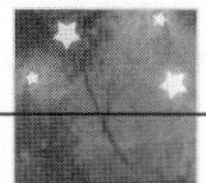

Phase Four: Historical Fiction

Analytical Reading of Linda Sue Park's *A Single Shard*

In this section we apply Adler and Van Doren's stages in analytical reading to Linda Sue Park's *A Single Shard*, the 2002 Newbery Medal book. As you read and analyze each of the stages, identify how the technique increases both analytical and critical reading ability. Also notice how the approach increases and improves involvement in discussion and writing about a book.

First Stage: Rules for Finding What a Book Is About

1. Identify and discuss the kind of literature and the subject matter in *A Single Shard*. This book is historical fiction. Writers of effective historical fiction must develop character's experiences, conflicts, and resolutions of conflicts that reflect what is known about the time period. The language, setting, and themes should be authentic for the time period. We must decide whether or not Park has developed a credible historical fiction book for a story set in twelfth-century Korea.

2. Briefly describe (summarize) the book. Park's book is set in Korea during the time when the celadon potters of Korea (918–1393 C.E.) created famous and beautiful pottery. The main character, the thirteen-year-old orphan boy Tree-ear, is fascinated by the potter's craft and dreams of making a pot of his own. When he is given the opportunity to work for a famous potter in Korea, he is given the most menial jobs. He discovers persistence is necessary if he is ever to gain his dream. As you read this book, notice how the sense of authenticity is developed through the author's use of Korean sayings and proverbs, descriptions of the process used for creating celadon porcelain, and stories told that reveal Korean history. How do all of these sayings, stories, and proverbs also help you understand how the author developed characterization and conflict?

3. List and outline the major parts of the book. (a) Tree-ear's parents die and he is taken care of by Crane-man, a homeless man who lives under a bridge. (b) Tree-ear asks a famous potter to allow him to work with him. (c) Tree-ear is given the most menial of tasks, but he is persistent and does not give up his dream. (d) Tree-ear watches and learns some of the secrets of the potter's trade. (e) Through stories Tree-ear learns the history of the potter's trade and the social structure of Korea. (f) Tree-ear is sent to the royal palace with a valued piece of celadon porcelain, but along the way he must overcome many obstacles. (g) Tree-ear finally succeeds and returns with an important commission to create the porcelain. (h) Tree-ear gains his dream and become Hyung-gu, a name that signifies respect, honor, and attachment to a family. As you read the book, consider how each of these major parts lead to the final fulfillment of Tree-ear's dream and to his important name change.

4. Define the problems the author has tried to solve. This book is mainly a story about a young man's search for identity and his quest to reach his dream. Along the way he must overcome obstacles such as society's attitudes toward a lowly orphan, following a course that allows him to learn the secrets of creating this beautiful pottery, and conducting an important mission to take a finished pot on a long and hazardous journey to the royal palace. As you read this book, ask yourself, "What are the major problems that Tree-ear must solve, and what does he do to overcome each problem?"

Second Stage: Rules for Interpreting a Book's Content

1. Identify and interpret the author's key words (Vocabulary). Ask the students to identify and discuss the meanings of words related to ceramics and the setting of the book. For example, What is the importance of the court of the Chinese emperor for this story set in Korea? What is a communal kiln, and why is it important? What does Tree-ear mean when he says he can read the mountains? What is a clear celadon color, and why is it important when creating the celadon glaze? What is the significance of the Buddhist beliefs in this story? What is a single shard, and why is such a small piece of pottery important in this story?

2. Understand the author's leading propositions by identifying and discussing the author's most important sentences. Read the following quote to students from an interview with Linda Sue Park (Johnson and Giorgis, 2003) in which she states what *A Single Shard* is really about:

> In huge general terms, I think people who have a passion for something are just happier people. To have something you're really interested in can provide you with many hours and days of pleasure. People who don't have that seem to be a little unanchored to me. In the broadest sense this is what is central to *A Single Shard*—that it's important to have something you're passionate about. Min, Tree-ear, and the Emissary all have something they're passionate about. The process is the passion. Doing it—the time you spend with it—that's the important thing. (p. 398)

Ask students to identify and discuss sentences and longer quotes that develop the importance of having a passion about something in *A Single Shard*.

3. Know the author's arguments by identifying them in the text. The author's arguments are related to the development of several themes in the text. For example, ask students to identify themes they discover in the text and to present evidence they believe are themes developed by Park. The following themes may be identified and discussed: Work gives a man dignity; stealing takes it away. A son is very important in Korean culture. Nature is very important and will provide balance in life. Patience is one of the most important values. The same wind that blows one door shut often blows another door open. Pride and foolishness are often close companions.

4. Determine which of the problems the author has solved and which have not been solved. Find out the author's solutions: ask the students to review the major problems identified in the text and discuss which of the problems are solved. If the problems have not been solved, which of the problems relate to the historical time period and to the culture? Could these problems have been solved in an authentic way during the time period and within the culture?

5. Do not begin criticizing the book until you have completed your interpretation. Ask yourself, What additional information do I need to know about the time period and the culture before I can make valid criticisms about the book?

6. When you disagree, do so reasonably. Ask the students to provide evidence when they disagree with a character's actions, the plot of the story, or the themes developed within the book.

7. Respect the differences between knowledge and personal opinion by giving reasons for critical judgments. Ask students to give their judgments related to the text. Students might analyze additional literature about the time period and the culture. Ask them to compare the books, especially for the authenticity related to problems of the time period and the culture. Numerous folktales about the culture are also told in this book. Students can search for and respond to additional folktales about early Korean culture.

Additional Activities to Enhance Phase Four

Here are some activities for children or young adult students related to this phase:

1. Jean Merrill's *The Girl Who Loved Caterpillars,* a picture book set in twelfth-century Japan, provides an interesting stimulus for creative writing. The author states that the second chapter to the original scroll has been lost. Consequently, you can speculate about what happened to the subject of the story—a wise woman who was interested in nature. Write your own version of the missing chapter and decide if the woman became a scientist or a philosopher, or if she became alienated from her family and society, or if she has some other fate.

2. Trace the molding of two cultures in two picture storybooks by Allen Say. *Grandfather's Journey* is an immigration story that focuses on a character's journeys: the first one from Japan to California and then a later one that takes him back to visit the Japan of his youth. *Tree of Cranes* is set in Japan and develops a story as the boy's mother, who was born in the United States, prepares a Christmas celebration that combines Japanese and U.S. cultural traditions.

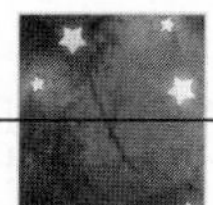

Phase Five: Contemporary Literature

Compare Biographies of One Biographical Character

Studying several biographies of the same individual allows students to evaluate and compare the accuracy of characterization in biographies. Students can also analyze plot, setting, and theme in biographies. For example, they could compare three biographies of Gandhi: Victoria Sherrow's *Mohandas Gandhi: The Power of the Spirit,* Glenn Alan Cheney's *Mohandas Gandhi,* and Doris and Harold Faber's *Mahatama Gandhi.*

To analyze plot in biographies, have students identify the pattern of action, locate examples of specific types of conflicts (person against self, person against person, person against nature, person against society), analyze why the biographer emphasizes those types of conflicts, consider why and how the conflicts relate to the biographer's purpose in writing, and locate examples of ways in which the biographer develops the readers' interest.

To evaluate setting in biographies, ask students to identify the various settings; identify the ways in which the biographer informs readers about the important details related to the time period; analyze how much influence the setting has on the plot and characters; find specific locations mentioned in the biography and locate these places on a map, in geography texts, or in other nonfiction sources; evaluate the authenticity of settings by comparing the information in various nonfiction sources; check the accuracy of dates and happenings in other nonfiction sources; and draw a setting as if it were a backdrop for a stage production (first evaluating whether or not there is enough information about the setting to complete a drawing).

To evaluate theme in biography, ask the students to find the primary, or main, theme in a biography and several secondary themes. Ask the students to consider how these themes are integrated into the biography, analyze whether or not the title of the biography reflects the theme, search for evidence of the biographical subject's ability to triumph over obstacles, identify and compare the themes developed in several biographies written about the same person, and compare the themes in biographies written for younger children with those written for young adults.

How Would Confucius, Buddha, or the Dalai Lama Respond to These Issues?

Ask students to search through current newspapers, magazines, or broadcast media to locate articles related to various Asian cultures. Ask the students to consider how people in the books they have read might respond to the issues and content in the articles. For example, many newspaper articles published in 2011 emphasize the importance of education in Asian cultures. Examples of articles that stress this value include:

Bajaj, Vikas. "Skipping Over Rote in Indian Schools." *New York Times* (February 18, 2011): B1, B7.

Friedman, Thomas L. "Serious In Singapore." *New York Times* (January 30, 2011): Week in Review, 8.

Kristof, Nicholas D. "China's Winning Schools?" *New York Times* (January 16, 2011): A10.

Kristof's article emphasizes one of the strongest connections between cultural values and educational attainment when he states, "An international study published last month looked at how students in 65 countries performed in math, science, and reading. The winner was Confucianism!" (p. A10). He reports that the top performers are Shanghai, Hong Kong, Singapore, and South Korea; all of these countries have a Confucian legacy that reveres education. (In comparison, the other top non-Confucian country was Finland. The United States ranked fifteenth in reading, twenty-third in science, and thirty-first in math.) Ask students to respond to Kristof's comment that, "Education thrives in China and the rest of Asia because it is a top priority" (p. A10). Ask the students to consider how Confucius would respond to these high educational aspirations. Remind the students that Russell Freedman's biography, *Confucius: The Golden Rule,* stressed that the main requirement for Confucius's students was a passion for learning. Ask the students to respond to Confucius's belief that education eliminates distinctions between the classes. Do they agree or disagree? Why or why not?

When reading Bajaj's article students may consider how and why a wealthy industrialist in India is helping government schools improve the education of the poorest children from the least educated families. Bajaj describes a curriculum in which teachers help students write their own stories, pursue their own projects, and enact poetry through oral presentations. From their reading of the biographies, how might Confucius or the Dalai Lama respond to this curriculum?

Looking at the five phases we studied in Asian literature, what support for education did you find in Chinese and Chinese American folklore, historical nonfiction, historical fiction, and contemporary literature? If you were to write an editorial about Asian values and high aspirations for education, what would you emphasize? Try to include the beliefs and values of both Confucius and the wealthy businessman from India who is spending money to help poor children obtain an education.

Additional Activities to Enhance Phase Five

Here are some activities for children or young adult students related to this phase:

1. Laurence Yep is one of the most prolific authors of Chinese American literature for young readers. His books integrate information about Chinese cultural heritage into the everyday lives of his characters. In addition to Yep's historical fiction books already discussed, read books such as *Child of the Owl; Star Fisher*; *Thief of Hearts*; and *Later, Gator*. Identify important recurring themes that are developed by the author. Are there any similarities in characterization, conflict, and setting? If so, what are these similarities? How does the author develop cultural knowledge and beliefs within his stories? Read information about the author and try to decide why he writes his stories.

2. Poetry with Asian or Asian American roots may be found that reflects traditional values and beliefs or contemporary concerns. Many of the Japanese poems, for example, reflect close relationships with nature. Using a poetry collection such as Demi's *In the Eyes of the Cat: Japanese Poetry for All Seasons*, discuss the various images of nature and various animals that live in nature. Are there similarities in the feeling about nature in the poetry and in the traditional literature? This book of poetry could also introduce a study of haiku. Search for and share additional examples of haiku and write your own haiku poetry. David Patneaude's *Thin Wood Walls* might be used as a model to show students how an author uses haiku poetry within a novel to help the character express various emotions, conflicts, and situations. Ask students to include poetry in their own writing or to choose a favorite book and insert haiku or another form of poetry within the text.

Visualizing Chinese Art

Symbolism is especially important in Chinese art, literature, and music. We have already noted that Holland Cotter (2003) found considerable symbolism in Chinese art, literature, and music that reveals the history of the culture. He sees coded images from nature in the arts. Through these media, artists and authors were able to express ethical dilemmas and provide guidance through their works. For example, wind-tossed bamboo and choppy waters speak of social and psychological crises. Bamboo used in art and literature is a symbol of embattled survival; it weathers the most devastating storm through its resilience. The long-lived pine tree is often found in art because it grows in harsh and inhospitable terrain. The evergreen is the most honored of trees because it is an appropriate subject for each of the seasons; it remains verdant throughout the year. It also symbolizes the virtue of the lofty scholar and his ideals. Students may notice how many paintings show lone scholars and lone pine trees together. Ask them to consider what this representation might symbolize.

Having students search through art and literature for these visual and literary symbols helps them understand some of the values associated with the ancient Chinese culture. As they find these symbols in art, they may also identify the symbols in folklore, poetry, historical fiction, and biographies about early personages.

Explain to the students that such visual representations as the bamboo and the evergreen had strong meanings in early Chinese culture. Various animals, both real and supernatural, also had meanings for the people. To accomplish this activity, provide as many examples of art books showing early Chinese art as possible. Drawings in Chinese folktales may also be used as the students consider whether or not the drawings in the folktales are authentic for an early Chinese culture. Ask the students to become detectives and to locate as many examples of the following symbols in art and literature as possible.

Symbol	Meaning	Example
Dragon	Divine or supernatural attributes; represents man	
Phoenix	Supernatural; represents woman or dragon's bride	
Eagle	Strength and bravery	
Wild geese	Spirit of freedom	
Hawk	Heroic image of man	
Cranes	Longevity and health	
Flowering plum	Hardiness and spring	
Orchid	Blooms in secluded valleys, has far-reaching fragrance; represents summer	
Chrysanthemum	Blooms at end of growing season; represents autumn	
Bamboo	Resilience that allows it to bend with the wind; represents winter	
Evergreen	Remains verdant throughout the year; represents virtue of lofty scholar and his ideals; symbolizes longevity and steadfastness under adversity	
Jade	Associated with scholarly traditions and permanence; Confucius concept of "Worthy Gentleman," which he likened to jade	
Lotus	Buddha seated in meditation on fully blooming lotus is symbol of Buddhist purity	
Bronze	In ritual vessels it symbolizes China's reverence for the past	

When students find examples showing these symbolic meanings, ask them to share them with the class and explain what these symbols represent in the art or literature and why they think the symbols are used in that particular instance.

The following websites may also be helpful for this activity:

http://www.travelchinaguide.com

http://www.metmuseum.org

http://www.originalsource.com

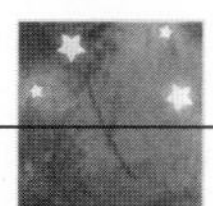

Writing Connections with Asian Literature

Each of the phases in the study of Asian literature includes numerous opportunities for motivating writing activities. For example, in Phase One, ask students to create a picture storybook from a single folktale found in an anthology. They should research the culture to create authentic illustrations, write an author's note that tells about the origins of the tale, state how they conducted research to authenticate their own illustrations, provide information about themselves as illustrators, and describe the techniques and media they used to complete the illustrations.

Also in Phase One they may write comparisons between Chinese and Japanese tales. How do the tales reflect similarities in the two cultures? How do the tales suggest differences? They may also research how Buddhist or Hindu religions are associated with cultural beliefs and values found in folklore from India.

As part of Phase Two, they may interview Asian Americans from the students' community and collect the stories they remember from their culture. Ask students to bind these stories together, include information about the tales, and provide information about the local Asian community.

As part of Phase Three, use the interview with Yo-Yo Ma in the *Smithsonian* magazine (Covington, June 2002) to motivate students to conduct their own research about the music and art they would use to depict one of the Asian countries and its culture. In a group they can focus on the culture during a specific time period, write their findings, and present their findings along with appropriate music and art. They could also listen to Yo-Yo Ma's music, "The Silk Road Project," and write their responses.

For Phase Four, there are numerous writing activities to accompany the analytical reading activity using Linda Sue Park's *A Single Shard*. Ask students to choose one of the following themes found in the book and to write their own story in which they develop one of these themes: Work gives people dignity; stealing takes it away; Nature is very important and will provide balance in life; Patience is one of the most important values; The same wind that blows one door shut often blows another door open; and Pride and foolishness are often close companions.

One of the most critical activities for Phase Five is to ask students to read two biographies about the same person and write a critical review. In the review the students should emphasize the biographers' techniques that made the biography successful or unsuccessful.

Survival strategies are developed and found in all of the phases of Asian literature. To bring the literature to contemporary issues, ask students to identify current news items about an Asian disaster or a social problem and to write a survival story about how they might use Asian cultural beliefs to survive. For example, in 2011 Japan experienced an earthquake, a tsunami, and a nuclear meltdown. But, news reports emphasized the heroism of many of the people and their will to survive and even to rebuild. Some students might choose to use Kimiko Kajikawa's *Tsunami!* as a model and write a survival story in which they use their imaginations to send out a warning that saves people.

REFERENCES

Baird, Merrily. *Symbols of Japan: Thematic Motifs in Art and Design*. New York: Rizzoli International, 2001.

Bajaj, Vikas. "Skipping over Rote in Indian Schools." *New York Times* (February 18, 2011): B1, B7.

Beer, Robert. *The Handbook of Tibetan Buddhist Symbols*. Boston: Shambhala, 2003.

Cai, Mingshui. "Images of Chinese and Chinese Americans Mirrored in Picture Books." *Children's Literature in Education* 25 (1994): 169–191.

Committee on Geographic Education. *Guidelines for Geographic Education*. Washington, D.C.: National Council for Geographic Education and the Association of American Geographers, 1983.

Cotter, Holland. "The World According to Some Glorious Chinese Misfits." *New York Times* (September 19, 2002): B34.

Council on Interracial Books for Children. "Criteria for Analyzing Books on Asian Americans." In *Cultural Conformity in Books for Children,* edited by Donnarae MacCann and Gloria Woodard. Metuchen, N.J.: Scarecrow, 1977.

Covington, Richard. "Yo-Yo Ma's Other Passion." *Smithsonian* 33 (June 2002): 82–85, 88.

Dalai Lama and Howard C. Cutler. *The Art of Happiness: A Handbook.* New York: Penguin/Putnam, 1998.

Degen, Natasha. "Non-Asians Show a Growing Interest In Chinese Courses." *New York Times* (November 29, 2006): C19.

Denton, Kirk A., ed. *China: A Traveler's Literary Companion.* Berkeley, CA: Whereabouts Press, 2008

Drury, John. *The Poetry Dictionary.* Cincinnati, OH: Story Press, 1995.

Egan, Timothy. "Little Asia on the Hill," "Education Life." *New York Times* 4A (January 7, 2007): 24–27, 35.

Fennelly, Katherine. "U.S. Immigration: A Historical Perspective." *The National Voter* 58 (February 2007): 4–7.

Freeman, Nancy K. "Look to the East to Gain a New Perspective, Understand Cultural Differences, and Appreciate Cultural Diversity." *Early Childhood Education Journal* 26 (1998): 79–82.

Friedman, Thomas L. "Serious in Singapore." *New York Times* (January 30, 2011): 8.

Gandhi, Indira. *My Truth.* New York: Grove Press, 1980.

GEO News Handbook (November 11–17, 1990): 7.

Guirand, Felix, ed. *New Larousse Encyclopedia of Mythology.* Translated by Richard Aldington and Delano Ames. New York: Crescent Books, 1987.

Gurjar, Nandita. "Literature from India." Paper presented at Texas A&M University. College Station: Texas A&M University, December 12, 1995.

Hickey, M. Gail. "'Back Home, Nobody'd Do That': Immigrant Students and Cultural Models of Schooling." *Social Education* 62 (November/December 1998): 442–447.

Holzman, Donald. "The Place of Filial Piety in Ancient China." *Journal of the American Oriental Society* 118 (April–June 1998): 185–199.

Johnson, Nancy J., and Cyndia Giorgis. "Interview with the 2002 Newbery Medal Winner, Linda Sue Park." *The Reading Teacher* 56 (December 2002/January 2003): 394–398.

Kao, Karl S. Y., ed. *Classical Chinese Tales of the Supernatural: Selections from the Third to the Tenth Century.* Bloomington: Indiana University Press, 1985.

Kristof, Nicholas. "China's Winning Schools?" *New York Times* (January 16, 2011): 10.

Leach, Maria, ed. *Funk & Wagnalls Standard Dictionary of Folklore, Mythology, and Legend.* New York: Harper & Row, 1972.

Lee, E. "The Chinese Exclusion Example: Race, Immigration, and American Gatekeeping, 1882–1924." *Journal of American Ethnic History* 21 (2002): 36–62.

Mackenzie, Donald. *India: Myths and Legends Series.* London: Mystic Press, 1987.

Marcus, Leonard S. "Talking with Authors." *Publishers Weekly* 247 (February 14, 2000): 98–101.

Marquis, Amy Leinbach. "The Other Prisoners of War." *National Parks* 81 (Spring 2007): 14–15.

McLeod, Melvin, ed. *The Best Buddhist Writing: 2010.* Halifax, NS: Shambhala Sun.

McLimans, Melissa. "Diaries of Discovery." University of Wisconsin *Friends of the Libraries Magazine* 50 (2010): 12–15.

Nivendita, Sister, and Ananda K. Coomaraswamy. *Hindus and Buddhists: Myths and Legends Series.* London: Mystic Press, 1987.

Norton, Donna E. *Through the Eyes of a Child: An Introduction to Children's Literature,* 5th ed. Upper Saddle River, N.J.: Merril/Prentice Hall, 2003.

Onishi, Norimitsu. "Affirmative Action: Choosing Sides." *New York Times* 4A (March 31, 1996): 26–29, 32–35.

_____. "In Japan's New Texts, Lessons in Rising Nationalism." *New York Times* (April 17, 2005): 4.

_____. "Japan's Textbooks Reflect Revised History." *New York Times* (April 1, 2007): 12.

O'Riley, Michael Kampen. *Art Beyond the West,* 2nd ed. Upper Saddle River, N.J.: Pearson/Prentice Hall, 2006.

Pang, Valerie Ooka, Carolyn Colvin, MyLuong Tran, and Roberta H. Barba. "Beyond Chopsticks and Dragons: Selecting Asian-American Literature for Children." *The Reading Teacher* 46 (November 1992): 216–224.

Ramanujan, A. K., ed. *Folktales from India: A Selection of Oral Tales from Twenty-Two Languages.* New York: Pantheon, 1991.

Reza. "Pilgrimage to China's Buddhist Caves." *National Geographic* (April 1996): 52–63.

Shantideva. *A Guide to the Bodhisattva Way of Life*. Ithaca, NY: Snow Lion Publications Shantideva Society 1997.

Swaraji, Paul. *Indira Gandhi*. London: Robert Royce Limited, 1985.

Temple, Charles. "Reading Around the World." *The Reading Teacher* 54 (2000): 312–315.

Tsunetomo, Yamamoto. *Hagakure: The Book of the Samurai*. Translated by William Scott Wilson. Tokyo: Kodansha, Int'l., 1979.

Tyler, Royal, ed. and trans. *Japanese Tales*. New York: Pantheon Books, 1987.

Wang, Gia-Zhen. *Auntie Tigress and Other Favorite Chinese Folktales*. Translated by Annie Kung. New York: Purple Bear Books, 2006.

CHILDREN'S AND YOUNG ADULT LITERATURE REFERENCES

Chinese Literature

Cole, Joanna. *Ms. Frizzle's Adventures: Imperial China*. Illustrated by Bruce Degen. Scholastic, 2005 (I: 7–10 R: 4). The teacher and her students travel back to China, 1000 A.D.

Compestine, Ying Chang. *The Runaway Wok: A Chinese New Year Tale*. Illustrated by Sebastia Serra. Dutton, 2011 (I: 5–8 R: 4). A poor family gains good fortune.

Czernecki, Stefan, reteller. *The Cricket's Cage: A Chinese Folktale*. Hyperion, 1997 (I: 5–8 R: 4). This is an illustrated version of the legend of the Forbidden City.

Demi. adapter. *Dragonkites and Dragonflies: A Collection of Chinese Nursery Rhymes*. Harcourt Brace, 1986 (I: all). A collection of twenty-two traditional nursery rhymes.

_____. *The Empty Pot*. Holt, 1990 (I: 5–9 R: 4). This folktale shows that honesty is important.

Freedman, Russell. *Confucius: The Golden Rule*. Illustrated by Frederic Clement. Scholastic/Levine, 2002 (I: all). This is a biography of the early scholar.

Heyer, Marilee. *The Weaving of a Dream: A Chinese Folktale*. Viking, 1986 (I: 8+ R: 5). This is a retelling of "The Chuang Brocade."

Hong, Chen Jiang. *The Magic Horse of Han Gan*. Translated by Claudia Zoe Bedrick. Enchanted Lion Books, 2006 (I: all). The tale is based on the traditional story about a Tang dynasty artist.

Lin, Grace. *Where the Mountain Meets the Moon*. Little, Brown, 2009 (I: 8+ R: 5). A girl seeks answers from the Old Man of the Moon.

Look, Lenore. *Ruby Lu, Empress of Everything*. Illustrated by Anne Wilsdorf. Simon & Schuster, 2006 (I: 5–9 R: 4). A girl faces changes in the family when her deaf cousin comes from China to live with the family.

Mah, Adeline Yen. *Chinese Cinderella and the Secret Dragon Society*. HarperCollins, 2005 (I: 10+ R: 5). The novel is set in the time of the Japanese invasion of China during the 1940s.

Mahy, Margaret, reteller. *The Seven Chinese Brothers*. Illustrated by Jean and Mou-Sien Tseng. Scholastic, 1990 (I: 5–8 R: 4). Watercolors complement this traditional folktale.

Major, John S. *The Silk Route: 7,000 Miles of History*. Illustrated by Stephen Fieser. HarperCollins, 1995 (I: 8–12 R: 6). The text and illustrations discuss different cities along the ancient Silk Route.

Muth, Jon J. *Zen Shorts*. Scholastic, 2005 (I: all). The book is developed around Zen, a Japanese word for meditation.

Namioka, Lensey. *Yang the Third and Her Impossible Family*. Illustrated by Kees de Kiefte. Little, Brown, 1995 (I: 8+ R: 4). This is a sequel to *Yang the Youngest and His Terrible Ear*.

_____. *Yang the Youngest and His Terrible Ear*. Illustrated by Kees de Kiefte. Little, Brown, 1992 (I: 8+ R: 4). A nine-year-old boy moves with his musical family from China to Seattle.

Phillip, Neil. *The Spring of Butterflies and Other Chinese Folktales*. Collins, 1985.

Sellier, Marie, Catherine Louis, and Wang Fei. *What the Rat Told Me: A Legend of the Chinese Zodiac*. North South, 2008 (I: all). The meaning of each sign is described.

Seeger, Elizabeth. *Pageant of Chinese History*. Longmans, 1934 (I: 8+ R: 5). Winner of the 1935 Newbery Honor.

I = Interest age range
R = Readability by grade level

Stone, Jeff. *The Five Ancestors: Tiger*. Random House, 2005 (I: 10+ R: 5). Historical fiction set in Henan Province, China, AD 1650.

Wallace, Ian. *Chin Chiang and the Dragon's Dance*. Atheneum, 1984 (I: 6–9 R: 6). A boy dreams of dancing on the first day of the Year of the Dragon.

Wang, Gia-Zhen. *Auntie Tigress and Other Favorite Chinese Folktales*. Translated by Annie Kung, Illustrated by Eva Wang. Purple Bear Books, 2006 (I: all). The author includes interpretive information to accompany three Chinese folktales.

Waters, Kate, and Madeline Slovenz-Low. *Lion Dancer: Ernie Wan's Chinese New Year*. Photographs by Martha Cooper. Scholastic, 1990 (I: 5–8 R: 4). A six-year-old boy performs his first lion dance.

Yee, Paul. *Tales from Gold Mountain: Stories of the Chinese in the New World*. Macmillan, 1990 (I: 10+ R: 5). Eight original stories are based on the experiences of Chinese immigrants.

Yep, Lawrence. *Child of the Owl*. Harper & Row, 1975 (I: 10+ R: 7). Casey learns to respect her heritage and to look deep inside herself.

_____. *Dragon's Gate*. HarperCollins, 1993 (I: 10+ R: 6). This historical novel takes place during the construction of the transcontinental railroad in the 1860s.

_____. *Dragonwings*. Harper & Row, 1975 (I: 10+ R: 6). In 1903, eight-year-old Moon Shadow helps his father build a flying machine.

_____. *Later, Gator*. New York: Hyperion, 1995 (I: 8–12 R: 5). This is a story of sibling rivalry.

_____. *The Rainbow People*. Illustrated by David Wiesner. Harper & Row, 1989 (I: 9+ R: 5). These twenty Chinese folktales were collected from Chinese Americans.

_____. *Star Fisher*. Morrow, 1991 (I: 10+ R: 6). In 1927, a Chinese American family experiences prejudice when they move to West Virginia.

_____. *Thief of Hearts*. HarperCollins, 1995 (I: 10+ R: 7). In this sequel to *Child of the Owl*, Casey faces issues related to cross-cultural understanding.

Young, Ed, trans. *Lon Po Po: A Red-Riding Hood Story from China*. Philomel, 1989 (I: all R: 5). The girl outwits the wolf in this version of the folktale.

_____. *The Lost Horse*. Harcourt Brace, 1998 (I: all). The folktale includes puppets.

_____. *Mouse Match*. Harcourt Brace, 1997 (I: all). The telling is done on a background that resembles a scroll.

_____. *My Mei Mei*. Philomel, 2006 (I: 4–8 R: 4). A Chinese American girl tells the story of her reactions to a newly adopted Chinese child.

India

Arnett, Robert. *India Unveiled*, 5th ed. Arman Press, 2006 (I: 10+ R: 8). Photographs and text provide a journey through India.

Buller, Laura. *A Faith Like Mine: A Celebration of the World's Religions Through the Eyes of Children*. DK, 2005 (I: 8–12 R: 5). The text includes an overview of Hinduism and Buddhism.

Chatterjee, Debjani. *The Elephant-Headed God and Other Hindu Tales*. Illustrated by Margaret Jones. Oxford University Press, 1992 (I: 8+ R: 5). This is a collection of twelve Hindu myths.

Cheney, Glenn Alan. *Mohandas Gandhi*. Watts, 1983 (I: 11+ R: 7). This biography emphasizes Gandhi's ideas as well as presents information about his life.

Chodzin, Sherab, and Alexandra Kohn, retellers. *The Wisdom of the Crows and Other Buddhist Tales*. Illustrated by Marie Cameron. Tricycle, 1998 (I: 8+ R: 6). A collection of Buddhist stories.

Cumming, David. *The Ganges*. Raintree Steck-Vaughn, 1994 (I: 8+ R: 5). The text provides an overview of one of the largest waterways in the world.

Demi. *Buddha Stories*. Henry Holt, 1997 (I: all). A collection of Jataka tales that reveal the teachings of the Buddha.

_____. *The Dalai Lama: A Biography of the Tibetan Spiritual and Political Leader*. Henry Holt, 1998 (I: all). A highly illustrated biography of the Tibetan spiritual leader.

Dharma Publishing Staff. *The Rabbit in the Moon: A Jataka Tale*. Illustrated by Rosalyn White. Dharma, 1989 (I: 6–9 R: 5). A rabbit is placed in the moon to show the world the power of selflessness and a pure heart.

Eaton, Jeanette. *Gandhi, Fighter Without a Sword*. Morrow, 1950 (I: 10+ R: 6). Winner of the 1951 Newbery Honor.

Ernst, Judith. *The Golden Goose King: A Tale Told by the Buddha*. Parvardigar, 1995 (I: 10+ R: 5). A goose's wisdom helps a king learn to rule wisely.

Faber, Doris, and Harold Faber. *Mahatama Gandhi*. Messner, 1986 (I: 10+ R: 6). The authors focus on the nonviolent philosophy of Gandhi in this biography.

Ganeri, Anita, and Jonardon Ganeri. *India*. Raintree Steck-Vaughn, 1995 (I: 8+ R: 4). This is a source of general information and key facts about the country.

Greene, Carol. *Indira Nehru Gandhi: Ruler of India*. Children's Press, 1985 (I: 8+ R: 4). This is a highly illustrated biography written for younger readers.

Hao, K. T. *Little Stone Buddha*. Illustrated by Giuliano Ferri. Translated by Annie Kung. Purple Bear Books, 2005 (I: 5–8). A stone Buddha searches for those who need him.

Hewitt, Catherine. *Buddhism*. Thomson Learning, 1995 (I: 9+ R: 5). The illustrated text presents history and beliefs associated with Buddhism.

Jaffery, Madhur, reteller. *Seasons of Splendour: Myths and Legends of India*. Illustrated by Michael Foreman. Atheneum, 1985 (I: 8+ R: 4). This is a collection of tales from the Hindu tradition.

Jendresen, Erik, and Joshua M. Greene. *Hanuman*. Illustrated by Li Ming. Tricycle, 1998 (I: 8+ R: 6). A tale based on Valmiki's "Ramayana."

Lewin, Ted. *Sacred River*. Clarion, 1995 (I: 6–10 R: 5). Watercolors depict a pilgrimage to Benares.

Masani, Shakuntala. *The Story of Indira*. Vikas, 1974 (I: 10+ R: 6). This is a carefully researched biography of Indira Gandhi.

McDermott, Gerald. *Monkey: A Trickster Tale from India*. Houghton Harcourt, 2011 (I: 5–8 R: 4). Monkey tricks Crocodile in a tale filled with irony.

Perkins, Mitali. *The Sunita Experiment*. Little, Brown, 1993 (I: 12+ R: 6). An eighth-grade girl discovers understanding of and respect for her Indian heritage.

Roth, Susan L. *Buddha*. Doubleday, 1994 (I: 6–9 R: 5). This picture book tells about the life of Prince Siddhartha, who became the Buddha, the Enlightened One.

Schomp, Virginia. *Ancient India*. Watts, 2005 (I: 10+ R: 5). This nonfiction book discusses the Indian culture including rulers, priests, and artisans.

Shepard, Aaron. *Savitri: A Tale of Ancient India*. Illustrated by Vera Rosenberry. Whitman, 1992 (I: 8–10 R: 5). This story appears within the Mahabharata, India's national epic.

Sherrow, Victoria. *Mohandas Gandhi: The Power of the Spirit*. Millbrook Press, 1994 (I: 12+ R: 7). This biography chronicles the life of the man who believed in peaceful resistance.

Tomlinson, Heather. *Toads and Diamonds*. Holt, 2010 (I: YA R: 6). Set in precolonial India, the story is a retelling of Perrault's tale.

Wangu, Madhu Bazaz. *Hinduism: World Religions*. Facts on File, 1991 (I: 9+ R: 5). This informational book presents the history, customs, and beliefs associated with Hinduism.

Whelan, Gloria. *Homeless Bird*. HarperCollins, 2000 (I: 10+ R: 5). A thirteen-year-old girl overcomes problems related to being abandoned after she becomes a widow.

Young, Ed. *Seven Blind Mice*. Philomel, 1992 (I: 4–8). This is a retelling of the moral tale from India: "The Blind Men and the Elephant."

Japan

Bang, Molly. *The Paper Crane*. Greenwillow, 1987 (I: 8+ R: 5). A paper crane brings success.

Blumberg, Rhoda. *Commodore Perry in the Land of the Shogun*. Lothrop, Lee & Shepard, 1985 (I: 8+ R: 6). This informational book describes Commodore Perry's diplomatic mission to open Japan to trade in the 1850s.

Bodkin, Odds, reteller. *The Crane Wife*. Illustrated by Gennady Spirin. Harcourt Brace, 1998 (I: all). Greed is punished.

Coerr, Eleanor. *Mieko and the Fifth Treasure*. Putnam, 1993 (I: 8+ R: 5). A young Japanese girl almost loses her gift for drawing when her hand is cut during the bombing of Nagasaki.

Demi, ed. *In the Eyes of the Cat: Japanese Poetry for All Seasons*. Translated by Tze-si Haung. Holt, 1992 (I: all). The poems are divided according to the seasons.

Feldbaum, Carl B., and Ronald J. Bee. *Looking the Tiger in the Eye: Confronting the Nuclear Threat*. Harper & Row, 1988 (I: 12+ R: 7). This book tells the history of nuclear weapons.

French, Fiona. *Little Inchkin*. Dial, 1994 (I: 4–8 R: 4). A small hero is rewarded by Lord Buddha.

Friedman, Ina R. *How My Parents Learned to Eat*. Illustrated by Allen Say. Houghton Mifflin, 1984 (I: 6–8 R: 3). This humorous story is about eating with chopsticks or knives and forks.

Haugaard, Erik Christian. *The Boy and the Samurai*. Houghton Mifflin, 1991 (I: 11+ R: 6). In feudal Japan, a young orphan helps a Samurai rescue his wife from a warlord.

Ichikawa, Satomi. *Here a Little Child I Stand: Poems of Prayer and Praise for Children*. Philomel, 1985 (I: all). The collection includes a Japanese and Hindu prayer.

Kadohata, Cynthia. *Kira-Kira*. Atheneum, 2004 (I: 10+ R: 6). Two Japanese American girls move from Iowa to Georgia.

______. *Weedflower*. Atheneum, 2006 (I: 10+ R: 5). The story of internment is told through the experience of a twelve-year-old Japanese American girl.

Kajikawa, Kimiko. *Tsunami!* Illustrated by Ed Young. Philomel, 2009 (I: all). The text is based on a man in 1854 who burned his harvest to warn the people.

Kodama, Tatsuharu. *Shin's Tricycle*. Illustrated by Noriyuki Ando. Translated by Kazuko Hokumen-Jones. Walker, 1995 (I: all R: 5). This story is set in World War II at the time of the bombing of Hiroshima.

Laurin, Anne. *The Perfect Crane*. Illustrated by Charles Mikolaycak. Harper & Row, 1981 (I: 5–9 R: 6). A Japanese tale tells about the friendship between a magician and the crane he creates from rice paper.

Lee-Tai, Amy. *A Place Where Sunflowers Grow*. Children's Book Press, 2006 (I: 10 R: 5). A Japanese American family is sent to the Topaz Relocation Center in Utah.

Levine, Arthur, reteller. *The Boy Who Drew Cats: A Japanese Folktale*. Illustrated by Frederic Clement. Dial, 1994 (I: 5–9 R: 5). The cats come to life to defeat a giant rat.

Levine, Ellen. *A Fence Away from Freedom: Japanese Americans and World War II*. Putnam, 1995 (I: 12+ R: 7). The book describes the experiences of Japanese Americans during this period.

Mannis, Celeste Davidson. *One Leaf Rides the Wind: Counting in a Japanese Garden*. Illustrated by Susan Kathleen Hartung. Puffin, 2002 (I: all). This is a collection of nature poems.

Maruki, Toshi. *Hiroshima No Pika*. Lothrop, Lee & Shepard, 1982 (I: 8–12). A powerfully illustrated picture book shows the aftereffects of the first atomic bomb.

Merrill, Jean, adapter. *The Girl Who Loved Caterpillars*. Illustrated by Floyd Cooper. Putnam, 1992 (I: 5–8 R: 5). The story is set in twelfth-century Japan.

Mochizuki, Ken. *Passage to Freedom: The Sugihara Story*. Illustrated by Dom Lee. Lee & Low, 1997 (I: 8+ R: 5). A biography of a Japanese man who saved many Jewish people.

Mosel, Arlene. *The Funny Little Woman*. Illustrated by Blair Lent. Dutton, 1972 (I: 6–8 R: 6). In a Japanese folktale, a woman steals a magic paddle.

Myers, Tim. *Basho and the River Stones*. Illustrated by Oki S. Han. Marshall Cavendish, 2004 (I: all). The poet is considered the father of the haiku form.

Nicholson, Dorinda Makanaoalani, ed. *Remember World War II: Kids Who Survived Tell Their Stories*. National Geographic, 2005 (I: 101). Survivors, including a Japanese American boy whose family was interned, tell their stories.

Nomura, Takaaki. *Grandpa's Town*. Translated by Amanda Mayer Stinchecum. Kane-Miller, 1991 (I: 3–7 R: 4). The text written in both Japanese and English follows a boy and his grandfather as they go around the grandfather's town.

Oppenheim, Joanne. *Dear Miss Breed: True Stories of the Japanese American Incarceration During World War II and a Librarian Who Made a Difference*. Scholastic, 2006 (I: 101). The text is in the form of letters written between a San Diego librarian and young people who are incarcerated.

Paterson, Katherine. *The Tale of the Mandarin Ducks*. Illustrated by Leo and Diane Dillon. Lodestar, 1990 (I: 5–10 R: 6). A couple is rewarded for their kindness to a pair of ducks.

Patneaude, David. *Thin Wood Walls*. Houghton Mifflin, 2004 (I: 10+ R: 5). A Japanese American is interned during World War II.

Preus, Margi. *Heart of a Samurai*. Amulet/Abrams, 2010. (I: 10+ R:5). Set in 1841, a Japanese youth is rescued by an American whaling captain.

Reibstein, Mark. *Wabi Sabi*. Illustrated by Ed Young. Little, Brown, 2008 (I: all). The haiku poem shows that we can find beauty in unexpected places.

Salisbury, Graham. *Under the Blood Red Sun*. Delacorte, 1995 (I: 8+ R: 5). A Japanese American boy and his best friend find their lives are disrupted by the bombing of Pearl Harbor.

San Souci, Robert D. *The Samurai's Daughter: A Japanese Legend*. Illustrated by Stephen T. Johnson. Dial, 1992 (I: 5–8 R: 5). The heroine slays a sea monster.

Say, Allen. *Grandfather's Journey*. Houghton Mifflin, 1993 (I: all). The immigration story of a Japanese American.

_____. *Kamishibai Man*. Houghton Mifflin, 2005 (I: 5–8 R: 5). An elderly Japanese storyteller is surprised by changes as he follows his old storytelling route.

_____. *Tree of Cranes*. Houghton Mifflin, 1991 (I: 5–8 R: 4). A Japanese boy's mother shares her California Christmas.

Sexton, Colleen. *Japan*. Scholastic, 2010 (I: 7–10 R: 4). An introduction to the country including maps, photographs, and further reading.

Sierra, Judy. *Tasty Baby Belly Buttons*. Illustrated by Meilo So. Knopf, 1999 (I: all). A girl battles the oni, whose favorite food is human navels.

Snyder, Dianne. *The Boy of the Three-Year Nap*. Illustrated by Allen Say. Houghton Mifflin, 1988 (I: all R: 6). A Japanese woman tricks her lazy son into working.

Spivak, Dawnine. *Grass Sandals: The Travels of Basho*. Illustrated by Demi. Atheneum, 1997 (I: all). The text includes both haiku and journal entries.

Stamm, Claus. *Three Strong Women*. Illustrated by Jean and Mou-sien Tseng. Viking, 1990 (I: 5–9 R: 4). Three women teach a wrestler lessons about the true meaning of strength.

Stanley, Jerry. *I Am an American: A True Story of Japanese Internment*. Crown, 1994 (I: 10+ R: 5). The author examines the experiences of Japanese Americans during World War II.

Tyler, Royal, ed. and trans. *Japanese Tales*. Pantheon, 1987 (I: 12+ R: 7). This is a large collection of tales.

Uchida, Yoshiko, reteller. *The Magic Purse*. Illustrated by Keiko Narahashi. Macmillan, 1993 (I: 6–9 R: 4). In this folktale, a courageous act brings rewards.

_____, reteller. *The Wise Old Woman*. Illustrated by Martin Springett. McElderry, 1994 (I: 8–10 R: 5). This folktale develops the theme that wisdom comes with age.

Yasuda, Yuri. *A Treasury of Japanese Folktales*. Translated by Yumi Matsunari and Yumi Yanaguchu. Illustrated by Yoshinobi Sakakura and Euchi Mitsui. Tuttle, 2010 (I: 8–10 R: 4). A collection of twelve stories.

Yep, Laurence. *Hiroshima*. Scholastic, 1995 (I: 10+ R: 5). The text describes the nuclear bombing.

Literature from Other Asian Cultures

Garland, Sherry. *The Lotus Seed*. Illustrated by Tatsuro Kluchi. Harcourt Brace Jovanovich, 1993 (I: 5–8 R: 4). A Vietnamese woman brings an important lotus seed with her to America.

Han, Suzanne Crowder. *The Rabbit's Escape*. Illustrated by Yumi Heo. Holt, 1995 (I: 5–8 R: 5). The text is told in both Korean and English.

_____. *The Rabbit's Judgment*. Illustrated by Yumi Heo. Holt, 1994 (I: 5–8 R: 5). This is an adaptation of a Korean variant of "The Tiger, the Brahmin, and the Jackal."

Hoyt-Goldsmith, Diane. *Hoang Anh: A Vietnamese-American Boy*. Photographs by Lawrence Migdale. Holiday, 1992 (I: 5–9 R: 4). The activities of a boy who now lives in California.

Lee, Lauren. *Korean Americans*. Cavendish, 1995 (I: 10+ R: 5). The author celebrates the contributions of Korean Americans.

McMahon, Patricia. *Chi-Hoon: A Korean Girl*. Photographs by Michael O'Brien. Caroline House, 1993 (I: 81). The text presents one week in the life of a Korean girl.

Nye, Naomi Shihab. *This Same Sky: A Collection of Poems from Around the World*. Four Winds, 1992 (I: all). This anthology includes poems from China, India, Japan, South Korea, and Vietnam.

Park, Linda Sue. *A Single Shard*. Houghton Mifflin, 2001 (I: 10+ R: 5). This historical fiction is set in medieval Korea.

Rose, Naomi C. *Tibetan Tales from the Top of the World*. Clear Light, 2009 (I: 7–10 R: 4). Three tales express the values of wisdom.

Shea, Pegi Deitz. *Tangled Threads: A Hmong Girl's Story*. Clarion, 2003 (I: 10+ R: 5). The main character is a thirteen-year-old orphan from Laos who faces challenges as she tries to assimilate into American culture.

Simmons, Walter. *Vietnam*. Scholastic, 2010 (I: 7–10 R: 4). An introduction to the country including maps, photographs, and further reading.

Yep, Laurence. *The Khan's Daughter: A Mongolian Folktale*. Illustrated by Jean and Mousien Tseng. Scholastic, 1997 (I: all). A shepherd boy accomplishes three trials to win the khan's daughter.

Young, Ed. *I, Doko: The Tale of a Basket*. Philomel, 2004 (I: all). This tale from Nepal has a theme related to the importance of caring for an elderly parent.

Chapter 6
Jewish Literature

To begin our exploration into Jewish literature, we must first understand the importance of literature to the Jewish people and then answer the question, What does it mean to be Jewish? Gloria Goldreich in her introduction to *A Treasury of Jewish Literature: From Biblical Times to Today* (1982) provides a historical background that stresses the importance of literature to a people who were denied a homeland for twenty-five centuries. From the time they were exiled by the Babylonians to the creation of the modern state of Israel in 1948, they were dispersed throughout the world. During this time, Goldreich emphasizes the importance of the prose and poetry of the people:

> [It] sustained them and ensured their survival as a people. The written word was the portable homeland of the Jews. They carried their precious books from country to country. Each generation added to this wondrous literature and taught it with gentleness and love. Reading and writing, the study of books, the weaving of words, are a form of worship for the Jewish people. To read the story of one's people means to become united with that people. (pp. 1–2)

In this chapter, we explore early writings inspired by the Torah and the Talmud (interpretative writings on the Bible), as well as the folklore of Yiddish-speaking people. We discuss the history texts and the historical fiction stories that present the history of the people. We examine contemporary stories that focus on Judaism today. Through folklore, historical fiction, biography and autobiography, poetry, and informational books, we discover the values, the beliefs, and the history of the Jewish people. Through the literature, we discover characteristics of the writing as well as the authors who bring this literary heritage to us.

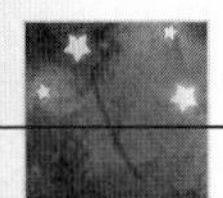

What Does It Mean to Be Jewish?

Who are the approximately 13 million Jewish people who live in the world today? Rabbi Morris Kertzer (1993) provides three definitions for Jewish people: religious, spiritual, and cultural definitions. Kertzer's religious definition is, "A Jew is one who accepts the faith of Judaism." The spiritual definition is, "A Jew is one who seeks a spiritual base in the modern world by living the life of study, prayer, and daily routine dedicated to the position that Jewish wisdom through the ages will answer the big questions of life—questions like, Why do people suffer? What is life's purpose? Is there a God?" The cultural definition is, "A Jew is one who, without formal religious affiliation, and possibly with little Jewish practice, regards the teachings of Judaism—its ethics, its folkways, its literature—as his or her own" (p. 7). Rabbi Kertzer adds to these definitions the fact that Judaism is not a race.

Jewish Timeline

1743 BCE	The Covenant with Abraham, beginning important period in Jewish history
11th Century CE	Rashi's commentary on the Pentateuch (first five books of Bible)
1492	Expulsion of 200,000 Jewish people from Spain during the Spanish Inquisition
1580	The *Maaseh Buch,* a popular book incorporating Talmudic tales and legends, which remained the most popular book in Yiddish for three centuries
1600	Elaboration on five books of Moses (Pentateuch) compiled
1700s/1800s	Awakening interest in the study of Jewish folklore
1884	Joseph Jacobs's application of principles of anthropology and folklore to Jewish literature, in articles published in the *Jewish Encyclopedia* and in *Studies in Biblical Archaeology*
1887	Moses Gaster's collecting and publishing of *Jewish Folklore in the Middle Ages*
Late 1800s and early 1900s	Years of emigration when many Jewish families sought to escape political, economic, and religious restrictions in Eastern Europe
1938	Archives of Yidisher Visnshaftleker Institute contained more than 100,000 items of Yiddish folklore
1938–1939	Abraham Berger's early survey of Jewish folklore
1933–1945	Years of the Holocaust: 1933, Hitler took power in Germany; 1935, Hitler reintroduced conscription; 1938, Hitler's armies began moving across Europe and the imprisonment of the Jewish people began; 1945 Allied forces defeated Germany
1973	Newbery Honor: Johanna Reiss's *The Upstairs Room*
1977	Caldecott Honor: Artist Beverly Brodsky McDermott, *The Golem: A Jewish Legend*
1982	Newbery Honor: Aranka Siegal's *Upon the Head of the Goat: A Childhood in Hungary, 1939–1944*
1985	Mildred L. Batchelder Award: Uri Orlev's *The Island on Bird Street*
1986	Mildred L. Batchelder Award: Roberto Innocenti's *Rose Blanche*
1990	Newbery Honor: Lois Lowry's *Number the Stars*
1990	Caldecott Honor: Illustrator Trina Schart Hyman for *Hershel and the Hanukkah Goblins*
1992	Mildred L. Batchelder Award: Uri Orlev's *The Man from the Other Side*
1993	Children's Book Award: Karen Hesse's *Letters from Rifka*
1994	Children's Book Award: Nelly S. Toll's *Behind the Secret Window: A Memoir of a Hidden Childhood During World War Two*
1995	*Anne Frank: The Diary of a Young Girl: The Definitive Edition,* including materials not found in the earlier diary
1996	Hans Christian Andersen International Medal: Uri Orlev
1996	Mildred L. Batchelder Award: Uri Orlev's *The Lady with the Hat*
1997	Caldecott Honor: David Wisniewski's *Golem*
1999	Scott O'Dell Award: Miriam Bat-Ami's *Two Suns in the Sky*
2005	Batchelder Award and Honor: Sylvie Weil's *My Guardian Angel* and David Chotjewitz's *Daniel Half Human and the Good Nazi*
2009	Caldecott Honor: Uri Shulevitz's *How I Learned Geography*
2010	Rabbi Adin Steinsaltz translates Talmud into modern Hebrew

As we explore the literature, we will discover the role of each of these definitions. As you read the various genres of literature, you will also discover basic Jewish values that thread through the literature. For example, Jews place considerable value on life. One of their sayings, l'Chayim, means "to life." Much of the literature from the biblical stories of the Exodus to the World War II Holocaust stories emphasize the importance of freedom. As a way to gain freedom, however, there is a focus on the need for human action. Rabbi Kertzer emphasizes that Judaism strikes a balance between human rights and the rights of other creatures, and even Earth itself. A milestone has been reached by Rabbi Adin Steinsaltz, who spent forty-five years translating ancient texts of the Talmud into modern Hebrew (Kershner, 2010).

Folklore and Ancient Stories of the Jewish People

The folklore of the Jewish culture transmits its essential values and beliefs. Ellen Frankel describes the characteristics of a Jewish tale when she states, "The trademark of the Jewish tale is its special point of view, a paradoxical blend of resignation and optimism. Many of our stories tell of heroes, masters of cunning and spiritual courage; other stories deflate their characters, recounting tales of failure, sexual trespass, intellectual conceit, spiritual arrogance, and foolishness. And it is precisely this double-edged vision that has been the secret of Jewish survival" (1997, p. 7).

History of the Collection of Folklore

In a survey of Jewish folklore, Abraham Berger (1938/1939) presents a history of the collecting, scholarly studying, and publishing of Jewish folklore. This history begins with Rashi's commentary on the Pentateuch (the first five books of the Bible), written in the eleventh century CE. An elaboration on the five books of Moses was compiled around 1600. The most popular book of this early period was the *Maaseh Buch,* first edited in 1580. This text incorporated Talmudic tales and legends. For three centuries, the *Maaseh Buch* remained the most popular book written in Yiddish.

Yiddish, according to David Bridger in *The New Jewish Encyclopedia* (1976), is second only to Hebrew as the most important of all languages spoken by Jewish people. According to Berger, the awakening interest in the study of Jewish folklore reached its height in the seventeenth and eighteenth centuries. In the nineteenth century, Moritz Steinschneider conducted extensive studies of Hebrew and Yiddish tales.

In the late nineteenth century, Joseph Jacobs applied principles of anthropology and folklore to Jewish literature in articles published in the *Jewish Encyclopedia* and in his *Studies in Biblical Archaeology* published in London in 1884. In 1887, Moses Gaster collected and published *Jewish Folklore in the Middle Ages*. Berger emphasizes that a strong interest in Jewish legends was found throughout the nineteenth century. The Talmud and Midrash were cited as demonstrating moral lessons or as unveiling important events and divine truths.

The romantic interest in folklore in Russia and Poland and the growing Jewish nationalism aroused additional interest in collecting Jewish folklore and using folklore to preserve the spirit of the Jewish people.

According to Weinreich (1988), considerable work in collecting and publishing Yiddish folklore is credited to the establishment of the Yidisher Visnshaftleker Institute—VIVID (The Institute of Jewish Research). By 1938, the archives of the institute contained more than 100,000 items including 32,442 proverbs, 4,989 folk beliefs, 4,673 children's tales, 4,411 folk songs, 3,807 anecdotes, 2,340 folktales, 1,000 customs, 630 songs without words, and 79 Purim plays.

Scholars choosing to conduct research, teachers selecting stories for telling, and retellers choosing materials have a rich source of literature. As we approach a study of Jewish folklore, we should heed Berger's (1938/1939) advice: "The Jewish folklorist of the future will have to be versed not only in the methods of general folklore, but also in the historic past of the people, so that he may be able to interpret Jewish folklore both as part of its environment and as a continuation of the traditional pattern" (p. 49).

Types of Folklore

Folklore is sometimes categorized by who tells the stories and for what purposes they are told. When evaluating tales of the Yiddish-speaking peoples of Eastern Europe, Weinreich (1988) identifies several of these important types and purposes. For example, comic and sentimental tales were told at weddings by entertainers known as *badkhomin*. Stories about the Jewish patriarchs and Elijah the Prophet were told by grandfathers to their grandsons as they waited in synagogues between early- and late-evening prayers. Wonder and magic tales were told by mothers and grandmothers to children in the home. Students told scary ghost and demon tales after their teachers left for evening prayers. Teachers told stories of God's wonders, and rabbis told parables to illuminate truths.

Folklorists and collectors of Jewish folklore such as Weinreich (1988), Ausubel (1946/1975), and Sherman (1992) have identified various types of tales and characteristics of the tales. For example, when analyzing Yiddish folktales, Weinreich identified the following types of tales: parables and allegorical tales that give listeners moral or spiritual instruction; children's tales, or kinder-mayselekh; wonder tales, or vunder-mayses, which have supernatural figures and helpers such as Elijah the Prophet, who acts like a fairy godmother; pious tales, which contain ethical messages or reflect the persecution of the Jews; humorous tales, which reflect absurd and inappropriate behavior especially of nitwits and pranksters; legends, which are mainly religious stories about spiritual leaders; and supernatural tales about ghosts, golems, and elves. Weinreich maintains that the inclusion of a Yiddish proverb or a citation from the Bible, Talmud, or Book of Prayers is one of the ways of changing a universal tale into a Jewish story.

Considerable Jewish traditional literature is based on sacred writings. Ausubel (1946/1975) emphasizes the influence of this early literature when he states, "sacred writings, such as the Talmud and Midrash, are almost inexhaustible repositories of the legends, myths, and parables of the Jewish people" (p. xviii). Ellen Frankel (1997) emphasizes the importance of these sacred writings:

> In time, a hierarchy arose that placed a higher value on the written text than on spoken tales. These written narratives begin with the Torah (literally, the Teaching), which comprises the Pentateuch and other books of the Hebrew Bible, and include stories drawn from the rabbinic anthology of law and lore known as the Talmud and the collective body of legends known as the Midrash. Although oral tales have often been regarded as the stepchildren of rabbinic authority, they have been lovingly embraced by the people, retold and singularly embellished by each community in the far-flung Jewish diaspora. (p. 9)

Cherie Karo Schwartz in her collection *Circle Spinning: Jewish Turning and Returning Tales* expands on the importance of the Midrash when she states that "Midrash fills the spaces between the letters, which are as holy as the words themselves. . . . Midrash creates expansive new views or connections" (p. vi). Consequently, many Midrash tales provide interpretations of the holy teachings. For example, one of Schwartz's tales, "The King's Jewel," uses a story to interpret a teaching from the Torah. Likewise, "The Most Precious Thing in the World" found in Ellen Frankel's *The Jewish Spirit: A Celebration in Stories & Art* is a tale from the Midrash that explains the importance of marriage.

As we discuss the literature, notice how each of the types of literature is represented and how the literature may be influenced by the sacred writings.

Examples of Jewish Folklore

In a review of Jewish folktales, Rahel Musleah (1992) identifies four elements that are found in Jewish folktales. First, a Jewish folktale includes reference to a Jewish place such as a synagogue or a wedding canopy. Second, the characters in a Jewish folktale include important historical characters such as King Solomon rather than an unknown king. Third, the stories are frequently set in a "Jewish time" such as a holiday or life-cycle event. Finally, the story includes a Jewish message that reveals values such as faith, learning, remembrance, hospitality, and family. The following sections give some examples of types of Jewish folktales. As you read them, look for the four elements cited by Musleah.

Wonder Tales Jewish wonder tales, like wonder tales from other cultures, are filled with supernatural characters and magical objects. The stories, however, may contain Jewish proverbs and characters or "markers" that identify them as Jewish. For example, in "How Much Do You Love Me?" in Beatrice Silverman Weinreich's *Yiddish Folktales* or Nina Jaffe's *The Way Meat Loves Salt: A Cinderella Tale from the Jewish Tradition,* readers will find characteristics of Cinderella tales, as well as Jewish markers. Cinderella characteristics include supernatural beings, attendance at a special function, a girl dressed in rags, a person of high regard, a search for the maiden, a test for the rightful owner of a shoe, and a magical object. There are, however, also various Jewish markers such as the importance of the rabbi and the rabbi's son, the character of Elijah the Prophet, the blessing over wine, the importance of cleanliness, and the reliance on visions seen through dreams.

Elijah the Prophet appears in these two variants of the Cinderella story. Elijah is found in numerous Jewish wonder tales: he takes the place of a fairy godmother or another supernatural helper. Several folktales in Howard Schwartz and Barbara Rush's *The Diamond Tree: Jewish Tales from Around the World* illustrate the importance of the powers of Elijah the Prophet and the magical characteristics of wonder tales. For example, in "Katanya," Elijah in disguise helps a worthy person in need. The title of this tale from Turkey means "God's little one" in Hebrew. In "The Magic Sandals of Abu Kassim," Elijah the Prophet, disguised as an old man, gives a generous, but needy man a pair of remarkable shoes.

The *Rooster Prince of Breslov* retold by Ann Redisch Stampler is a humorous Yiddish folktale about a prince who insists on crowing like a rooster. The king and queen offer gold to anyone who can cure him. When the likely candidates—a doctor, the magicians, and the sorcerers—fail the challenge, it is a frail old man who finally succeeds. Through this experience, the prince learns compassion and eventually becomes a wise ruler. The author includes background information about the folktale including the source of the tale as being from Rabbi Nachman of Breslov who lived from 1772 to 1810.

Leslie Kimmelman's *The Little Red Hen and the Passover Matzah* is an example of a folktale variant in which the folktale is changed to reflect a Yiddish setting, holiday, humor, and vocabulary. In this retelling, the hardworking hen complains about her lazy friends who refuse to help her make matzah but appear at the Passover Seder ready to enjoy the hen's hard work. All ends happily when the friends are forgiven and do the dishes as payment for their previous lazy actions. The text includes information about the holiday, the history of the occasion, and a recipe for matzah. Both the Prince of Breslov and the Little Red Hen reflect the values of compassion, forgiveness, and wisdom. They also show the importance of using humor to teach cultural values.

Humorous Tales and Fools and Simpletons Many of the Jewish folktales are pious and moralistic, as well as witty and ironic. They frequently make an ethical point and present a lesson of right conduct. Examples of this characteristic are found in Margot Zemach's *It Could*

Always Be Worse. Zemach relates the story of nine unhappy people who share a small one-room hut. The father desperately seeks the advice of the rabbi, who suggests the father bring a barnyard animal inside the hut. A pattern of complaint and advice continues until most of the family's livestock is in the house. When the rabbi tells the father to clear the animals out of the hut, the whole family appreciates its large peaceful house.

In the stories of fools and simpletons, the characters demonstrate innocent stupidity. This type of character is found in several selections in Isaac Bashevis Singer's *Stories for Children*. For example, in "The Elders of Chelm and Genendel's Key," the elders, including Gronam Ox, the head of the community council, and Dopey Lekisch, Zeinvel Ninny, Treitel Fool, Sender Donkey, Shmendrick Numskull, and Feivel Thicwit, solve the problem of the lack of sour cream by passing a law that from then on water will be called sour cream and sour cream will be called water. Fools and silly actions are also found in Francine Prose's *The Angel's Mistake: Stories of Chelm*.

Advice from a rabbi is a frequent story plot technique that both develops the ridiculous situation and leads to the moral of the story. Joan Rothenberg's *Yettele's Feathers* is a cautionary tale against spreading rumors and gossip. When the situation becomes extreme and no one will speak to Yettele Babbelonski, she asks the rabbi for advice. When Yettele declares that words are like feathers and not like rocks because words and feathers cannot hurt anyone, the rabbi tells her to cut off the top of her largest goose-feather pillow and bring it to him. When the wind snatches the pillow from her arms, she is lost in a blizzard of feathers. Now the rabbi tells her he will help her after she retrieves all of the feathers. After Yettele becomes extremely fatigued trying to gather the feathers, she concludes that in a lifetime she could never put all the feathers back into the pillow. Now the rabbi uses her own words to teach the moral of the story: "And so it is with those stories of yours, my dear Yettele. Once the words leave your lips, they are as impossible to put back as those feathers" (p. 31).

Jewish folklore is life affirming. Even though many of the people lived through persecution and the poverty of ghettos, their stories are an affirmation of life and a defiance against the world's cruelties. Many stories such as Isaac Bashevis Singer's *Mazel and Shlimazel, or the Milk of a Lioness* illustrate a moral triumph even in what appears to be certain defeat. The story ends optimistically and teaches an important lesson for life. Singer's *Mazel and Shlimazel, or the Milk of a Lioness* pits Mazel, the spirit of good luck, against Shlimazel, the spirit of bad luck. To test the strength of good luck versus bad, the two spirits decide that each of them will spend a year manipulating the life of Tam, a bungler who lives in the poorest hut in the village. As soon as Mazel stands behind Tam, he succeeds at everything he tries. Even Princess Nesika is in love with him. Just as Tam is about to complete his greatest challenge successfully, Mazel's year is over, and an old bent man with spiders in his beard stands beside Tam. With one horrible slip of the tongue encouraged by Shlimazel, Tam is in disfavor and condemned to death. Shlimazel has won. But wait! Mazel presents Shlimazel with the wine of forgetfulness, which causes Shlimazel to forget poor Tam. Mazel rescues Tam from hanging and helps Tam redeem himself with the king and marry the princess. Tam's success is more than good luck, however: "Tam had learned that good luck follows those who are diligent, honest, sincere and helpful to others. The man who has these qualities is indeed lucky forever" (p. 42).

In *Kibitzers and Fools: Tales My Zayda Told Me* Simms Taback includes short tales that are both humorous and life supporting. The collection includes thirteen brief traditional tales that are made more humorous through the illustrations. Each tale concludes with a Jewish saying that is illuminated through the story and the illustrations. For example, "The Sign" is a tale about a fish peddler who puts up a sign only to change the sign because of advice from people who pass by his sign. After he changes his sign five times, he is left with no sign at all until the sixth kibitzer tells him to put up a sign if he wants to attract any customers. The story concludes with a saying: "A kibitzer can be a pain in the neck. But more than one can make you moishe kapoir (all mixed-up)!" (unnumbered).

Tales of Ghosts and Goblins Supernatural spirits in Jewish folktales range from restless spirits known as *dibbuks* to enormous human-made creatures, or golems, created to protect the Jewish community of Prague. Many of these stories include holy people who are able to cast demons into uninhabitable places or foil evil spirits. Some of the supernatural beings like goblins and demons are evil; others, like some ghosts and the golem, are beneficial.

Eric Kimmel's *Hershel and the Hanukkah Goblins* is an example of a frightening tale in which spiritual forces overcome evil. In addition, the story contains many characteristics of Jewish folktales: the setting is a village synagogue during a Jewish holiday; there are Jewish symbols including a menorah, Hanukkah candles, and potato latkes; there are Jewish names such as Hershel and Queen Esther. In this scary tale, Hershel outwits a series of menacing goblins until he finally faces the dreaded King of the Goblins. Now Hershel uses the power of the menorah and the Hanukkah candles to outwit the goblin and remove his frightening power. The theme of the story reveals the triumph of Hanukkah.

A section titled "Tales of Ghosts and Other Strange Things" in Josepha Sherman's *Rachel the Clever and Other Jewish Folktales* contains several ghost tales. Some of the stories develop beneficial ghosts; in others, the ghosts are frightening or even evil. Many of these ghost stories, however, reflect strong Jewish values such as the importance of keeping a promise and the need for a rabbi to say proper funeral prayers.

"The Golem of Prague" is one of the best known stories about a beneficial supernatural being. The story set in Prague, Czechoslovakia, tells about the chief rabbi who fears for his congregation and creates a giant man out of clay. This golem, a huge silent creature, protects the Jewish people until King Rudolf issues a decree that "None of his people was ever again to spread rumors about the Jews, on the pain of banishment" (p. 96). At the point in the tale when the golem is no longer needed, the rabbi speaks holy and magical words over him. After this prayer, the golem returns to lifeless clay and is hidden under a pile of books. The tale ends with a feeling of hope for future times when the Jewish people might need assistance: "And who knows? For all anyone can tell, the golem is sleeping there still, waiting for the time when he will be needed once more" (p. 97). You may compare this version of the tale with Barbara Rogasky's *The Golem*, Isaac Bashevis Singer's *The Golem*, and David Wisniewski's *Golem*.

Clever Folks and Survivors Stories focusing on clever folk may have complicated bits of argumentation, puzzles, and word play. Riddle stories are popular among Jewish storytellers. For example, "The Clever Daughter: A Riddle Tale," in Weinreich's *Yiddish Folktales*, is a tale in which a nobleman asks three questions: What is the fastest thing in the world? What is the fattest thing in the world? And what is the dearest thing in the world? It is only the innkeeper's daughter who can help her father answer the questions.

"The Bishop and Moshke: Another Riddle Tale" is also found in *Yiddish Folktales*. In this tale, Moshke saves himself from a thrashing by the bishop by answering three questions given by the king: Where is the middle of the Earth? How many stars are in the sky? What will I be thinking when you come back to see me? Moshke tricks the bishop, dresses in the bishop's clothes, and presents himself before the king where he answers the king's questions in such a clever way that the king allows Moshke to thrash the bishop. Now Moshke becomes the king's chief counselor. Many of the Jewish tales show that clever characters tend to survive.

Nina Jaffe and Steve Zeitlin's *While Standing on One Foot: Puzzle Stories and Wisdom Tales from the Jewish Tradition* retells stories in two parts. The problem is developed in the first part, and the resolution is provided in the second. The two parts are separated with a question that reinforces the role of wisdom in Jewish folklore.

Myths and Legends with Biblical Sidelights According to the Torah, the world began with "Yehi Or!" (Let there be light!). In *The Jewish Spirit: A Celebration in Stories & Art*, Frankel

(1997) tells the story of "The Beginning—Traditional Midrash." Notice in the beginning of this tale how the Torah is introduced and the world as we know it is created:

> Before the heavens and the earth were made, while all still whirled in the chaos of first things, God fashioned the Torah. Eons before the earth cooled and life burst forth upon its fertile soil, the letters of the Torah blazed forth, black fire upon white fire, lighting up the entire universe with its glory.
>
> And then God created a world. But alas! It was not a perfect world, and so God destroyed it. Nine hundred and seventy-four generations sprang forth and perished, and still God labored toward perfection. Until at last God understood that the lower world would always be incomplete and flawed. So God spread over this last created world the Divine Wings of mercy and goodness and shielded it from the harsh glare of heaven's own justice. And so, this world did not perish like the others. It sparkled radiantly in the blackness, a blue-green gem in the diadem of God's love. And God saw that it was a good world. (p. 16)

Many of the stories in Jewish legend include biblical characters. According to Ausubel (1946/1975), "In the entire history of the Jewish people there was no personality that left its stamp on the Jewish consciousness as indelibly as Moses. The folk regarded him not only as its greatest hero, its supreme prophet, its lawgiver and its ruler, but also as its teacher. That is why for three thousand years Jews have referred to him as Mosheh Rabbenu (Moses, Our Teacher)" (p. 477).

Therefore, it is not surprising that many Jewish stories include the heroic character of Moses. Miriam Chaikin's *Exodus* is adapted from the biblical story. The text dramatizes such occurrences as discovering Moses in the bulrushes, the voice of God in the burning bush, the ten plagues sent to the Egyptians, the parting of the Red Sea, and the giving of the Ten Commandments. Warwick Hutton's *Moses in the Bulrushes* is a heavily illustrated retelling of the finding of the infant Moses by the pharaoh's daughter. Barb Rosenstock's *The Littlest Mountain* is a *pourquoi* tale that explains why Mount Sinai was chosen as the site for the Ten Commandments. The theme of the story reveals the value of being humble as other mountains compete for the honor. It is only Mount Sinai that tells God that whichever mountain he chooses will be the best one. The various stories of Moses reflect a strong Jewish theme about the importance of freedom. Eric A. Kimmel's *Wonders and Miracles: A Passover Companion* includes seventeen references to Moses. "Moses and Pharaoh" tells about the baby Moses being found by the Pharaoh's daughter and "When I Went Out of Egypt" is based on the first Passover and the Exodus from Egypt.

Two collections of literature are retellings of Midrash stories, a collection of biblical events and stories. Jan Mark's *God's Story: How God Made Mankind* progresses from the first seven days of creation through the story of King Solomon and the promise of the Messiah. The author's introduction provides valuable information about the background of the stories. This collection may be compared with Miriam Chaikin's *Clouds of Glory: Legends and Stories about Bible Times*. Chaikin emphasizes the elements of a story that make up a Midrash.

The White Ram: A Story of Abraham and Isaac, a highly illustrated book by Mordicai Gerstein, is another story based on a Midrash. This tale goes back to the white ram that God made to be sacrificed on the altar in exchange for Isaac, Abraham's son. This book, which emphasizes the importance of unselfish acts, is dedicated to "our fellow animals from whom we take and receive so much" (unnumbered).

Texts may focus on women in biblical times. Sandy Eisenberg Sasso's *But God Remembered: Stories of Women from Creation to the Promised Land* includes legends about Lilith, who tradition tells us was Adam's first wife, and other little known female figures such as Serach, the granddaughter of Jacob, and the five daughters of Zelophehad, who come to Moses after their father dies and ask to inherit their father's land. The characteristics of these women reflect many of the important values found in Jewish folklore: the love for family; the desirable characteristics of grace and wisdom; the importance of music and Psalms to impart knowledge and understanding; the role of hope, forgiveness, and God in Jewish history; and the requirement of kindness to a stranger, as well as the importance of freedom.

The folklore discussed in this section reflects the values and beliefs of the people. Most of the stories include a message that shows the importance of such values as faith, learning, hospitality, knowledge, cooperation, and charity. We conclude our discussion of the folklore of the Jewish people by applying some of the insights into an example in which we authenticate a folklore selection that does not include source notes. To authenticate this example, we need to apply the values, beliefs, and characteristics discovered through our study of Jewish folklore.

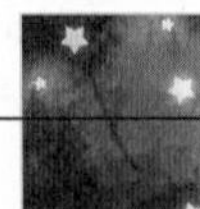

Early History of the Jewish People

Both nonfiction books and historical fiction texts available for children and young adults provide a vivid history of the Jewish people. The books also reinforce the strands of cultural beliefs and values developed through the study of Jewish folklore.

Many of the informational books, especially those written for younger readers, focus on specific times or places. Interesting comparisons may be made by analyzing picture books that focus on a common subject. For example, Karla Kuskin and Neil Waldman have written books associated with the history of Jerusalem. Kuskin's *Jerusalem, Shining Still* begins with the building of the temple by King David and proceeds through the tumultuous history of the city. The author includes the role of Babylonians, Greeks, Romans, Persians, Muslims, Egyptians, Turks, and Crusaders in the history of the city. The author concludes with the Six-Day War that returned Jerusalem to the Jewish people. Notice how the author concludes the book on a positive theme:

> For three thousand years this city has been battered and burned, and then built up, rebuilt and built again. . . . Three thousand years have passed, and still Jerusalem shines. (p. 27)

In *The Golden City: Jerusalem's 3,000 Years,* Waldman also focuses on this sacred city. He includes information about the early conflicts. To trace historical change, Waldman's watercolor illustrations are labeled with both time and place. He also includes biblical texts. Mark Podwal's *Jerusalem Sky: Stars, Crosses, and Crescents* compares Jerusalem as a home for Jews, Christians, and Muslims. As you analyze these books, consider the impact of the different types of illustrations, the content covered, and the moods created by each of the texts and the illustrations.

Another time period that had great impact on Jewish history is 1492. Norman H. Finkelstein's *The Other 1492: Jewish Settlement in the New World* details the history of the Jewish people who were expelled from Spain in 1492. There is information about the Spanish Inquisition, anti-Semitism during the period, and the movement of people and ideas as the Jewish people searched for a new location in which to live. The author stresses that during the expulsion, 200,000 Jews left Spain with only their religion and their culture. The final chapter chronicles the positive Jewish experience in the American colonies. The text includes a bibliography of books and articles and an index. Additional information about the Jewish experience in 1492 and a comparison with life in other parts of the world is available by reading *The World in 1492* by Jean Fritz, Katherine Paterson, Patricia and Fredrick McKissack, Margaret Mahy, and Jamake Highwater. For example, topics related to Judaism are discussed in sections on Europe, Asia, and Africa.

Alice Hoffman sets her historical fiction for young adults during the time of the Spanish Inquisition. In *Incantation,* Hoffman develops the relationship between two friends. One, however, is a Jew whose family pretends to be Catholic to escape persecution. The author describes the horrific experiences of many Jews, the strength of the Jewish teenager as she tries to save herself and her grandmother, and the possibility of hope as the heroine is saved by the love of a Christian.

Applying Knowledge Gained about Jewish Folklore

Folklore in which the original sources are not identified may be authenticated, at least partially, by analyzing the authenticity of the values, beliefs, situations, and characteristics of characters found in the folklore. For example, in an effort to authenticate the values, beliefs, situations, and believability of characters found in Isaac Bashevis Singer's "A Tale of Three Wishes" from *Stories for Children,* we can identify the important cultural elements in Singer's tale and then search for these elements in other sources such as Rabbi Joseph Telushkin's *Jewish Wisdom* (1994), Nathan Ausubel's commentaries in *A Treasury of Jewish Folklore* (1946/1975), and Rabbi Irving Greenberg's *The Jewish Way: Living Holidays* (1993).

An analysis of Singer's tale reveals that the story is philosophical in nature with both moralistic and witty elements. The story takes place in a town that has all of the things a town should have, including a synagogue, a study house, a poorhouse, a rabbi, and a few hundred inhabitants. The main characters are named Shlomah, Esther, and Moshe. The three wishes in the story include a desire to be as wise and rich as King Solomon, to be as learned in religion as the famous Rabbi Moshe Maimonides, and to be as beautiful as Queen Esther. Part of the story takes place on Hoshanah Rabbah, the last day of the feast of Tabernacles. On this miraculous night, the children see angels, seraphim, cherubim, fiery chariots, and the ladder from Jacob's dream. When the children squander their wishes, they discover the consequences of foolish actions. They also discover the most important lessons of all: how to gain wisdom, scholarship, and beauty of the soul. The sources for their growing wisdom include the Bible, the Talmud, and the Torah.

All of these features found in "A Tale of Three Wishes" can be authenticated using other sources. For example, according to Ausubel (1946/1975) the features of Jewish folklore that distinguish it from other bodies of folklore include the following: (1) it is philosophical and subtle, pious and moralistic, witty and ironic; (2) it is almost always ethical, pointing a lesson of right conduct, ceaselessly instructing, even when the tale is being entertaining or humorous; (3) it is life affirming; and (4) it includes mention of Heaven and Earth, natural and supernatural, and spiritual and material.

"A Tale of Three Wishes" has all of these qualities. The three characters learn a moral lesson in a witty and ironic manner. There is a strong moral lesson when the characters misuse their wishes in a foolish way. In "A Tale of Three Wishes," the moral lesson is developed through the knowledge of an old man, when he states,

> You were the ones who tried to play tricks on heaven. No one can become wise without experience, no one can become a scholar without studying. (p. 11)

As a consequence of their foolish actions, the three characters in the story finally discover the true and moralistic means of attaining their desires—wisdom, scholarship, and beauty. The values and beliefs expressed in these quotes from "A Tale of Three Wishes" are similar to the Jewish values and beliefs identified in other sources.

Biblical and historical references are found in the story, including Jewish names and the mention of holy days. The characters in "The Tale of Three Wishes" include Shlomah, Esther, and Moshe. All of these names are found in Jewish history and legend. The Jewish Queen Esther is known in literature for both her beauty and her virtue. Portions of "The Tale of Three Wishes" are set on the holy night of Hoshanah Rabbah. According to Rabbi Greenberg (1993), Hoshanah Rabbah (Great Hosannas) is the final day of Sukkot and a special day of rejoicing in the temple. This holy night is also associated with the studying of the Torah. The custom grew for the people to stay up all night learning the Torah. This is also the day when the people begged for forgiveness from the king and the king finally granted them mercy. In "The Tale of Three Wishes," it is this holy night on which wishes may be granted.

The lessons discovered and the morals developed in "The Tale of Three Wishes" are characteristic of Jewish culture. As a consequence of foolish actions, the characters finally discover they must work to gain wisdom, scholarship, and beauty of the soul. Jewish scholars testify to the importance of all three characteristics. According to Rabbi Telushkin (1994), wisdom and scholarship are of the utmost importance because, "[i]n traditional societies, elders are respected for their ties to the past and for the wisdom they transmit. . . . As regards scholars, the older they become the more wisdom they acquire. . . . But as regards the ignorant, the older they become, the more foolish they become" (pp. 249, 250).

Wisdom and virtue are also characteristics eventually gained by the characters in "A Tale of Three Wishes." Ausubel (1946/1975) also emphasizes the importance of wisdom and virtue. He states that the wise man has always been the ideal of Jewish tradition and folklore. It is knowledge and reason

(*continued*)

that lead him to wisdom, and virtue is the highest wisdom. Ausubel stipulates that knowledge comes before wisdom and that he who lacks knowledge lacks everything. In addition, knowledge of the Talmud and the Torah are of vital importance.

All of these cultural beliefs and values are found in "A Tale of Three Wishes." Even though there is no information about the original source identified in the text, the cultural authenticity of the story may be authenticated through other sources.

Elizabeth George Speare's Newbery Award winner *The Bronze Bow* is the most highly acclaimed historical fiction novel written for children about the early Jewish people. Speare's text focuses on Israel during Roman rule. She portrays the harshness of the Roman conquerors by telling the story through the eyes of a boy, Daniel bar Jamin, who longs to avenge the death of his parents. (The boy's father was crucified by Roman soldiers, and his mother died from grief and exposure.) Daniel bar Jamin's bitterness intensifies when he joins a guerrilla band and nurtures his hatred of the Romans. His person-against-self conflict comes to the turning point when he almost sacrifices his sister because of his hatred. Speare encourages readers to understand Daniel's real enemy. When Daniel talks to Jesus, both Daniel and readers realize that hatred, not Romans, is the enemy. In fact, the only thing stronger than hatred is love. Speare shows the magnitude of Daniel's change when he invites a Roman soldier into his home at the close of the story. It is interesting that this theme, along with the importance of wisdom, is also stressed in many of the selections of folklore discussed earlier.

My Guardian Angel by Sylvie Weil, the winner of France's Prix Sorcières for children's literature, is another example of a text that has high literary quality and an accurate historical setting. The historical setting places the book in Troyes, France, in 1096 at the time of the Crusades when Crusaders moved through the town on the way to the Holy Land. The plot allows the twelve-year-old Jewish heroine, Elvina, to hide one of the Crusaders when he decides to leave the Crusades. While Elvina hides him she answers his questions about the Jewish culture. The author develops a theme that it is possible for both Christians and Jews to understand and respect each other. It is a strong love for learning that ties the two young people together. Both the text and the author's afterword reinforce the theme that helping others may result in gratitude and protection. The author explains the importance of the actions of the Jewish leaders in Troyes that saved them from the anti-Jewish hatred and destruction that occurred, especially in Germany, as the Crusaders marched toward the Holy Land. A glossary of terms provides additional information about the Jewish culture.

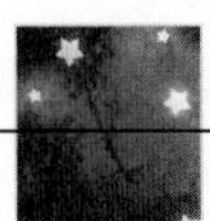

Years of Emigration and Immigration

The next important time period developed in Jewish literature focuses on the years of emigration in the late 1800s and early 1900s, when many Jewish families sought to escape the political, economic, and religious restrictions placed on them. Books written about this time period emphasize the search for sanctuary, freedom, and a better life. The literature also develops the destructive forces associated with anti-Semitism and the horrors and dangers experienced by many Jewish people as they sought freedom. The characters and themes show the importance of inner strength, which allows families to take great risks to escape persecution and to create new lives.

According to Dorothy and Thomas Hoobler's *The Jewish American Family Album,* about 2.5 million Jewish immigrants arrived in the United States between 1880 and 1924. Most of these immigrants came from Eastern Europe, particularly Russia. This nonfiction book provides descriptions of families as they leave Europe, arrive in the United States, begin new lives, and become part of U.S. life. Historical photographs and firsthand descriptions add to the authenticity of the book. As you read this book you will notice from Elizabeth Hasanovitz's experiences how her description of life in Russia before World War I and her desire for education and freedom mirror the conflicts, settings, and themes found in many historical fiction books written about this same time period. Many excerpts from this book may be used for comparisons and for authentication of historical fiction.

Escaping anti-Semitism in Czarist Russia, searching for personal identity in a new land, and working hard to raise money to bring family members to America are all themes Sheldon Gardner develops in *The Converso Legacy*. The author bridges Samuel's experiences in Russia with his new concerns in America through a dream that provides a flashback between programs in Russia and an anti-Semitism attack against him in La Rosa, New Mexico. The historical fiction novel follows Samuel across America from his arrival in New York until he reaches his final destination in frontier New Mexico. Along the way he faces problems of survival in a land where he has great hopes but little knowledge. The author uses letters from Samuel to his parents in Russia to tell about his journey and the people he meets who help him. There is a person-versus-person conflict as he faces Salvadore de Navarro in a showdown to help farmers sell their corn at a profit. The author includes other immigrants who have come to America to escape persecution or poverty. For example, the priest who fled Ireland helps Samuel understand that other groups have suffered oppression and that help will come from God if your goal is just. Through Samuel's Jewish religion, his best friends discover their own family secret: their ancestors escaped Spain during the Inquisition and out of fear, kept their Jewish identity secret. To add authenticity, the author describes several Jewish holidays and biblical stories such as the story of Moses, which shows how the Lord strengthened Moses and will also strengthen Samuel.

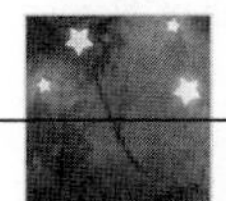

The Holocaust in Children's and Young Adult Literature

In 1933, Adolf Hitler took power in Germany, and Germany resigned from the League of Nations. In 1935, Hitler reintroduced conscription of German soldiers and recommended rearmament, contrary to the Treaty of Versailles. Along with a rapid increase in military power came an obsessive hatred of the Jewish people. In March 1938, Hitler's war machine began moving across Europe. Austria was occupied, and imprisonment of Jews began. World War II became a reality when the Germans invaded Poland on September 1, 1939.

The 1940s saw the invasions of Norway, Belgium, and Holland; the defeat of the French army; and the evacuation of British soldiers from Dunkirk. The literature written from the start of the invasions through the defeat of Hitler's forces in 1945 includes many tales of both sorrow and heroism.

This period from January 30, 1933—beginning with the rise of the Nazis to power—through May 8, 1945—ending with the Allied defeat of Nazi Germany—is considered the most tragic period of Jewish history and is called the Holocaust. Approximately six million Jews—including one million Jewish children under the age of eighteen—were killed during this period.

Authors who write informational books, biographies and autobiographies, and historical fiction set in World War II often focus on the history of the Holocaust and the experiences of Jewish people in hiding and in concentration camps. Because the literature is frequently written by people who lived similar experiences to those whom they write about, the stories tend to be emotional. The authors often create vivid conflicts as they explore the consequences of war and prejudice by having characters ponder why their lives are in turmoil, by describing the characters' fears and their reactions to their situations and to one another, and by revealing what happens to the characters or their families as a result of war. As might be expected, the themes of these stories include the consequences of hatred and prejudice, the search for religious and personal freedom, the role of conscience, and obligations toward others.

Why is it important to learn about the Holocaust and to discover any lessons learned from this time period? On the sixty-fifth anniversary of the liberation of Auschwitz and Dachau, Samuel Pisar, a survivor of Auschwitz, reflected on the lessons learned from the Holocaust. On such a dark anniversary he reminds us how often we vacillate in response to natural disasters, racial hatred, religious intolerance, or terrorism. But, the anniversary also reminds us "that we have managed to stave off the irrevocable; that our chances for living in harmony are, thankfully, still intact" (2010, p. A19).

Educational and Political Background of the Time of the Holocaust

Several of the biographies and autobiographies as well as historical fiction novels discussed in this chapter mention the importance of education in the lives of the protagonists. This is especially true in the autobiographies of persons who were in hiding. For example, Nelly S. Toll in *Behind the Secret Window: A Memoir of a Hidden Childhood During World War Two* dreams of and draws pictures associated with attending school. She hopes that one day she will attend school like her mother.

Eleanor H. Ayer's *Parallel Journeys* allows readers to understand the role of books and education, especially through the viewpoint of Hitler youth: one is Jewish, and the other a member of a German youth organization. By using alternating chapters to tell the story of each, Ayer allows readers to understand two very different experiences. Notice in the following example how Ayer introduces attitudes toward school and books. Alfons Heck, the German youth, introduces his memories in this way:

> From our very first year in the Volksschule or elementary school, we received daily doses of Nazism. These we swallowed as naturally as our morning milk. (p. 1)

Later, he describes the massive book burning during which at least 70,000 books that were censored by the Reich were burned. He also describes how the Jewish children were singled out for special treatment by the teachers and then were no longer permitted to attend school. Compare this book burning with Meg Wiviott's *Benno and the Night of Broken Glass*.

To get a better understanding of what authors describe in books, let us go back to Germany in the 1930s and 1940s and try to recreate the educational climate during the Nazi rule. As we progress through these examples, try to picture what was happening in German education that also encouraged the Nazi attitude toward the Jewish people and, consequently, helped to lead to the Holocaust. You might consider what your attitudes would be if you were a Nazi youth or if you were a Jewish student before the Jewish students were no longer permitted to attend school.

According to Hans Mauer in *Jugend und Buch im Neuen Reich* (1934), the goals of the Reich Youth Library and Hitler Youth Organization included the following: First, books should arouse an enthusiasm for the heroes of sagas, legends, and history; for the soldiers of the great wars; and for the führer and the New Germany. These books should strengthen youth's love of the fatherland and give them ideals by which to live. Second, books should show the beauty of the German landscape. Third, books should focus on the fate of children of German ethnic groups living abroad. Such books should emphasize that German youth yearn for the Third Reich. Fourth, books should deal with the love of nature and promote nature crafts. Fifth, books should relate old German myths, folktales, and legends in a language reflecting the original folk tradition. Sixth, books should give practical advice and help to the Hitler Youth.

Christa Kamenetsky (1984) researched the role of literature in developing the National Socialist (Nazi) indoctrination, the literature plan for the seventh grade, and censorship principles of Hitler's Germany. Each of these findings provide broader insights into the role of books in Nazi Germany and the increasing prejudice against the Jewish people. As you read each of these descriptions, try to imagine the impact on education and the children.

To indoctrinate youth in the National Socialist Movement, the Reformed School Curriculum in literature for German schools included Nordic themes in literature, poetry, drama, and ritual with an emphasis on folktales, myths, legends, and sagas. In language, the curriculum emphasized the wisdom of the ancestors through such sources as proverbs, sayings, and place names. In geopolitics, the curriculum focused on the historical rights for eastward expansion and the spiritual character of the Nordic race. In history, the curriculum included heroic themes in German history, German fighters, German thinkers, German conquests, and German peasants and settlers.

The most revealing of these areas is the list of censorship principles advocated by the Nazi party. As you read this list, pay particular attention to these principles and think about how the principles would have affected the Jewish people:

1. Removal of books that contradict the Nordic Germanic attitude. This includes books that show unheroic Germanic characters, pacifistic themes, or weaknesses in German history.
2. Removal of books that develop the wrong attitude toward Jews. Books should not portray Jewish people as noble protagonists or Germans as treacherous villains.
3. Removal of books that present cooperation among different races or interracial marriages.
4. Removal of books that accept the imperialism of the pope or place the monastic life over the value of a life dedicated to the service of Germany.
5. Removal of books written by Jewish authors or by people who express views that dissented with those of the Nazi regime. (The works of seventy Jewish writers were withheld from children. The works of forty dissidents were withheld.)
6. Removal of books for reasons of national self-preservation and national security. (The Nazi party determined these security risks.)
7. Removal of books that represent sentimental clichés and moralistic tales because these books had no bearing on promoting the heroic ethics needed for the young team of the future.

As you read examples of the literature discussed in the next sections, consider how these censorship rules could influence students. You will also have a greater understanding of Ayer's biographical character in *Parallel Journeys* when he mentions that more than 70,000 books were burned that might be considered threatening.

Informational Books about the Holocaust In this section, we discuss the informational books, historical fiction, and biographies and autobiographies written about the Holocaust. According to Leslie Barban (1993), this is a very important subject that may be ignored by parents, teachers, and librarians. She stresses the consequences of silence about the subject, citing the growth of neo-Nazi groups and the apparent increase in anti-Semitism feelings. Her article titled "Remember to Never Forget" includes lists of recommended informational books, fiction and picture books, biographies and autobiographies; discussion suggestions; and activities to accompany Holocaust literature. It provides a valuable resource for anyone using Holocaust literature in a classroom.

As for evaluations of any informational books, the accuracy of the facts is extremely important in evaluations of informational books about the Holocaust. Highly emotional periods in history are difficult to present objectively. Many of the books on the Holocaust rely heavily on photographs that depict the horrors of the time period. Often photographs are more appropriate than drawings because they clarify the text and illustrate the happenings described in the text. For example, Chana Byers Abells's *The Children We Remember* presents black-and-white photographs from the Yad Vashem Archives in Jerusalem. The photographs contrast people's early lives with their later experiences in the Holocaust. The photographs leave little question about the fate of the Jewish people and the horrors they suffered.

David A. Adler's *We Remember the Holocaust* is based on remembrances of survivors of the Holocaust, most of whom were children and teenagers at the time. The chapter headings provide a vivid introduction to the text that follows. For example, "I remember people carrying around tremendous bundles of money"; "They wanted everyone to know who the Jews were"; "Tell them I was there, I'm real. It happened."

The information in Susan D. Bachrach's *Tell Them We Remember: The Story of the Holocaust* was researched using materials, photographs, and documents from the United States Holocaust Memorial Museum. The text is divided into three parts: Nazi Germany; the "Final Solution"; and Rescue, Resistance, and Liberation. In addition to photographs and detailed information, the text includes maps, a chronology of events associated with the Holocaust, suggestions for further reading, a glossary, and an index. The suggestions for further reading are divided according to general overviews, specialized nonfiction topics, biographies, fiction, memoirs, and art. This list is also divided into two sections: one for younger readers and one for more advanced readers.

Seymour Rossel approaches his book *The Holocaust* with an historian's detachment. He traces Adolf Hitler's rise to power; describes the harassment, internment, and extermination of many Jewish people; and discusses the Nuremberg trials of the Nazis. Rossel effectively quotes from original sources, such as diaries and letters, to allow readers to visualize the drama and draw their own conclusions.

Milton Meltzer's *Rescue: The Story of How Gentiles Saved Jews in the Holocaust* develops another side of the Holocaust and shows that many people risked their lives to help the Jewish people. This book is very important to help readers authenticate historical fiction stories such as Lois Lowry's *Number the Stars*, which is based on the resistance movement.

There are several valuable reference books that are not written for children or young adults. The information in the books, however, can easily be shared with students. For example, Sharon Keller's *The Jews: A Treasury of Art and Literature* (1992) includes beautiful reproductions of Jewish paintings. A section of the book includes art and literature associated with the Holocaust. *Marc Chagall and the Jewish Theater* (Guggenheim Museum, 1992) provides reproductions of Chagall's works that were first displayed in the Jewish Theater and were then left to decay in basements as the Holocaust continued.

The Cat with the Yellow Star: Coming of Age in Terezin is a collaboration between Susan Goldman Rubin and Ela Weissberg, a survivor of Terezin. The text covers Ela's experiences before, during, and after the war. The author adds historical authenticity through the use of photographs. Interestingly, Ela played in the children's opera Brundibar when it was performed by the Jewish children at Terezin. Compare this with Ruth Thomson's *Terezin: Voices from the Holocaust.*

William Kaplan and Shelley Tanaka's *One More Border* follows the Kaplan family as they escape from Europe and eventually reach Canada. By describing the role of the Japanese consul in helping them gain visas, the author develops the theme that many people helped Jews, even at the risk to their own lives and reputations.

Historical Fiction A considerable portion of Holocaust literature written for children and adolescents is classified as historical fiction, although the stories may be based on experiences of the author or experiences of family or friends. The authors of these books usually encourage readers to see, feel, and experience the frightening person-against-society conflicts in which they place their heroes and heroines.

Although most of the books written on this subject are for slightly older readers, there are several interesting picture storybooks that are appropriate for all readers. These books provide an introduction to the Holocaust and allow interesting comparisons. The setting for Roberto Innocenti's *Rose Blanche* is a time in Germany when a young girl's curiosity leads her to the country outside of her town where she discovers a concentration camp and the people who live behind barbed wire. The somber-colored illustrations and text depict a time of danger and hardship but also a time when the girl's unselfish actions lead her to try to help the Jewish people.

Jo Hoestlandt's *Star of Fear, Star of Hope* is a book of friendship and terrible memories. The text begins in a compelling style: "My name is Helen, and I'm nearly an old woman now. When I'm gone, who will remember Lydia? That is why I want to tell you our story" (p. 2, unnumbered). The narrator tells her story set in France during the German occupation. Her best friend is Lydia, a Jewish girl who must wear a star. Unfortunately, the close relationship of the two girls ends on Helen's birthday when Lydia, fearing for her parents, goes home to warn them about the Nazis who are rounding up the Jews. Unable to understand why Lydia leaves her on her birthday, Helen calls out, "You're not my friend anymore." This is Helen's last encounter with Lydia because the family then disappears. The story concludes on a note of both hope and sadness as Helen hopes that Lydia lived and reads this story to her granddaughter because she retains her hope.

Karen Hesse's *The Cats in Krasinski Square* is based on a true story about the Jewish Resistance during World War II. To outwit the Gestapo and their dogs in 1943, the Resistance members let cats loose in the Warsaw train station. The dogs chased the cats rather than their human Jewish prey. The author includes an historical note about the Jewish Resistance members who fought the Nazis in the Warsaw ghetto.

Doreen Rappaport's *The Secret Seder* is also based on a true experience. The author develops a theme showing that people will take considerable risks to practice their religion. The family, which is hiding in a small town in France, risks exposure by attending a Seder in a hidden mountain cabin because "We promised Grandpa that we would celebrate all the holidays, no matter what" (unnumbered). The author includes additional information about the Jewish experience, the Passover and other books about the Passover, and Holocaust experiences. Elka Weber's *The Yankee at the Seder* presents the importance of a religious celebration during another period of strife. Based on a true story, the author shows the importance of overlooking differences following the Civil War.

As you examine these picture books about the Holocaust, compare the themes, the style, and the illustrations. What are the messages? Which ones seem the most appropriate to you? Why?

Brundibar, retold by Tony Kushner and illustrated by Maurice Sendak, is another highly illustrated book appropriate for all ages. The book is based on a Czech opera that was performed fifty-five times by the children of Terezin, a Nazi concentration camp. The illustrations and the text include political overtones as two young children try to obtain milk for their sick mother. Unfortunately, they are thwarted by Brundibar, an organ grinder who is drawn as a sinister character complete with mustache. Clues to the location of the book are found in illustrations that look like a town square in the Czech Republic, the depiction of a Jewish cemetery, and Jewish symbols. By translating slogans, readers discover "work makes one free." The colors in the illustrations range from soft pastel shades when the children interact with love to their sick mother to more violent colors that reflect the dangers of the time period. Even though the children, with the help of a chorus of children, raise money for milk and Brundibar is sent away, the book ends with possible foreshadowing for the future:

"Nothing ever works out neatly—
Bullies don't give up completely.
One departs, the next appears,
and we shall meet again my dears!
Though I go, I won't go far—"

(unnumbered)

You may compare *Brundibar* with Monique Polak's *What World Is Left*. This historical fiction, based on true events, focuses on a teenager and her family who are sent to Terezin and their struggles to survive in this "model" camp. The author includes more information about how the Nazis created an elaborate hoax to convince the world and the Danish Red Cross that the Jews were prospering at Terezin. The author also includes a bibliography and selected websites.

Most of the historical fiction selections about the Holocaust are written for older students. These stories have strong person-versus-society conflicts. For example, Uri Orlev in *The Island on Bird Street* uses actions of the character and descriptions of the society to encourage readers to understand the nature of that society. Notice in the following quote how Orlev uses actions to let readers understand the danger that the Jewish boy faces in the Warsaw ghetto:

> I walked on the dark side of the street, away from the moonlight, trying to hug the walls of the houses as closely as I could. "Stop to listen." (p. 36)

The author uses descriptions of the men who come to the hidden bunker and the reactions of the boy and the people who have been hiding in the bunker. For example, the Germans and the policemen shout loudly as they gather the hidden people. The people stumble, but even the children stop crying after shots are fired. The boy considers how strange it is that these people all lived in his building without his knowing them. He also concludes that he will never be taken away by the Germans.

Trust in and loyalty toward a parent are strong motivational forces in *The Island on Bird Street*. It is a survival story set in the Jewish ghetto of Warsaw, Poland. The book chronicles Alex's experiences as he turns a bombed-out building into a refuge while he waits for his father's return. Orlev develops the symbolism of a lonely island, on which Alex, like Robinson Crusoe, must learn how to survive, and the terrifying historical background of the Holocaust, in which Alex witnesses the capture of his Jewish family and friends, experiences fear and loneliness, and nurses a resistance fighter's wounds. The book concludes on a note of hope. Alex's father returns, finds Alex where he promised to wait, and takes Alex to the forests to be with the partisans who are resisting the Nazis. Like Orlev's hero, Orlev spent the years 1939 to 1941 in hiding in the Warsaw ghetto.

Orlev's *The Man from the Other Side* is based on true experiences of a journalist who helped his stepfather smuggle food through the sewer to sell to Jewish people in the Warsaw ghetto. This is another vivid book that allows readers to glimpse the Jewish experience during World War II.

In *Milkweed*, Jerry Spinelli's winner of the Scott O'Dell Award for Historical Fiction, readers may trace and discuss the meaning of the symbolism developed through the title, *Milkweed*. For example, notice how the author relates the milkweed plant to the theme of survival. The author introduces milkweed by relating the puffs from milkweed to angels and the purpose for angels to help people in times of trouble. The author then indicates that milkweed puffs are like angels and that Janina is the protagonist's angel (pp. 142–143). The story continues by relating actions to the milkweed. For example, Janina happily blows milkweed pods on her mother's grave (p. 151). The author uses a simile: "I thought she would sail forever like a milkweed puff on an endless breeze" (p. 186). At the conclusion, the importance of the survival theme is again related to the milkweed. When the children look at the brilliant orange of the maple trees the author states, "The year is gorgeous in its dying. The milkweed does not change colors" (p. 207). The protagonist then plants a milkweed away from the maple tree because milkweed plants need the sun.

Several historical fiction books focus on the Jewish people and the Gentiles who helped them during the Holocaust. Annika Thor's *A Faraway Island* follows Stephie and her younger sister Nellie as they are evacuated from Nazi Austria to Sweden. Unfortunately, their parents are not allowed to leave. The author uses many comparisons to allow readers to understand the extreme changes in Stephie's life. For example, to show the magnitude of the Nazi invasion on Stephie's life, she contrasts Stephie's beautiful home and her happy family life in Austria with the cramped housing quarters they are forced to live in and the fear that is part of their life. She also compares the changes in Stephie's school experience as she goes from praise for being the top student in her class to ridicule and prejudice after the Nazi invasion.

Comparisons are also made between Stephie's former life in Austria with her experiences on the island. For example, the author contrasts the tone of the High Holy Days at the synagogue in Austria with the more somber revival meetings in the Pentecostal church on the island. Even music has a different meaning. Instead of the music Stephie loves, she discovers that secular music is considered sinful. The author develops both person-versus-society and person-versus-person conflicts as Stephie faces prejudice and anti-Semitism. She also faces person-versus-self conflicts as she wonders about the fate of her parents and realizes that she cannot help them. By the end of book, however, Stephie discovers that many of the people on the island are kind and generous. The author shows Stephie's change of attitude as she realizes that she is not at the end of the world, as she originally believed. Instead, she has friends who love and respect her. The Author's Note reveals one of her purposes for writing this book: she wanted to "contribute to a better understanding of the vulnerable situation in which refugee children continue to live" (p. 247).

In *Tropical Secrets: Holocaust Refugees in Cuba* Margarita Engle presents her historical fiction about a refugee who escapes from Germany in verse form. The author tells the story through two points of view. Daniel is the young, Jewish boy who escapes to Cuba from Nazi Germany. He dreams of being united with his parents someday in New York, but he does not know what has happened to them. Paloma is the Cuban girl who befriends Daniel and helps fight the anti-Semitism her father and his German associates express. The Author's Note in Engle's text expresses her purpose in writing the book: she states that she wants to show the necessity of becoming the kind of person who will help refugees of any faith in times of need. Notice the similarity in purpose between the authors of *A Faraway Island* and *Tropical Secrets*. You may wish to compare the strategies and the effectiveness of each author in revealing the purpose.

Gregory Maguire's *The Good Liar* uses an interesting technique by introducing the book as a class project in which children write or talk to someone who experienced World War II. The remainder of the book is the response sent to the children by an artist who at the time was a young boy living in France. The experiences of the family during the German occupation are told through the viewpoint of the boy, who is not aware his mother is hiding Jewish refugees in the crawl space under their home.

The hiding in David Chotjewitz's *Daniel Half Human and the Good Nazi* results from a complex person-versus-self conflict when a teenage Nazi sympathizer discovers that his mother is Jewish. At this discovery, Daniel goes through a series of reactions. At first he feels shame, which causes him to rebel against his parents and try to keep his heritage a secret. This decision becomes very difficult as he witnesses the atrocities and the changes happening to society under Nazi rule. This Batchelder Honor Award book develops complex issues of both person-versus-society and person-versus-self conflicts. At the end of the story, Daniel faces one of his hardest decisions.

Miriam Bat-Ami's *Two Suns in the Sky* develops parallel voices to express points of view of an American girl and a Jewish boy from Yugoslavia. The setting for this book is also the refugee camp in Oswego, New York. The parallel-voice approach allows the author to explore the many sides of the refugee experience. For example, early in the book when writing from the viewpoint of Chris, the American girl, the author explores the local and national society's attitudes toward the refugees by having Chris read editorials and comments from the newspapers. When writing from the viewpoint of Adam, the Jewish refugee, she presents historical information and insights into the historical conflicts influencing the Jewish people. The author reinforces many of the themes and conflicts developed in the book by introducing each chapter with quotes from former refugees or other historical personages.

As you read these historical fiction books about the Holocaust, you will discover that the important themes found in World War II literature are all found here: people seek freedom from religious and political persecution, prejudice and hatred are destructive forces, moral obligation and personal conscience are strong forces, freedom is worth fighting for, and family love and loyalty help people endure catastrophic experiences.

Biography and Autobiography First-person accounts of an incident are among the most powerful portrayals of the Holocaust experience. Certainly, *Anne Frank: The Diary of a Young Girl: The Definitive Edition* is among the most widely read autobiographies of the Holocaust. The diary, written by Anne Frank while she was in hiding in the attic of a house in Amsterdam, provides an intimate view of family life during the Holocaust.

The following entry from the diary is an excellent example of the power of Anne Frank's story:

> Friday, October 9, 1942
>
> Dear Kitty,
>
> Today I have nothing but dismal and depressing news to report. Our many Jewish friends and acquaintances are being taken away in droves. The Gestapo is treating them very roughly and transporting them in cattle cars to Westerbork, the big camp in Drenthe to which they're sending all the Jews. Miep told us about someone who'd managed to escape from there. It must be terrible in Westerbork. The people get almost nothing to eat, much less to drink, as the water is available only one hour a day, and there's only one toilet and sink for several thousand people. Men and women sleep in the same room, and women and children often have their heads shaved. Escape is almost impossible; many people look Jewish, and they're branded by their shorn heads. (p. 54)

Through her diary, Anne Frank reflects not only growing fear but also love for life. This ability is highlighted in Patricia Hampl's review of the book published in the *New York Times Book Review* (1995). Hampl states, "The 'Diary,' now 50 years old, remains astonishing and excruciating. It is a work almost sick with terror and tension, even as it performs its miracle of lucidity. . . . All that remains is this diary, evidence of her ferocious appetite for life. It gnaws at us still" (p. 21).

You may compare the impact of Anne Frank's autobiography and its content with two biographies of Frank written for younger readers: Johanna Hurwitz's *Anne Frank: Life in Hiding* and Ruud van der Rol and Rian Verhoeven's *Anne Frank: Beyond the Diary*. The authors of these books develop strong feelings of advocacy for Anne Frank and the Jewish people, as well as attacks against the developing attitudes of anti-Semitism and the experiences of the Jewish people in the concentration camps. You may also consider how these two books may differ because the authors know more about the outcomes of the Holocaust than were known by Anne Frank when she wrote her autobiography. Also compare the diary with Sid Jacobson's *Anne Frank: The Anne Frank House Authorized Graphic Biography.*

You may also compare Anne Frank's autobiography with Livia Bitton-Jackson's *I Have Lived a Thousand Years: Growing Up in the Holocaust.* The autobiography focuses on the life of a thirteen-year-old Hungarian girl and the experiences of her family as they live in ghettos, forced labor camps, and in both Auschwitz and Dachau. Readers understand the severe consequences of the experiences when she is finally liberated and someone assumes Livia is sixty years old.

An effective author's style may be one of the most important literary elements used to increase understanding of the Jewish experience during World War II. In *No Pretty Pictures: A Child of War,* Anita Lobel, a future Caldecott Honor winner, develops her own life experiences during the years in Krakow, in hiding in the countryside, while living in the ghetto, and during internment in various concentration camps. Lobel does not complete her autobiography, however, with liberation. Instead, she tells about her life of recuperation in Sweden following her imprisonment by the Nazis. Lobel uses an especially effective writing style to allow readers to understand the full meaning of the changes in her life.

In the second part of her autobiography—which is set in Sweden—Lobel uses contrasting descriptions of settings, personal responses to food, and emotional reactions to help readers understand the differences. For example, notice in the following quote how Lobel helps readers visualize the changes in her life by contrasting settings: "The sheets on my bed were so white, so clean. . . . These were miraculous pleasures after the filthy bunks barely filled with hay and burlap." (p. 130)

Lobel contrasts the memories brought on by such simple things as smells, sounds, bus rides, gates, weather, and announcements. Through these contrasts, readers also gain an understanding of the fear and suspicion that became a part of Lobel's life and how difficult it was for her to overcome her suspicious reactions. Lobel creates a many-sided character by contrasting and describing her own reactions and conflicting person-versus-self conflicts. By the conclusion of the autobiography, the author has developed a strong character who understands her own need for self-realization, especially through her artwork.

To provide additional information about anti-Semitism and Hitler's treatment of Europe's Jews, read James Cross Giblin's biography *The Life and Death of Adolf Hitler* (2002). This text, which won the Robert F. Sibert Medal, provides sources for learning about such actions as the Final Solution, the Holocaust, the concentration camps, and the removal of Jews from jobs and schools. Readers can compare Giblin's text with the autobiographies and biographies of people living during the Holocaust. Labeled photographs add to the understanding of this time period. The text includes a glossary of German words and terms, source notes by chapter, and an extensive index.

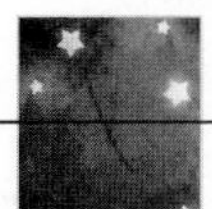

Jewish Poetry

Jewish poetry ranges from the words of the Psalms and Proverbs found in the Writings (the third section of the Hebrew Bible) to expressions of fear, horror, and hope for life written during the Holocaust, as well as to contemporary poetry that expresses longings for peace and stability.

The best known poetry is probably the poetry written in Psalms and Proverbs. When writing about this poetry, Gloria Goldreich (1982) declares that the Psalms and Proverbs offer advice on how individuals can live moral and just lives. Herbert G. May and Bruce M. Metzger (1973/1977) provide the following classifications for the Psalms: hymns, in which individuals express acts of praise; laments, in which individuals seek deliverance from illness or false accusation, or the nation asks for help; songs of trust, in which people express their confidence in God's readiness to help; thanksgiving, in which an individual expresses gratitude for deliverance; sacred history, in which the nation recounts the story of its past; royal psalms, which are used during special occasions such as coronations or royal weddings; and wisdom Psalms, in which the individual meditates on life.

ISSUE Holocaust Literature

Three important issues are discussed in journals and in informational books written for adults in relation to the topic of the Holocaust: (1) How should authors write about the Holocaust? (2) How should the Holocaust be taught in schools? (3) How can people be prepared to answer the claims of those who deny the Holocaust?

Hazel Rochman (1992) provides an interesting discussion about how authors should and should not approach writing about the Holocaust. In a review of Ruth Minsky Sender's *The Holocaust Lady* (1992), Rochman maintains that even though this book is much discussed, it is an example of how authors should not write about the Holocaust. Rochman states, "The writing here is sentimental and self-centered, full of cliché about 'horror, pain, and degradation.' On almost every page, at least once, her tears glide, glisten, or roll gently down her cheeks, and/or her heart skips a beat; people read her work with quivering hands, their faces distorted with pain" (p. 46). In contrast, Rochman discusses books such as Ida Vos's *Hide and Seek* (1991) and Art Spiegelman's *Maus: A Survivor's Tale* (1991), which are written in a controlled style that has greater power. As you study books about the Holocaust, decide which styles are most effective for presenting this time period.

Two other authors present issues that are important when reading and discussing Holocaust literature. Wilson Frampton (1991) argues that although Holocaust education is vital to our understanding of both the past and the future, the subject is not found in many school curricula and is inadequately covered in history textbooks. Frampton states,

> In summary the issue of Holocaust education will continue to percolate. It's a topic identified by many but comprehended by few. The revisionists are producing massive literature that denies the Holocaust ever existed. When a student is confronted with this 'type' literature will he or she have the ability to recognize the underlying message or will the student fall prey and assume the revisionist point of view? The literature of the revisionists is dedicated toward discrediting the Holocaust as nothing more than a 'Jewish myth.'" (pp. 34–35)

In her book *Denying the Holocaust: The Growing Assault on Truth and Memory,* Deborah Lipstadt (1994) presents the strategies that people use when they deny the existence of the Holocaust and discusses the claims of the deniers. She concludes her book with a chapter on "Twisting the Truth." The section in which she discusses the documentation of *The Diary of Anne Frank* and the strategies that deniers use to claim the book was written after the war are of particular interest to anyone interested in literature about the Holocaust.

One response to deniers of the Holocaust is a German proposal "to make Holocaust denial a crime throughout the European Union and to ban the display of the swastika (to some a 5,000-year-old symbol of peace)" (p. 53). This article in *The Economist* (2007) asks questions such as "Holocaust denial is profoundly wrong. But should it be illegal?" and "Where might it end?" These questions are important, as students consider the consequences of various viewpoints including legal censorship and punishable actions.

As you read these articles and books, ask yourself these questions: What is your viewpoint on the writing style of Holocaust literature? How is the Holocaust taught in schools today? How should the Holocaust be taught? What is your answer to people who would deny the existence of the Holocaust?

One of the most famous Psalms is Psalm 100. As you read this poem, notice that it is a hymn calling for all nations to praise the Lord:

PSALM 100

Make a joyful noise to the Lord, all the lands!
Serve the Lord with gladness!
Come into his presence with singing!
Know that the Lord is God!
It is he that made us, and we are his;
We are his people, and the sheep of his pasture.
Enter his gates with thanksgiving, and his courts with praise!

Give thanks to him, bless his name!
For the Lord is good;
His steadfast love endures for ever,
And his faithfulness to all generations.

Many of the values and beliefs presented in earlier literature in this chapter are apparent when reading the Proverbs, which are attributed to Solomon, the son of David. The quest for wisdom and knowledge are found throughout Proverbs. For example, Proverbs 1, verse 2, admonishes "That men may know wisdom and instruction." Proverbs 2, verse 2 teaches the need to be "attentive to wisdom" and include "your heart to understanding." Chapter 2, verses 8, 9, and 10 states that those who guard the paths of justice and preserve the way of God's saints can expect the following:

Then you will understand
righteousness and justice
and equity, every good path;
for wisdom will come into your
heart,
and knowledge will be pleasant
to your soul; . . .

Just as the Psalms include hymns of praise, there are songs that are sung during traditional Jewish holidays. Jeanne Modesitt's *Songs of Chanukah* is a collection of fourteen songs sung during this eight-day holiday. The book includes an introduction to each song that states when it would be sung or explains the meaning of the song. The text includes musical arrangements for piano and chords for guitar.

Some of the Jewish poetry is similar in nature to the Yiddish folktales presented in this chapter. For example, Mani-Leib's *Yingle Tsingl Khvat* is a humorous poem that tells the story of a shtetl, a little village, in which the rainy autumn continues until the village is so muddy that neither people on foot or on horseback can reach the market. The poem reveals how Yingle Tsingl solves the villagers' problem by bringing winter to the town. The poem contains many elements of Yiddish folktales, including a synagogue; a rebbe, who is a plucky and daring hero who is brave and adventurous even though he is small; and a magic object.

Poetry written during the Holocaust contains similar themes as those found in the historical fiction and biography with Holocaust settings. One of the best collections of poetry written by children during this period is . . . *I Never Saw Another Butterfly . . . : Children's Drawings and Poems from Terezin Concentration Camp, 1942–1944*, edited by Hana Volavkova. As you read the following poem, notice what the child misses and how the child expresses the desolation of the ghetto:

THE BUTTERFLY

The last, the very last,
So richly, brightly, dazzling yellow,
Perhaps if the sun's tears would sing
against a white stone. . . .

Such, such a yellow
Is carried lightly 'way up high.
It went away I'm sure because it wished to
  kiss the world good-bye.
For seven weeks I've lived in here.
Penned up inside this ghetto.
But I have found what I love here.
The dandelions call to me
And the white chestnut branches in the court.
Only I never saw another butterfly.
That butterfly was the last one.
Butterflies don't live in here,
  in the ghetto.

1942 Pavel Friedmann (p. 39)

Notice in this next example, that even though there is a feeling of fear, there is still a strong feeling of Jewish pride and dignity:

I AM A JEW

I am a Jew and will be a Jew forever.
Even if I should die from hunger,
  never will I submit.
I will always fight for my people,
  on my honor.
I will never be ashamed of them,
I give my word.
I am proud of my people,
  how dignified they are.
Even though I am suppressed,
I will always come back to life.

Franta Bass (p. 57)

Contemporary poets continue to develop themes that are similar ones in the earlier poems as searching for God and the need for peace. Sandy Eisenberg Sasso suggests in her poem *In God's Name* that people may call God by different names, but all of the names such as "Creator of Light," "Shepherd," and "Redeemer" are all really the same name.

In *The Matzah That Papa Brought Home*, Fran Manushkin uses the structure of a cumulative rhyme to tell about a family preparing for and celebrating the Passover Seder. The poem begins with the *matzah* (unleavened bread) that Papa brought home and is expanded with new verse ele-

"The Butterfly" by Pavel Friedmann and "I Am a Jew" by Franta Bass from *I Never Saw Another Butterfly* by U.S. Holocaust Memorial Museum, edited by Hana Volavkova. Copyright © 1978, 1993 by Artia, Prague Compilation © 1993 by Schocken Books. Used by permission of Schocken Books, a division of Random House, Inc.

ments relating to the Passover Seder as they shared: the asking of the four questions; the counting of ten plagues; the singing of the "Dayenu," which has fourteen verses; the dipping of bitter herbs; the sipping of the matzah ball soup; the hunting for and finding the *afikoman*, which is a piece of matzah hidden at the start of the Seder; the opening of the door for Elijah in the hope that the prophet will come and bring peace to the people of the earth; and the hugging and saying "Next year in Jerusalem." The poem ends on this joyous note, which has a special meaning to Jewish people who were scattered around the world for centuries and could not return to Israel. Both the cumulative poem and the illustrations convey feelings of family closeness, as well as of excitement as the family looks forward to the days of the Passover and to the experiences they will remember.

Several of the poems included in Naomi Shihab Nye's anthology *The Same Sky: A Collection of Poems from Around the World* are written by authors from Israel. These poems reflect contemporary conflicts, especially the conflict between war and peace. Poet Yehuda Amichai declares that he is influenced by the ethics of his father and by the cruelties of war. This conflict is developed in his poem "Wild-peace" as he searches for a peace that comes quickly like wildflowers and in "Jerusalem," in which he considers the two sides of the conflict and what people do to try to convince each other that they are happy. James Berry's *Around the World in Eighty Poems* is another collection of poems from various countries. "When I Was a Child" is by Israeli poet Yehuda Amichai who contemplates a boy's thoughts as he lies by the seashore and looks out at the world.

Karen Hesse uses eight periods in Jewish history to reinforce the meaning of Hanukkah in *The Stone Lamp: Eight Stories of Hanukkah Through History*. The historical time periods range from the Crusades to the assassination of Yitzhak Rabin. An explanation of each time period is followed by a free verse written from a child's viewpoint. Brian Pinkney's illustrations add to the feelings about Hanukkah.

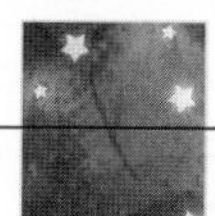

Contemporary Jewish Literature

The literature written about Jewish experiences after the Holocaust differs considerably depending on the age of the intended audience. Picture storybooks develop themes about relationships and the importance of family or depict important holidays in the life of the Jewish community. Books written for older audiences may describe the experiences of survivors from the Holocaust as they learn to live in a new land, follow characters who experience anti-Semitism, or develop the conflicts felt by Jewish characters when they live in non-Jewish environments.

Lisa Silverman (2007), the director of the Sinai Temple Blumenthal Library in Los Angeles, provides the following advice for adults choosing and sharing the many examples of Holocaust literature with children and young adults: "Parents, teachers, and librarians need to use these books with sensitivity. Even a child who is an excellent reader may not be ready to understand a book's content or the graphic nature of some illustrations. Adults are compelled to confront the subject of evil in our world and explain it to children in our care. We hope that children understand that we do this not to scare them, but to teach. The importance of this literature, besides the inherent history lesson, is that it can be used to convey values—the value of social justice and moral courage, problem solving, and resisting prejudice. . . . Clearly the Holocaust should not be hidden from children" (p. 62).

Picture Storybooks

Many of the books for younger readers explain the importance of various Jewish customs, holidays, and celebrations. Both Barbara Goldin and Patricia Polacco authored books about Sukkot, also called The Feast of Tabernacles or the Festival of Booths, a week-long holiday in September or October that is a reminder of generations of homelessness. To celebrate Sukkot, Jewish people build little huts, or sukkah. Sukkot marked the forty years that Israelites wandered in the desert, before they entered the Promised Land. In Goldin's *Night Lights: A Sukkot Story*, a young boy helps the family build the sukkah. Through the preparation, the author reveals the history of the celebration. Two of the main characters, Daniel and Naomi, also overcome their fear as they look through the branches and stalks that form the roof of the hut and realize the stars and moon that light the night are the same stars and moon that the early wanderers in the desert and farmers in the field saw through their sukkah roofs.

Books written by Roni Schotter, Stephanie Spinner, and Eric A. Kimmel focus on Passover and Hanukkah. Schotter's *Passover Magic* follows a family and their relatives as they prepare for and celebrate the Passover with the traditional Seder. The author's note presents additional information about the Passover and the history of the Jewish people as they escaped from slavery. This information includes the significance of various symbolic foods. Spinner's *It's a Miracle: A Hanukkah Storybook* is framed around a young boy who is chosen as the Official Candle Lighter. Each night as he lights the candles, his grandmother tells stories about family life. The text includes a brief retelling of the Hanukkah legend. Jill McElmurry's illustrations add a humorous touch to the stories. Kimmel's *A Hanukkah Treasury* includes stories, recipes, and games.

Hanukkah and Christmas both feature in Michael J. Rosen's *Elijah's Angel: A Story for Chanukah and Christmas*. In this story of friendship between Michael, a nine-year-old Jewish boy, and Elijah, an elderly African American wood carver, the person-versus-self conflict

A Featured Book for Young Adults

The Book Thief by Markus Zusak is a highly recommended book for young adults and is also on *The New York Times* Children's Best Sellers listing. On April 15, 2007, it was number four on the list of chapter books and remained on the list for fifty-one weeks. The book, narrated by Death, is set in Nazi Germany. The heroine is Liesel Meminger, a girl who believes strongly in the power of words and that books have the ability to feed the soul. The title of the book is based on Liesel's attraction to books. Consequently, she steals books from the Nazi book burnings and discovers that the mayor's wife has an irresistible collection of books that may be secretly stolen.

The theme, books have the power to nourish the soul, is highlighted as Liesel comforts neighbors as she reads from the stolen books during bombing raids and reads to a Jewish man who is hidden in her basement. As you read the book, you may trace the author's development of these powerful themes and the development of the conflicts as seen through Death's viewpoint.

The author develops an interesting technique to relate words, conflict, and characterization. When Liesel discovers a dictionary, the author relates words and their meanings to the developing conflict. For example, you may trace how the following meanings relate to both developing conflict and characterization: Happiness (p. 358), Forgiveness (p. 368), Angst-Fear (p. 375), Word (p. 382), Opportunity (p. 386), Misery (p. 391), Silence (p. 398), and Regret (p. 401).

As you read the book, also consider why the author chose to tell the story through Death's all-seeing point of view. You may speculate about the meaning of the following comment made by Death toward the conclusion of the book:

> Yes, I have seen a great many things in this world. I attend the greatest disasters and work for the greatest villains. But then there are other moments. There's a multitude of stories (a mere handful, as I have previously suggested) that I allow to distract me as I work, just as the colors do I pick them up in the unluckiest, unlikeliest places and I make sure to remember them as I go about my work. *The Book Thief* is one such story. (p. 549).

You may also consider what the narrator means by the following conclusion to the book:

> A Last Note From Your Narrator:
> I am haunted by humans. (p. 550)

This is a complex book that tells a powerful story about World War II, the fate of both German citizens and Jewish residents, and the consequences of war and hatred. It could also lead to thoughtful discussions among older students who are studying World War II or are reading about the possible consequences of current international conflicts.

To add an American point of view about World War II, older readers could view the video or DVD production, *Franklin Roosevelt and World War II*. The film includes comments by historians and journalists as well as clips showing various political leaders and the war in Europe.

develops when Elijah gives Michael a carved angel as a gift for Christmas. Michael now tries to decide if it is all right to have a Christmas angel in a Jewish home. The story has an ecumenical ending as the boy's parents tell him the angel represents friendship, "And doesn't friendship mean the same thing in every religion?" (p. 21). The ecumenical theme is strengthened at the close of the story when Michael gives his friend a menorah and the Jewish family finds candles lit on the menorah that is placed in the window of Elijah's shop.

In Roni Schotter's *The Boy Who Loved Words*, the author creates a character, Selig, who delights in discovering new words, especially the way they sound and even taste. As a result of his love for words, he hoards words on scraps of paper and keeps them in his pockets. After he dreams that a Yiddish Genie tells him to use this passion for words, he discovers that his words can help people who need them. For example, a poet who needs a word to complete a poem, a baker who needs a descriptive term for his goods, and an elderly man who needs a positive description about how he walks. The descriptive words are italicized in the text and defined in the glossary. This is an excellent book to encourage a love for language.

Books for Older Readers

Novels for older readers may focus on the lives of characters and their families after they escape from the Holocaust and settle in a new country. Some of these stories are filled with happy experiences; others include the tragic outcomes of prejudice and anti-Semitism.

In a study that looks at Holocaust survivors, Helmreich (1990) identifies two different types of responses by those who came to the United States. In the early responses are a buoyant quality in which the refugees want to emulate the spirit of earlier "pioneers" who came to the United States. In contrast, journal entries of social workers tell about immigrants who had difficulty adapting to the relatives and friends who welcomed them to the new land and to the struggle to find adequate housing and decent jobs. In addition, some of the immigrants experienced anxiety, depression, and paranoia. These survivors were surrounded by a broad cross section of the U.S. population who knew little about the Jewish culture and their previous experiences. Helmreich points out that the Jewish immigrants faced two problems as they tried to assimilate into life in the United States: (1) they had been weakened physically and psychologically by their experiences, and (2) they had little or no English and were unfamiliar with U.S. culture. The survivors brought with them, however, a desire to preserve Jewish culture and to raise the level of Jewish consciousness to new heights. Many of these immigrants brought with them a need to remember the Holocaust and a strong support for Israel.

Many of the characteristics identified by Helmreich are also found in realistic fiction. Sonia Levitin's characters in *Silver Days* and *Annie's Promise* face severe changes in their lives as Papa works desperately hard to make a living and Mama, formerly a lady from a well-to-do background, takes on menial jobs to help support her family. The author uses contrasts between life in prewar Germany and life as Jewish immigrants in the United States to develop the understanding of changes in their life.

Nonfiction books for older audiences may focus on important celebrations or on other cultural information. Books about the Jewish coming of age have been written by Eric A. Kimmel and Barbara Diamond Goldin. Kimmel's *Bar Mitzvah: A Jewish Boy's Coming of Age* describes the importance of being thirteen, the history of the bar mitzvah, and the responsibilities that accompany this ceremony.

Kimmel develops the meaning of the bar mitzuah experience and the history associated with it. Kimmel tells his readers that now they understand what it means to become bar mitzvah and become part of the ancestors who go back to the time of Abraham. In *Bat Mitzvah: A Jewish Girl's Coming of Age*, Barbara Diamond Goldin uses a similar approach to describe the ceremony and preparation for the Jewish girl's coming of age.

How Do You Spell God? Answers to the Big Questions from Around the World is an interesting comparative text designed to answer questions about different religions. Rabbi Marc

Gellman and Monsignor Thomas Hartman answer questions in nineteen chapters. The title of each chapter is based on a question answered in that chapter. Some of these questions include: What's a religion? How are religions the same? How are religions different? How do you spell God? What questions does each religion want to answer the most? Can I talk to God? In addition to Jewish and Christian answers, the book provides basic information on other organized religions including Hinduism, Buddhism, Confucianism, Shinto, and Islam.

Current nonfiction books also provide answers to questions about Israeli conflict. Mitch Frank's *Understanding the Holy Land: Answering Questions About the Israeli-Palestinian Conflict* focuses on contemporary issues. Students may compare the current nonfiction books about this conflict with news sources in newspapers and journals. For example, an article in *The Economist* (January 13, 2007) is titled "Second Thoughts About the Promised Land." The article provides interesting topics for discussion.

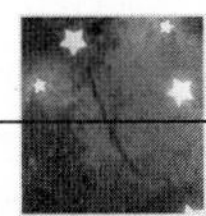

Survival

Let us begin our discussion of survival in Jewish literature with a search for the survival motif in picture books. Many picture books reflect survival in the greatest times of need, whether the survival is from slavery in Egypt as expressed in books about the Passover or later survival during the Holocaust. The story of Moses and the Exodus from Egypt is the focus of Josh Hanft's *The Miracles of Passover*. Survival is expressed in the belief that God will deliver the people from slavery. Seymour Chast's illustrations include flaps that readers lift to identify the plagues on the Egyptians and the meanings of the special foods that are eaten during the Passover Seder.

More detailed explanations of the Passover and accompanying survival strategies are presented in Seymour Rossel's *The Storybook Haggadah*. The text, written in both Hebrew and English, follows a family celebration, including the Bible verses that explain how God freed the people from slavery in Egypt. This is a good beginning for survival themes in Jewish literature because many of the themes in the Haggadah are also found in other examples of Jewish literature. For example, a promise must be kept (God remembers his promise to the people and assists them during their Exodus); a long-range plan may be necessary for survival (Joseph is sold into Egypt, but he eventually saves his family from starving); the greatest miracles may be hidden in little things (Moses sees the burning bush); when freedom calls, the people must hurry to answer (the unlevened bread reminds people that during the Exodus the people could not wait for the bread to rise); and songs (singing lifts the spirits in times of stress) and an open door are important during the Passover Seder (doors are open to show strangers that a celebration is happening and to invite the prophet Elijah into the home).

The importance of inviting strangers to the Passover Seder is developed in Elka Weber's *The Yankee at the Seder*. This book, based on a true story, is set in Virginia following the Civil War. When a Jewish Union soldier is invited into the home of a Confederate family for the celebration, the author shows that the Seder allows people to overlook differences and to celebrate what they have in common. The boy in the family discovers that this is one of the most important survival strategies.

Julie Gruenbaum Fax (2010) states that books and art have offered Jewish people both expression and escape from the Nazi horrors and the challenges of assimilation. Escaping from Nazi horrors through art and music is shown in *Brundibar*, retold by Tony Kushner and illustrated by Maurice Sendak. This highly illustrated text presents an opera first performed by doomed children in the model Nazi concentration camp of Theresienstadt. Unfortunately, this model camp was also a way station for Auschwitz. The opera was performed fifty-five times by a cast of imprisoned children. The cast changed, however, because the children were sent to Auschwitz and new arrivals took their places. Even in this terrible environment, there are

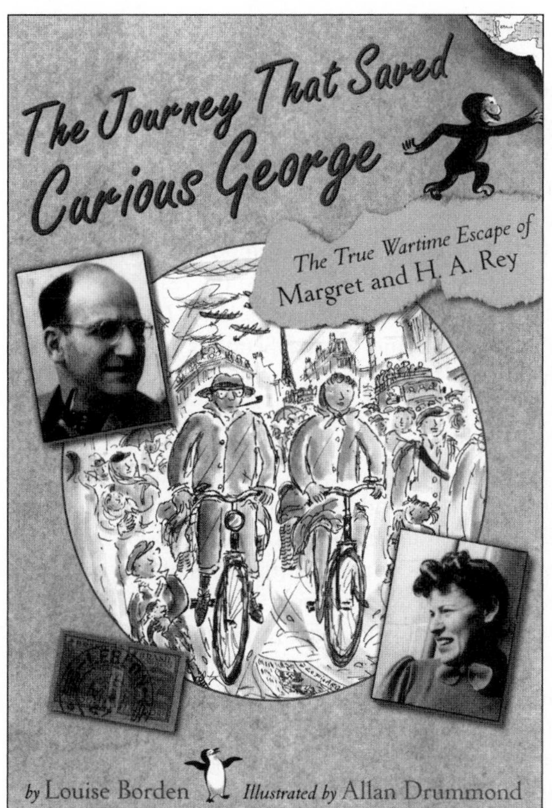

Survival for these Jewish authors is made possible by a children's book.

Cover from *The Journey That Saved Curious George: The True Wartime Escape of Margret and H. A. Rey,* by Louise Borden. Front Jacket art © 2005 by Allan Drummond. Reprinted by permission of Houghton Mifflin Harcourt Publishing Company. All rights reserved.

positive strategies for survival: for example, helping others makes people happy, singing lifts the spirits, friends make us strong, and bravery helps overcome bullies. Unfortunately, the book ends with the message that bullies do not give up; they will return.

The poetry book *. . . I Never Saw Another Butterfly . . . : Children's Drawings and Poems from the Terezin Concentration Camp, 1942–1944* is another example of the work of imprisoned children in Theresienstadt. Between 1942 and 1944, 15,000 children passed through the concentration camp; fewer than 100 survived. Although many of the poems and drawings express fear, it is remarkable that many of them express courage and optimism required for survival. For example, even though the author of "The Butterfly" is imprisoned, he finds spiritual comfort in nature through the dandelions and white chestnut branches that call to him. Other poets reflect looking out at the distant world and remembering home, dreaming of childhood, or listening to favorite stories. One poet believes that justice sweetens pain and woe, while another stresses that toughness allows the body to survive. A primary strategy for survival that several poets express is not to lose faith or hope.

A happier escape from Nazi horrors is the focus of Louise Borden's *The Journey That Saved Curious George: The True Wartime Escape of Margret and H. A. Rey.* The characterizations of these two authors and illustrators reveal their survival strategies. For example, they are curious about the world, feel free to speak their minds, and are skillful at writing and illustrating. In 1940, they develop careful plans to flee imprisonment in Europe by trying to reach freedom in America. Their plans include documents and currency. Their greatest survival document is their manuscript for *Curious George,* which convinces authorities that they are not spies but authors of children's books. Their lack of fear and sense of adventure are revealed as they build a bicycle and travel through France, Spain, and Portugal and then across the Atlantic to Rio de Janeiro, and finally to New York. According to the author's note, "It is my way of honoring their creativity and their courage during a dark time in history for many countries of Europe" (p. 3). It is interesting to read the various "Curious George" books and to discover how closely the mischievous monkey uses many of the survival strategies believed important by the authors.

Memories of Survival by Esther Nisenthal Krinitz and Bernice Steinhardt provides a bridge between picture books that develop survival skills during Europe in WWII and challenges of assimilation. Here are stories of survival lived by the author Esther Krinitz along with the embroidered pictures she created. Survival during her early life included creating new identities for herself and her sister, hiding in attics during Nazi raids, and joining the Polish army. The book begins with her childhood in Poland and concludes with coming to America in 1949. The author states, "For Esther, coming to America meant that she would never again be persecuted for being Jewish" (p. 63).

Another life story featuring survival and escape is developed in Uri Shulevitz's Caldecott Honor book, *How I Learned Geography.* This story is based on the author's childhood experiences as his parents flee Poland in 1939 to live in Turkestan (now Kazakhstan in Central Asia). Even though the family is very poor and often hungry, his father returns from the market with a huge map that covers an entire wall with color. It is this map that ignites Schulevitz's imagination and allows him to travel the world. He survives his experience because of his fascination with strange-sounding names, burning deserts, snowy mountains, wondrous temples, and cities with tall buildings. He survives by spending hours in his fantasy flights rather than thinking about hunger and misery. The Author's Note expands on the autobiographical nature of the book.

Although not escaping from a dangerous world, Max in Maurice Sendak's *Where the Wild Things Are* uses his imagination and a fantasy flight to escape from his personal anger. When Max becomes furious with his mother he is sent to bed without his supper. Now his imagination changes his bedroom into the land of wild things where he is empowered by becoming king. This experience allows him to overcome his anger; he returns to the reality of his bedroom where a hot meal is waiting. In Anita Silvey's *Everything I Need to Know I Learned from a Children's Book* (2009) children's author Marc Brown points out that Sendak's book determined the course of his career; it showed him the potential of becoming an illustrator and an author of children's books.

Historical fiction, biography and autobiography, and information books written for older students are filled with many instances of Jewish survival strategies. Books set in WWII during the Holocaust are filled with both terrible devastation and heart stopping instances of heroism and striving for survival. *The Book Thief* by Markus Zusak is "A Featured Book for Young Adults" in this chapter. It is also a book that includes numerous instances of survival. Even the introduction by Death, the narrator, states that the story is about a perpetual survivor, one who seems to stay out of the grasp of Death. According to Death, this story is about one of the humans who is worthy of surviving. When searching for survival strategies we can locate strategies used by the heroine, Liesel Meminger; her foster father, Papa Hubermann; and Max Vandenburg, the Jewish refugee who is hiding in their basement.

As the title of the book suggests, Liesel's strategies relate to obtaining books and reading them. One of the themes the author develops is that words and books can save lives. Liesel develops her strategy early in the story when she obtains her first book and then strives to learn to read and write. She is so fascinated by books that she begins stealing them from Hitler's bonfires of burning books. This is a dangerous activity that requires nerve, stealth, speed, and luck. Liesel's reading helps both herself and her family to survive as she reads the books to distract them during bombing raids. She also reads to Max as he hides in the basement. She feels the power of words every time she deciphers a new word or constructs a sentence.

Papa also has specific survival strategies that help the family during these dangerous times. Papa gains Liesel's trust and affection through his kindness and his understanding that she is a lonely girl who needs love. He also uses music to help the family survive as he plays his accordion to help overcome Liesel's nightmares. Papa understands Liesel's needs and teaches her to read; this activity again shows the power of words. Papa's actions toward the Jewish refugee show that to survive, promises and secrets must be kept.

Max's survival strategies begin with finding Papa, the person whose life was saved by a Jew during WWI. Max hopes that Papa will keep his promise to help save another Jew. Max's survival strategies also relate to books and writing. He has a copy of *Mein Kampf* that saves him from suspicion; however, when he is away from the Nazi guards he paints over pages from this book and writes a positive story for Liesel. Through many lonely and dangerous hours while in hiding, he listens to Liesel read the various books that she has taken from the burning fires.

Survival strategies found in biographies set during this time period are especially revealing. Dorit Bader Whiteman's *Lonek's Journey: The True Story of a Boy's Escape to Freedom* is about an eleven-year-old Jewish boy and his family who escape Nazi-occupied Poland in 1939 only to be captured by the Russians and sent to a labor camp in Siberia. As the text begins, readers are introduced to the family's survival strategies as they collect and hide valuables that might be needed in a hasty flight. As the German solders approach, father tells the family to never give up hope and if captured, they must try to escape to freedom. Even after the family is captured and placed on a train to Siberia they have one goal: to survive. To maintain some pride and dignity in this gulag, father tries to make their shack more livable and Lonek scrounges for wild berries and mushrooms to keep his family from starving. His mother realizes that the family's survival requires making the children feel secure.

Unfortunately, Lonek is separated from his family. Eventually he is placed in an orphanage. Fortunately, he is one of the 1,000 Jewish children who are rescued. His journey of survival covers thousands of dangerous miles until he eventually reaches freedom in Palestine (later to become Israel). As he crosses the Red Sea he thinks about the earlier rescue of Moses and his people as they cross the same body of water. As the children arrive they are met by cheering Jewish residents who celebrate the miracle that these 1,000 children survived. As the text concludes, Lonek stresses one of his most important survival strategies: Never waste food. Bread is more precious than gold!

As you read this book you may decide why a middle school librarian identified this book as a favorite book with boys. The emotions expressed by the characters may also be so believable because as a child the author escaped from Nazi-occupied Vienna in 1938. You might compare this book with Annika Thor's *A Faraway Island*, translated from the Swedish by Linda Schenck Delacorte, in which two Jewish sisters escape from Nazi-occupied Austria to live with two different families on a remote island. Part of the survival strategies in Thor's book deal with overcoming prejudice.

Is It Night or Day? by Fern Schumer Chapman is another historical novel based on a factual event. One thousand Jewish children were rescued from Nazi Germany and placed in foster homes in America in a program endorsed by Eleanor Roosevelt. The heroine of the story is twelve-year-old Edith, a character based on the experiences of the author's mother who traveled from Germany to America. As in many of the historical fiction stories, Edith attempts to raise money to help her parents escape. Although she cannot save her parents, she discovers that pride in being Jewish is a factor of survival. This is demonstrated through the actions of sports hero Hank Greenberg, who is proud to be Jewish.

The Bat-Chen Diaries: Selected Writings by Bat-Chen Shahak provides a more contemporary setting for survival strategies. The author is an Israeli teenager who kept a diary from her early childhood until, at the age of 15, she is killed by a suicide bomber in Tel Aviv's Dizong Center. Her diary begins with the belief that life is the most beautiful gift of all, and no one has the right to take it away. Throughout her writing she expresses her strongest survival strategy: There should be no more wars and people should be able to live in peace with other countries. Her survival strategies are all very positive. For example, writing and music are happy experiences; look at a glass as being half full and not half empty; measure friends by the way they treat you in times of trouble; imagination helps answer the hard questions; and freedom, liberty, hope, faith, and trust are vital for survival. Her writings express the belief that the Holocaust taught that her people could no longer live among foreigners; they must be able to live in their own land where they have complete rights as individuals and as a people.

This analysis of survival strategies in Jewish literature indicates a common thread that extends from the early deliverance from slavery at the time of Moses to the horrors of the Holocaust and the dangers of living in a country where terrorists make life unpredictable. Authors stress such survival strategies as retaining hope and faith, even in times of peril. Characters understand that promises must be kept, secrets must not be revealed, and long-range plans may be required for survival. Characters also use personal strategies to help them survive. For example, they may rely on books to help them escape, use their imaginations to fantasize, and write their own poems and stories that help them remember. All of the characters reveal that courage is important. They also express a desire for the elimination of war and the striving for peace. Many of the books stress the need to have a homeland where they can live in safety or to emigrate to a country where they will experience freedom.

Summary

In this chapter, we have analyzed the folklore and ancient stories of the Jewish people and identified the values, beliefs, and types of stories found in the literature.

Many of the folklore selections reflect the values and beliefs of the people including messages that show the importance of such values as faith, learning, hospitality, knowledge, cooperation, and charity. Various examples of Jewish folklore were discussed, including wonder tales, humorous tales, tales of ghosts and goblins, clever folks and survivors, and legends with biblical sidelights.

We considered literature, both nonfiction and fiction, that provided a vivid history of the Jewish people and the years of emigration and immigration. The nonfiction books cover important periods in Jewish history and may focus on historical change in locations such as Jerusalem. Books that create vivid images of fleeing Europe in the early 1900s depict the importance of and trauma associated with developing a new life in a new land.

We discussed literature about the Holocaust including historical fiction, biography, and autobiography. The most emotional literature of the Holocaust is told through the point of view of authors who either lived through the experience or had friends or family members who told their stories to the authors.

Finally, we considered contemporary works. Through this literature, we discovered threads that proceed from the earliest folklore through poetry and contemporary literature. Through analyzing survival strategies we discovered threads for survival that proceed from the earliest traditional literature to contemporary works.

Suggested Activities for Developing Understanding of Jewish Literature

1. Develop a timeline of Jewish history. Identify literature that relates to important occurrences. Discuss why you believe the literature is a good example of the period.

2. Choose a value found in Jewish folklore and collect examples of literature that exemplify that value. Discuss how the value is developed through the folklore. Sources such as Rabbi Joseph Telushkin's *The Book of Jewish Values* (2000) or *A Code of Jewish Ethics: You Shall Be Holy* (2006) may provide sources for values.

3. Two examples of a Cinderella-type tale were discussed in the chapter ("How Much Do You Love Me?" in Beatrice Silverman Weinreich's *Yiddish Folktales* and Nina Jaffe's *The Way Meat Loves Salt: A Cinderella Tale from the Jewish Tradition*). Locate additional tales that are similar to those found in other cultures. How is the variant similar to the tales from other countries, and how does the tale develop a Jewish perspective?

4. Identify the major Jewish holidays such as Hanukkah, Passover, Purim, Rosh Hashana, and Yom Kippur. Why are these holidays important for the Jewish people? How are the holidays portrayed in books for children? How are they described in adult texts? What are the similarities and differences? Why might there be differences?

5. Read Eleanor Ayer's *Parallel Journeys* and compare the points of view of the Jewish girl who survived the Holocaust and the German youth who grew up as part of the Hitler

Youth Organization. Discuss how the goals of the Reich Youth Library and the school curriculum discussed in this chapter might have influenced German youth.

6. Identify and compare the authors' development of characters, conflict, settings, and survival strategies in books about Holocaust survivors. What, if any, are the differences between these books and books about Holocaust victims? Examples to consider include Lola Rein Kaufman's *The Hidden Girl: A True Story of the Holocaust*; Monique Polak's *What World Is Left*; Elly Berkovits Gross's *Elly: My True Story of the Holocaust*; and Laura Hillman's *I Will Plant You a Lilac Tree: A Memoir of a Schindler's List Survivor.*

7. *Anne Frank, The Diary of a Young Girl: The Definitive Edition* is the most famous example of a journal written by a Jewish child who did not survive the Holocaust. Rutka Laskier's *Rutka's Notebook: A Voice from the Holocaust* has been called "The Polish Anne Frank." Read the two examples and compare the description of the Holocaust, the person-versus-self and person-versus-society conflicts, and the survival strategies used by the main characters.

8. Choose a Jewish person who is the subject of biographies and, if possible, who has also written an autobiography. Compare the information in the literature. What are the points of view expressed? Analyze the authenticity of each title.

9. Compare the values and beliefs developed in Jewish folklore with the values and beliefs expressed in Jewish poetry. What similarities do you find? If there are differences, how do you account for the differences?

10. Search one of the following websites. Report your evaluations of the website to your class:

    United States Holocaust Memorial Museum: For Teachers. http://www.ushmm.org/education/foreducators.

    Holocaust Denial: An Online Guide to Exposing and Combating Anti-Semitic Propaganda: http://www.adl.org/holocaust/introduction.as. ADL: Anti-Defamation League

Involving Children with Jewish Literature

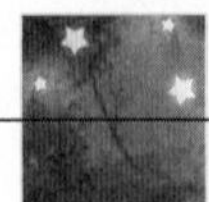

Phase One: Traditional Literature

As discussed in this chapter, the Jewish folklore transmits the essential values of the culture, provides a portrait of the people, offers an understanding of the Jewish heritage, and furnishes links to both the biblical and historical past.

Storytelling

As developed earlier in our discussion of Jewish folklore, the tales that may be chosen for oral storytelling reflect centuries of this tradition. Ellen Frankel (1997) provides an interesting motivation for and introduction to the importance of oral storytelling. She states,

> For the Jewish people, uprooted so often from home throughout the long centuries of a restless history, stories have served to orient and guide us back into a familiar path. Like other portable baggage of Jewish tradition—an elaborate code of laws, the Hebrew language, the prayerbook, the Jewish calendar, and a comprehensive ritual life—stories are easily packed, carried, and unpacked when our people reach the next watering hole. All it takes is a teller, a listener, and a moment to catch our breath. (pp. 8–9)

Jewish Storytelling Festival To develop a Jewish Storytelling Festival, review the various examples of Jewish folklore discussed earlier in this chapter.

Wonder Tales
Humorous Tales and Fools and Simpletons
Tales of Ghosts and Goblins
Clever Folks and Survivors
Myths and Legends with Biblical Sidelights

Ask the students to read examples of each type of folklore. The class may choose one type of folklore and each student may develop a story for telling that reflects that type of folklore. Or they may select a broader festival, divide according to each type of folklore, and select and develop a story within that type for oral retelling. Whichever approach is used, they should investigate the background of the story and the story type, prepare an introduction to the story, and practice the story for an oral presentation.

As part of the Jewish Storytelling Festival, students should also collect and display examples of books that include Jewish folklore. They may also display a Jewish folklore web as part of their Jewish Storytelling Festival. Other student projects such as comparisons between Jewish Cinderella tales with Cinderella tales from other cultures and plot diagrams may be included as part of the display.

Webbing the Values Found in Jewish Folklore

Begin this webbing activity by acquiring as many examples of Jewish folklore as possible. As students read the folklore, have them develop a web showing its important characteristics. Figure 6.1 is an example of a partial web about Jewish folklore developed with students.

As students add to the web, ask them to discuss the importance of the values, the historical characters, and the references to places and people.

FIGURE 6.1 Web Showing Traditional Jewish Values Found in Folklore

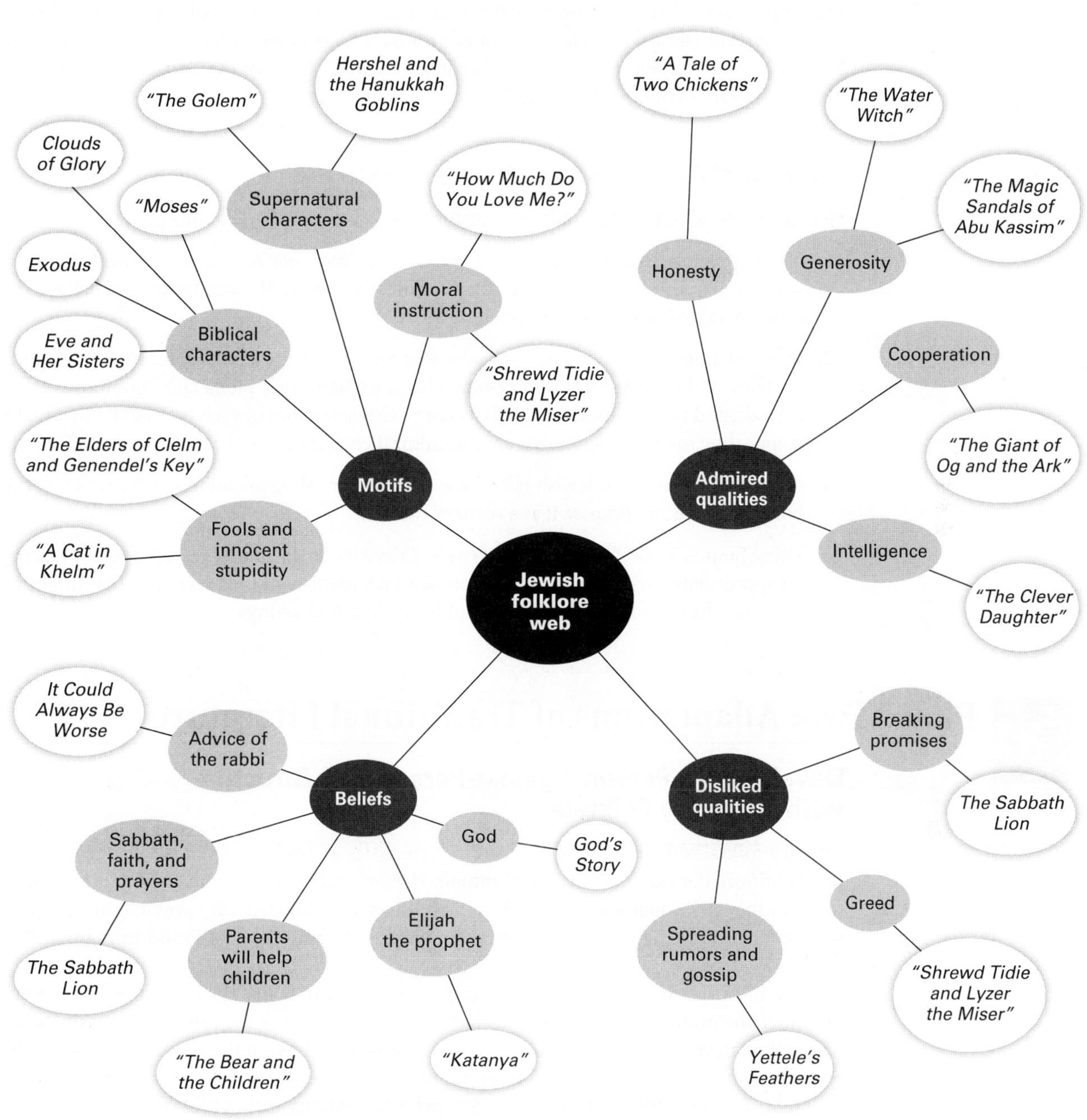

Comparing Three Versions of *The Golem*

Students may read and compare the illustrations and the texts in three versions of the Golem story: David Wisniewski's *Golem*, Barbara Rogasky's *The Golem*, and Isaac Bashevis Singer's *The Golem*. Students may read all three texts and compare the power of the writing, consider the quality of the information provided in the author's or illustrator's notes, and view and discuss the impact of the illustrations. They may also consider why Wisniewski's illustrations were chosen as one of the ten best illustrated books of the year and presented with the Caldecott Medal, and why the Isaac Bashevis Singer's text (Singer was a recipient of the Nobel Prize) was chosen as an American Library Association "Notable Book," a *School Library Journal* "Best Book of the Year," a *New York Times Book Review* "Notable Children's Book of the Year," and a *New York Times* "Outstanding Book of the Year."

Additional Activities to Enhance Phase One

Here are some activities for children or young adult students related to this phase:

1. Compare Nina Jaffe's *The Way Meat Loves Salt: A Cinderella Tale from the Jewish Tradition* with Cinderella stories found in other cultures. What are the similarities? What are the differences? What makes Jaffe's retelling a Jewish folktale?
2. Make an annotated bibliography of tales that may be categorized as parables and allegorical tales, children's tales or kinder-mayselekh, wonder tales, pious tales, humorous tales, legends, and supernatural tales. What are the characteristics of each type of tale that make it appealing to the reader? What are the cultural contributions of each type of tale?
3. Many of the humorous Jewish tales are especially appealing to children. Choose a favorite humorous tale and prepare it as a readers' theater.
4. Using Simms Taback's *Kibitzers and Fools: Tales My Zayda Told Me* as a model for placing an appropriate saying at the conclusion of a tale, identify or create sayings that might be placed at the end of folktales that do not have identified sayings.

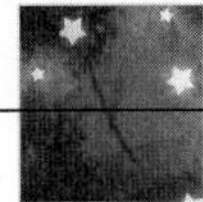

Phase Two: Adaptations of Traditional Literature

Developing a Person-Against-Person Plot Structure with a Literary Folktale

Literary folktales include many of the characteristics of traditional tales told through the oral tradition. For example, Eric A. Kimmel's *Hershel and the Hanukkah Goblins* is similar to many of the traditional Jewish folktales. In addition, the plot structure provides an excellent source for developing a person-against-person plot structure that is found in many of the folktales.

Plots in stories frequently follow a triangle, a structure in which the beginning of the story identifies the problem, introduces the characters, and describes the setting. Increasing conflict is then developed until the story reaches a climax. Following the climax there is usually a turning point incident, followed quite rapidly by an end of conflict or a resolution of the problem. To show this conflict, you might present students with a plot diagram similar to that in Figure 6.2.

Ask the students to think about some stories they know follow this type of plot structure. For example, they can retell "The Three Billy Goats Gruff" or "Goldilocks and the Three Bears" and decide how the story follows this diagram. Asking students to act out one of these stories will help them understand and appreciate the developing conflict. After students have retold or acted out a familiar story, have them place the incidents from the story on the plot diagram.

Select a Jewish folktale—a traditional or a literary retelling—that has a strong plot development that can be shown on such a plot structure. For example, *Hershel and the Hanukkah*

FIGURE 6.2 A Plot Diagram

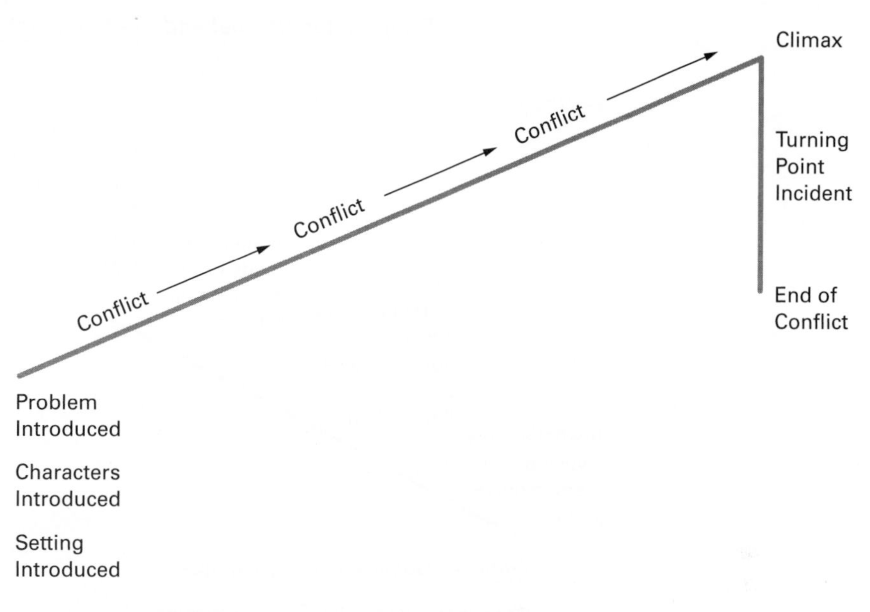

Goblins is a literary folktale similar to many Jewish folktales. The story is set in a village during Hanukkah. Hershel, the main character, enters the village and discovers the people are unable to celebrate Hanukkah because wicked goblins haunt the synagogue. To rid the village of goblins, someone must spend eight nights in the old synagogue, light the Hanukkah candles each night, and convince the king of the goblins to light the candles on the eighth night. Hershel declares he is not afraid of the goblins and offers to rid the village of them. The plot develops as Hershel uses his wits and common materials to trick increasingly fearsome goblins and light the candles. The progression continues until on the eighth night, Hershel tricks the king of the goblins into lighting the Hanukkah candles. At this point the spell is broken and all of the households celebrate Hanukkah in their homes. The author develops the theme that even common materials may be used in uncommon ways if a person uses those materials with wit and intelligence.

Introduce *Hershel and the Hanukkah Goblins* to the students. Show the illustrations and ask the students to respond to the mood of the story and to consider what type of problem and conflict might be in the story. If desired, you may read the author's endnote, in which he provides information about the Hanukkah celebration.

Read the story aloud to the students. Before placing the incidents on the plot diagram, encourage the students to provide their personal responses to the story. Now draw a blank plot diagram on the board or an overhead transparency and ask the students to identify elements from the story that can be placed on the plot diagram. For example, a group of third-grade students identified the information found in Figure 6.3 (Norton & Norton, 2003).

After the students complete the plot diagram, ask them to consider what they think the theme is or the message the author is giving. The third-grade students who completed this activity decided the themes were (1) it is important to use one's wits and intelligence, and (2) even common objects may be used to outwit the enemy if they are used with intelligence. Have the students defend their choice of themes by identifying what happened in the story to

FIGURE 6.3 A Plot Diagram of *Hershel and the Hanukkah Goblins*

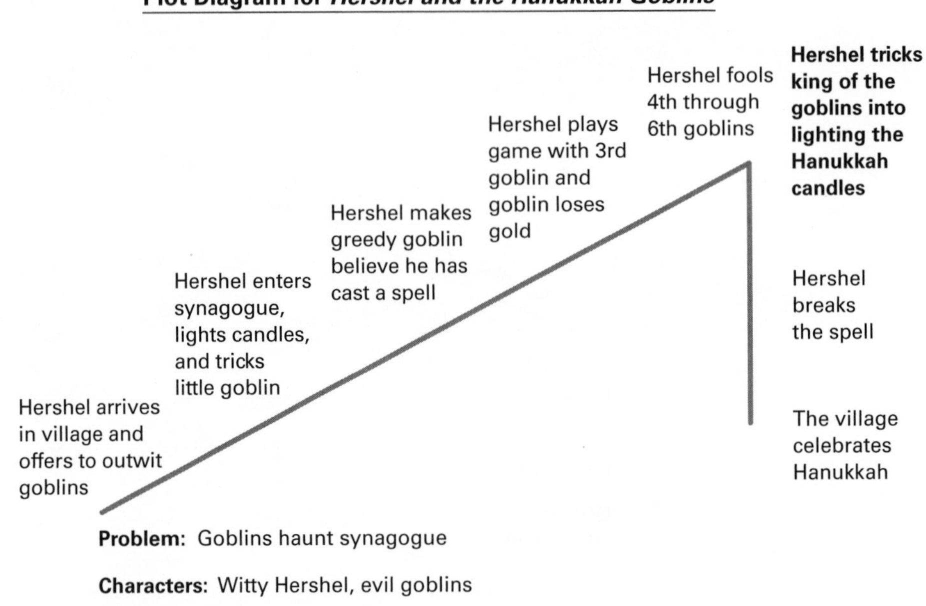
Plot Diagram for Hershel and the Hanukkah Goblins
Hershel arrives in village and offers to outwit goblins
Hershel enters synagogue, lights candles, and tricks little goblin
Hershel makes greedy goblin believe he has cast a spell
Hershel plays game with 3rd goblin and goblin loses gold
Hershel fools 4th through 6th goblins
Hershel tricks king of the goblins into lighting the Hanukkah candles
Hershel breaks the spell
The village celebrates Hanukkah
Problem: Goblins haunt synagogue
Characters: Witty Hershel, evil goblins
Setting: Country village during winter. Time of Hanukkah

make them important. For example, all of Hershel's actions show the importance of wit and intelligence. In a search for common objects used to outwit the enemy, Hershel crushes a hard-boiled egg, which is part of his lunch, to make the little goblin believe he can crush rock. He uses pickles and the second goblin's greed to make it believe he has cast a spell on the pickle jar in which the goblin has caught its fist. He uses a dreidel and his wits to play a game with the third goblin and force the goblin to lose gold. He uses Hanukkah candles to trick the king of the goblins into lighting some candles so Hershel will believe the goblin really is fierce and the king.

Additional Activities to Enhance Phase Two

Here are some activities for children or young adult students related to this phase:

1. Search for cultural evidence related to the Jewish tradition in Trina Schart Hyman's illustrations for Eric A. Kimmel's *Hershel and the Hanukkah Goblins.*
2. Select important motifs, themes, and values found in Jewish folklore, and create your own literary folktale. Students might Consider what makes Leslie Kimmelman's *The Little Red Hen and the Passover Matzah* Jewish.

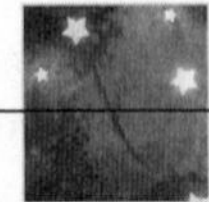

Phase Three: Historical Nonfiction

Historical nonfiction includes books that depict the early centuries of the Jewish people, biographies and autobiographies, and the early years of immigration and emigration.

Prepare Timelines and Maps Showing Early Jewish History

Students might read books such as Karla Kuskin's *Jerusalem, Shining Still* and Neil Waldman's *The Golden City: Jerusalem's 3,000 Years* and then develop a timeline showing important dates and happenings in Jewish history.

Following the reading of Norman H. Finkelstein's *The Other 1492: Jewish Settlement in the New World*, ask students to prepare a world map that shows the expulsion routes of some of the 200,000 people who left Spain.

Additional Activities to Enhance Phase Three

Here are some activities for children or young adult students related to this phase:

1. Get heavily illustrated adult sources such as Sharon R. Keller's *The Jews: A Treasury of Art and Literature* (1992), Therese and Mendel Metzger's *Jewish Life in the Middle Ages: Illuminated Hebrew Manuscripts of the Thirteenth to the Sixteenth Centuries* (1982) or Chapter 8 in Penelope Davies et al.'s *Janson's History of Art: The Western Tradition* (2011). Develop shadow boxes, collages, or other pictorial representations of various time periods. For example, using *Jewish Life in the Middle Ages*, focus on topics depicted and illustrated in the following chapters: "The Jewish Quarter," "The House," "Costume," "The Professional Life of the Jewish Community and Its Place in the Medieval City," "Family Life," and "Religious Life."
2. Two highly illustrated informational books, Neil Waldman's *The Golden City: Jerusalem's 3,000 Years* and Karla Kuskin's *Jerusalem, Shining Still* provide a history of the city. Compare and evaluate the books by answering these questions: (1) Are the facts accurate? How do you know if the facts are accurate? (2) What are the qualifications of the author to write the book or of the illustrator to illustrate the book? (3) How do the illustrations help or not help readers understand the subject? (4) How does the organization of the book help or not help the reader develop understanding of the subject? (5) Does the author encourage the readers to become involved in the subject?
3. Informational books about Jerusalem frequently include information about the Western Wall, which are the remains of an outer wall of the Second Temple, destroyed 2,500 years ago. Conduct research to discover the history of and the importance of this wall. This activity could be expanded to include other walls that have been important in history. For example, *The Talking Walls* by Margy Burns Knight includes the Western Wall in Jerusalem, in addition to the Great Wall of China, the granite walls of Great Zimbabwe in Africa, and the Cuzco walls in the Andes of Peru, and the Vietnam Veterans Memorial in Washington, D.C. In addition, the book discusses other kinds of walls, such as carvings in the cliffs near India's Bay of Bengal, paintings on the outside walls of an Egyptian house, and the paintings of Diego Rivera found on walls throughout Mexico. This comparative study allows students to discover the importance of walls throughout history and within a diverse group of cultures.

Phase Four: Historical Fiction

The majority of historical fiction books written for children and Holocaust. This topic is found in both picture storybooks and in combine a study of historical fiction with that of biography and aut develop a clearer understanding of this time period.

The majority of recent published articles on teaching Jewish literature also focus on developing instructional strategies and units around the subject. For example, Margaret Lincoln (2006) emphasizes using the resources of the United States Holocaust Memorial Museum in Washington, D.C. and taking advantage of its online workshops and lesson plans. She identifies the following websites that are useful for classroom use:

The Museum Fellowship Teaching Resources Website
http://mandelproject.us/index.html
The online version of Life in Shadows
http://www.ushmm.org/museum/exhib/online/hiddenchildren
The Holocaust Museum's downloadable teaching resources
http://www.ushmm.otg/education/foreducators/resource
Guidelines for Teaching about the Holocaust workshop
http://www.ushmm.org/education/foreducators/guidelines

Kathleen Baxter (2006) identifies Holocaust literature that should be used in classrooms. She believes: "Older elementary students and many middle schoolers will be riveted by these compelling accounts of courage and resilience told by and about young people who, in another time, could have been their neighbors" (p. 37).

The modeling activity developed in this section presents considerable background information. Providing background information is frequently necessary because students may not have enough prior knowledge to understand the conflict in the books.

Developing Understandings of Holocaust Literature through Modeling

Reading researchers identify modeling as one of the most effective ways to increase comprehension of text. For example, Dole, Duffy, Roehler, and Pearson (1991) emphasize modeling to help teachers explain the mental reasoning involved in performing various reading tasks. Early and Ericson (1988) declare that research shows that teachers neglect modeling the process and explaining or describing what students should do during a comprehension lesson. They stipulate that modeling is especially important when teaching students to make inferences. Modeling encourages readers to think about why they are responding personally to literature or a question in a certain way. Norton (1992, 2003) has developed modeling approaches designed to help students understand the inferences authors use when developing characterization and applying figurative language. Making inferences about the characters through their actions, dialogues, and thoughts is difficult for many students.

Developing the Modeling Strategy To prepare for the modeling lesson, first identify a skill and analyze the requirements needed to implement it. For example, gaining meaning through inferred characterization requires that readers go beyond the information provided in the text; use clues from the text to hypothesize about a character's feelings, actions, beliefs, values, and so on; and use background knowledge gained from other experiences. Next, you need to identify a text and portions of the text from which characterization can be inferred.

Using the text, plan ways to review the students' prior knowledge (schema) related to both the literary element and the setting, conflict, or historical happenings for the book. For example, you could develop a "review" to illustrate how authors imply characterization in literature through such devices as narration, dialogue, character's actions and thoughts, and even more subtle ways such as symbolism and figurative language. To introduce the setting or time frame for a story, use supports such as maps, pictures, films, historical timelines, picture books, and news articles that encourage students to identify prior knowledge, develop new understandings, and increase their abilities to respond to the characters and conflicts developed in the story. Activities such as brainstorming what is known, identifying images or feelings associated with a word or topic, and listing and answering questions about topics are additional ways to activate prior knowledge.

When you teach the modeling strategy you introduce or review the specific literary element that will be modeled and introduce the text. Then you model the whole sequence by reading from the text, stopping at an appropriate place and asking the inference question, answering the question, providing evidence that supports the answer, and exploring your reasoning process. This last part is extremely important because it allows you to explain how the task was approached. It also allows for an aesthetic response as you explain your personal feelings, past experiences, and previous knowledge that entered into the thought processes. Finally, when the students understand the process, they join in by answering questions, citing evidence, and exploring their own thought processes.

Modeling Example of Inferring Characterization The book example in this modeling lesson focuses on the 1990 Newbery Award book, Lois Lowry's *Number the Stars*. This historical fiction novel is set during the Holocaust. As you prepare this modeling activity, first identify the requirements for effective reasoning so students understand those requirements. For this lesson, students must be aware that effective inferencing requires them to go beyond the information the author provides in the text. They must use clues from the text to hypothesize about a character's emotions, beliefs, actions, hopes, and fears. Students must also be aware that authors develop characters through dialogue, narration, and characters' thoughts and actions. Share examples from literature or create your own and then ask the students to provide examples that show how they can make discoveries about characters.

Explain to the students that they will first listen to you read an excerpt from a book, ask a question, answer the question, provide evidence from the story that supports the answer, and share your reasoning process. You should also explain that after students listen to you proceed through the sequence, they will use the same process to answer questions, identify evidence, and explore their own reasoning process. You should discuss the meanings of evidence and reasoning and encourage students to consider how they use evidence and reasoning in their own lives. Students should realize that their own experiences, prior knowledge, emotions, and reactions are important parts of their reasoning process.

Then emphasize the importance of this activity by asking students to explain why it is important to be able to make inferences about characters in literature. Encourage students to discuss how understanding characterization makes a story more exciting, enjoyable, and believable. Students should also understand they can employ characterization in their own writing.

Next, plan a way to introduce *Number the Stars* to students. The review of prior knowledge or the development of new knowledge about the Holocaust is extremely important for students to understand the settings and conflicts presented in *Number the Stars*. For example, to introduce the setting you can use a map of Europe on which students locate the important places in World War II. Ask students to locate the countries of the European Allies and the Axis Powers. They should locate the setting for the book (Copenhagen, Denmark) and the route taken by 7,000 Jews who were smuggled by the Danish Resistance across the sea to Sweden.

Students will also require background information about the events in the 1940s that created the plot and conflict developed in *Number the Stars*. To provide additional background information about the Holocaust, you could read excerpts from Barbara Rogasky's *Smoke and Ashes: The Story of the Holocaust* and Milton Meltzer's *Rescue: The Story of How Gentiles Saved the Jews in the Holocaust*. These books reinforce the reasons for the actions and terror the characters in *Number the Stars* express.

Provide the first modeling example. Read orally from the beginning of the book through the section: "Annemarie had heard it often enough before, but it had never been directed at her until now" (p. 2).

Ask, "What do Annemarie's actions and feelings reveal about her?" Provide your own answer such as the following: "I think that Annemarie is normally a happy girl. I think that Annemarie is also experiencing a time when she feels considerable fear." Then provide the evidence from the text: "Annemarie's actions and responses when she races her friends indicate that she normally responds with laughter and enjoys the activities associated with playing with her friends and exploring the neighborhood. When she hears the soldier use the German word 'Halte!', her reactions change from laughter and joy to those associated with fear. The descriptions such as her heart seemed to skip a beat are associated with this fear." Now, provide your own reasoning to reach the answer: "As I read this story, I could first feel the joy associated with carefree children as they race laughingly through their familiar neighborhood. I know from my own experience the feelings of joy and happiness that occur when winning such a race. The author, however, develops a total change of attitude as within two paragraphs Annemarie goes from the normal laughing girl to one of such fright that her heart seems to skip a beat. The mood changes so drastically that I believe Annemarie is experiencing extreme fear. I believe that Annemarie may be experiencing this fear for the first time because she does not remember such words being directed at her."

At this point, verify that the students understand the procedure. If they do not, model another example. When the students understand the process, let them join the discussion by providing answers, evidence, and reasoning. It is advisable to let older students write brief answers to the questions, evidence, and reasoning before the discussion. These notes will increase the quality of the discussion that follows each question. This procedure should be flexible and encourage students to provide numerous responses and reasons.

Continue reading the book aloud until you come to the next logical discussion point. Interesting inferences and discussions could result following the interaction with the soldiers and response to the encounter: "When they were almost home, Ellen whispered suddenly, 'I was so scared' " (p. 5).

Ask these questions: "What do the soldiers' actions reveal about them? What do Ellen and Annemarie's responses reveal about them and the nature of the conflict?" Ask the students to answer the questions, provide the evidence, and explore their reasoning processes. Encourage a range of ideas. The students may use background information gained from the introduction to the book to expand their reasoning processes.

Number the Stars includes many additional opportunities for inferred characterization activities. Longer stories, such as *Number the Stars*, lend themselves to discussions according to chapters. Students can read or listen to and discuss several chapters each day. After each session, ask the students to summarize what they know about the characters and their developing conflict. Ask them, "What do you want to know about these characters?" To increase interactions with the text, you may ask students to write personal responses to each of the characters or to consider how they might have reacted if they were in the same position.

After students have been involved in modeling and discussion activities, they should have many opportunities to read, discuss, and respond to additional books in which the authors use inferences to develop characterization. The following books are useful for extending understanding of both the Holocaust and for modeling characterization. Shorter picture storybooks include Jo Hoestlandt's *Star of Fear, Star of Hope* and Margaret Wild's *Let the Celebrations Begin!* Longer novel-length books include Uri Orlev's *The Island on Bird Street*, Johanna Reiss's *The Upstairs Room*, and Ida Vos's *Hide and Seek*.

Analytical Reading of Miriam Bat-Ami's *Two Suns in the Sky*

The following series of lessons uses Adler and Van Doren's (1972) stages in analytical reading and applies those stages to the 1999 Scott O'Dell Award for Historical Fiction, Miriam Bat-Ami's *Two Suns in the Sky*. The following example provides an in-depth analysis of how to discuss, analyze, and criticize this book:

1. Classify the book according to kind and subject matter. To begin this activity, ask the students to read or listen to the extensive Author's Note on pages 215–218. In the Author's Note, Bat-Ami describes the Emergency Refugee Shelter at Fort Ontario, Oswego, New York. She also describes how she conducted research, interviewed people, and wrote a historical fiction account of the experience of a Jewish refugee boy, Adam, and an American girl, Chris, who lived near the refugee camp.

   After reading the Author's Note, ask the students to consider why they believe the book won the Scott O'Dell Award for Historical Fiction. What does this award signify about the type and quality of the literature? What does historical fiction mean? What part of the book needs to be historically accurate? How much of the story can be fictional?

2. Briefly state what the book is about. Before reading and discussing this book, make sure students understand the experiences of Jews and Jewish refugees during World War II. You might develop a list of what the students know and what they need to know to understand the book.

   Another needed area for understanding is point of view. Explain to the students that authors may tell their stories through various points of view. Who tells the story will influence how the characters are developed and even perceived by others. Tell the students that Bat-Ami uses a parallel-voice approach to explore the many sides of the refugee experience. For example, early in the book when writing from Chris's point of view, the author explores the local and national society's attitudes toward the refugees by having Chris read editorials and comments from the newspapers. When the author writes from the Jewish boy's point of view, she presents both feelings of the refugees and historical background about their experiences, especially with anti-Semitism.

3. List and outline the major parts of the book. Each chapter is introduced with quotes from former refugees or other historical personages. Ask students to preview the book by reading and discussing these various quotes. For example, they can discuss and list the major happenings in the book that proceed from the first quote:

   > "My friends:
   >
   > "Yesterday on June 4, 1944, Rome fell to American and Allied troops. The first of the Axis capitals is now in our hands. One up and two to go!"
   >
   > President Franklin Delano Roosevelt (p. 11)

   to the final quote:

   > "They left, and it was sad. I mean for me, it was very sad. I was so upset in a way over them all going. It was going to be a whole new life for me."
   >
   > Geraldine Rossiter, Oswegonian (p. 206)

4. Define the problems the author has tried to solve. The text includes considerable person-versus-society conflict as the first refugees face anti-Semitism in Europe and

then in the United States as they face attacks against immigrants. As the story progresses and the townspeople began to respect the refugees, they also accept them. In addition, the Jewish characters learn to love America, its customs, and its people.

5. Identify and interpret the author's key words (vocabulary). Ask the students to identify words that are political in nature. The words might be used by characters when they want to promote a cause or in contrast when they want to attack an ideological principle.
6. Understand the author's leading propositions by identifying and discussing them in the text. Ask the students to contrast and discuss the attitudes of many of the townspeople as reflected in quotes from Chris's point of view such as "Dad hates all immigrants. He hates anything that doesn't come directly from America" (p. 49). They may contrast these quotes with Adam's point of view such as "That was the fourth day of June 1944. Rome was liberated, and I continued to ask myself what it would be like, this picture of a boy who was free: Yes, we are free!" (p. 20).
7. Know the author's arguments by identifying them in the text. Ask the students to trace the attitudes of the Jewish refugees and the attitudes of the people in the town. Ask the students to find quotes that suggest these arguments.
8. Determine which problems the author has solved and which are not solved. Ask the students to answer this question by tracing changes in point of view and history of the country. For example, Roosevelt's declaration about what has been learned: "And so today, in this year of war, 1945, we have learned lessons. . . . We have learned that we must live as men, and not as dogs in the manger. We have learned to be citizens of the world, members of the human community" (p. 134). Discuss this quote with the students and ask them to consider whether or not the lessons have been learned. Have the Jewish refugees learned lessons about America? Have the townspeople learned lessons about the refugees? They may relate Roosevelt's quotation to current world events. Why do the students believe the world has either learned or not learned these lessons?
9. Do not begin to criticize the text until you have completed your interpretation. What do you still need to know before you can give your judgment? How will you obtain this information?
10. What areas of the book cause you to disagree with the author? If you disagree, why do you disagree?
11. Give your reasons for your critical judgments of the text and the author's techniques. Ask the students to emphasize the authentication of the historical happenings and the impact of using parallel viewpoints.

Additional Activities to Enhance Phase Four

Here are some activities for children or young adult students related to this phase:

1. Historical fiction is a means of translating the information in textbooks into vivid spectacles of human drama. Choose a social studies or history text appropriate for students of a certain age. Compare the coverage of the Holocaust in the history or social studies textbook with that found in historical fiction. If possible, find passages in historical fiction that develop similar settings and conflicts described in the social studies or history textbooks. Discuss the impact of two different presentations.

2. Newspaper articles frequently stress the courage of German citizens who helped Jewish people during World War II. Search for articles that express this point of view. For

example, Peter Schneider (2000) introduces an article titled "Saving Konrad Latte" in the *New York Times Magazine*, in this way: "For every Jew who was saved, dozens of Germans performed everyday acts of heroism to make it possible. This man's saviors proved that obedience wasn't the only option" (p. 53). Read the articles, and then discuss various options that might have been possible during this period and the consequences of these options.

3. The heroism of diplomats who helped Jewish people escape is the subject of Richard C. Holbrooke's book *Diplomat Heroes of the Holocaust* (2007) and Peter Steinfels's review of the book (2007). Young adults may choose to investigate the actions of one of these heroes such as Feng Shan Ho, China's Consul General in Vienna; Jan Zwaartendijk, honorary Dutch Consul General in Kaunas and Chiune Sugihara; Raoul Wallenberg, envoy sent from Sweden with the backing of Franklin D. Roosevelt to protect Jews in Budapest; and Aristides de Sousa Mendes, Consul General in Bordeaux, France. You may choose to discuss the consequences of Steinfels's conclusion: "The book also recognizes that the inherent tension between a diplomatic profession resting on following instructions and the moral demands arising from unforeseen and overwhelming human suffering has not gone away. In his introduction to the book, Mr. Holbrooke mentions refugees from Vietnam and Darfur" (p. A12).

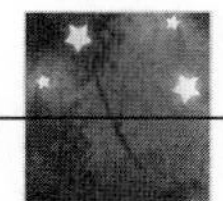

Phase Five: Contemporary Literature

Informational books, biographies and autobiographies, and fictional titles are all found in contemporary literature. Some of the biographies and autobiographies provide literature that may be related to the Holocaust. Several of the contemporary fiction stories develop the lives of characters after they survive their experiences and move to Israel or to the United States.

Analyzing Author's Style to Develop an Understanding of the Holocaust

In *No Pretty Pictures: A Child of War,* Anita Lobel uses such literary devices as symbolism, similes, metaphors, and comparisons to develop both a believable and vivid autobiography. As students read *No Pretty Pictures: A Child of War*, ask them to identify and discuss examples of especially vivid writing style. Ask them to relate the appropriateness of various examples of author's style to their knowledge of the Holocaust. The following section illustrates this process.

Symbolism To have students explore symbolism, ask questions such as the following: what is the importance of the missing furs and empty cupboards in this quote? "'They took my furs . . .' And all the silver. The open cupboards of the dining room armoire were bare" (p. 6).

The author uses many even more powerful but more subtle symbols. For example, ask students to consider what the author means by each of these terms and the symbolism of no light, leafless trees, and no blue in the sky in the following passage: "A barren area with no light. With leafless trees and no blue in the sky" (p. 9).

Similes and Metaphors Ask the students to consider what the author means by each of these examples of figurative language: Comparing the Jewish strangers to the contents of a boiling pot on page 47, comparing the heroine to a yelping dog on page 81, and comparing words to sleeping beauties on page 132.

There are many additional activities that may be accomplished to study Lobel's writing style. For example, students can find and discuss the author's use of contrasting settings and emotions as she compares her life after liberation with that in captivity or in hiding. They can trace her use of war words and peace words and how these words reflect the conflict and her changing attitudes.

Additional Activities to Enhance Phase Five

Here are some activities for children or young adult students related to this phase:

1. Identify common themes found in Jewish poetry and trace the themes through folklore and other types of literature. Develop an oral presentation of favorite poems.
2. Study poetry, using Samuel Totten's (1998) suggestions for using reader response.
3. Develop an illustrated dictionary or encyclopedia that develops the importance of various Jewish customs, holidays, and celebrations. If possible, interview Jewish people about the importance of these subjects and include these firsthand reports in the texts.
4. Investigate the role of the bar mitzvah and the bat mitzvah in the lives of thirteen-year-old Jewish youth.

How Would Anne Frank Respond to Current Issues in the Media?

Ask students to search newspapers, magazines, or broadcast media to discover current issues or news items that relate to the Jewish people. Ask them to consider how people in the books they have been reading might respond to the concerns or issues presented in the articles. For example, the following three articles published in 2011 relate to the Holocaust:

Kimmelman, Michael. "Auschwitz: Telling Its Story to a New Generation." *New York Times* (February 19, 2011): A1, A3.

Rothstein, Edward. "Making the Holocaust the Lesson on All Evils." *New York Times* (April 30, 2011): C1, C5.

Santos, Fernanda. "E-Mail About Book Questioning the Holocaust Shakes a School." *New York Times* (January 26, 2011): A18.

Use these articles with autobiographies to ask: "How would Anne Frank, Livia Bitton-Jackson, or Anita Lobel respond to the points in these articles?" For example, Kimmelman's article focuses on changes to be made by 2015 in the educational exhibits at the Auschwitz concentration camp. This extermination site from WWII attracts more than one million visitors a year. The article questions: How should the exhibit relate to people who no longer have an understanding of World War II and to the terrible consequences for the Jewish people living under Nazi rule? According to the article, the new exhibits would describe the process of extermination by leading visitors through the victims' experiences and would include a section that shows the daily dehumanization of the Jewish people. According to the article this exhibit must "engage young people so they leave feeling what the director called 'responsibility to the present' " (p. A3). It is hoped that the exhibit will change people so that they will lead more ethical lives.

After reading one of the autobiographies of a Holocaust victim or survivor discussed in this chapter, ask the students to speculate about how the autobiographical character might respond to the goals of the Auschwitz exhibit. They could provide suggestions for an exhibit that would educate visitors and help them lead more ethical lives. What is the most important message that visitors might take away from the exhibit?

Rothstein's article discusses the Museum of Tolerance in Los Angeles and questions the expansion of the museum into lessons on broader tolerance within a Holocaust exhibition that features Anne Frank and photographs of survivors. Rothstein states: "Though Yad Vashem in Israel and the United States Holocaust Museum in Washington have remained relatively immune to such sweeping moralizing, in most institutions and curriculums, the Holocaust's lessons are clear: We should all get along, become politically active and be very considerate of our neighbors. If not, well, the differences between hate crimes and the Holocaust—between bullying and Buchenwald—are just a matter of degree" (p. C5). Ask the students to consider the major role of Holocaust museums and to debate the impact of the messages presented through the museums. If possible, suggest that students visit a museum.

Santos's article focuses on the responses of parents who received an e-mail from the parent of a third-grade student in New York City. The e-mail pictured the cover of a book titled *Debating the Holocaust*. The cover showed a Nazi flag at the top and a Star of David at the bottom. According to Santos, the author of the e-mail belongs to a group that debates whether accounts of the Holocaust are exaggerated. Parents responded to the e-mail by contacting the Anti-Defamation League. The league's regional director called the writer of the e-mail a "hard-core Holocaust denier who has promoted his beliefs through mass e-mail mailings that are not always wanted" (p. A18). Ask students to consider how the autobiographical characters might respond to this e-mail writer? What do they believe is the appropriate response to such e-mails?

Ask the students to summarize the various issues that they find in the media and to consider responses of literary characters. Interesting discussions may also relate to topics such as those found in Joseph Berger's "At a Yeshiva University Fair, a Wealth of Jewish Books and Social Encounters" (*New York Times*, February 11, 2011, p. A23). This article reinforces the value of education and reading for "People of the Book." Another value expressed by many literary characters is to live in a homeland that is free from war. Articles such as Bernard Avishai's "The Israel Peace Plan That Almost Was and Still Could Be" (*The New York Times Magazine*, February 13, 2011, pp. 36–41, 48, 50) provide valuable insights into this wish for survival and suggest topics for discussion. When relating current issues to values and beliefs of the culture, students should provide support for their responses by presenting quotes from the literature.

REFERENCES

Ausubel, Nathan, ed. *A Treasury of Jewish Folklore*. New York: Crown, 1946, 1975.

Avishai, Bernard. "The Israel Peace Plan That Almost Was and Still Could Be." *The New York Times Magazine* (February 13, 2011): 36–41, 48, 50.

Barban, Leslie. "Remember to Never Forget." *Book Links* 2 (March 1993): 25–29.

Baxter, Kathleen. "Nonfiction Booktalker: Hidden Shadows." *School Library Journal* 52 (June 2006): 37.

Berger, Abraham. "The Literature of Jewish Folklore: A Survey, With Special Reference to Recent Publications." *Journal of Jewish Bibliography* 1 (October 1938/January 1939): 12–20, 40–49.

Berger, Joseph. "At a Yeshiva University Fair, a Wealth of Jewish Books and Social Encounters." *New York Times* (February 11, 2011): A23.

Bridger, David, ed. *The New Jewish Encyclopedia*. New York: Behrman House, 1976.

"Charlemagne/Slippery Slope." *The Economist* 382 (January 27, 2007): 53.

Davies, Penelope, et al. *Janson's History of Art: The Western Tradition,* 8th ed. Upper Saddle River, N.J.: Prentice Hall, 2011.

Dole, J. G., L. Duffy, L. Roehler, and P. D. Pearson. "Moving from the Old to New: Research on Reading Comprehension Instruction." *Review of Educational Research* 61 (1991): 239–264.

Early, Margaret, and Bonnie O. Ericson. "The Act of Reading." *Literature in the Classroom: Readers, Texts, and Contexts*, edited by Ben F. Nelms. Urbana, Ill.: National Council of Teachers of English, 1988.

Fax, Julie Gruenbaum. "A Jewish History Picture Show." *Hadassah* 92 (October/November, 2010): 78–82.

Frampton, Wilson. "Holocaust Education and the Need for Consistency." *Jewish Education* 59 (Spring/Summer 1991): 31–35.

Frankel, Ellen, ed. *The Jewish Spirit: A Celebration in Stories & Art*. New York: Stewart, Tabori & Chang, 1997.

Goldreich, Gloria. "Children Reading Our Stories." *Hadassah* 92 (October/November 2010): 88–92, 94–96.

_____, ed. *A Treasury of Jewish Literature: From Biblical Times to Today*. New York: Holt, Rinehart and Winston, 1982.

Greenberg, Rabbi Irving. *The Jewish Way: Living Holidays*. New York: Touchstone, 1993.

Guggenheim Museum. *Marc Chagall and the Jewish Theater*. New York: Guggenheim Museum, 1992.

Hampl, Patricia. "A Review of *Anne Frank: The Diary of a Young Girl: the Definitive Edition*." *New York Times Book Review* (March 5, 1995): 21.

Helmreich, William B. "The Impact of Holocaust Survivors on American Society: A Socio-Cultural Portrait." *Judaism* 39 (Winter 1990): 14–27.

Holbrooke, Richard C. *Diplomat Heroes of the Holocaust*. New York: KTV and the Rabbi Arthur Schneier Center for International Affairs of Yeshiva University, 2007.

Kamenetsky, Christa. *Children's Literature in Hitler's Germany*. Columbus: Ohio University Press, 1984.

Keller, Sharon R. *The Jews: A Treasury of Art and Literature*. New York: Macmillan, 1992.

Kershner, Isabel. "Life's Work Is a Talmud Accessible to All Jews." *New York Times* (November 19, 2010): A9.

Kertzer, Rabbi Morris, revised by Rabbi Lawrence A. Hoffman. *What Is a Jew?* New York: Macmillan, 1993.

Kimmelman, Michael. "Auschwitz: Telling Its Story to a New Generation." *New York Times* (February 19, 2011): A1, A3.

Lincoln, Margaret. "Witness to History." *School Library Journal* 52 (February 2006): 54–57.

Lipstadt, Deborah. *Denying the Holocaust: The Growing Assault on Truth and Memory*. New York: Plume/Penguin, 1994.

Mauer, Hans. *Jugend und Buch im Neuen Reich*. Leipzig: Lehmanns Verlag, 1934.

May, Herbert G., and Bruce M. Metzger. *The New Oxford Annotated Bible with the Apocrypha: An Ecumenical Study Bible*. New York: Oxford University Press, 1973, 1977.

Metzger, Therese, and Mendel Metzger. *Jewish Life in the Middle Ages: Illuminated Hebrew Manuscripts of the Thirteenth to the Sixteenth Centuries*. Secaucus, N.J.: Chartwell Books, 1982.

Musleah, Rahel. "Rediscovering the Jewish Folktale." *Publishers Weekly* 239 (September 21, 1992): 42–43.

Norton, Donna E. *The Impact of Literature-Based Reading*. Upper Saddle River, N.J.: Merrill/Prentice Hall, 1992.

_____, and Saundra E. Norton. *Language Arts Activities for Children,* 5th ed. Upper Saddle River, N.J.: Merrill/Prentice Hall, 2003.

Pisar, Samuel. "Out of Auschwitz." *New York Times* (January 29, 2010): A19.

Rochman, Hazel. "How Not to Write about the Holocaust." *Booklist* 89 (October 15, 1992): 416.

Rothstein, Edward. "Making the Holocaust the Lesson on All Evils." *New York Times* (April 30, 2011): C1, C5.

Santos, Fernanda. "E-Mail About Book Questioning the Holocaust Shakes a School." *New York Times* (January 26, 2011): A8.

Schneider, Peter. "Saving Konrad Latte." *New York Times Magazine* (February 13, 2000): 52–57, 72–73, 90, 95.

"Second Thoughts About the Promised Land." *The Economist* 382 (January 13, 2007): 53–54.

Sender, Ruth Minsky. *The Holocaust Lady*. New York: Macmillan, 1992.

Sherman, Josepha. *A Sampler of Jewish American Folklore*. Little Rock, Ark.: August House, 1992.

Silverman, Lisa. "Bearing Witness Through Picture Books." *School Library Journal* 53 (March 2007): 62–66.

Silvey, Anita, ed. *Everything I Need to Know I Learned from a Children's Book*. New York: Roaring Brook, 2009.

Spiegelman, Art. *Maus: A Survivor's Tale*. New York: Pantheon, 1986, 1991.

Steinfels, Peter. "In the Era of the Holocaust, 29 Who Made a Difference." *New York Times* (February 3, 2007): A12.

Telushkin, Rabbi Joseph. *The Book of Jewish Values*. New York: Bell Tower, 2000.

_____. *A Code of Jewish Ethics: You Shall Be Holy*. New York: Bell Tower, 2006.

_____. *Jewish Wisdom: Ethical, Spiritual, and Historical Lessons from the Great Thinkers*. New York: Morrow, 1994.

Totten, Samuel. "Using Reader-Response Theory to Study Poetry about the Holocaust with High School Students." *The Social Studies* 89 (January/February 1998): 30–39.

Vos, Ida. *Hide and Seek*. Boston: Houghton Mifflin, 1991.

Weinreich, Beatrice Silverman, ed. *Yiddish Folktales*. Translated by Leonard Wolf. New York: Random House/YIVO Institute for Jewish Research, 1988.

CHILDREN'S AND YOUNG ADULT LITERATURE REFERENCES

Abells, Chana Byers. *The Children We Remember*. Greenwillow, 1986 (I: all). Photographs are from the archives of Yad Vashem, Jerusalem, Israel.

______. *We Remember the Holocaust*. Holt, 1989 (I: 10+ R: 7). Survivors of the Holocaust describe their experiences.

Ayer, Eleanor H., with Helen Waterford and Alfons Heck. *Parallel Journeys*. Atheneum, 1995 (I: 12+ R: 7). A biography of a Jewish Holocaust survivor and a German youth.

Bachrach, Susan D. *Tell Them We Remember: The Story of the Holocaust*. Little, Brown, 1994 (I: all). Information from the United States Holocaust Memorial Museum.

Bat-Ami, Miriam. *Two Suns in the Sky*. Front Street/Cricket, 1999 (I: 12+ R: 6). A Jewish boy in an American refugee camp becomes friendly with a girl who lives near the camp.

Berry, James, selected by. *Around the World in Eighty Poems*. Illustrated by Katherine Lucas. Chronicle, 2002 (I: all). This collection of poems includes a poem from Israel.

Bitton-Jackson, Livia. *I Have Lived a Thousand Years: Growing Up in the Holocaust*. Simon & Schuster, 1997 (I: 12+ R: 6). An autobiography based on the author's experiences in ghettos, labor camps, and Auschwitz.

Chaikin, Miriam. *Clouds of Glory: Legends and Stories about Bible Times*. Illustrated by David Frampton, Clarion, 1998 (I: 9+ R: 5). This is a retelling of Midrash stories.

______, adapter. *Exodus*. Illustrated by Charles Mikolaycak. Holiday House, 1987 (I: all R: 5). This adaptation follows Moses as he leads his people from slavery in Egypt.

Chapman, Fern Shumer. *Is It Night or Day?* Farrar Straus & Giroux, 2010 (I: 8–12 R: 5). Children are rescued in a program endorsed by Eleanor Roosevelt.

Chotjiewitz, David. *Daniel Half Human and the Good Nazi*. Translated by Doris Orgel. Atheneum, 2004 (I: 14–18 R: 7).

Engle, Margarita. *Tropical Secrets: Holocaust Refugees in Cuba*. Holt, 2009 (I: all). A Jewish boy is befriended by a Cuban girl.

Finkelstein, Norman H. *The Other 1492: Jewish Settlement in the New World*. Scribner's, 1989 (I: 10+ R: 6). This book describes the story of Jewish people as a consequence of their expulsion from Spain in 1492.

Frank, Anne. *Anne Frank: The Diary of a Young Girl: The Definitive Edition*. Edited by Otto H. Frank and Mirjam Pressler. Translated by Susan Massotty. Doubleday, 1995 (I: 12+ R: 6). This autobiography of Anne Frank's years in hiding in the Netherlands contains material not included in the earlier edition.

Frank, Mitch. *Understanding the Holy Land: Answering Questions About the Israeli-Palestinian Conflict*. Dial, 2006 (I: 10–YA R: 6). A nonfiction book about current conflicts.

Frankel, Ellen, ed. *The Jewish Spirit: A Celebration in Stories & Art*. Stewart, Tabori & Chang, 1997 (I: all). This adult source includes numerous stories and art work.

Fritz, Jean, Katherine Paterson, Patricia McKissack, Fredrick McKissack, Margaret Mahy, and Jamake Highwater. *The World in 1492*. Illustrated by Stefano Vitale. Henry Holt, 1992 (I: 81). This book includes sections written by different authors.

Gardner, Sheldon. *The Converso Legacy*. Pitspopany Press, 2004 (I: 12–18 R: 6). The protagonist escapes the anti-Semitism of Czarist Russia.

Gellman, Rabbi Marc, and Monsignor Thomas Hartman. *How Do You Spell God?: Answers to the Big Questions from Around the World*. Morrow, 1995 (I: 10+ R: 7). This informational book provides basic information on various organized religions.

Gerstein, Mordicai. *The White Ram: A Story of Abraham and Isaac*. Holiday House, 2006 (I: 6–10 R: 5). This story is adapted from a Midrash tale.

I = Interest age range
R = Readability by grade level

Giblin, James Cross. *The Life and Death of Adolf Hitler*. Clarion, 2002 (I: 10+ R: 6). This biography provides considerable history of the Jewish people under Hitler.

Goldin, Barbara Diamond. *Bat Mitzvah: A Jewish Girl's Coming of Age*. Illustrated by Erika Weihs. Viking, 1995 (I: 10+ R: 5). This informational book describes the ceremony that marks a Jewish girl's coming of age.

_____. *Night Lights: A Sukkot Story*. Illustrated by Louise August. Harcourt Brace, 1995 (I: 4–8 R: 5). A boy overcomes his fears as he learns about the meaning of Sukkot.

Gross, Elly Berkovits. *Elly: My True Story of the Holocaust*. Scholastic, 2009 (I: 10+ R: 5). A story about a Holocaust survivor.

Hanft, Josh. *The Miracles of Passover*. Illutrated by Seymour Chwast. Blue Apple, 2007 (I: 6–10 R: 5). The author explains the symbolism of Passover.

Hesse, Karen. *The Cats in Krasinski Square*. Illustrated by Wendy Watson. Scholastic, 2004 (I: all). This picture storybook is developed from a true incident at a train station in Warsaw during World War II.

_____. *Letters from Rifka*. Henry Holt, 1992 (I: 10+ R: 6). A Jewish girl and her family flee Russia in 1919.

_____. *The Stone Lamp: Eight Stories of Hanukkah Through History*. Illustrated by Brian Pinkney. Hyperion, 2003 (I: 7–10). Poetry reflects children's viewpoints of Jewish history.

Hillman, Laura. *I Will Plant You a Lilac Tree: A Memoir of a Schindler's List Survivor*. Atheneum, 2005 (I: 12–YA R: 5). A survivor tells her story.

Hoestlandt, Jo. *Star of Fear, Star of Hope*. Translated from the French by Mark Polizzotti. Illustrated by Johanna Kang. Walker, 1995 (I: 7–10 R: 3). Nine-year-old Helen tells the story of the disappearance of her friend during the Holocaust.

Hoffman, Alice. *Incantation*. Little, Brown, 2006 (I: YA R: 6). This story of persecution is set during the Spanish Inquisition.

Hoobler, Dorothy, and Thomas Hoobler. *The Jewish American Family Album*. Oxford University Press, 1995 (I: 101). A nonfiction book focuses on the lives of many Jewish immigrants.

Hurwitz, Johanna. *Anne Frank: Life in Hiding*. Illustrated by Vera Rosenberry. The Jewish Publication Society, 1988 (I: 8–12 R: 5). This is a simpler version of the life of Anne Frank.

_____. *Moses in the Bulrushes*. Atheneum, 1986 (I: 4–8). This picture book version focuses on the discovery of the infant Moses by the pharaoh's daughter.

Innocenti, Roberto. *Rose Blanche*. Stewart, Tabori & Chang, 1985 (I: all). A young German girl discovers a concentration camp outside of her town.

Jacobson, Sid. *Anne Frank: The Anne Frank House Authorized Graphic Biography*. Illustrated by Emie Colon. Hill and Wang, 2010 (I: 10–YA R: 6). The book traces Anne's history.

Jaffe, Nina. *The Way Meat Loves Salt: A Cinderella Tale from the Jewish Tradition*. Illustrated by Louise August. Holt, 1998 (I: 5–8 R: 4). A musical score is included in this version.

_____, and Steve Zeitlin. *While Standing on One Foot: Puzzle Stories and Wisdom Tales from the Jewish Tradition*. Illustrated by John Segal. Holt, 1993 (I: 10+ R: 5). Problems and resolutions are presented in two-part stories.

Kaplan, William, and Shelley Tanaka. *One More Border: The True Story of One Family's Escape from War-Torn Europe*. Illustrated by Stephen Taylor. Douglas & McIntyre, 1998 (I: 8+ R: 4). This photobiography tells of a family's escape.

Kaufman, Lola Rein, and Lois Metzger. *The Hidden Girl: A True Story of the Holocaust*. Scholastic, 2010 (I: 8–12 R: 4). The story of a Holocaust survivor.

Kimmel, Eric A. *Bar Mitzvah: A Jewish Boy's Coming of Age*. Illustrated by Erika Weihs. Viking, 1995 (I: 10+ R: 5). This informational book describes a Jewish boy's coming of age.

_____, ed. *A Hanukkah Treasury*. Illustrated by Emily Lisker. Holt, 1998 (I: all). This is a collection of stories and activities.

_____. *Hershel and the Hanukkah Goblins*. Illustrated by Trina Schart Hyman. Holiday House, 1989 (I: 4–9 R: 5). Hershel outwits the goblins that haunt the synagogue.

_____. *Wonders and Miracles: A Passover Companion*. Scholastic, 2004 (I: all). This is a large collection of stories and art.

Kimmelman, Leslie. *The Little Red Hen and the Passover Matzah*. Illustrated by Paul Meisel. Holiday, 2010 (I: 4–8 R: 4). A folktale variant reflects a Yiddish setting.

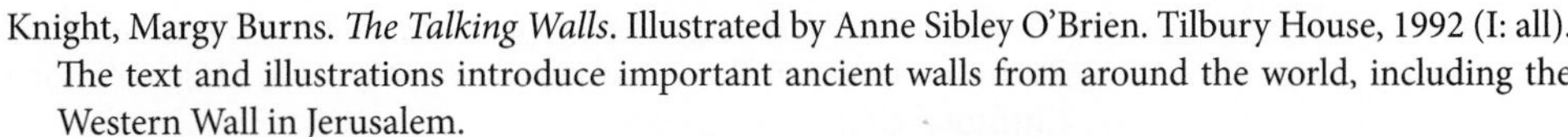

Knight, Margy Burns. *The Talking Walls*. Illustrated by Anne Sibley O'Brien. Tilbury House, 1992 (I: all). The text and illustrations introduce important ancient walls from around the world, including the Western Wall in Jerusalem.

Kushner, Tony, *Brundibar*. Illustrated by Maurice Sendak. Michael Di Capua/Hyperion, 2003. (I: all). The book is based on an opera performed at Terezin.

Kuskin, Karla. *Jerusalem, Shining Still*. Illustrated by David Frampton. Harper & Row, 1987 (I: 8–10). This picture book provides historical information about Jerusalem.

Laskier, Rutka. *Rutka's Notebook: A Voice from the Holocaust*. Time Books, 2008 (I: 12–18 R: 5). This book may be compared with Anne Frank's diary.

Levitin, Sonia. *Annie's Promise*. Atheneum, 1993 (I: 12+ R: 6). This is the third book about the Platt family.

_____. *Silver Days*. Atheneum, 1989 (I: 12+ R: 6). These are additional experiences of the family introduced in *Journey to America*.

Lobel, Anita. *No Pretty Pictures: A Child of War*. Greenwillow, 1998 (I: 10+ R: 6). This is an autobiography written by the author of many children's books.

Lowry, Lois. *Number the Stars*. Houghton Mifflin, 1989 (I: 10+ R: 6). The Danes try to save their Jewish citizens in 1943.

Maguire, Gregory. *The Good Liar*. Clarion, 1999 (I: 9+ R: 5). A French boy tells about his experiences when his mother hides Jewish refugees.

Mani-Leib. Translated by Jeffrey Shandler. *Yingle Tsingl Khvat*. Illustrated by El (Lazar) Lissitzky. Moyer Bell Limited, 1986 (I: all). This poem is written in Yiddish and English.

Manushkin, Fran. *The Matzah That Papa Brought Home*. Illustrated by Ned Bittinger. Scholastic, 1995 (I: 3–8). This cumulative rhyme describes the Passover Seder.

Mark, Jan, reteller. *God's Story: How God Made Mankind*. Illustrated by David Parkins. Candlewick, 1998 (I: all). These stories are retellings from the Old Testament.

Meltzer, Milton. *Rescue: The Story of How Gentiles Saved Jews in the Holocaust*. Harper & Row, 1988 (I: 10+ R: 6). Non-Jewish individuals help Jewish people during World War II.

Modesitt, Jeanne, compiler. *Songs of Chanukah*. Illustrated by Robin Spowart. Musical arrangements by Uri Ophir. Little, Brown, 1992 (I: all). A collection of fourteen songs.

Nye, Naomi Shihab, ed. *This Same Sky: A Collection of Poems from Around the World*. Four Winds, 1992 (I: all). This collection of poems from sixty-eight different countries includes four poems from Israel.

Orlev, Uri. *The Island on Bird Street*. Translated by Hillel Halkin. Houghton Mifflin, 1984 (I: 10+ R: 6). A twelve-year-old Jewish boy survives in the Warsaw ghetto.

_____. *The Lady with the Hat*. Houghton Mifflin, 1995 (I: 12+ R: 5). A Holocaust survivor moves to Israel.

_____. *The Man from the Other Side*. Houghton Mifflin, 1991 (I: 10+ R: 6). A boy and his father help bring supplies to the Jewish people in the Warsaw ghetto.

Podwal, Mark. *Jerusalem Sky: Stars, Crosses, and Crescents*. Doubleday, 2005 (I: all). The text and illustrations introduce sites that are sacred to Jerusalem.

Polacco, Patricia. *The Keeping Quilt*. Simon & Schuster, 1988 (I: 5–8 R: 5). This picture story-book tells the story of the importance of the quilt to four generations of Jewish women.

Polak, Monique. *What World Is Left*. Orca, 2008 (I: 8–12 R: 5). This historical fiction is about a family sent to Terezin.

Prose, Francine. *The Angel's Mistake: Stories of Chelm*. Illustrated by Mark Podwal. Greenwillow, 1997 (I: all). The stories about the people of Chelm include silly actions.

Rappaport, Doreen. *The Secret Seder*. Illustrated by Emily Arnold McCully. Hyperion, 2005 (I: 5–9 R: 4). A family takes considerable risks to take part in a celebration.

Reiss, Johanna. *The Upstairs Room*. Crowell, 1972 (I: 11+ R: 4). This is based on a true story of a Jewish girl's experience hiding from the Nazis.

Rogasky, Barbara, adapter. *The Golem*. Illustrated by Trina Schart Hyman. Holiday House, 1996 (I: 10+ R: 5). A clay giant is brought to life.

_____. *Smoke and Ashes: The Story of the Holocaust*. Holiday House, 1988 (I: 10+ R: 6). This is a history of the 1933–1945 Holocaust.

Rosen, Michael J. *Elijah's Angel: A Story for Chanukah and Christmas*. Illustrated by Aminah Brenda Lynn Robinson. Harcourt Brace Jovanovich, 1992 (I: 5–8). A Jewish boy is in conflict over accepting a Christmas gift.

Rosenstock, Barb. *The Littlest Mountain*. Illustrated by Melanie Hall. Lerner, 2011 (I: 5-8 R: 4). A *pourquoi* tale explains why Mount Sinai was the location for the Ten Commandments.

Rossel, Seymour. *The Holocaust*. Watts, 1990 (I: 12+ R: 7). This history proceeds from the Treaty of Versailles to the rise of Hitler to the Nuremberg trials.

_____. *The Storybook Haggadah*. Illustrated by Janet Zwebner. Pitspopany, 2006 (I: all). Written in Hebrew and English, the text follows a family celebration.

Rothenberg, Joan. *Yettele's Feathers*. Hyperion, 1995 (I: 5–8 R: 6). A highly illustrated folktale about a widow who learns a lesson about gossiping.

Rubin, Susan Goldman, and Ela Weissberg. *The Cat with the Yellow Star: Coming of Age in Terezin*. Holiday, 2006 (I: 8–12 R: 4). Historical photographs add to this tale about Terezin's children.

Sasso, Sandy Eisenberg. *But God Remembered: Stories of Women from Creation to the Promised Land*. Illustrated by Bethanne Andersen. Jewish Lights, 1995 (I: 8+ R: 7). The text includes legends about four women who lived during biblical times.

_____. *In God's Name*. Illustrated by Phoebe Stone. Jewish Lights, 1994 (I: all). Written in poetic form, this book describes a diverse group of people's search for the name of God.

Schotter, Roni. *The Boy Who Loved Words*. Illustrated by Giselle Potter. Random House, 2006 (I: 6–10). A boy finds a purpose for his love of words by helping others who need the words.

_____. *Passover Magic*. Illustrated by Marylin Hafner. Little, Brown, 1995 (I: 5–8). A young girl and her family celebrate Passover.

Schwartz, Cherie Karo. *Circle Spinning: Jewish Turning and Returning Tales*. Illustrated by Lisa Rauchwerger. Hamsa, 2002 (I: 8–YA). This is a collection of folklore based on the Midrash.

Schwartz, Howard, and Barbara Rush, retellers. *The Diamond Tree: Jewish Tales from Around the World*. Illustrated by Uri Shulevitz. HarperCollins, 1991 (I: 8+ R: 5). This collection of fifteen tales includes sources and commentary on each tale.

Sendak, Maurice. *Where the Wild Things Are*. Harper & Row, 1963 (I: 4–8 R:6). A young boy has a fantasy experience.

Shahak, Bat-Chen. *The Bat-Chen Diaries*. Translated by Diana Rubanenko. Ka-Ben/Lerner, 2008 (I: all). An Israeli teenager keeps a diary.

Sherman, Josepha, ed., reteller. *Rachel the Clever and Other Jewish Folktales*. August House, 1993 (I: 9+ R: 5). This is a collection of forty-six tales.

Shulevitz, Uri. *How I Learned Geography*. Farrar Straus & Giroux, 2008 (I: all). A highly illustrated text about using maps to learn about the world.

Siegal, Aranka. *Upon the Head of the Goat: A Childhood in Hungary, 1939–1944*. Farrar, Straus & Giroux, 1981 (I: 10+ R: 7). Nine-year-old Piri experiences the Holocaust.

Singer, Isaac Bashevis. *The Golem*. Illustrated by Uri Shulevitz. Farrar, Straus & Giroux, 1982, 1996 (I: 101). A giant is shaped from clay.

_____. *Mazel and Shlimazel, or the Milk of the Lioness*. Illustrated by Margot Zemach. Farrar, Straus & Giroux, 1967 (I: 8–12 R: 4). The spirit of good luck and bad luck have a contest.

_____. *Stories for Children*. Farrar, Straus & Giroux, 1984 (I: 10+ R: 5). This is a collection of thirty-seven stories retold by the Nobel Prize–winning author.

Speare, Elizabeth George. *The Bronze Bow*. Houghton Mifflin, 1961 (I: 10+ R: 6). A Jewish boy rebels against Roman rule during the time of Jesus.

Spinelli, Jerry. *Milkweed*. Knopf, 2003 (I: 12–YA R: 6). A young orphan tells a story set in Nazi-occupied Warsaw.

Spinner, Stephanie. *It's a Miracle: A Hanukkah Storybook*. Illustrated by Jill McElmurry. Simon & Schuster, 2003 (I: all). A young boy is chosen as Official Candle Lighter while his grandmother tells family stories.

Stampler, Ann Redisch, reteller. *The Rooster Prince of Breslov*. Illustrated by Eugene Yelchin. Clarion, 2010 (I: 5–8 R: 4). This is a Yiddish folktale.

Taback, Simms. *Kibitzers and Fools: Tales My Zayda Told Me*. Viking, 2005 (I: all). Each of these Jewish tales is accompanied by a saying.

Thomson, Ruth. *Terezin: Voices from the Holocaust*. Candlewick, 2011 (I: 10-YA R: 5). Many artists were forced to assist Nazi propaganda.

Thor, Annika. *A Faraway Island*. Delacorte, 2009 (I: 10–14 R: 5). Two refugees are evacuated from Nazi Austria to Sweden.

Toll, Nelly S. *Behind the Secret Window: A Memoir of a Hidden Childhood During World War Two*. Dial, 1993 (I: all R: 5). The text and illustrations tell the autobiography of a girl in Poland.

Van der Rol, Ruud, and Rian Verhoeven. *Anne Frank, Beyond the Diary: A Photographic Remembrance*. Translated by Tony Langham and Plym Peters. Viking, 1993 (I: 81). Photographs and maps provide a graphic accompaniment to the biography.

Volavkova, Hana, ed. . . . *I Never Saw Another Butterfly . . . Children's Drawings and Poems from Terezin Concentration Camp, 1942–1944*. Schocken, 1993 (I: all). This collection of poems was written by children during the Holocaust.

Vos, Ida. *Hide and Seek*. Translated by Teresse Edelstein and Inez Smith. Houghton Mifflin, 1991 (I: 8+ R: 5). A Jewish girl describes her years of hiding in Nazi-occupied Holland.

Waldman, Neil. *The Golden City: Jerusalem's 3,000 Years*. Atheneum, 1995 (I: 8–12 R: 5). This illustrated nonfiction book traces the history of Jerusalem from the time of King David through the Six-Day War in 1967.

Weber, Elka. *The Yankee at the Seder*. Illustrated by Adam Gustavson. Tricycle Press, 2009 (I: 6–10 R: 5). Two enemies experience peace during war.

Weil, Sylvie. *My Guardian Angel*. Translated by Gillian Rosner. Scholastic, 2004 (I: 9–12 R: 5).

Weinreich, Beatrice Silverman, ed. *Yiddish Folktales*. Translated by Leonard Wolf. Pantheon, 1988 (I: 12+ R: 6). This is a large collection of Yiddish folklore that includes annotations to the tales, notes, bibliography, and glossary.

Whiteman, Dorit Bader. *Lonek's Journey: The True Story of a Boy's Escape to Freedom*. Star Bright, 2005 (I: 10–15 R: 5). A boy escapes to freedom in Palestine.

Wild, Margaret. *Let the Celebrations Begin!* Illustrated by Julie Vivas. Orchard, 1991 (I: all). Lighter colors project a less somber mood for a Holocaust story.

Wisniewski, David. *Golem*. Clarion, 1996 (I: all). This 1997 Caldecott Medal winner includes notes about the origins of the legend.

Wiviott, Meg. *Benno and the Night of Broken Glass*. Illustrated by Josee Bisaillon. Lerner, 2010 (I: 8–10 R: 4). Told through the viewpoint of a cat who experiences Kristallnacht.

Zemach, Margot. *It Could Always Be Worse*. Farrar, Straus & Giroux, 1977 (I: 5–9 R: 2). A small hut seems larger when all the animals are removed.

Zusak, Markus. *The Book Thief*. Knopf, 2005 (I: 14+ R: 7). A Jewish man is protected by a German family during World War II.

sam Barakat's *Tasting the Sky: A Palestinian Childhood*, another book written for young adults. A 2010 article in *School Library Journal* includes both websites and recommended titles for books: "Resources for Teaching about Islam" includes nine websites (p. 36); "SLJ's Recommended Titles" includes eleven titles for books that range from first grade to young adult (p. 37).

Discovering the backgrounds of authors who place their stories in Middle Eastern settings illustrates how closely many of them base their stories on firsthand experiences. For example, Suzanne Fisher Staples, author of *Shabanu: Daughter of the Wind* and the sequel *Haveli*, worked as a UPI correspondent in Asia, including Pakistan and Afghanistan. While she was in Pakistan, she became involved with the nomads of the Cholistan Desert. This is the setting for the characters and plots developed in her books.

Gaye Hicyilmaz, author of *Against the Storm*, lived in Turkey for many years. Her book was inspired by a true incident reported in the Turkish press. Rafik Schami, author of *A Hand Full of Stars,* was born in Damascus, Syria. Judith Heide Gilliland, co-author of *Sami and the Time of the Troubles* and *The Day of Ahmed's Secret*, lived in Beirut for several years. Many of the authors of the adult texts, such as the folklore sources discussed later in this chapter, are literature and folklore scholars. Some of these books, however, have been criticized for cultural inaccuracies in either text or illustrations (Iskander, 1997).

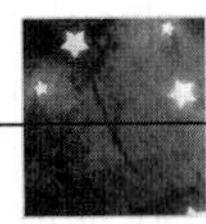

Values Identified in the Culture and Literature

One of the ways to help us evaluate and to authenticate the literature from a culture is to identify some of the values that scholars from the culture believe are important. Because the current scholarship emphasizes values of Islamic literature, in this section we discuss these values. For example, when discussing Islamic literature for children, Tasneema Khatoon Ghazi (1997) stresses the importance of stories about khalifahs, prophets, and scholars that teach values related to respect for parents and teachers, kindness to servants, and the rewards of perseverance. After identifying how these values are developed in several books, she concludes, "The values introduced in these stories, however, are universal and can be taught to any child. They emphasize the importance of truth, generosity, leading an unpretentious life, and finding pleasure in simple things" (p. 9).

Writers who stress the importance of Islamic values in literature frequently emphasize the ethical concerns that are included in books. For example, Khorana (1997) states, "books for children serve as integrating forces and are intended to provide an ideological base for youth" (p. 3). She emphasizes the need for literature that transmits the traditions to the next generation.

Several writers in the journal *Islamic Horizons* also mention the need for retaining and teaching Islamic values especially as Muslims move into non-Islamic nations. Abdul Basit's (1998) article in which he stresses integration without losing Muslim identity identifies the following Islamic values: extended family systems in which parents and others in this family exercise control over the young, strong sexual mores, adherence to religious faith anchored in a belief in one God and traditional moral values, and importance of family or community goals over personal goals. Khaliijah Mohammad Salleh (1997) emphasizes the roles of men and women in the value system of society and how these roles are defined by religion and tradition. For example, "men are the protectors and maintainers of women because Allah has given them more strength. While men are reminded of their responsibility, the women too are reminded of theirs: that the righteous women are devoutly obedient and guard their chastity in their husband's [*sic*] absence" (p. 57).

Several scholars stress the importance of folklore in developing both cultural identity and value systems. For example, Mansooreh Rai (1997) states that in Iran there is now a search for cultural identity through the study of Iranian folklore, music, painting, sculpture, and architecture. Rai also emphasizes her belief in the need for authentic cultural literature: "To prevent cultural invasion from Western countries through music, movies, and books, and to establish a peaceful dynamic society in harmony with Islamic values, we should trust in the miracle of children's literature to effect change and the implication of its rise and fall on the cultural development of a nation" (p. 33).

As you read and evaluate literature from the Middle East, especially literature that includes Muslim people and Islamic values, search for these values. If the values are there, how do authors develop these values? How are they shown in literary elements associated with conflicts, plots, characterization, and themes?

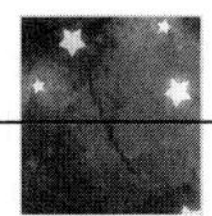

Folklore and Ancient Stories from the Middle East

From our definition of the Middle East and the various countries that lie within this region, it is understandable that the folklore comes to us from many different sources and time periods and is influenced by various religions.

History of Collection

The influence of Muhammad and his followers is apparent in the purposes for collecting Arabic folklore. According to Inea Bushnaq in *Arab Folktales* (1986), the collection of Arab tales began as early as the eighth century when Arab philologists of the Abbasid era, who were centered in Baghdad, collected tales and poetry recited by professional bards. Bushnaq states, "The collectors' purpose was to equip themselves with all the knowledge to be had about the prophet's time, the better to write scholarly commentaries on the Koran" (p. xxiii). Problems resulted, however, because of differences between written language, the language of the Koran, and spoken Arabic, which often did not include words found in dictionaries.

In 1704, *The Arabian Nights or The Thousand and One Nights* was translated from the Arabic into French by Antoine Galland (Leach, 1972). This translation introduced the Persian tales into Europe. Between 1885 and 1888, Sir Richard Francis Burton, the British Consul in Trieste, translated *The Thousand Nights and a Night* from Arabic to English and published the tales in sixteen volumes (Burton, 1985). Burton's translation is a primary source for many retellings in English. (Susan Fletcher identifies Burton's book as her guide for the writing of *Shadow Spinner,* discussed later in this chapter.) Mary Ellen Brown and Bruce A. Rosenberg (1998) conclude,

> The 1001 Nights has played important roles in both the folk and literary traditions as a conduit for oral tales across linguistic and literary traditions, as an inspiration for other medieval frame tales, and as the raw material for many imaginative prose works, both in the East and the West through its diverse ancestors and descendants. It epitomizes the interaction between folk and literary narrative. (p. 635)

An increased interest in collecting the tales occurred in 1900 when Enno Littman, an archaeologist on an expedition, collected tales through an Arab friend. In 1910, Hans Schmidt published 200 tales. Collections of Arabic tales began to appear in French, English, German, and Italian academic journals. These journals were intended for study by Arab specialists and linguists (Bushnaq, 1986).

Types of Tales

Collectors of the folklore categorize the stories according to specific types. For example, Burton (1985) identifies the following three types of stories found in *The Thousand Nights and a Night:* classic fables, fairy tales based on some supernatural agency, and stories based on historical fact or anecdote.

According to Bushnaq, the favorite type of animal story in Arabic is a trickster tale in which two animals, or a human and an animal, try to outwit each other. These tales usually end with a punch line that is wise and witty. For example, "The Cat Who Went to Mecca," an animal tale from Syria, concludes, "'Never mind the pilgrimage,' said the king of the mice.' He may pray like a Hajji, but he still pounces like a cat'" (p. 216).

Religious Tales and Moral Instruction The Egyptian myth "The Sun-God and the Dragon: God Ra the Creator" is found in Virginia Hamilton's *In the Beginning: Creation Stories from Around the World.* According to Hamilton, "the myth is taken from Egyptian Mortuary Texts and is part of a temple ritual. Some of the ritual was a dramatic presentation of the conflict between God Ra and the dragon Apophis. The myth is thought to come from ancient Thebes. . . ." Instead of riding in a chariot, the sun-god Ra traveled the heavens in a boat called Millions of Years, starting in the morning in the east, and at sunset, disappearing into the underworld of the Underneath Sky. The lesser god Osiris was the moon-god and the Judge of the Dead. Isis was Osiris's sister and the patron goddess of women. Horus was the son of Osiris and Isis and the savior of mankind.

Some of the religious tales reflect the common ground between Islam and Christianity. Shulamith Levy Oppenheim's *Iblis*, a retelling of a story thought to date back to the ninth century BCE, is both a creation story explaining the beginnings of humankind and our troubles, and a cautionary tale showing the dangers of disobeying God's orders. You may compare this variant of the Adam and Eve story with the Christian story. In the Islamic version, the teller reveals that Adam and Eve lived in Paradise for 500 years during which time Iblis, the great Satan, tried to enter Paradise, but the entrance to Paradise was protected by the flaming sword of the angel Ridwan. In his desire to enter Paradise, Iblis flatters the peacock, who sends out a serpent who was created a thousand years before man and was Eve's favorite companion. Iblis tricks the serpent into allowing him to enter Paradise and convinces Eve she should eat from the forbidden tree. After they eat the fruit, God commands that Adam, Eve, and the animals that led them into disobeying God depart from Paradise. The peacock lost his melodious voice, the serpent lost her feet, and Iblis was cast back into the torments of all eternity. Adam was expelled from Paradise through the gate of Repentance so he would never forget how Paradise might be regained. Eve was expelled through the gate of Grace. The serpent and the peacock were exiled through the gate of Wrath. Iblis was hurled out through the gate of Damnation.

Muhammad is very important in traditional tales and other literature from the Middle East. "A Nest and a Web" is retold by Geraldine McCaughrean in *The Silver Treasure: Myths and Legends of the World.* According to McCaughrean, "In AD 622, Muhammad moved from Mecca to Medina, on a journey called the Hejira or migration. It marks year one of the Muslim calendar. This is a story told about that journey" (p. 128). The tale ends, "And eloquent Mohammad went on to weave a web of words that captured the hearts and souls of millions" (p. 41).

Tales of Wit and Wisdom According to Josepha Sherman in her collection *Trickster Tales: Forty Folk Stories from Around the World*, "Although the Arab world has no true animal or supernatural tricksters, it has its share of human tricksters instead. One of these clever folks is Djuba. Sometimes odd events put him at a loss—but only for a very short time. Soon enough, Djuba finds a clever way out of whatever problem has been thrown his way" (p. 58). Sherman's "Duba's Guests: A Tale from Morocco" reveals how he uses his wits. Sherman includes an Author's Note that reveals the sources for the tales and comments about interpretation.

"The Clever Minister's Daughter," in Inea Bushnaq's *Arab Folktales*, is an example of a tale of wit and wisdom. In this story from Syria, a minister's daughter answers two series of three questions asked by the king. In so doing, she proves her worth and she marries the king. After she identifies the most precious stone as the millstone, the sweetest sound as the call to prayer, and water, after God, as the most lifegiving, she saves her father's life and he becomes father to the queen.

As you read additional tales, try to discover some of the characteristics, values, and beliefs discussed in this folklore. For example, you may find that many of the Bedouin tales reflect generosity, hospitality, and the importance of family, ancestry, and birth. The characters frequently show pride, independence, and self-sufficiency. Tales of the magical and the supernatural frequently develop the importance of wit and wisdom and the importance of Allah. Enchanted characters, magical spells, and trickster animal characters are found in many of the tales of magic. Many tales from Egypt include the cycle of life, death, and rebirth. Religious tales frequently suggested a common ground between Islam and Christianity.

Modern Fantasy Based on Legend Hilari Bell bases her story *Flame* on an ancient Persian legend of Rostam, Tahmineh, and Sorahb. *Flame* is the first volume in a series of books that she titles "The Book of Sorahb." The book's setting, a fantasy land of Farsala, reflects a time when it is being threatened by invasions from the Hrums, a group of people closely resembling soldiers of the Roman Empire. These threats develop considerable conflict between the people of Farsala and the invading forces. Older readers will probably enjoy the detailed descriptions of military tactics used by both sides in this clash.

The themes and characterizations relate to the importance of staying free and the need for survival during this frightening time. The three main characters also reflect different social classes within Farsala. Consequently, there is considerable person-against-society conflict. Soraya, a daughter of the noble House of the Leopard, is accustomed to the advantages of the

ISSUE Comparing Illustrations in Folklore

Early editions of Arabic folktales and more modern editions provide the basis for interesting comparisons. The various versions of "The Thousand and One Nights" provide interesting comparisons of their illustrations. For example, a facsimile edition of *Arabian Nights: The Book of a Thousand Nights and a Night* translated by Sir Richard Burton was published in 1985. This edition includes sixteen illustrations by Albert Letchford that were included in the first edition published in the late 1800s. The illustrations in this adult version of the tales may be compared with Edmund Dulac's illustrations for *Sindbad the Sailor and Other Stories from the Arabian Nights* first published in 1914 and reissued in 1986. According to the text, Dulac's art was inspired by Persian miniaturists of the fifteenth century.

Illustrations in the older editions may also be compared with more recent editions of various stories from "The Arabian Nights." For example, comparisons might include Sheila Moxley's illustrations for Neil Philip's *The Arabian Nights*, Eric A. Kimmel's illustrations for *The Tale of Aladdin and the Wonderful Lamp: A Story from the Arabian Nights*, and A. E. Jackson's illustrations for *Ali Baba and the Forty Thieves and Other Stories*.

You might consider the following evaluation criteria for the illustrations (Norton, 2011, p. 115):

1. The illustrator's use of visual elements—line, color, shape, texture—and certain artistic media should complement or even extend the development of plot, characterization, setting, and theme in the text.
2. The design of the illustrations—individually and throughout an entire book—should reinforce the text and convey a sense of unity that stimulates aesthetic appreciation.
3. The artistic style chosen by the illustrator should enhance the author's literary style.
4. The illustrations should help the readers anticipate the unfolding of a story's action and its climax.
5. The illustrations should convincingly delineate and develop the characters.
6. The illustrations should be accurate in historical, cultural, and geographical detail, and they should be consistent with the text.

This final point dealing with historical, cultural, and geographical detail is especially important when evaluating the illustrations if the books are to provide accurate cultural information. Nonfiction books showing art from the ancient cultures may be used to help with this authentication process. These books are discussed in this next section.

highest social order. Her father is the commander of the troops who are responsible for stopping the invaders. After his death, however, she discovers she must use some new powers that she learns from a peasant woman if she is to avenge her father's death.

Jiaan, her half brother by a peasant mother, is subject to ridicule by members of the higher social classes. It is his military abilities, however, that will help save the land after his father's death. In his quest for self-discovery he realizes he must forget the person-against-society conflicts that have ruled his life if he is to save his land from conquest and all his people from slavery.

The hardest journey of self-discovery is completed by the peddler, Kavi, who progresses from a traitor and a spy to the realization he cannot be part of a conquering army that takes people into slavery. This realization is particularly difficult for Kavi because he has been wounded by members of the higher social classes and because of his wounds his livelihood was taken away from him. He must overcome considerable hatred toward the ruling classes if he is to help all the people of Farsala. The author develops three credible characters who each face and must overcome conflicts related to both the oncoming army and their own social class biases.

An analytical reading of literature activity is developed in the "Involving Children with Literature from the Middle East" section. There are also ideas for using the book in "Writing Connections."

Early History

Nonfiction informational books provide excellent sources for learning about a culture and for authenticating the illustrations and texts in fictional works. Numerous books written for juvenile audiences provide interesting information about the early history of the people living in the Middle East. Some of the books written for adult audiences provide excellent sources for authenticating illustrations and texts.

Books about the ancient Egyptian culture are especially valuable and informative if they include both historical information and photographs of architecture and artifacts. For example, the adult book *The Ancient Egyptian Book of the Dead,* translated by R. O. Faulkner and edited by Carol Andrews (1985), provides valuable information to accompany the folklore about Osiris and Isis and other gods and goddesses of ancient Egypt. The translations in this text came from the collection of Egyptian funerary papyri found in the British Museum. The text explains the purposes for the sheets of papyrus covered with magical texts and illustrations, which the Egyptians placed with their dead. They were used to help the dead pass through the dangers of the Underworld and attain an afterlife in the Field of Reeds, the Egyptian heaven. The text traces the dates of the papyri and discusses the purposes for the various spells found on the papyri. Many of the accompanying illustrations are in full color and provide a visual interpretation of the beliefs of early Egyptians.

David M. Rohl's *Pharaohs and Kings* (1995) provides another adult source for the history, culture, and geography of ancient Egypt. The photographs may be used to supply useful information for any age group.

Informational books about ancient Egypt written for juvenile audiences may present the history of the people or focus on specific subjects such as the building of the pyramids, creating mummies, or exploring the tombs. Because several sources discuss the same subjects, readers may compare the effectiveness of each of the books. As you read informational books, consider such areas as the accuracy of the facts and the ability of the author to separate facts and theory; the quality of the illustrations and the ability of the illustrations to clarify the text; the organization of the text; the ability of the text to increase interest in the subject and to encourage analytical thinking; the style of the writing; and the quality of the aids such as maps, graphs, indexes, glossaries, and lists for further reading.

Ancient Cultures of Egypt

Informational books should encourage analytical thinking by allowing young readers to become involved in solving problems and observing carefully. Andrew Haslam and Alexandra Parsons's *Ancient Egypt* encourages reader involvement because the text includes step-by-step directions for making models, clothing, objects, and foods related to ancient Egypt. In addition, the text provides a brief introduction to ancient Egypt and then examines different aspects of the civilization such as religions, family life, communications, and geography.

Stewart Ross's *Egypt in Spectacular Cross-Section* provides an introduction to this ancient civilization through labeled drawings and detailed pictures that illustrate such features as an Egyptian harbor, a temple, a palace, and a pyramid.

Timelines are another feature that authors use to clarify information about historical times. Viviane Koenig's *The Ancient Egyptians: Life in the Nile Valley* includes a timeline, as well as an introduction to the people including their work, social and economic lives, and religious traditions. Readers obtain a feeling for the different types of people who made up ancient Egypt—including craft workers and artists, scribes and scholars, and pharaohs who ruled the land. The text includes a list of further reading, a glossary, and an index.

Pyramids, Mummies, and Searching the Tombs Books on building the pyramids provide insights into ancient Egyptian beliefs in the ancient gods and the afterlife.

A step-by-step description of the process of construction of the Great Pyramid of Giza is a highlight of Peter Chrisp's *Pyramid*. In addition, the author describes funeral ceremonies and the process of mummification. Full-color photographs and reproductions of artifacts found in the pyramid add to the interest of the reader.

Ideas in informational books should be broken down into easily understood component parts. Authors often use an organization that progresses from the simple to the more complex, or from the familiar to the unfamiliar, or from early to later development. In *Into the Mummy's Tomb: The Real-Life Discovery of Tutankhamun's Treasures,* Nicholas Reeves introduces the topic with a prologue that relates history to more current events. This prologue introduces a mystery in which two secret locked cupboards in Highclere Castle in England reveal ancient Egyptian treasures that were hidden after the discovery of Tutankhamun's tomb. The text then proceeds in chronological order, beginning with "The Hidden Steps, Cairo, Egypt, 1907" and concluding with "The Tomb's Secrets, Hampshire, England, 1988." Numerous photographs and maps complement this historical progression. *Tutankhamun: The Mystery of the Boy King* is written by Zahi Hawass, the Director of Excavations at the Giza Pyramids. This highly illustrated text presents an account of the discovery of the tomb. The text reveals recent medical examinations of the mummy. Hawass's *Curse of the Pharaohs: My Adventures with Mummies* includes the author's experiences with the dangers associated with excavating tombs including crumbling rocks, germs, and snakes. The text includes photographs, reproductions of works, and discoveries of grave robbers caught in the tombs during earlier times.

James Putnam's *Mummy* describes the principles, history, and ceremonies associated with the preservation of bodies. The text includes numerous labeled photographs that illustrate topics covered including what mummies are, the Egyptian Book of the Dead, the process for creating mummies, and Egyptian concepts of the afterlife. The section on the mummy and the god Osiris can help in understanding the folklore. The author includes comparisons with other mummies such as Greek and Roman mummies, mummies from the Andes, and animal mummies. In an interesting section Putnam discusses the treasures of Tutankhamun and the curse of the mummy.

James Cross Giblin's *The Riddle of the Rosetta Stone: Key to Ancient Egypt* describes the process used to decipher the hieroglyphs found on the Rosetta Stone, which had been written in Greek, hieroglyphs, and another Egyptian script. It was the finding of this stone that eventually made possible the translations of the ancient hieroglyphs. The illustrations clarify the text by showing the techniques used by the scholars. For example, Giblin shows how Champollion assigned letters to all of the hieroglyphs and thus made it possible to read the ancient symbols. Notice in the following quote how Giblin helps readers follow a spatial organization as they also view the stone: "At the top are fourteen lines of hieroglyphs—pictures of animals, birds, and geometric shapes. Below them you can make out thirty-two lines written in an unfamiliar script" (p. 7). Giblin's *Secrets of the Sphinx* provides background information about the Sphinx, hieroglyphic writing, Egyptian religion, and recent excavations. He includes ancient legends associated with the Sphinx.

Students who are interested in searching for the art of ancient Egypt or conducting additional research can read Emily Sands's *Egyptology: Search for the Tomb of Osiris*. The following note from the publisher provides an intriguing motivation for students to conduct research and determine what parts of the text are accurate: "This book is the facsimile of a journal supposedly written in 1926. As there is scant evidence to backup this claim, it must be enjoyed solely on its own merits" (inside cover).

The text is highly illustrated with numerous examples of letters and booklets that may be opened and read, and posters that might be found during the 1920s. These posters are supported with facts about the subject. For example, a poster advertising a hat that will allow wearers to stay cool is accompanied by a twelve-month temperature chart for four cities in Egypt; temperatures for Aswan in June range from 76 to 108 degrees. A poster advertising a walking tour of Egypt is accompanied by a chart showing international distances in miles from places such as New York to Cairo. All of these numbers could be authenticated by readers. Additional authentication opportunites are found in booklets showing hieroglyphs, archaeological tools, rules for games of Senet, drawings of coffins, and an example from *The Egyptian Book of the Dead*.

Ancient Cultures of Other Middle Eastern Areas

Just as for the early Egyptian culture, there are informational books that allow readers to glimpse the arts, architecture, and lifestyles of other cultures in the Middle East. For example, several adult sources provide excellent illustrations and accompanying text that could be valuable for any age group. *The Art and Architecture of Islam 1250–1800* by Sheila S. Blair and Jonathan M. Bloom (1994) is a comprehensive text that includes sections on the architecture and arts in Iran under the Ilkhanids, the Timurids, and the Safavids and Zands. The text is organized in chronological order and divided into two major periods: 1250–1500 and 1500–1800. The photographs, many in color, provide a source for authenticating the illustrations in juvenile books. *Islam: Art and Architecture,* edited by Markus Hattstein and Peter Delius (2004), is an extensive source that includes more than 1,000 photographs and essays written by twenty international scholars.

Three additional adult sources include sections on ancient Middle Eastern cultures. Jay A. Levenson's *Circa 1492: Art in the Age of Exploration* (1991) includes a section on the art from Islamic empires. Color photographs and accompanying text present such artifacts as a Turkish lantern, a Koran binding, a Koran fragment, a Koran chest, a ceremonial kaftan, and various swords from the Ottoman Empire. This text is especially useful because it allows readers to compare the art in different cultures of the world including Europe and the Mediterranean, the Orient, and the Americas. H. W. Janson's *History of Art* (1995) includes sections on ancient Persian art and Islamic art. The Islamic art chapter includes photographs of mosques, mausoleums, statuary, drawings, and manuscripts. David Piper's *The Illustrated History of Art* (1994) includes sections on Iranian art and Islamic art from Syria, North Africa, and Turkey. These sources are valuable for identifying characteristics of the early art of these cultures.

Photographs, maps, and diagrams highlight the content of James Barter's *The Ancient Persians*. The text, part of the Lost Civilizations Series, integrates research by ancient historians and modern archaeologists. Charts, diagrams, and maps also add to an understanding of life in the Arabian Peninsula in James E. Lindsay's *Daily Life in the Medieval Islamic World.*

Juvenile Informational Literature Several books written for younger audiences present the history of peoples of the Middle East and their cultures. Fiona Macdonald's *A 16th Century Mosque* provides detailed information about the architecture in the ancient Arabic world and yields insights into the role of religion in art and architecture. The text describes the mosques built in the sixteenth century in and around Istanbul, Turkey. Most of these mosques were built for Sultan Suleyman the Magnificent, the ruler of the Ottoman Empire; they were designed by the architect Sinan Pasha, who lived from 1491 to 1588. The text discusses Sinan's career at Suleyman's court and his accomplishments in building the mosques, which are considered some of the finest achievements of Islamic art. Detailed colored drawings with labels help readers follow the text. The text includes topics such as the first mosque, mosque styles, workers' lives, and the Ottoman Empire. The text concludes with an overview of mosques around the world.

David Macaulay's *Mosque* includes detailed illustrations showing the creation of a structure modeled after examples built between 1540 and 1580 in Istanbul, Turkey, by Sinan, the most famous architect of the Ottoman Empire. In an interview on NPR's *Weekend Edition* (November 9, 2003), Macaulay took the interviewer through a mosque and described how he developed his book. As you read the text and look carefully at the illustrations, do you agree with Macaulay's goal of capturing God's light and showing an individual experience between "you, your prayer mat, and God"? He stated that the sacred buildings inspired him and the events of September 11 motivated him to write *Mosque.* Macaulay believes the buildings shown in his illustrations "represent the best of what a community can create." Macaulay's text includes a glossary to help readers understand the terms.

Mokhtar Moktefi and Veronique Ageorges's *The Arabs in the Golden Age* presents the history, social life, and customs of Islamic peoples. In the introduction, the authors emphasize the importance of the Islamic religion on daily life, culture, and art:

> Islam was the creative force behind the religious, military, and cultural prominence of the Arabic empire during the Golden Age, which began with the spread of the teachings of the prophet Muhammad in the early eighth century and endured roughly into the mid-thirteenth century. Decorative arts—weaving, glassmaking, tile-work, pottery, inlaid carvings in stone, plaster, and metal—had never been so beautiful. Many people, for the first time, could read. Thousands of hand-tooled, leather-bound books were filled with calligraphy so well executed that it rivaled the beauty of the miniatures accompanying the stories, poems, religious teachings, and learned treaties. (p. 5)

This text helps students realize the importance of the arts in the Islamic world, as well as providing illustrations demonstrating their beauty.

Peter and Ruth Mantin's *The Islamic World: Beliefs and Civilizations 600–1600* provides an informative introduction to the beliefs associated with the Islamic religion, the rise of Islam, and the founding of Islam by Muhammad, the Prophet of Allah. Maps, photographs, and illustrations clarify the discussion about different aspects of Islam. The accuracy of information in this text written for juvenile audiences may be authenticated through such adult sources as John Alden Williams's *The Word of Islam* (1994) and Mostafa Vaziri's *The Emergence of Islam: Prophecy, Imamate, and Messianism in Perspective* (1992).

In her biography *Muhammad,* Demi focuses on the prophet born in Mecca in 570 AD. The author presents the life and basic teachings of the man who, at the age of forty, received his first revelation from Allah. His recorded words are in the Koran and became the foundation of the Islamic faith. Demi illustrates her biography in the style of Persian miniatures. Islamic tradition forbids pictorial representations of Muhammad; consequently, Demi represents his image as a golden silhouette. She also provides a bibliography and art references.

Kathryn Lasky's *The Librarian Who Measured the Earth* is a biography of Eratosthenes, the chief librarian in Alexandria, Egypt. His calculations made over 2,000 years ago provided a measurement for the size of the earth that is only 200 miles different from our calculations today. This biography describes a man who strove for knowledge and used his curiosity to make remarkable discoveries. Kevin Hawkes's illustrations give a flavor of this time period. The author's notes, an afterword, and an author's bibliography, and an illustrator's bibliography provide additional information and add to the authenticity of the text.

Fictional Storybooks Set in the Ancient Middle East Authors of fictional picture storybooks with settings in the ancient Middle East frequently focus on people from early cultures or develop stories that are similar to the folklore set in the ancient civilizations. Robert Sabuda's *Tutankhamun's Gift* is a fictionalized biography about the life of the son of Pharaoh Amenhotep III, an Egyptian ruler. In the notes on the text, the author states that facts from such ancient civilizations as Egypt are both difficult to determine and debated by scholars. In this tale of Tutankhamun's ascendancy to pharaoh in the mid-1300s BCE, the author highlights the role of the young ruler, who proclaims, "I shall rebuild the temples and fill them with monuments to the gods . . . I shall lead the people of Egypt through their suffering and tears so they believe in themselves" (p. 25, unnumbered).

Shulamith Levy Oppenheim's *The Hundredth Name* is similar to a folktale because it is set "far back in time" in Muslim Egypt. This literary folktale has an emphasis on Allah as its young hero tries to discover, through his camel, the hundredth name for Allah. The spiritual quality of the tale is reinforced through the hazy illustrations, painted in acrylics on gessoed linen canvas, that allow the grain to show through the paint.

Appointment is a picture storybook adaptation of W. Somerset Maugham's "Appointment in Samarra." In this Arabic tale set in Baghdad, death in the disguise of an old woman searches for Abdullah the servant. There is a strong sense of fate when Abdullah tries unsuccessfully to escape death by leaving Baghdad to travel to Samarra. In a surprise ending, Maugham shows we cannot escape death, or our fate. Death's appointment with the servant is actually in Samarra and not in Baghdad. Roger Essley's double-page illustrations in desert tones add to the feeling of a hot, dry country.

Historical Fiction Set in the Ancient Middle East Susan Fletcher's *Shadow Spinner* is set in ancient Persia during the time of Shahrazad and the telling of the tales for "The One Thousand and One Nights." The Author's Note reveals that she used Richard F. Burton's English translation of *The Book of The Thousand Nights and a Night* as her guide. The heroine of her story is Marjan, a crippled serving girl who has the ability to spin her own stories. Marjan becomes involved with Shahrazad's problems when Marjan is overheard telling a story that is new to Shahrazad. At this point, Marjan enters the harem to assist Shahrazad in her quest for new stories; subsequently, Marjan is forbidden to leave the harem and becomes part of palace intrigue. Through the descriptions of the palace, the city, and the harem, readers discover many of the details associated with the setting in the ancient Middle East.

Fletcher uses an interesting technique to introduce both the themes in the book and the importance of storytelling. Each chapter is introduced with a section titled "Lessons for Life and Storytelling." For example, notice in the following quote how Fletcher develops the power found in words and stories: "In the old tales, there is power in words. Words are what you use to summon a jinn, or to open an enchanted door, or to cast a spell" (p. 194). Many of these chapter introductions would be interesting to use as part of a storytelling project. Fletcher also provides additional information in the Author's Note when she discusses the background of the book.

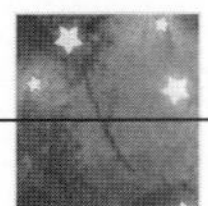

Contemporary Literature with Middle Eastern Roots

Nonfiction children's literature that emphasizes the Middle East typically focuses on religious aspects of the culture, the geography and the people, and conflicts. Poetry and fictional literature often focuses on the human struggle as characters overcome conflicts with society or within themselves.

Informational Books

Laura Buller's *A Faith Like Mine: A Celebration of the World's Religions through the Eyes of Children* may be useful as a comparative study. There is an introduction to the beliefs of Islam including a discussion of beliefs, practices, and traditions. The book includes photographs and quotations from children as the author presents related subjects such as ways of worship and family celebrations. The text includes overviews of Buddhism, Christianity, Hinduism, Judaism, and Sikhism. Maps, glossary, and index provide support for the text.

To help adults understand the complexities of the Islamic faith and the current struggles in the world related to Islam and the West, it is helpful to read books written for adult audiences such as Vartan Gregorian's *Islam: A Mosaic, Not a Monolith* (2003). Gregorian, president of the Carnegie Foundation, traces Islam's origins, its spread from the Middle East and North Africa to Spain and Russia, and the more recent division between people who want to retain traditional values and beliefs and those who consider themselves modernists.

Informational books by Tricia Brown, Lat, and Said Hyder Akbar and Susan Burton focus on experiences of Muslim youth. Brown's *Salaam: A Muslim American Boy's Story,* a book written for younger children, shows Imran's experiences with family and friends. The text shows that Salaam is very much like other American young people: he eats peanut butter and jelly sandwiches and dreams of becoming a rock star. The text also presents a simplified discussion about the tenets of Islam. Lat's *Kampung Boy,* written for middle- and upper-elementary students, presents a nostalgic view of a Muslim boy growing up in a Malaysian village during the 1950s. It suggests that this way of life may be rapidly disappearing. Akbar and Burton's *Come Back to Afghanistan: A California Teenager's Story,* written for young adults, tells about a teenager's experiences as he joins his father in returning home to Afghanistan after the fall of the Taliban in 2001. As he travels around the country, he provides accounts of his experiences for public radio's "The American Life." This book, written for an older audience, presents issues related to the Middle East.

These three books provide interesting comparisons. Readers may consider the content, the forms of presentation, and any issues discussed by each author. The book written for young adults presents considerable observations about Afghan life, politics, and issues related to the war. An adult book, Bernard Lewis's *What Went Wrong?* (2002), provides interesting subjects for discussions that could accompany Akbar's experiences.

Come Back to Afghanistan: A California Teenager's Story may also be compared with the memoir of a Palestinian woman during the Six-Day War and its aftermath in Ibtisam Barakat's *Tasting the Sky: A Palestinian Childhood.* What, if any, are the similarities between experiences in the Afghan war and the 1967 war? How does the Palestinian woman describe her experiences since coming to the United States?

Elizabeth Ferber's biography *Yasir Arafat: The Battle for Peace in Palestine* provides added insights into the conflict in the Middle East. The biography traces Arafat's political career and provides background information on the history of the Arab–Israeli conflict. The biography includes chapter notes and a chronology. Black-and-white photographs illustrate the text.

Jeanette Winter's *The Librarian of Basra: A True Story from Iraq* is another biography in which the biographical character dreams of peace. This librarian has a specific challenge: what

ISSUE Issues Surrounding Contemporary Islamic Literature and Culture

Two issues seem to dominate the discussions about contemporary Islamic cultures and consequently may influence the literature. First, what is the role of women in the culture? How is the role of women depicted in current literature? How might the role of women be depicted in future literature? Second, what is the impact of Westernization on Islamic culture?

Paul Wiseman (2004) begins his article about women's rights: "Conservative leaders want to take us back 200 years, 24-year-old says" (p. 6A). Wiseman reports that many educated urban women are organizing, signing petitions, and holding public protests to demand their rights. In contrast, conservative Islamic leaders want to outlaw civil courts overseeing marriage, divorce, inheritance, and family matters, and replace these courts with religious courts run by clerics. Wiseman clarifies the cultural issue for women when he states, "Women's groups feared that individual religious judges would impose Saudi- or Iranian-style rulings that strip women of rights they had enjoyed under Saddam's more secular government" (p. 6A). Wiseman develops both sides of the issues related to women by quoting women whose beliefs represent the traditional role of women in an Islamic society and women who represent the struggle for equality.

Westernization is another issue that influences Islamic culture. Neil MacFarquhar (2004) titles his article "A Kiss Is Not Just a Kiss to an Angry Arab TV Audience." MacFarquhar reports various reactions to a Middle Eastern version of "Big Brother," the latest import of Western reality television in the Arab world. The television show showed a social kiss between a young man and a young woman. Parliament members "called the show an assault on traditional values, and last Friday a few prayer leaders led 1,000 protesters chanting 'No to indecency!'" (p. A3).

As might be expected, there are spokespeople on both sides of the Westernization of Islamic culture. Fundamentalists view many of the Western-type television shows as "Sodom and Gomorra." In contrast, owners of commercial television stations and creators of the shows believe they have programs that have the potential of selling to millions of new viewers.

As you read articles about women's rights and the influence of Westernization on Islamic culture, consider how these issues may impact Islamic literature. What consequences do you believe might result from either of these issues? Try to identify any of these issues as they are developed by authors of contemporary literature. How might information related to current issues influence how you would authenticate a piece of contemporary literature?

will she do to safeguard the national treasury of over 30,000 books in time of war? Winter reveals how Alia Muhammad Baker, chief librarian of Basra's Central Library, rescued 70% of the library's collection prior to the burning of the library. This picture storybook depicts the importance of a woman's actions when she dreams of peace "and dreams of a new library. But until then, the books are safe—safe with the librarian of Basra" (unnumbered).

As you read these contemporary books, consider the views on stereotypes identified by William J. Griswold et al. (1975) and Rita M. Kissen (1991). Do you find the stereotypes identified by these researchers? Has the literature changed since the study conducted by Griswold et al.? How are the conflicts depicted? What, if any, are the biases in reporting these conflicts?

Poetry

One of the more extensive sources of poetry from the Middle East for children is Naomi Shihab Nye's anthology *This Same Sky: A Collection of Poems from Around the World.* In her introduction, Nye states her motivation for editing this collection:

> Poetry has always devoted itself to bringing us into clearer focus—letting us feel or imagine faraway worlds from the inside. During the Gulf War of 1991, when the language of headline news seemed determined to push human experience into the 'sanitized' distance, I found myself searching for poems by Iraqi poets to carry into classrooms. Even if the poems had been written decades earlier, they helped to give a sense of human struggle and real people living behind the headlines. (p. xii)

This collection includes poetry from Saudi Arabia, Kuwait, Pakistan, Iraq, and Lebanon, as well as from many other countries throughout the world. Many of the themes in the poetry are universal. For example, in "A Sailor's Memoirs," a poem by Muhammad al-Fayiz from Kuwait, the poet longs to give peace—peace to the Gulf breeze, peace to sandy shores, peace to returning ships, and peace to quiet dwellings. In "A Dream of Paradise in the Shadow of War," a poem by Muneer Niazi from Pakistan, the poet remembers the poignant melodies of the nightingale's song, people returning home, and a village wilderness turned into a perfumed garden. In "A Pearl," a poem by Fawziyya Abu Khald from Saudi Arabia, the poet remembers a gift, symbolic of truth and love, passed down from grandmother to mother and finally to the poet. The fact the poems in the anthology reflect universal needs is highlighted by the titles of the anthology's, sections: Words and Silences, Dreams and Dreamers, Families, The Earth and Sky in Which We Live, Losses, and Human Mysteries.

The Space Between Our Footsteps: Poems and Paintings from the Middle East, a collection of poetry also selected by Naomi Shihab Nye, includes both poems and paintings from the Middle East. The selections represent the works of more than 100 poets and artists from nineteen Middle Eastern countries. In her introduction to the anthology, Nye provides considerable information about the importance of poetry in the Middle East. Nye also provides a discussion of the themes that are found in the poetry. For example, affection for children and family, longing for innocent days, love for homeland, grief over exile, and regard for the natural world and for one another can all be found in the poetry. As you read the poems and look at the art, try to identify these themes.

Several additional anthologies of poetry include at least a few poems from the Middle East. Satomi Ichikawa's *Here a Little Child I Stand: Poems of Prayer and Praise for Children* includes an Islamic prayer to Allah by Add Al'Aziz Al-Dirini. Ruth Gordon's anthology *Under All Silences: The Many Shades of Love* includes several poems from Egypt and Persia. The Egyptian poems are translated from ancient hieroglyphic texts written about 1500 BCE. The Persian texts are also translated from ancient sources in the 1200s. In one of these ancient Persian poems, the poet wonders about Solomon and all his wives and the Soul. Two poems from ancient Egypt are also included in Kenneth Koch and Kate Farrell's *Talking to the Sun: An Illustrated Anthology of Poems for Young People.*

Contemporary Realistic Fiction

Picture storybooks written for younger children include stories about personal development and pride, trying to live in a city when there is conflict, and keeping the memory of a beloved brother alive. These books may be criticized for inaccuracies or stereotypes, or they may be acclaimed for positive representations. For example, as you read *The Day of Ahmed's Secret* by Florence Parry Heide and Judith Heide Gilliland, set in Cairo, Egypt, analyze the content and illustrations to decide which is more important: the themes of personal development and pride in work or Sylvia Iskander's (1997) analysis that "the flaw lies in the lack of cultural accuracy in text and illustrations?" (p. 13).

In contrast, Iskander's analysis of Heide and Gilliland's *Sami and the Time of the Troubles* concludes that this text and the illustrations by Ted Lewin "present an accurate portrait of life in war-torn Lebanon" (p. 15). This story depicts a family trying to survive in the basement shelter as guns and bombs shake the walls. Notice how the authors introduce the conflict and suggest the influences on a young boy's life and why it is a time of troubles: "It is a time of guns and bombs. It is a time that has lasted all my life, and I am ten years old." As the family huddles in the basement, Sami thinks about the quiet days when it is safe to be outside and he remembers all of these pleasant experiences. Ted Lewin's illustrations allow readers to visualize the contrasts between the basement shelter and the pleasant times when there are no bombs. The front and endpapers introduce the true nature of the conflict by showing the results of a car bomb in a once-quiet neighborhood.

Several picture books written for younger children describe various elements of religion or important holidays. The protagonist in Maha Addasi's *Time to Pray* is a young girl who visits her grandmother in the Middle East. While there, she learns about her religion and discovers ways that she can pray at home since she cannot attend a mosque. This is a bilingual story told in English and Arabic. Several picture books have settings around the preparation for and the celebration of Ramadan. Maha Addasi's *White Nights of Ramadan* is set in Kuwait and focuses on preparations for Girgian, a holiday celebrated during the month of Ramadan. In Hena Khan's *Night of the Moon: A Muslim Holiday Story*, a seven-year-old Pakistani American girl takes part in a family celebration. In Na'ima B. Robert's *Ramadan Moon*, a girl explains what happens during Ramadan, including praying, reading verses, and doing good deeds.

The Bedouin folktales reflected the pride, independence, and self-sufficiency of the nomadic characters. These same characteristics are found in Sue Alexander's *Nadia the Willful.* Nadia is the young daughter of a Bedouin sheik who lives with her family in the desert. The Bedouin values of pride and independence are especially strong in Nadia when she refuses to allow the family to forget her favorite brother who has been lost in the desert. Nadia does not obey when her father tries to hide his grief by decree that no one will utter Hamed's name again. In a satisfying ending, Nadia makes her father realize that the only way he can retain his son Hamed is to remember him and talk about him. Nadia's actions not only stress determination, they also develop the power of love and remembrance.

Books for older readers develop themes related to the importance of childhood memories and friendships, the necessity for surviving in a dangerous world, and the searching for personal identity within a culture that may not respect women's roles.

The theme of the importance of memories and friendship is developed in Vedat Dalokay's *Sister Shako and Kolo the Goat: Memories of My Childhood in Turkey.* This book, which won the 1995 Mildred Batchelder Honor Award, is a personal remembrance of the former mayor of Ankara, Turkey. In it, he lovingly recalls his childhood in rural Turkey and his special friendship with a widow and her remarkable goat, Kolo. The author develops many of the values and beliefs identified in the folklore. For example, the importance of hospitality is shown when the new goat comes into the family unexpectedly and is considered a "Guest of God" because "[i]f a traveler needs shelter or food, he knocks at the door of any house along the way. The host offers him whatever he needs" (p. 14).

Dalokay develops many of these Turkish values as he remembers Sister Shako's thoughts and advice about subjects such as holy places and death. For example, Sister Shako states her beliefs about death when she states that after death she will be in the rain, the wind, and the rivers. She also hopes, "May death come nicely, smoothly, without pain, without suffering" (p. 58). To clarify understanding, the text includes footnotes that describe various customs and beliefs presented in the story. The cultural nature of the text is reinforced by regional words, idioms, sayings, and descriptions of traditions of eastern Turkey.

Surviving in a dangerous world is a theme developed in several books set in the Middle East. Rafik Schami's *A Hand Full of Stars* places the hero in the political turmoil of modern Damascus. Showing how dangerous society can be, the story follows a teenager who wants to become a journalist within this suppressed society. His wishes come true when he and his friends begin an underground newspaper. After reading this book, you may speculate about the symbolism in the title. The author states at the end of the book what *A Hand Full of Stars* means: "The Hand is the hand of Uncle Salim, always there to guide the narrator: in the saddest moments, it points the way out of despair. Like the stars that illuminate the dark night sky, the Stars in the hand stand for hope" (endnote).

Applying Knowledge of Cultural Values and Beliefs to *Shabanu: Daughter of the Wind*

The 1990 Newbery Honor book, Suzanne Fisher Staples's *Shabanu: Daughter of the Wind,* provides strong literary elements of character, conflict, and theme, as well as examples of cultural beliefs. Consequently, the book provides a good source for identifying values and beliefs and for relating those values and beliefs to the plot and characterization in the story. Two articles may help students of children's literature as they read and analyze this book: Suzanne Fisher Staples's "Writing about the Islamic World: An American Author's Thoughts on Authenticity" (1997) and Laurie A. Brand's "Women and the State in Jordan" (1998).

Shabanu: Daughter of the Wind is a story about a Muslim family who live in the Cholistan Desert in Pakistan. The main character, Shabanu, is the youngest of two daughters in a nomadic extended family. She has learned she cannot determine the direction of her life, and this causes her person-against-self and person-against-society conflict. As a Muslim, her father has complete authority over her, and she is struggling to accept his decisions regarding her future.

As you read the following list of lifestyles, values, and beliefs found in the book, try to authenticate them with what you have learned about an Islamic culture that is influenced by the Quran (Koran) and the threads of the culture identified in the folklore. The family in this story closely adheres to the mandates of their religion. Some of the lifestyle descriptions, values, and beliefs mentioned in the story include the following:

Sons are more important than daughters.
Marriages are arranged by the families, and are encouraged to take place as soon as a girl reaches puberty.
Poetry has a strong history in this culture.
Girls must be veiled once they reach puberty.
A woman can be killed for tarnishing the family's honor.
When children are small, they can go anywhere.
Sexual segregation begins at puberty.
A girl who is not married by age 16 is a disgrace.
Wrestling is an acceptable recreational activity for men.
The ritual of the dead includes facing the body toward Mecca, washing the body, and wrapping it in a shroud.
Burial must be quick, to send the soul on its way.
Children do not fast during Ramadan, the month of fasting.
During Ramadan, no eating or drinking is allowed until sundown.
Muslims must be up before the sun rises.
Parents decide what is best for their children.
A child's happiness is less important than the family's honor.
A bride price is a common practice with arranged marriages.
Muslim men are permitted four wives; women, one husband.
A woman's place is in the home.
Parents are due the utmost respect.
A child is not to question a father's decision.
A "light beating" is permissible if a woman is disobedient.

As you authenticate the lifestyles, values, and beliefs identified in the book, try to decide if the book is or is not authentic for a nomadic people of the Islamic faith. What is your evidence that the book is or is not authentic?

Inner-city survival provides the setting and conflict in Gaye Hicyilmaz's *Against the Storm,* set in Ankara, Turkey. This story shows the consequences of urban poverty when Mehmet and his family arrive in Ankara and find themselves trapped in a shantytown that is quite different from the wonderful city the family has heard about. This becomes a story of friendship and determination when Mehmet receives the help of a streetwise orphan and uses his own courage to find a way out of this environment. Hicyilmaz's story is vivid because she lived in Turkey for many years. According to the endnotes, "It was here that she was struck by the way children in particular are forced to suffer the effects of poverty and how poverty destroys the very fabric of society. Her novel was inspired by a true incident reported in the Turkish press" (endnotes).

The setting in Suzanne Fisher Staples's *Under the Persimmon Tree* is Afghanistan in 2002. The main characters are a rural Afghani girl and an American woman who has converted to Islam. In this wartime book, Staples explores the personal losses faced by the characters because of war. You may compare this book with Deborah Ellis's *Parvana's Journey.* In Ellis's

A Featured Book for Upper Elementary and Middle School Students

Kathy Henderson's *Lugalbanda: The Boy Who Got Caught Up in a War* provides exemplary sources of information for this traditional legend from Iraq. The author describes the ancient Sumerian culture and how the original tale was translated from clay tablets believed to be between 4,000 and 5,000 years old. These tablets were discovered during the nineteenth-century excavations, but were not deciphered until the 1970s.

The legend is about a young prince who becomes ill while traveling with his brothers and his father's army as they march to war. When he is left alone in a cave to hopefully recover, he sees and tames the ferocious Anzu bird who has great powers to grant wishes. After he feeds the Anzu's chick and treats it like a princling, Lugalbanda asks for and is rewarded with legendary capabilities: strength in legs so they will never tire, arms that never feel weak, and the abilities to dance like sunlight, leap like flame, and dart like lightning. These capabilities make it possible for the prince to save his father's army.

The language of the legend has the cadence of an oral story. For example, "In the Lullubu Mountains, where no cypress trees grow, where no snakes slither and no scorpions scurry, where the prince slept and the night was dark" (p. 36). Throughout the book, Henderson uses language that creates a strong visual experience.

In legendary format, warnings and requirements are given if the hero is to successfully help his father in this time of need and war. First, the Anzu bird warns the prince not to tell anyone about his new gifts. Second, the prince gives his word of honor and promises the Anzu bird that he will keep his word and also honor the Anzu bird after the prince returns to his country. The prince then promises his father, the king, that he will give the message to the goddess Inana who has always protected the king. Third, the goddess tells the prince the actions the king must do to be successful in battle. Fourth, the goddess gives a warning to the king. He must not destroy the warring city; he may only bring back worked metals, fabled stone carvings, and craftsmen who can teach their skills to the king's people.

The themes in this legend are also found in many tales that focus on cultural heroes. Two themes are very important. First, a hero must keep promises. This theme is developed through the actions of of the prince and the promises given to the Anzu bird, to the king, and to the goddess. Second, it is desirable to strive for peace. This theme is developed when the king promises the goddess that if he and his army are brought safely home, he will lay down his spear, break his shield, and make an end to war. A theme for peace is also developed when the king does not destroy the enemy city, but restores the city and makes sure that the treasures and craftsmen are safe. The conclusion of the story verifies these themes as the prince grows up in peace, becomes the next king of his country, creates beautiful carvings and statues to honor his promise to the Anzu bird, and has singers sing songs about the Anzu bird and storytellers tell the story again and again so that no one will forget.

book, a thirteen-year-old girl searches war-torn Afghanistan for her family. Are there any similarities in characterizations, conflicts, and survival techniques? What are the themes of the two books? As you read these books you will notice how many of the books written for older readers have the importance of striving for survival in a dangerous world. Notice how the authors develop these themes and suggest the personal characteristics that make survival possible. Are there any similarities among the books, the authors' points of view, and the themes developed in the books?

Survival

Suzanne Fisher Staples's Newbery Honor book *Shabanu: Daughter of the Wind* is one of the best sources for analyzing survival strategies in contemporary realistic fiction that is not set during wartime. In a story set in present-day Pakistan, the heroine faces personal and social conflicts as she tries to balance her own desires with the traditional roles in which a female is not considered important and must adhere to her father's decisions. This role of the female is introduced early in the novel as Shabanu states that Muslim girls are taught at an early age that their childhood homes are only temporary; their real homes are the ones they go to after they marry. To reinforce the role of the father in a girl's life, Staples describes the anger expressed by Shabanu's father when he tells her not to ever disobey him and her mother warns her, "You must learn to obey even when you disagree" (p. 28). In this environment Shabanu discovers both the strength of her will and its limitations. She also realizes that if she does not marry a good man, she will need to be strong and independent. Shabanu's survival strategies are very realistic for the role of women, as shown when she tells her sister, who is preparing for her own marriage, to wake up and prepare for what comes next.

Shabanu's survival strategies are the strongest when she finds she must prepare for her own marriage to a much older man who has three wives already. Her father ignores Shabanu's pleas to allow her to make her own decisions. The author develops the attitudes of the father when he maintains that the marriage will uphold the family's honor. Readers discover Shabanu's inner survival strategies as she considers advice from several wise women. They tell her to make her strength of independent thinking work for her and not against her. She must keep the secrets of her soul locked in her heart, keep her inner reserves hidden, trust herself, and be wise. This advice goes completely against the beliefs of her father, who maintains that intelligence does not help a woman. As Shabanu ponders the advice of the wise women she realizes that she could learn to read and write and even play the flute. She knows that she will survive if she keeps her own counsel and keeps her happiness deep in her heart.

VOICES OF IRAQI REFUGEES

CHILDREN OF WAR

DEBORAH ELLIS

Interviews reveal the stresses associated with war.

Cover from *Children of War: Voices of Iragi Refugees*, by Deborah Ellis. Reprinted by permission of House of Anansi Press, Inc.

Students of children's literature may compare the roles of women in current Pakistan with the roles portrayed in the Batchelder Award winner *The Shadows of Ghadames* by Joelle Stolz. This is a historical fiction novel set in nineteenth-century Libya. The author focuses on the secret role of women as they live with men in two different worlds. Readers discover the challenges for a girl who wants to gain some of the advantages that males receive, such as learning to read. The father in this novel has a much different attitude than Shabanu's father as he agrees that she should learn to read and he overcomes his wife's concerns when he says, "Only weak men are afraid of a woman who can read! . . . Don't worry. You'll learn and you'll find a husband because the times are changing" (p. 117). Note that learning to read and write is considered a survival strategy by both Suzanne Fisher Staples and Joelle Stolz. Why is that such a survival strategy? What is the current role of education in the lives of women living in the Middle East? The two books are set in two different centuries. Have attitudes toward education for women changed in Pakistan or in Libya during these time periods? Use current news articles to justify your responses.

Many current books about the Middle East, especially those written for older readers and young adults, have Middle Eastern settings and conflicts in which the protagonists must survive under the most dangerous circumstances. If the books are set in America, the characters may face a society with stereotypical views of their culture, or if Muslim, their religion. Many of the books reflect the newspaper reports, and the titles could be headlines in any major newspaper. To strengthen the authenticity of these books, we discover that many are nonfiction remembrances or are interviews with people who are trying to survive.

Deborah Ellis's books are based on experiences of real people and their will to survive. For example, *Parvana's Journey* follows a thirteen-year-old girl as she searches through war-torn Afghanistan for her family. *Three Wishes: Palestinian and Israeli Children Speak Out* focuses on interviews with young people who range in age from eight to eighteen. *Off to War: Voices of Soldiers' Children* includes interviews with children of Canadian and American soldiers who are fighting in Afghanistan and Iraq. *Children of War: Voices of Iraqi Refugees* includes interviews with young people who fled Iraq and are refugees living in Jordan. This final book includes the conflicts they endured and the values and beliefs that made survival possible. Consequently, we will use this book for an in-depth look at survival strategies that the young people use as they face person-versus-person (soldiers versus civilians), person-versus-society (Christians versus Muslims, Iraq versus America, women versus the new regime), and person-versus-self (fear of death, lack of trust for people who were former friends) conflicts.

The survival strategies are similar to those found in many wartime stories. Some of the survival strategies relate to living in a dictatorship such as joining a political party when told, having no choice about taking military training, and needing to retain papers that allow you to move around. Other survival strategies relate to safety during times of war such as taking threats seriously, searching for safe places to hide, and realizing that it is foolish to tease people who could easily shoot you. Some survival strategies relate to personal well-being such as having trusted friends and family, relying on past pleasures such as writing and drawing to remind one of what is beautiful in life, and saving photographs because they are important possessions. Some survival strategies relate to the future, such as seeking asylum in the United States or Canada and realizing that an education is most important for survival in the future.

One of the final interviews presents a strategy for all people to survive. Yeman states: "I wish American kids could understand that we have many things in common. Really, we are not different. They don't need to be afraid of us" (p. 124).

An Unexpected Light: Travels in Afghanistan by Jason Elliot, winner of the Thomas Cook/Telegraph Travel Book Award, is an adult novel that is part travelogue, history, personal quest, and reflections on the joys and perils of the author's journey through Afghanistan in the late 1990s. Throughout his journey, Elliot discovers strategies that helped the people survive war with Russia, the resulting poverty, and intertribal rivalries. For example, he interacts with people who, even if living in poverty, express spirits of openness and generosity. To answer complex questions, the people frequently quote poetry, tell stories about past heroes, and almost always stress their adherence to the will of Allah.

The people's use of analogies to present their views was shown when a tribesman told Elliot why people have negative attitudes toward the United States. According to the tribesman, these attitudes go back to 1989 when the people felt the United States abandoned them after they had helped the United States fight Russia. The Afghan used the following analogy to show feelings for a former ally: It felt like a pot placed on a fire and left to boil long after the water had disappeared (the Russians withdrew from the country) and a man helped to the top of a tall building and then having the stairs removed from under him, leaving him stranded (American aid withdrawn). They felt like crippled victims of the cold war.

As readers of cultural literature and news articles about Afghanistan, we may wonder if these feelings of abandonment still influence current relationships. A 2011 article partially answers this question. The article is titled "U.S. Ambassadorial Nominee Warns of Risk of Abandoning Afghanistan" (June 9, 2011). In the article, Miller and Knowlton quote Robert C. Crocker, the nominee for ambassador to Afghanistan, warning the Senate Foreign Relations Committee: "The United States had abandoned Afghanistan once before, after the war with the Soviet Union in 1989 with disastrous consequences—the rise of the Taliban" (p. A7). What do you believe will be the outcome of the war in Afghanistan? What strategies might allow both the United States and Afghanistan to survive this crisis? Try to answer this question as you read news articles and listen to reports about the war and troops stationed in Afghanistan.

Demi's biography *Muhammad* depicts the life of the prophet and includes holy utterances that were revealed to him, written down by scribes, and became the text for the Koran. Demi includes Muhammad's teachings and beliefs that stress how people should live. These utterances provide strategies for life and survival that are based on Muhammad's values and beliefs, including honesty in business transactions, equality among rich and poor, respect for freedom of thought and speech, and dignity and respect for all people.

Biographies about the lives of contemporary individuals also reveal survival strategies. For example, the young boy in James Rumford's *Silent Music: A Story of Baghdad* longs for peace in wartime Baghdad. He tries to forget the bombs falling on the city by practicing his calligraphy. *Listen to the Wind: The Story of Dr. Greg & Three Cups of Tea* by Greg Mortenson and Susan L. Roth, is a highly illustrated book based on the life of the man who helped to build schools in Pakistan. This book features the stages used to build the first school and suggests the survival strategies he used to build the schools and provide education for the village. The first stage shows that he gains the cooperation of everyone: they work together to build a bridge that can carry the supplies needed to build the school. The cooperation continues as mothers carry water to mix the cement, men place the stones for the classroom walls, and children add fragments of stones to the cement to make the walls stronger. The importance of education is shown as the children learn to write, do arithmetic, read books, and explore maps. The book concludes with photographs that show people working during different stages of construction. (There is controversy around the work of Greg Mortenson, as discussed later in this chapter.)

Summary

In this chapter, we have discussed the traditional literature and identified values and beliefs found in the folklore from various cultures and countries in the Middle East. For example, we found that the Bedouin tales reflect generosity, hospitality, the importance of family, ancestry, and birth. Pride, independence, and self-sufficiency are important values. In this chapter, folklore was discussed in the following categories: Bedouin tales, tales of magic and supernatural, animal tales, and religious tales and moral instruction.

We discussed informational and fiction books that depict the ancient cultures. Books about the ancient cultures are especially valuable and informative if they include both historical information and photographs of ancient architecture and artifacts. Informational books that encourage analytical thinking by allowing young readers to become involved in solving problems and observing are especially meaningful. Fictional books about ancient cultures either typically focus on stories about people who might have lived in the ancient Middle East, such as a stone carver, or are fictionalized biographies of early rulers. Authors of fiction frequently build stories on the folklore such as found in "The One Thousand and One Nights."

Poetry is an important part of the literature from the various Middle Eastern countries. Many of the values found in the folklore, such as closeness of family and love for homeland, are reflected in the poetry. The poetry discussed is from both ancient and contemporary cultures.

We concluded the chapter with a discussion of the survival strategies found in Middle Eastern literature.

Suggested Activities for Developing Understanding of Literature from the Middle East

1. Compare the values and beliefs found in folklore from ancient Egypt and from Islamic cultures. Find examples of folklore that depict these values and beliefs.

2. Trace the emergence of Islamic beliefs in the folklore.

3. Locate an article about the exploration of ancient Egyptian tombs and artifacts such as Terence Walz's "The American Experience in Egypt: A Retrospective Chronicles Two Centuries of Exploration" (1996). How does an article like this one written by the executive director of the American Research Center in Egypt compare to the information found in other informational books about ancient Egypt?

4. Locate a picture storybook in which the illustrator has depicted the early Islamic culture. Authenticate the illustrations by referring to art books that include photographs of Islamic art and architecture. Does the illustrator of the picture storybook develop an accurate feeling for the culture? Why or why not? *Islam: Art and Architecture* (2004), edited by Markus Hattstein and Peter Delius, is very useful for this activity. The large, heavily illustrated text written for adult audiences "follows the historic development of the Islamic regions and their ruling dynasties, and illustrates their greatly varied forms of artistic expression from the birth of the religion to the present day" (front cover). The text includes more than 1,000 photographs and diagrams that are extremely useful when authenticating picture storybooks and illustrated informational books. Andrew Lawler's "Reconstructing Petra" (2007) follows archaeologists as they work to uncover information about Petra, the capital of Jordan's powerful trading empire 2,000 years ago.

5. Read a novel written for adults such as Jean P. Sasson's *Princess: A True Story of Life Behind the Veil in Saudi Arabia* (1992). Compare the novel with Suzanne Fisher Staples's *Shabanu: Daughter of the Wind,* a book written for younger readers. What are the similarities and what are the differences in the culture, values, and lifestyles depicted?

6. *Children of War: Voices of Iraqi Refugees* by Deborah Ellis is analyzed in the "Survival" section in this chapter. She also interviewed children of American and Canadian military personnel in *Off to War: Voices of Soldiers' Children.* Read both books and compare the survival strategies the children expressed. What are the differences and the similarities? Try to account for differences and similarities. Use newspaper and media sources to authenticate the responses of the two groups.

7. Collect news articles about the Middle East. Do you identify any of the stereotypes reported in the earlier study discussed in this chapter? Do you identify any of the conflicts found in literature about the Middle East? If so, what are the major conflicts found in newspaper articles? You might consider news articles such as the following:

Elliott, Andrea. "A Cleric's Journey Leads to a Suburban Frontier." *New York Times* (January 28, 2007): 1, 24. This article describes the experiences of an imam in America.

Power, Carla. "A Secret History." *The New York Times Magazine,* (February 25, 2007): 22–24. The author makes this observation and asks this question: "In the Middle Ages, many Islamic scholars were women. Will their rediscovery have an effect on Muslim women today?" (p. 22).

Involving Children with Middle Eastern Literature

As we discovered in the previous sections, literature from the Middle East includes literature from a wide range of countries—from Egypt and Turkey to Saudi Arabia, Yemen, and Iran. The literature also includes the influences of the Islamic faith. In this section, we follow the same five phases used with literature from other cultures in previous chapters.

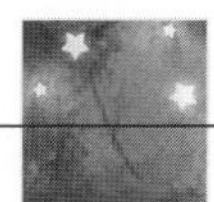

Phase One: Traditional Values in Folklore

You may begin your study of the cultural characteristics of folklore from the Middle East by collecting a number of folktales, myths, and legends from the various countries. As you read the literature, identify the geographic location of the tale on a map. Developing a web of the folklore and the respected values and disliked qualities is an excellent way to begin this study. The web in Figure 7.1 is an example of one developed by students following the reading of the folklore.

Study the information on the web. The respected values include wit and wisdom, generosity, hospitality, friendship, and protection for those in your care. The disliked qualities include jealousy and disobeying God's orders. The beliefs include a belief in Allah, a belief in death and revival, and a belief in fate. The motifs include magical spells, trickster animals, and moral instruction. Also notice that by identifying locale, students can compare both similarities and differences. For example, they will discover that the ancient Egyptians believed in fate and revival after death as reflected in such myths as the myth of Isis and Osiris. They will also discover that many respected values are closely related to the geography of the culture. For example, the Bedouin people who lived a nomadic life in the desert emphasized the importance of hospitality and generosity especially to those who are under their care. Lead discussions in which students consider each of these values and motifs.

Additional Activities to Enhance Phase One

Here are some activities for children or young adult students related to this phase:

1. Compare Eric A. Kimmel's Egyptian version of Snow White, *Rimonah of the Flashing Sword: A North African Tale,* with Snow White tales from other cultures. What are the characteristics of this tale that make it Egyptian? What are the characteristics that make it similar to other Snow White tales?

2. Compare Neil Philip's variant of the Cinderella story in *The Arabian Nights* or Rebecca Hickox's *The Golden Sandal: A Middle Eastern Cinderella Story* with Cinderella tales from other cultures. What are the characteristics of the tale that make it Arabic? What are the characteristics that make it similar to other Cinderella tales?

3. Ehud Ben-Ezer's *Hosni the Dreamer: An Arabian Tale* is described as being based on an old Arabian folktale. Read and analyze the tale and evaluate Uri Shulevitz's illustrations. What evidence can you find that this is based on an Arabian folktale? Are the illustrations authentic for the culture and the location?

4. Make a collection of openings and closings found in folklore from various areas of the Middle East. Are there any generalizations that can be made about the folklore style?

FIGURE 7.1 Web Showing Traditional Values Found in Folklore from the Middle East

- **Middle East folklore web**
  - **Motifs**
    - Magical spells
      - *"The Enchanted Horse"*
      - *"Rimonah of the Flashing Sword"*
    - Need for moral instruction
      - *"The Camel and the Mouse"*
      - *"Ibis"*
    - Trickster animals
      - *"The Cat Who Went to Mecca"*
  - **Admired qualities**
    - Wit and wisdom
      - *The Three Princes*
      - *"The Clever Minister's Daughter" (Syria)*
    - Hospitality
      - *"The Boy in Girl's Dress" (Bedouin)*
      - *"The Duty of the Host" (Saudi Arabia)*
    - Protection for those in one's care
      - *"The Enchanted Horse"*
    - Respect for parents
      - *"The Enchanted Horse"*
    - Generosity
      - *"The Last Camel of Emir Hamid" (Bedouin)*
  - **Beliefs**
    - Fate
      - *"Isis and Osiris" (Egypt)*
    - Allah
      - *"The Fisherman and the Jinni"*
    - Death and revival
      - *"Isis and Osiris"*
  - **Disliked qualities**
    - Disobeying God's orders
      - *Ibis (Islamic)*
    - Jealousy
      - *The Arabian Nights*

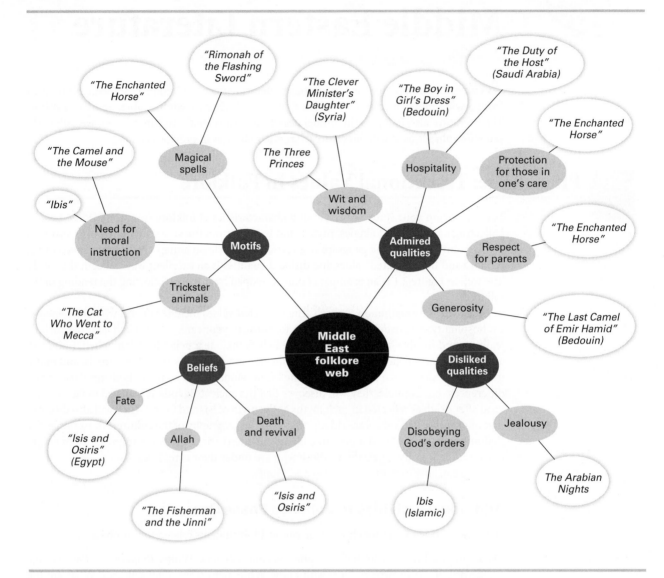

5. Using the religious tales such as Shulamith Levy Oppenheim's *Iblis,* search for the common ground between Islam and Christianity. What are the Islamic influences depicted in *Iblis?*

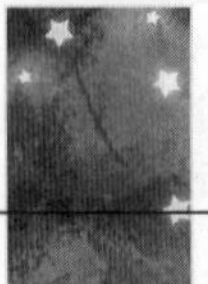

Phase Two: Narrowing the Folklore to the Literature of One Country

If desired, you may develop separate webs for topics such as "Folklore from Egypt," "Bedouin Folklore," or "Arabic Folklore." Now students can do an in-depth study of one of the areas. They should locate the places where the folklore originated on a map. They could also relate the themes and motifs in the folklore to the geography of the locations.

They may choose illustrated versions of folktales from one area and authenticate the cultural, geographical, and historical accuracy of the illustrations. Another excellent activity that provides a pleasurable culminating activity for a study of the folklore of the culture is to develop a storytelling activity in which students prepare stories for telling by investigating the background of the stories, discovering the traditional storytelling styles, and telling the tales to an audience.

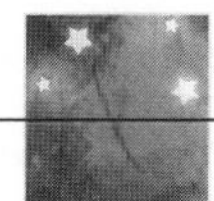

Analytical Reading of Hilari Bell's *Flame*

The example of literature for this activity, based on Adler and Van Doren's (1972) steps, is Hilari Bell's *Flame*. The author uses an ancient Persian legend to motivate her writing of a fantasy that includes the retelling of the legend. The fantasy landscape is reminiscent of ancient Persia, and the conflict includes a military quest that resembles the conquests by the Roman Empire. There are also three strong characters who are on their own quests for self-discovery and to save an ancient land. Let's now use Adler and Van Doren's analytical method to discuss, analyze, and criticize this book.

1. Identify and discuss the kind of literature and the subject matter in *Flame*. This book is fantasy. Writers of fantasy develop plots by encouraging readers to believe in the fantasy world. Authors need readers to suspend disbelief to accept the possibility the story could happen. As we read this book we must decide if and how Bell creates a plot that readers believe is possible, characters and situations that seem probable to readers, and settings that provide detailed descriptions of the world of the fantasy.

2. Briefly describe or summarize the book. In this volume, part of the Book of Sorahb series, Bell develops the fantasyland of Farsala, which is under attack by the Hrums. Three characters are developed who themselves are on a quest of self-discovery. The author follows the development of various conflicts within Jiaan, a peasant boy who is actually the son of the country's major commander and must eventually take over his father's quest to save the country. The second character, Soraya, is the daughter of the commander who develops her special abilities so she can avenge her father's death. Finally, there is Kavi, a trader who is trapped into being a traitor and spy until he realizes he cannot be part of actions that place the people into slavery.

3. List and outline the major parts of the book. The author uses an interesting technique that helps readers understand the framework for the story and the developing conflict, characterization, and themes. The text opens with a map of Farsala that helps readers believe this is a real country. The map traces the Great Trade Route that is important in the story. Alternating chapters focus on each of the main characters: Jiaan, Soraya, and Kavi. An outline of each character's development and plot of the story could focus on the characters' changes within the chapters and how the characters reach their final self-discovery and realize they have responsibilities. At appropriate locations in the book, the author retells portions of an ancient Persian legend about Rostam, Tahmineh, and Sorahb. In the legend, Sorahb is a hero, a warrior who comes to Farsala's aid when the need is the greatest.

4. Define the problem the author has tried to solve. The major problems relate to the themes: it is imperative to retain and even fight for personal freedom, the survival of the spirit is extremely important, and we all have a responsibility toward our fellow beings. The increasing conflict focuses on the invasion of the land that might result in slavery of the people. The author develops these problems by describing both person-versus-society and person-versus-self conflicts. The person-versus-self conflicts are crucial as readers decide how credibly each character faces his or her conflict.

5. Identify and interpret key words. Some of the words and phrases that could be identified and discussed include sacrifice, Iron Empire, Great Trade Route, peasants, Time's Wheel, Tree of Life, Flame of Destruction, ancient legends, Djinn, the leopardess, and traitor.

6. Identify and discuss the most important sentences in the text.

Sentences that describe the attitudes between peasants and nobility. There are numerous references to social class differences.

Sentences that describe contrasts between the Farsala and the invading Hrums. These include both attitudes about the ruling people and comparisons between approaches to military tactics.

Sentences that depict references to Time's Wheel.

Sentences that depict the person-versus-self struggle of each character as they approach their own self-discovery.

Sentences that foreshadow the plot and conflict that will probably develop in Volume 2 of "The Book of Sorahb."

7. Know the author's arguments by identifying them in the text. A search for sentences that reveal the author's themes helps identify the author's arguments:

p. 28: "Time's Wheel spun all things, from the Tree of Life down into the Flame of Destruction, but there is no sense in tempting it to turn."
p. 66: Jiaan's father emphasizes the confidence and trust he has in Jiaan by placing his daughter's safety in his care.
p. 210: "She would have to return to the desert after all. A deghass recognized a debt of honor."
p. 336: "Conquest involved more than fighting—there must be other ways to resist. He'd find those ways."
p. 344: The legend reveals that a champion for the people will appear when needed.

8. Determine which of the problems the author has solved and which have not been solved. Readers can decide whether or not each of the characters solved their own quest for self-discovery and if they faced their person-versus-self conflicts. Because this is a first volume in a continuing saga, readers will realize that the major problem of the Hrum invasion will be a continuing quest. They can decide, however, whether or not the author has developed a framework in which the problem will be solved.

9. Criticism. Before developing critical judgment of the text, readers should understand the text. Here are some concerns:

a. This text has references to a Persian legend. How does the author's insertion of the legend aid understanding of the plot, culture, and characters?
b. The Hrum invading culture developed in the text has close relationships with the Roman Empire. How effective is this comparison?

10. When you disagree with the author, do so reasonably. For example, are there any parts of the story that do not allow suspending disbelief? Why?

11. Respect the difference between knowledge and personal opinion by giving reasons for critical judgments.

Additional Activities to Enhance Phase Two

Here are some activities for children or young adult students related to this phase:

1. Find folktales from a specific country of the Middle East that do not have extensive author's notes, or your teacher will provide them for you. Develop author's notes or illustrator's notes that might accompany each of the books. Several books provide examples

of source and author's notes developed by authors or retellers of folklore. For example, in Eric A. Kimmel's *The Tale of Ali Baba and the Forty Thieves,* Kimmel provides background information about the tale, including a reference to an eleventh-century sheikh and a location in modern Teheran where the tale might have taken place. Lise Manniche's *The Prince Who Knew His Fate* includes extensive notes, maps, and sketches of figures in the Egyptian Museum, Cairo. There is also a listing of meanings of terms from the early Egyptian culture. This latter book includes eight pages of supporting information titled "About the Story and the Illustrations." Kathy Henderson's *Lugalbanda: The Boy Who Got Caught Up in a War* is an epic tale from ancient Iraq. The author includes four pages of "Notes on the Story." These notes identify the source of the original tale, explain how she adapted the tale for contemporary readers, and provide a map showing ancient Sumer.

2. Extend the storytelling activity into a "Storytelling Festival from _____." Ask students to focus on the stories from one area, practice the stories using an appropriate storytelling style, and include music that might provide background for the stories.
3. Ask students to choose a folktale from a specific area that does not include illustrations. Have students either draw authentic illustrations or choose illustrations from art books that could be used to illustrate the text.

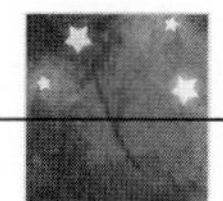

Phase Three: Historical Nonfiction

There are numerous nonfiction informational books about various locations in the Middle East; consequently, the books provide excellent sources for evaluating informational books and comparing texts written about the same subjects. Guidelines developed by the National Science Teachers Association (1992) provide selection and evaluation criteria for informational books that may be used for this activity. For example, this organization recommends the following criteria:

1. All facts should be accurate.
2. Stereotypes should be eliminated.
3. Illustrations should clarify the text.
4. Analytical thinking should be encouraged.
5. The organization should aid understanding.
6. The style should stimulate interest.

Before students discuss and apply these criteria to informational books, you may ask the students to suggest their own guidelines for selecting and evaluating nonfiction books. After they provide their suggestions and reasons for the guidelines, you may compare their guidelines with those developed by the science association.

Next, select a group of informational books that develop similar topics and tell the students they will use the guidelines to evaluate each of these books. For example, you might choose Zahi Hawass's *Tutankhamun: The Mystery of the Boy King* and *Curses of the Pharaohs: My Adventures with Mummies* and James Cross Giblin's *Secret of the Sphinx*. Students might authenticate Emily Sand's *Egyptology: Search for the Tomb of Osiris* to decide how much of the book is accurate. Students might compare the worlds developed in James Barter's *The Ancient Persians* with the life depicted in James E. Lindsay's *Daily Life in the Medieval Islamic World.*

Students could develop a chart with the evaluative criteria and then include information from the text that show if the text meets or does not meet the guidelines. For each book, they may summarize the coverage found in the books, as well as how well it meets each of the criteria. As students develop and use their evaluative criteria, they should compare the accuracy of the facts found in the texts. If they discover discrepancies, they have an opportunity to use other references to try to discover which text is correct.

Additional Activities to Enhance Phase Three

Here are some activities for children or young adult students related to this phase:

1. Several of the informational books encourage reader involvement by including step-by-step directions for making models or other items. Choose a book such as Andrew Haslam and Alexandra Parsons's *Ancient Egypt*, and follow the directions for making models, clothing, objects, or foods. Give a demonstration to the class or to a group.
2. Develop a list of criteria for evaluating maps in informational books. Select a group of informational books that include maps and evaluate the maps. Rate them and qualify the texts from best to worst. Provide your reasoning for each rating.
3. Select several nonfiction books that present the art and architecture of the Islamic world. Identify characteristics of the art. Search illustrated folklore, and identify any similarities between the art and architecture in the nonfiction books and those found in the folklore.

Phase Four: Historical Fiction

Many of the historical informational books just discussed may be used to provide sources so that students can write fictional accounts of people's lives. According to Robert Sabuda in the Author's Note to *Tutankhamun's Gift*, a fictionalized biography about the life of the Egyptian ruler who came to the throne as a child during the mid-1300s BCE, "Historical facts from ancient civilizations such as Egypt's are often difficult to determine and are much debated by scholars" (notes on the text). Consequently, Sabuda uses information that he could find on ancient Egypt to write a fictionalized biography about the young ruler.

After students have researched the early periods of the Middle Eastern cultures, ask them to select a time period and a location. Then have them write a historical fiction story about the time period and a person who may or may not have actually lived during this period. For example, Mary Stolz uses an actual monument built to honor a pharaoh of Egypt to write a fictional story about a stone carver who may have worked on the Sphinx. After the students have written their fictionalized stories, ask them to write an author's note that provides historical background and that supports the actual historical information in the book.

Additional Activities to Enhance Phase Four

Here are some activities for children or young adult students related to this phase:

1. Many of the poems selected by Naomi Shihab Nye in *The Space Between Our Footsteps: Poems and Paintings from the Middle East* provide glimpses into the history of either a person or a people. Some of the poems provide happy memories; others focus on cultural conflicts caused by war or consequences of political disagreements. Choose a poem and use the poem to develop a historical fiction or an illustrated book that uses ideas developed in the poem.
2. Compare the characteristics of and the themes developed in Shulamith Levy Oppenheim's *The Hundredth Name* with folklore that has Islamic characteristics.

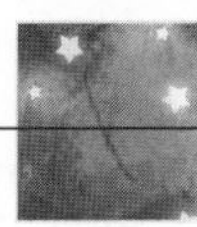

Phase Five: Contemporary Literature

Identifying and Analyzing Resources for Teaching about Islam

The October 2010 issue of *School Library Journal* includes a number of websites that may be used to help teachers and librarians select materials and develop curriculums that teach students about Islam. Select one or more of these sources. What are each website's goals? What information about Islam would students gain after following one of these curriculums? Evaluate the value of each of the websites and present your findings to your class. The following are websites included in the *School Library Journal* article (p. 36):

Elementary Grades:

Access Islam, Thirteen.org http://bit.ly/du9wlC. The text includes ten lessons about Islamic holidays, cultures, and traditions.

Children's Book Study Guides: The Librarian of Basra and Alia's Mission: Saving the Books of Iraq, Morningside Center for Teaching Social Responsibility. http://bit.ly/9ROIZN. Suggests ways to discuss the books with children.

Information on Islam, Woodland Junior School, Kent, England. http://bit.ly/9ah91J. Focuses on history lessons.

Middle School:

Extra Credit Study Guide, Andrew Clements. http://bit.ly/cdUr2t. A study guide for a book discussion.

Geometry and Islam, Asia Society. http://bit.ly/acBiKU. Describes a student activity that includes Islamic textiles and architecture.

Teaching on Controversial Issues: Guidelines for Teachers, Morningside Center for Teaching Social Responsibility. http://bit.ly/cLepPO. A teacher's guide for teaching issues.

High School:

NYC Muslim Community Center: Why There? Why Not? Morningside Center for Teaching Social Responsibility. http://bit.ly/9S23wf. Guidelines for discussing the proposed mosque.

Islam, Empire of Faith, PBS Educational Resources. http://to.pbs.org/aJC2en. Five lessons for grades 6–12.

National Geographic, The World of Islam. http://bit.ly/d7nZob. Information about Islam with links to additional source.

What are the strengths and weaknesses of each of the websites? Is there enough accurate information for you to develop a lesson using this information? Why or why not? What are the messages that each of the developers wants to convey to students?

How Might Muhammad Respond to Articles about Education in the Middle East?

Characters in three of the books discussed in the "Survival" section of this chapter emphasize the value of education. The heroines in Suzanne Fisher Staples's *Shabanu: Daughter of the Wind* and in Joellie Stolz's *The Shadows of Ghadames* both express the desire to learn to read and write even though their cultures do not believe in the value of educating females. Several of the personages interviewed in Deborah Ellis's *Children of War: Voices of Iraqi Refugees* state that obtaining an education is most important for survival in the future.

Although according to Demi's biography of *Muhammad*, he had no formal education, he memorized sacred words and had scribes write them down. He did maintain that all men and women, black and white, rich and poor, must be treated with dignity and respect. According to *Listen to the Wind: The Story of Dr. Greg & Three Cups of Tea* by Greg Mortenson and Susan L. Roth, Mortenson believes so strongly in education that he raised money and personally helped build schools in areas in Pakistan that did not have access to education.

The topic of education in the Middle East, especially the education of females, lends itself to research, discussion, and debate. After discussing the role of education in several of the books, students may search for articles that suggest the current role of education and the availability of schools in various Middle Eastern countries. For example, the following provide interesting points for discussion:

Rivera, Kay, and Taimoor Shah. "Filling Classes with Learning, Not Fears." *New York Times* (June 30, 2011): A4.

Kristof, Nicholas D. "'Three Cups of Tea,' Spilled." *New York Times* (April 21, 2011): A21.

The article reported by Rivera and Shah states, "'Since March 21, the beginning of the Afghan calendar year, education officials have recorded 20 school-related attacks,' said Gul Agha Ahmadi, a spokesman for the Ministry of Education" (p. A4). Attacks can include the burning of schoolhouses, kidnappings, threats, forced school closings, and the killing or injuring of students or teachers. According to the spokesperson, this is an improvement from the previous two years when there were twice as many attacks. The journalists go on to report that the decrease in attacks is notable because the banning of girls from schools was one of the symbols of the Taliban's rule from 1996 to 2001.

After sharing articles such as this one, ask the students to consider questions such as: Why is education considered so dangerous, especially for women? How might one of the characters from the books they have read respond to the burning of schoolhouses? Would the characters from the books, those who maintained that education is important, be happy or sad from the discussions in this article? Ask the students to support their viewpoints.

The Kristof article is a response to charges that Greg Mortenson misstated how he started building schools, exaggerated about the number of schools he built, and misused money his charity collected. Kristof presents the facts of these accusations and then presents his own viewpoint in which he states that Mortenson was right about the big things: "He was right about the need for American outreach in the Muslim world. He was right that building schools tends to promote stability more than dropping bombs. He was right about the transformative power of education, especially girls' education. He was right about the need to listen to local people—yes over cup after cup of tea—rather than just issue instructions" (p. A21). The journalist continues that he worries that scandals such as this will leave Americans disillusioned and cynical and will ultimately leave countless children in Afghanistan without an education. He concludes that Mortenson's books may or may not have been fictionalized, but there is no question that "American donors and Afghan villagers were able to put aside their differences and prejudices and cooperate to build schools—and a better world" (p. A21).

This article could lead to an interesting debate as students discuss the advantages of education and consider how the need for a formal education for both males and females may be crucial in the twenty-first century. They may also consider how Muhammad might respond to these issues about education if he were living today.

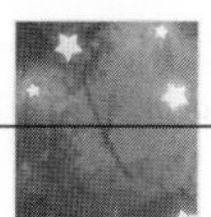

Visualizing Middle Eastern Art

The illustrations in David Macaulay's *Mosque* are modeled after examples of structures and art created between 1540 and 1580 in Istanbul, Turkey. Using sources of art that depict a similar time period such as Sheila S. Blair and Johnathan M. Bloom's *The Art and Architecture of Islam, 1250–1800* (1994), and Markus Hattstein and Peter Delius's *Islam: Art and Architecture* (2004) ask students to find photographs of mosques and art works similar to those depicted by Macaulay. What are the similarities, what are the differences? The art book is also divided between Part I: 1250–1500 and Part II: 1500–1800. Ask students to compare the art and architecture of these two time periods.

Another activity that helps students understand the art of the Middle East is to ask them to search newspaper and magazine articles that focus on art such as Holland Cotter's "In 16th-Century Iran, a Dynasty Hunts a Signature Style" (*New York Times,* October 17, 2003) and Alain Zivie's "Guardian of the Sun God's Treasure" (*National Geographic,* November 2003). Using such articles, ask students to describe the cultural values depicted in the art. How are these cultural values similar or different from those developed in the literature? Additional magazine articles that reflect art in the Middle East include Don Belt's "Petra: Ancient City of Stone" (*National Geographic,* December 1998); A. R. William's "Death on the Nile" (*National Geographic,* October 2002); and Alain Zivie's "A Pharaoh's Peace Maker" (*National Geographic,* October 2002).

Students may find articles that describe the destroying of art objects or the looting of archaeological sites during the 2003 Iraq war. These articles frequently depict the sorrow that accompanies the loss of ancient art. One such article is Andrew Lawler's "Beyond the Looting: What's Next for Iraq's Treasures?" (*National Geographic,* October 2003). Ask students to debate the destroying and stealing of art by looters and the attempts to regain the art. They may consider why ancient art is important in preserving a culture. What do we learn about a culture through the art? They could also relate this activity to their own culture. What would they consider important to retain for their grandchildren? What artifacts are the most important for their culture? What do they learn about their culture from these artifacts? This type of activity could be expanded to museums in the United States and discussions of the various museums found in Washington, D.C., as part of the Smithsonian Institution, or in the students' hometowns. For example, the Smithsonian Institution is referred to as the nation's museum or even the nation's attic. What type of artifacts would students expect to find there? Why is the Smithsonian Institution free for visitors? Why do they think the government and other individuals make these museums accessible?

Additional Activities to Enhance Phase Five

Here are some activities for children or young adult students related to this phase:

1. Newspapers such as the Sunday edition of the *New York Times* include many features that could be used to model a newspaper about contemporary Middle Eastern cultures. For example, search through a newspaper and list the various features that might be in a newspaper, such as the following: international, national, and state news; editorials; arts and leisure; travel; magazine; business; and sports. There could also be special features such as in-depth coverage of education, fashions, foods, and book reviews. Students can choose features they would like to investigate, select editors and reporters for each feature, and publish the newspaper.

2. Use a book such as Richard Wormser's *American Islam: Growing Up Muslim in America* as an example of a book that describes the lives of young people in the United States. If

possible, interview people who came to the United States from one of the Islamic countries. Compose a list of questions, conduct interviews, and share these responses with the class.

REFERENCES

Adler, Mortimer J., and Charles Van Doren. *How to Read a Book*. New York: Simon & Schuster, 1972.

Andrews, Carol, ed. *The Ancient Egyptian Book of the Dead,* translated by R. O. Faulkner. New York: Macmillan, 1985.

Arberry, A. J., trans. *The Koran Interpreted*. New York: Macmillan, 1955.

Armstrong, Karen. *Muhammad.* New York: HarperCollins, 1992.

Barack, Lauren. "Islam in the Classroom." *School Library* 56 (October 2010): 34–37.

Basit, Abdul. "Islam in America: How to Integrate Without Losing Muslim Identity." *Islamic Horizons* 27 (March/April 1998): 32–34.

Bayat, Mojdeh, and Mohammad Ali Jamnia. *Tales from the Land of the Sufis*. Boston: Shambhala, 1994.

Belt, Don. "Petra: Ancient City of Stone." Photographs by Annie Griffiths Belt. *National Geographic* (December 1998): 116–133.

Blair, Sheila S., and Johnathan M. Bloom. *The Art and Architecture of Islam 1250–1800*. New Haven, Conn.: Yale University Press, 1994.

Brand, Laurie A. "Women and the State in Jordan." *Islam, Gender and Social Change,* edited by Yvonne Yazbeck Haddad and John L. Esposito. New York: Oxford University Press, 1998: 100–123.

Brown, Mary Ellen, and Bruce A. Rosenberg, eds. *Encyclopedia of Folklore and Literature*. Santa Barbara, Calif.: ABC-CLIO, 1998.

Burton, Sir Richard F., trans. *Tales from the Arabian Nights: Selected from the Book of a Thousand Nights and a Night*. New York: Excalibur, 1985.

Bushnaq, Inea, ed. *Arab Folktales*. New York: Pantheon, 1986.

Cotter, Holland. "In 16th-Century Iran, a Dynasty Hunts a Signature Style." *New York Times* (October 17, 2003): B34.

Crossette, Barbara. "A Manual on Rights of Women under Islam." *New York Times* (December 29, 1996): 5.

Delong-Bas, Natana J. *Wahhabi Islam*. New York: Oxford, 2004.

Denny, Frederick M. *Islam: Religious Traditions of the World*. New York: HarperCollins, 1987.

Elliot, Jason. *An Unexpected Light: Travels in Afghanistan*. New York: Picador, 2001.

Elliott, Andrea. "A Cleric's Journey Leads to a Suburban Frontier." *New York Times* (January 28, 2007): 1, 24.

Ghazi, Tasneema Khatoon. "Islamic Literature for Children Adopts the English Language." *Bookbird* 35 (Fall 1997): 6–10.

Gregorian, Vartan. *Islam: A Mosaic Not a Monolith*. Washington, D.C.: Brookings Institution, 2003.

Griswold, William J., et al. *The Image of the Middle East in Secondary School Textbooks*. New York: Middle East Studies Association, 1975.

Hattstein, Markus, and Peter Delius, eds. *Islam: Art and Architecture*. New York: Konemann, 2004.

House, Karen Elliot. "Five Best." *The Wall Street Journal* (November 11–12, 2006): 10.

Iskander, Sylvia. "Portrayals of Arabs in Contemporary American Picture Books." *Bookbird* 35 (Fall 1997): 11–16.

Janson, H. W. *History of Art*, 5th ed. New York: Abrams, 1995.

Khorana, Meena G. "To the Reader." *Bookbird* 35 (Summer 1997): 2–3.

Kissen, Rita M. "The Children of Hagar, and Sarah." *Children's Literature in Education* 22 (1991): 111–119.

Kristof, Nicholas S. "'Three Cups of Tea,' Spilled." *New York Times (*April 21, 2011): A21.

Lawler, Andrew. "Beyond the Looting: What's Next for Iraq's Treasures?" *National Geographic* 204 (October 2003): 58–75.

_____. "Reconstructing Petra." *Smithsonian* 38 (June 2007): 42–49.

Leach, Maria, ed. *Funk & Wagnalls Standard Dictionary of Folklore, Mythology, and Legend*. San Francisco: Harper & Row, 1972.

Levenson, Jay A. *Circa 1494: Art in the Age of Exploration*. New Haven, Conn.: Yale University Press/ Washington, D.C.: National Gallery of Art, 1991.

Lewis, Bernard. *What Went Wrong?* New York: Oxford, 2002.

Little, Greta. "The Changing Image of Arabs in Hostage Dramas." *Booklist* 35 (Fall 1997): 28–30.

MacFarquhar, Neil. "A Kiss Is Not Just a Kiss to an Angry Arab TV Audience." *New York Times* (March 5, 2004): A3.

Norton, Donna E. *Through the Eyes of a Child: An Introduction to Children's Literature*, 8th ed. Boston: Pearson/Allyn & Bacon, 2011.

Piper, David. *The Illustrated History of Art*. New York: Crescent Books, 1994.

Power, Carla. "A Secret History." *The New York Times Magazine* (February 25, 2007): 23–24.

Publishers Weekly 250 (November 10, 2003): 62.

Rai, Mansooreh. "The Iranian Revolution and the Flowering of Children's Literature." *Bookbird* 35 (Fall 1997): 31–33.

Rivera, Ray, and Taimoor Shah. "Filling Classes with Learning, Not Fears." *New York Times* (June 10, 2011): A4.

Rochman, Hazel. *Against Borders: Promoting Books for a Multicultural World*. Chicago: American Library Association, 1993.

Rohl, David M. *Pharaohs and Kings*. New York: Crown, 1995.

Salleh, Khaliijah Mohammad. "Islam in America: The Role of Men and Women in Society." *Islamic Horizons* 26 (January/February 1997): 57.

Sasson, Jean P. *Princess: A True Story of Life Behind the Veil in Saudi Arabia*. New York: Morrow, 1992.

School Library Journal. 44 (November 2003): 134, 162.

School Library Journal. "Resources for Teaching about Islam." 56 (October 2010): 36.

School Library Journal. "SLJ's Recommended Titles." 56 (October 2010): 37.

Staples, Suzanne Fisher. "Writing About the Islamic World: An American Author's Thoughts on Authenticity." *Bookbird* 35 (Fall 1997): 17–20.

Vaziri, Mostafa. *The Emergence of Islam: Prophecy, Imamate, and Messianism in Perspective*. New York: Paragon, 1992.

Walz, Terence. "The American Experience in Egypt: A Retrospective Chronicles Two Centuries of Exploration." *Archaeology* 49 (January/February 1996): 70–72, 74–75.

Weekend Edition, National Public Radio (November 9, 2003).

William, A. R. "Death on the Nile." Photographs by Kenneth Garrett. *National Geographic* 202 (October 2002): 2–25.

Williams, John Alden. *The World of Islam*. Austin: University of Texas Press, 1994.

Wiseman, Paul. "Iraqi Women Juggle Freedom, 'Moral Duty.'" *USA Today* (March 8, 2004): A6.

Zivie, Alain. "A Pharaoh's Peace Maker." Photographs by Patrick Chapuis. *National Geographic* 202 (October 2002): 26–41.

_____. "Guardian of the Sun God's Treasure." Photographs by Kenneth Garrett. *National Geographic* 203 (November 2003): 52–59.

CHILDREN'S AND YOUNG ADULT LITERATURE REFERENCES

Addasi, Maha. *Time to Pray.* Translated by Nuha Albitar. Illustrated by Ned Gannon. Boyds Mills, 2010 (I: 6–10 R: 4). A girl learns about her heritage when she visits her grandmother.

_____. *The White Nights of Ramadan.* Illustrated by Ned Gannon. Boyds Mills, 2008 (I: 6–10 R: 4). Set in Kuwait, the story describes Girgian, a Muslim celebration.

Akbar, Said Hyder, and Susan Burton. *Come Back to Afghanistan: A California Teenager's Story.* Bloomsbury, 2005 (I: 12+ R: 6). A teenage boy and his father travel around Afghanistan.

Alexander, Sue. *Nadia the Willful.* Illustrated by Lloyd Bloom. Pantheon, 1983 (I: 7–10 R: 5). A Bedouin girl teaches her father about the importance of remembering a lost son.

I = Interest age range

R = Readability by grade level

Barakat, Ibtisam. *Tasting the Sky: A Palestinian Childhood.* Farrar, Straus & Giroux, 2007 (I: 12+ R: 6). This nonfiction book is a memoir of childhood experiences during the Six-Day War.

Barter, James, *The Ancient Persians.* Gale, 2005 (I: all). Photographs, diagrams, and maps introduce this ancient civilization.

Bell, Hilari. *Flame.* Simon & Schuster, 2003 (I: 10+ R: 5). A fantasy based on a Persian legend.

Ben-Ezer, Ehud. *Hosni the Dreamer: An Arabian Tale.* Illustrated by Uri Shulevitz. Farrar, Straus & Giroux, 1997 (I: 6–8 R: 5). The author identifies the story as being based on an old Arabian folktale.

Brown, Tricia. *Salaam: A Muslim American Boy's Story.* Photographs by Ken Cardwell. Holt, 2006 (I: 5 – 8 R: 4). Photographs show the life of an American Muslim boy.

Buller, Laura. *A Faith like Mine: A Celebration of the World's Religions Through the Eyes of Children.* DK, 2005 (I: 9+ R: 5). The text includes a section on Islam.

Bushnaq, Inea, ed. *Arab Folktales.* Pantheon, 1986 (I: 12+ R: 7). This is a large collection of Arabic folklore.

Chrisp, Peter. *Pyramid.* DK, 2006 (I: 9+ R: 5). Extra-large illustrations present the Great Pyramid of Giza.

Dalokay, Vedat. *Sister Shako and Kolo the Goat: Memories of My Childhood in Turkey.* Translated by Guner Ener. Lothrop, Lee & Shepard, 1994 (I: 10 R: 5). In this 1995 Mildred Batchelder Honor book, the former mayor of Ankara recalls his childhood and his friendship with a widow and her goat.

D'Adamo, Francesco. *Iqbal: A Novel.* translated by Ann Leonori. Simon & Schuster, 2003 (I: 8+ R: 5). A bonded servant in Pakistan helps children working in a carpet factory.

Demi. *Muhammad.* McElderry, 2003 (I: all). This heavily illustrated biography presents the life of the Muslim leader.

Dulac, Edmund, illustrator. *Sindbad the Sailor and Other Stories from the Arabian Nights.* Hodder and Stoughton, 1914; Omega, 1986 (I: 121). This is a reissue of a book published in 1914.

Ellis, Deborah. *Children of War: Voices of Iraqi Refugees.* Groundwood, 2009 (I: 12–YA). Nonfiction, interviews with refugees living in Jordan.

_____. *Off to War: Voices of Soldiers' Children.* Groundwood, 2008 (I: 12–YA). Nonfiction, interviews with children of military personnel from Canada and the United States.

_____. *Parvana's Journey.* Groundwood, 2002 (I: 12+) A thirteen-year-old girl searches for her father in Afghanistan.

_____. *Three Wishes: Palestinian and Israeli Children Speak Out.* Groundwood, 2004 (I: 12–YA). Interviews with young people.

Ferber, Elizabeth. *Yasir Arafat: The Battle for Peace in Palestine.* Millbrook, 1995 (I: 12+ R: 7). This is a biography about the Palestinian leader.

Fletcher, Susan. *Shadow Spinner.* Atheneum, 1998 (I: 10+ R: 6). This historical fiction novel is set in the time of Shahrazad.

Giblin, James Cross. *The Riddle of the Rosetta Stone: Key to Ancient Egypt.* Crowell, 1990 (I: 10+ R: 6). The informational text follows the process used to decipher the ancient hieroglyphs.

_____. *Secrets of the Sphinx.* Illustrated by Bagram lbatouline. Scholastic, 2004 (I: 8–12 R: 6). The author discusses scientific research associated with the Sphinx.

Gordon, Ruth, ed. *Under All Silences: The Many Shades of Love.* Harper & Row, 1987 (I: 91). The anthology includes several Egyptian and Persian poems.

Hamilton, Virginia, reteller. *In the Beginning: Creation Stories from Around the World.* Illustrated by Barry Moser. Harcourt Brace, 1988 (I: 81). This collection of myths includes "The Sun-God and the Dragon," a tale from Egypt.

Haslam, Andrew, and Alexandra Parsons. *Ancient Egypt.* Thomas Learning, 1995 (I: 8–12 R: 4). This informational text includes directions for making models related to ancient Egyptian civilization.

Hawass, Zahi. *Curses of the Pharaohs: My Adventures with Mummies.* National Geographic, 2004 (I: 8–12 R: 6). The author describes his excavations, including the dangers.

_____. *Tutankhamun: The Mystery of the Boy King.* National Geographic, 2005 (I: 8–12 R: 5). This nonfiction is written by the director of excavation at the Giza pyramids.

Hawes, Louise. *Muti's Necklace: The Oldest Story in the World.* Illustrated by Rebecca Guay. Houghton Mifflin, 2006 (I: all). A folktale from Egypt.

Heide, Florence Parry, and Judith Heide Gilliland. *The Day of Ahmed's Secret.* Illustrated by Ted Lewin. Lothrop, Lee & Shepard, 1990 (I: 6–9 R: 4). A picture storybook set in Cairo.

_____. *Sami and the Time of Troubles.* Illustrated by Ted Lewin. Clarion, 1992 (I: 6–9 R: 4). A Lebanese boy and his family live in a basement shelter.

Henderson, Kathy. *Lugalbanda: The Boy Who Got Caught Up in a War.* Illustrated by Jane Ray. Candlewick, 2006 (I: 9+ R: 4). This is an ancient legend.

Hickox, Rebecca. *The Golden Sandal: A Middle Eastern Cinderella Story.* Illustrated by Will Hillenbrand. Holiday House, 1998 (I: all). A tale from Iraq.

Hicyilmaz, Gaye. *Against the Storm.* Little, Brown, 1992 (I: 10+ R: 6). A boy learns about survival in Ankara.

Ichikawa, Satomi. *Here a Little Child I Stand: Poems of Prayer and Praise for Children.* Philomel, 1985 (I: all). A collection of prayers from many countries and cultures.

Khan, Hena. *Night of the Moon: A Muslim Holiday Story.* Illustrated by Julie Paschkis. Chronicle, 2008 (I: 6–9 R: 5). A seven-year-old Pakistani American girl learns about the celebration.

Kimmel, Eric A., adapter. *Rimonah of the Flashing Sword: A North African Tale.* Illustrated by Omar Rayyan. Holiday House, 1995 (I: 5–9 R: 5). An Egyptian version of the Snow White tale.

_____. *The Tale of Aladdin and the Wonderful Lamp: A Story from the Arabian Nights.* Illustrated by Ju-Hong Chen. Holiday House, 1992 (I: 6–9 R: 5). Retold from the Arabian Nights.

_____. *The Tale of Ali Baba and the Forty Thieves.* Illustrated by Will Hillenbrand. Holiday House, 1996 (I: 6–9 R: 5). The folktale is from the Arabian Nights.

_____. *The Three Princes: A Tale from the Middle East.* Illustrated by Leonard Everett Fisher. Holiday House, 1994 (I: 6–9 R: 5). A princess challenges three princes.

Koch, Kenneth, and Kate Farrell, eds. *Talking to the Sun: An Illustrated Anthology of Poems for Young People.* Metropolitan Museum of Art and Holt, Rinehart and Winston, 1985 (I: all). This anthology of poems illustrated with works of art includes two poems from ancient Egypt.

Koenig, Viviane. *The Ancient Egyptians: Life in the Nile Valley.* Illustrated by Veronique Ageorges. Millbrook, 1992 (I: 8+ R: 5). The informational book discusses the people, including their work, social and economic lives, and their religious traditions.

Lasky, Kathryn. *The Librarian Who Measured the Earth.* Illustrated by Kevin Hawkes. Little, Brown, 1994 (I: 9+ R: 5). This is an illustrated biography about the chief librarian in Alexandria.

Lat. *Kampung Boy.* Roaring Brook, 2006 (I: 9+ R: 4). Set in the 1950s, the text describes the life of a Muslim boy in a Malaysian village.

Lindsay, James E. *Daily Life in the Medieval Islamic World.* Greenwood, 2005 (I: 12–YA R: 7). The text uses charts, diagrams, and maps to describe life in the Arabian Peninsula from the sixth century to the thirteenth century.

Macaulay, David. *Mosque.* Houghton Mifflin, 2003 (I: all). This informational book focuses on detailed drawings showing the architecture of a mosque.

Macdonald, Fiona. *A 16th Century Mosque.* Illustrated by Mark Bergin. Peter Bedrick, 1994 (I: all). Detailed illustrations show the mosques built in Istanbul.

Manniche, Lise. *The Prince Who Knew His Fate.* Philomel, 1981 (I: all). The story is translated from hieroglyphs.

Mantin, Peter, and Ruth Mantin. *The Islamic World: Beliefs and Civilizations 600–1600.* Cambridge University Press, 1993 (I: 10+ R: 7). This informational book includes formation on the rise and influence of Islam.

Maugham, W. Somerset. *Appointment*, adapted by Alan Benjamin. Illustrated by Roger Essley. Simon & Schuster, 1993 (I: all). A servant cannot escape a fateful death.

McCaughrean, Geraldine. *The Silver Treasure: Myths and Legends of the World.* Illustrated by Bee Willey. Simon & Schuster, 1998 (I: all). The collection includes a tale from the Middle East.

Moktefi, M. *The Arabs in the Golden Age.* Illustrated by Véronique Ageorges. Millbrook Press, 1992.

Morrison, Ian A. *Middle East.* Steck-Vaughn, 1991 (I: 9+ R: 5). This book surveys the geography, languages, history, and culture of the region.

Mortenson, Greg, and Susan Roth. *Listen to the Wind: The Story of Dr. Greg & Three Cups of Tea.* Illustrated by Susan L. Roth. Dial, 2009 (I: all). A picture book about Mortenson's experiences.

Nye, Naomi Shihab, ed. *This Same Sky: A Collection of Poems from Around the World.* Four Winds, 1992 (I: 9+). This anthology includes poetry from Saudi Arabia, Kuwait, Pakistan, Iraq, and Lebanon.

_____. ed. *The Space Between Our Footsteps: Poems and Paintings from the Middle East.* Simon & Schuster, 1998 (I: all). An anthology of poems and paintings.

Oppenheim, Shulamith Levy. *The Hundredth Name.* Illustrated by Michael Hays. Boyds Mills, 1995 (I: 4–8 R: 4). An Egyptian boy tries to discover the hundredth name for Allah.

_____, reteller. *Iblis.* Illustrated by Ed Young. Harcourt Brace, 1994 (I: all). This is an Islamic version of Adam and Eve.

Philip, Neil, reteller. *The Arabian Nights.* Illustrated by Sheila Moxley. Orchard, 1994 (I: 8+ R: 5). Shahrazad saves her life by telling the king a different story every night.

Putnam, James. *Mummy.* Photographs by Peter Hayman. Knopf, 1993 (I: 9+ R: 5). The book describes the principles and ceremonies associated with the preservation of bodies.

Reeves, Nicholas. *Into the Mummy's Tomb: The Real-Life Discovery of Tutankhamun's Treasures.* Scholastic, 1992 (I: 8+ R: 5). This book traces Howard Carter's discovery of the tomb.

Robert, Na'ima B. *Ramadan Moon.* Illustrated by Shirin Adi. Frances Lincoln, 2009 (I: 5–9 R: 4). A girl explains what happens during Ramadan.

Ross, Stewart. *Egypt in Spectacular Cross-Section.* Illustrated by Stephen Biesty. Scholastic, 2005 (I: 8–12 R: 5). Labeled drawings show ancient Egyptian architecture.

Rumford, James. *Silent Music: A Story of Baghdad.* Roaring Brook, 2008 (I: 5–8 R: 4). A boy learns to survive in Baghdad.

Sabuda, Robert. *Tutankhamun's Gift.* Atheneum, 1994 (I: all). This highly illustrated text gives a fictionalized account of the possible childhood and early life of the man who became leader of Egypt.

Sands, Emily. *Egyptology: Searching for the Tomb of Osiris.* Candlewick, 2004 (I: all). A highly illustrated text shows many different aspects of early Egyptian culture.

Schami, Rafik. *A Hand Full of Stars.* Translated by Rika Lesser. Dutton, 1990 (I: 12+ R: 6). In this story set in Damascus, a boy becomes involved with an underground newspaper.

Sherman, Josepha, reteller. *Trickster Tales: Forty Folk Stories from Around the World.* Illustrated by David Boston. August House, 1996 (I: all). The collection includes tales from ancient Babylonia, Morocco, Egypt, Iraq, and Turkey.

Staples, Suzanne Fisher. *Haveli.* Random House, 1993 (I: 12+ R: 6). This is a sequel to *Shabanu: Daughter of the Wind.*

_____. *Shabanu: Daughter of the Wind.* Knopf, 1989 (I: 12+ R: 6). A girl in Pakistan asserts her independence.

_____. *Under the Persimmon Tree.* Farrar, Straus & Giroux, 2005 (I: 10+ R: 5). A rural Afghani girl's and an American woman's lives intertwine in Afghanistan in 2001.

Stolz, Joelle. *The Shadows of Ghadames.* Delacorte, 2004 (I: 10+ R: 6). The author focuses on the secret life of women.

Van Allsburg, Chris. *The Garden of Abdul Gasazi.* Houghton Mifflin, 1979 (I: 5–8 R: 5). A boy enters a magic garden.

Winter, Jeanette. *The Librarian of Basra: A True Story from Iraq.* Harcourt, 2005 (I: 6–9 R: 4). A biography about a librarian who saves many of the books prior to the Iraq war.

Wormser, Richard. *American Islam: Growing Up Muslim in America.* Walker, 1994 (I: 12+ R: 6). The book describes the lives of American teens who follow the Islamic religion.

Author/Title Index

Subject Index